THE
SUPERPOWER
MYTH

The Use and Misuse
of American Might

Nancy Soderberg

WILEY

John Wiley & Sons, Inc.

Published by John Wiley & Sons, Inc., Hoboken, New Jersey
Published simultaneously in Canada

For general information about our other products and services, please contact our Customer Care Department within the United States at (800) 762-2974, outside the United States at (317) 572-3993 or fax (317) 572-4002.

Wiley also publishes its books in a variety of electronic formats. Some content that appears in print may not be available in electronic books. For more information about Wiley products, visit our web site at www.wiley.com.

Library of Congress Cataloging-in-Publication Data:

Soderberg, Nancy E., date.
 The superpower myth : the use and misuse of American might / Nancy Soderberg.
  p. cm.
 Includes index.
 ISBN 0-471-65683-6 (cloth)
 1. National security—United States. 2. United States—Military policy. 3. United States—Foreign relations—1989– 4. World politics—1989– 5. Soderberg, Nancy E., 1958– I. Title.
 UA23.S52626 2005
 355′.033073—dc22

                                                                              2004017099

Printed in the United States of America

10 9 8 7 6 5 4 3 2 1

To Richard, Jake, and Elizabeth

CONTENTS

FOREWORD

by Bill Clinton

When I became president in 1993, the cold war had just ended with freedom's victory. As the world's only superpower, how were we to use our vast military, economic, political, and moral power? Could we build a New World Order? Would our primary policy be isolationism, unilateralism, or cooperation?

As one of the first senior officials from my administration to evaluate our country's foreign policy over the past decade, Nancy Soderberg delivers in *The Superpower Myth* an insightful and intriguing analysis of the decisions we made, the way we made them, and the impact they had. Because the post–cold war world was increasingly interdependent, our country could not afford to withdraw from the world's problems; neither could we solve them on our own. Instead we had to strengthen the institutions—and habits—of international cooperation, while preserving our ability to act alone if necessary to protect America's security. We pursued the following objectives:

- reconciling the United States to its principle cold war adversaries, Russia and China, in a way that advanced stability, economic opportunity, and freedom;
- building a Europe that for the first time was united, free, and democratic by expanding NATO and supporting the expansion of the European Union;
- working to end religious, racial, ethnic, and tribal warfare in the Middle East, Northern Ireland, Bosnia, Kosovo, East Timor, and several African nations;
- working to contain the spread of weapons of mass destruction through expansion of the Nunn-Luger program, agreements with North Korea, ratification of the Chemical Weapons Convention and indefinite extension of the Nuclear Non-Proliferation Treaty;
- putting the United States at the center of new institutions of economic and security cooperation, including the World Trade Organization, NAFTA, the APEC leaders meeting, the Summit of the Americas, the Kyoto Climate Change treaty, the Comprehensive

Test Ban Treaty, the Millennium Debt Relief initiative, and more effective initiatives by the IMF and the World Bank;

- increasing America's capacity to prevent and punish terrorist attacks through law enforcement, intelligence, and military efforts.

As I said, our philosophy was to cooperate whenever we could and to act alone when necessary. For example, acting in concert with allies, we joined with NATO to strike Serbian forces in Bosnia and Kosovo and established new trade networks and security agreements. Acting alone, we struck at al Qaeda in Afghanistan and Sudan, provided critical financial aid to Mexico and Russia, and opened markets to African countries.

We believed the United States should proceed in a way that would serve our interests not only in the present but also in a future in which we might not be the sole economic, political, and military superpower. Therefore, working with other nations on treaties like the Kyoto Accord or working with the United Nations and other organizations would benefit America in the long run, even as we had to grapple with the frustrations that such cooperation inevitably involves.

Pursuing this course helped to advance our security interests and to bring more prosperity and freedom to the developed world and new trade and investment to the developing world, where more people moved out of poverty than in any comparable period in history and life expectancy went up while infant mortality dropped. Meanwhile, for the first time in history, over half the world's people lived under governments they voted into power.

Throughout the 1990s, we developed constructive relationships among the major adversaries of the cold war: Russia, China, Europe, and the United States. China came into the World Trade Organization. NATO expanded. We fought terrorism hard, preventing attacks at home and abroad and bringing many terrorists to justice. We built a strong international coalition to rein in the proliferation of weapons of mass destruction. Genocide and ethnic cleansing were ended in the Balkans. There were over seven years of progress toward peace in the Middle East, until the current period of violence began in September 2000. Peace was brought to Northern Ireland. We did not succeed in our efforts to get Osama bin Laden and the other top al Qaeda leaders, but we did roll up over twenty al Qaeda cells and prevent serious attacks planned for the 1999–2000 millennium weekend.

Despite that record of progress, serious threats to our security, economy, health, and environment remain, alongside enormous opportunities—alleviating poverty, putting all the world's children in school, creating millions of high-paying jobs in the clean energy and biotechnology fields, and using medical advances to conquer the spread of AIDS and other deadly diseases.

I believe we must meet those challenges and seize those opportunities by refining and improving the approach that resulted in so much progress during the 1990s, a strategy that increases our security and is based on building a world with more partners and fewer terrorists. In this interdependent but not yet integrated world, we cannot possibly kill, jail, or occupy all of our potential adversaries. Therefore, we should work with other nations whenever we can, acting alone only when we have to—not the other way around.

Our goal must be to build a world of shared responsibilities, shared benefits, and shared values. We cannot meet that goal by going it alone. Whether by trade or travel, by immigration or information technology, by common cultural experiences or scientific endeavors, or by shared vulnerabilities to terrorism or disease, we simply cannot escape each other. Like it or not, our fates are bound up with one another.

The United States must convince other nations that it is in their interest to join us to meet these new, complex challenges that know no borders, while setting the standard for democracy, economic integration, and stability. No nation can ignore global warming or HIV/AIDS; at the same time, no nation can defeat them alone. No nation can ignore terrorism *or* defeat it alone. We can retain our unique identities and the diversities of our peoples and cultures, but we will have to build a shared future rooted in our common humanity.

Nancy Soderberg rendered extraordinary service to the United States through her contributions to the development and effective implementation of our nation's foreign policy during my administration, and she has done so again in writing *The Superpower Myth*. It makes a rich contribution to American history and offers valuable lessons for our country's future.

ACKNOWLEDGMENTS

This book would not exist without extraordinary support and encouragement from many people. It had never occurred to me to write a book, but toward the end of the Clinton administration, many friends and colleagues urged me to write about my time advising the president on the Irish peace process. In November 2000, I began doing so. Over the next four years, the book went through many incarnations, first expanding to an evaluation of President Clinton's foreign policy and finally to a study of the use and misuse of force since the cold war. Throughout that evolution, the wise counsel and support of many proved invaluable.

I owe my wonderful agent, Andrew Stuart, a large debt of gratitude for believing in this first-time author and in pushing me to write the book I did not know I had in me. I also owe much to my first-rate editor, Eric Nelson, whose brilliant guidance throughout the development of the book took it to an entirely different level. Several people provided crucial early guidance and support. As they have throughout my life, Cynthia Ballard and the late Wilson Ballard guided me to do better than I ever thought I could. Let me thank Alice Mayhew and Hannah Pakula for reading my embarrassing first drafts and yet still encouraging me to continue. Arthur Schlesinger Jr. and David Callahan helped convince me I could actually write a book more than they will ever know. I am especially indebted to Charlie Euchner, who taught me how to tell a story and write a book. James Steinberg offered instrumental new conceptual ideas and gave generously of his time and wise counsel.

Writing this book while balancing a full-time job with the International Crisis Group (ICG) was a challenge and required great indulgence by and support from ICG, in particular its president, Gareth Evans, and my colleagues. For their support throughout this process I am forever grateful. They include: Samina Ahmed, Suliman Baldo, Deepti Choubey, Carole Corcoran, Amitabh Desai (and Ingrid Alvarez), Stephen Ellis, Nick Grono, Amy Hunter, Jahn Jeffrey, Robert Malley, Tim Moriarty, Vikram Parekh, John Prendergast, Connie Robinson, Catherine Sanger, Robert Templer, Stephen Townley, Nicholas Whyte, and Mariyan Zumbulev.

I was also blessed with a string of dedicated, smart, hardworking—and fun—researchers, including: Alex Barker, Eric Bartz, Lesley Bourns,

Courtenay Dunn, Barbara Feinstein, Jennifer Gregoire, Richard Hazelwood, Natasha Kindergan, Francesco Mancini, Aaron Niedermayer, Angela Stene, Radha Vij, and Christian Westra. I am also indebted to three very talented writers who helped me at key stages, Heather Hurlburt, Ivan Ikman, and Frederik Wesslau. Without them, this book would simply not exist. I am also especially grateful to those who answered my call for emergency help toward the end, as well as to Jennifer, Ami, Radha, and most of all Kate for rising to the challenge way beyond the call of duty.

Many friends and colleagues took the time to read and comment on the book, edit various sections, and provide me guidance that gave the book more depth than I could have ever produced on my own. I am enormously grateful to each of them: Steve Andreasen, Commander Steve Brock, Simon Chesterman, Captain James R. Craig, Steve Croskrey, Steven Donziger, Tom Duffy, Susan Falvella-Garraty, NYPD Captain Frank Dwyer, Larry Garber, Andrew Hillman, Anthony Lake, Bill Lynn, Sean McCormick, Cobb Mixter, Steve Naplan, Conor O'Clery, Dan Poreman, Jeff Ratner, Michael Riordan, Charity Robey, Gary Saymore, Gayle Smith, Steve Solarz, Stephen Townley, Peter Vrooman, Kael Weston, and Richard Wilcox.

As a former senior government official, I am constrained by what I can talk about. Walking that line was made easy with the exquisite guidance and patience of the White House's National Security Staff's Records Management Team, including William Leary, Rod Soubers, and Mike Smith. They painstakingly reviewed for clearance successive drafts of the ever-changing manuscript. Over the last four years, I have imposed far too many demands on the staff of the National Archives, who generously lent me their time, offices, and guidance as I went through my notes from my time at the National Security Council. I want to thank Nancy Smith, Kate Dillon McClure, Beth Fidler, John Laster, and Doug Thurman for their extraordinary support.

My family provided me a constant source of support throughout the process, reading various drafts and offering frank comments only one's family can say. My parents Lars and Nancy Soderberg, my sister Sigrid Pinsky, and my brothers Lars and John Soderberg are all very much a part of this book. I would not be in public service if not for their values of right and wrong and for their enthusiastic participation in my life in politics and government. I am especially grateful to Jake and Elizabeth Bistrong for their indulgence of my taking over their playroom over the last year and in helping me with ideas and research for the book.

And, to Richard—for everything. I could never have done it without you.

Introduction

We are the children of your sacrifice.

—President William Jefferson Clinton speaking to the veterans of World War II,
Pointe du Hoc, Normandy, June 6, 1994

The helicopters took off from the USS *George Washington* carrier and flew toward the famous Pointe du Hoc, which loom over the beaches of Normandy. President Bill Clinton, congressional veterans, and other VIPs were heading to the commemoration ceremony of the fiftieth anniversary of D-Day. Clinton had just finished a ceremony in the carrier's hanger bay honoring the navy's role in the invasion of Normandy. He had thrown a wreath into the sea as the *Navy Hymn* played. A twenty-one-gun salute was followed by taps. Jets flew overhead, one soaring off alone in the "missing man" formation. As the third-ranking official of the National Security Council at the White House, I had been invited to join the presidential party to assist with any foreign policy issues that might arise during the trip.

I looked out the helicopter's small window. There, emerging from the morning mist, were the cliffs that American and allied soldiers had climbed to save Europe exactly fifty years before. As we flew over the foaming sea, I tried to imagine the fear that they must have felt, and the courage they demonstrated, as they took this same route on June 6, 1944, the turning point in World War II. My generation—the sons and daughters of the World War II generation—had heard countless stories of American bravery that day, how wave after wave of young soldiers had waded ashore, even after seeing thousands of their buddies before them gunned down by Nazi soldiers on the cliffs above. A book most of us had read as children, *The Diary of Anne Frank*, described how Europe talked "day and night" about the invasion. We had learned in school how the Army Rangers scaled the cliffs as the soldiers above shot at them and cut their ropes. But with the "can-do" attitude that became legendary that day, the young Americans took charge and won the battle, and eventually the war.

1

The president's helicopter motorcade landed on the edge of the Normandy American Cemetery at Pointe du Hoc honoring those who had died that day, including some ninety-four hundred American soldiers. A group of Frenchmen, some dressed in their old World War II uniforms, came out to welcome us. The president walked over to address the eight thousand Normandy veterans who had returned to the battle site for the anniversary. In one of the most moving speeches of his presidency, Clinton told the story of how the soldiers had gone "onto the beaches below and up these unforgiving cliffs."

"Bullets and grenades came down upon them, but by a few minutes after seven, here, exactly here, the first Rangers stood," Clinton said. "Today let us ask those American heroes to stand again." I watched as the veterans, slowly, one after another, stood. Almost all were over seventy years of age—some in wheelchairs, others on respirators—and they took what seemed like hours to stand. But stand they would. For this generation understood, honored, and was prepared to make the sacrifices necessary for its time. World War II was a defining challenge for the United States. The battle at Normandy defined America's role as an emerging superpower that would last the next two generations.

I listened as Clinton spoke of soldiers' individual acts of bravery, calling attention to their descendents in the audience. "We look at this terrain and we marvel at your fight. We look around us and we see what you were fighting for. For here are the daughters of Colonel Rudder. Here are the son and grandson of Corporal Bargmann. Here are the faces for which you risked your lives. Here are the generations for whom you won a war. We are the children of your sacrifice." Clinton closed with a call for action: "You completed your mission here. But the mission of freedom goes on; the battle continues. The 'longest day' is not yet over." It was one of Clinton's most poignant speeches as president. It was a reminder to all Americans of their country's great achievements, a reminder of their role as defenders of democracy around the world. Such a moment of sacrifice would not come again until September 11, 2001.

Having defeated fascism in Europe, Americans had signed up to fight the cold war. Over the next four decades, the U.S. military remained poised to defend the gains made during the great World War II campaigns fought by the veterans of that generation. Any actions abroad, be they in Africa, Latin America, or the moon, were directed through the prism of that war. The American people understood the need and sacrifices required to sustain that legacy. America engaged in the largest nation-building exercise in history—the rebuilding of the vanquished Germany and Japan—and hundreds of thousands of its soldiers remain today in those countries to keep that peace. The next generation of American soldiers deployed to contain the Soviet Union. A single guiding threat monopolized America's attention, confined the spectrum of policy options, and framed the standards for justifying the use of force and support of or opposition to governments abroad, which were viewed as pawns in their superpower struggle. All of America's might—political, economic, moral, and military—was directed to face the challenge of the Soviet Union. And it succeeded. The rival super-power collapsed in 1989.

As I surveyed the sea of aged veterans listening to the president's speech, I thought about the challenges facing the soldiers of my time. After the fall of the Berlin Wall, Americans believed their need for sacrifice lessened and expected to reap the benefits of peace. When Bill Clinton took the oath of office on January 20, 1993, America was uncertain of its role in the world. The United States, suddenly the lone superpower, was adrift on how to face the new era of risk, challenge, and opportunity. In this new world, challenges were increasingly unconventional conflicts within the borders of states, rather than the bipolar interstate strife of the post–World War II era. They often occurred in areas considered beyond the sphere of U.S. interest, places such as Haiti, Bosnia, Somalia, and Rwanda. The post-Vietnam generation was reluctant to engage in such "minor" conflicts around the globe. The United States was not prepared to use force in conflicts that appeared similar to Vietnam, outside what America saw as its "strategic" area of interest.

These conflicts and the growing transnational threats, such as weapons proliferation and terrorism, demanded new responses—but most Americans did not yet understand the gravity of these new threats. The challenge required new forms of cooperation, new alliances, and new goals that took years to develop. The Clinton administration, to solve the dilemmas that greeted it, had to develop a new understanding of the potential possibilities and limits of military force. As the children of the sacrifice of Normandy, the new pres-ident and his team knew their task was to realign a superpower.

During his eight years in office, President Clinton did just that. He devel-oped a policy of U.S. engagement that largely met the challenges of his time and charted a reasoned course for America to meet the challenges of the twenty-first century. The key question in American foreign policy concerned how, and whether, to engage in these new conflicts. In redefining America's role, Clinton had to reject two myths about that role: isolationism and the world policeman. Having won the cold war, many Americans felt they could safely withdraw from the world. Others felt that America's preponderance of power made the world's problems America's responsibility.

Clinton faced stiff opposition in developing a foreign policy that did not fall victim to these myths. When the Republicans gained power in the House of Representatives in 1994, the isolationists gained the power of the purse and used it to curtail Clinton's efforts to manage conflicts, engage in peacekeeping, and support multilateral efforts, including arms control and protecting the environment. Clinton also had to overcome the world police-

man myth of America's omnipotence, omniscience, and thus omniresponsibility. Because America had unparalleled military, economic, and moral
power, Clinton faced the expectation that he would engage in and even
solve the world's conflicts, not just in the more recent crises in Haiti, the
Balkans, and the myriad of conflicts in Africa, but also in long-festering
problems such as North Korea, Cyprus, India and Pakistan, and the Middle
East. Yet, the superpower was far from able—or willing—to engage everywhere. Defining where and how to engage was an essential challenge of
Clinton's presidency.

World War II remained the gold standard for the use of force. Little
support existed—in Congress, in the administration, in the military, and
among the American people—for the deployment of U.S. troops into the
new world disorder. Facing these political restraints, Clinton sought to
engage diplomatically in various conflicts, while reserving the use of force
for areas of clear strategic interest, such as Iraq, Korea, and defending
Europe. Thus, his early initiatives and successes were limited to those in
which mediation could achieve progress, such as in Northern Ireland and
the Israeli-Palestinian conflict. Those nonstrategic areas that required the
use of force were deferred, or remained failures.

Early in Clinton's presidency, the process of exploring alternatives to
force made the administration appear weak and indecisive. However, the
crises in Somalia, Haiti, and Bosnia provided the crucible from which the
administration developed a more forceful and mature strategy that would
endure. The loss of eighteen rangers in Somalia in late 1993 was Clinton's
"Bay of Pigs." The tragedy shocked him into following his instinctual leadership, challenging traditional foreign policy paradigms, and forging a bold
approach of force and diplomacy that was to mark his administration, first
in Haiti and eventually in the Balkans.

In challenging the two myths of the superpower prevalent during his
presidency, the myth of isolationism and the myth of world policeman,
Clinton pursued new forms of engagement, using force prudently and diplomacy effectively to promote stability, democracy, and respect for human
rights in parts of the world previously considered beyond U.S. strategic interests. He defined a new kind of foreign policy by taking initiatives in areas,
primarily the Balkans, requiring diplomacy backed by force and coupled with
the use of peacekeeping and nation-building, which became the harbinger
of the 1990s. Clinton combined the idealist and realist facets of his public
philosophy to create a moral, assertive, and reliable strategy of engagement
to meet the challenges presented by failing states no longer propped up by
cold war alliances. Realigning the superpower to meet these new and unpre-
dictable threats will prove to be one of Clinton's lasting legacies.

Over the course of his eight years in office, Clinton developed a new
national willingness to use force to confront brutality and violence in areas

now deemed in America's interest. Thus, the country would continue to act in Europe, the Middle East, and North Korea, but it would also engage selectively in promoting democracy and freedom and developing international support for combating the emerging threats of infectious diseases, drugs, environmental degradation, weapons of mass destruction, and terrorism. Clinton acted in concert with America's friends and allies around the world so that they, too, would share in the burdens of engagement. American diplomacy developed a new momentum to promote democracy and freedom, but with the United Nations and troops from around the world to help shoulder the burden. By 2000, the United States was accepted by most nations as working for, and an indispensable leader in, the search for progress.

President George W. Bush came to office challenging the very core of Clinton's engagement, seeking to reduce American engagement in the search for peace in the world's conflicts and with international bodies and norms. During his 2000 campaign for the White House and his first nine months in office, Bush's foreign policy advisors struggled to press their divergent views on the new president. On one side were the realists who sought to continue the first president George H. Bush's overall moderate, less ambitious approach to foreign policy. On the other side were the hegemons, largely from the Reagan era, who promoted today's dangerous myth that, as the lone superpower, America could—and therefore it should—use its military strength to force the world to bend to its wishes and counter the emergence of any rival to its power. Bush soon fell victim to the hegemon's myth.

The cold war had constrained the hegemons in the 1980s. In the early 1990s, the first president Bush largely ignored them and dismissed their arguments as fringe. During the first nine months of the second Bush administration, there was open warfare between the two camps of realists and hegemons. The result was confusion over the foreign policy of the United States, especially toward the great powers, Russia and China, as well as the Middle East and North Korea, and confrontation with allies over U.S. engagement with international norms that had been developed over the last fifty years.

The murder on September 11, 2001, of three thousand Americans in New York, Washington, D.C., and on the flight downed in Pennsylvania thrust the use of force to the forefront of American foreign policy. The United States suddenly was vulnerable, a target for its wealth, culture, and overwhelming military strength. As had the World War II veterans on the beaches of Normandy, the American people joined together to defend their freedoms after the attacks of September 11. They answered the call to duty to protect the country from additional terrorist attacks. Like World War II and the cold war, September 11 will define America's interests and actions in the decades ahead.

At first, the world stood by the United States. The North Atlantic Treaty Organization (NATO) for the first time invoked Article V of its charter, stating that the attacks on the United States constituted an attack on all members. The UN passed a sweeping antiterrorism resolution mandating an end to support for terrorists across the globe. A strong international coalition supported the overthrow of the Taliban in Afghanistan after its leaders refused to hand over Osama bin Laden. Evoking President John F. Kennedy's famous words at the Berlin Wall, the world declared "we are all Americans now."

Bush's first actions following September 11, 2001, involved an international approach, gaining strong support from other countries for invading Afghanistan and for rebuilding the peace. Following the overthrow of the Taliban, the United States had a choice. It could decide to continue to rally the support of the world in meeting the post–September 11 challenge of terrorism, while mindful of America's many other interests and responsibilities; or it could chose the path of seeking American hegemony in which the United States attempted to meet these challenges largely on its own, with coalitions of like-minded countries, rather than working with alliances and international bodies and norms, agreeing to the compromises as a necessary but manageable cost. Force would be a resort of first use, not last; diplomacy a matter of convenience, not necessity.

The realistic, internationalist approach advocated by Secretary of State Colin Powell and others lost out to the hegemons' approach soon after September 11. The president's decision to go to war against Iraq despite the lack of any imminent threat and the opposition of most of the rest of the world will prove to be the test of the validity of the hegemons' view of America's role as a superpower. Putting aside the failure to find weapons of mass destruction and the failure to achieve their other goals of the war, such as democratizing the Arab world and promoting a lasting settlement of the Arab-Israeli conflict, the war against Iraq tests the belief that America does not need allies or the United Nations to meet today's challenges.

The Bush administration's chief hegemons—Richard B. Cheney, Paul Wolfowitz, and Richard N. Perle—were born of the Reagan administration, while Donald H. Rumsfeld harkens back to the Ford era. In the 1970s and 1980s, these men all shared the belief that American military might and unilateral decision making could protect American interests far more effectively than seeking to lead America's allies in shaping norms, treaties, and constraints on the international community, and therefore America as well. Until September 11, they had never had a chance to test their theories.

In many ways, the administration of President George W. Bush is an unrestrained continuation not of his father's administration but that of Ronald W. Reagan. The similarities are striking beyond a recycling of the personalities. Each came to office with a conviction that the previous

Democratic administration had led the country astray from the real national interest. Pragmatism would be replaced with clarity of vision, moral purpose, and dogged consistency of purpose. In rhetoric and diplomacy, each saw the world in terms of black and white, good and evil. Both administrations had little regard for the views of America's allies in pursuit of their goals. Both presidents presided over enormous increases in military spending which, coupled with tax cuts, drove the nation deeply into debt and high unemployment.

While the invasion of Iraq is the most vivid example of the hegemon's myth, myriad actions have put America on a course of collision with much of the rest of the world. Al Qaeda is regenerating and poses a continuing threat to Americans. North Korea may now be capable of producing as many as eight nuclear weapons, yet U.S. policy remains adrift. The Iranian nuclear threat is increasing, but U.S. policy lacks the support of key U.S. allies. International norms and treaties are frayed and America's alliances are weakened.

The approach has put America at risk. Today's threats are global and will only be met through strong, unified, international action. With its $10 trillion economy, $1 trillion worth of exports, armed forces of nearly 1.4 million, a $410 billion defense budget, consistent Nobel Prize winnings, and omnipresent culture across the globe, America certainly can survive on its own. The question, rather, is at what cost? Is there a more responsible way for America to protect its interests abroad? Should we continue Bush's essentially unilateral hegemonic approach or return to a tougher policy of engagement that will galvanize other nations to follow? Which course will inspire today's children to honor the sacrifices made not only on the beaches in Normandy but also on September 11?

This book is not a memoir; instead, it provides an account of America's recent foreign policy, told from my standpoint as a 1992 Clinton campaign aide, a National Security Council official at the White House from 1993 to 1996, an ambassador to the United Nations from 1997 to 2001, and, currently, as a foreign policy advocate for the nonprofit International Crisis Group. The book brings the reader behind the scenes, using recently declassified personal notes and other documents and first-hand interviews at the most senior levels of government. To date, no insider of the Clinton White House has discussed the broad challenges involving the use of force and diplomacy faced by his administration. Thus, the book provides insight into the decision-making process all presidents face, a process that can be ad hoc, disorganized, and certainly based on less than full information. Often, decisions involve having to choose among options that are all unappealing. In addition, while presidents rarely make foreign policy decisions for reasons of political expediency, they are always constrained by whether the American public and thus the Congress support these decisions. Hence, the reader must be conscious of the American public's view of foreign policy and how it impacts a president's decision.

Certainly, there are many others who contributed in far more signifi-cant ways to President Clinton's foreign policy than I did. But only a few were privileged to work closely with him and his team from 1992 to 2001. I was a rare witness to, and at times a participant in, the high-level challenge of charting a new course for American foreign policy. This book attempts to challenge the all-too-common view of Clinton's foreign policy written primarily by outsiders who have failed to appreciate the foreign policy sub-tleties, challenges, and accomplishments of America's forty-second presi-dent. It will also present the challenges faced by President George W. Bush. In analyzing America's forty-third president, the book places his actions in the context of the lessons that have been learned since the end of the cold war and the attacks of September 11, 2001. These lessons provide an endur-ing guidepost to the challenges faced by America in 2005 and to President Bush as he begins his second term.

This book aims to be a testament to the importance of getting right America's leadership role and responsibility in the world. While September 11 demonstrated America's vulnerability, it may also galvanize the public to support a deeper engagement with the rest of the world that will not only make America safer but also help future leaders meet the many challenges of the twenty-first century, a world far more complex than at any time in human history. Although we know the legacy of those who died in Normandy, perhaps the legacy of those who died in the World Trade Center, the Pentagon, and aboard the plane that crashed in Pennsylvania will be America's firm commitment to engage and lead in today's world with, as Clinton called for in 2004, "wisdom as well as strength." Such a course will require visionary leadership by the president of the United States at home and abroad. It also requires a well-balanced use of America's vast economic, political, moral, and military resources to lead our friends and persuade our enemies to follow the United States in meeting the challenge of enhancing security, democracy, and prosperity.

1

Things Fall Apart

Things fall apart; the centre cannot hold;
Mere anarchy is loosed upon the world,
The blood-dimmed tide is loosed, and everywhere
The ceremony of innocence is drowned.

—W. B. Yeats, "The Second Coming"

It was March 13, 1993. The principals—the cabinet-level officials responsible for national security policy—gathered in the Situation Room on the
ground floor of the West Wing. Having grown up with the movie *Dr.
Strangelove*, I assumed the Situation Room would be a large hall covered
with maps, high-tech gadgets, and phone lines connected not only to the
Russians but to other key world leaders as well. In fact, the room is small
and unassuming, large enough for a rectangular shiny wooden table that
seats about ten people comfortably and another twenty chairs along the
wood-paneled walls. The table has one chair taller than the rest, in theory
reserved for the president but most often used by the chair of the meeting,
usually the national security advisor. The Cabinet Room is the only other
room with a taller chair reserved for the president—one of the few vestiges
of British royal tradition.

This particular principals' meeting turned out to be one of the most
memorable—and, at over four hours, one of the longest—of my time at the
White House. Three of the many issues discussed, the Middle East, Haiti,
and Bosnia, required decisions on difficult questions, especially whether and
how to use ground troops. As the third-ranking official at the National
Security Council, my job was to help manage the foreign policy agenda.
First as staff director, then as deputy assistant to the president, I sat in
on most of the National Security Council (NSC) meetings throughout
Clinton's first term, and then regularly from my position at the United
Nations for the second term.

That day, Clinton, who had been president less than two months, made his first decision to deploy troops—to the Golan Heights, should there be a peace agreement between Israel and Syria. The group discussed the continued threat of Saddam Hussein and briefly discussed but rejected the use of force to return Haitian President Jean Bertrand Aristide to power. For the first time, the group grappled with inserting U.S. ground troops into Bosnia, in this case following an agreement among the parties. In addition, the principals had their first discussion about the use of force to bring about compliance by President Slobodan Milosevic of the former Yugoslav Republic, with the demands of the international community. The meeting began the process that would eventually lead to the use of force to back up American diplomacy more than two years later. It would also begin to develop a new foreign policy for America as the lone superpower, one that deployed not only America's vast, unrivaled military power but also its economic, diplomatic, and even moral strength.

The discussion set up a personal and policy dynamic that was to last through each of the participant's tenure in the administration. National Security Advisor Anthony (Tony) Lake tried to keep the conversation moving toward a conclusion. His *very* subtle humor offered comic relief to those sophisticated enough to get his jokes. Secretary of Defense Les Aspin raised repeated questions about the advisability of drawing the military into messy situations. His bombastic manner and failure to always be fully up on his brief alienated his colleagues and many at the Pentagon. He would often, however, be the first to ask the tough questions. For instance, that day he asked the key question, "Is the United States prepared to go to war in the Balkans?"

Chairman of the joint Chiefs of Staff Colin Powell threw cold water on plans to involve the United States in the Balkans or any other "nonstrategic" situation, opposing the use of air power to achieve political aims and, at times, holding back key bits of information. The CIA Director James Woolsey offered "doom and gloom" scenarios that often failed to take into consideration key nuances. Ambassador to the United Nations Madeleine Albright repeatedly pushed for more robust uses of force. Leon Fuerth, the vice president's national security advisor, would raise seemingly arcane points but, after navigating a very circuitous route, laid down important issues for consideration and pushed, with Albright, for the use of force to back up diplomacy. Deputy National Security Advisor Samuel (Sandy) Berger was always good for a bit of needed humor and for reminding his colleagues of the overall objectives of the president. While the principals did not realize it at the time, the discussion on whether to offer U.S. troops to support a Middle East peace agreement would prove to be the easiest discussion regarding that deployment.

If I were Israeli, I'd make damn certain there were Americans up there

Sitting to Lake's right, Secretary of State Warren (Chris) Christopher brought the group up to date on his negotiations in the Middle East. The United States had long played a leading role in trying to forge peace agreements between Israel and its neighbors. In 1979, then president Jimmy Carter had brought Israeli prime minister Menachem Begin and Egyptian president Anwar Sadat together at Camp David. Yet, progress had eluded both presidents Reagan and Bush.

Christopher saw new opportunities for peace on two tracks: between Israel and the Palestinians and between Israel and Syria. Reserved, courteous, disciplined, and a little stiff, Christopher always dressed in a suit and tie. Passed over for secretary of state by Carter, Christopher had kept the post in his crosshairs for twelve years. I barely knew him as he had played virtually no role in foreign policy during Clinton's campaign. To my surprise, during the transition Clinton asked him to be secretary of state.

Building on his predecessor's policy, Christopher had been working to get an interim agreement between the Palestinians and Israelis that would give the Palestinians some form of increased self-rule and would mandate an incremental withdrawal of Israeli troops from the occupied territories. It now looked as though progress were possible. On the peace process with Syria, the Israelis were showing new flexibility and appeared willing to consider returning the Golan Heights, taken in the 1967 war. That meant the possibility of peace between Israel and Syria.

Christopher explained that Israeli Prime Minister Yitzak Rabin was prepared to take "significant steps" before April 28 that might help induce the other Arabs to come around. The Israelis were looking at Palestinian elections to "choose someone there and give some legitimacy," as well as land "usage and management, but not sovereignty during the interim stages." As negotiations went forward, there could be some improvement in human rights conditions. Christopher also said Rabin had put dual citizenship on the table. While the proposal needed to be further developed, Christopher described it as "very encouraging."[1]

Those in the room nodded in agreement. "The two main tracks are mutually reinforcing," said Lake, referring to the Syrian and Palestinian tracks. He then asked about the politically sensitive issue of the status of the Palestine Liberation Organization (PLO), which in 1993 remained on the U.S. list of terrorist organizations. "I don't envision dealing with the PLO," replied Christopher. "They know what they have to do. The Brits and the Belgians have started negotiations with the PLO. . . . I wouldn't close the door forever. If we could find a way to deal with them, it would be simpler.

But we can't do so until it is OK with the Israelis." Little did he know that in six months—to the day—PLO Chairman Yasir Arafat would walk into the White House.

On the Syrian track, Christopher was continuing discussions regarding peace between Israel and Syria in exchange for a full Israeli withdrawal from the Golan Heights. Christopher explained cautiously that he thought there was a chance to get Syrian president Bashir al-Assad to agree to peace with Israel "in exchange for a full Israeli withdrawal from the Golan." Christopher laid out the U.S. approach, "full withdrawal for full peace." He was seeking an umbrella agreement that would set out these guidelines, followed by sequential steps to achieve the peace. But there was a catch, noted Christopher. "Assad understands the apex of full withdrawal for full peace. Therefore, it is necessary to tell him we're prepared to guarantee security through the UN—where the United States will play a major role for providing security on the Golan Heights. The *sine qua non* is a U.S. general in charge." That meant thousands of U.S. troops on the Israeli-Syrian border. Christopher wanted the authority to make Assad just such an offer.

President Clinton and Vice President Gore had joined the group to discuss the deployment of U.S. troops in the Golan. Listening carefully to Christopher's explanation, both Clinton and Gore agreed that Christopher should make the offer to Assad. Clinton was concerned about the congressional reaction, knowing how little support existed for the deployment of U.S. troops abroad. "If I tell him [Assad] I'll enforce security on the Golan Heights," Clinton asked the group, "do I need to have talked to Congress?" The principals decided they did not have to inform Congress further, as the Hill had already been briefed on letters of assurance on border security "according to U.S. Constitutional practices." While perhaps a stretch, no one wanted to risk a leak on an issue of this magnitude. A nasty debate in Congress over the deployment of troops to the Golan could have scuttled the deal.

Describing Rabin as a "flinty, taciturn man," Christopher said that Rabin really wanted "answers, especially regarding security arrangements on the Golan." Clinton also understood the troops had to be "real combat troops, not blue helmets," referring to UN peacekeepers. "If I were Israeli, I'd make damn certain there were Americans up there."

Offering to put U.S. troops on the Golan to guarantee security on the border between Israel and Syria was the first decision Clinton made to deploy troops abroad. It was the simplest decision he would face regarding U.S. troops—and also one that would not be implemented, as Assad ultimately never made the deal. There was no disagreement on the benefits to the United States of an Syrian-Israeli peace, long considered a strategic U.S. goal. No one winced when Powell later came back with an estimate of a U.S. battalion[2] in the Golan for twelve years at the cost of "a couple of million" a year. The president's response to Powell's estimate was, "I think it is worth it."

The use of American troops to help implement peace in the Middle East was far less controversial than whether to deploy troops in the nonstrategic areas in conflict in 1993. These tougher decisions, ones that, unlike Syria, would ultimately be implemented, involved the use of force to back up American diplomacy in what *New York Times* columnist Leslie Gelb termed "teacup wars," those areas deemed during the cold war as not worthy of U.S. involvement, such as Somalia, Haiti, and Bosnia. Yet, as a superpower now free from the burden of containing the Soviet Union, the United States was increasingly called upon to *do something* to stem these conflicts. Clinton understood the need for U.S. leadership in such crises and during the campaign had challenged President George H. W. Bush to restore democracy to Haiti and end the war in the Balkans. He now struggled to find a way to do so as the new president.

Not your father's Democrat

In developing his foreign policy positions, Clinton had to redefine not only America's role in the post–cold war era but also Democratic foreign policy after nearly a quarter century of Republican presidents. The only hiatus had been Jimmy Carter's four-year presidency that, in foreign policy, was largely remembered for the success of the Camp David peace accords, but also for a perceived weakness because the Soviets had in 1979 invaded Afghanistan on his watch and because of his unsuccessful efforts to free the American hostages in Iran. The Democratic Party was perceived as weak on defense and unwilling to use force. On the other hand, Nixon's recognition of China, Reagan's increase in defense spending, tough Central American anti-communist policies, and invasion of Grenada created an image of toughness, and President George H. W. Bush's 1989 invasion of Panama and 1991 ouster of Iraqi forces from Kuwait, together with the recent collapse of the Soviet Union, had all helped to shape the image of a successful Republican foreign policy. In fact, Republicans seemed invincible.

During the campaign, Clinton trailed President Bush 15 percent to 63 percent in perceived ability to conduct foreign policy.[3] Clinton sought to neutralize that deficit by taking many centrist positions, not only because he believed them appropriate but also because he hoped to win back the so-called Reagan Democrats who had abandoned the Democratic Party for more than a decade. Clinton called for "the world's strongest defense, ready and willing to use force, when necessary." Recognizing the concern of conservatives that the United States not overextend its forces, he advocated the selective use of U.S. influence, saying that "America's challenge in this era is not to bear every burden, but to tip the balance." Although he did propose modest cuts in defense spending to "plow those savings back into jobs right here at home," Clinton endorsed force modernization and increased support for soldiers and their families. He supported many of Bush's positions such as aid to the former Soviet Union, engagement in the Middle East peace process, and arms sales to Saudi Arabia.[4]

Clinton aggressively and successfully challenged the Republican foreign policy on a range of issues, especially its failure to adapt to the new international relations wrought by the end of the cold war. He likened the Republican claim of having won the cold war to the "rooster taking credit for the dawn." He pressed for "an America that will never coddle tyrants, from Baghdad to Beijing, an America that champions the cause of freedom and democracy, from Eastern Europe to Southern Africa, and in our own hemisphere in Haiti and Cuba." On Haiti, he had pledged to reverse Bush's policy of returning Haitian refugees and to work for the restoration of the deposed President Aristide. On Bosnia, he had challenged his predecessor's unwillingness to use America's economic and military strength to pressure the Serbs to end their aggression against the Muslim population. Both positions would take years to implement—and although we did not yet realize it—U.S. ground troops. First, the new team had to find its footing.

The team

Clinton's foreign policy team drew largely from the ranks of Carter's team— the only Democratic president since 1968. Thus, the newly appointed officials had been out of power, and in many cases out of Washington, for twelve years. They were not attuned to the rigors of the new twenty-four-hour news cycle or the harsh partisan politics that pervaded the Congress. The team had the right instincts but faced a steep learning curve in the new ways of Washington. Most importantly, they faced the daunting task of charting a new American foreign policy in the post–cold war era.

The ultimate reserved Protestant New Englander, Tony Lake brought to the campaign an intense intellectual rigor and a centrist approach to the use of force, which was appreciated by Clinton. Slight of build, with wispy graying brown hair, and large academic glasses, Lake was a well-liked and respected professor of international affairs at Mount Holyoke College in Massachusetts. A self-described neo-Wilsonian, Lake believed that the United States should use its moral, military, economic, and political strength to engage and promote a more just, stable world. As a young Foreign Service officer, Lake had requested to go to Vietnam. He rose quickly through the ranks and served as head of Policy Planning at the State Department under Carter. Lake had been given the plum task of serving as Henry Kissinger's special assistant in the early 1970s but had resigned over the Cambodian invasion and other issues. Kissinger subsequently tapped his phone. Lake's slightly stern way put off some people, yet his intellect and loyalty to his staff and colleagues earned him respect and support.

Having met Clinton two decades earlier, Sandy Berger was one of his closest advisors during the campaign and throughout their eight years at the White House, first as deputy national security advisor and, in the second term as national security advisor. A New Yorker with a quick wit, Berger had a strong sense of the political realities of foreign policy. Berger shared Lake's belief in the need for U.S. engagement abroad, a strong U.S. military, and support for human rights. He and Lake complemented each other well, as Berger brought a less academic and more political approach to the table. A Washington trade lawyer, Berger had served as Lake's deputy at policy planning in the Carter State Department and had been a speechwriter for George McGovern during his 1972 presidential campaign. During that campaign Berger met Clinton, and the two had kept in touch over the years. It was Berger who asked his friend Lake to join the campaign.

I joined the Clinton campaign with a decade of experience in foreign affairs, including the Walter Mondale and Michael Dukakis presidential campaigns and six years as a Congressional staffer. I had studied for a graduate degree in international relations at Georgetown University, where I met Professor Madeleine Albright, who would become the Clinton administration's ambassador to the United Nations and the first woman to serve as secretary of state. A refugee from the former Czechoslovakia, Albright was the hawk of the administration, always pressing for stronger U.S. action against repression, especially in Europe. Albright helped me get an internship on Mondale's 1984 campaign. I started as a delegate counter in Mondale's tight battle for the nomination with Senator Gary Hart. I never left politics.

After Mondale suffered his devastating electoral loss, I joined the foreign policy staff of Senator Ted Kennedy of Massachusetts for six years, with a brief break for the Dukakis campaign in 1988. Perhaps the most influential senator in U.S. history, Kennedy was an effective leader on every key issue of the day. That's where I found a place in the "issue network" of foreign policy that gave me invaluable contacts that served as a counterweight to the bureaucracy once I got to the White House. Such activists are closer to events on the ground than are government officials. A champion of human rights causes, Kennedy and his staff had access to dissidents around the world, many of whom later came to power, including activists in the Soviet block, democracy advocates in Asia, Solidarity leaders, including Lech Walesa in Poland, the Kurds in northern Iraq, and human rights activists in Central America. He negotiated with Soviet leaders to secure the release of political prisoners and Soviet Jews and met with the world's best-known living political prisoner, Nelson Mandela, shortly after his release from prison. Thus, I had a front-row seat during much of the world's transition from dictatorship to democracy.

When I was offered the job as director of foreign policy for the campaign, Kennedy urged me to take it, proclaiming, "Clinton's going to win." I responded that he was dreaming, a hopelessly romantic Democrat. Kennedy shook his head. "I may be a romantic, but Clinton's going to win. Bush's numbers are inflated and the economy will be the issue, not the Gulf War." Kennedy said that Clinton understood the need to move the party to the center. He predicted that Clinton would co-opt the Republicans on their toughest issues—crime, health and education, and especially the economy. "Clinton's going to do it," he said. "I'm running for reelection and won't be doing much on foreign policy. Take the job." Ten months later I became the third-ranking official on the National Security Council, with an office in the West Wing.

Isn't there supposed to be a honeymoon?

By any standard, Bill Clinton's first few months in office were not good ones. Much of the problem was of his own making, certainly, but he was also right in claiming that it originated with the ambitious agenda of change—in health care, in welfare, in taxes, and in the deficit—that he and his wife sought to implement. Washington's large federal bureaucracy and the Congress did not want to change and the administration underestimated the resistance its agenda would meet. Right on substance but naive about Washington, Clinton's team was a combination of Arkansas outsiders, senior people who were out of touch with the new Washington, and eager thirtysomethings who brought the passion of the campaign to the halls of government but not the experience of governing. The clash of agendas was combustible.

The first hundred days of a presidency are supposed to include a long honeymoon during which Congress supports the new president as he assembles his team, lays down a broad agenda, and begins to set in motion his own priorities. Yet, in President Clinton's case, the honeymoon evaporated within weeks of his taking office. Two of his nominees for attorney general were embroiled in scandal and withdrew, and he was forced to drop the middle-class tax cut. White House meetings went on for hours, and the president was always running late. He seemed to have abandoned his foreign policy campaign positions on everything from Bosnia, to Haiti, to Northern Ireland. Clinton's campaign promise to lift the Pentagon's ban on gays in the military exploded in the press, in Congress, and in the Pentagon. The controversy eroded much of the goodwill of the honeymoon and severely damaged Clinton's early relations with the Pentagon. In contrast to most presidents, who enjoy approval ratings of over 50 percent during their first four months in office,[5] Clinton's overall job approval rating dropped 10 percent from April to May, from 55 to 45 percent. On foreign policy, it plummeted from 63 percent in February to only 38 percent in June.[6]

There was trouble on many fronts. Congressional Democrats and Republicans were building a coalition to block the passage of the North American Free Trade Agreement (NAFTA). A resurgent old-guard communist network increasingly threatened Clinton's budding ally, Russian president Boris Yeltsin. In Iraq, president Saddam Hussein was again making worrisome moves against Kuwait. Only on the Arab-Israeli conflict were things looking up, with renewed hope for progress on both the Palestinian and Syrian tracks. It didn't help matters that Clinton's political advisors were telling the press that Clinton was only paying sporadic attention to foreign policy and that he had conceded that his campaign positions had been "naive." Clinton's younger, more media-savvy domestic advisors wanted to keep the focus on the economy and paid little attention to foreign policy. The administration thus failed to lay the groundwork with the press and Congress that it would take time—and a lot of work—to implement the new agenda.

What we encountered in January 1993 was a changed world. The new team was slow to realize that implementing a new agenda in foreign policy would require rewriting the fifty-year-old rules of the game. Struggling with the dueling forces of isolationism and pressures to be the world's policeman, Clinton tried in his first two years to define America's proper role as the lone superpower. Conflicts that for years and even decades had been suppressed by superpower standoffs could no longer be ignored. Humanitarian catastrophes that might previously have failed to garner much attention now made the nightly news. With satellites, cheap airfares, the Internet and the global financial market, events in Colombia, Rwanda, or Cambodia were no longer so far away.

The 1991 Gulf War had changed Americans' perception of war as no longer requiring significant casualties. But it had not increased public or Congressional enthusiasm for the United States serving as the world's policeman. Nor had it entirely erased the legacy of Vietnam from U.S. thinking about the use of force. Yet, the victory of our troops in Iraq in 1991, and even more importantly, the resurgence of our institutions and values across formerly communist Eastern Europe, raised global expectations that we would police the world.

The new team in the White House was slow to realize that, behind public expectations of a peace dividend and global calls for U.S. leadership, behind the isolationists' eagerness to declare victory and come home, and the hegemons' desire to continue the old fight, lay a need to rewrite the rules on the use of force and diplomacy. Gone were the overwhelming threats of the Soviet Union and communism, Adolf Hitler and fascism. The Gulf War had been won. Calls increased for America to engage in the myriad new post–cold war conflicts emerging, particularly in the Balkans. Yet, Americans saw no reason for, and certainly didn't support, going to battle over the "teacup" wars. Yet, because America had the power to intervene in such conflicts, much of the world looked to the remaining superpower for leadership and for such intervention. In this new era, the new president would have to expand the arena in which he would contemplate the use of force. It would also take time and a strong public campaign to win the support of an isolationist Congress and a skeptical American public.

In his early years as president, Clinton seemed paralyzed, unable to realize his high-minded rhetoric. Meanwhile in Bosnia, the UN–led efforts seemed only to be rewarding Serb aggression, rather than protecting the rights of the besieged Muslims. The Yugoslav leader Milosevic was on a rampage, committing the worst crimes in Europe since World War II, yet no one moved seriously to stop him. The nightly news showed horrific pictures of Bosnian women and children running for cover in "Snipers' Alley" in Sarajevo as Serbs picked them off like rabbits.

Clinton had been forced to reverse his campaign pledge not to return Haitian refugees when more than a hundred thousand Haitians prepared to come to the United States following his inauguration. Graphic pictures of U.S. Coast Guard ships returning wet, bedraggled Haitian refugees provided real-life images of presidential flip-flopping. The UN–led negotiations seeking the return of Aristide were failing, and Aristide remained in Washington as black America rallied to his cause.

Resolution of the Bosnia and Haiti crises would ultimately require the use of force to back up Clinton's more robust policies. While the American people and Congress disagreed at the time, Clinton understood early on that restoring democracy in Haiti and ending another war in Europe were in America's interest. Yet, in 1992, the use of force in these "nonstrategic" internal conflicts, especially the deployment of U.S. ground troops, had no support—not in Congress, not in the Pentagon, and not among the American public. Changing that attitude would prove to be Clinton's toughest foreign policy challenge during his first two years.

Yes, Minister

Any new president struggles with Washington's bureaucratic behemoth to implement his foreign policy and to realize his campaign positions. Clinton's difficulties in changing long-standing policies after twelve years of Republican rule quickly became apparent. Much of policy is run on auto-pilot—because "it's always been done that way." For instance, late one night in the early days of the administration, I was sitting in my new office reviewing a routine cable meant to instruct our delegation to a UN human-rights committee in Geneva on how to vote on a resolution criticizing Indonesia's human rights violations. The only problem was that it instructed our government to support the repressive Indonesian regime, not the human rights initiative. Although it was 11 P.M., I called the NSC staff person in charge of human rights, Eric Schwartz, who had not seen the cable. It appeared that no one had thought to check whether the new administration supported Bush's policy. We changed the instructions and told our delegation to support the human rights resolution. I wondered how many other "old" policies were still being carried out without the new team's knowledge.

In other instances, we faced outright resistance from the bureaucracy. For example, the president had decided to recognize Angola, on Tony Lake's recommendation. For the prior seventeen years, Washington had supported the rebel leader, Jonas Savimbi, in his fight to topple the Marxist government, which had stayed in power with Soviet and Cuban support. With the Soviet Union gone and the Cuban troops out of Angola, the policy no longer made sense, especially after the government of Angola signed a new peace agreement with the rebels, even though Savimbi had refused to sign it. In one of the more blatant diplomatic stalling efforts, despite the president's decision to recognize Angola, the State Department steadfastly refused to do so.

Our inquiries concerning a plan to implement the president's decision were met with collective mumbles. The situation reminded me of the constant stalling of a fictitious British minister's civil servant in the comedy, *Yes, Minister*. Each time Lake inquired at the State Department as to when the diplomatic announcement of the new policy could be expected, officials would simply reply, "We are working on it, sir." Eventually, the president, tiring of the delay, simply announced the decision during a meeting on May 19 with South African antiapartheid leader Archbishop Desmond Tutu, leaving the State Department to pick up the pieces. "Today," the president said simply, "I am pleased to announce the United States' recognition of the Government of Angola. This decision reflects the high priority that our administration places on democracy."

Realigning a superpower

For two generations, American foreign policy had been defined by the balance of power between the two cold war superpowers. For the prior four generations, it had been defined by the fight to protect our allies in Europe and Asia. Conflicts fit neatly into these two frameworks or were ignored. Absent the Soviet threat, Americans saw little reason to engage abroad. Isolationism is a strong force in the United States. With the luxury of two large oceans to the east and west, and two good neighbors to the north and south, absent a direct threat, Americans prefer to keep to themselves. Overall, the pre–September 11 myth of America's invincibility persisted, fostering an alarming disinterest in what transpired overseas.

Certainly, when threatened, Americans have always risen to the challenge and fought for their interests. But it took an attack on Pearl Harbor that killed twenty-four hundred and wounded another twelve hundred Americans to generate the public support necessary for President Franklin D. Roosevelt to enter World War II. The attacks of September 11, 2001, shook the public out of its post–cold war isolationist shell and destroyed the myth that America was not vulnerable and need not engage abroad. However, in 1993, there was no such call to battle. Americans were more concerned about their jobs and mortgages than any conflict thousands of miles away. In the glow of having won the cold war, Americans felt they could rest on the assurance of the security its superpower status provided.

In addition, the perception of war was changing from one that required great sacrifice to a new immunity from the cost of war, one that did not affect most Americans' lives. While sixteen million Americans had served in the Second World War, only 468,000 soldiers had served in the first Gulf War. Nearly 300,000 Americans died in battle during World War II, compared to 148 battle deaths in the 1991 Gulf War. The ground war lasted just four days. Indeed, most Americans had watched it on television from an emotional distance and did not directly know anyone who had fought in the conflict.

Our parents and grandparents, including my own uncle and father, had jumped at their chance to fight in World War II and in Korea. The fifties generation initially volunteered to go to Vietnam, hoping for similar glory. But the new generation coming of age in the 1990s had no great enemies to fight and had understood the ultimate futility of the war in Vietnam. In the period between the end of the cold war and September 11, 2001, Americans would support only a short, relatively painless war, particularly to preserve easy access to cheap oil, or nearly cost-free interventions in Grenada and Panama, or the bombing of Libya. But they saw no reason to engage much beyond America's shores, especially with the use of ground troops. As one senior military official described the public's perspective, "If we put ourselves into operations voluntarily, or in efforts to stop war or provide humanitarian assistance in far-off lands, then casualties would be far less acceptable."[7] It took the terrorist attacks of 2001 to galvanize support for the large deployment of ground troops again. In 1993, Vietnam-style entanglements were out. Colin Powell's doctrine of overwhelming force used in the first Gulf War was in.

Yet, the world in 1993 was not that simple. The end of the cold war had brought to a head long-festering historical conflicts and created power vacuums that could not be ignored. The global technology revolution would bring with it new threats of terrorism, proliferation, and infectious disease. In 1992, Clinton and his advisors faced competing pressures. One, isolationism, argued that America was not vulnerable and need not engage. The other, that of omniresponsibility, was that the lone superpower, freed from the constraints of the cold war, could now solve all the world's conflicts, that it was omniscient and omnipotent. Yet, as Clinton said many times, the United States cannot be the world's police. Not only could it not deploy troops to solve every problem but also there was no public support for such engagement abroad. Clinton, unlike his predecessor, rejected these myths, developing a realistic foreign policy that rejected both the isolationists and calls to act everywhere.

Clinton faced strong resistance to his efforts. Officials in the Pentagon and in the Congress—as well as in much of the administration—viewed the "lesser" conflicts as someone else's problem, or not really much of a problem at all. In 1993, deploying troops into such "nonstrategic" areas as Bosnia or Haiti, particularly absent a political agreement, remained off-limits. At the time, Clinton and his team honestly thought negotiations and sanctions would restore Aristide to power in Haiti and force a change in Serbian behavior in Bosnia. The result was a failed cocktail: American diplomacy *not* backed up by force. It would be nearly two years before Clinton and his principals began to get the balance of force and diplomacy right. The superpower would finally use its full range of military, political, economic, and moral strengths to meet the new challenges.

We don't have a dog in this fight

The toughest challenge in early 1993 was how to use America's vast powers to end the war in Bosnia. Yugoslavia's president, Marshal Tito, had held the country together by promoting a brand of socialism with more freedom than its Soviet neighbors, buoyed by economic support from the West following Tito's break with Stalin. As the cold war ended, Yugoslavia disintegrated into five entities, triggering violence in all but Macedonia. Croatia, Bosnia, Slovenia, and the former Yugoslavia (Serbia and Montenegro, including Kosovo) all suffered violence. In Bosnia, the three constituent nations of the multiethnic state, including Muslims, Croats, and Serbs, failed to agree on creating an independent, unified Bosnia. The Serbs refused to take part in a referendum supporting independence and instead declared a Serb republic within Bosnia. As the fighting spread, the Serb leader, Slobodan Milosevic, sought to create ethnically pure areas by expelling and murdering the Croats and Muslims who lived there. He unleashed a brutal campaign of ethnic cleansing against Bosnia, seeking to carve out Serb-only enclaves that would join his own Serb state. Bosnia struggled to remain a multiethnic single state. The more powerful Serbs were succeeding.

At the time, the UN, U.S., and European leaders failed to grasp the need to stand up to the Serbs, believing all parties shared some of the blame for the war. The UN secretary-general Boutros Boutros-Ghali later admitted that he had felt that "no party in Bosnia was free of at least some of the blame for the cruel conflict."[8]

Clinton instinctively understood that the United States had a direct interest in ending the war in Bosnia. Allowing it to rage could ignite the ethnic and sectarian tensions that had lain dormant for the past four decades. Bosnia was not the only country threatened by war; Macedonia, Greece, Hungary, and Slovakia, all faced risks of a spillover of irredentist claims. And Clinton knew that America would be called upon to respond to those crises as well.

By 1993, the war in Bosnia was on the front pages of newspapers across the country. The Serbs, led by Milosevic, were systematically targeting ethnic Bosnian areas in an attempt to take over the country. Communities were being shelled, and civilians were being murdered, raped, and rounded up into camps reminiscent of those used by the Nazis during the Holocaust.

Clinton had inherited a weak U.S. position on the issue. President Bush, excessively confident after his victory in the Gulf, preferred to let the Europeans handle Bosnia. Bush's abdication of responsibility proved a terrible misreading of the situation and made a mockery of his so-called "vision thing." In 1991, I had asked a member of his National Security Council staff, Bob Hutchings, why the Bush administration wasn't addressing the Bosnia crisis when the situation so clearly demonstrated the need for the implementation of the New World Order that Bush had called for. He replied that the United States couldn't solve all the world's problems. "We're going to leave this one to the Europeans," he said confidently. Secretary of State James Baker's similar comment—that "we don't have a dog in this fight"—symbolized that administration's wrong-headed take on the issue.

In contrast, Clinton understood the threat to American interests posed by another war in Europe—the risk of historical tensions erupting well beyond Bosnia—and understood America's responsibility to help end the suffering. During the campaign, he had advocated tightening the sanctions against Serbia, including freezing assets and weapons sales, an oil embargo, and expelling Serbia from international organizations. He had urged that European and U.S. naval forces in the Adriatic should be given authority by the UN Security Council to stop and search ships violating the arms embargo. He had called on the international community to take steps to charge the Milosevic regime and those responsible for the slaughter of innocent civilians with crimes against humanity. He also had endorsed a no-fly zone and its enforcement, while agreeing with the Bush administration's opposition to putting ground troops into a possible "quagmire" in Bosnia. While he did not do so publicly, Clinton had long wanted to endorse lifting the arms embargo on Bosnia's Muslim population but was reluctant to do so over the opposition of the Europeans. "If we aren't going to come in and help them, then we ought to at least let them fight for themselves," he argued privately on numerous occasions.

As the situation continued to deteriorate throughout the 1992 summer, Clinton issued a carefully crafted statement that "the United States should take the lead in seeking UN Security Council authorization for air strikes against those who are attacking the relief effort. The United States should be prepared to lend appropriate military support to that operation. Air and naval forces adequate to carry out these operations should be visibly in position." Sitting in the Situation Room in March 1993, Clinton now had the chance to implement that policy. It would take a difficult period of trial and error before he developed a way to do so.

We have learned the proper lessons of history

As the principals sat around the table in March 1993, they thought a tougher negotiating strategy would succeed in ending the war. The use of force, however, remained controversial. The strongest opponent to force in Bosnia came from the Pentagon, and especially from the chairman of the joint Chiefs of Staff, Colin Powell. He, as did most of the military's leadership, saw Bosnia as a test of whether his generation had learned the lessons of Vietnam. The senior officers in the 1960s "knew the war was going badly," Powell later wrote in his 1995 memoir. "Yet they bowed to groupthink pressure and kept up pretenses. . . . Many of my generation . . . vowed that when our turn came to call the shots, we would not quietly acquiesce in half-hearted warfare for half-baked reasons that the American people could not understand or support. If we could make good on that promise to ourselves . . . then the sacrifices of Vietnam would not have been in vain."[9]

As a Gulf War hero and the most experienced member of Clinton's team, no one was in a position to challenge him. Unlike the cabinet, chairmen of the joint chiefs are appointed for a set two-year term, usually renewed once. When Clinton took office, Powell had nine months to go in his term. The president was wary of a political challenge from Powell in 1996. The first black chairman of the joint Chiefs of Staff *and* the first black national security advisor, Powell always posed difficulties for the president. A tall, handsome man who radiates power, Powell is warm, friendly, and loves a good joke. He tried hard to be a team player, but it soon became obvious his heart was not in it. As he had risen to power within Republican administrations, he could never be a full part of Clinton's team. He was always polite but often slightly condescending and at times testy with his colleagues, including the president.

News organizations were actively polling Powell against the president. One poll claimed by a three-to-one margin that Americans thought Powell would do a better job than Clinton in foreign affairs. In a race for president, Powell would beat Clinton 42 to 38.[10] As a national hero, Powell always considered himself above the fray—and it showed.

He had already made his views known publicly in the politically charged atmosphere of October 1992 in an op-ed in the *New York Times*. Normally, chairmen of the joint chiefs do not go public with their views. But Powell was different. Responding to a press story that had accused the Bush team of dithering, Powell fired off an article, declaring, "You bet I get nervous when so-called experts suggest that all we need is a little surgical bombing or a limited attack." Cautioning against deeper military involvement in Bosnia, Powell declared the military had "learned the proper lessons of history, even if some journalists have not."[11] Powell stuck to his line in the 1995 memoir: "Whenever the military had a clear set of objectives, . . . as in Panama, the Philippine coup, and Desert Storm, the result had been a success. When the nation's policy was murky or nonexistent—the Bay of Pigs, Vietnam, creating a Marine 'presence' in Lebanon—the result had been disaster. In Bosnia, we were dealing with an ethnic tangle with roots reaching back a thousand years." Powell equated the Bosnians with the North Vietnamese: "The harsh reality has been that the Serbs, Muslims, and Croatians are committed to fight to the death for what they believe to be their vital interests." "The West," he continued, "has wrung its hands over Bosnia, but has not deemed it a vital interest or matched their commitment." Powell then argued that no president could "likely sustain the long-term involvement necessary to keep the protagonists from going at each other's throats all over again at the first opportunity."[12]

It was this colossal misreading of the situation, shared by most U.S. officials in 1993, that kept the United States from acting sooner in Bosnia.

What would be the consequences to the Serbs of noncompliance?

Instead of using force to end the carnage in Bosnia, the administration sought to push the diplomatic front harder. In March 1993, there were signs that diplomacy might succeed in getting the Serbs to end their drive to take over much of Bosnia. In the Situation Room, Lake began the principals' discussion by explaining to his colleagues that forty-eight hours earlier, chances had been slim that the Serbs would sign a peace agreement in Bosnia. But now there were indications that Milosevic might be prepared to do so. The agreement called for a ceasefire within seventy-two hours, removal of the "heavy weapons" that were being used to attack civilians in Sarajevo, the opening of routes, and unimpeded UN operations.

Explaining it could be a "cynical ploy," Lake said there was "a chance there will be progress, and therefore we need to think about implementation." The United States needed to decide on whether to send troops to Bosnia to help secure the agreement. In February, the administration had stressed that the United States would send ground troops *only* in the event of a comprehensive peace settlement.[13] It now looked like that chit might be called in. Lake wanted to secure a "yes" from the principals but knew he faced strong opposition from the Pentagon—as well as from Congress and, of course, the American public. Members of Congress were insisting that having "won" the cold war, the United States should stay home. The public was also reluctant to send troops abroad.

Clinton had not expected to have to address so quickly the issue of whether to deploy U.S. troops to Bosnia in the event of a settlement. Milosevic, having apparently changed his mind about signing the proposed peace agreement during a meeting with French President Mitterrand, now indicated that he might actually sign the agreement. That posed two dilemmas for the United States. First, how would the administration know whether Milosevic's signing was anything more than a cynical ploy for him to buy time as he sought to achieve his goal—swallowing up all of Bosnia? Second, if the signing were real and could be tested, the United States would be called upon to put troops on the ground to help implement the peace. Was it willing to do so?

Secretary of Defense Les Aspin was the first to speak up. "What *exactly* are we talking about?" he asked. "If we are talking about a signing, especially a cynical one, that leaves us with an *enormous* problem," he said, hands flailing. Shirt rumpled, tie loosened, his top button undone, Aspin was the antithesis of the ship-shape military he now ran. A brilliant military expert, he knew as much about weapons systems and force levels as the generals in the room. His problem was that he alienated them with his unorthodox and sloppy management style. But on Bosnia, he shared his military colleagues' skepticism.

Aspin went on to outline the key problem, one that the United States would struggle with for the next two years: the United States had never "sorted out" whether it was "for enforcing and implementing an agreement." He pointed out that if the United States tried to implement an agreement that the Serbs had signed only as a tactical ploy to gain time, we would be in for a "*major* military undertaking." Aspin was asking the key question: was the United States prepared to go to war in the Balkans to enforce a peace? He clearly was not for that course of action, nor were the uniformed officials in the Pentagon.

No one expected Milosevic to sign an agreement for other than short-term tactical reasons. CIA director Woolsey chimed in to say that "no one believes" that if the three parties (Croats, Bosnians, and Serbs) sign, "they'll observe what they sign." As Aspin and Powell stalled on any discussion of ground troops, Lake argued in frustration, "I don't think any of us ever believed this would be a self-enforcing agreement. We are all talking about enforcing the agreement and that would require ground forces." In a reference to the "Powell Doctrine" of only using force overwhelmingly, Lake pointed out in this case we would not need two hundred thousand ground troops. "We need to take a careful look at doing it," he explained, arguing there would only be a brief window of opportunity to move to support an agreement if one were reached.

Four key issues blocked the administration from taking action: suspicion that the Serbs would never live up to their commitments, in effect a "sincerity test"; the lack of an exit strategy, which might lead to another Vietnamese-style quagmire; U.S. aversion to "ownership" of the Balkan problem; and the question of whether to use force to bring about Serb compliance. The last question was the toughest one of all.

As would be the case for the next eight years, Leon Fuerth first raised the question no one wanted to discuss: "What would be the consequences to the Serbs of noncompliance?" Madeleine Albright quickly joined in, arguing that "we should start thinking about the threat of the use of force." Otherwise, we would "weave ourselves out of the game." Powell dismissed Albright's repeated calls that we use force to back up diplomacy as naive. He later wrote in his memoir that her calls for the use of force almost gave him an aneurysm. Albright's position would ultimately prevail.

No one had yet come to terms with the need to use force to back up diplomacy. No one had an answer to Leon Fuerth's key question of whether we would force compliance, especially if the Serbs failed to end the deadly use of heavy artillery. Expressing growing frustration with the weak European position on Bosnia, Fuerth pointed out, we had to "get the allies to endorse that this time we mean business."

Powell immediately seized on Fuerth's point and wasn't about to let it pass. "What about Leon's point?" he asked, as Lake tried to bring the discussion to a close. Lake replied that Fuerth was asking how we could use the threat of air strikes or other means to encourage the parties to comply. "No," replied Powell, "I heard more. What I heard was that if any party hasn't complied, American military power will be used to force them to comply."

This was Powell's moment to live up to the promise he had made after Vietnam. This time, he would stop the quagmire before it started. He would block the limited use of force in the Balkans. Throughout his tenure as Clinton's chairman of the joint Chiefs of Staff, Powell argued repeatedly that any such action would be tantamount to going to war with Serbia. If we go that route, he argued, "We have to be prepared to go to war with Serbia. If so, let's do it. But don't use 'additional measures.' Don't fall in love with air power because it hasn't worked." To Powell, air power would not change Serb behavior, "only troops on the ground could do that."

Despite Powell's reluctance, officials in the Pentagon over the next few months did develop plans for the use of air power against Serb artillery in the event of noncompliance. The process, however, was a difficult one. "If you are asking me what kinds of forces will be needed, it all depends on whether people are serious about these kinds of issues" was a typical Powell response. The Pentagon dragged its feet in developing the military plans for Bosnia and raised numerous objections. For instance, Admiral David E. Jeremiah, vice chairman of the joint Chiefs of Staff, argued—rightly—that

U.S. troops would not "get in and out with a 'quickie' operation." Knowing the United States would need a quick insertion of troops to solidify the agreement, the Pentagon insisted that it would "take weeks, months to get a force in there."

The Pentagon's early estimates of the number of troops required to help implement an agreement involved a range of twenty thousand to forty thousand troops. Senior military leaders were quick to point out that any such deployment would require a call-up of the reserves, which would be politically unpopular, especially for a new president wanting to focus on domestic issues so early in his term. Interestingly, at this stage, Powell did not object to the command structure that was envisioned—a U.S. general on the ground reporting through the French and the Germans back to the United States.

The principals discussed using "tactical air strikes that will have an effect on the instruments of war." In other words, the strikes might be used to take out the heavy weapons of the Serbs, but not to force the Serbs to the negotiating table. "Short of war," Lake summed up the policy in that early principals' meeting in 1993. In the end, the Serbs reneged on the agreement shortly thereafter, so the urgency of making a decision on whether the United States would send troops to enforce an agreement dissipated. But the crisis did not.

Tell, don't ask

I first noticed that Clinton was beginning to challenge his own government's approach on Bosnia on May 10, 1993. I walked down the aisle of Air Force One and into the president's spacious office to give him his daily intelligence briefing. Each morning, except Sunday, Clinton received the Presidential Daily Brief (PDB), a short document prepared by the CIA on important developments around the world. Access to the document is restricted to only a very few top officials in order to keep the sensitive information from leaking. Normally, eight to ten one- to three-page memos made up the PDB. Short additional memos were often provided separately as well. I had first started taking the PDB to Clinton during the transition in Little Rock. As the NSC staff person traveling with the president that day, my job was to bring him the PDB and other foreign policy updates.

We were on our way to Cleveland where he was scheduled to give an address on the economy, and then on to Chicago where he was to talk to high school students the following day. But foreign policy was on the president's mind as he sat behind his rectangular desk on Air Force One. Funding for these planes—two identical reconfigured 747s—had been pushed through Congress by Ronald Reagan at a cost of $266 million. There was a kitchen, a senior staff room with four first-class-style chairs, a big conference room with a TV, and two types of sections in the back: one for staff with a variety of work tables and a basic business-class section for the press. In the flying Oval Office, on the wall to the president's left were two large, clumsy phones, the dial-up kind in use in the 1970s, although these had no dials. One was beige for secure calls and the other was white for open communications. Unlike commercial flights, on which one can call directly with a credit card, Air Force One phones can only be used through a tedious process involving a "signal" operator back in Washington. The president had a portable stereo on the shelf behind him, together with a variety of CDs— classical, country, and pop music. His draft speech was spread out on the desk as he rewrote it.

As I entered, he stopped working on the speech and looked up at me, his eyes flashing. I knew the look. It meant he was not happy about something. I handed him the usual review of the morning's intelligence reports, but he ignored the papers.

"I think Chris is wrong," he said. He was referring to the secretary of state and his recent failed mission to convince our European allies to support our new "lift and strike" policy, which called for lifting the arms embargo against the Bosnians and supporting air strikes if Serb attacks continued. Unwilling to put U.S. troops on the ground, Clinton and his advisors had agreed to push for the new policy as a way of tipping the balance back in favor of giving the Bosnians a fighting chance. The Christopher trip had failed. The Europeans, with troops on the ground, rejected the approach.

"He's wrong not to push just because the Europeans wouldn't go along," complained the president. This was the first time I had heard him criticize the respected Christopher. I responded that he still had the option to push for the policy. He needn't give up just because Christopher's trip had not succeeded in getting the Europeans on board.

"You mean do it unilaterally?" he asked, clearly indicating he was considering such a course. "Probably not unilaterally," I said. "But if you really push, I'd bet you can get the Europeans to go along." Clinton was tired and testy, complaining that he did not think we were moving in the right direction on the Bosnia policy. As so often was the case when Clinton did not like the policy he had adopted, he began testing new ideas, calling his friends, and mulling over a variety of other options, complaining about his poor choice of options throughout. He would talk to anyone who happened to be in the room—and today, it happened to be me.

Clinton had ample reason to be testy. Still wedded to acting in concert with Europe, the administration—and the president—had decided to dispatch Secretary Christopher to seek support for the new, more robust approach, "lift and strike." The Europeans believed the policy might undermine their diplomatic efforts and put their own troops at risk of retaliation by Serbs. The Christopher trip had furthered the image of the Clinton administration as weak and vacillating on foreign policy. But the policy's failure also galvanized Clinton.

An hour later, Clinton called me to the front of Air Force One to continue the discussion. This time, he was in the private front cabin, a smaller room in the nose of the plane with two couches and a small desk, again with secure and nonsecure phones. The president's back was hurting and he was on the floor doing stretches throughout the conversation. He again pressed me on what I thought he should do. I again said that he should push for what he believed in. The "lift and strike policy is a good one, and we shouldn't take no for an answer," I urged. Clinton had long wanted to lift the arms embargo and was frustrated by European inaction. "If I were a Bosnian, I'd want to be able to decide whether I wanted to go down fighting. Some things are worth fighting and dying for," he had told British prime minister John Major in an earlier call on April 18. A few weeks later, he had erupted when I had shown him a cable from our embassy in London saying Major was inclined toward air strikes only and not a lifting of the arms embargo. "That's crazy," the president fumed. He was convinced lifting the embargo was the right thing to do, especially since the United States was not prepared to enter the war. But the Europeans were not going along.

The problem with the policy, however, was larger than just a failure to push the Europeans. The administration was not yet ready to link the use of force to diplomacy to end the war. In addition, the president and his team still opposed putting ground troops into Bosnia other than to help implement a peace settlement. Without American troops on the ground, the United States was poorly placed to push the Europeans to support a policy that would put *their* troops at risk. We were thus hostage to the weaker European approach, and they opposed bombing Serb targets. By midsummer 1993, it was clear that the effort to work out a common approach with the Europeans was failing, and the situation on the ground in Bosnia was getting worse, with CNN photos of the siege of Sarajevo and horrible suffering on the nightly news. The president told Lake he should look at all options on Bosnia—including for the first time the use of American ground troops.[14] He began to cross the Rubicon of a new use of force.

In July 1993, Lake followed up on the president's request and asked Secretary of Defense Aspin to take a serious look at how many troops it would take to end the siege of Sarajevo. The earlier discussions of whether to put ground troops into Bosnia to implement a peace agreement were supplanted by discussions of how to use force to achieve an end to Serbian aggression in Bosnia. The Pentagon's first response to the request was a plan requiring an estimated seventy thousand to eighty thousand troops to protect Sarajevo.[15] After Christopher and Lake visited the Pentagon to press for options involving fewer ground troops, the Pentagon suggested that the more limited goal of protecting relief supplies to Sarajevo could perhaps be achieved with twenty-five thousand.[16]

While the president had in principle authorized a discussion of ground troops, in practice, no one was ready to make such a politically unpopular decision. In the spring and summer of 1993, the American public was deeply skeptical of any involvement of U.S. ground troops in Bosnia. Only 16 percent of Americans felt that a moral desire to stop atrocities in Bosnia was a "very good reason" to authorize air strikes against Serbian forces.[17] They opposed U.S. participation in a UN peacekeeping operation 49 percent to 44 percent.[18]

No one had figured out a way to use ground troops effectively without "owning the problem" and bogging down U.S. troops in Bosnia for the foreseeable future. In discussing the issue with his colleagues in May, Powell had complained that, "unlike in Desert Storm," there was "no way to seize the initiative" in Bosnia, it "doesn't have the clarity of Desert Storm." While saying that it "doesn't mean we shouldn't act," Powell proceeded to lay out the case for why the United States should not act. "The only real way to stop the Serbs is to go in and take over Serbia with several hundred thousand troops. . . . Go in with a force to kick their butt. There is no certain or clear objective. The only way to do this is on a large scale." With strong congressional opposition to the use of ground troops in Bosnia, and only one principal—Madeleine Albright—supporting the option, discussion of the use of ground troops quickly petered out. The new, more robust policy would rely instead on tougher American leadership and the use of air power alone.

Lake decided to seek to change U.S. policy in two fundamental ways. First, while he continued to oppose a total break with the Europeans, Lake felt more American leadership could lead to more progress. Rather than *ask* the Europeans their views, we would *tell* them what the American president had decided to do and invite them to join. This time, rather than consult as Christopher had, Lake "informed" the allies that the president had decided on this course of action, and that the president expected NATO to act in accordance with that decision. The new assertiveness was dubbed "Tell, don't ask" in a play on the policy on gays in the military in a front-page story in the *New York Times*.[19] With the United States in the lead, the allies quickly, if somewhat grumpily, lined up and supported the new policy.

Second and most importantly, rather than just use air power to alleviate the Serb siege of Sarajevo and other Muslim enclaves, Lake linked the use of air power directly to the diplomatic track. Lake later explained, "The idea was, if we're going to use power for the sake of diplomacy, let's relate it directly to the diplomacy."[20] The United States would conduct air strikes against the Serbs if they continued the "strangulation" of Bosnian safe areas or refused to negotiate a settlement. Like pornography, Lake explained, we would "know it when we saw it" when asked to define strangulation. In addition, Lake left his responses to the Europeans vague regarding what the president would do if the Europeans failed to take our lead.[21]

Thus, for the first time, American force would be used to back up American diplomacy in the Balkans. Building on the principals' discussion of the previous March, Leon Fuerth finally got an answer to his question, "Would the U.S. force compliance?" The answer was suddenly yes, but with air power and not ground troops. The goal was to use air power to force the Serbs to commence serious negotiations.

Throughout the fall, the United States worked to make the threat real. The goal was to gain the agreement of the allies to issue an ultimatum to the Serbs to withdraw their forces around Sarajevo and stop shelling the city, or face bombing attacks against those forces. At the NATO summit at the end of the year, Clinton got his "Sarajevo ultimatum." The effort eased the situation—but only for a while.

The air strikes that eventually followed—NATO's first combat operation in its forty-five years—were viewed as "pinpricks" and ultimately divided NATO. The air strikes put in question the neutrality of the troops on the ground and were eventually called to a halt. United Nations peacekeepers were killed and taken hostage. Murders of thousands of Bosnians continued. Maintaining European solidarity and the neutrality of the peacekeeping operation became the goal, not the end of the war. The problems of the dual chain of command in which both the UN and the commander on the ground had to approve military action (dubbed the "dual-key" arrangement) and other coordination issues continued to hamper progress. Negotiations for a peace went nowhere. The Serbs continued their attacks on the UN safe areas, coming close to overrunning the town of Bihac in 1994.

Although the new "Tell, don't ask" approach brought new U.S. leadership to the Bosnia problem and helped in Sarajevo, the crisis continued as long as Washington was unwilling to use sustained force to bring about a broad final agreement to end the war. Through the eight years that followed, the Clinton administration would use force successfully and sustainedly, and bequeath to its successor the foundations of a twenty-first-century world in which the United States could count on widely accepted rules to constrain others and broad support for the use of force when those rules failed and the threat justified force. That approach ended some conflicts and successfully managed others. It was first forged and tested in the killing fields of Bosnia. Not until the summer of 1995 would Clinton decide to put the full weight of the U.S. military behind efforts to end the war there.

2

Crossing the Rubicon

If General McClellan isn't going to use his army,
I'd like to borrow it for a time.

—Abraham Lincoln, in response to the general's reluctance
to use the army in the Civil War

An early morning call from the Situation Room woke me on Sunday, October 3, 1993. "Ma'am," the young man said, "I am calling to inform you that we have early reports that several U.S. soldiers were killed in Somalia during a confrontation with Somali forces." The information was sketchy, but at first it appeared to be a minor skirmish, not unlike those of the past prior months.

The Situation Room is staffed by individuals, largely from the Pentagon and CIA, who are "detailed" to the White House. They monitor cables from around the world as well as the media, and they serve as a first-alert network for the president and senior White House officials. Lake, Berger, and the White House chief of staff were the first to be alerted. A variety of other staff, including myself, were notified as needed. Over the years, I received many middle-of-the-night calls alerting me to coups, military actions, deaths of leaders, and other significant events—the most bizarre in 1994 when a small Cessna airplane crashed into the White House. Some of the calls were unnecessary interruptions of what was always too short a sleep. For instance, when Turkey's president Turgut Ozal died in April 1993, Berger quipped to the "Sitroom" staff, "Now, what exactly am I supposed to do about that at two o'clock in the morning?"

Somalia represented a shift from the cold war Vietnam-era conflicts to the challenge of failed states in the post–cold war era. Throughout that cold war, the only reason to engage in developing-country conflicts was to contain the Soviet Union. In the proxy wars in Central America, Africa, and Asia, physical U.S. involvement was limited, and the UN was called upon to play a supporting role in peace negotiations and, above all, humanitarian operations. The failures in Vietnam had made Americans wary of interventions, especially once the cold war was won.

The world had gotten used to viewing these conflicts through a superpower lens rather than analyzing their underlying local dynamics. And the world was wholly unprepared for how vicious and tenacious they could be without any superpower involvement, or to understand that, if history had ended, as some believed, someone had forgotten to inform the local combatants. The United States soon found it could not ignore these festering situations. They were America's problem, too.

Somalia, and Haiti shortly thereafter, also introduced the concept of "failed states" as a national security problem. Absent the cold war, a state whose government had largely ceased to function had been viewed as merely a humanitarian problem. Now it became painfully clear that, in an age of satellite television, cheap guns, and jet airplanes, the very weakness of states like these could harm U.S. power and prestige—whether they were ninety miles from our shores, like Haiti, or thousands of miles away, like Somalia.

The situation in Somalia had become more tense over the prior summer. In one of his last acts as president, George H. W. Bush had sent twenty-eight thousand troops to help stop the famine in Somalia. By the fall of 2003, the United States had gradually reduced its presence and was in the process of transferring the mission to the UN. While originally designed to feed the starving people and depart, the mission quickly became immersed in the fractious political struggle in a country that lacked a functioning central government. The prior June, soldiers led by the most powerful Somali warlord, General Mohamed Farah Aideed, had attacked a UN contingent of Pakistani soldiers, killing twenty-four. The UN Security Council demanded the apprehension of those responsible for the attacks and the disarmament of all factions. The United States, as the strongest member of the UN force, took the lead and commenced a raid against Aideed's forces. While the United States had suffered a handful of casualties, overall the mission appeared on track for a successful handover to the United Nations. With the October raid, it took twenty-four hours for the administration to realize a tragedy was under way.

While Clinton kept an eye on the unfolding events in Somalia, his main concern at first was with events in Moscow. Russian President Boris Yeltsin was under siege from communist hard-liners who had seized the parliament building and threatened to bring down his government. Anti-Yeltsin forces were fighting police and military units in the streets of Moscow. Protesters were ramming trucks and launching rocket-propelled grenades into government buildings. Having declared a state of emergency, Yeltsin sent in military reinforcements. White House officials watched CNN since it managed to get information about the crisis faster than the information coming from the U.S. embassy in Moscow, much to Tony Lake's great frustration. "Why aren't the embassy guys out there in front of the Parliament with CNN?" he complained. "When I was in Vietnam, we would be everywhere."

By Monday, October 4, CNN was running split scenes of the dual crises in Moscow and in Somalia. The Russia crisis ended well. Clinton, who had taken an instant liking to the Russian president's gutsy political style, stood by Yeltsin throughout the crisis, including when he ultimately quelled the uprising with the use of force. But the crisis in Somalia did not end well. By Monday morning, it was clear that the raid to confront Aideed had gone horribly wrong. There were shocking images of the body of an American soldier being dragged through the streets of Mogadishu to the cheers of crowds of Somalis. Another American, Chief Warrant Officer Michael Durant, was being held captive. Ultimately, eighteen U.S. soldiers were killed and seventy-four wounded. Hundreds of Somalis were killed. The images were sickening and our hearts went out to the families of the dead men, as they undoubtedly saw them on TV as well. Later, the administration would learn that a little-known Saudi terrorist named Osama bin Laden had been involved in the attacks.

The president was in California at the time to address the AFL-CIO convention in San Francisco. Lake kept him informed by phone of the unfolding tragedy. Secretary of Defense Aspin was recommending an immediate *increase* in the number of troops in Somalia, as the troops on the ground needed enhanced protection at once. After discussing the issue with Aspin by phone, Clinton approved the increase, announcing the decision to reporters at midday at the San Francisco Hilton.

The president arrived back in D.C. on Tuesday, October 5, and met with his national security advisors. He was deeply angry, at himself, at the Pentagon, at the United Nations, and at his own foreign policy team. Fuming, he asked how this disaster could have happened, and why he had not known that we had started a war with the warlord Aideed, complaining we had turned our policy over to the UN. He felt he had not been involved enough in the decision to shift to a strategy to arrest Aideed, and that no one had warned him such a disaster was a possibility. Colin Powell had told him the previous June that the effort against Aideed had been a success. How had this happened? Lake offered to resign, although in the end the casualty would be Secretary of Defense Aspin, who was harshly criticized for failing to provide requested defensive items, especially tanks, to the troops in Somalia. Although later reviews found that providing the tanks would not have helped, Aspin never recovered and was forced to resign. He was eventually replaced by his deputy, the respected William Perry.

Clinton's anger rarely showed in public; the Somalia crisis was an exception. For instance, during a press conference the following week with Turkish prime minister Tansu Ciller, a reporter asked the president to respond to recent criticism levied by former president Bush, former secretary of defense Dick Cheney, and former secretary of state James Baker, who had called the president's actions in Somalia "naive" and accused him of having allowed "mission creep." The president lost his composure and lashed out at his predecessor. "It may have been naive for anyone to seriously assert in the beginning that you could go into a situation as politically and militarily charged as that one, give people food, turn around and leave, and expect everything to be hunky dory."[1]

The president sought to explain the crisis to the American people from the Oval Office on Wednesday, October 7 at 5:02 P.M. "Until June, things went well, with little violence. The United States reduced our troop presence from twenty-eight thousand down to less than five thousand, with other nations picking up where we left off. But then, in June, the people who caused much of the problem in the beginning started attacking American, Pakistani, and other troops who were there to keep the peace.

"So now we face a choice. Do we leave when the job gets tough, or when the job is well done? Do we invite a return of mass suffering or do we leave in a way that gives the Somalis a decent chance to survive?" Recently, General Colin Powell said this about our choices in Somalia: "Because things get difficult, you don't cut and run. You work the problem and try to find a correct solution."[2] In this case, working the problem meant beefing up U.S. forces while they withdrew and handed off the operation to the United Nations.

It was no accident that the president referred to General Powell. Clinton wanted to ensure that he stood closely with the Pentagon as the crisis was managed. He also wanted to remind the American public that General Powell, considered an American hero, had been intimately involved with the decision to "work the problem." Clinton had not yet established his own military credentials; thus, he wanted to stay close to Powell.

In the press, in Congress, and among the pundits, many were calling for an immediate withdrawal from Somalia. Senator Robert Byrd circulated a resolution that would have cut off all funds for the operation by the end of the year, telling the president: "Let's vote and get out."[3] In some of Clinton's most contentious meetings to date, he met with congressional leadership to avoid such legislation, a congressional directive that the United States cut and run. Senators George Mitchell, Robert Dole, Sam Nunn, and John Warner put forward a compromise, which was ultimately adopted, calling for the forces to withdraw no later than March 31, 1994. In a series of tense meetings with congressional members, the president argued that a quick withdrawal would make U.S. soldiers targets around the world.

Although Clinton chose the more difficult political route and resisted a quick pullout, to this day, most observers believe the United States hightailed it out of Somalia following the deaths of the U.S. soldiers. While the American troops did leave on March 25, 1994, it did so in an orderly fashion; the plan had always been for the United States to leave and hand over the mission to the UN. In fact, the United States and UN missions, totaling thirty-seven thousand troops from twenty-eight countries, saved an estimated quarter of a million Somalis from starvation, at the cost of 130 peacekeepers and $1.6 billion. The United States continued to push the UN to take a stronger role in finding a political solution for what remains today essentially a state without a central government.[4]

"Don't worry. We'll have the troops out by January 20."

The evolution of U.S. policy toward Somalia provides a case study of the failure to get the balance of force and diplomacy right. It also served as a harsh wake-up call to Clinton and his team of the need to manage more closely the Pentagon and America's use of force. Following Bosnia, Somalia represented the second test of the "New World Order" about which former President Bush had often spoken. And it was the mirror image of Bosnia, where the United States refused to use force or deploy troops. In Bosnia, the United States would pursue diplomacy as well as the use of force. In Somalia, the United States would ultimately decide neither the use of force nor the deployment of troops was warranted. Both issues would be central to Clinton's difficulties in defining the appropriate use of force in the post–cold war era.

Following the death of the U.S. soldiers in October 1993, Lake asked me to pull together a summary of what the internal NSC process had been in an attempt to reconstruct where mistakes had been made. What I found was troubling. The policy had been largely left in the hands of midlevel officials as it shifted from a humanitarian mission, to feed starving civilians, toward a military effort to capture the warlords who were threatening the peacekeepers. While Lake had kept the president informed verbally and in writing, the principals never sat down among themselves, or with the president, to review the shift. The Pentagon's more robust plans, designed to respond to the attacks on the Pakistani forces, had been accepted without higher-level interagency review by those more sensitive to the political implications of initiating military operations against one of the factions.

The problems had started in the fall of 1992. Responding to the images on CNN of hundreds of thousands of Somalis starving to death, President Bush had agreed just before Thanksgiving to send in troops to secure the capital, Mogadishu, and the supply roads, in what officials described at the time as "a Desert Shield/Storm way of handling Somalia." Blinded by the ease of the Gulf War, Bush severely underestimated the difference between expelling an army from Kuwait and sending troops into a civil war. Stunningly, Bush made the decision without consulting the next president of the United States. When I called Bush's national security advisor Brent Scowcroft from Little Rock after Bush's decision had been leaked to the press, he told me in words that would later prove to be breathtakingly naive: "Don't worry. We'll have the troops out by January 20."

The Bush administration envisioned a combat phase, during which they would clear strategic areas and destroy the warlords' heavy equipment, followed by the withdrawal of the U.S. combat force before January 20. The troops would then be replaced by a peacekeeping force, with the United States perhaps maintaining an offshore naval presence. When Berger asked in November 1992, "What's to prevent the warlords from coming back after the combat force leaves?" Scowcroft replied, "We'll be destroying their capability and deterring them." At the time, Scowcroft told Berger they expected "that the combat phase of this mission could be completed within two weeks, using helicopter gunships to destroy heavy equipment, with the expectation that the 'thugs' will melt into the desert."

Bush had failed to understand the need to address the political vacuum in Somalia—and so had Clinton. Throughout history, military success could be measured in terms of military goals, particularly between the two cold war superpowers. Suddenly, military success depended on progress on local parties' political steps, not on a superpower's military prowess. Although Clinton decided U.S. interests in Somalia were insufficient to keep troops in a country without a functioning government, later he determined U.S. interests in Bosnia required that U.S. forces remain in place until the political parties fulfilled their obligations under peace agreements, while sharing that decade-long effort with the UN and European allies.

The administration had fallen into the trap of believing the myth of the superpower—first, that it could easily exercise absolute power in Somalia, and second, when it chose to get out fast, that it could withdraw without broader, painful consequences. The U.S. withdrawal from Somalia, even though it was orderly, left the impression that America could be driven into retreat. President Reagan's withdrawal from Lebanon following the 1983 bombing of the Marine barracks apparently fed that impression as well. Bin Laden certainly came to believe terrorism against America could impact its behavior.

But Somalia in many ways taught the administration important lessons for the role of a superpower in confronting failed states. Somalia became the model for future conflicts: a failed state, a power vacuum, armed factions, and enough chaos to make military power almost impotent. Failed states would also threaten America as havens for terrorists to plot attacks on our embassies and our cities. When the two Black Hawk helicopters went down in Somalia, it was clear that a new approach not based in a military solution was needed.

Clinton's Bay of Pigs

On October 19, 1993, I sent a memo to Lake outlining what the NSC process on Somalia had been since Clinton took office. Overall, the NSC had held a total of thirty-eight Principals Committee meetings on foreign policy and sixty Deputies Committee meetings. But on Somalia, Lake had never convened a Principals Committee meeting, although there had been nine Deputies Committee meetings run by Berger. This contrasted with eighteen principals' and twelve deputies' meetings on Bosnia. On Haiti, there had been four principals' and five deputies' meetings. In fact, the first time the president met formally with his advisors on Somalia was after the death of the U.S. soldiers. The main reason there had been no Principals Committee meetings was that the operation seemed to be going well. The mission seemed on track for transfer to the UN, with U.S. forces scheduled to be out by early to mid-1994.

In his memos to the president, Lake emphasized that Somalis would have to "take the opportunity afforded them by our actions." Instead, the Somalis failed to seize their opportunity. They resumed the war for influence and saw the UN forces as blocking their goals. There was little debate and no disagreement in the UN or the United States at the time over the need for a swift and strong reaction to Aideed's attack on the UN forces. In part because of this general agreement, the issue was never critically analyzed in the way it might have been, had there been some discord. Thus, over the next two months, in a decision the UN secretary-general would later call "an abominable mistake,"[5] U.S. and UN policy shifted from giving the Somalis humanitarian assistance to a military campaign to apprehend the man responsible for the attacks against the Pakistanis: General Aideed. Perhaps most importantly, this shift in policy occurred just as the majority of U.S. forces was preparing to withdraw and hand the key security tasks over to other, less capable forces taking over the UN mission. The shift left U.S. and other forces vulnerable to attack, a crucial fact the administration failed to grasp at the time.

The military operations were developed by Powell's staff and forwarded in writing by General Powell to Undersecretary of Defense Frank Wisner, the Pentagon's third-ranking civilian. The plans outlined a four-phase operation to begin June 12. They involved:

1. a draw-down of the UN forces from Mogadishu
2. an attack on one of Aideed's radio stations by a company of the "Quick Reaction Force," supported by attack helicopters, in order to disable the stations and take control of them
3. an attack on Aideed's compound
4. an effort to "clean up" Aideed's enclaves throughout Mogadishu.

On June 12, in a predawn strike, UN planes and helicopters blasted the Mogadishu radio station controlled by Aideed, as well as weapons storage sites and an abandoned cigarette factory used by Aideed. The radio station had been broadcasting anti–UN propaganda and had incited Somali gunmen to ambush the Pakistani peacekeepers. Clearly misunderstanding the complex situation in Mogadishu, the Pentagon repeatedly briefed the administration that its operations were going well. Such optimism prompted Powell to brief the president on June 17 that the Somalia operation to undermine the capacity of Aideed to wreak military havoc in Mogadishu was "over and that it was a success."[6] Based on Powell's briefing, the President declared publicly at a press conference the same day—three and a half months before the deaths of the U.S. soldiers in Somalia—that the "United Nations, acting with the United States and other nations, has crippled the forces in Mogadishu of warlord Aideed and remains on guard against further provocation. Aideed's forces were responsible for the worst attack on UN peacekeepers in three decades. We could not let it go unpunished."[7]

The UN asked the United States to provide Special Forces, known also as Rangers, to help "track down and arrest" Aideed. The request was rejected as the administration wanted to minimize the impression that this was a U.S. operation. Lake informed the president of the decision in a written memo. By July, however, the UN's requests for U.S. Special Forces to assist in the apprehension of Aideed had become more urgent, and the man Lake and Berger had sent to Somalia as "our guy," former deputy national security advisor Admiral Jonathan Howe, pressed hard for the UN—and the United States—to take action against Aideed. Believing those in Washington should trust the "man on the ground," administration officials supported Howe's recommendation. United Nations Ambassador Albright and the new U.S. special envoy for Somalia, Ambassador Robert Gosende, strongly endorsed the request.

The Deputies Committee, led by Sandy Berger, debated the request for a month, and then, on August 16, approved a new four-part plan:

1. to continue the effort to apprehend Aideed
2. to pursue the idea put forward by Ethiopia of forced exile
3. to urge and assist the UN to seek the arrest of Aideed and his deputies
4. to press the UN for a plan for a hand-off from the United States to the UN.

U.S. forces had been reduced to forty-two hundred, while UN forces totaled roughly twenty thousand. About four hundred Special Forces were deployed to Somalia on August 24 as part of a UN–led force intended to quell Aideed's "disruptive faction." Eighteen of these soldiers lost their lives in Mogadishu six weeks later.

As the military actions escalated, Lake had realized he needed to get more involved and pressed Berger to ensure there was a sound political strategy to back up military action. President Clinton stressed the need for a political plan during his meetings with UN Secretary General Boutros-Ghali in September. Indeed, in the last Deputies Committee meeting before the deaths of the U.S. soldiers, there was discussion of the need to push the UN to develop a stronger political plan for Somalia and for dealing with Aideed following his arrest, including possible detention in a third country. But this came too late for the eighteen who died that October.

The Somalia tragedy shocked Clinton into taking control of his foreign policy and his bureaucracy. In some ways, it represented Clinton's own Bay of Pigs in that he had inherited a flawed plan and then had failed to question adequately the military plans of the Pentagon. He never again failed to be personally engaged in asking the tough "what if" questions and satisfying himself that the political situation had been adequately taken into account in planning military operations. It was also the first of several harsh lessons on the failures of the UN system and the inability of UN peacekeepers to fight a war.

Never again would President Clinton allow U.S. forces to take part in an *enforcement* operation under UN command. But it would take some more tough lessons before the administration learned that the only way to ensure that the parties on the ground fulfill their obligations was to threaten—and use force if necessary—if they failed to live up to their agreements. Eventually, that tactic would be applied in Bosnia and Kosovo. But first, Clinton had to put to rest the legacy of Vietnam.

Exorcizing the ghosts of Vietnam

Although it had been over for two decades, the shadow of the Vietnam War still limited support for American intervention abroad and complicated Clinton's relationship with the foreign policy establishment and the military leadership. Senator James Jeffords, the Vermont Republican who later switched parties, made clear the establishment's overriding fear: "We're all scared to death of public reaction to things that have a Vietnam overtone."[8]

Using force to back up diplomacy in "nonstrategic areas" was a radical concept in 1994. Unlike the interstate conflicts of the past, those facing Clinton posed new, complex military and political challenges. There were no clear military objectives and any exit strategy depended on political progress of the parties, not action of the U.S military. The political aftermath of the loss of American lives and prestige in Vietnam still lingered in the debate over the appropriate use of force. The Pentagon resisted any hint of military engagement in any similar "quagmires." The U.S. public and Congress also strongly opposed the deployment of troops outside any "strategic" areas. The Vietnam quagmire propelled Colin Powell to ensure Desert Storm would be conducted with overwhelming force and kept the United States from a more flexible response in the Balkans for years. Americans did not feel vulnerable; terrorism was a distant threat. Thus, military engagement was based on the myth of America's invincibility at home and a belief it need not engage in far-off places.

Clinton's victory in 1992 represented the rise to power of the Vietnam generation, in effect the victory of the "sixties kids" over the established so-called wise men who had run foreign policy since the 1950s. The men in uniform resented that Clinton and many of his peers had avoided the war most of them had fought in and believed the rhetoric that Democrats were soft on defense. They viewed the conflicts of the 1990s through the lens of Vietnam, vehemently opposing *any* military involvement in places like Bosnia where no clear-cut victory was in sight. Furthermore, many were suspicious of the new president and his lack of military service, efforts to avoid the draft, and his minor protests in the 1960s against the Vietnam War. Having yet to establish his credentials as commander in chief, Clinton was reluctant to challenge the Pentagon's narrow support for the use of force.

Clinton understood the painful impact of Vietnam; he wanted the country—and the Pentagon and Congress—to move beyond it. He was also under considerable pressure from the business community, State Department, and key congressional players, particularly Vietnam veterans, to lift the embargo. But even stronger pressure against moving forward came from groups of veterans and their families who felt that normalizing relations with Vietnam would take pressure off the Vietnamese to cooperate on accounting for the missing American soldiers from the war. Two thousand two hundred thirty-eight U.S. soldiers remained unaccounted for from the war. Although more than six thousand soldiers remain unaccounted for from the Korean War and more than seventy-eight thousand from World War II, the drive to bring back remains of those left behind in the only war America has ever lost remained a passion for a small but politically powerful sector of American society. Many towns in the United States still fly a flag honoring those missing, and Clinton understood that he needed to show progress by the Vietnamese on the issue before he could move toward normalizing relations.

Therefore, he began early on to press the Vietnamese to account for those soldiers still missing in action (MIA) or still considered prisoners of war (POW). While only fringe elements believed Vietnam might still be holding live U.S. soldiers,[9] most of the family-and-veteran groups were convinced that Vietnam was holding back on the return of remains. Clinton was in no hurry to move on the politically sensitive issue.

"This is the war we lost and I want it to end with dignity."

Support for the normalization of relations with Vietnam came from an unlikely pair—two Vietnam veterans, Senators John Kerry of Massachusetts and John McCain of Arizona. The two pressed Clinton to move forward repeatedly, first on June 11, 1993, in the Oval Office.

Kerry, a Democrat, made an impassioned twenty-five-minute non-stop plea. "We come here with the feeling that this is a compelling moment, a delicate moment in Vietnam. . . . If you move now, you can maximize getting back larger continued cooperation. If you delay, you create a higher mountain for us to climb," arguing that Vietnam might reduce its help on the POW/MIA issue. "There are," Kerry continued, "regional security interests and Cam Rahn Bay. You can get a regional security arrangement to see U.S. ships using the bay again and playing a major hand in the China region. That's what we fought for—to maintain our projecture."

Next spoke John McCain, who was no friend of Clinton's. A staunch conservative Republican, he had been shot down over Vietnam on October 26, 1967, by a surface-to-air missile. After spending five years in a Vietnamese prison, McCain catapulted into national politics. He has one of the Senate's most conservative voting records; he opposes abortion, big government, and high taxes. But he has demonstrated his independence by also taking on his own party to fight for campaign finance reform and partnering with Democrats on centrist issues like the environment. Vietnam was one of those issues about which McCain felt passionately—and he was willing to spend some political capital to achieve his goal.

"It is in our national interest to move forward. The situation in Vietnam is becoming unstable. The Chinese are moving in on the Spratley Islands," McCain explained.[10] "It's where the oil is. We need an economically stable Vietnam. They are cooperating, not totally but they do make a reasonable point regarding their 300,000 MIA's."[11] McCain warned that if we didn't move, "the hardliners will prevail." Dismissing those who believed the Vietnamese were in a conspiracy to hold back remains of Americans, McCain joked, "I understand every day more and more why they dug up Zachary Taylor," referring to the debate over whether to exhume the remains of former President Taylor to investigate consistent rumors he had died of poisoning in 1850.[12]

Conversations with Kerry and McCain changed Clinton's mind. He and his advisors had been discussing a slower timetable, conscious of the possible political fallout with the family-and-veteran groups. Lake sought a balance between those concerns and the desire to bring the Vietnam era to a close. "This is a public issue in the truest sense of the word," Lake said at one principals' meeting in 1993. "My little town flies an MIA flag. This is the war we lost and I want it to end with dignity." In the end, Clinton eased some financial restrictions that fall, lifted the embargo in February 1994, and normalized relations in 1995. As Clinton announced that last historic decision, John McCain stood stoically at his side.

By lifting the embargo, Clinton began the process of putting the Vietnam War behind himself and the country; everything else—normalization of relations, appointment of an ambassador—came in time. As Senator Larry Pressler of South Dakota, another Republican Vietnam veteran, said after the embargo was lifted, "The Vietnam War is finally over."[13] In doing so, Clinton showed political strength in taking on the difficult issue and began to move the political debate over the use of force past those centered on Vietnam-like quagmire situations, especially at the Pentagon and in Congress. With the issue behind him, Clinton was now freer to develop a new doctrine for the use of force to back up his diplomacy in the post–Vietnam War era. He did so first in Haiti.

The challenge of Haiti, a failed state, required policymakers to take on the myths of the early 1990s. Although isolationists would call for Clinton to ignore these conflicts, and Colin Powell would oppose the use of force, the Haitian refugees turning up in Florida were living examples of the need for the United States to engage. The belief that the United States could turn its back on Haiti evaporated as "their problem" quickly became "everyone's problem." The Haiti crisis also points to the growing role that nonstate actors—refugees, terrorists, gangsters, corporations, NGOs, and protestors—had begun to play in foreign policy.

The last straw

Just one week after the tragedy of Somalia, the administration walked straight into one of its worst public relations disasters: Haiti. The political negotiations for the return of Haitian president Jean Bertrand Aristide had concluded on July 3, 1993, with an agreement signed on Governors Island in New York City by President Aristide and Haiti's military rulers. The United States had brokered the deal, which stipulated that Aristide would return to power on October 30, 1993. The military and police forces in Haiti were to take a series of steps to pave the way for Aristide's return; the United States agreed to send in trainers for the security forces and engineers to rebuild the infrastructure.

Hopes were high for a political solution to this three-year stalemate that would not only return the democratically elected leader to Haiti but also enable the president to make good on one of his campaign commitments— to return Aristide to power and reverse Bush's policy of forcibly returning refugees. As part of the negotiations, Aristide had called for a lifting of the tough international sanctions imposed following his ouster and an amnesty for the military junta. The Governors Island agreement called for the return of Aristide and the departure of the junta as soon as the parliament passed a bill separating the military from the police. It also invited the international community to send six hundred military advisors to help train the police and army during that transition. U.S. Navy construction troops—two hundred so-called "Seabees"[14]—were to professionalize the army and build military housing, while the French and Canadians were to create a police force independent from the military. Although the troops were lightly armed for their own protection, they were not a force designed to go anywhere they were not wanted.

And as it turned out, they were not wanted. On October 11, the USS *Harlan County*[15] docked in Port au Prince with the initial Seabee trainers on board. The junta had organized a mob to demonstrate against the arrival of the trainers and prevented them from disembarking. The junta's soldiers and police stood aside as about fifty demonstrators surged onto the dock— a clear sign the junta was reneging on its part of the Governors Island Agreement. The USS *Harlan County* had no choice but to turn around and leave the port, as it was not equipped to fight its way into port, nor was that its mission. But that image came to symbolize the weakness of the Clinton foreign policy—an image that came to represent his early presidency. It certainly helped prompt Gary Trudeau to portray Clinton as a talking waffle in his cartoon *Doonesbury*.[16]

While the image of the USS *Harlan County* turning around was disastrous from a political point of view, the mistake had not been in that act. The problem had been that the ship had not been backed up by force that would be used if the Haitian military backed out of the agreement. But in the fall of 1993, the administration had no intention of using U.S. ground troops to restore President Aristide to power. Nor was Aristide asking for such action, fully conscious of the fact that his legitimacy would evaporate were he to ride back to power on the back of the U.S. military.

So, the weapon of choice to respond to the debacle was tough sanctions, with a strong U.S. presence nearby, "over the horizon." On October 14, the UN Security Council voted to reimpose stiff sanctions on Haiti within a week, including an embargo on oil imports, if the junta failed to comply with its commitments under Governors Island. In addition, the administration imposed unilateral sanctions, revoking visas and freezing the junta's and its supporters' assets, and ordered six destroyers to patrol the waters off Haiti to assist in the enforcement of the sanctions. Clinton also ordered an infantry company to be on standby at Guantanamo Naval Base in Cuba to send a signal that, this time, the United States meant business about enforcing sanctions and protecting the one thousand Americans living in Haiti.

But Clinton didn't have a plan "B" if the sanctions failed to secure the departure of the junta. Increasingly, the option of using U.S. troops to oust the militia crept into the discussion. The Haitian military leaders seemed to be brushing off the threats of the international community. There were indi-

cations they considered the naval blockade a bluff and that they were prepared to wait out the international community. As the sanctions tightened,
the junta indicated that it was prepared to endure them rather than agree
to negotiate Aristide's return. As the discussions shifted to the possibility
of the U.S. military taking action to restore Aristide to power, the CIA intensified its disinformation campaign against Aristide.

The CIA had long been mistrustful of Aristide, who was a radical, mys-
tical, Catholic priest. Always more sympathetic to the ruling elite, the CIA
accepted too easily the propaganda of Aristide's opponents. The CIA's personal profiling of Aristide as a psychotic nut was a textbook case of the politi-
cization of intelligence. It was a lesson that I never forgot when given their
assessments, although I found most were professional and useful when not
generated in a highly politicized environment.

The CIA's report was leaked to the press in August, causing an uproar
among Aristide's supporters. An August 3, 1993, front-page *New York Times*
article summarized what had been circulating for years on Aristide. "A classified Central Intelligence Agency psychological profile prepared after his
ouster in September 1991 portrayed a man prone to severe mood swings.
The report suggested that he suffered from depression and may have had
nervous breakdowns, and it concluded that he was capable of saying one thing
one day and the reverse the next day without being aware of any inconsis-
tencies."[17] Although the CIA later admitted the sources for the report were
second-hand and had never been verified, at the time, the principals were
understandably nervous about restoring such a man to the presidency.

Small and thin, Aristide was soft-spoken and gentle. He wore glasses
too big for his small head; his eyes were large and piercing. Contrary to
his reputation as a firebrand, he engaged easily in conversation and had a
quick sense of humor. His first meeting with President Clinton the prior
March was cordial and friendly, without a hint of the fiery oratory for
which he was famous in Haiti; however, Aristide's patience soon began to
run thin since, in his view, the negotiations were failing. I became a bit of
a sounding board for him during these months. It was clear to him the
military leaders in Haiti were stonewalling the international community—
and doing so with impunity.

"I can't lie and tell them," referring to the people of Haiti, "to trust
President Clinton," Aristide complained to me in the late evening of April
26, 1993. "If President Clinton does not stop his dilatory process, I cannot tell my people to trust him. It has been three months for President
Clinton but it has been nineteen months for us. Meanwhile, we are losing
people in Haiti. In another four years, this will be another 'read my lips' for
President Clinton," referring to President Bush's broken pledge not to raise
taxes. Aristide argued that Clinton "could do it," meaning secure the departure of the junta through tougher diplomacy. He urged the United States

to freeze the assets of the coup leaders, suspend visas, and block the ship-
ment of oil. The UN envoy was negotiating the "continuation of the military in power," he complained. The way was not being paved for his return.

Throughout 1993 and 1994, the principals discussed the possibility of
holding elections in Haiti without Aristide, meaning democracy without
Aristide. Skepticism of him remained high, but the president always stuck
by the goal of returning him to power. Clinton put the reports of Aristide's
psychotic nature in perspective, even commenting that many considered
President Lincoln to be slightly crazy. "He may have been crazy, but he was
a hell of a president."[18] Just after a meeting in the Oval Office on December
6 with Aristide and Prime Minister Robert Malval, the president turned to
Tony Lake and Sandy Berger and asked if he and Aristide were "singing out
of the same hymnal." Throughout the prior year, Berger had always
reminded his skeptical colleagues that Aristide had a strong democratic mandate. Berger pushed back on repeated efforts to restore democracy to Haiti
without Aristide. He also was a master at making his point through humor.
"He's singing from different pages, Mr. President," replied Berger, "but
it's the same hymnal."

Even before the *Harlan County* debacle, Lake had begun to push the
president to use force to restore Aristide. He had first done so in the spring
of 1993 and again in April 1994, only to be rebuffed by Clinton, who still
hoped to make progress through diplomacy and sanctions.[19] After *Harlan
County*, Lake again pushed for the use of force as the only way to restore
Aristide. "We need to make clear," Lake said early on, "that there will be
trouble if they try it again. It may not mean less Americans but lots more."
In fact, that is exactly what it would eventually take—lots more troops in
the form of the 82nd Airborne.

A new chairman at the Pentagon

In October 1993, General John Shalikashvili attended his first Principals
Committee meeting and was greeted with warm applause. Unlike most civilian senior officials of the U.S. government, the chairman of the joint Chiefs
of Staff has a two-year term that is normally renewed, regardless of whether
it coincides with the U.S. electoral cycle.[20] Thus, Colin Powell's term had
overlapped with Clinton's for nine months. Clinton had been of two minds
about Powell's departure. He had proven a steady hand in planning the
retaliatory strike against Iraq earlier that year after an assassination attempt
against former President Bush. Overall, Powell had been a voice of reason
on foreign policy. But he had also hindered the new team's efforts to think
creatively about how to use America's overwhelming military might in new
conflicts. Powell's departure freed the administration from his overwhelm-

ing opposition to more flexible uses of force and engagement in areas he considered beyond America's interest.

The arrival of "Shali," as he was called, heralded a new era of cooperation with the Pentagon. For the first time, discussion of new approaches to the use of force was possible. A Polish immigrant who spoke with a thick accent despite having arrived in the United States as a young man, Shali understood the need for global U.S. leadership, which at times had to rely on force. No doubt his own personal connection to the suffering of the Poles during World War II prompted him to be more aggressive in urging the use of force to back up U.S. diplomacy. He had been commander of U.S. forces in Europe and had impressed Clinton with his plainspoken, honest willingness to help him think through the day's tough problems. On Haiti, he demonstrated a willingness to think out of the box on the use of the military to back up diplomacy.

Throughout 1993 and 1994, Clinton sought every way *other than* the use of force to oust the junta in Haiti and restore Aristide to power. Administration officials worked to get Security Council approval for tighter trade sanctions, a ban on travel by military leaders, their families, and their supporters, and on all commerce to and from Haiti except food, medicine, cooking oil, and journalistic supplies. The United States also revamped the diplomacy, including the appointment of a new envoy, William H. Gray III, and reversed the policy of direct return of refugees without first hearing their claims for asylum. While the sanctions succeeded in preventing the indulged wives of the junta from shopping in Miami—a sanction that placed surprisingly real pressure on the regime—the overall policy was failing and, as the months passed, the difficult solution only became clearer. Clinton could not succeed as long as he kept force off the table.

In April 1994, it became evident that the relationship with Aristide was deteriorating as political pressure was mounting on the administration to restore him to power. He began to threaten to play the "immigration card," and unleash hoards of Haitian boat people who would clog the shores of Florida. He called the negotiations seeking his return "a cynical joke."[21] He also deployed his political backers in Hollywood and the Congress to good effect. In late March, Julia Roberts, Robin Williams, Danny Glover, Paul Newman, and Joanne Woodward, who were the president's guests at a White House St. Patrick's Day gala, signed a protest letter that ran in the *New York Times*. Randall Robinson, executive director of the lobbying organization TransAfrica, launched a hunger strike on April 21, tragically ignoring the ongoing Rwandan genocide. He called the U.S. policy of returning Haitian refugees "cruel and . . . profoundly racist."[22] Six members of Congress protested in a closed-off area outside the White House and were arrested.

By early May 1994, the status quo was unacceptable. The political pressures to restore Aristide to power were growing and it was increasingly clear that diplomacy alone would fail. Thus, the principals finally started to grapple with the probable need to use force to restore President Aristide to power. On May 7, the principals sat around the long table in the Cabinet Room with the president and vice president. A smaller group had just finished a meeting in the Situation Room on the crisis in Korea and had moved up to the Cabinet Room for the "Foreign Policy Team" meetings that had become part of the administration's modus operandi in the wake of Somalia.

Lake opened the discussion in his understated way, saying it would be "useful" to make a decision on the use of force as the group worked through the options, including what type of force would be considered and whether it would be unilateral or multilateral. "We have to be clear," Lake said, "so we don't end up in a Somalia situation where we take on more than the UN is willing to do, posing the question of whether the United States should make its willingness to put troops on the ground contingent on the UN's willingness to create a UN follow-on force." Drawing on his experience with the "Tell, don't ask" policy with regard to Bosnia, Lake knew we would have to show a willingness to use force unilaterally before the UN would follow. It was a key turning point for the administration—it realized the power of the lone superpower. When the United States acted, others would follow. That principle would guide much of the rest of Clinton's foreign policy.

Clinton, having learned the lessons of Somalia, asked the tough questions. "What are the objectives of intervention? We can clearly throw them out of power and disarm their forces. We get back to Panama if the idea is to apprehend individuals," he continued, referring to President Bush's military action in 1989 to put the elected president in power and apprehend the dictator Manuel Noriega on drug charges. (Noriega eluded U.S. forces for a week.) "Depending on how we define it, it can get more complicated. What, specifically, is the military objective?"

"The goal is not to apprehend individuals," Shalikashvili replied. Rather, he continued, "it is to disarm and neutralize the military and police force. Our track record is no good on apprehending individuals." I thought of that comment years later when the second President Bush personalized the 2001 war in Afghanistan, claiming we would get Osama bin Laden "dead or alive" and when Iraq's Saddam Hussein eluded more than one hundred sixty thousand coalition forces for eight months.

"We need to separate the goals," Shalikashvili continued. "We need to neutralize their forces to create the conditions for Aristide's return. Beyond that, it is tricky because we have to maintain order until another force can take over the function. The mission is to retain that security until our forces are replaced by an international force or until the internal forces are rebuilt." Thus, Shali was the first to articulate the new way in which force would be used in the "new conflicts" in the 1990s. He was also the first military leader to understand that in the post–cold war conflicts, winning the peace would be just as important as winning the war. Should the policy side fail, U.S. forces would have no exit strategy.

Shali said that it would initially take eighteen thousand troops, but then only seven thousand to stabilize the situation. He then set forth the toughest issue, saying he and "the Chiefs," as the heads of the military branches were dubbed, were in a difficult situation. "We can't deliver you a plan on how to get out." The room fell silent. There were no Haitian troops capable of providing security and UN forces likely would be incapable of coping with the volatile political situation.

Without an exit strategy, support for the operation from Congress would be dead on arrival.

Diplomacy backed by force

Finally, toward the end of June, the administration confronted the fact that it had to decide whether it would use force to back up its diplomacy. The United States had confronted the myths of failed states not affecting U.S. national security. In the past, force had been used to back rebellions or expel invading armies. Whereas the hegemons would use diplomacy to justify force, Clinton used force to back up diplomacy. In doing so, he began to lay the foundation of a new realist foreign policy of the twenty-first century.

Meeting in the Situation Room on June 28, 1994—first at 10 A.M. and then again at 4:30 P.M.—the principals argued about the Haiti endgame. Skepticism of Aristide remained high. There were rumors of narcotics trafficking involving Aristide, including one that a Colombian cartel had sent Haiti a transshipment of cocaine. The drug dealers had reportedly met with Aristide in 1990. There was concern that if he were returned, Aristide would allow Haiti to be used as a transshipment point.

"Are we going to restore democracy but not Aristide?" Lake argued that to change the policy "fundamentally at this stage would be misguided." Clinton's new secretary of defense, William Perry, disagreed. "Let's change the way we restore democracy. Delete Aristide." Ultimately, the principals agreed to support Aristide's return, but the lack of an "exit strategy" for U.S. troops remained problematic. Their departure would depend on political progress on the ground in Haiti.

The exit strategy thus became giving the Haitians a window of opportunity to build a more stable political system. David Gergen, the communications guru who had joined the administration to help shape its message, understood the political problem of getting troops stuck in a Haiti quagmire. "What are the chances of our troops getting stuck?" he asked. "Ninety-seven to ninety-eight percent," replied Lake, "but let's give them a fair chance to succeed and then we can bring them home." "We can't homogenize Somalia and Haiti so close. We can't walk away from Haiti the way we did in Somalia. We have to give the new president a fair opportunity," said Christopher. "Let's give it at least six months," suggested Lake.

Clinton did not want the United States to shoulder the burden of restoring democracy to Haiti alone. American public opinion remained opposed to any invasion. Sixty-one percent of Americans believed that the United States did not have a responsibility to do anything to restore democracy to Haiti.[23] Thus, before approving the military invasion on August 26, Clinton pushed for and received a United Nations Security Council resolution authorizing a multinational force to restore Aristide to power. It was unprecedented for the United States to seek UN authorization for the use of force in its own hemisphere. Doing so, however, reflected the new reality of the conflicts Clinton faced. The American public did not support the action and did not want to shoulder the burden alone. By getting UN support, Clinton not only demonstrated to the American people that the action had the support of the world, he also shifted much of the burden to America's allies. Such burden sharing would become a new hallmark of American foreign policy. While the world looked to the lone superpower to tackle every crisis, the United States had to set the course of the international community but then could share the burdens of keeping the peace.

Much like it would do in 2003 prior to the invasion of Iraq, the administration sought to highlight the human rights abuses of the regime to help convince the public of the merits of an invasion. The State Department released a report on September 13 that alleged violence committed by the junta was even worse than that of "the notorious regime of Papa Doc Duvalier," Haiti's former brutal ruler. The report said: "The de facto Government promotes general repression and official terrorism. It sanctions the widespread use of assassination, killing, torture, beating, mutilation, rape and other violent abuse of innocent civilians, including the most vulnerable, such as orphans."[24]

Then, on September 15, Clinton delivered a nationally televised address, announcing that the United States would use force to oust the military leaders of Haiti. He also sent a delegation, which included Jimmy Carter, Senator Sam Nunn, and the now retired General Colin Powell, to try diplomacy one last time. Knowing Carter would likely push for more time for negotiations, Clinton set a firm deadline for the team: the junta had until one minute after midnight, Monday, September 19 to agree to leave by October 15 or the United States would invade Haiti.

The team arrived in Port au Prince on Saturday, September 17. Jimmy Carter had laid out for the junta that the invasion was inevitable, trying to induce the military leaders to leave Haiti peacefully and take advantage of an amnesty the United States was prepared to offer to avoid bloodshed.

"We will not go," General Raoul Cedras, leader of the junta, declared, adding such a step would be unconstitutional and "a stain on our integrity." The next day at 9:00 A.M., Carter, Nunn, and Powell asked for more time, resisting Clinton's instructions for them to leave at noon if they had no deal. Clinton told them no. The two thousand paratroopers from the 82nd Airborne were already preparing for the invasion set for just after midnight. Sixty-one aircraft would take off from Fort Bragg, N.C., for Haiti at 5 P.M.

Back in Haiti, the negotiating team pushed the Haitians harder. Powell leaned across the table at Cedras. "Let me make sure you understand what you're facing," Powell explained. As Cedras's spirits sank, Powell ticked off the U.S. force already on its way: two aircraft carriers, two and a half infantry divisions, twenty thousand troops, helicopter gunships, tanks, and artillery.[25] The junta still refused to budge.

The scene in the Oval Office on Sunday morning, September 18, 1994, was chaotic as President Clinton received news of the negotiators' progress, with too many aides and officials rushing in and out. Clinton's foreign policy advisors huddled around the famous Oval Office desk once used by President Kennedy. They included Sandy Berger, Tony Lake, Deputy Secretary of State Strobe Talbott, and Secretary of Defense Bill Perry. I ran into Madeleine Albright standing in the hallway. She asked me whether she should join the others, not having been formally asked to attend. "No one else has been invited, either. Just go in," I advised. These were the days before Chief of Staff Panetta had succeeded in limiting who had access to the Oval Office. Clinton's political advisors were there as well, with George Stephanopoulos joining the others in pushing for Clinton to hold firm to his deadline. In Haiti, the junta was stalling.

Then at 4:00 P.M., the mood changed in Haiti. Brigadier General Philippe Biamby, one of the junta leaders, burst into the room where Powell was pressing Cedras, announcing, "The invasion is coming!" The Haitians had learned from a source at Fort Bragg that American paratroopers were getting ready to board their aircraft at 5:00 P.M. Suddenly, the reality of the U.S. invasion sank in. Shortly afterwards, the junta agreed to depart.[26] Clinton called the invasion off.

The next day, September 19, after some more haggling, Clinton's negotiators had a new deal in hand and the first three thousand of an eventual twenty thousand U.S. troops peacefully landed on the shores of the small island nation, without a shot being fired. On October 10, the leader of the military junta resigned. On October 15, after three years in exile, Aristide returned to Haiti, greeted by wild supporters—and high expectations of a new Haiti.

The return to power of Aristide provided the Haitians an unprecedented opportunity to create a new society. At first, progress looked possible. Aristide stepped down from office after his term ended in February 1996, the first-ever transition between two democratically elected presidents in the country. Four and a half years later, in November 2000, Aristide was reelected by an overwhelming margin—92 percent of the voters. The United States successfully transferred its peacekeeping mission to the United Nations, which took it over in March 1995 with a force of 6,000 military personnel, including 2,400 U.S. troops, and 850 civilian police. The policy did protect the key American interest—stemming the tide of refugees arriving on the beaches of Florida—and improved the human rights situation.

The United States rightly gave Aristide and the other Haitian politicians an opportunity to make a functioning democracy. Yet, the Haitians ultimately failed to take advantage of what the international community had provided. Although the Haitian people were certainly better off under democratic governments, Aristide failed to rise above the brutal Haitian politics. He could have used his enormous popular power to build a democratic and moderate center, but instead he used it to undermine his political opponents and seek total power. In the end, Aristide was never able to rise above the two hundred-year-old Haitian dynamic of needing total power to survive. The result was the continuation of Haiti's fractured society, gross abuses of human rights, utter poverty, and political instability. Disputes over the 2000 elections kept the parliament from functioning and further polarized the political parties. Rumors persisted of corruption, drug dealing, and political murders by Aristide and his supporters.

Haiti remains the least developed country in the Western Hemisphere and one of the poorest in the world. According to the 2003 UN Human Development Index, Haiti now ranks 150 out of 175. In 2002, its GNP per capita was $425, 80 percent of the population lived below the poverty line, and more than two-thirds of the labor force lacked formal jobs.[27] As one observer summarized it, "the case of Haiti seemed to show that the international community can put nations into the process of transition, but effecting the transition depends on the indigenous leaders and political class."[28]

The international community, too, bears responsibility for some of the failures. Creating a new political climate and building civic institutions take time, yet the world was in a rush to get out of Haiti. There was little appetite in Washington or the United Nations for a sustained presence in Haiti. International assistance never matched the needs in Haiti. Congress pushed for an early end to the U.S. and UN missions. For instance, on October 6, 1994, both the House and Senate had approved a nonbinding resolution urging the "prompt and orderly withdrawal" of U.S. troops from Haiti.[29] Senate GOP leader Robert Dole said on *Meet the Press* in November, "How long does it take to train a police force? They've had enough time."[30] The UN mission ended in February 2000, well before the political situation had stabilized adequately. The last U.S. troops left Haiti in January 2000.[31]

President Bush took office determined not to follow Clinton's policy of engagement in Haiti, as he and his advisors had long been opposed to Aristide's return. In protest over Aristide's failure to resolve the contested 2000 parliamentary and presidential elections, President Bush froze all aid to Haiti, including $500 million in emergency humanitarian aid from the United States, World Bank, and other international organizations. Without U.S. bilateral and international assistance, Aristide had no chance of governing successfully, and as one observer described it, Haiti's economy "went into a tailspin."[32] The Bush administration pushed him out of office in March 2004.

But, back in 1994, the restoration of Aristide to power set in motion a new use of America's political and military power that will prove enduring over time. For the first time, a U.S. president had considered force not to defeat direct threats to Americans, such as fascism or communism, but rather to defend American principles—respect for democracy and human rights—and interests—and stability in its own hemisphere. America's strategic interests were broadened to include humanitarian catastrophes in traditionally nonstrategic areas. Diplomacy backed by force would be used in such areas now deemed to be in this broader sense of U.S. interest. But given the more diffuse U.S. interests at stake, the administration sought to share the burden. U.S. troops would thus enforce the peace until the job could be handed over to the United Nations and eventually local security forces. The new role of the lone superpower—leadership coupled with burden-sharing—had begun to emerge. A new awareness of the tools the United States had and how to deploy them was developing. The United States would be prepared to use force and persuade others to help in keeping the peace. It would also begin using the full power of its superpower diplomacy, first in promoting peace in the Middle East and Ireland.

3

Go as Peacemakers

Our problems are man-made, therefore they can be solved by man.

—John F. Kennedy

I sat in the middle of the VIP section among three thousand guests on the South Lawn of the White House. It was a crisp, sunny, fall day, September 13, 1993, and the United States' unique position as the only superpower was on display for the world to see. President Clinton gently pressed the two reluctant warriors, Israeli prime minister Yitzak Rabin and PLO chairman Yasir Arafat, toward peace. "Go in peace. Go as peacemakers," he urged. Then, stepping up behind them, he placed one hand gently on each of their backs and prodded them together. Their historic handshake, with Clinton between them, heralded a new era of hope in the Middle East.

Although the pageantry was for the Middle East peace signing, the ceremony marked a significant step in Bill Clinton's evolution from politician to statesman. He had been willing to invest prestige and political capital in a conflict that had eluded resolution for most of the century. It is difficult today, following the collapse of the Middle East peace process, to remember just what a tremendous achievement that handshake on the South Lawn was in 1993, together with the progress made over the next seven years. Through his personal commitment, Clinton demonstrated what could be accomplished when an American president chose to exercise strong leadership in the world and engage reformers willing to work for peace. The collapse of the peace process in 2000 showed the limits of that power as well.

Most importantly, however, the signing ceremony and the seven years of progress signify how the United States in the post–cold war era had become indispensable in international affairs. No other country is capable of underwriting peace between Israel and the Palestinians. The United States, given its unique standing, is able to set the international agenda and to shape events in the world. Military might is a crucial component of America's power and, if used wisely, can effectively back diplomacy. But power is not merely about the size or the number of one's guns. It is also about enticing and persuading others to act.

President Clinton put America's diplomatic, economic, and moral power to use in 1993 when he embarked on peacemaking missions in two of the world's most intractable violent conflicts: Northern Ireland and the Israeli-Palestinian conflict. In both cases, the United States' engagement in the conflicts provided much-sought-after legitimacy for leaders who were willing to distance themselves from terrorism. The Irish Republican Army (IRA) and the Palestine Liberation Organization (PLO) had been largely ostracized in the West because of their terrorist tactics and their opposition to the 1991 Gulf War. With the end of the cold war and the rise of a truly global economy, leading figures in the two groups sought political legitimacy, which only the United States could bestow.

These two conflicts, and both the successes and failures the Clinton administration encountered in trying to resolve them, have a great deal to say about the role of the lone superpower. In both cases, what was at stake was clearly more than humanitarianism, more even than the strong concerns of ethnic diasporas in the United States. Poverty, violence, and instability in Northern Ireland increasingly seemed out of step with the aims of a Europe coming closer together politically and economically after the end of the cold war. In the Middle East, too, peace seemed to promise economic opportunity and a chance for the region's lagging economies to solve their own social tensions by jumping into the global economy. At the same time, it was already clear in the early 1990s, at least to those who chose to look, that the road to solving a whole range of the region's deeper problems—poverty, support for terrorism, lack of democratization—ran through the Israeli-Palestinian conflict.

These were both long-running conflicts, apparently so violent and entrenched that diplomatic approaches risked seeming naive. But the Clinton administration came to understand that the United States had unique tools and opportunities to help the parties move forward: historic ties with the peoples concerned, a reputation for fair dealing, and overwhelming military but also economic might that could speak to the aspirations, not just the fears, of citizens on both sides of the divides.

Successes in Northern Ireland and the Middle East were hard-won, imperfect and, in the case of the Middle East, only temporary. They did not fit the hegemons' vision of an America perfectly able to impose its will. They embroiled the United States in other countries' affairs far too much for the isolationists' liking. But they produced the periods of reduced violence and the greatest economic progress that either region had seen in decades. They lifted U.S. prestige to soaring levels because the United States had overwhelming power and was using it for broader good. Economically and politically, too, they brought benefits that far outweighed the risks involved. They helped lay the groundwork for a new global concept of peacemaking, and new trust of the United States in that role.

The United States is in a unique position to use incentives such as political legitimacy and economic growth to further diplomatic processes. As the sole remaining superpower, the United States can impart legitimacy upon international actors, for instance, through granting them access to the White House. Such recognition is a highly coveted asset that can substantially enhance the position of a leader at home. Moreover, with its dynamic $10 trillion economy, the United States can stimulate growth through investment, assistance, and trade. Where peace is beginning to take root, economic support can make a significant contribution to ensuring that peace holds. American economic statecraft can be an effective diplomatic instrument by raising peoples' standard of living and demonstrating the tangible, everyday benefits to peace. By providing hope for a better future, such investment can be the key to an end to violence.

These two conflicts involved two areas Americans agreed were of strategic interest—Europe and the Middle East. They were also violent. America's growing concern with terrorism in the 1990s gave them a particular urgency. Since the 1960s, some thirty-three hundred people had been killed in the Northern Ireland conflict; the Arab-Israeli conflict had involved costly wars in 1967 and 1973, with the constant possibility of another. The first Palestinian intifada, which means "uprising" in Arabic, erupted in 1987 and had killed and injured twenty thousand people by 1993.[1] The violence and animosity that evolved over the decades of conflict had fostered such distrust between the parties that meaningful direct negotiations were close to impossible. Thus, only an outside party—the United States—could bring negotiations to fruition. Although the Middle East process ended in 2000, it will only move forward once again with U.S. leadership.

There is no accommodating al Qaeda, which seeks to drive infidels out of the Islamic world; their demands are not negotiable. In contrast, there are clear political solutions to the Irish and Palestinian conflicts that negotiations can reasonably be expected to achieve. The PLO and the IRA viewed themselves as freedom fighters seeking liberation of their own people. In the Middle East, Israeli and Palestinian aspirations could be met with two states, its people living within secure borders, although agreeing on the details of those terms remains a massive challenge. In Northern Ireland, a political solution that recognized the rights of both traditions would ultimately bring the violent conflict to an end, although implementation of the peace agreement continues to stall because of continuing distrust and bigotry.

By mid-1993, leaders on both sides in both conflicts turned to the United States, the only country capable of helping the parties negotiate lasting peace. Russia and Europe had little to offer the parties and were preoccupied with internal matters. Russia was struggling to manage the collapse of the Soviet empire. Battling crippling inflation during its transition to a market economy—inflation reached 28 percent in January 1993—Moscow was trying to secure a $43 billion aid package from the world community. Europe was grappling with unification, an unemployment rate above 10 percent, and global economic uncertainties.[2] Europe's and Russia's political and economic frailties prevented them from fully engaging as effective peace brokers. Only the United States was powerful enough—militarily was not necessary, but rather economically and politically—to serve as the indispensable peace broker in the Middle East and Northern Ireland. All parties wanted to be on the side of the superpower.

Clinton instinctively understood the role that the United States could play as peacemaker. Within six months of his presidency, he was gaining the strength and confidence necessary to lead the United States both at home and abroad. In August 1993, Clinton narrowly won the passage of his budget, which was perhaps the most important vote of his presidency since the victory laid the foundation for the economic growth that became the hallmark of his presidency. He also took on Congress to win congressional passage of the controversial North American Free Trade Agreement (NAFTA), which Congress approved in December of 1993.

As Clinton's domestic agenda took shape, he forged a new role for the United States abroad as peacemaker. His early success in the Middle East and Northern Ireland was possible because of diplomatic persuasion, economic enticement, and the moral credibility the United States brought to each peace process.

We don't make peace with our friends but with our enemies

Following the 1991 Gulf War, President Bush made good on his promise to engage in the search for peace in the Middle East. He launched his talented secretary of state, James Baker, to press for progress through two diplomatic channels: one between Israel and Palestine, and another between Israel and its neighboring Arab states. In October 1991, following the Gulf war, the United States and the Soviet Union cohosted an historic meeting in Madrid between Israel, Palestine, and several European and Arab nations. It was the first time Israeli and Palestinian leaders negotiated face-to-face. Baker stressed that peace should come directly from those leaders—not from the United States—and that any peace would have to ensure both Israeli security and some level of Palestinian self-determination.[3] The Bush team had teed up an historic opportunity for peace.

The Oslo process had its origins in a research project on the living conditions in the Palestinian territories by a Norwegian organization[4] headed by a former government minister, Terje Roed-Larsen. Through the project, he and other Norwegian officials had been able to cultivate extensive contacts with Israelis and Palestinians, which had in turn led to secret talks. Not a member of the European Union (EU), Norway was particularly well placed to act as mediator because it was perceived by Israel as not having the pro-Palestinian bias of the EU countries. While Norway's neutrality enabled it to play the role of mediator and catalyst; only the United States was economically and politically powerful enough to help implement a peace accord.

Through the secret talks, the Norwegians had managed to secure agreement between Israeli and Palestinian officials to recognize the other side's right to exist and to take a set of steps leading to a two-state solution to the conflict. The mutual distrust between the parties, however, entailed that the parties needed the United States to endorse what became known as the Oslo Accords. Norwegian foreign minister Johan Holst and Israeli foreign minister Shimon Peres contacted Secretary Christopher and the State Department's point man on the Middle East, special Middle East coordinator Dennis Ross, in mid-August 1993 for help.

Soon after Clinton became president in early 1993, Christopher and Ross had begun pushing for peace in the Middle East along two tracks: peace between Israel and Syria and peace between the Israelis and the Palestinians. Early on, the Syrian track turned out to be a nonstarter since Syrian president Hafez al-Assad had declined several gestures from America and Israel. The talks in Norway, on the other hand, had provided the necessary opening for making peace between the Israelis and the Palestinians. But the parties needed the United States to make the deal.

The secrecy around the talks, in which for the first time Israel agreed to recognize the PLO as a party to the negotiations, allowed for potentially difficult contacts between Israelis and Palestinians. In August, the parties agreed to a "Declaration of Principles," which aimed for a two-state solution. The declaration was carefully constructed as a step-by-step plan that included mutual recognition, security cooperation, and the concept of land-for-peace in which Israel returns land it won in the various wars in exchange for peace. The agreement also called for the further development of Palestinian institutional capacity through the Palestinian Authority. The most contentious issues—borders, settlements, refugees, and the status of Jerusalem—were to be negotiated in a permanent status agreement by May 1999.[5]

These initial steps toward peace were possible because of a confluence of historical factors. In late 1992, the collapse of the Soviet Union, which had been a strong military and financial backer of the PLO, weakened the organization and widened the opportunity for peace. During the cold war, Moscow had sided with Arab nations and many developing nations in sup-

porting the PLO in order to counterbalance the United States and its support for Israel. Now, suddenly, it could no longer count on Moscow's backing. In addition, it had lost financial patronage from Kuwait and Saudi Arabia
because the organization had aligned itself with Saddam Hussein in the first
Gulf war.

Thus, the PLO was searching for recognition and legitimacy as international, political, and financial backing plummeted. On his part, Rabin had
concluded that without the PLO, efforts to create a capable Palestinian government would continue to fail. Rabin also knew that Washington's support was crucial to the implementation of any peace deal. While neither side
trusted the other, they each would trust commitments the parties made to
the United States, not only in signing the Declaration of Principles but also
in developing the confidence-building measures as the process was implemented. In addition, Rabin knew he would need visible and strong U.S.
support for any negotiations with the PLO. Hence, the United States
became the crucial peacemaker.

Knowing that Arafat craved the credibility that entering the White
House would give him, Clinton saw an opportunity to provide political support to Rabin and to prod Arafat to renounce terrorism by offering to host
a gala signing ceremony of the Declaration of Principles. The political benefit of the dramatic breakthrough in the Arab-Israeli peace process was not
lost on the president and his advisors. At the time, however, it was not clear
that Israeli prime minister Rabin would agree to attend such a high-profile
event with a terrorist. He only reluctantly had supported the Oslo process,
which had been led by more left-leaning fellow Labor party officials, Shimon
Peres and Yossi Beilin.[6]

On September 9, 1993, President Clinton called Rabin from Air Force
One to offer warm congratulations on the breakthrough and to try to convince him to come to Washington. "We've taken a very, very dramatic decision," Rabin told the president in his famous husky voice. "It is not so easy
for us. People can't overcome easily the many years of terrorism and killing."
But Rabin understood the moment. "On the other hand, people realize the
time has arrived to make peace." And then, in words President Clinton
would quote often, Rabin commented, "We don't make peace with our
friends but with our enemies." He explained that he had "concluded that
of the options, this is the one we had to take. It is the first time in a hundred years an agreement has been reached between Palestinians and Jews.
Israelis look forward to symbolic, dramatic change that will take place on
Monday," September 13, the scheduled signing day.

Rabin, of course, did come. He was understandably reluctant to appear
on stage with a man he and most Israeli citizens viewed as an enemy of
Israel and a committed terrorist. Until this time, dealing with Arafat had
been off-limits to the United States, but Secretary Christopher had been

working on a clear renunciation of terrorism by Arafat in exchange for the privilege of coming to the White House. The efforts succeeded on September 9, 1993, the same day Clinton called Rabin, when Arafat issued a statement recognizing Israel and renouncing "the use of terrorism and other acts of violence."[7]

Four days later, Arafat walked through the doors of the White House and, for the first time, met with a U.S. president. The negotiations, covering every detail, lasted until the final moments. Arafat only reluctantly acceded to the Secret Service demand that he not wear his omnipresent pistol. Just before the ceremony, National Security Advisor Tony Lake advised the president how to do a jujitsu grasp with his arm to avoid any effort by Arafat to embrace Clinton in front of the cameras.

The grand signing of the Declaration of Principles on the South Lawn of the White House showed Clinton for the first time as a statesman—and it demonstrated the power of the United States to make peace between sworn enemies. The ceremony was attended by thousands of Clinton's friends and supporters, including the Jewish and Arab American communities. Clinton's words "Go in peace. Go as peacemakers" would remain a theme throughout the rest of his presidency.

Success in the short run

Following the Oslo Accords, the United States led a series of negotiations throughout the 1990s that was designed to build toward a fulfillment of the Declaration of Principles. With Secretary of State Warren Christopher shuttling repeatedly to the region, Clinton secured a number of agreements and declarations between Israel and the Palestinians, as well as with Jordan, that heralded an era of unprecedented peace in the region.

On May 4, 1994, Israelis and the Palestinians signed the Gaza-Jericho Agreement, also known as the Cairo Accord, which led to the establishment of the Palestinian Authority (PA), headed by Yasir Arafat. The PA pledged to combat terror and prevent violence. Furthermore, the Cairo Accord laid out the guidelines for implementing the Oslo Accords, with final status negotiations beginning in May 1996 and concluding three years later in May 1999. President Clinton also encouraged a resolution of the wider Arab-Israeli conflict. In July 1994, he invited King Hussein of Jordan and Prime Minister Yitzhak Rabin to the White House to sign the Washington Declaration, in which both pledged their commitment to peace in the region. The 1994 Nobel Prize was awarded to Prime Minister Rabin, Foreign Minister Shimon Peres, and Chairman Yasir Arafat.

Next, on September 24, 1995, the Interim Agreement on the West Bank and the Gaza Strip, also known as "Oslo II" or the "Taba Agreement" was signed in Taba, Egypt, and countersigned four days later in Washington,

D.C. The agreement organized the West Bank and Gaza into three areas, introduced the concept of safe passage between Gaza and the West Bank, and provided the Palestinians with self-rule in a number of towns and villages. Areas "A", "B," and "C" were categorized according to the varying degree of control given to the PA.[8]

Don't let it happen

On November 4, 1995, Israeli prime minister Yitzhak Rabin spoke to tens of thousands of people gathered in Tel Aviv's Square of the Kings of Israel to support the peace process. As he finished his remarks, he declared that "there is now a chance for peace, a great chance, and we must take advantage of it. . . . I have always believed that the majority of the people want peace and are ready to take a chance for peace."[9] Tragically, those would be the last words Rabin spoke in public. As Rabin left the gathering, a Jewish fundamentalist law student, Yigal Amir, walked up to Rabin from behind and shot him several times at point-blank range. The far right in Israel opposed Rabin's efforts to make peace; sadly, with the death of Rabin, the Oslo peace process lost its best hope for success and began to die as well. Amir later explained his actions, saying "A Jew who turns over his land and people to enemies—Halachic law allows him to be killed," referring to traditional Jewish law and teachings.[10]

Speaking in the Rose Garden shortly before 6 P.M., Clinton deplored the loss of his friend and partner in peace. Following the news that Rabin had been shot, he spent the day chipping golf balls on the White House putting green, unable to work, as he prayed Rabin would survive. Visibly shaken, Clinton pledged to continue to press for the legacy of peace Rabin had left behind. Quoting Rabin's words spoken at the White House only the month before, Clinton said, "We should not let the land flowing with milk and honey become a land flowing with blood and tears. Don't let it happen."[11]

Despite deep engagement by President Clinton, the persistent efforts of Secretaries of State Christopher and Albright, and the talented special Middle East coordinator, Dennis Ross, over the next four years, the parties failed to heed Rabin's warning. During the election period following his assassination, there was a wave of terror attacks. Clinton and his Middle East team tried to show the parties the path of peace by organizing an extraordinary summit of twenty-three Arab leaders in Sharm el-Sheik, Egypt, in March 1996, to support the peace process. While U.S. presidents normally refrain from endorsing candidates abroad, Clinton openly backed the Labor Party's candidate Shimon Peres, a strong supporter of the Oslo accords, to replace Rabin. It did not work. A man opposed to the Oslo process, Benjamin Netanyahu of the Likud Party, won the election in 1996, capitalizing on a spate of violence and Peres's lackadaisical campaign. While Netanyahu said he would abide by the Oslo process he had inherited, he did little to implement it. There was some progress during his three years in office. Netanyahu did agree to redeploy troops from Hebron in 1997, where a little-noticed peacekeeping operation has been deployed ever since. Netanyahu and Palestinian officials also agreed to clarify issues regarding the implementation of Oslo II at Wye River, Maryland, in October 1998. The economic front improved as well.

Throughout the Oslo process, the United States, together with Europe, used its economic clout to help promote and maintain momentum. Economic aid was used extensively as an incentive to keep the parties moving toward peace and demonstrate to the population the tangible benefits of peace. For instance, following the Oslo signing, the United States presented an aid package of $500 million for the West Bank and Gaza. Beginning in 1993, the United States provided $75 million a year to assist the Palestinians. In 2000, Congress approved $400 million in supplemental assistance to the United States Agency for International Development (USAID) for its activities in the occupied territories to facilitate the Wye Accord between Israel and the Palestinians. Between 1993 and 2002, USAID funding to the occupied territories totaled $1.1 billion, making the United States the largest bilateral donor to the Palestinians.[12] For a while, there was hope that Oslo would be fulfilled.

Yet, following Rabin's death, the Oslo process stalled. Its interim steps lagged and Palestinian violence escalated. The Palestinians objected to the lack of release of their prisoners, of a halt to Israeli settlements, of Israeli troop redeployments out of Palestinian areas. On the Israeli side, support for a peace process eroded as Arafat's commitment to peace came increasingly into question. They felt betrayed by the PLO's continuing incitement to violence in the media and in the classroom, and the failure of the PLO to live up to its other Oslo commitments such as limits on the police force and weapons. Peace got a last chance following the election in May 1999 of Labor's Ehud Barak, who came to office determined to pick up where Rabin had left off.

Recognizing that the failure to implement the Oslo timetable risked an end to the peace process and a resumption of hostilities, Clinton pushed both sides to resume final status negotiations again in Sharm el-Sheik, Egypt, in September 1999. At second Sharm el-Sheikh talks, Barak and Arafat signed the Sharm el-Sheikh Memorandum, which reiterated the need to put the timetable of the 1998 Wye River agreement back on track, but no concrete commitments were made. As Clinton's presidency drew to a close in 2000, the parties had yet to enter into, much less conclude, negotiations on the permanent status agreement called for in May 1999 by the Oslo Accords. Seeking to put the full weight of the United States behind the search for peace, in the final months of his presidency Clinton decided to take the risk of pushing the parties to the table.

During fifteen intense days in July 2000, Clinton, with the strong support of Israeli prime minister Barak, led negotiations between Barak and PLO Chairman Arafat at Camp David, not coincidentally the site of President Carter's historic 1978 negotiations which led to the 1979 peace treaty between Israel and Egypt. Aided by Secretary of State Albright (who had replaced Christopher in 1997), Dennis Ross, and their first-rate team, Clinton took the unprecedented step of putting forward his own concepts and proposals, although he did so only orally. Clinton had to shuttle between the two leaders, as Barak refused to negotiate personally with Arafat. Despite the efforts, the talks ended without agreement, with both Clinton and the Israelis blaming Arafat for the breakdown, although Arafat had warned Clinton the summit was likely to "explode in the President's face."[13]

Shortly thereafter, the Palestinians resumed their campaign of violence, the intifada, largely abandoning negotiations. Subsequent investigations found a "confluence of circumstances and frustrations"[14] were the cause of the new uprising. Overall, the Palestinian leadership endorsed the second intifada as an ill-conceived way to pressure Israel to leave the occupied territories. The Palestinians violently protested the controversial visit of Ariel Sharon, one of Israel's most hard-line politicians at the time and the leader of the opposition Likud Party, to the Temple Mount, a holy site to both Jews and Muslims. The protests initially involved Palestinian youths throwing Molotov cocktails and stones at Israeli soldiers and police. They soon escalated into a street war between Israeli forces and Palestinian security officials and gunmen and eventually to Palestinian suicide bombers targeting Israeli civilians. This second intifada continues today.

On December 23, 2000, amidst the increasing violence, Clinton outlined "parameters" that he felt could serve as the basis for the long-sought two-state solution. The Palestinians would have close to 100 percent of the West Bank territory, although 1 to 3 percent would be swapped for Israeli settlement land, and the 3.5 million Palestinian refugees would have the right to return to Palestine,[15] although, for the most part, not Israel. Jerusalem would be divided between the two sides, with each exercising sovereignty over the holy sites in Old Jerusalem.[16] Tragically, Clinton left office on January 20, 2001, without an agreement, even on his parameters.

The parties continued negotiations without Clinton between January 21 and January 27, 2001, in Taba, Egypt, where they came to significant understandings on key issues of territory, Jerusalem, refugees, and security. Specifically, it was agreed that the June 4, 1967, borders would remain, and the two sides would share a divided Jerusalem as their capital, with each side having control over certain neighborhoods in the city. They also came to common understandings, although not formal agreements, on issues of refugee return and control of holy sites.[17] Although the sides came as close as they ever had to a final peace settlement, the Taba talks ended in failure. In the snap elections Ehud Barak called on February 6, 2001, the Israeli public, reeling from the intifada, elected the hawkish Ariel Sharon with 62.5 percent of the vote. The peace process has been essentially suspended ever since.

The causes of the breakdown in the peace process in the fall of 2000 will remain the subject of historical disagreements. Certainly, the death of Israeli prime minister Rabin on November 4, 1995, dealt a severe blow to the process. Had he lived, the Oslo process might have succeeded as Rabin had the vision, political courage, and strength to press for progress on both sides and perhaps achieve a settlement, including a Palestinian state by the end of the decade. Another consideration was the lack of constructive involvement of the Arab states in actively pushing Arafat to make peace. Saudi Arabia, Egypt, and Syria, which opposed a peace that did not include a return of the Golan Heights, were noticeably absent in actively supporting a peace process during the 1990s.

One key lesson from the failure of Oslo is the difficulty in meeting the people's expectation of improvements to their daily lives. Particularly when the superpower is involved, citizens assume that following a peace process their daily lives will vastly improve. Such is the case today in Iraq. Certainly, during some periods of the Oslo process, Palestinians enjoyed improved prosperity and relative calm in the occupied territories—in no small part thanks to U.S. economic assistance and $1.5 billion in international assistance.[18] There were improvements in banking and construction. The Palestinian economy enjoyed a 4 percent growth rate in 1998, and employment was up over 7 percent in the first six months of 1999.[19] Israel's economy also improved substantially. By early 2000, unemployment had dropped to 1.3 percent, the lowest rate in thirty-two years.[20] As the head of USAID in Gaza Larry Garber explained, "In the last two years before the outbreak of the intifada, the massive investments were paying off. There was more hope than ever in the fall of 2000 for the Palestinians to enter the global economy."[21]

During the lagging Oslo political process, the daily lives of the Palestinians did not improve sufficiently to deter them from a return to violence. For success, this process must allow people to feel the benefits of peace and experience a significant improvement in their lives. But the standard of living for the Palestinians in the occupied territories remained abysmal. Throughout most of Oslo, their economy suffered and their unemployment rate remained high—20 percent in 1995, a significant increase from 5 percent in the 1980s. From 1992 to 1996, real per capita GDP declined by one-third.

Since the second intifada began in September 2001, the lives of the Palestinians have deteriorated significantly. Support for negotiations in Israel has evaporated.

Palestinian unemployment in 2003 was as high as 50 percent, with up to nine hundred thousand Palestinians prevented from getting to work by Israeli road closures established for security reasons. Sixty percent of the population in the West Bank and Gaza live under the World Bank's poverty line of $2 a day. The cost in human terms is high. Since 2000, over 3,200 Palestinians and over 970 Israelis have been killed, and 27,000 Palestinians and 6,500 Israelis have been injured.[22] Increasingly, terrorist groups are growing in influence and will vastly complicate the peace process whenever it resumes. The terrorist organization Hamas, for instance, is increasingly providing social services to Palestinians and growing in popularity.[23]

Both sides blame each other for the failure. Israelis lambasted the Palestinian stonewalling at Camp David, charging that Arafat walked away from a generous agreement and was unwilling to engage or offer constructive proposals. Former Israeli prime minister Barak claimed that Arafat lacked "the character or will" to compromise and never intended to secure a peace. "He did not negotiate at all. He just kept saying 'no' to every offer, never making any counterproposals of his own."[24] Palestinians refute this charge, claiming that they warned the United States in advance that the summit was "insufficiently prepared."[25] The Palestinians had entered the talks reluctantly and ultimately accused Israel of offering a proposal that would not yield a viable Palestinian state, although most observers agree that both Barak and Clinton did offer Arafat exactly that. Others disagree. Terje Roed-Larsen, who had in 1999 been appointed UN special coordinator for the peace process, noted, "It's a terrible myth that Arafat and only Arafat caused this catastrophic failure. All three parties made mistakes . . . no one solely is to blame."[26]

Had Clinton and Barak more time in office, or had Clinton's successor picked up where he left off, perhaps more progress could have been made. Had Arafat been willing to negotiate in the final days of Clinton's and Barak's time in office, a peace most likely could have been reached. Many now question whether Arafat was ever serious about renouncing violence and making peace with Israel. By the end of the summit, most Israelis were convinced that the Palestinian leadership had rejected the most generous offer yet made by Israel. Many believe Arafat decided instead to return to violence. As a result, according to one report, "they seriously questioned whether the Palestinians had truly accepted the two-state solution and Israel's right to exist."[27]

Most of Clinton's negotiating team aggress that Arafat was not prepared to make peace. Dennis Ross explains Arafat was "a decision-avoider, not a decision-maker. . . . By never fully deciding, he avoided exposure and possible opposition, and he preempted his colleagues from revealing to people like me or the Israelis what the ultimate concessions might be."[28] James Steinberg, who was integrally involved in the negotiations during Clinton's eight years in office, said, "There was no harm in his taking interim steps, but he was never going to sign a final deal. He does not believe in a two-state solution. He is certainly not willing to give his life for it. He kept the ball moving down the field but would never accept that there was a finish line."[29]

In fact, Arafat reportedly told Clinton at Camp David, "I can sign this deal, but you will have to come to my funeral." Former President Clinton summarized the failure, "Perhaps he simply couldn't make the final jump from revolutionary to statesman. . . . Arafat never said no; he just couldn't bring himself to say yes."[30] In June 2002, following President Bush's efforts to ostracize him, Arafat said he accepted the peace plan Clinton put forward at the end of his term. Most viewed the comment as cynical, for Arafat knew President Bush and Sharon had taken Clinton's proposals off the table.[31]

Since President George W. Bush took office in 2001, the United States has rejected any serious engagement in the peace process, and progress has stalled on all fronts. The Bush administration proposed a road map, involving reciprocal steps leading to the creation of a poorly defined "provisional" Palestinian state in 2005. It has failed, however, to foster a return to negotiations and is, in the words of Ariel Sharon, "effectively dead."[32] Instead, President Bush's policy has been simply to lend his full support to Prime Minister Sharon's increasingly hardline strategy toward the Palestinians and to disengage from efforts to resume meaningful negotiation.

For his part Arafat refused to stem the violence and undermined efforts to establish a functioning Palestinian leadership. While the Palestinians have selected several prime ministers who ostensibly were to take over the functions of the governing Palestinian Authority, Arafat retained the real power and blocked any meaningful reforms. By 2004, he had lost all credibility; neither the Israelis nor the United States would deal with him. They considered him part of the problem, not the solution. As of this writing, Arafat lay dying in a Paris hospital. His death will enable new Palestinian leadership to emerge and perhaps pave the way for new negotiations.

Israel has taken increasingly strong measures against the Palestinians in an effort to protect themselves from their continuing terrorism including the increased use of women and children as suicide bombers blowing up Israeli civilians. To prevent Palestinian infiltration, Israel built a Berlin Wall–type security fence along the West Bank, a move supported by 80 percent of Israelis. Increasingly, Israel is resorting to assassinating Palestinian leaders who are considered behind the terror attacks, including the founder of Hamas, Sheik Ahmed Yassin, in March 2004 and his replacement, Dr. Abdel Aziz Rantisi, the following month. One observer described the effort as "mowing the grass." Recognizing the steps will not end terrorism, officials believe it will slow it.[33] While the United States opposed such a move, Sharon made it clear that Arafat could have been targeted as well.

In April 2004, Israeli prime minister Ariel Sharon dramatically changed the political landscape by announcing that Israel would no longer wait for the Palestinians to negotiate a peace and that he would instead move forward with a series of unilateral steps. He declared Israel would, on its own, withdraw from Gaza and retain some of the West Bank settlements. He also made it clear that the Palestinian refugees do not have the right to return to Israel. President Bush, with an eye to the November 2004 elections, broke with longstanding U.S. policy against unilateral measures and endorsed the plan as "historic and courageous."

In the end, the United States will have to engage once again, directly and at the level of the president, in the search for peace between Israelis and Palestinians. Without sustained U.S. engagement in the search for peace, the situation will continue to worsen. The continued suicide bombings have eviscerated the support for the peace process in Israel; neither Prime Minister Sharon nor any successor will make peace with the Palestinians until a more responsible post-Arafat leadership emerges. The Arab leaders must play a constructive role as well, pushing for reforms and a Palestinian commitment to peace.

The parties are so polarized, it will take time before they return to final-status negotiations. Given the ongoing violence, it may even take a generation. But in the meantime, the United States must push for progress and an end to the violence. Like the overused analogy of a bicycle, it falls over if it does not keep moving forward.

It remains to be seen whether the parameters Clinton put on the table will still be viable after years of violence. It is noteworthy, however, that the December 2003 Geneva Accord—an unofficial joint Israeli-Palestinian draft peace accord with no official standing—mirrors most of Clinton's parameters and has gained cautious yet widespread support from Israelis, Palestinians, and the international community.[34] The accord, which was a private initiative that built on the progress made at Taba, calls for a nonmilitarized Palestinian state in the West Bank and Gaza in return for peace with Israel. The Palestinians would have sovereignty over the Arab neighborhoods in East Jerusalem, their holy sites in Jerusalem, particularly the Al-aksa mosque, and their capital in the Arab neighborhood of East Jerusalem. Some heavily populated West Bank settlements would be part of Israel, in exchange for an equivalent amount of land going to Palestine. Most of the Palestinian refugees would have the right of return to Palestine, but not Israel, or the right to receive compensation. Polls indicate that 53.3 percent of Israelis and 55.6 percent of Palestinians support the broad approach of the Geneva Accord initiative.[35] Thus, while growing more difficult by the day, the opportunity for peace remains, if only the Israeli and a new Palestinian leadership will seize it, and if the president of the United States will help them reach it.

Taking risks for peace: The Gerry Adams visa

In the fall of 1993, I began receiving calls from my contacts in the Irish-American community who said that the IRA was considering a ceasefire and a negotiated settlement to the conflict in Northern Ireland. Although not all of the IRA leadership agreed, some, in particular Gerry Adams, the president of Sinn Fein, the IRA's political wing, increasingly questioned whether a quarter century of violence was really achieving the IRA's goals. Its own children were coming of age, and many IRA members were asking whether they wanted the next generation to repeat their lives of violence and long prison terms. The time had come to explore alternatives.

Although the United States has a long history of negotiating in the Middle East, the issue of Northern Ireland had always been off-limits to American administrations. Governments on both sides of the Atlantic felt that the issue was best left to London and Dublin. Especially during the cold war, Washington did not want to risk alienating Downing Street over a "second tier" issue that the UK government saw as an internal affair. But with the cold war over, the United States was more willing to risk a rift if such an effort could contribute to peace and end terrorism in Northern Ireland. Thus, Clinton's first break with the UK came not, as many expected, on the issue of Bosnia but rather on Northern Ireland.

In the Northern Ireland conflict—as in the Middle East conflict in 1993—the United States began its role as peacemaker after the fighting parties reached agreement on broad principles of cooperation. The British prime minister John Major took a more moderate approach to Northern Ireland than his predecessor, Margaret Thatcher. She had notoriously exclaimed, "Never!" when asked if she would negotiate with the IRA, and instead let the IRA activist Bobby Sands die while on a hunger strike.[36] Major, who came to office in 1990, recognized the benefits of negotiations. He also saw in his Irish counterpart, Albert Reynolds, a partner with whom he could work toward a solution to the conflict. On December 15, 1993, Major and Reynolds put forward a "Joint Declaration" in which the British government committed itself to abide by the wishes of the majority of the citizens of the North, and the Irish government renounced its claim to the North until the people agreed to change its status.[37]

The new British recognition of the right of self-determination for the citizens of Northern Ireland addressed the key demand of the predominantly Catholic Nationalist community, namely that Northern Ireland could join Ireland. Equally, the predominantly Protestant Unionist community insisted there would be no change in the status without the consent of the majority, which happened to be Unionist. The Republic of Ireland, for its part, undertook to alter its constitution to abandon its claim on the six provinces of the north, a key demand of the Unionist community, which wanted Northern Ireland to remain part of the United Kingdom.

Significantly, by addressing the Nationalist community's main complaints head-on, the Joint Declaration challenged the IRA's argument that violence was the only recourse to achieving the goals of a British withdrawal and unification with Ireland. It also lent important support to the more moderate Nationalist Party, the Social Democratic and Labour Party (SDLP), which opposed violence. The door for peace opened. But, as with the Middle East Declaration of Principles, the parties could only negotiate if a third party joined the process to bridge the gap of distrust. The United States stepped in to be the indispensable intermediary among the parties. President Clinton also had a personal interest in the conflict dating back to his student days as a Rhodes Scholar at Oxford, when he watched the beginning of the "troubles." Clinton had always felt that the United States could play a peacemaking role between these two close U.S. allies. As president, he would get that chance.

Engaging a terrorist

In late 1993, Gerry Adams wanted to visit IRA strongholds in the United States, both to underscore his primacy as a political leader and to press for support for a possible IRA ceasefire. However, he was barred from entering the United States because of his support for terrorism, and there was significant opposition within the Clinton administration to issuing a waiver that would allow his entry.[38]

While there was no concern that Adams would engage in acts of terrorism during a visit to the United States, there was real trepidation in U.S. law enforcement circles that he would use the visit to raise funds in the United States, and thus increase the overall lethal capacity of the IRA. Bomb detonators, recently purchased by IRA supporters in Phoenix, Arizona, had already begun showing up in terrorist attacks. There was a particular concern that the funds would be spent on "stinger" missiles, which could be used to shoot down aircraft. The visa request came as the threat of terrorism was becoming an increasing focus of the U.S. government, especially following the first World Trade Center bombing in early 1993. Letting a known leader of a key terrorist organization into the United States was strongly opposed by every relevant department of the U.S. government.

The informal network of Irish activists and political leaders that I had come to know while working with Kennedy in the Senate proved invaluable to developing a successful policy on Northern Ireland at the White

House. Their information served as an important counterweight to the pro-British State Department and the FBI, which accepted without review London's analysis of the situation. Part of the "special relationship" between the United States and Britain involves an agreement that the countries will not spy on each other. This meant that the United States had virtually no independent intelligence on, or analysis of, the peace process in Northern Ireland.

In asking for background on Adams, I was given the British line. While probably accurate in the broad sense, the analysis neither indicated the existence of divisions within the IRA nor suggested that key leaders were prepared to end violence. Despite his denials, Adams was believed to be central in the IRA structure, probably a leading member of the Provisional Army Council, the highest authority in the IRA, which meant that he would have had direct knowledge of any planned IRA terrorist operation. A friend told me in 2004 that Northern Ireland's police force, the Royal Ulster Constabulary (RUC), claimed to have Adams on tape approving a murder, although while I was in government, I never heard such an accusation. Adams had strong political backing among Irish American business and political leaders and received significant funding from the Irish American community. Adams had also developed strong links to the Democratic Party, especially in cities such as New York, Chicago, and Boston with large Irish American constituencies.

In order to gain a more nuanced idea of what was happening in Northern Ireland, I often sought the advice of John Hume, the most respected Nationalist leader. Known as the "Martin Luther King of Northern Ireland," he had led nonviolent protests in the 1970s and created the SDLP, the political party of Nationalists opposed to violence. Hume had been engaged in a secret dialogue with Gerry Adams since 1986, always keeping me briefed on the progress while I was in Senator Kennedy's office, and later when I was at the White House. Hume probably knew Adams better than anyone outside the inner circle of Sinn Fein and IRA officials.

In the fall of 1993, I invited Hume to lunch in the White House "mess," a windowless basement room covered in dark wood paneling in the West Wing. Over soup and sandwiches, Hume told me that elements within the IRA were moving toward peace and advised me to follow those events closely. By the time we spoke again, after the Joint Declaration in mid-December, he argued that granting Adams the visa would facilitate the peace process in light of the new atmosphere. The fact that Hume was now recommending that the president take such a step caught my attention as he had an astute sense of the peace process. I also knew much of Irish America would follow his lead.

Clinton was under considerable pressure from all sides over the visa issue. Saying no to the visa would cause an uproar among some of the president's closest political allies in Congress and Irish America, largely supportive of Adams. While saying yes would please Clinton's political and financial supporters, it would also enrage the president's Cabinet—including Secretary of State Christopher, FBI Director Louis Freeh, and Attorney General Janet Reno.

Clinton's political and congressional advisors in the White House, as well as many political appointees of Irish origin, were naturally in favor of the visa and as much engagement as possible. But no NSC or State Department official favored those steps. The sole exception was Jean Kennedy Smith, the ambassador to Ireland and Ted Kennedy's sister, who understood that Adams was serious about moving the IRA toward peace. But to do so, he needed the support of the United States.

Irish America mobilized to pressure Clinton to engage Adams. Members of Congress and leading financial backers of the president called, wrote, and cajoled the president to give Adams the political support he would need to convince the IRA to declare a ceasefire and enter into negotiations. In early November 1993, Ted Kennedy, who had long opposed the IRA's use of violence and thus a visa for Adams, changed his view and threw his considerable political weight behind Adams' request. He was soon followed by nearly two dozen other senators and former New York governor Mario Cuomo. In early January 1994, a leading New York businessman, William Flynn, and George Schwab, who, with Flynn, ran the respected National Committee on American Foreign Policy, sent invitations to five leaders from Northern Ireland, including Adams, to a "peace" conference in New York starting on January 31. Clinton was forced to make a decision.

A win-win situation

Clinton was due to decide the issue on Sunday morning, January 30, 1994, a day before the peace conference began. Lake's British counterpart, Roderic (Rod) Lyne, realized that Clinton was close to giving Adams the visa and made a final attempt to prevent it from happening. He called Lake and reminded him that Adams was a leading figure in the IRA, which had murdered not only thousands of its own countrymen, but also one member of the royal family, one cabinet minister's wife, two close advisors to Margaret Thatcher, two members of parliament, two British Ambassadors, and—to hammer home the point—"small children in shopping centers."

Clinton called Lake from the White House residential quarters around 11:00 A.M. and Lake asked me to pick up on one of the extensions in his West Wing office. For about a half an hour, we went through the arguments with the president on why he should grant the visa. Clinton threw at us the arguments of Secretary of State Christopher, CIA Director Woolsey,

Attorney General Reno, and FBI Director Freeh: What if Adams comes here and IRA violence increases? What if he fails to deliver a ceasefire? How can we stop him from fundraising? Won't the British stop cooperating with us on Bosnia if we cross them on this? Can't we wait until Adams goes further?

Lake and I walked him through the objections, refuting each point. We argued that giving Adams the visa was a win either way for the president. If it helped foster a ceasefire, then Clinton's actions would be vindicated. If Adams failed to deliver a ceasefire after Clinton had risked such political capital on him, then Clinton would be in a strong position to turn Irish America against Adams and undermine the IRA.

Ultimately, it was this "win-win" logic that persuaded the president to move forward. His instincts had long urged him to take the plunge into Irish politics, and now was his chance. He ended the phone call with a simple, "OK, let's do it."

Diplomacy and dollars

In New York, Adams gave a straightforward speech at the peace conference and took part in a whirlwind of press conferences and television shows, including *Larry King Live*. Although nothing substantive happened, the trip gave Adams the political clout he needed to engage in peace at home.

As expected, the visit caused a furor at 10 Downing Street. Major refused to take Clinton's calls for several days and the British tabloids were full of malicious headlines such as "Slimy snake Adams spits venom for Yanks" and "Why don't the Yanks keep their noses out of Ulster?"[39] Yet, the Adams visit put pressure on both the IRA and the United Kingdom to make progress in the negotiations. Prime Minister Major accelerated political talks among the parties, and Adams came under increased pressure from Irish America and the Irish government to deliver the ceasefire that he sought.

Eight months later, on August 31, 1994, the IRA declared a ceasefire. The loyalist paramilitaries, linked to the Unionists, followed suit in October. Through a dance of engagement with Adams that continues today, the United States pressed him to enter the political process and end IRA violence. Clinton used increased access to the White House and senior government officials as incentives, eventually meeting with Adams himself in November 1995 during his historic visit to Belfast.[40] Clinton reached out to the Unionist politicians in the same fashion, inviting Ulster Unionist Party leader David Trimble to the White House.[41] As with Yasir Arafat, access to the White House bestowed political legitimacy on Adams and Trimble, thus increasing their political power at home and helping them to move forward toward peace.

Unlike in the Middle East conflict, America's economic might proved decisive in fostering the peace process in Northern Ireland. The skillful use of economic incentives ensured that momentum was not lost. The conflict in Northern Ireland had caused immense economic deprivation: in 1988, unemployment in Northern Ireland was at 17.9 percent compared to 9.3 percent in the rest of the United Kingdom.[42] The deprivation fueled the sectarian conflict as unemployment levels in the Nationalist community were much higher than in the Unionist community. For instance, unemployment among Catholics reached 34 percent in 1987, up from 17 percent in 1971. In some Catholic neighborhoods in West Belfast, unemployment was as high as 80 percent.[43]

Clinton also put considerable effort into promoting trade and investment in Northern Ireland. If the United States could spur economic growth, the next generation of potential terrorist recruits might choose a job instead. Clinton sent Commerce Secretary Ron Brown on several trips to Ireland and Northern Ireland to promote economic growth. The White House also organized a Trade and Investment Conference in May 1995, inviting all the political parties from Northern Ireland. For the first time ever, members of Nationalist and Unionist parties gathered under one roof at the Sheraton Hotel in Washington. Drinking at the bar late into the morning, men who literally had spent years plotting ways to kill each other now joined together to discuss how to create more jobs in both communities. Although inconceivable in Northern Ireland, it was possible for these sworn enemies to meet each other under the cover of a United States–sponsored event designed to create more jobs back home.

Clinton's focus on the concept of "commercial diplomacy" gave an important boost to the peace process. Suddenly, people could feel the benefits of peace. Northern Ireland has been the fastest growing regional economy in the UK in recent years.[44] Between 1992 and 2000, GDP increased by 26 percent in Northern Ireland, and unemployment fell by 40 percent in the same period.[45] By focusing on jobs, Clinton began to show the parties that the peace process was not a zero-sum game but one in which all sides could benefit. That shift in mentality proved crucial to progress. In contrast to the Middle East peace process, the economic benefits in Northern Ireland solidified support for that process and kept the pressure on the political leaders to preserve the peace.

Former senator George Mitchell was appointed by Clinton in 1995 to be special advisor to the president and secretary of state for economic initiatives on Ireland. While initially brought in to increase U.S. trade and investment in the region, Mitchell ultimately became the key mediator in the peace process. His years as Senate majority leader had instilled in him the patience and vision necessary to bring the negotiations to fruition. After an extraordinarily difficult session, Mitchell succeeded in securing an historic peace agreement among the parties on Good Friday, April 10, 1998. As chair of the talks, Mitchell masterfully kept the parties negotiating despite their mutual animosity and suspicion. When John Hume and David Trimble received the 1998 Nobel Peace Prize for the agreement, many felt George Mitchell should have shared in the honor.[46]

President Clinton's personal commitment in the Northern Ireland peace process, as in the Middle East process, was vital in keeping the negotiations going. He repeatedly called the parties, staying up all night to see the talks through. In a speech in 2000, Irish prime minister Bertie Ahern told President Clinton that "the success of the peace process . . . would not have been possible without you."[47] The role of the United States also became critical in building confidence among the parties. While neither side trusted any commitments made to each other, any commitment made to the United States, especially the president, could be trusted.

Today, the peace process remains a difficult one, with the Northern Ireland self-governing institutions suspended over lack of agreement between the Unionists and the Nationalists over issues such as whether the IRA has sufficiently disarmed. Unionists remain deeply opposed to any steps toward a united Ireland. While overall the peace is holding, frustration over the lack of progress is growing. In the November 2003 elections, the hardliners gained ground, with the hardline Democratic Unionist Party led by the Reverend Ian Paisley, and the party linked to the IRA, Gerry Adams' Sinn Fein, won over the more moderate parties, including John Hume's party, the Social Democratic and Labour Party, and David Trimble's Ulster Unionist Party. Yet, a return to violence appears unlikely, as the benefits of peace, an end to the killings, and an increase in economic prosperity continue to outpace the frustratingly slow political progress.

The U.S. role in the Northern Irish and Middle East peace processes demonstrates the political, economic, and moral power of the United States. As the sole remaining superpower, America has the political standing to give the parties confidence in each other through the commitments they have made to the United States. They might mistrust each other but not the United States. These are not simply "altruistic" actions. Peace in the Middle East and Ireland are in the interests of the United States. Links to the IRA and terrorists in Libya, the Basque regime in Spain, and Colombia are now broken. With a resumed peace process, the destabilizing Arab-Israeli conflict would also reduce hatred of the United States abroad and lessen terrorist recruitment.

As a superpower, the United States cannot solve or engage in every conflict. But well-timed and well-chosen engagement can be the catalyst to bring about peace. As president, Clinton also engaged in numerous other conflicts around the world and appointed a record fifty-five special envoys.[48] He used American diplomacy assertively to resolve or prevent conflicts, not only in the Middle East and Northern Ireland but also to calm tensions between Greece and Turkey and to avoid a potential nuclear war between

India and Pakistan. He also played a critical role in lesser-known disputes, such as helping to negotiate an end to the conflicts between Peru and Ecuador and between Eritrea and Ethiopia.

In countries where the United States has historic ties and unique influence on the leaders, superpower diplomacy can make the difference between war and peace. In some cases, however, diplomacy is a necessary but not sufficient condition for peace. At times, the use or threat of force must back up the diplomacy. Nowhere was that fact clearer than in the wars in Bosnia and Kosovo.

4

Force and Diplomacy

Make war that we may live in peace.

—Aristotle

Around 6:30 P.M. on July 14, 1995, I received an odd call from the president's secretary, Betty Curry. "The president asks that you join him on the putting green," she said. Sandy Berger and White House Press Secretary Michael McCurry were also instructed to join President Clinton. While I wasn't exactly sure where the putting green was located, I headed toward the Rose Garden, and nearby I saw the president chipping golf balls.

"I'm getting creamed on Bosnia," he fumed. War was raging in the Balkans. Three weeks earlier, seventy-one civilians had been killed when a bomb exploded in a crowded downtown area in Tuzla, a town in northeastern Bosnia. The UN and NATO had responded by authorizing air strikes against Serbian ammunition bunkers. In turn, the Serbs took four hundred UN personnel hostage, using a number of them as human shields to prevent further strikes. The Serbs humiliated the UN personnel, handcuffing them to possible targets and cutting the electricity supply to Sarajevo.[1]

"Why aren't you all giving me better options? Chirac at least has some new ideas," Clinton continued, referring to the newly elected French president Jacques Chirac's suggestion to put a ten-thousand-strong Rapid Reaction Force (RRF) on the ground to provide greater protection for the UN peacekeepers. Clinton had been pushing his advisors to come up with new policy options on Bosnia for months. He was annoyed that Chirac had seized the initiative—and the limelight—with a proposal to send an initial one thousand RRF troops to protect Gorazde, a UN protected zone called a "safe area" east of Sarajevo. Calling for a "firm, yet limited military action," Chirac wanted the United States to provide air cover and lift for the troops.[2] Clinton thought the RRF proposal was ill-conceived since it relied on the flawed and weak UN rules of engagement. As the war raged, the efforts of the UN peace-keepers were increasingly futile as there was no peace for them to keep. The blue helmets were treated as pawns on the battlefield, and their presence some-times made them complicit in the ethnic cleansing. Lacking an alternative, Clinton did not want to block the European effort, and he agreed to provide the RRF with financial assistance, military lift, military equipment, logistics assistance, and intelligence support.[3] But as expected, the troops failed to make a meaningful difference in stopping the Serb attacks.

As the president practiced his stroke, Sandy and I explained that all his advisors agreed on the need for new thinking and that Tony Lake was devel-oping some "blue sky" options, meaning all current assumptions were sub-ject to review, including the use of ground troops. Clinton knew of Lake's effort but wanted immediate answers. Two and a half years into his presi-dency, Clinton was still struggling to end the war in Bosnia—or find a way he could neatly walk away. He had unsuccessfully tried limited military air strikes, high-level negotiations, tough sanctions to press Serb compliance, and UN resolutions condemning the parties' failure to live up to their agreements. In addition, political pressure was mounting as the man who would challenge him for the presidency in 1996, Senator Robert Dole, gathered support for a resolution to lift the arms embargo against the Bosnians.[4] Although the president was sympathetic to lifting the embargo, he understood that doing so would put the UN troops at risk and would likely unleash a Serb initiative to gain as much ground as possible before the Bosnians rearmed.

With Bosnia, as with many crises, officials clung to the hope that a solu-tion could be found through diplomatic avenues. Throughout the Bosnian war, various UN, EU, and U.S. envoys shuttled through the region to bro-ker peace, with occasional tactical successes that offered the promise of an end to the war.[5] Yet, hopeful periods in the negotiations ultimately only bought the Serbs more time for their offensives and delayed Clinton's deci-sion to use force. By 1995, it was clear that negotiations on piecemeal issues were failing. Only a comprehensive negotiation—and only diplomacy backed by force—would end the war. Only the United States could secure that peace.

While some have criticized Clinton's use of force in Bosnia and in Kosovo a few years later as unnecessary humanitarian interventions, both actions were in fact central to America's national security interests, espe-cially ensuring regional stability in Europe. Mindful of the fact that seven decades earlier, violence in the region had triggered a world war, Clinton recognized that Milosevic's dream of Greater Serbia and his campaign of ethnic cleansing could have grave consequences for the rest of Europe if left unchecked. Policymakers had very real concerns: the potential for Europe cleaving along Christian-Muslim lines, unchecked flows of drugs, guns, and people through a no-man's land in southeastern Europe, and the unwanted economic consequences of war and instability in the heart of Europe. Standing on the sidelines had by 1995 damaged the United States' prestige and moral authority. Especially in the new globalized age, the superpower was expected to act in the face of Europe's obvious inability to stem the slaughter of innocent civilians on the continent that had pledged "never again" just fifty years before.

The step from these diffuse but real national interests to a sound mix of force and diplomacy proved very difficult, both for the United States and our European allies, who had even more immediate interests at stake. Both political parties and the American public struggled, not always rationally, between their deep revulsion at what they saw on their television screens and an equally deep reluctance to commit U.S. ground troops. In 1995 the United States was prepared to fight against the Soviet Union, but not to use force commensurate with its more diffuse interests in the Balkans. That meant a deep reluctance to put U.S. ground troops into the conflict and an overreliance on a failed peace process.

Yet, in Bosnia, as in Somalia and Haiti, the United States confronted an adversary that would not be dissuaded without the use of force. Ultimately, the successful use of force—and the U.S.–led negotiations that ended the Bosnian wars after four long years—set the stage for a new understanding of America's place in the world to emerge.

Peacekeepers without a peace to keep

Throughout early 1995, the Serbs continuously exposed the ineffectiveness of UN peacekeepers and the inability of the international negotiations to stop the war. The United Nations had been given a mandate to "deter attacks" on six safe areas established in May 1993 in Bosnia and Herzegovina. While the UN presence no doubt saved some lives through its delivery of humanitarian assistance and by deterring some Serb attacks, ultimately an estimated twenty thousand people, primarily Muslims, were killed in and around the safe areas. During its three-year presence from February 1992 to March 1995, the UN peacekeeping operation suffered a total of 167 fatalities.

The worst atrocities occurred in Srebrenica in July 1995, two years after it was ironically designated as the world's first United Nations safe area. Early in the morning of July 6, the Bosnian Serb Army launched its attack on the town, populated mostly by Muslims. Knowing they were no match for the two thousand advancing Serb forces, the six hundred lightly armed

Dutch peacekeepers, led by Colonel Ton Karremans, repeatedly asked for air strikes against the Serb forces.[6] At first, the UN forces were ordered not to return fire and withdraw. It soon became clear that a massive assault on Srebrenica was under way as the Serbs heavily shelled the town. Confusion at the UN and NATO headquarters regarding the situation on the ground, concern that military action would endanger UN troops, and a desire to keep the UN "neutral" in the war delayed any decision on air strikes until after the Serbs had entered Srebrenica in mid-July. Only then did NATO act, targeting two Serb vehicles and dropping two bombs. The Serbs immediately threatened to kill the Dutch peacekeepers if there were further air strikes. There were none.

The Serb attack on Srebrenica became the single most brutal slaughter in Europe since World War II. Twenty-three thousand women and children were rounded up and expelled from the town to non-Serb areas of Bosnia. The Serbs detained between four thousand and five thousand men and in the early morning hours of July 14, they loaded them into vehicles and transported them to what would become extermination sites. Over the next two to three days the Serbs systematically shot them. Up to eight thousand people are still missing and presumed murdered.[7]

News of the atrocity quickly leaked out, first by eyewitness accounts from refugees who saw the deportations and suspected the worst, then by survivors of the executions who had managed to escape. Human Rights Watch recorded the testimony of one eyewitness to the massacres. The Serbs, he said, picked out Muslims, interrogated them, and made them dig pits. "During our first day, the Cetniks [Serbs] killed approximately five hundred people. They would just line them up and shoot them into the pits. The approximately one hundred guys whom they interrogated and who had dug the mass graves then had to fill them in. At the end of the day, they were ordered to dig a pit for themselves and line up in front of it. . . . [T]hey were shot into the mass grave. . . . At dawn . . . [a] bulldozer arrived and dug up a pit . . . and buried about four hundred men alive. The men were encircled by Cetniks: whoever tried to escape was shot."[8]

By early August, Clinton and his advisors were shown haunting photos from U.S. spy satellites. The photos, which the administration soon made public,[9] showed large patches of freshly bulldozed earth around Srebrenica. As I looked at the photos in the White House Situation Room, there was little doubt that the mounds of earth contained the bodies of the thousands of missing males from Srebrenica. Albright used the photos in the Security Council in her efforts to press for tougher action. "This is clearly a case that needs to be investigated by the war crimes tribunal," she said after the meeting.[10]

Following the fall of Srebrenica, the Serb military leaders made clear their intention to eliminate the other UN safe areas. They quickly surrounded the town of Zepa and, as the architect of the massacre, war criminal General Ratko Mladic, said, "By the autumn, we'll take Gorazde, Bihac and in the end Sarajevo and we'll finish the war."[11] Clinton had to make a decision: either involve the United States directly in the effort to end the war, or give up and leave the Bosnians to fend for themselves. The Serb forces, led by Slobodan Milosevic of the former Yugoslav Republic, were succeeding in carving out pieces of Bosnia for his expansionist plan. The multiethnic state of Bosnia was at risk.

The battleground shifts

Ultimately, events on the battlefield shifted in the Bosnians' favor and paved the way for direct U.S. involvement in the war. In early August, the Serbs suffered a military loss that triggered their willingness to negotiate an end to the war. In neighboring Croatia, the nationalist leader, President Franjo Tudjman, had sought to regain a Serb-controlled area called the Krajina after it had been seized by Milosevic's forces following Croatia's declaration of independence in 1991. The United States turned a blind eye to the action, understanding that it would help pressure the Serbs to negotiate. Weakened by NATO's bombing campaign and focused on having the sanctions lifted, Milosevic was willing to sacrifice the Krajina. Serb forces fled the region, and two hundred fifty thousand Serbian civilians were driven out of their homes, many of whom had been there for centuries. Croatian forces conducted their own ethnic cleansing operation as brutally as the Serb forces did against the Croats and Muslims, including summary executions.[12]

Within three days, the Krajina was in Croatian control and the tide of the war had shifted. Prior to the offensive, the Bosnian Serbs had controlled roughly 70 percent of Bosnia. By September, they controlled roughly 49 percent, with the Croats and Bosnians together controlling 51 percent.[13] The shift on the battlefield made it possible for the United States to use these percentages as the basis for negotiations in the endgame strategy.

By the summer of 1995, Clinton had realized that more half measures would not end the war. He had already tried the threat and use of limited air strikes against the Serbs: in 1993 to stop the Serb "strangulation" of Sarajevo; in February 1994 to insist that the Serbs withdraw their heavy weapons following the shelling of the Markala marketplace in Sarajevo; in April 1994 against Serb forces attacking the Muslim enclave of Gorazde; in November 1994 as a response to Serb attacks against the western Muslim enclave of Bihac; in May 1995 to press the Serbs to withdraw heavy weapons from around Sarajevo; and following the Serb attack on Tuzla.[14] These "pinprick" strikes ultimately were ineffective as they failed to change significantly the battlefield and were not linked to any comprehensive effort at diplomacy. The Krajina gave Clinton an opening to change that equation.

To make a difference, Clinton knew he would have to take not only the unpopular step of using American ground troops in Bosnia but also using force to back up American diplomacy. Only 3 percent of Americans considered Bosnia a major foreign policy issue, with 19 percent calling for the United States to "stay out of affairs of other countries." A mere 6 percent saw U.S. foreign policy as an important issue at all.[15] The crisis was also affecting the president's political standing as he began to prepare for his reelection campaign. Clinton's approval rating on foreign policy issues had dipped as low as 39 percent by June 1995, with 53 percent disapproving.[16]

Despite the opposition of the American people to engagement in the Balkans, Clinton decided in December 1994 to pledge between twenty thousand and twenty-five thousand U.S. troops to assist a UN troop withdrawal if needed. Putting troops directly into the conflict remained off-limits, but the need for American ground troops to implement a new policy was increasingly clear. As the situation continued to deteriorate in mid-1995, Clinton began to prepare the public for a possible deployment of ground troops in Bosnia. He reiterated his commitment to assist NATO at the U.S. Air Force Academy on May 31 and again in a radio address on June 3.[17] The policy of assisting in a withdrawal of the UN put the United States in the awkward position of being willing to use troops in a failure, but not in a successful peace. Soon America would also decide to put its full weight, including U.S. troops, behind the search for peace. Clinton and his team prepared a new diplomatic strategy—a comprehensive negotiation to end the war. This time, the diplomacy would be backed by airpower.

Endgame

In late June 1995, Lake began to draw up the endgame of the war in Bosnia.[18] In doing so, he turned his own principals' interagency process on its head: rather than develop options and recommendations among his colleagues, which would then be discussed with the president, Lake developed a strategy with a small NSC team, made sure the president was on board with the general approach, and only then went to his colleagues. As Lake described the new policy, building on his early "Tell, don't ask" approach, he made it "clear to the allies that they had no veto over our approach; we would act with or without them." Lake also used a carrot-and-stick approach on all the combatants, making it clear the Muslims would be pressured as well, to convince the parties it was "in all their interests to settle."[19]

The presence of the UN peacekeepers had become a hindrance to tougher international action, as they provided ready hostages for the Serbs. Thus, Lake pushed for an agreement: if the final, high-level U.S. effort for a negotiated end failed, the United States would press to get the UN out, lift the embargo, and help the Bosnians fight for themselves. The superpower, as part of the "lift, arm, train, and strike" strategy, would provide this and other support to the Bosnians, including enforcement of the no-fly zone and air strikes, for a nine-month period while the Bosnians gained strength to defend their territory. Should the Bosnians use U.S. air cover to start a new offensive, the United States would simply lift the embargo and leave them to their own fate. Up to twenty-five thousand U.S. ground troops would be used, either to help the UN withdraw or to support a peace settlement. It was a high-risk effort, but one Clinton was prepared to take. "The situation underscores the need for robust airpower," Clinton said to his advisors on July 18. "The United States can't be a punching bag in the world anymore."[20]

Lake received key support from the Pentagon in July. Responding to Chirac's proposal to send RRF troops to Gorazde, Chairman of the joint Chiefs of Staff Shalikashvili traveled to Paris to deflect the ill-conceived proposal. His effort proved crucial in developing, for the first time since Vietnam, the use of airpower to achieve political aims. Shali argued that the one thousand RRF troops Chirac proposed to send to Gorazde would be too vulnerable unless NATO first destroyed the Serb air-defense systems that could attack the troops. Thus, Shali pushed for a "devastating" air attack against the Serbs rather than sending in the troops. He also argued that the UN forces had to be withdrawn to avoid more hostage-taking.

Shali's proposals for air strikes were adopted at an "international crisis meeting" of foreign and defense ministers of NATO and Russia, called by British prime minister John Major in London on July 21.[21] At the London conference, the United States agreed with its allies that NATO would respond to an attack on the safe areas—or a clear preparation to do so—with a significant air campaign throughout Bosnia. The allies also streamlined the cumbersome process that had hindered the decision to use force. The "dual keys" to authorizing close air support were now placed in the hands of local military men—the UN commander on the ground and NATO's regional commander, rather than political leaders in New York and Brussels. On August 1, NATO further refined the proposals, announcing that any attack or threat of attack on the safe areas would be "met with the firm and rapid response of NATO's airpower."[22] There was agreement to use force only to protect the safe areas. Washington or Europe had not yet decided to use force to end the broader war.

In a series of intense meetings between August 7 and August 9, Lake worked with his colleagues to build support for a diplomatic strategy to complement Shali's and now NATO's military strategy. Lake wanted one that would push for a negotiated end to the war but preserve the essence of the multiethnic Bosnian state. Knowing he already had Clinton's blessing for a United States–led comprehensive negotiating endgame effort, Lake pushed the strategy through the policy process in Washington. In the end, the president formally approved it, although the State Department and the Pentagon had deep reservations. Secretary Christopher had called Clinton from abroad to argue that the plan was too ambitious and unlikely to gain the support of the allies; Secretary of Defense Perry warned of a Vietnam-like quagmire. Only UN Ambassador Madeleine Albright fully endorsed Lake's approach.[23] With Clinton's blessing of the plan, Lake left the night of August 9 to secure the support of Europe, Turkey, and Russia.

Having followed a strategy of "muddling through" the Bosnian quagmire since 1992, the Europeans had begun to accept that only the use of force could end the nightmare. The recent Serb defeat in the Krajina, the failure of the pinprick air strikes to bring lasting Serb compliance, the Srebrenica massacre, the humiliation of the UN troops, and the new determination from Washington all came together to bring about support for the new policy. As Lake told his colleagues on his trip to Europe, the "big dog" had barked; once the United States made its position clear, the Europeans followed. The endgame was teed up.

On August 14, 1995, Lake met in London with Richard Holbrooke, then assistant secretary of state for European affairs, to hand off the mission. While tempted to negotiate the endgame himself, Lake understood that the national security advisor's role was broader than what such an intense and specific task required. Thus, Holbrooke took over from Lake and began one of history's most intense and brilliant negotiations. America was now prepared to use forceful air strikes against Serb forces and weaponry to compel Milosevic to agree to a negotiated settlement.

The test came on August 28, when a Serb artillery shell hit a crowded marketplace in Sarajevo, killing thirty-eight civilians and wounding eighty-five. The atrocity triggered Shali's policy that had been endorsed in London. That night, the UN and NATO each turned their "keys," launching the largest NATO military action in its nearly fifty-year history. "Operation Deliberate Force" began on August 30 and did not end until September 14. It involved over 3,500 aircraft sorties, thrusting 1,026 bombs against 48 Bosnian Serb targets.[24]

Still seeking a negotiated settlement, the UN requested and was granted a halt in the campaign. The UN demanded a negotiated pullback of the Serb's heavy weapons used to shell Muslim cities, an end to attacks on safe areas, and an end to attacks on and freedom of movement of international personnel. The UN commander, General Bernard Janvier, set out the demands in writing to the indicted Serb leader, Ratko Mladic, including a deadline of 11 P.M. Monday, September 4, for withdrawal of heavy weapons. The operation had to be completed quickly, Janvier insisted, or "air and military attacks will be resumed." The UN also passed the demand on to Milosevic in Belgrade.[25]

The negotiations failed after Mladic, calling NATO worse than Hitler, rejected the UN demands. With the strong urging of the new negotiator,

Richard Holbrooke, who told his colleagues in Washington, "Give us bombs for peace,"[26] the NATO campaign resumed on September 5, with ninety aircraft attacking Serb military targets in Bosnia. The attacks over the next several days included Tomahawk cruise missiles and the radar-guided missiles made famous by the Gulf War, which had an important psychological impact on the Serbs. In all, NATO conducted eleven days of bombing, interrupted by a three-day pause for UN negotiations. The air campaign tipped the balance for Holbrooke.

Throughout the NATO bombing, Holbrooke and his team had been conducting intensive shuttle diplomacy around Europe, meeting with NATO and European leaders as well as Milosevic. Holbrooke had lost three members of his negotiating team in an accident along the dangerous road to Sarajevo, including one of my NSC colleagues, Nelson Drew.[27] The tragedy drove Holbrooke even harder to secure an agreement as an honor to their legacy. In Geneva on September 8, he secured the Joint Agreed Principles Agreement from the foreign ministers of the three warring parties, Croatia, Bosnia, and Serbia, in the first high-level meeting among the three in two years.[28]

On September 13, as NATO planes were bombing Bosnian Serb territory, Holbrooke and his team met with Milosevic, Mladic, Karadzic, and an array of Bosnian Serbs in Milosevic's villa outside Belgrade. Recognizing the meeting as their "moment of maximum leverage," Holbrooke and his team pressed the Serbs to agree to a ceasefire, repeatedly threatening to walk out when the Serbs stalled by denouncing the NATO actions. After ten hours of negotiations, at 2:15 A.M. on September 14, the Serbs signed the United States–drafted agreement that they cease all offensive operations, remove all heavy weapons from the safe areas, open land routes out of Sarajevo, and open the Sarajevo airport. As Holbrooke later summed up, the mistake of the West over the past four years had been treating the Serbs as "rational people with whom one could argue, negotiate, compromise, and agree. In fact, they respected only force or an unambiguous and credible threat to use it."[29]

The bombing was also suspended on September 14, but Holbrooke kept open the threat of resuming it until he secured a formal ceasefire agreement. On September 20, UN and NATO officials announced that the Bosnian Serbs had met their demands, including the withdrawal of heavy weapons around Sarajevo. Thus, "the resumption of air strikes is currently not necessary."[30] Operation Deliberate Force formally ended the next day. Over three thousand "air sorties" had attacked more than sixty targets. The three-year siege of Sarajevo had ended.[31] The use of force finally brought Milosevic to the negotiating table.

Dayton negotiations

In his memoir, *To End a War*, Holbrooke provides an intriguing, detailed history of the negotiations at the Wright-Patterson Air Force Base in Dayton, Ohio. The talks, which took place between November 1 and November 21, involved a complicated set of negotiations among the leaders from the three former Yugoslav republics (the Republic of Bosnia and Herzegovina, the Republic of Croatia, and the Federal Republic of Yugoslavia). The talks also involved negotiations of leaders of the two new entities within Bosnia (the Republic of Bosnia Herzegovina and the Serb Republic).

In the end, the parties chose peace, agreeing to preserve Bosnia's multi-ethnic state, with the Republic of Bosnia Herzegovina (made up of Croats and Muslims) holding 51 percent of the territory to the Serbs' 49 percent. The presidency rotated among the three ethnic groups and ceded strong power to the two federal entities, the Republic of Bosnia Herzegovina and the Serb Republic. The delicate balance of power in the federal government was severely challenged by the strong nationalist leaders, Franjo Tudjman of Croatia and Slobodan Milosevic of the Federal Republic of Yugoslavia.

The negotiations left difficult questions unresolved and created new problems. In Holbrooke's view, the serious flaw in Dayton was that it left two separate, opposing armies in one country, one for the Serbs and one for the Croat-Muslim Federation, although disarming the parties at the time of Dayton was not possible.[32] The Dayton constitution provided for "an extreme degree of decentralization," as one analyst describes it, failing to resolve whether Bosnia's future lies in reintegration or further separation.[33] By the fall of 2004, nine years after Dayton, nationalists in both Bosnia and Croatia had shown only sullen acquiescence in the political reforms pushed by the international community. To this day, nationalist politicians in Belgrade continue to undermine the agreement, driving a separatist agenda in the Serb Republic and in Kosovo. As the respected International Crisis Group (ICG) found, "The Serbian government continues to hamper the effort by stalling reforms, thereby undermining the overall political progress that can be achieved."[34] Although imperfect, Dayton was the best peace that could have been reached at the time. Strong international leadership remains key to continuing its evolution and implementation.

The successful conclusion of the Dayton Peace Accord demonstrated the power of American diplomacy backed by military force. Only an American diplomat—and only one with Holbrooke's tenacity and brilliance—could have brought the war to an end, and Holbrooke succeeded because he could rely on American military power. Although U.S. negotiators angered their European and UN colleagues by limiting their role at Dayton, they had no other choice. German foreign minister Klaus Kinkel blasted the United States for giving the impression "that Europeans contributed nothing." He vowed not to allow "European participation [to be] pushed into the background."[35] But the weak, multiparty negotiations the Europeans had pursued between 1991 and 1995 led to the lowest common denominator of success, and the parties could always play the differences among the Europeans off one another for a weaker deal. With the United States in charge, the Balkan parties had less room to exploit those differences.

Not only did United States–led negotiations and air power bring the parties to the negotiating table, sixty thousand United States–led NATO troops secured the peace on the ground in Bosnia. The administration wrongly estimated the original time frame of one year for the troop deployment. Concerned Congress would not fund the Bosnia deployment without an exit strategy and wanting to set clear military goals following Somalia, the administration set an arbitrary deadline that was thought to be feasible at the time but proved to be wildly inaccurate. The troops proved essential at keeping the peace as the implementation of Dayton lagged. Rather than one year, 1,580 U.S. troops (out of a total of about 7,000 NATO troops) remain in Bosnia today, with the Europeans set to take over the mission in 2005.[36] Despite many differences, the United States had worked in partnership with Europe throughout the crisis, and today the Europeans are shouldering the bulk of the burden.

The United States–led peace in the Balkans underscored the role of America as the lone superpower. In 1995, Europe was not ready to step up to the plate, while the United States could not step back and expect others to achieve its aim of a peaceful Europe. The success of the United States–led negotiations pushed back on the isolationist forces at home and also demonstrated that the United States did have a role to play, as policeman at least, in Europe. Ultimately, by working with Europe and the United Nations to forge an international response, the resolution of the Bosnian crisis underlined that the world did not resemble the hegemons' view that the United States does not need international partners.

The lessons of the Bosnia crisis helped craft a new way forward for American foreign policy, and it shaped a new perception of the UN's ability to use force. The stark lesson is that the United Nations peacekeepers cannot fight a war, nor can they enforce a peace. Throughout the atrocities at Srebrenica, for instance, UN troops never fired at attacking Serb units. The UN forces were lightly armed and placed in indefensible positions; furthermore, they were outnumbered and overpowered by Serb forces that had the support of armor and artillery.[37] United Nations troops were reluctant to use force, believing that action would make them participants in the war and undermine what the UN saw as its core mission: the provision of humanitarian assistance. The UN also feared losing control of the military action once it turned its "key" as well as reprisals against the peacekeepers.[38]

Central to the inability of the UN is this strong reluctance to use force. Secretary-General Boutros Boutros-Ghali had spoken against a "culture of death," supporting only nonmilitary methods in the search for peace. Thus, when the Europeans provided UN troops with a heavily armed rapid reaction force, the UN argued against using it. It was only after Dayton that the UN recognized that "the Bosnian Serb war aims were ultimately repulsed on the battlefield, and not at the negotiating table."[39]

In its frank 1999 assessment of the tragedy of Srebrenica, the UN put forward the key lessons from the Bosnian quagmire that still shape the body's approach to crises. The report states that "peacekeeping and war fighting are distinct activities which should not be mixed. . . . Peacekeepers must never again be deployed into an environment in which there is no ceasefire or peace agreement." While saying the UN cannot fight the world's wars, the UN report challenged the international community to use force to stop ethnic cleansing. "The cardinal lesson of Srebrenica is that a deliberate and systematic attempt to terrorize, expel or murder an entire people must be met decisively with all necessary means. . . ."[40]

In May 2003 the International Criminal Tribunal for the Former Yugoslavia began a trial against four military officers in charge of the Bosnian Serb army in Srebrenica. They were all charged with crimes against humanity, complicity to commit genocide, and violations of the laws or customs of war. One was sentenced in December 2003 to seventeen years in prison and another, who had pleaded guilty in May 2003, received a twenty-seven-year prison term. As of this writing, of the other two officers, one has been sentenced and the other is still in trial proceedings. Although the two men most responsible for the massacre, Radovan Karadzic and Ratko Mladic, were indicted by the Tribunal on July 24, 1995, for genocide and crimes against humanity, both remain at large.

Kosovo

The world proved it had learned from the Bosnian crisis when Slobodan Milosevic began to foment yet another war in the Balkans. In early 1998, Milosevic accelerated a policy of repression and intimidation of Kosovo-Albanians in Kosovo, a province that had enjoyed large autonomy until the end of the cold war. Kosovo, the site of an historic battle in 1389 by the Serbs against invading Turks, has long been a symbol of Serb nationalism, although it was inhabited largely by ethnic Muslim Albanians by the end of the twentieth century. In 1989, Milosevic had revoked the province's autonomy in his nationalist bid for power. During the 1990s, Belgrade's violent measures in the small province fueled aspirations for independence and fostered the emergence of the Kosovo Liberation Army (KLA), a small insurgency group.

The brewing conflict reached a critical moment in March 1998 when Serb forces and paramilitary groups massacred fifty-eight Kosovars. From then on, violence quickly escalated with large-scale Serb operations against Kosovar civilians and the KLA. Serb forces drove some three hundred thousand Kosovar Albanians from their homes, of whom fifty thousand took refuge in nearby hills, at risk of death in the coming winter. Kosovar refugees began pouring over the borders as Serb forces ethnically cleansed the province. In 1992, the first president Bush had warned Milosevic—in the so-called "Christmas warning"—that the United States would use force against the Serbs if they provoked a conflict in Kosovo, a threat the Clinton administration reiterated when it took office in 1993. Having watched Milosevic's brutal actions in Bosnia, the international community knew only too well the risk faced by the civilian population. The question now was whether the international community would take action and whether Clinton would make good on his warning to Milosevic.

In September 1998, as a response to the violence in Kosovo, the Security Council passed Resolution 1199, which recognized that the situation constituted a threat to regional peace and security, demanded a ceasefire, a withdrawal of Serb forces attacking civilians, and a negotiated solution to Kosovo. At the time, I was serving as one of the ambassadors to the United Nations responsible for the Security Council, having left the White House at the end of Clinton's first term. In negotiating the resolution, I had been instructed by Washington to seek inclusion of a reference to Chapter VII of the UN Charter, a first step toward the authorization of the use of force. Russia, in particular, opposed any use of force against its traditional ally in Belgrade and thus argued against the use of Chapter VII. Sitting in the private "informal" chamber across the hall from the Security Council, I listened as the Russian and Chinese delegations passionately argued against any use of force. The sophisticated Russian ambassador, Sergey Lavrov, spoke in Russian, although he could speak near perfect English. One of the UN's most talented diplomats who was appointed Russia's foreign minister in March 2004, Lavrov could oscillate between a suave European diplomat supporting the need to end the violence in the region and a Soviet-era apparatchik. He was reminiscent of Khrushchev pounding the table in the General Assembly when defending the Serb actions.[41]

Following a flurry of calls between Washington and Moscow, Russia voted reluctantly for the resolution, publicly declaring it did not consider it a resolution to authorize force. The UN Security Council adopted Resolution 1199 in a 14 to 0 vote, with China abstaining, fearing a precedent that might lead to international interference in its own affairs. It contained the Chapter VII reference and defined the situation as a "threat to peace and security in the region." In an example of how convoluted the negotiations in the UN can get, Russia had refused to accept a reference to "international" threat and blocked the inclusion of an authorization of "all necessary means," to counter the threat, UN–speak for the authorization of the use of force.

As he would do regarding Iraq in November 2002, in explaining Russia's vote, Lavrov insisted that "there is nothing in this resolution which authorizes the use of force." The colleague with whom I tag-teamed the Security Council, Ambassador A. Peter Burleigh, made it clear that the United States interpreted the resolution differently. "Planning at NATO for military operations if these efforts do not succeed is nearing completion," he said after the vote, adding that "the international community will not stand idly as the situation in Kosovo deteriorates."[42] As with the 2003 Iraq debate in the United Nations, the language in many UN resolutions contains a sophisticated ambiguity that enables each country to put its own interpretation on it. In this case, however, the resolution's broad support and tough U.S. rhetoric clearly put Belgrade on notice that this time the United States would not wait two years before acting decisively to stop ethnic cleansing in Europe.

That fall, Clinton took the lead in pressing Milosevic to negotiate a peace in Kosovo or face NATO air strikes against Serbia proper if he did not halt the atrocities in Kosovo. As the Serb obstruction continued, one Serb diplomat even joked, "A village a day keeps NATO away,"[43] underscoring the Serbs' initially successful efforts to anticipate and adapt to U.S. political constraints on sending troops into combat in the Balkans. In early October, Clinton again sent Richard Holbrooke to negotiate with Milosevic, who stalled on accepting the demands until October 13 when NATO issued activation orders for air strikes against Yugoslavia, to begin in ninety-six hours. Milosevic agreed later that day to comply with the demands set out in UN Resolution 1199 under which Serb forces in Kosovo would be garrisoned and refugees would be allowed to return. He also agreed to admit unarmed international monitors into Kosovo to verify compliance and to complete negotiations on a political framework by November 2, 1998. The Security Council endorsed the Holbrooke-Milosevic Agreement on October 24, again under the Chapter VII provision. Yet, with only unarmed observers and no international troops capable of enforcing the agreement, it was short lived. On January 15, 1999, following three days of artillery shelling, Serb forces entered the village of Racak in southern Kosovo and executed forty-five people.[44]

By early 1999, it became evident that the United States had to bring an end to Milosevic's war in Kosovo with the threat—and possible use—of military action. While no one brought up ground troops, Albright proposed to her colleagues in Washington that Milosevic be given an ultimatum to accept the proposed interim settlement, enforced by NATO troops, or face an air campaign. By January 20, President Clinton had agreed to the new approach and Albright set off on a diplomatic blitz to gain allies' endorsement. The results were impressive. On January 26, she secured Moscow's agreement, on January 29, that of the European allies and the formal endorsement of the Contact Group,[45] and finally that of NATO, which announced on January 30 its intention to use force to compel compliance should either the Serbs or the Kosovars reject the proposal. Despite the strong opposition of China and Russia, UN Secretary-General Kofi Annan, who had succeeded Boutros-Ghali in 1997, had urged NATO to endorse the approach, declaring that the wars of the 1990s had not "left us with any illusions about the need to use force, when all other means have failed. We may be reaching that limit, once again, in the former Yugoslavia."[46]

With the use of force to back up diplomacy clearly established, Secretary of State Madeleine Albright began negotiations on February 6, 1999, in Rambouillet, France, for a political settlement between Serb and Kosovo-Albanian leaders. The proposal on the table provided for the KLA's disarmament, the withdrawal of Serb forces under the supervision of NATO troops, and substantial autonomy for Kosovo—leaving its final status to be resolved at a later date. As with Dayton, annexes provided for a new constitution, elections, and military and civilian implementation provisions. Much of the negotiations focused on what type of security guarantees the international community was prepared to undertake and what the parties would accept. The Kosovars wanted a substantial military presence, ideally with U.S. troops, in the province; for the Serbs such a presence was anathema. Reluctant to commit to ground troops, it was not until February 13 that Clinton announced that the United States would participate in such a force.

Albright made it clear to the Kosovar representatives that they had little choice but to take the deal or otherwise face abandonment by the international community. The Kosovars finally signed on March 18. The negotiations, however, broke down after the Serbs refused to accept the plan, considering the Kosovo autonomy provision and the presence of foreign troops on Serb territory too great an intrusion on their territorial sovereignty. The United States then made good on its Christmas warning, and NATO initiated air strikes on March 24 against Yugoslavia to force compliance with the terms of Rambouillet.[47]

Russia had endorsed the political strategy but strongly opposed the use of force, and indicated that it would veto any Security Council resolution authorizing it. Hence, to avoid a situation in which the Security Council explicitly rejected an authorization to use force, no further resolution was circulated by the NATO members in the Council. Russia, however, made the mistake of presenting a resolution condemning the campaign. The move backfired as twelve of the fifteen Security Council members voted against it, demonstrating strong, if indirect, support for the campaign. Thus,

NATO's war in Kosovo was initiated without explicit UN Security Council authorization, although the military action was endorsed by NATO, the UN secretary-general, and a large part of the international community. In addition, the campaign's political goals were supported by a series of previous UN Security Council resolutions and by all the key leaders in Europe, thus guaranteeing, in stark contrast to the war against Iraq in 2003, strong international support for the policy's implementation once the military campaign ended.

Although the United States and its NATO allies anticipated that a short, intense bombing campaign would quickly coerce Milosevic to the negotiation table, Belgrade instead hastened its ethnic cleansing of Kosovo, expelling most of the Kosovar Albanian population from their homes. In all, nearly three-fourths of the prewar population of 1.8 million ethnic Albanians were driven from their homes. Eight hundred thousand were forced out of the country; another five hundred thousand were internally displaced.[48]

Having seen the use of force work quickly in Haiti, and having watched Milosevic capitulate in 1995 to the bombing campaign, administration officials wrongly assumed Milosevic would soon give in to the latest NATO campaign. Officials underestimated the fact that Kosovo was the cradle of Serb nationalism—the ideology that ensured Milosevic's hold on power. In addition, Clinton and his advisors took the ill-advised step of publicly ruling out the use of ground troops in the conflict. "I do not intend to put our troops in Kosovo to fight a war," Clinton declared on March 24 in his address to the nation on the eve of the bombing campaign. Clinton and his advisors, believing grounds troops would not be necessary, wanted to avoid an unnecessary fight with a Congress that remained skeptical over the action in Kosovo. The House of Representatives, in fact, voted on April 29 to prohibit ground forces in the region without prior congressional approval and was divided on supporting the air war. The American people were also divided on the issue, with 46 percent supporting U.S. ground troops and 45 percent opposed.[49]

The statements ruling out ground troops served to embolden Milosevic during the bombing campaign and probably forced a longer bombing campaign than might have otherwise been necessary. During a White House meeting on April 21, Blair pushed Clinton to put ground troops on the table. While stopping short of committing to do so, he left the door open. "When we fight, we fight to prevail," Clinton said, vowing to continue the campaign "for as long as it takes."[50]

As the campaign dragged on, NATO commanders, in particular the supreme allied commander, General Wesley Clark, pushed for an escalation of the bombing, often over the objections of a skeptical Pentagon and NATO allies. British prime minister Tony Blair also pushed particularly hard for a ground invasion. By late May, NATO launched as many as three hundred strike sorties a day, a ten-fold increase from the war's first week, against the Serbs' air-defense network, infrastructure, command centers, airfields, main army units, and heavy weapons. Some purely political targets, such as the Socialist Party headquarters, were taken out as well. In a stunning mistake, NATO bombed the Chinese embassy in Belgrade on May 7, believed by the CIA to have been a Serb military communications facility. But the escalation of the attacks continued. Clark, recalling the words of General MacArthur, "There is no substitute for victory,"[51] also pushed to keep the option of using ground forces on the table. Clinton eventually shifted his position and issued a call up of thirty-three thousand reservists on April 27.

Throughout the campaign, Russian president Yeltsin had pressed for an immediate end to the bombing. Yet, by April, he realized his efforts had little support, and he launched his former prime minister, Viktor Chernomyrdin, on a seven-week mission to find a way to end the war, in effect accepting NATO's policy that Milosevic comply with its demands. On May 6, the Group of Eight (G8) industrialized nations, including Russia, issued a statement of principles intended to serve as the basis for an end to the war, including a ceasefire, a pullout of Serb military and police forces, an international security presence, full return of refugees, and participation at a later date in negotiations to determine the final status of Kosovo. On May 18, Clinton announced publicly for the first time that the allies "will not take any option off the table," indicating that ground troops were a possibility.[52] Traveling to Belgrade on May 27, Chernomyrdin told Milosevic, who was indicted that same day by the International Criminal Tribunal, that Moscow believed NATO would launch a ground invasion if he failed to meet NATO's demands calling for an end to the repression and violence in Kosovo, the withdrawal of Serb forces, the return of refugees, and an international civil and security presence.

A troika of Clinton's deputy secretary of state, Strobe Talbott, Finnish president Martti Ahtisaari, and Chernomyrdin presented the international community's core demands to Milosevic on June 2. With Russia now supporting NATO's position, Milosevic understood that he had no choice but to comply. Milosevic began to pull his forces out of Kosovo, and air strikes were suspended on June 10. The campaign, named Operation Allied Force, had lasted for 78 days and consisted of more than 38,400 air sorties, including nearly 10,500 air strikes against Serb targets. Not one Allied fatality occurred.[53] Although the campaign initially failed to deter Milosevic's ethnic cleansing of Kosovo, most of the Albanians returned after Serb troops withdrew.

Two days after the campaign ended, in a surprise move Russian troops, in armored vehicles with the name of the NATO operation "KFOR" newly painted on the sides,[54] took over the airport in Kosovo without informing

NATO. Although this caused a minor diplomatic spat, in the end, Moscow became more cooperative, providing four thousand Russian troops to the stabilization effort. On June 12, peace-enforcing troops from NATO and non-NATO countries entered Kosovo. Within five days, twenty thousand troops had been deployed as part of the force that would eventually reach forty-six thousand from thirty-nine countries, including the twelve thousand European RRF troops and twenty-five thousand U.S. troops.[55] As Bosnia had painfully demonstrated, UN troops could not perform such an enforcement mission. Rather, the United Nation's role would be to create the institutions and local capacity of a multiethnic, inclusive society of Kosovo-Albanians, Kosovo Serbs, and other minorities, protected, as in Bosnia, by a stabilization force. About twenty thousand NATO troops, including twenty-five hundred U.S. troops, remained in Kosovo in 2004. In addition, thirty-eight hundred international civilian police forces and military observers are operating under the UN.[56] In contrast to the United States having to go it mostly alone in Iraq in 2003, thirty-four nations remain in Kosovo five years after the war. Less than 10 percent of the force is American.[57]

Today, although the Kosovars are living free from the violence of Serb troops, the failure of the international community to resolve the final status of Kosovo remains a source of instability for the region. Belgrade's ongoing goal of regaining control of the territory, or at least the Serb parts, fuels fear and extremism in the province. The tensions caused by four and a half years of very slow progress erupted in mid-March 2004 when mobs of Albanian youths, extremists, and criminals went on a rampage that escalated into ethnic cleansing of Serb villages and neighborhoods, leaving nineteen people dead, nearly nine hundred injured, and forty-five hundred displaced. The violence was the worst since the end of the NATO bombing campaign and served to justify Serbian fears of repression by the Albanian community. It demonstrated the need for the Albanians to provide responsible leadership in ensuring respect for the Serb minority community, more accommodation of their needs, and support for the return of Serb refugees.

The international community mistakenly believes that negotiating the final status will foster instability rather than resolve its underlying causes. The insistence on "standards before status," that Kosovo meet certain international standards before resolving its final status, has failed. The international community must now move forward on resolving the final status of Kosovo, making it clear that the province will never return to Belgrade's rule. The problematic UN mission should transfer to the Europeans who should be more willing to take charge of issues on the continent. Full independence, however, can only come once Kosovo has met these international standards, including respect for the Serb ethnic minority.[58] Ultimately, the international community will remain in Kosovo until its status is resolved, most likely becoming an independent Kosovo that must guarantee the rights of the Serbs that remain, although some territorial shifts cannot be ruled out. The sooner such negotiations on final status begin the better.

Superpower lessons

Building on the lessons of Haiti and Bosnia, the intervention in Kosovo set the stage for a new American foreign policy and a new division of labor among the international institutions. The UN would be left to political negotiations where there is a peace to make and to peacekeeping when there is a peace to keep. The UN and regional organizations other than NATO would focus on institution and capacity building, and NATO and coalitions of capable forces, led by the United States, would take on the wars, or so-called enforcement operations.

To date, the United States remains the leading force capable of such enforcement. Although the Europeans have taken steps to develop a force capable of intervention and enforcement, called the "rapid reaction force," political divisions continue to hamper its effectiveness. European governments have failed to spend the necessary money on equipment or to agree among themselves on how to act independently of NATO. As one former British air marshal noted, "The thing is a total mess."[59]

The Europeans, through the Organization for Security and Cooperation in Europe (OSCE) and the United Nations are, however, capable of providing critical assistance in developing local governance institutions, providing international police, and training indigenous police forces. In a lesson that would resurface following the 2003 war with Iraq, the peacekeeping efforts of the 1990s have shown that international forces must remain in place, not only until military tasks are completed but also until the indigenous political will and structures exist to support a stable government and a local security force to keep the peace. Thus, the "exit strategy" for the international community depends on a political evolution that can take decades.

The experience in Haiti, Bosnia, and Kosovo shattered the myth Clinton faced at the end of the cold war that the United States could retreat into isolationism. The United States' interests and values demanded leadership and involvement. In response, Clinton developed a new use of force to back up a new American diplomacy in areas previously considered beyond America's strategic interest. The instability created by ethnic strife and violence in areas central to U.S. interest, such as Europe and the Western Hemisphere, were now seen as impacting U.S. security and worthy of U.S. military and political engagement, with ground troops being an absolute last resort. America's view of its own interests in the Balkans had shifted from Secretary of State James Baker's dismissal that "we don't have a dog in that fight" to a recognition that war in the Balkans threatened America's core interest in stability in Europe, the credibility of American commitments, and even NATO's very survival.

During this period, Clinton also struggled to overcome the other myth of the 1990s, that the U.S. should, because many believed it could, be the world's policeman. Clinton made clear that America's commitment to engage militarily was not limitless; the deployment of ground troops into combat remained reserved for the major strategic threats, such as a resurgent Russia, Iraq, or potential enemies in Asia. Beyond these areas, Clinton calibrated U.S. engagement depending on the level of U.S. interest. Thus, in Haiti and the Balkans, the threats to those interests were sufficient to propel engagement but sufficiently diffuse to justify the complex and difficult effort to work with U.S. allies, rather than seek to go it alone. As will be explored in a later chapter, America's interests in Africa were even more diffuse, making the United States all the more reluctant to engage in the continent's conflicts.

Rejecting both myths of isolationism and omniresponsibility, Clinton sought a balance of engagement that reflected the United States' role as the lone remaining superpower, one that would later prove more effective than the approach naively sought by President George W. Bush, who believes the hegemonic myth. Over the first two years of his presidency, Clinton redefined a new use of force and diplomacy aimed at protecting a broader view of America's interests and maintaining broad international support. He also sought to use America's strengths to protect and promote America's broader interests on the world stage during a time of unprecedented challenge and opportunity.

The doctrine search

Every American president tries to elaborate a "doctrine" that defines certain core priorities of U.S. foreign policy. President Monroe put the world on notice not to interfere in the Western Hemisphere. The Truman Doctrine stipulated that the United States would "contain" the spread of communism in the world. Reagan's doctrine called for support of anti-Communist forces, or "freedom fighters," around the globe. Clinton, however, struggled to come up with a principle that could be called the "Clinton doctrine."

Throughout Clinton's eight years as president, his administration had difficulty defining its overall foreign policy goals to an American public still used to the single goal of containing the Soviet Union. Tony Lake tried to base U.S. foreign policy on expanding democracy around the world, but this focus proved too narrow. Madeleine Albright put forward "assertive multilateralism," but the awkward term was too UN–focused and failed to reflect the occasional need to go it alone. Clinton took great solace in reread-ing the biography of President Harry Truman by David McCullough[60] and openly compared the difficulties he was facing in defining a post–cold war foreign policy to Truman's struggles in developing new rules following the end of World War II. "During the immediate post WWII years," Clinton often mused, "everyone thinks we knew what to do." Pointing out that there had been a two-year hiatus before Truman set America's direction with the Truman Doctrine, Clinton said during the height of the Bosnia crisis, "by Truman's standard, I'm not doing so badly."

Clinton was not alone in struggling to come up with a guiding foreign policy principle as the United States emerged as the lone superpower. Historians, politicians, and pundits also wrestled with the problem through-out the 1990s. Grand theories of international relations, such as Francis Fukuyama's *End of History* claimed all would embrace Western democratic values, thus ending conflict, while Samuel Huntington's *The Clash of Civilizations* predicted that religious and cultural divides would exacerbate conflict.[61] Yet, neither theory would be borne out by the events of the 1990s. At the same time, the demise of the Soviet Union also prompted many in Congress to call for a withdrawal by the United States from international engagement. For example, Senator Jesse Helms, who chaired the Senate Foreign Relations Committee, repeatedly argued that the United States should leave the United Nations.[62]

Clinton and his advisors, however, understood the need for U.S. lead-ership abroad to protect America's interest. But the complex nature of inter-national relations following the cold war belied defining a simple formula on which to pursue a foreign policy. While the cold war had been charac-terized by a bipolar system, the post–cold war era was characterized by dis-order. Civil wars, ethnic conflicts, failed states, rogue states, and international terrorism were just some of the threats that had to be thwarted. In particular, a single principle that would guide American policy amidst such an array of threats proved impossible.

In the post–cold war era, there is simply not one monolithic threat or theory that justifies endorsing a single issue or policy over all others. Even the attacks of September 11, 2001, failed to provide a lasting new context for a simple doctrine. President George W. Bush initially tried "You're either with us or against us" in an effort to coach America's goal as fight-ing evil. Yet the complexities of world affairs soon undermined this Manichean doctrine approach and more subtle policies had to be pursued. Later, Bush tried the policy of "preemptive self-defense" believing the United States could act alone to reshape the world. But this myth proved dangerous to America's interests. A more sophisticated, complex, and nuanced policy is required.

Clinton's foreign policy legacy

Clinton eventually gave up on the search for a summary of his foreign policy that "could be put on a bumper sticker" and instead defined it in a set of principles that guided his policies and America's engagement. Although rejected by President Bush in his first term, they continue to offer lasting guiding principles to which the United States is likely to return in Bush's second term as reality sets in.

The United States needed to meet the international challenges with the full array of diplomatic, economic, and military tools, prepared to lead but also able to garner support. Unlike his successor, Clinton understood that success often meant extensive diplomacy before, or along with, the use of force. In this new world, most of America's goals—security, economic prosperity, and the extension of the core freedoms Americans value—would be achieved most often not by force or duress but rather by persuasion and coalition building. This, too, would make it easier to count on the help of others. Clinton thus embarked on building foundations of an international system that today helps constrain the negative acts of others, build positive and reinforcing support for democracy, the rule of law, and provide joint action where response to violence is needed.

Clinton established a broad U.S. foreign policy that embedded U.S. interests firmly in the international community. His approach can be summarized in five key tenets:

1. ensuring that the cornerstone of U.S. national security remained its alliances with Europe and Asia
2. ensuring that its relationship with the other key powers, especially Russia and China, was built on principled and constructive interaction
3. recognizing that local conflicts have global consequences and therefore must be resolved before they escalate and harm vital interests
4. addressing the new dangers accentuated by the technological advances and permeability of borders
5. integrating and expanding economic markets globally to advance both U.S. interests and democratic values.[63]

Clinton also understood the need to retool the American military to meet the challenges of the post–cold war warfare. He learned the lessons of the early failures of the 1990s in Bosnia, Somalia, and Haiti and ensured that his successor had a military that would win wars in both Afghanistan and Iraq. Above all, Clinton recognized the need for America's leadership in meeting the new challenges. By the end of his presidency, these policies would all produce major accomplishments that offered future administrations a sound blueprint for America's engagement abroad. Following the attacks of September 11, these policies continue to offer a guidepost to protect America's interest. Building on his accomplishments, Clinton's successors should pursue a policy of tough engagement, with zero tolerance for terrorism and proliferation of weapons of mass destruction.

On the eve of the twenty-first century, President Clinton understood that, confronted with the technology revolution, global trade, and the threat of global terrorism, the United States must rely on a global system of international treaties and laws. Rather than needlessly restrain the United States, as opponents charged, such a system widened the net of countries more likely to play by the rules. In this way, Clinton worked to strengthen and reform the major institutions established in the aftermath of World War II. He led the world effort to strengthen its international financial architecture to include emerging economies, to enhance transparency in governments and financial institutions, and to create stronger regulations on lending countries. He pressed for reform of the International Monetary Fund (IMF) to achieve transparency, accountability, and more equitable lending practices. As global trade exploded from $4 billion a year when Clinton took office to approximately $6.6 trillion when he left, Clinton supported more than three hundred bilateral and regional free- and fair-trade agreements.[64] Clinton's efforts to promote global trade culminated in the establishment of the World Trade Organization (WTO) in January 1995 with the goal of reducing tariffs, settling trade disputes, and enforcing global trade rules.

Ultimately, managing the challenges of globalization required greater international engagement and strong U.S. leadership. As outgoing national security advisor Sandy Berger noted in 2000, "Globalization does have qualities that we can harness to advance our enduring objectives of democracy, shared prosperity, and peace. . . . Some of the world's most positive recent developments have occurred because of how we chose to use that influence, not because globalization preordained them."[65]

Clinton also lent U.S. support to a variety of international human rights and arms-control treaties. On the human rights front, the Clinton administration helped establish the Office of the United Nations High Commissioner for Human Rights and cosponsored subsequent resolutions for human rights improvements in China, Russia, Cuba, Iran, and Iraq.[66] Clinton also backed international arms control to prevent nuclear proliferation and terrorists' access to weapons of mass destruction. He secured Russian president Boris Yeltsin's agreement on the Start II Arms Control Treaty in 1993, an agreement that would cut both countries' nuclear warheads by almost 50 percent over ten years. Clinton also pressed for the treaty's formal approval, which the Senate and Russian Duma granted in 1996 and 2000, respectively. He also signed the Comprehensive Test Ban

Treaty that bans all underground nuclear testing, although the Senate rejected the international treaty in October 1999.

As Clinton developed these global standards, he worked to unite Europe following the fall of the Berlin Wall, one of his most important achievements. He strongly supported the new democracies, especially by bringing them in as partners in the transatlantic structures. Clinton revitalized, adapted, and expanded NATO to include the Czech Republic, Hungary, and Poland. He launched the Partnership for Peace military training-and-exercise program to help prepare the new democracies of Central Europe for possible membership in NATO. He also negotiated a new, more stable structure for conventional forces in Europe through the Treaty on Conventional Armed Forces in Europe that created a new, highly stable, transparent set of limitations on conventional forces.

Clinton also focused on bringing the key powers, such as Russia and China, into the fold. In the wake of the cold war, Russia's reformers faced an internal struggle against the hard-line former communists. Clinton threw his full support behind the reformers, strongly supporting President Boris Yeltsin as he sought to create a market-based democracy. Clinton also sought to bring Russia into the international architecture as a way of reinforcing the reform movement, including pressing Russia's inclusion in the Group of Seven (G-7) industrialized nations, making it the G-8. Clinton furthermore worked to establish a strong partnership between NATO and its former adversary, Russia. With the NATO–Russia Founding Act in 1997, Russia began a new cooperative relationship with NATO, despite its objections to NATO's expansion to the nations of Eastern Europe. For the first time since World War II, Russian and American troops served side by side, in both Kosovo and Bosnia.

Similarly, Clinton spent a great deal of effort to manage the opportunities and risks with the other great power, China. Recognizing the uncertainties about China's future, Clinton sought to engage the leadership on global issues, while pressing Beijing on key issues of concern, such as human rights, nonproliferation, regional cooperation, and ensuring stability in the Taiwan Strait and North Korea. He also sent tough signals when necessary, including the dispatch of naval forces to the strait in 1996 to counter China's threatening military exercises.

He also worked to bring China into the world community, leading the effort to secure China's entry into the WTO. Clinton agreed to normalize the United States–China trade relationship, the most significant change in dealings between the two countries since normalization in 1979. Believing that U.S. interests are best served by a secure, stable, open, and prosperous China, Clinton viewed that country as a "strategic partner" and sought China's entry into the international arms-control and trade system, one that would enforce the rule of law for the Chinese people. As Sandy Berger explained, "Just as NAFTA helped erode the economic base of the one-party rule in Mexico, participation in WTO . . . can help promote change in China."[67]

By firmly embedding U.S. policy in international law and institutions, Clinton succeeded in pressing other nations to follow suit. He helped bring closer to reality the Wilsonian ideal of a global set of rules to which nations adhere, thus encouraging others to play by the rules and share the burden of international responsibilities. While working within the international system where possible, Clinton also recognized that at times America would have to use force, including unilaterally, to protect and defend its interests, particularly against Saddam Hussein and Osama bin Laden, as will be explored in later chapters.

Whether through the use of force, diplomacy, or economic power, Clinton understood the need for the United States to lead the world as the "first nonimperialist superpower."[68] To do so, he had to persuade the American people and leaders around the world to overcome their fear of ceding some sovereign authority in order to create a functioning global system of rules, regulations, and burden sharing. As summed up by Clinton's deputy secretary of state, Strobe Talbott, "In a fashion and to an extent that is unique in the history of Great Powers, the United States defines its strength—indeed its very greatness—not in terms of its ability to achieve or maintain dominance over others, but in terms of its ability to work with others in the interests of the international community as a whole."[69]

Clinton's successor would challenge this approach at its very core.

5

A Realistic Foreign Policy?

We have learned that our own well-being is dependent on the well-being of other nations far away. We have learned to be citizens of the world, members of the human community.

—Franklin D. Roosevelt

The Republican Party never accepted Clinton's policy of modern Wilsonian foreign engagement. Conservatives criticized Clinton for intervening too willingly, and too slowly; for avoiding moral clarity while using troops for humanitarian missions beyond the national interest; and for constraining America by building international treaties and coalitions while shirking the country's responsibility to lead the world. Senator Bob Dole jibed at a "pattern of neglect, delay and indecision,"[1] Senator Chuck Hagel spoke of a void in foreign policy leadership because of "a president who is not engaged, not all that interested."[2]

Accuracy aside, the criticisms were a symptom of a deeper malaise that settled in conservative foreign policy circles at the end of the cold war. With communism vanquished, only one issue united Republicans on international affairs: a common hatred of Bill Clinton's approach. They ignored the lessons of the 1990s and instead sought to maintain the cold war simplicity of containment. It was difficult for officials trained in the dark arts of "Kremlinology" and nuclear strategy, looking beyond the framework they inherited for thinking about the world. States, rather than nonstate actors, were the paramount concern. Nuclear weapons, missile defenses, and unfinished business from the cold war—Korea, China, Taiwan, and Cuba—continued to be perceived as the principle challenges. In the process of conceptualizing America's new role in the world, deep divisions emerged—and remain—in conservative foreign policy circles. Three groups began to promote very different ideas about America's future as a superpower.

Although no single perspective is entirely distinct, there are three broad camps: the realists, the isolationists, and the hegemons.

The traditional realpolitik outlook—cold realism, attention to the "balance of power," and cautious action in the pure self-interest of the state—was the dominant policy perspective in Republican foreign policy circles in 2000. It was personified by former secretaries of state Henry Kissinger, James Baker, and former national security advisor Brent Scowcroft. They had sought détente and accommodation during the cold war; now they rejected Clinton's use of force in conflicts and regions outside of what they defined as America's national security interests. The military interventions in Somalia, Haiti, and the Balkans were considered a distraction, squandering power, prestige, and resources. The interplay of great nations was their prism on the world; the ebb and flow of influence and power that *really* determined the fate of America. Interests not morals would determine management of the threats posed by Russia, China, and other emerging powers. For security, America should rely on containment and deterrence, backed by uncompromising assurances to respond to acts of aggression against the national interest.

The patriarch of that establishment, Henry Kissinger, perhaps articulated the realists' perspective on Clinton's foreign policy most lucidly in his book *Does America Need a Foreign Policy?* Kissinger accused Clinton and his administration of having "recoiled from the concept of national interest and distrusted the use of power unless it could be presented as being in the service of some 'unselfish' cause—that is, reflecting no specific American national interest." Kissinger dismissed Clinton's generation as pursuing an approach of "self-indulgence or self-righteousness of the protest period." The statesman who was so influential in shaping policy through the Nixon and Ford administrations (but has not been in government since) believed that this generation had "not yet raised leaders capable of evoking a commitment to a consistent and long-range foreign policy. Indeed, some of them question whether we need any foreign policy at all."[3] In a post–cold war setting, Kissinger was again advocating pragmatism over morals, the deliberate manipulation of power in realizing clearly defined national interests. The superpower should be engaged, but not distracted.

To the flanks of the realists, traditionally on the periphery of power, were the isolationists and the hegemons. Republican isolationists, who had been discredited since World War II, resurfaced in the mid-1990s. They despised Clinton's international engagements and, especially, his desire to strengthen international institutions and norms. The disintegration of the Soviet Union, according to the isolationists, was an opportunity to declare victory, withdraw from foreign entanglements, and turn inward. The isolationists became increasingly powerful following the 1994 midterm elections, which saw the Republicans take control of both houses of Congress for the first time in forty years. Senators, such as Jesse Helms, the ultimate isolationist, and Newt Gingrich, also partly a budding hegemon, exerted enormous influence on foreign policy, undermining White House efforts to manage effectively America's new role in the world.

Having run on its "Contract with America,"[4] the new isolationist leadership in Congress pressed to implement its extreme agenda: pushing legislation to bar presidents from putting U.S. combat troops under the command of a foreign officer or the UN, voting against sending peacekeeping troops to the Balkans, demanding a U.S. withdrawal from Haiti, seeking to prevent the WTO from being able to compel changes in American consumer and environmental laws, opposing efforts to pay U.S. back dues to the UN, and denouncing the war in Kosovo. Their star would wane with the realization toward the end of the decade of the need for U.S. engagement. September 11 ended the debate—America had to engage with the world.

A new rationale for our role in the world

The hegemons drew their experience, and ideology, from Ronald Reagan's era. While constrained from acting in the 1980s by the cold war realities, under President Reagan's strong and simple leadership, officials got a taste of the potential for American hegemony and never lost sight of that dream. For most of the mid-1990s, the hegemons were considered a fringe voice, spending most of their time ruminating in right-wing think tanks, such as the American Enterprise Institute, and writing in journals such as the *Weekly Standard*. Their defining characteristic was a steadfast confidence in the global benefits of American supremacy. This perspective was succinctly described by William Kristol and Robert Kagan in a 1996 article in *Foreign Affairs*: "American hegemony is the only reliable defense against a breakdown of peace and international order. The appropriate goal of American foreign policy, therefore, is to preserve that hegemony as far into the future as possible. To achieve this goal, the United States needs a neo-Reaganite foreign policy of military supremacy and moral confidence."[5]

Often confused with the more moderate and somewhat bipartisan neoconservatives (whom Clinton had actively courted), the hegemons are a more extreme, largely Republican group. In their eyes, proactive supremacy not only would defeat the known threats but also would prevent the emergence of future challenges. The danger was not exhausting economic resources—they argued we were blessed with abundance—but a loss of political will at the critical moment. Politicians should educate the electorate on America's responsibilities, encourage a stronger military, an immediate missile-defense system, and act with an unflinching moral courage abroad. America was the overwhelming world power and could simply bend the world to its will. To the hegemons, the election of President Bush provided them with their opportunity for power and to implement their ambitions radical agenda.

In 1997, the hegemons launched The Project for a New American Century (PNAC) to promote many of their priorities. Among the twenty-five individuals who signed the statement of principles advocating "a Reaganite policy of military strength and moral clarity," were Donald Rumsfeld, Dick Cheney, Paul Wolfowitz, and Governor Jeb Bush. The group set forth many policies that would later be adopted by President George W. Bush. It emphasized the "need to increase defense spending significantly if we are to carry out our global responsibilities today and modernize our armed forces for the future." It previewed the myth that a stronger military, largely on its own, would preserve and extend "an international order friendly to our security, our prosperity, and our principles." Foreshadowing the doctrine of preemption, the PNAC declared that "it is important to shape circumstances before crises emerge, and to meet threats before they become dire."[6] The signatures of Powell, Armitage, Scowcroft, and the patriarchs of the realist establishment were conspicuous in their absence.

One key goal of the group was the removal of Saddam Hussein from power in Iraq. In a January 1998 letter to President Clinton, the group argued that, with the sanctions against Iraq collapsing and inspectors blocked, "in the not-too-distant future we will be unable to determine with any reasonable level of confidence whether Iraq does or does not possess such [weapons of mass destruction]." Claiming the current policy of containment through sanctions was "dangerously inadequate," the group called for the removal of Saddam Hussein from power. They claimed it was "difficult if not impossible to monitor Iraq's chemical and biological weapons production." In an argument the Bush administration would use for going to war in 2003, the letter stated that existing UN resolutions provided the necessary authority for the use of force, and that pursuing unanimity in the Security Council would be misguided. Two of the signers would become the top two officials at the Pentagon in 2001, Donald Rumsfeld and Paul Wolfowitz. Another, Richard Perle, would head the Defense Policy Board.[7]

The hegemons did not argue simply for the maintenance of American economic and defensive strength. No American advocates anything less. The hegemons believe in unrivalled American power, maintaining global preeminence through dominating militarily the regional politics of Europe, Asia, and the Middle East. South America and Africa are largely ignored. The United States should act with a near monopoly of every manifestation of power in areas of American interest. This was the vision articulated in the controversial 1992 "Defense Planning Guidance," a classified Pentagon policy paper, now issued biannually, that maps out America's military strategy, serving as guidance for planning future defense spending.

In March 1992, an early version of the document, drafted in the office of then under-secretary of defense for policy Paul Wolfowitz, was leaked to the press. The first such paper since the end of the cold war, it argued that the United States' "dominant consideration" should be to prevent the reemergence of a new rival. This goal "requires that we endeavor to prevent any hostile power from dominating a region," convincing allies and enemies "that they need not aspire to a greater role." It went on to state that the United States "will retain the preeminent responsibility for addressing selectively those wrongs which threaten not only our interests, but those of our allies or friends, or which could seriously unsettle international relations."[8] The document caught the attention of Secretary of Defense Cheney, who told the author of the document, Zalmay Khalilzad, "You've discovered a new rationale for our role in the world."[9]

Yet, in 1992, such a rationale had little support. When it was leaked to the press, the document was sharply criticized. Official spokespersons distanced the administration from the paper, claiming that key officials—even Paul Wolfowitz—claimed not to have read the draft. President George H. W. Bush's centrist, realist approach rejected such extreme ideas for orienting America after the collapse of the Soviet Union. The hegemons, as with Reagan, were never afforded real power by the first president Bush. Following September 11, 2001, the second president Bush would give them just that.

The compassionate conservative

In the 2000 election campaign, foreign policy was not a personal strength of Governor George W. Bush. When the word "Taliban" was put to him as part of a verbal Rorschach test for *Glamour* magazine, Governor Bush merely shook his head in silence. Prompted on their repressive Islamic credentials, Bush replied "Oh, I thought you said some band. The Taliban in Afghanistan! Absolutely. Repressive."[10]

Bush's presidential campaign pledged to implement a moderate platform of "compassionate conservatism." Most expected him to endorse the foreign policies of his father—pragmatism, caution, and multilateralism. Notwithstanding the rhetoric common in political campaigns, the younger Bush's approach to foreign policy seemed tempered and internationalist, broadly aligned to the Kissingerian realist tradition. Gearing up to a presidential campaign in 1999, Bush, referring to himself as a "clear eyed realist" spoke of a need to "reject the blinders of isolationism, just as we refuse the crown of empire. Let us not dominate others with our power—or betray them with our indifference."[11]

The campaign message attempted to overcome any questions about Bush's experience and grasp of policy by portraying him as a skilled chief executive, with good instincts and good advisors. Selection of Dick Cheney as his vice president was designed to further reassure voters that the new team could handle foreign policy. Bush's limited international experience—he had rarely left America—made crucial the selection of a running mate with a capable reputation in the foreign arena. Dick Cheney's background as a former White House chief of staff, six-term congressman, secretary of defense, and as head of Halliburton, a major construction and energy services company, brought the valuable weight of experience to the Bush ticket.

A diverse group of foreign policy advisors was assembled to train the candidate, predominantly made up of midlevel former Bush-, Reagan-, and even Ford-era officials. Although occasionally consulted, the moderate and more experienced Brent Scowcroft and James Baker were noticeably absent from the team. The group, dubbed the "Vulcans" after the statue of the Roman god of metalworking in former NSC Soviet advisor Condoleezza Rice's hometown of Birmingham, Alabama, was a mix of realists and hegemons.

This balance was reflected in the cochairs of the group. Called the "quarterback" of the Vulcans, Condoleezza Rice was on leave from her position as provost of Stanford University. Mentored by Scowcroft at the NSC and Madeleine Albright's conservative father, Joseph Korbel, at the University of Denver, Rice was thoroughly schooled in the realist tradition. "Even those comfortable with notions of the 'national interest' are still queasy with a focus on power relationships and great-power politics" she wrote during the campaign in *Foreign Affairs* magazine. "The reality is that a few big powers can radically affect international peace, stability, and prosperity . . . capable of influencing American welfare for good or ill."[12] Her cochair, Paul Wolfowitz, the former Bush undersecretary of defense for policy whose office was responsible for the controversial 1992 Defense Planning Guidance paper, was convinced of the need to use a strong military posture to promote stability, challenge tyranny, and initiate democratic reform. Other hegemons included Dov Zakheim, a former defense official in the Reagan administration, and Richard Perle, another Reagan-era defense official. On the moderate, realist end of the spectrum were Robert Blackwill, a Bush NSC European and Soviet advisor, Richard Armitage, and Stephen Hadley, both of whom had served as assistant secretaries in the first president Bush's Defense Department.

During the campaign, the Vulcans mapped out a conservative and assertive foreign policy, founded in the realist tradition, and dismissive of Clinton's internationalist, moral engagements. Rice wrote that the Bush team would tackle the sense of drift in American foreign policy by "maintaining a disciplined and consistent foreign policy that separates the important from the trivial." True to the tenets of realism, Rice believed the "crucial task for the United States is to focus relations with other powerful states."[13] Under a Bush presidency, America would adopt an assertive and muscular approach to potential rivals, a position made patently clear with regard to the new enemy China, which was, in the words of Bush, to be "a competitor, not a strategic partner."[14] While uncompromising in their approach to rogue states—calling for the United States to use whatever resources it can to "remove" Saddam—Rice still emphasized the methodical realism that would define the new approach. "These regimes are living on borrowed time, so there need be no sense of panic about them. Rather the first line of defense should be a clear and classical statement of deterrence."[15]

Bush argued for a strong military, used carefully and deliberately to support a clearly defined national interest. Avoiding the more extreme policies, Bush laid out a foreign policy approach during the campaign largely following that of his father. The vision of hegemons was overridden by more pragmatic concerns.

"We don't need to have the 82nd Airborne escorting kids to kindergarten."

Throughout the 2000 campaign, Bush repeatedly dismissed Clinton's efforts to address the conflicts of the 1990s, as ad hoc, failing to set clear strategic priorities and straying from America's national interest. "Foreign policy in a Republican administration will most certainly be internationalist," Rice explained. "But it will also proceed from the firm ground of the national interest, not from the interests of an illusory international community."[16] Bush and his team reserved special criticism for Clinton's policies of peacekeeping and nation building. "I don't think nation-building missions are worthwhile," Bush declared during a debate with Vice President Al Gore at Wake Forest University in North Carolina. "I think our troops ought to be used to fight and win war," he said.[17] The Vulcans saw the military as a lethal tool for fighting and winning wars. The military had no role in politics, policing, or civil affairs. It was certainly not designed to build nations. Rice memorably remarked, "Carrying out civil administration and police functions is simply going to degrade the American capability to do the things America has to do. We don't need to have the 82nd Airborne escorting kids to kindergarten."[18]

Despite having agreed with Clinton's decisions to intervene in the Balkans, Bush called for an immediate review of overseas deployments leading to a timely and orderly withdrawal of U.S. troops from deployments such as Kosovo and Bosnia.[19] Vice presidential candidate Dick Cheney and Rice echoed that line, emphasizing the need for the Europeans to take over the Balkan missions, claiming U.S. forces abroad were in need of relief. Misunderstanding the danger to U.S. interests of the war in Bosnia, in particular the possibility of similar historical conflicts erupting in much of Europe, many of Bush's advisors shared Henry Kissinger's view that "the

United States has no national interest for which it must either risk lives or deploy forces to bring about a multiethnic state in Bosnia, or permit itself to be tied forever to a political quagmire."[20]

More for missile defense, more for everything

For decades, the Republicans have derided Democratic support for the military. Bush was no exception. In a September 1999 speech, criticizing the Clinton administration for asking the military to "do more with less," the candidate Bush called for increasing funds for the military, decreasing the volume of deployments, and improving overall morale. "If elected, I will set three goals: I will renew the bond of trust between the American president and the American military. I will defend the American people against missiles and terror. And I will begin creating the military of the next century." He pledged to add a billion dollars in salary increases for the military in his first budget, to earmark at least 20 percent of the procurement budget for acquisitions in military technology, and to add another $20 billion between 2001 and 2006.[21] In addition, in September 2000, he called for spending $45 billion of a projected budget surplus on defense over 10 years.[22] *The Weekly Standard* perhaps best summed up Bush's basic approach on defense: "We need to spend much more on our armed forces. We need more money for readiness, more for R&D, more for procurement, more for troops, more for missile defense, more for everything."[23]

The key issue for hegemons was the need to build a national missile defense (NMD). Ever since Ronald Reagan endorsed the goal of an NMD—dubbed "Star Wars" by critics—the Republican Party has been intent on building such a system. It fit well into the cold war fixations with nuclear war, surprise attack, and maintaining strategic advantage. It was the logical extension of an old-world threat into a new-world environment, meeting the priorities of isolationists and hegemons alike.

Although Republicans had dismissed his efforts, Clinton had also recognized the political and practical need to develop such a system. But he had insisted that funding for such a program be contingent on a system that actually worked. Tearing up solid and durable international treaties for what critics had referred to as an umbrella with holes—or a pork barrel in space—was unwise, certainly before a working system had been developed. During his presidency, Clinton spent about $1.6 billion on NMD and budgeted an additional $10.3 billion in fiscal years (FY) 2001 to 2005 to support the possible deployment of the initial national missile-defense architecture. In 2000, he ultimately decided against deploying the system, citing technological deficiencies—a difficult decision in an election year. Richard Perle, a former Defense Department official closely associated with promoting the Star Wars scheme, belittled Clinton's program as "a system so modest and ineffective (even when it works) as to be useless for all but political purposes," and calling for a system "that will do more than defend Vice-President Gore's election prospects."[24]

Candidate Bush enthusiastically endorsed the call for NMD in September 1999. In a keynote speech at the Citadel he declared that he would deploy an antiballistic missile system at the earliest possible date and that he would withdraw from the 1972 Anti-Ballistic Missile Treaty (ABM) if Russia refused to agree to the sweeping amendments that were necessary. The potential of the unproven technology would trump the demonstrated value of the international treaty that had restrained the arms race for almost three decades.

Throughout his campaign in 2000, Bush argued that the United States should lead the world with humility. American omnipotence since the end of the cold war had sparked resentment. Bush thought he understood why. "If we're an arrogant nation, they'll view us that way, but if we're a humble nation, they'll respect us," he answered in one of the presidential debates. When asked about the United States' role in the world, Bush replied "I just don't think it's the role of the United States to walk into a country and say, we do it this way, so should you. . . . I think the United States must be humble and must be proud and confident of our values, but humble in how we treat nations that are figuring out how to chart their own course."[25] Rice explained that "America can exercise power without arrogance and pursue its interests without hectoring and bluster."[26]

The new team

George W. Bush became the forty-third president of a bitterly divided United States of America. Throughout December 2000, the country was gripped by the legal battle over whether Bush or Gore had won the crucial state of Florida and thus the White House. On December 12, the Supreme Court intervened—seen as a blatant political act by the Gore camp—and gave the election to Bush. Bush became president by 537 votes cast in Florida. Whether Gore actually won the race continues to be a matter of debate for his supporters and historians.

The race was not supposed to be so close. American voters, used to the effervescent Clinton, never warmed to Gore, considered less charismatic than his own cardboard cutout. His shunning of the departing but still enormously popular President Clinton because of the Monica Lewinsky scandal cost him key support in several states. Although he was the most influential vice president in American history, on his own Gore failed to capture the heart of American voters, although he actually received a higher percentage of the popular vote than did Bush.[27]

Bush initially emphasized unity in the wake of the bruising electoral battle, stressing the need for a bipartisan approach. Speaking in the chamber of the Texas House of Representatives, chosen as a symbol of bipartisan cooperation, Bush said, "I hope the long wait of the last five weeks will heighten a desire to move beyond the bitterness and partisanship of the recent past. Our nation must rise above a house divided." A month later, on January 20, 2001, George W. Bush stood on the steps of the Capitol and took the oath of office. He told America he intended to build a "single nation of justice and opportunity." Americans expected Bush to follow through on that pledge and pursue moderate, bipartisan policies at home and abroad.

A president's decisions on his cabinet are the most important of the early days in office. The officials are the instrument, good or bad, competent or ineffectual, for shaping his legacy. Bush appointed a diverse cabinet in terms of race, gender, and ideology. It reflected a wide range of philosophies and backgrounds, including three women, four African Americans and Hispanics, two Asian Americans, and even one Democrat. This is not to say that there were not some unashamedly divisive decisions. The appointment of John Ashcroft as attorney general, given his extreme positions on abortion, the role of religion, and civil liberties, belied Bush's lack of commitment to the campaign platform of "compassionate conservatism."

Vice President Dick Cheney was immediately a powerful presence in the new Bush administration. His vast experience in government and business stood in stark contrast to the thin resume of the new president. Throughout the early days of the administration, the contrast in experience between the president and vice president sparked gossip and jokes. *Time* magazine called Cheney a "man in charge" and repeated the popular Washington joke: "We have to keep Dick Cheney healthy. Otherwise it will be the first time in history that the No. 1 will have to take over."[28]

In 1992, Dick Cheney was viewed as a traditional conservative, not the hegemon he is seen to be today. Cheney's voting record as a congressman from Wyoming was steadfastly conservative; he voted against gun control; against using any public finds for abortion, even to save the life of a woman; against the release of Nelson Mandela from prison, calling the ANC a terrorist organization; against the creation of the Department of Education; against funding voluntary AIDS testing and research. As defense secretary under the first president Bush, he had, albeit reluctantly, initiated the spending cuts necessary to realign the Pentagon at the end of the cold war. Notably, during the 1991 Gulf War, he counseled against the march on to Baghdad, explaining, "Once you've got Baghdad, it's not clear what you do with it. It's not clear what kind of government you would put in place of the one that's currently there now. Is it going to be a Shi'a regime, a Sunni regime or a Kurdish regime? . . . How much credibility is that government going to have if it's set up by the United States military when it's there? How long does the United States military have to stay to protect the people that sign on for that government, and what happens to it once we leave?"[29] There were, however, some early signs of the more extreme views Cheney holds. As one of his colleagues from the Ford administration described him, "Whenever his private ideology was exposed, he appeared somewhat to the right of Ford, Rumsfeld, or, for that matter, Genghis Khan."[30]

Seldom do vice presidents reach the White House with no presidential aspirations. Knowing he lacked the political base for a big future in the White House and with serious heart trouble, Dick Cheney focused not on his political future but in advancing his hegemon agenda. Initially, he fought—and lost—a major power play on foreign policy. The role of the national security advisor has long been to chair the Principals Committee, the cabinet-level national security interagency group that develops and ensures implementation of the president's foreign policy. Cheney sought that role for himself, an extraordinary challenge to tradition, and probably wholly unrealistic, given the domestic-policy demands on any vice president. In the end, Bush sided with Condoleezza Rice. Cheney, like his predecessors, was free to attend the Principals Committee meetings as he desired. Despite the setback, the vice president was successful in doubling his national security staff and enhancing his power in the interagency development and implementation of policy. In another break with precedence, he sat in on Rice's weekly lunches with Secretary of Defense Rumsfeld and Secretary of State Powell.

Bush's appointments for national security advisor, Condoleezza Rice, and secretary of state, Colin Powell, were seen as moderate. At the time, Rice was assumed to be a realist, as Brent Scowcroft was considered one of her mentors. While she had no experience in government outside of the cold war environment, observers expected her to follow a Scowcroft-like approach. Her close relationship with the president, built through the campaign, protected her from power plays from her older, more experienced colleagues. Rice was the first woman and second African American (after Colin Powell) to hold the post. As an advisor on the Soviet Union and East European affairs at the National Security Council from 1989 to 1991, Rice had developed close ties to the Bush family and had remained in touch once she left government for a new job as provost at Stanford University. She was also able to secure coveted spots on corporate boards, such as Chevron, which named a tanker after her. During the campaign, Rice developed a close personal relationship with George Bush. A devout Presbyterian, Rice is famously disciplined, fastidious, and punctual. She is also an accomplished pianist, ice skater, and avid National Football League fan. Despite her impressive resume and reputation, Rice took over the powerful White House job with only a few years of experience actually in government.

Although her parents were Republicans, Rice initially registered as a Democrat, later switching parties because she felt the Democrats were soft on defense. She reportedly became a Republican after Jimmy Carter's remark in 1980 that he was "shocked" by the Soviet Union's invasion of Afghanistan; Rice was shocked that anybody would be shocked by the invasion.[31] Those of us working on presidential campaigns in the early 1980s assumed she was a Democrat, as she had informally advised Gary Hart in his 1984 bid for president. Later, when Madeleine Albright, James Steinberg, and I were working together on the Dukakis campaign in 1988, we were all surprised when Rice turned down Albright's invitation to assist on the campaign, declaring politely she was a Republican.

Powell was extremely popular across the country, widely regarded as a moderate general, celebrated for his determination to use force cautiously and overwhelmingly. While Powell had not been a close advisor during the campaign, his support for Bush was a crucial reassurance to voters. He made a number of significant public appearances during the tight campaign that were designed to reassure voters that Bush would support engagement on foreign policy and to reinforce the view of Bush as a compassionate conservative. General Powell had charisma and experience. He was also a war hero, a former national security advisor, and a chairman of the joint Chiefs of Staff. He was expected to be a dominant force, a skilled manager, a convincing public spokesman, and a voice of reason. The United States should lead, Powell said, "not by using our strength and position of power to get back behind our walls but by being engaged in the world."[32]

The only surprise in the foreign policy cabinet came at the Pentagon. Donald Rumsfeld, a staunch conservative on foreign policy whose career had been intertwined with that of Cheney since the Nixon administration, was chosen as defense secretary. When Rumsfeld was asked to be defense secretary—for the second time—it had been almost a quarter of a century since he had last been in government. At age sixty-eight, Rumsfeld brought vast government and business experience to the Bush team and a reputation as a ferocious bureaucratic operator. Elected to the House of Representatives in 1962, he resigned in 1969 to join the Nixon administration. He served briefly as U.S. Ambassador to NATO before returning to serve as chairman of the transition to the presidency of Gerald R. Ford following Nixon's resignation. After a stint as White House chief of staff, Rumsfeld, at age forty-three, became under Ford the youngest secretary of defense in history. Under President Bush, he also became the oldest.

In the private sector, Rumsfeld built a successful career in business, serving as the CEO, president, and chairman of a series of pharmaceutical, high-tech, and biotech companies. He periodically took on various public service posts, including a brief stint as President Reagan's special envoy to the Middle East in 1983 and as a member of a variety of commissions. In 1998, he chaired the Commission to Assess the Ballistic Missile Threat, known as the Rumsfeld Commission, and in 2000, he chaired one on the need to exploit space more aggressively.

Rumsfeld was supportive of increases in defense spending, opposed to arms control, and an enthusiastic advocate of a national missile defense. Although his work on various commissions had maintained his policy credentials, his age and the fact that he was a longtime rival of the senior president Bush made his selection a surprise to many. As President Ford's chief of staff in 1975, Rumsfeld had orchestrated Bush's shift from U.S. ambassador to China to director of the CIA. Rumsfeld, who at the time had presidential ambitions of his own, saw the move as a way to put the elder Bush into a politically unattractive position. Once Bush was at the CIA, Rumsfeld, reminiscent of his later actions in hyping the threat from Iraq, never hesitated to voice his view that the agency had grossly underestimated the level of Soviet military spending. Rumsfeld lost out to Bush for the vice presidential slot at the Republican convention in 1979. Many years later, Rumsfeld asked Richard Allen, Reagan's national security advisor, why Reagan and his advisors had overlooked his own credentials. Allen explained, "Because I didn't happen to have your phone number handy, and I did have Bush's."

Many openly wondered how Rice, significantly younger than the rest and the first woman in the post, could manage such an experienced team. Bush was confident: "General Powell's a strong figure and Dick Cheney's no shrinking violet, but neither is Don Rumsfeld, nor Condi Rice. I view the four as being able to complement each other."[33]

In early 2001, the polarization among the principals began to emerge with the appointment of the second and third tier of officials at the State and Defense departments. Paul Wolfowitz was appointed as deputy secretary of defense. Wolfowitz, the former dean of the School of Advanced International Studies at Johns Hopkins University, was the intellectual guiding force of the administration. Wolfowitz completed a doctorate in political science at Chicago University, taking courses with the famous nuclear strategist Albert Wohlstetter. His education imbued him with a sense of the importance of politics, of foresight, moral courage, and the need for preventive action against tyranny and the senseless brutality of man. In government he had been closely involved in monitoring policy on Iraq, from the Carter administration—where he counseled that the U.S. should be more cautious of its ally Saddam Hussein—to the first Gulf war, where he advocated that U.S. forces should continue to Baghdad and sharply criticized the decision not to support the Shia revolt in 1992. Other hard-line appointments included Douglas Feith as undersecretary of defense for policy and Richard Perle, nicknamed the "Prince of Darkness," as chairman of the Defense Policy Board, an advisory group to Secretary Rumsfeld.

Although his philosophy is more sophisticated than that of the pure hegemons, Wolfowitz brought a moral, more intellectual dimension to their thinking that provided them justification for their policies. A neo-Wilsonian, or some would say democratic imperialist, he views the responsibility of the United States as the world's sole superpower is to rid the world of evil. Wolfowitz believes that a world more resembling America, with the universal benefits of democracy, freedom, and self-determination, will pose less of a threat to America. He explains, "If people are really liberated to run their countries the way they want to, we'll have a world that will be very congenial for American interests."[34] Wolfowitz's framing of the hegemons' aggressive actions in "soft" Wilsonian terms gave their foreign policy a perceived moral legitimacy that helped propel it to the forefront after September 11.

Although Powell was able to select a moderate, Richard Armitage, as his deputy, the White House pressed a number of hard-line appointments on him. John Bolton, notorious for his poisonous words against the very principle of an international law, was appointed undersecretary of state for arms control and international security, sending waves of concern through the international community. The White House also sought to bring back many officials caught up in the scandals of President Reagan's controversial Central American policies. They pushed Otto Reich, an ultraconservative Cuban American who had been involved in illegal propaganda activities involving the use of public funds to promote the Reagan administration's Latin America policy in the 1980s, for the post of assistant secretary of state for Western Hemispheric affairs.[35] The Senate never confirmed him. Elliott Abrams, convicted of withholding information from Congress in the Iran-Contra affair in 1991 but later pardoned by the first president George Bush, was chosen by Rice first to head the National Security Council's office for democracy, human rights, and international operations, and was later appointed senior director for Near East and North African affairs.[36]

The ABC rule

As with any new team, there were early miscues and uncoordinated policy statements. There was also a steep learning curve—the Republicans had been out of office for two terms, and the world had not waited for them. As with all new presidents, the challenge of reconciling the easy rhetoric of opposition to the realities of policy implementation would take time. For the first nine months, the new team struggled with the constraints and potential of governing as the world's lone superpower.

Bush set out quickly to distance his policies from Clinton's, prompting some to claim his policies followed an "ABC" rule—anything but Clinton. "If Clinton was pushing hard for it," related one former diplomat, "their instinct was to pull way back."[37] Bush and his advisors immediately sent out signals that this administration would be less involved in many international conflicts. Bush eliminated more than a third of the fifty-five special envoy posts that Clinton had created to work the many conflicts around the globe, including those for Haiti, Congo, Cyprus, and the Balkans.[38] Bush made it clear that he would "wait to be asked"[39] before engaging in the Northern Ireland peace process. Publicly disagreeing with his secretary of state, Bush rejected efforts at reconciliation with North Korea and distanced himself from involvement in Middle East negotiations.

A very public ideological battle among the principals emerged in the first nine months. Powell won the first round on Iraq. During the presidential debates, Bush had derided Clinton's policy in Iraq as a "total failure."[40] While Rumsfeld and Wolfowitz came to office determined to oust Saddam Hussein, in early 2001 such an option remained off the table. Instead, the administration sought to improve the decade-old containment of the regime. Powell's first initiative as secretary of state was to secure agreement at the United Nations for a tougher sanctions regime against Iraq.

By 2000, the post–Gulf War consensus on sanctions in the Security Council had disintegrated. France and Russia pressed for sanctions to be lifted as they simultaneously negotiated contracts worth tens of billions of dollars in oil and infrastructure industries with the Saddam Hussein regime. The Russian oil company Lukoil had won a contract in 1997 to develop Iraq's West Qurna field, a concession valued at $3.7 billion.[41] France was Iraq's third-largest trading partner and had a large stake in the Iraqi oil industry. Total Fina Elf was developing Iraq's Majnoon and Nahr Umar fields, valued by some as high as $650 billion.[42] In addition, Saddam Hussein had succeeded in undermining international support for the sanctions by shifting the blame for the suffering of the Iraqi people from himself to the sanctions, while diverting billions of dollars intended for humanitarian purposes. United Nations inspectors had been absent since 1998 and there was growing frustration over the tedious process of approving any sale of equipment to Iraq through the UN sanctions committee. Thus, Powell sought to revamp the sanctions effort by easing the sanctions against Iraq in exchange for a tougher control over exports with a military use. These so-called "smart sanctions" forbid military imports while allowing for trade in humanitarian goods. The UN would scrutinize so called "dual-use" goods, namely those that could be used for both military and civilian purposes. Additional goals were to freeze bank accounts and prohibit the travel of targeted persons.

While Powell quickly secured the agreement of others on the Security Council for an easing of the sanctions, he failed to reach agreement on the tougher controls on military or dual-use items. Powell's efforts did not please the hard-liners in the administration. Paul Wolfowitz, for instance, told members of the European parliament that Powell was not the last word on Iraq policy.[43] Richard Perle dismissed the effort, declaring, "Improved sanctions or smarter sanctions, none of them are going to end the threat from Saddam Hussein."[44]

"We came in together, and we will leave together."

A sharp dose of reality rapidly quelled any hopes various officials harbored to reduce American peacekeeping commitments. The claim that peacekeeping operations placed an inordinate strain on the military was false. By January 2001, there were virtually no U.S. troops serving in UN peacekeeping operations; only 44 soldiers served in such operations, primarily as military advisors; another 865 served in the Sinai, not under the UN. The United States did participate in the 65,000-strong NATO forces keeping peace in Bosnia and Kosovo, providing 11,400 U.S. troops to those operations. Thus, of the 1.4 million U.S. troops, only 12,300 were deployed in peacekeeping missions. The Balkan missions cost $3.5 billion in FY 2000, slightly more than 1 percent of the $280 billion defense budget. Said Wesley Clark, the army general who commanded the war in Kosovo, "When allies are putting in more than 80 percent of the effort, there is not much room for an argument about burden-sharing. If we want to be part of this, we can't do much less.[45]

Conflicting and confusing signals about peacekeeping operations began to emanate from Washington shortly after Bush took office. At the first opportunity, Secretary of Defense Rumsfeld raised the possibility of withdrawing the U.S. troops from the Sinai. The U.S. military presence, which had its origins in the Camp David Accords of 1978, supervised the implementation of the treaty in which Israel returned the Sinai to Egypt. In separate meetings with Egyptian president Hosni Mubarak on April 3 and Israeli prime minister Ariel Sharon on March 19, Rumsfeld—apparently without consultation with the State Department or the White House—said that "the United States has had troops in the Sinai Desert between Israeli and Egypt for twenty years. It was a good thing to do at the beginning, but now may be the time to pull them out."[46] The State Department swiftly squashed any prospect of a withdrawal. Powell told a Senate subcommittee hearing: "It's not a very exciting mission, and it costs something. At the moment, however, we have an obligation to Israel and Egypt to support this multinational force."[47]

In March 2001, Rumsfeld declared that the administration had no plans to put troops into Macedonia or to send more peacekeepers to Kosovo, despite NATO's calls for such support in the face of renewed tensions. He then pushed to pull American peacekeepers out of Bosnia, claiming "the military job was done three or four years ago."[48] On Macedonia, Powell pushed back, leaving the door open to U.S. troop participation in a possible NATO operation to disarm ethnic Albanian fighters as part of a settlement plan.[49] Similarly on U.S. troops in Bosnia and Kosovo, Powell declared in May 2001 at a meeting of NATO foreign ministers that "we went into this together, and we'll come out together."[50] Talk of discord between the

Defense and State departments was rife. When challenged on the disagreements over troop withdrawals from Bosnia Rumsfeld replied, "I am not having trouble with Colin on it. But is it true that I am pushing it? Yes."[51]

In July 2001, on his first trip to Kosovo, Bush finally settled the debate in the administration. "We will not draw down our forces in Bosnia or Kosovo, precipitously or unilaterally," he said, speaking at a U.S. military base. "We understand that America's contribution is essential both militarily and politically." The administration was forced to reconcile its political belief that the military should be used for fighting wars with the reality that peacekeeping commitments were vital for securing America's interests abroad. Bush repeated Powell's earlier comments: "We came in together, we will go out together."[52] Bush also settled the dispute on U.S. troops going to Macedonia: "I take no option off the table in terms of the troops. We're a participant in NATO."[53] In August, three hundred to five hundred U.S. troops were deployed to Macedonia to assist a contingent of thirty-five hundred NATO troops.[54]

In another attack on peacekeeping, in June 2001, Secretary Rumsfeld decided to close the Peacekeeping Institute at the Army War College in Carlisle, Pennsylvania. Clinton had created the institute in 1993 to address the lack of peacekeeping preparedness in the army. It was the only agency of its kind in the U.S. military. Yet, following the massive peacekeeping efforts in Afghanistan and Iraq, in July 2003 the Pentagon officials revived the Institute as the Peacekeeping and Stability Operations Institute. In fact, the administration doubled the number of staff and increased the original budget of $200,000.[55]

Strategic competitors not partners

The administration came to office intending to instill "tough realism in our dealings with China and Russia."[56] But again, reality intruded. In March 2001, the largest spying scandal erupted since Ronald Reagan expelled eighty diplomats in 1986. The Bush administration gave four diplomats ten days to leave the country, a formal expulsion for directly "running" Robert Hanssen, a former senior FBI counterintelligence expert accused of spying for Russia. Hanssen had been passing highly classified information to the Russians since 1979, including the identities of at least four Russian agents who were spying for the CIA and FBI. Three of the men he exposed were executed. An additional forty-six diplomats were asked to leave by the summer in an attempt to reduce the number of Russia's U.S. intelligence operations.

Although Washington was clearly justified in demanding the expulsions, the large numbers set a tense new tone for relations between the former cold war rivals. In response to the spy incident, Moscow did not hold back its criticism. Russian foreign minister Igor Ivanov called the move "a hostile act, aimed at increasing tension in Russian-American relations . . . the policy of those trying to push mankind and the United States toward the Cold War and confrontation will fail."[57] Coupled with Rumsfeld's assertion that the Russians were acting as "active proliferators" of nuclear missile technology to rogue states, the actions of Washington fueled deep anxiety in Moscow. Sergei Ivanov, President Putin's closest aide, warned that the U.S. administration was returning to its Reagan-era view of Russia as "the evil empire that keeps trading in rockets, and spying everywhere."[58]

A similarly blunt approach marked the Bush administration's tone with China. A Bush campaign speech at the Reagan Library in 1999 had already set Beijing on edge. He called China "an espionage threat to our country" and "a competitor not a strategic partner," pledging to "help Taiwan defend itself."[59] Once in office, Bush faced an early crisis with his new competitor. Early one morning in April 2001, over the South China Sea, a U.S. Navy electronic surveillance EP-3E aircraft collided with a Chinese F-8 fighter jet in international airspace. While the Chinese fighter crashed into the sea, the U.S. aircraft made an emergency landing on Hainan Island off the coast of China without first asking for permission. The Chinese, incensed, refused the United States access to the twenty-four crew members or the plane. But the problem lay not just with recovering the American crew. The plane contained some of the United States' most sensitive and sophisticated spying equipment. Bush faced his first test in crisis diplomacy.

The administration immediately escalated the incident to the Oval Office, rather than giving quiet diplomacy a chance. The day after the crash, the president told the Chinese to give "immediate access" to the crew members, saying he was "troubled" by the lack of a timely Chinese response. Later that day, speaking in the Oval Office, Bush was even blunter: "We expect there to be contact, as soon as possible, with our crewmembers. And we expect that plane to be returned to us."[60] He introduced a style that was to become a hallmark of his early approach to sensitive diplomatic tasks. No outward sign of compromise, finesse, patience, or understanding—he simply "expected" foreign leaders to accede to his demands.

Predictably, the tensions rapidly escalated. The Chinese foreign minister Tang Jiaxuan demanded an apology and said that the United States had "displayed an arrogant air, used lame arguments, confounded right and wrong, and made groundless accusations against China."[61] Although still refusing to apologize, Bush sent a letter to the missing pilot's wife, expressing "regret" over the incident. Vice President Cheney said that "the notion that we would apologize for being in international air space . . . is not something we can accept." By April 9, Bush was warning that relations with China could "become damaged," and administration officials were suggesting that the United States could withdraw its support for China's bid to host the 2008

Summer Olympics as well as cancel a visit to Beijing that Bush had planned for October 2001.[62]

Ten days after the crash, Washington backpedaled. The United States said that it was "very sorry" for the death of the Chinese pilot and "very sorry" that the navy plane had entered Chinese airspace and made an emergency landing without Chinese permission. The Chinese released the crew the same day, although the plane—in pieces—was not returned until June. While resolved peacefully, the incident left Sino-American relations on rocky ground. It was also Bush's first lesson on the need for sophisticated diplomacy, not Oval Office diktats.

On the heels of this tense standoff, Bush stepped into one of China's most sensitive concerns, arms sales to Taiwan. United States' policy toward Taiwan has involved a sophisticated and deliberate ambiguity ever since President Nixon recognized China in 1972. Since that time, the United States has pledged to assist in Taiwan's defense in a series of agreements embodied in the Taiwan Relations Act of 1979. Taiwan has a strong lobby on Capitol Hill and decisions on arms sales have long been a delicate balance between ensuring Taiwan's defense needs and taking China's concerns into consideration.

Early in his presidency, Bush's advisors and supporters on Capitol Hill urged him to substantially upgrade U.S. arms sales to Taiwan. Improvements to China's navy and air force fostered the view among administration aides that the United States needed to assert its right of passage in the Taiwan Strait and recalibrate the military balance. Wolfowitz and Armitage had signed a letter before taking office in which they urged the United States to say explicitly that it would defend Taiwan.[63] On April 24, 2001, Bush approved the largest package of arms sales to Taiwan in almost ten years, estimated at $4 billion, which included items such as four Kidd-class destroyers, twelve P-3C Orion aircrafts, eight diesel submarines designed to counter blockades and invasion, and an Avenger surface-to-air missile system. Despite pressure from Rumsfeld and others, Bush decided not to provide Taiwan with the Arleigh Burke destroyers, which were most vehemently opposed by China. The editorial page editor of the conservative *Washington Times* seethed that "China won the first round with the Bush administration."[64]

Besides the arms sales, Bush seemed to alter the United States' long-standing position on Taiwan. Asked if he felt the United States had an obligation to defend the island, Bush replied, "Yes, we do, and the Chinese must understand that." Asked if that meant using the full force of the American military, he replied "Whatever it took to help Taiwan defend herself."[65] The remark created a firestorm of protest as Bush appeared to be substantially changing the U.S. commitment to Taiwan, long shrouded in ambiguity with the intention of restraining Taiwanese actions. His aides rushed to correct the record, saying Bush was not changing U.S. policy. "Nothing has changed in our policy," insisted State Department spokesman Philip Reeker. "Our policy hasn't changed today. It didn't change yesterday. It didn't change last year. It hasn't changed . . . I think he reiterated what we've always said."[66] Bush was unapologetic: "I think that the Chinese are beginning to learn what my administration meant when I said on the campaign trail that we'd be strategic competitors."[67]

Defense budget

Vice President Dick Cheney and Secretary of Defense Donald Rumsfeld led the charge to transform the military. Rumsfeld signaled his intention to pursue dramatic reforms in the way the nation's armed forces were organized, emphasizing that the Pacific Ocean was the most likely theater of major U.S. military operations. Defense policy would shift from keeping the peace in Europe and deterring the Soviet Union to a new orientation more wary of China and requiring a new emphasis on "long-range power projection." To counter the threat of missile proliferation, he called for cutting spending on older weapons systems and placing greater emphasis on acquiring planes, ships, and vehicles that have radar-evading stealth capabilities.[68] Rumsfeld's internal review relied on outside consultants and retired generals, frustrating the senior military officers at the Pentagon.[69] Rumsfeld raised further concerns when he said he would consider outer space as a potential battlefield of the future.

During the campaign, Cheney had promised the armed forces that "help is on the way," echoing traditional Republican charges that the Democrats are weak on defense.[70] Yet, once in office, the administration proposed no major change in the defense budget, arguing it could pay for the new systems of Rumsfeld's transformation by replacing older systems and reducing the size of the force. The administration's focus was not on increasing defense spending, but on securing passage of the president's tax cut. White House spokesman Ari Fleischer claimed that the Bush administration was not going to "throw money in the direction of defense" before it figured out its long-term strategy.[71] The administration basically followed Clinton's defense budget, in part because time restrictions constrained efforts to develop a different plan. Bush reportedly failed to inform his defense secretary of the decision not to seek more Pentagon funding.[72]

Again a gap began to emerge between campaign rhetoric and the reality of governing. The trumpeted force transformation "to use this window of opportunity to skip a generation of technology"[73] was drastically moderated. Existing weapons systems were maintained, the combat force structure was hardly touched, and overseas deployments were not reduced. As one analyst noted, the 2001 review "contained the fewest programmatic and force-structure initiatives of any of the four major U.S. defence reviews since the Cold War ended (since it contained virtually none) . . . Rumsfeld had essentially settled on a conservative quadrennial defence review document."[74] The rhetoric of the review, however, rejected Clinton's strategy of engagement, or "preventive defense," and instead put forward a policy that divided the world into those for and those against the United States. Defense policy would be designed to reassure allies and to dissuade, deter, or if necessary, defeat enemies. Little nuance existed for countries such as Russia, China, and India.[75]

Some modest increases in funding were implemented. In February 2001, the Bush administration proposed a budget for Defense of $310.5 billion, a slight increase from $296 billion when Clinton left office but in line with Clinton's proposed $310 billion for the 2002 budget. In June, Rumsfeld added $5.6 billion through a supplemental appropriation request, and then an additional $18.4 billion, almost entirely devoted to added training, spare parts, and military pay. In total, before September 2001, the Bush administration proposed a budget that was approximately $25.5 billion higher than Clinton's proposal for FY 2002.[76] In protest for the failure to do more, an editorial in *The Weekly Standard* offered "some unsolicited advice for two old friends, Donald Rumsfeld and Paul Wolfowitz: resign."[77]

Much of the rhetoric surrounding defense issues ignored the state of the military when Clinton left office. Clinton had already focused on ensuring adequate resources for readiness and modernization. For the fiscal year 2000 budget, he sought an increase of more than $12 billion for readiness and modernization, as well as $112 billion more in the first long-term sustained increase in defense spending in over a decade, including funds for personnel, readiness, modernization, and facilities. The Pentagon had first discussed expanding the range of military resources to include precision strikes, highly developed protection of forces, and precisely focused logistics. In 1997, Secretary of Defense William Cohen had described, in the *Quadrennial Defense Report*, a new operational concept called "precision engagement," meaning real-time information on the target and a more precise delivery, with increased survivability for all forces, weapons, and attack platforms.

As retired General Wesley Clark wrote in 2003, "The vision of transformation—a high-tech battlefield, viewed through an array of sensors, with battles fought and won by precision strikes and slimmer ground component, which the Bush administration and especially Donald Rumsfeld have trumpeted, had in large part already become a reality when they took office in 2001."[78] In private, the senior military officials were seething at Rumsfeld's high-handed tactics and lack of knowledge of the changes that had been made since he last served in Washington. Senior military officers who sought to brief him on issues, from NATO enlargement to activities in the former Soviet Union, found it "stunning that for someone as smart as he is, he was just not engaged." "We call him Rip Van Winkle," one then serving four-star general told me on September 10, 2001. "He's so stunned that the world had changed in the last thirty years."[79]

National missile defense and the ABM Treaty

For the first months in office, the administration was consumed with the goal of developing and deploying the NMD. It was the core element of the administration's answers to the challenge of America's new superpower status. The justification was a complicated amalgam of cold war threat legacies, a belief that states still posed the greatest danger to the United States and a confidence that America could use technology to defend itself from the world while simultaneously consolidating an unassailable strategic advantage. Once again, Rumsfeld exaggerated the problem, putting forward a worst-case scenario. The threat from hostile states like Iraq, Iran, and North Korea "is broader, more mature and evolving more rapidly" than previous estimates, concluded the 1998 bipartisan commission—the Commission to Assess the Ballistic Missile Threat to the United States—headed by Donald Rumsfeld. The problem was that, in order to provide sufficient protection against such missile attacks, an enormous number of technical and political difficulties would need to be overcome.

The main political obstacle to the deployment of a missile defense system was the 1972 Anti-Ballistic Missile Treaty, which restricted deployment of antimissile defenses. Its purpose was to limit the superpowers' ability to protect themselves from a massive retaliatory strike, thereby maintaining an effective deterrent against any side attempting a first strike of nuclear weapons. The theory of Mutual Assured Destruction (MAD) held that stability was enhanced if both sides were assured of destruction if either attacked. According to MAD logic, rational actors would not commit mutual suicide.

To supporters of NMD, the end of the cold war signaled their chance to realize the goal of a Star Wars missile defense. The MAD theory of restraint no longer applied as the menace now came from states unlikely to be deterred by any threat of a massive retaliation. Thus, the ABM Treaty no longer mattered. They argued it had to be amended or scrapped to allow the United States to build a defense shield to protect against the new emerging threat. Supporters of the ABM Treaty, in contrast, argued that it served as the cornerstone of arms control. Thus, if the ABM Treaty were scrapped, a nuclear arms race might ensue as nations, especially Russia and China, sought to build up a nuclear offensive capability that could overwhelm a new U.S. defensive capability. "That's the real problem here," said the chairman of the senate foreign relations committee Senator Joseph Biden, "China will speed up. And I just saw the Indian ambassador, who nodded and said that would put pressure for India to do the same. And then, of course, the Pakistanis match the Indians. Pretty soon, you've started another arms race."[80]

Recognizing the growing threat of a missile attack from rogue nations or terrorists, Clinton had supported efforts to develop a national missile defense, but one that would preserve the ABM Treaty. In July 1999, Clinton signed into law the National Missile Defense Act of 1999, stating that "it is the policy of the United States to deploy as soon as technologically possible an effective national missile defense system."[81] Clinton's proposal included possible deployment beginning in 2005 of a system that would include one hundred ground-based interceptors deployed in Alaska, an ABM radar station in Alaska, and five upgraded early-warning radars.[82] He also planned a second site beginning in 2010 or 2011 that would include additional interceptors and radars. The goal was to provide a fifty-state defense against emerging threats from both North Korea and the Middle East, focused on the most "immediate and certain" threat, North Korea.

Clinton had cautiously discussed possible amendments to the ABM treaty with Russian president Vladimir Putin and achieved an acknowledgment of the problems involved—a sign of potential future progress. Supporters of a more robust NMD system were not impressed, belittling Clinton's program and criticizing his policy of seeking answers that would be consistent with the ABM Treaty. The veteran diplomat Jeane Kirkpatrick said that "the ABM Treaty is a very, very, very damaging treaty for us. So much of it has to be changed to allow missile defenses that it is not realistic."[83]

Bush was determined to amend—substantially—or withdraw from the ABM Treaty. Following two failed tests in 2000, Bush declared that he remained "confident that, given the right leadership, America can develop an effective missile defense system."[84] Arguing that the cold war policy of Mutual Assured Destruction was obsolete, Bush called for "new concepts of deterrence that rely on both offensive and defensive forces."[85] Rejecting the MAD theory, Rice explained that "peace is not the absence of war, stability is not a balance of terror . . . we cannot cling to the old order like medieval scholars clinging to a Ptolemaic system even after the Copernican revolution. We must recognize that the strategic world we grew up in has been turned upside down."[86] Bush outlined his proposals in May 2001 at the National Defense University outside Washington, D.C., declaring that the ABM Treaty was outdated. He stated that the thirty-year-old pact did not "recognize the present or point us to the future. . . . No treaty that prevents us from addressing today's threats, that prohibits us from pursuing promised technology to defend ourselves, our friends, and our allies is in our interests or in the interests of world peace."[87]

Initially, Bush sought to negotiate a new security framework. High-level delegations, comprised of deputies from the NSC, State, and Defense, were dispatched to Europe, Asia, Australia, and Canada, pressing for agreement on abandonment of the ABM Treaty. The aim was to create "a new framework for security and stability that reflects the world of today."[88] The delegations returned empty-handed. Rice visited Moscow to encourage Russia's cooperation. It was not forthcoming. President Bush's own discussions with President Putin and other world leaders were met with skepticism.

Indeed, far from ameliorating opposition to the initiative, the Bush administration's diplomacy provoked resistance. Russian defense minister Marshal Igor Sergeyev thought scrapping the ABM Treaty merely reflected an American "desire to achieve strategic domination of the world."[89] Yet, Bush pressed ahead. During a trip to Europe in June 2001, he explained that he wanted the ability to explore all the options, saying that the "ABM Treaty is a relic of the past. It prevents freedom-loving people from exploring the future."[90] Allies looked on with deep and growing concern as the treaty that had been the foundation of nuclear stability for nearly thirty years came under threat.

Needless unilateralism

The U.S. effort to abolish the ABM Treaty was the most high-profile effort to distance the administration from international arms-control regimes. But within his first year in office, Bush distanced himself from a host of other pacts and policies as well. One of Bush's first acts as president was to send a memorandum to the administrator of the United States Agency for International Development (AID) reinstating the so-called "Mexico City Policy." First announced by President Reagan in 1984 at a population conference in Mexico City, the policy required nongovernmental organizations to agree, as a condition for receiving federal funding, that they would neither perform nor actively promote abortion as a method of family planning abroad, even with their own funds. The ruling had been used to cover speaking out in favor of legal abortion and providing information to women about their medical options, including abortion. International agencies had strongly objected to the provision, dubbed the "gag rule," as it was viewed as interfering with the advice a doctor or counselor could provide women.

A hot-button issue for liberals and conservatives, the policy had been rescinded by President Clinton on his second day in office, January 22, 1993. Two days into his presidency, on January 22, 2001, the same day Bush sent a message of appreciation to participants in the March for Life, reinstating the policy, he said, "It is my conviction that taxpayer funds should not be used to pay for abortions or advocate or actively promote abortion, either here or abroad."[91] Coupled with a later decision in April 2001 to object to the UN Convention on the Rights of the Child and a UN conference on the issue over a reference in the draft communiqué to "reproductive health services," the Mexico City action sent a strong signal to conservatives that Bush would defend their positions; it also sent a strong signal around the world that this president would put concerns of religious conservatives first and make decisions with virtually no consultation.

The administration quickly distanced itself from many UN efforts. Particular loathing was reserved for the International Criminal Court (ICC), which was considered to undermine U.S. sovereignty and foreign policy. Clinton had signed the ICC treaty in the last days of his presidency, prompting Senator Jesse Helms, the powerful Chairman of the Senate Foreign Relations Committee, to declare: "The decision will not stand. I will make reversing this decision, and protecting American men and women in uniform from the jurisdiction of this kangaroo court, one of my highest priorities in the new Congress."[92] In May 2002, the Bush administration took the unprecedented step of "unsigning" the treaty. A few months later, the American Service Members Protection Act became law, withdrawing military aid to countries that have ratified the ICC statute, and authorizing the use of force to free American citizens being held by the World Court in The Hague.

In July 2001, the administration's representative, Undersecretary of State John Bolton, stunned delegates at a UN small arms control conference when he declared the U.S. opposition to the purely voluntary effort to "prevent, combat, and eradicate" the illicit trafficking of small arms and light weapons. Bolton essentially gave a stump speech for the National Rifle Association, claiming incorrectly that it might interfere with the constitutional right to bear arms. Just as troubling was the decision of the United States to pull out of efforts to secure support for a legally binding verification regime of the Biological and Toxins Weapons Convention (BWC), which committed signatories never to develop, produce, or stockpile biological agents or toxins for military purposes. Although the treaty has been in force since U.S. ratification in 1975, concerns persisted over the lack of enforcement and verification provisions, and negotiations were ongoing to address them. The draft provision would "put national security and confidential business information at risk,"[93] according to the chief U.S. negotiator.

International consternation over these unilateral spasms would be compounded by what the administration was about to announce. On June 11, 2001, President Bush walked out to the Rose Garden at 11:10 A.M. to announce the multiyear international effort of Kyoto dead. Calling the Kyoto protocol "fatally flawed in fundamental ways," Bush pledged that instead he would work to develop an "effective and science-based response to the issue of global warming."[94] Little could have infuriated European governments more. The treaty was one of the continent's most cherished achievements, disregarded on the eve of the president's first trip to Europe.

Years of negotiations, kick-started at the Rio Earth Summit in 1992 by the albeit reluctant attendance of President George H. W. Bush, were shattered. Kyoto called for the United States and other industrial nations to reduce carbon dioxide and other heat-trapping pollutants to below 1990 levels, setting the first binding limits on emissions of carbon dioxide and other heat-trapping gases that scientists say are contributing to global warming and threaten disastrous climate change. Reaching the Kyoto accords in 1997 had been an arduous process. But as Americans emit the greatest amount of greenhouse gases, accounting for 26 percent of the world's output, Kyoto was essentially unworkable without U.S. leadership.[95]

Opponents of Kyoto argue that the accords fundamentally place an unfair burden on the United States and that economic growth can help solve, not cause, environmental problems. While Bush's father and Clinton shared many of those concerns, they ultimately calculated that it was important to stay at the negotiating table to press for improvements.

The diplomatic repercussions were quickly felt. A statement from the European Parliament declared, "We are appalled that the long-term interests of the majority of the world population are being sacrificed for short-term corporate greed in the United States."[96] One of London's leading papers declared Bush's policy was a "Taliban-style act of wanton destruction."[97] France's environmental minister, Dominique Voynet, said, "Mr. Bush's unilateral attitude is a scandal."[98] Taken aback by the outcry, White House Chief of Staff Andrew Card made a rare admission, "We did not do a good job setting the stage for the obvious discussion of the flaws of Kyoto."[99] Even the reserved Powell said, "I would have done it differently."[100]

At the July 2001 Bonn meeting on the issue, Undersecretary of State Paula Dobriansky tried to explain the position, stating, "The Bush administration takes the issue of climate change very seriously and we will not abdicate our responsibility." Her remarks prompted spontaneous booing in the conference hall. Bush sought to mollify European supporters by pledging to come up with a plan for the next international conference on global warming in Morocco the following October 2001. But in the wake of the September 11 attacks, the administration set aside its review of alternatives to Kyoto. Undersecretary of State Dobriansky, the head of the U.S. delegation in Morocco, "arrived at the conference with no new offers and largely stayed in the background while the talks proceeded haltingly."[101]

Much of the difficulties of the Bush administration position on Kyoto was its failure to consult with, much less inform, allies of its intention to declare the treaty dead, in a manner one former diplomat called "needless unilateralism."[102] Bush's rejection of Kyoto was in fact a gratuitous slap at environmentalists. The pact was stalled over objections from Canada, Japan,

Russia, and Australia. The treaty was far from entering into force as it had yet to be ratified by many countries.[103] Voted down in the Senate by a margin of 95 to 0, the practical difficulties were in the short term insurmountable. Had the Bush administration simply ignored the treaty, the practical impact would have been the same. Instead, Bush chose to rile the world.

Bush fundamentally rejected the Clinton approach of seeking change and improvements through participation in international treaties. President Bush hoped that withdrawing from the negotiations would force the international community back to the drawing board to seek an agreement more favorable to the United States. Yet, the administration's handling of Kyoto, the ABM Treaty, the BWC, its 2002 declaration that it opposed the Comprehensive Nuclear Test Ban Treaty, and its visceral opposition to the International Criminal Court left America's allies stunned and fearful of a unilateralist United States that would ignore their concerns. By August 2001, an overwhelming majority of Europeans described Bush as a unilateralist, concerned only with U.S. interests. More than seven in ten of those surveyed said Bush acted solely based on U.S. interests in making decisions. Only two out of ten thought he took Europe into account when making decisions. Europeans expressed little confidence in Bush. Only 20 percent of French, 30 percent of the British, and 33 percent of the Italians answered in an August 2001 poll that they had a fair degree of confidence or better in Bush's conduct of world affairs.[104]

"Europeans expected the smack of firmer leadership from the new administration in Washington, but have been taken aback," wrote *The Economist*. "So far it seems all smack and little leadership."[105]

His foreign policy is going to be based on reality

Bush's first nine months in office were difficult ones, as are those of many presidents whose primary experience is serving as governors. In 1977, Jimmy Carter created a firestorm when he said that he wanted to pull U.S. forces out of South Korea. Certainly, Clinton's early months were not his best. The nine months prior to September 11 of George W. Bush's term set the United States on a collision course with much of the rest of the world. How it would have evolved, without the tragedy of September 11, is difficult to evaluate.

By September 10, 2001, Bush's team remained in disarray. Overall, Powell set out an internationalist approach to promoting America's interest, which involved working with allies, but he was repeatedly overruled by the White House, with the active support of Secretary of Defense Rumsfeld, Vice President Cheney, and increasingly, National Security Advisor Rice. Bush's much-vaunted secretary of state had been publicly reversed over policy toward North Korea, engaging in the search for peace in the Middle

East, and had lost repeated internal battles on how to approach negotiations on a host of other international treaties and policies. Certainly, having ascended to the post with "an almost godlike reputation," as one senator put it, Powell would naturally be taken down a notch or two. Bush's political advisor Karl Rove criticized him, saying of Powell, "It's constantly, you know, I'm in charge, and this is all politics and I'm going to win the internecine political game."[106] But by September 2001, Washington watchers were openly speculating whether Powell would quit. *Time* magazine's September 10, 2001, issue had Powell on the cover asking, "Where have you gone, Colin Powell?"

Rumsfeld's star had also been tarnished. He lost his bid for significant new resources for defense, was forced to backtrack on his opposition to peacekeeping troops abroad, and had lost the support of much of the uniformed military. Speculation swirled that he would be asked to leave. On September 10, for instance, *Fox News* participants were openly asking, "Is Rumsfeld to be taken seriously? After all, there are rumors swirling in Washington that he might soon quit or be asked to quit."[107] Even Vice President Dick Cheney was coming under increasing criticism, primarily for his secretive Energy Task Force and his refusal to sever all financial links with his former company, Halliburton.[108]

The first nine months were characterized by the administration attempting, at times arrogantly, almost always abrasively, to fit an inappropriate template on a reluctant world. After causing a great deal of anguish abroad, reality had slowly tempered many impractical campaign promises. The constraints of government acted to contain extreme solutions. Neither the impulses of the realists, nor the hegemons, had prevailed in shaping the policy of the new president. The United States had not pulled its troops out of the Balkans or withdrawn from any other overseas deployment. It was still seeking to gain Russia's agreement in altering or eliminating the ABM Treaty, and it had begun to engage with its allies over key issues, such as trade. Defending the administration against charges it was harkening back to the cold war, Fleischer stated, "The message the president is sending is that his foreign policy is going to be based on reality. . . . He's going to have a realistic approach to foreign policy."

Reality would hit on September 11, 2001. Everything was about to change.

6

A New Breed of Terrorists

*The ruling to kill Americans and their allies—civilian and military—
is an individual duty for every Muslim who can do it in any country
in which it is possible to.*

—Manifesto of the International Islamic Front for Jihad against Jews and Crusaders, led
by Osama bin Laden, February 23, 1998

As with the assassination of President Kennedy in 1963, all Americans remember where they were when they heard the news of four hijacked planes crashing into the World Trade Centers in New York, the Pentagon, and a field in Pennsylvania. I happened to be in Belgrade, Yugoslavia, driving past the remnants of buildings bombed during the 1999 Kosovo campaign. Around three o'clock in the afternoon, one of my colleagues got a cell phone call and learned that a plane had crashed into the World Trade Center. I dismissed the report as yet another wild Serbian conspiracy rumor.

When we arrived at the United States embassy shortly afterwards for a scheduled meeting with the ambassador, William Montgomery, we saw a plane hitting one of the towers on CNN. Suddenly, we realized it was not a replay but rather a second plane hitting the second tower. Stunned, we watched as people jumped from the burning towers, and then, within two hours, the two buildings collapsed.

From Belgrade, it was impossible to grasp the horror occurring in Manhattan. It looked more like a bad Japanese Godzilla movie than real life. But it was all too real. Terrorists had attacked America at its core. That day, three thousand people died in the attacks, more than at Pearl Harbor or any other single terrorist incident worldwide.[1]

As I flew back to JFK Airport a week later, the smoke was still pouring out of the World Trade Center site. The New York City skyline without the Twin Towers looked like a 1950s postcard in which the Empire State Building was New York's tallest building. America had to respond.

See you at the White House

As it became frighteningly clear that America was under attack—and it was impossible to know whether there would be further attacks—President Bush darted around the country, looking like a man on the run. His day had begun normally, in a Sarasota, Florida, elementary school. Suddenly, everything had changed. The myth that America was beyond terrorists' reach was shattered.

Back in Washington, Vice President Cheney was rushed by the Secret Service from his West Wing office to the Underground Shelter Presidential Emergency Operations Center below the White House East Wing. The center, built during the cold war, is designed to provide the president and his top officials a reinforced, secure location with the key equipment for continuing the functions of government in a crisis.[2] In 1993, when the Secret Service had shown me the facility shortly after I joined the White House, I was struck by the 1950s feel of the area. Thick steel doors, like those that slam shut in the 1960s show Get Smart, are opened and closed as one winds through the thin corridors filled with canned and dried goods, military-style bunk beds, and chemicals for toilets. A compact Situation Room, mostly a conference room with secure phones and videoconferencing facilities, provides officials with a place to meet. A small bedroom and living room are available for the president or his senior officials, if needed, and a zigzagging tunnel leads outside the White House. The exact location of the exit remains classified. In showing me the door to the outside, the Secret Service agents referred to it as the "Monroe Tunnel." I realized they meant Marilyn, not President James Monroe. Rumors were that President Kennedy has used it to sneak the star into the White House. I never asked whether the comment was myth or reality.

From this underground vestige of the cold war, Cheney maintained communications with the president and other key government officials. Resisting suggestions that he evacuate the area, the vice president remained in the bunker throughout the entire first day of the nation's new war.[3]

After hours of issuing statements and darting across the country, Bush rejected the Secret Service's warnings to stay away from the White House and decided to return home and lead the country. He called his wife, Laura, to say, "I'm coming home, see you at the White House."[4] Once home, he also quickly became a voice of reassurance and strength for the traumatized American people. Nine months into his presidency, George W. Bush began acting like the nation's commander in chief.

Speaking to an America still unsure whether the attacks were over, President Bush set the framework for a global alliance against the war on terror, declaring: "America and our friends and allies join with all those who want peace and security in the world, and we stand together to win the war against terrorism." Foreshadowing his later diktat of "You're either with us or against us," President Bush warned terror-coddling nations that "we will make no distinction between the terrorists who committed these acts and those who harbor them. . . ."[5] The following day as he met with his national security team, President Bush declared, "This enemy attacked not just our people, but all freedom-loving people everywhere in the world. The United States of America will use all our resources to conquer this enemy. We will rally the world."[6]

"Ich bin ein New Yorker."

The world quickly answered that call. Within twenty-four hours, the international community, which had derided President Bush's policies and actions, came together in an unprecedented and moving show of support for America. Sounds of the United States' national anthem resounded from Buckingham Palace, the streets of Paris, and at Berlin's Brandenburg Gate. South Korean children gathered in prayer at the American embassy in Seoul and prayers of sympathy flowed from the mosques in Cairo. Condolences were sent to the United States from Africa, Latin America, and throughout the world. France's leading newspaper, *Le Monde,* headlined *"Nous sommes tous Americaines,"* (we are all Americans). Thousands of Germans gathered around the Brandenburg Gate proclaiming and unfurling banners that read, *"Ich bin ein New Yorker."*

The citizens of Slovakia floated paper boats bearing the message "We are all in the same boat" in ponds and lakes around the country. Members of the Masai tribe in Kenya presented gifts of cattle and beadwork in the form of an American flag to a United States embassy official, but only in May 2002 when the news of the tragedy finally reached the isolated tribe. Even football players in Iran paused in a moment of silence before a match. Chinese children laid memorials at the American embassy in Beijing. Offers of assistance from police, firemen, and investigatory officials flowed in from around the world.

The Atlantic alliance divisions over Bush's missile defense policy, Kyoto, and unilateral rejection of many international conventions were set aside as European leaders resolved to stand with the United States and against the war on global terrorism. German chancellor Gerhard Schroeder called the attacks "a declaration of war against the entire civilized world."[7] French President Jacques Chirac, perhaps Bush's harshest critic, declared that the French "are entirely with the American people."[8] In a personal telegram to President Bush, Russian president Putin stated, "Such an inhuman act must not go unpunished. . . . The entire international community should unite in the struggle against terrorism."[9] The European Union's High Representative for Common Foreign and Security Policy Javier Solana and

NATO Secretary-General Lord George Robertson vowed to stand with the United States. NATO made good on the pledge and invoked the collective defense provision of NATO's charter, Article V, for the first time in history, declaring the September 11 attacks to be an attack on all members.[10]

Abandoning his eight months of deriding the international community, Bush recognized he needed its support to win the war against terrorism. He quickly transformed the outpouring of international solidarity into concrete action. His first port of call was the United Nations. Despite the previous nine months of acrimony, the United Nations member states and Washington worked together, with historic unity and speed, to pass sweeping counterterrorism resolutions. On September 12, 2001, the United Nations Security Council unanimously adopted Resolution 1368, urging member states "to redouble efforts to prevent and suppress terrorist attacks" and emphasizing that "those responsible for aiding, supporting or harboring the perpetrators, organizers and sponsors of these acts will be held accountable."[11] The same day, the United Nations General Assembly passed a parallel resolution.[12]

The United States quickly developed a number of measures to implement that pledge and took them to the United Nations. On September 28, the United Nations Security Council passed Resolution 1373, the most sweeping counterterrorism measure in history. Reaffirming the right to self-defense in the face of international threats, the resolution called on all states to "refrain from organizing, instigating, assisting or participating in terrorist acts" while deciding that all states shall "freeze without delay" the financial assets or economic resources of terrorists and their collaborators, and "deny safe haven to those who finance, plan support or commit terrorist acts." In November, the General Assembly passed another resolution that provided the necessary assistance to states that lacked the technical capacity or resources to implement the counterterrorism measures outlined in Security Council Resolution 1373. The Security Council put its most able diplomat, British ambassador Sir Jeremy Greenstock, in charge of the committee to implement the resolution.

International praise for President Bush and support for his efforts were nearly universal. As one German official put it, "Something rather extraordinary has happened, and the reaction of the administration thus far, contrary to some fears that existed, was so different, so cautious and stressing the need to act with others." As a result, at least for now "the image of the cowboy shooting from the hip is gone."[13]

At home, Congress and the American public were unified in approval for the president's response to the terrorist attacks. On September 14, Congress approved a resolution, 98 to 0 in the Senate and 420 to 1 in the House, authorizing the president to take military action to "use all necessary and appropriate force against those nations, organizations . . . that planned, authorized, committed or aided the terrorist attacks that occurred on Sept. 11, 2001."[14] The Senate confirmed Bush's nominee for the United Nations, Ambassador John Negroponte, on September 14, after having held up the nomination when it was made the previous March over objections to his role in President Reagan's 1980s policy toward Central America. Gone was the debate about isolationism that had raged during the 1990s. America was no longer invincible. The hegemons retreated into temporary silence as the administration rallied domestic and international support, their early calls for action against Iraq put aside.

On October 8, 2001, the top congressional leaders of both parties issued an endorsement of President Bush's decision to begin military strikes in Afghanistan, declaring that "we stand united with the president and with our troops and pledge to work together to do what is necessary to bring justice to those terrorists and those who harbor them."[15] On October 12, the Senate approved 96 to 1 a bill giving the government increased surveillance and investigative powers to fight terrorism, including provisions previously rejected such as new powers on wiretapping, money laundering, and computer surveillance.[16] By November 1, 89 percent of the public approved of Bush's handling of the attacks since September 11, the highest public approval rating of any American president in the post-Vietnam era.[17] Never before had a United States president had such universal support at home and abroad. At that brief moment, the world was truly united.

But this war, so suddenly the foremost item on the American foreign policy agenda, had been a decade in coming, starting with Osama bin Laden's arrival in Sudan in 1991. Throughout the years that followed, United States officials failed to understand the full magnitude of his threat, failed to coordinate the information it did posses, and failed to disrupt effectively bin Laden's ability to attack America. Repeatedly, public and congressional support for more aggressive action came only *after* Americans had died. The 2002 Joint Congressional Inquiry into Intelligence Community Activities Before and After the Terrorist Attacks of September 11, 2001 found that, "neither President Clinton nor President Bush nor their National Security Councils put the government or the Intelligence Community on a war footing before September 11."[18] Why did America not act sooner?

A very different threat

In 1993, when President Clinton came into office, the recognized threat from terrorism was not al Qaeda but state-sponsored terrorism and possible diversion of weapons of mass destruction, especially from the former Soviet Union. Americans had been targeted, but only abroad, primarily by Middle Eastern groups.[19] Clinton sought to fight the threats of his day primarily by stemming the proliferation of weapons of mass destruction, resolving conflict among and within nations, and promoting sustainable development, a key component of stability. In September 1993, in his first speech to the United Nations General Assembly, he spoke of the threat of terrorism, including weapons of mass destruction. Pledging to make nonproliferation one of his highest priorities, Clinton announced to the assembled United Nations delegates a series of aggressive steps to control nuclear, biological, and chemical weapons, including a ban on the production of nuclear materials for weapons, a comprehensive ban on nuclear testing, and a call for the ratification of the Chemical Weapons Convention. He also proposed steps to thwart the proliferation of ballistic missiles, including pushing the missile technology control regime to conform to a set of global rules. He sought a new set of export controls in the United States to stop deadly technology from falling into the wrong hands.

During his presidency, Clinton succeeded in implementing many of these efforts. They no doubt made America safer from the very real possibility that weapons of mass destruction could fall into the hands of terrorists. With the exception of the sarin gas attack in the Tokyo subway on March 20, 1995, by the Japanese religious cult whose leader, Aum Shinrikyo, believes the end of the world is near, none of the terrorist attacks since the end of the cold war have involved weapons of mass destruction. State sponsors of terrorism did not transfer such weapons to terrorists; North Korea's nuclear program was largely halted; Saddam Hussein's efforts to amass such weapons were contained; and in 1999, Libya finally handed over two key suspects in the 1988 bombing of Pan Am Flight 103.[20]

But the attacks of September 11 still occurred. Historians will spend decades determining why and whose fault the attacks were. Clinton did not go to war early against Afghanistan—probably the only sure way to have eliminated the threat of Osama bin Laden. The Bush administration failed to see the imminent threat, despite obvious warnings. Understanding what went wrong is important to understanding the perceived threats, the missed signals, and why Americans felt invulnerable.

By and large, before September 11 Americans felt safe, and as a consequence, were reluctant to take strong measures against terrorism or terrorists. The story of antiterrorism efforts in the 1990s is one of dedicated men and women slowly putting together pieces of a complex puzzle, a response that mustered U.S. and global resources to meet a global threat, but—in retrospect—that underestimated the strength, patience, imagination, and determination of the enemy. It is also the story of an American public coming very slowly to terms with the idea that terrorism was the primary threat to America as each new incident—from the 1993 World Trade Center bombing to Oklahoma City, to the attack on a military compound in Saudi Arabia, to the embassy bombings in Africa, the millennium plot, and finally the USS *Cole*—

increased public and congressional willingness to respond. Ultimately, it is the story of how too many people, in too many agencies, in both the Republican and Democratic parties, believed that the old rules still held sway—that a great nation could only be threatened by a great adversary, and that the United States could stand proudly aloof from the world without being endangered by it. Antiterrorism efforts in the 1990s were making headway against this myth within the U.S. government, but no one understood the imminence of the threat. Finally, America was vulnerable as a transition of power occurred from one political party to the other. As with all new administrations, the new Bush team took time to set its own priorities. Yet in doing so, the Bush administration did not heed its predecessor's warnings on the threat from al Qaeda. That threat had emerged over many years.

World Trade Center 1

At 12:18 P.M., on February 26, 1993, a powerful bomb exploded in the underground garage of the World Trade Center in Manhattan, killing six people and injuring more than a thousand. This was the first ever terrorist attack on American soil, and it was carried out, it was later discovered, by terrorists with links to bin Laden.

A terrorist had parked a Ford van rented from Ryder in the garage, filled with a homemade fertilizer-based explosive weighing nearly fifteen hundred pounds. The blast, with a velocity of detonation of nearly fifteen thousand feet per second, left a crater 125 feet across and six stories deep, with hundreds of cars twisted like tin cans among the rubble. The wounded struggled out of the buildings amidst thick, billowing smoke. Thousands of others, stunned and panicked, fled into the streets of Manhattan's financial sector in a scene many New Yorkers would remember on September 11, 2001. The explosion shook the Twin Towers from bottom to top and caused pieces of the ceiling of the PATH station underneath the towers to crash down on frightened commuters. The idea was to bring down the entire tower by destroying the foundation.

United States officials would later discover the ringleader of the plot was a Palestinian-Pakistani named Ramzi Yousef. He had ties to bin Laden, although bin Laden has not been tied directly to the first World Trade Center bombing. The links among the terrorists would strengthen only later. Yousef fled the United States after the bombing and lived in Pakistan at a guesthouse funded by bin Laden, where he was eventually arrested.[21] Yousef had other connections to bin Laden. Mohamed Jamal Khalifah, the alleged financier of the scheme, was bin Laden's brother-in-law. In addition, U.S. authorities would later learn that one of Yousef's uncles, Khalid Shaykh Mohammed, would become one of al Qaeda's most senior leaders and be considered the mastermind of September 11.

While Yousef initially escaped justice, the four others involved in the plot were quickly arrested, brought to trial, and in March 1994 were convicted and sentenced to 240 years each. One of the men convicted had in his possession a document that bore the heading "the Basic Rule." Later translations showed that the heading was actually "al Qaeda," or "The Base," bin Laden's terrorist network. Yet, at the time, government officials did not pursue any broader links implied by the fact that the bombers had links to Pakistan and Afghanistan. It would be another three years before officials realized that a nascent al Qaeda had begun to emerge from the Afghan mujahedeen fighters bin Laden—and the United States—had supported. It would also be years before U.S. officials linked bin Laden to attacks on U.S. forces in Yemen in 1992 and Somalia in 1993.[22]

Part of the reason the first World Trade Center bombing did not trigger a stronger response was that other, more deadly plots were uncovered and prevented shortly afterwards, fueling the impression that the United States was capable of foiling the terrorists. In June 1993, an aggressive FBI operation dubbed TERRSTOP thwarted a massive plot, called "Day of Terror," to blow up the Lincoln and Holland Tunnels and the United Nations, and to assassinate New York Senator Alfonse D'Amato and the United Nations Secretary-General, Boutros-Ghali. The central figure in the plot was the blind sheikh, Omar Abdel al-Rahman, the spiritual leader of both Gamat al Islamiya and Egyptian Islamic Jihad.[23] Al-Rahman was sentenced in 1995 to multiple life sentences. While no link with bin Laden has been established to the Day of Terror plot, bin Laden did have ties to the blind sheikh. Some believe Abdel al-Rahman was a role model for bin Laden; in addition, Rahman's son was involved with al Qaeda.[24]

As the 2002 Joint Inquiry later found, it took "some time" for U.S. officials to recognize the emergence of a "new breed" of terrorists, individuals without state sponsors, loosely organized, favoring an Islamic agenda, and with an "extreme penchant for violence." In fact, it would take until 1995 for the intelligence community to recognize the shift and incorporate it into their analyses.[25]

Gaping holes in the United States

The 1993 World Trade Center bombing prompted a new effort to strengthen counterterrorism measures. Ambassador-at-Large for Counterterrorism Thomas McNamara sent to the White House on March 8, 1993 a list of "proactive, counterterrorism initiatives" the president could take, previewing many essential steps that would not be taken until after September 11. Among them were proposed summary exclusion for aliens who arrive after destroying travel documents, examining visa and screening practices, elevating the criminal penalties for acts of terrorism to a capital one, and expanding the definition of material support provided to terrorists to include all fundraising and training overseas.

In the longer term, McNamara proposed the appointment of a blue-ribbon panel to examine counterterrorism and border security and a review of U.S. domestic aviation security standards. He also suggested the administration explore the use of microscopic particles, called taggants, that enable the tracing of the source of materials after an explosion. While Clinton pressed for these recommendations, many were blocked by Congress until the Oklahoma City bombing two years later, others until the attacks of September 11, and even some today remain blocked.

The NSC also reviewed the existing system of coordinating information on possible terrorists. There were serious problems. The NSC official in charge of tracking terrorism, Richard (Dick) Clarke, saw gaping holes in the U.S. visa system. One example was that the government had arrested a suspect in the first World Trade Center bombing, Mohammed Salameh, and discovered that his six-month visitor's visa had expired five years earlier. To make matters worse, he had been granted a visa despite the fact he was on a list of people to be excluded for involvement with terrorist groups. Another was that, despite being on the State Department watch list for suspected involvement in the assassination of Egyptian president Anwar Sadat, the blind sheikh Rahman had been permitted to enter the United States in 1990, apparently because his name was misspelled. The INS had given him permanent residency status in April 1991.[26] He was later convicted for involvement in the Day of Terror plot.

In a meeting with Anthony Lake, Clarke explained that consulates abroad granted visas without checking the current terrorist data. The State Department maintained a file but many Middle Eastern consulates were not connected to that online database. "Thus, visas are issued without checking the current database," Clarke told Lake. "Moreover, the current database does not check alternative spellings and there is no system which tells a consular section that an application has been denied elsewhere." Clarke also highlighted the fact that current law did not consider membership in a terrorist organization as grounds for denying a visa or the right to fundraise in the United States. Thus, known terrorist groups were free to operate cells and raise money in the United States, including the Shining Path in Peru, the IRA, and Hamas.

Dick Clarke's career tracked the post–cold war rise of concern about terrorism. A career civil servant, he was deputy assistant secretary of state for intelligence during the Reagan administration and assistant secretary of state for political-military affairs, moving under George H. W. Bush to an antiterrorism niche at the White House where he worked until his retirement in 2003.[27] During the 1992–1993 transition, he was one of the few officials at the NSC that its transition team, led by Madeleine Albright, had recommended to Lake that he keep on. In 2001, Condoleezza Rice made the same decision, keeping Clarke on because he was viewed as a fighter you wanted on your team.

To respond to the growing threat of terrorism, the principals set up a coordinating group on counterterrorism, run by a "core group" at the level of the assistant secretary of state, including State, Defense, Justice, joint Chiefs of Staff, the CIA, the FBI, a vice presidential representative, and the NSC. Dick Clarke chaired it. The group would meet within two hours whenever a member requested a meeting. Throughout the 1990s, the group met regularly, often on short notice, and continued to do so up to September 11. The group met several times a week between July and August 2001.[28]

In a memo to Lake, Clarke summarized the challenges in 1993: "The general impression of the group is that any terrorist who wants to can enter and stay in the U.S. without the U.S. government even making much of an effort to prevent it. They can do, and do, operate cells in the U.S. often with little or no law enforcement surveillance." In a classic Clarke bureaucratic move, he then asked Lake whether he preferred Clarke to wait for agency views or to have the group develop recommendations. Lake chose the latter, more proactive option.

Over the next two years, the administration developed a variety of counterterrorism measures, including the freezing of the assets of thirty Middle East terrorist groups in January 1995. The most sweeping effort was the Omnibus Counterterrorism Act of 1995, submitted to Congress on February 9, 1995. The bill increased federal jurisdiction over terrorist cases, the authority to deport terrorists, and the authority to prevent terrorist fundraising in the United States. The bill languished in Congress, criticized by the right as too liberal and by the left as an attack on Americans' civil liberties. Anthony Lewis, for instance, in a *New York Times* op-ed, argued that "the Clinton Administration proposed a piece of legislation that in important respects would take us back to . . . the 1950s."[29] On the right, opposition was strong as well, led by Gun Owners of America, the NRA, and right-wing conservatives with a vehement distaste for the federal government. Opponents rallied behind Newt Gingrich's efforts to stop the bill, stating that people in rural areas especially had justifiable reasons to fear the federal government's tightened criminal code.[30]

Oklahoma City

On April 19, 1995, a truck bomb, a combination of fuel and fertilizer, blew up the Alfred P. Murrah Federal Building in Oklahoma City. The blast killed 168 people, including 19 children. Photos of the blown-out building immediately brought back images of the bombing of the Marine barracks in Lebanon that had killed 241 American soldiers a decade before.

At 9:00 A.M., when the Situation Room staff brought to me a "two red dots" alert, meaning urgent, relaying news reports of the bombing, the first suspects were Middle Eastern extremists who had begun using car bombs in the 1980s.[31] Shortly after the bombing, authorities arrested one unsuspecting, unfortunate man, a Jordanian American, who was flying from Oklahoma City to Jordan. He was questioned by British immigration officials at London's Heathrow Airport, briefly detained, and then flown to the United States to speak with federal officials. Federal investigators, however, soon turned to an American, Timothy McVeigh, who had been incensed over the FBI's 1993 assault on the religious cult Branch Davidian compound in Waco, Texas in which more than eighty of the cult members had been killed, including seventeen children. Within forty-eight hours of the bombing, Timothy McVeigh was in custody.

While it was a relief of sorts that Middle Eastern groups had not perpetrated the act on American soil, it was perhaps more frightening to all its citizens that an act of such magnitude could occur on U.S. soil and be carried out by one of their own. Four days after the bombing, I accompanied President Clinton to the memorial service for the victims, a scene I would recall six years later while watching the mourners of the September 11, 2001, victims. I had gone to high school in nearby Tulsa and wanted to take part in the official mourning. The stadium was packed with families, among them Governor Frank Keating and his wife, the evangelist Billy Graham, and President and Mrs. Clinton. Everywhere I looked, distraught families held on to each other as well as the hundreds of stuffed teddy bears that had been donated by a department store chain and sent by Brenda Edgar, the wife of Governor Jim Edgar of Illinois.

The bombing made us all pause. Just prior to my departure for Oklahoma City, I received an e-mail from the NSC senior director for intelligence George Tenet, who would later become director of central intelligence. We had known each other since our days in the Senate, when Tenet had worked first for Republican Senator John Heinz of Pennsylvania and then for Democratic Senator Dave Boren of Oklahoma, a rare feat of bipartisan staffing that later helped propel Tenet to the top of the CIA and to serve both Clinton and Bush. A friend of Tenet's, Dan Webber, was in his office across the street from the Murrah building in Oklahoma City when the bomb went off. His son was across the street at the Murrah day-care center. "He immediately ran across the street to try and find his son," Tenet, who also had a young son, wrote me in the e-mail. "The image of a young father wondering whether his young son was dead or alive is more than most of us can even think of let alone experience."

The son, a twenty-month old baby, had miraculously survived, although he was in critical condition with compound fractures in one arm and a broken lower jaw. He had also lost portions of both eardrums and already undergone two operations. "I tell you all this," Tenet wrote, "because our work here is often so clinical—pursuing terrorists and other thugs who have taken action against people we often do not know. In this instance, working to do everything we can to find the evil people who perpetrated this heinous crime has taken on greater meaning."

The fight against terrorism was just beginning in earnest.

The war on terrorism begins

It took an act on American soil that killed more than a hundred people to create the support within the administration, the Congress, and among the public for real action to combat terrorism. The threat was now not only those terrorists and rogue states that might acquire weapons of mass destruction, it was also from organized groups that could threaten America with simple but deadly conventional weapons.

Following Oklahoma City, Clinton set up an interagency response team under the direction of his chief of staff, Leon Panetta, to coordinate the federal government's response to a future terrorist attack. He also sought to strengthen the ability of the government to prevent those attacks. On April 24, the administration announced a series of new steps, including funding for research to enhance the use of court-authorized electronic surveillance of terrorist and other criminal activities; creation of a special FBI counterterrorist and counterintelligence fund; increased FBI access to disclosures by consumer-reporting agencies, such as hotels; and directing the attorney general to chair a cabinet committee to conduct a vulnerability review of federal facilities and report its recommendations in sixty days.

The president also asked federal law-enforcement agencies to reassess their needs in the fight against domestic terrorism. On May 1, 1995, the president sent to Congress another bill designed to strengthen the counterterrorism bill he had submitted the prior February, the Antiterrorism Amendments Act of 1995. The legislation would, among other things, set up a new Domestic Counterterrorism Center headed by the FBI and a thousand new agents, prosecutors, and other federal law-enforcement personnel to investigate, deter, and prosecute terrorist activity.

On April 24, 1996, a year and five days after the Oklahoma City bombing, before a group of survivors and family members of those slain by the terrorists, President Clinton signed into law the country's first comprehensive antiterrorism bill. Dubbed by Clinton a "mighty blow" against terrorism, the bill included most of the provisions of Clinton's earlier legislative proposals. The Antiterrorism and Effective Death Penalty Act of 1996 prohibited U.S. foreign assistance to governments that assist terrorists, required microscopic detection devices in plastic explosives called "taggants," required foreign air carriers in the United States to use the same security measures used by American carriers, facilitated quicker deportation of alien terrorists, and made it a crime to provide material support to designated terrorist organizations.[32] It banned fund-raising in the United States for designated terrorist organizations and made it easier to bar terrorists from entry into the United States. Later, in October 1997, Secretary of State Albright designated thirty foreign terrorist organizations, making it illegal for U.S. citizens and institutions to provide funds or other material support to these groups.[33] Al Qaeda was not yet on the list. Interestingly, the IRA and PLO were also exempted, as both organizations had moved toward peaceful methods.[34]

In debating the bill, however, Congress had blocked several key provisions Clinton had sought. It refused to expand electronic surveillance to include "roving" authority to intercept wire, oral, and electronic communications.[35] It also exempted black and smokeless powder from the requirement to add detection taggants to explosives.[36] Many of these provisions would be enacted only after September 11, 2001. The USA PATRIOT Act of 2001, signed into law on October 26, 2001, authorizes roving wiretaps and expands electronic surveillance. The provision on identification taggants, however, has yet to be implemented, due to objections from the National Rifle Association and explosive makers, which object to the cost of such measures. The NRA claims that taggants will lower the quality of gunpowder, and that federal law-enforcement agencies are too untrustworthy to conduct an impartial taggant study.[37]

However, despite Oklahoma City, terrorism in those early days was still not seen as the threat it is today. As Leon Panetta described the mood in Clinton's first term, "Clinton was aware of the threat and sometimes he would mention it . . . [but the big issues were] Russia, Eastern bloc, Middle East peace, human rights, rogue nations and then terrorism."[38] And as George Stephanopoulos, Clinton's former senior policy advisor, said, "It wasn't the kind of thing where you walked into a staff meeting and people asked, what are we doing today in the war against terrorism?"[39] But as the threat from Osama bin Laden emerged, that would begin to change.

Bojinka: The explosion

The kind of lethal threat al Qaeda posed began to become clear in 1995, months before the Oklahoma City bombings. The first real clue to its global reach occurred in the Philippines. On a Friday night in January 1995, a call came in to the Manila Police Station No. 9, alerting the officers that smoke had been spotted coming from the top floor of a building just down the street. Aida Fariscal, the watch commander, went to investigate. Upon entering the room from which the smoke emanated, Fariscal found a horde of bomb-making equipment. While she was in the room, one of its occupants, Ahmed Saeed, returned; he was apprehended. But Ramzi Yousef, his coconspirator and the mastermind of the 1993 World Trade Center attack, got away.

The prime target that day was the Pope John Paul II, due to visit Manila. The room held a costume that might have permitted an assassin to get close enough to the Pope to detonate a bomb. But there was far too much sophisticated bomb-making materiel for the attack on the Pope to have been the only objective. Among the materials found in the room were four floppy disks, one of which declared that "all people who support the U.S. government are our targets."[40]

In what would later prove to be an indication of September 11, one file on a laptop found in the room indicated a plan to hijack eleven large commercial airplanes and blow them up over the Pacific. Also on the computer was a set of United States airline schedules, including the itineraries of eleven flights between Asia and the United States. On the itineraries were marked times like "SETTING: 9:30 P.M. to 10:30 P.M. TIMER: 23HR. Bojinka: 20:30–21:30." Bojinka is a slang word for "explosion" in many dialects of Arabic.[41] In December 1994, Yousef had practiced smuggling a small bomb onto a plane, successfully exploding a contact lens case filled with nitroglycerin under the seat of a Philippines Airline flight to Tokyo, killing the unfortunate Japanese passenger who was in the seat where Yousef had planted the bomb.[42] The eleven U.S. airliners were to be blown up over the ocean on January 21, only two weeks away.

Under interrogation, Saeed disclosed information that further foreshadowed the September 11 attacks. He had attended flying schools in Texas, New York, and North Carolina, and he was supposed to acquire a small plane and crash it into CIA headquarters. Yet, because Saeed was charged only for his involvement in the airline plot, the plans to crash a plane into the CIA headquarters were not placed in the FBI's investigatory files, where they might have helped alert U.S. officials prior to the September 11 attacks.[43]

Released in 2004, the 9/11 Commission Report on the terrorist attacks found bin Laden's involvement in Bojinka to be "at best cloudy."[44] But the links among al Qaeda operatives were building. On Yousef's computer was a list of cell phone numbers; one of them belonged to Wali Khan Amin Shah, a third conspirator in the Bojinka plot, who had ties to bin Laden's brother-in-law's money-laundering network. Following the 1993 World Trade Center bombing, the United States led a worldwide manhunt for Yousef, including printing matchbooks with his photograph on the cover and offering a $25 million-dollar award for his arrest.

He was arrested in Islamabad, Pakistan, in February 1995, betrayed by another al Qaeda member, and with his coconspirators is serving a life sentence in a U.S. federal prison. A major terrorist ring had been destroyed, yet bin Laden continued to build his network against the United States.

The rise of Osama bin Laden

In the early 1990s, U.S. officials saw Osama bin Laden as a major financier of terrorism, but not someone who ran a terrorist network himself. Bin Laden was the focus of a joint Saudi-Egyptian investigation, which revealed in May 1993 that he used his business interests to funnel money to Egyptian extremists. Also in 1993, he financed the travel of hundreds of Afghan war veterans to Sudan for terrorist training. In July 1995, a member of Egyptian Islamic Jihad claimed that bin Laden had helped fund a group and was witting of specific terrorist attacks against Egyptian interests. Mustafa Hamza, the head of Gamat al Islamiyah (GI) behind the June 1995 assassination attempt against Egyptian President Mubarak, worked in late 1994 as a key executive for bin Ladin's Wadi al-Aqia company. By late 1995, bin Laden was said to be a key financier behind the Kunar camp in Afghanistan, a terrorist training camp for Egyptian Islamic Jihad and GI's members.[45]

Arab countries began to focus increasingly on bin Laden. The governments of Egypt, Algeria, Libya, Morocco, and Yemen all accused him of financing militant Islamic groups on their territory. As early as 1993, Yemeni officials described bin Laden as the founding father of Yemeni Islamic Jihad, the organization responsible for the attack against American soldiers billeted in Yemen the prior year. By April, U.S. intelligence officials agreed that bin Laden had "almost certainly played a role" in that attack.[46]

As bin Laden's terrorist network became clear, the Saudis shunned him. In February 1994, he was banished from his family and Riyadh revoked his Saudi citizenship for behavior that "contradicts the Kingdom's interests and risks harming its relations with fraternal countries." Bin Laden became an ardent opponent of the Saudi regime, forming an advisory and reformation committee based in London that as of July 1995 had issued more than three hundred fifty pamphlets critical of Saudi government.

In 1991, bin Laden had relocated to Sudan, where he was welcomed by National Islamic Front (NIF) leader Hassan al Turabi, a pro-Islamist military junta leader who had seized power in Sudan in 1989. It was not clear exactly when bin Laden started his business operations in Sudan, although in a 1994 interview, bin Laden claimed to have surveyed business and agricultural operations in Sudan as early as 1983. He quickly formed symbiotic business relationships with wealthy NIF members by undertaking civil infrastructure development projects on the regime's behalf, such as the road linking Khartoum and Port Sudan.

Bin Laden had four wives whom he kept in four separate residences in Khartoum. He lived as a semirecluse under heavy guard, concerned he might be kidnapped by a hostile government or assassinated by an Islamic extremist group adhering to religious precepts more extreme than his own. Bin Laden reportedly began fearing for his personal safety in early 1993 after media reports began detailing his support for terrorist groups, such as Egyptian al Gamat al Islamiyah and Yemeni Islamic Jihad. As hard as it is to believe today that bin Laden was viewed as too moderate by some extremists, his fears were reinforced by a February 1994 attack against one of his personal residences in Khartoum by the al-Takfir wa al-Hijra, an Islamic extremist group that deemed bin Laden "an unbeliever and a heretic."

Why can't we pick him up?

As early as 1993, bin Laden came to the attention of U.S. officials as his links to the financing of terrorism began to come to light. Anthony Lake recalls repeatedly questioning CIA Director Woolsey about him early on. Over the next several years, we all started asking questions about the elusive man who figured in the doings of so many terrorist groups. For instance, in early December 1995, I asked my morning CIA briefer for background on who bin Laden was, who supported him, and what he was trying to accomplish. The CIA's answer was troubling, describing bin Laden as "one of the most significant sponsors of Islamic extremist activities in the world today." He had developed a close relationship with radical Islamic leaders such as the Sudanese leader Hassan al Turabi, the Afghan prime minister Gulbuddin Hikmatyar, and Yemeni Islaah Party faction leader Abd al Majid al Zandani. He supported those seeking to topple moderate secular states in the Middle East, such as Egypt and Algeria. I sent the memo to Richard Clarke, the NSC official responsible for terrorism, and two colleagues handling legal and intelligence issues with the notation, "Why can't we pick him up in Europe? Can we look at seizing his assets?" Officials throughout the government began to ask the same questions.

By January 1996, the State Department was putting briefings on bin Laden in their morning summaries, widely distributed throughout the government (although in the materials I saw, the first mention of al Qaeda did not appear until the following month), recognizing that bin Laden's freedom of action made "him a threat in his own right to Western and moderate Arab interests."

United States officials now believed bin Laden to have been involved in the 1994 attacks against cinemas in Amman, Jordan; Ramzi Yousef's Manila-based plot in January 1995 to bomb U.S. airlines and to assassinate the Pope; the bombing the previous summer in France by Algerian extremists; and the July kidnapping of Western hostages, including one American, in Indian-held Kashmir. There was suspicion that he was also involved in the November 1995 bombing that destroyed a building where the United States trained the Saudi National Guard, killing seven, including five Americans; and the June 1995 attempt on Egyptian president Mubarak's life.[47] The Saudi king, Fahd Ben Abdel Aziz, reportedly had dispatched three officers of the Saudi Ministry of Interior General Investigation to London in early July 1995 to determine whether bin Laden had been involved.[48]

On November 13, 1995, two explosions rocked the Office of Program Management at a Saudi Arabian National Guard building in Riyadh, killing five Americans and injuring over sixty people. Deployed in 1990 to protect Saudi Arabia following Iraq's invasion of Kuwait, more than five thousand U.S. soldiers and airmen remained in the country in 1996. An FBI investigative and forensic team was immediately dispatched to assist in the investigation, which had netted four suspects, and eventually the bombing was tied to bin Laden although the 9/11 Commission Report found "nothing proves that bin Laden ordered this attack."[49] However, the subsequent Saudi investigation was conducted mostly behind closed doors. The four young suspects, Sunni Saudis, three of whom were veterans of the conflicts in Afghanistan, Bosnia, and Chechnya, were quickly beheaded, but not before mentioning bin Laden as one of three Islamists who had influenced them.[50]

Just six months later, at about 10:00 P.M. on June 25, 1996, a tanker truck loaded with five thousand pounds of plastic explosives blew up in front of the Khobar Towers, a residential complex in Dhahran, killing nineteen and injuring hundreds of soldiers and civilians. The bomb was larger than the one that destroyed the federal building in Oklahoma City a year before, and more than twice as powerful as the 1983 bomb used at the Marine barracks in Beirut.

This time, the administration wanted to ensure that the Saudis cooperated in the investigation. But while the Saudis ostensibly welcomed FBI Director Louis Freeh and his investigators, they denied him access to evidence and witnesses, fearful of their public learning of Shia Muslims attacking the Holy Land and nervous the United States might use the information to retaliate against Iran. Although the FBI was eventually granted access to witnesses, whom the Saudis eventually arrested, the cooperation by the Saudis was never enthusiastic or complete.[51] Iran, in cooperation with Saudi Hizbollah, was believed to be behind the Khobar bombing although the 9/11 Commission Report found there are also signs that al Qaeda played some role, as yet unknown.[52] Stunningly, the administration learned that the Saudis had failed to inform it that they had recently discovered an Iranian plot, working with Saudi Hizbollah, to attack a U.S. military facility in Saudi Arabia.[53]

The bombings in Saudi Arabia underscored the vulnerability of the Saudi regime to terrorism. But bin Laden quickly emerged as the more serious threat to America. On August 23, 1996, he issued a religious declaration of war, a fatwa, entitled "Declaration of War against the Americans Occupying the Land of the Two Holy Places." Exhorting his followers to fight against "the enemy," the Americans and the Israelis, to "do whatever

you can, with one['s] own means and ability, to expel the enemy, humiliated and defeated, out of the sanctities of Islam."[54] The United States was
in a war but did not yet realize it.

A potential deal on bin Laden?

In 1996, the administration stepped up pressure on the government of
Sudan to hand over bin Laden as well as end its support for other groups
including Hizbollah, Egyptian Islamic Jihad, Hizbollah, Hamas, Palestinian
Islamic Jihad, Abu Nidal, and Gamat al Islamiya. The government also
trained and dispatched fighters to support the nascent Eritrean Islamic Jihad
and several Islamist movements in southern Ethiopia. There were also indications the Sudanese leadership had been involved in the attempt to assassinate Egyptian president Hosni Mubarak in 1995. The three suspects in
the Mubarak assassination attempt were believed to be in Sudan. Sudan's
sponsorship of Muslim terrorists legitimized the government in the eyes of
hard-line Muslim regimes like Iran, a state that helped bankroll Sudan after
it defaulted on its debts.

Since September 11, there has been much discussion about whether
hardliners in the Clinton administration missed the possibility of cutting a
deal with Sudan for a handover of bin Laden. The former U.S. ambassador
to Sudan, Timothy Carney, charged in 2001 that the Sudanese "were opening doors, and we weren't taking them up on it. The U.S. failed to recip-
rocate Sudan's willingness to engage us on serious questions of terrorism."[55]
Yet, as ambassador in 1996, Carney's own messages back to Washington
said something very different. For instance, he summed up his meetings
with Sudanese officials by writing the "Sudanese still are not willing to admit
the extent of their support for terrorism and the United States probably will
gain limited results from the dialogue which will revolve around protracted
haggling over who is and is not a terrorist. Bashir will need a significant quid
pro quo to give him political cover to take the steps the United States is
requesting." In other messages, he accused Sudanese officials of "lying and
tapdancing." Carney still argued, however, that "the United States has little to lose by continuing these efforts and there is a potential for a deal on
[bin Laden]."[56] The facts demonstrate otherwise.

In early 1996, the administration developed a list to spell out clearly the
steps Sudan should take as a way of demonstrating its seriousness. The list
included extradition of the three suspects who sought refuge in Sudan following the Mubarak assassination attempt, expulsion from Sudan of Gamat
al Islamiya and Hamas terrorists, and information on activities of Iranian
MOIS in Sudan, as well as information on key terrorist figures, such as Imad
Mugniya, a key Hizbollah leader responsible for the 1983 bombing of the
Marine barracks in Beirut, Abu Nidal, the mastermind of the downing of a

TWA flight from Greece to Israel in 1974 and a leading Palestinian terrorist responsible for hundreds of deaths over two decades, and Osama bin Laden. The list also sought the detention or extradition to Saudi Arabia of Osama bin Laden and the names, dates of arrival, departure, destination, and passport data on the mujahedeen that bin Laden had brought to Sudan.[57]

At the United Nations, the United States pressed for sanctions against Sudan if it failed to hand over the three suspects in the Mubarak assassination attempt. After Sudan failed to comply with repeated UN deadlines, the United Nations Security Council passed Resolution 1054 in April 1996, which restricted Sudanese diplomatic personnel and Sudanese government officials' travel. On August 16, 1996, the Security Council also passed Resolution 1070, threatening to impose a flight embargo against Sudan unless it complied with UN resolutions 1044 and 1054 within 90 days. Although Sudan failed to comply, the Security Council never moved to implement Resolution 1070. The debate on Sudan coincided with increasing opposition to the sanctions in Iraq, thus raising the bar for any additional sanctions. In addition, the states involved feared they, too, might one day be the target of sanctions. Egypt, under pressure from other Arab countries, failed to push for action despite having been the original impetus for the sanctions because of Sudan's complicity in the assassination attempt against President Mubarak. Russia, France, and China expressed their reluctance to use more sanctions in implementing UN policy.[58] In the end, Security Council members failed to agree on a date for the new embargo to go into force.[59] In 1997, the United States implemented its own trade embargo and assets freeze against the government of Sudan starting in 1997.[60]

Despite numerous promises of progress, the Sudanese never seriously acted on the list. By 1998, Sudan was still providing training, travel, safe haven, and financial assistance for al Qaeda, Hamas, and Hizbollah. In 1999, U.S. officials were still concerned that Khartoum was cozying up to pariah regimes, including Iran, Iraq, Libya, and North Korea. From 2000 to 2001, the United States had a team stationed full time in Khartoum with the express mission to gather intelligence that Sudan promised to share. No useful information was forthcoming. As recently as 2001, Sudanese officials were found involved in a plot to bomb the U.S. embassy in New Delhi.[61]

United States officials held repeated meetings with Sudanese officials from 1996 to 2000, but at no time did they receive any concrete actions addressing Sudan's role in terrorism and certainly no credible offer on bin Laden. As Sandy Berger has since recounted, "We never turned down anything from the Sudanese," explaining that the Sudanese repeatedly argued, "if you just ease up on us, we'll help you."[62]

It is important to remember that in 1996, bin Laden was considered a major financier of terrorism, not an active terrorist himself. And, as Dick

Clarke explained in his memoir, the United States could have obtained an indictment for bin Laden in 1996 had there been any chance the Sudanese would have handed him over. The Sudanese had, in fact, handed the notorious terrorist Carlos the Jackal to French intelligence in 1994, a terrorist with whom there was no ideological link. But, as Clarke points out, the chance that the Sudanese leadership would hand over its benefactor and fellow radical Muslim to the United States was nil.[63] The 9/11 Commission Report found no credible evidence that Sudan offered to hand bin Laden over to the United States.[64]

The only real discussion of a deal on bin Laden involved whether Saudi Arabia would take him back. Secret negotiations between the CIA, Sudan, and Saudi Arabia attempted to reach an arrangement whereby Sudan would hand over bin Laden into Saudi custody.[65] In a number of discussions in early 1996, Sudanese officials discussed with U.S. officials the possibility of striking a deal on Osama bin Laden in which the Saudis would pardon him and then take him back. Bin Laden reportedly said he would not go unless the Saudis released religious prisoners. In the end, however, the Saudis never reached a deal with bin Laden as Saudi officials refused to accept bin Laden back.[66]

There is some dispute over how heavily the United States leaned on Saudi Arabia in efforts to get them to accept bin Laden. As one official later commented, "We were not about to have the president make a call and be told no."[67] In 1996, even with American pressure, the Saudis are unlikely to have taken bin Laden back. As bin Laden was sufficiently well connected, and sufficiently popular, the Saudi royal family was unwilling to take serious measures against one of their own.

On May 18, 1996, Sudan expelled bin Laden. He flew to Afghanistan.

The bin Laden initiative

By early 1996, the CIA initiated "The bin Laden Initiative." Its goal was "to undermine the financial support to terrorism provided by [Osama bin Laden] and to lay the groundwork to bring him to justice." The plan was to identify bin Laden's "points of vulnerability and deny him financial resources." The method was to "use all appropriate means to discredit bin Laden, his financial institutions and disrupt his future fund-raising capabilities." The director of Central Intelligence's Counterterrorist Center (CTC) created a special unit with ten to fifteen officials to focus solely on bin Laden, which over the next five years had expanded to roughly forty officials at the time of September 11, 2001.[68] For this group, the CIA sought individuals with knowledge of Arabic languages and advanced technical skills such as computer, photography, and communications. It also conducted new training in advanced technology, including computers, digital photography, and surveillance. Thus, from 1996 on, the United States was actively targeting bin Laden and his network.

The initial task of the CTC unit was to examine terrorist financing and determine to what extent bin Laden posed a significant threat. As time passed, it focused more exclusively on bin Laden and his terrorist network.[69] The unit initially had fewer than twenty people and included operations officers, analysts, and desk officers who directed field operations overseas for intelligence collection or disruption, working through the CIA's Directorate of Operations (DO). Although staff was added to the unit and more case officers were assigned to the field, by the spring of 2001, the CTC did not have sufficient staff to digest the vast quantities of information and develop targeting strategies. As the Joint Congressional Inquiry found, the unit was clearly stretched for people, not money.[70]

The focus on bin Laden was part of a broader antiterror intelligence effort. In 1995, the administration had established broad guidance for highest intelligence priorities in the new post–cold war era. Presidential Decision Directive 35 set forth the priorities, placing terrorism among them, ranging from Tier 0 to Tier 4. Within these new guidelines, the CIA developed a multifaceted plan to combat terrorism: get inside four high-priority terrorist organizations; prepare a compelling plan to undermine Osama bin Laden's finances to support terrorism; intensify operations against the terrorist activities of Hizbollah and the Iranian Ministry of Intelligence and Security (MOIS); expand into Islamic extremist activities in at least one new country; render at least two international terrorists into the custody of law enforcement authorities; and dramatically improve the CIA's knowledge of at least one important terrorist group.

Over the next few years, the United States developed a new counterterrorism policy aimed at reducing terrorist capabilities by termination of financial support to terrorists groups, the closure of terrorist offices and training facilities, and the arrest and punishment of terrorist criminals. Regarding state sponsors of terrorism, the policy called for a termination of aid, and active use of methods to disrupt and reduce capabilities of terrorist groups and state sponsors. The White House increasingly focused on the rising threat from terrorism—and bin Laden in particular. Clinton sought out terrorists hiding overseas, arresting and bringing back suspects from Egypt, Pakistan, the Philippines, and elsewhere for trial. He supported the extradition and return of terrorists to governments seeking them for the prosecution and negotiation of new arrangements if necessary. The administration blocked al Qaeda financial transactions and frozen Taliban assets of $255 million in 1998 and 1999 and banned the Afghan national airline. Additionally, Clinton boosted the Health and Human Services' bioterrorism budget from $16 million in 1998 to $265 million by the end of his term, and increased FEMA's WMD–response budget more than 500 percent over the last three years of his administration.[71] Meanwhile, bin Laden was preparing to attack America.

African embassy bombings

At 10:35 A.M. and 10:39 A.M. on August 7, 1998, al Qaeda struck America in an audacious, deadly, and well-coordinated attack against two U.S. embassies in Africa. With 415 miles between the two cities and four minutes separating the explosions in Dar es Salaam, Tanzania, and Nairobi, Kenya, suicide bombers drove trucks packed with TNT explosives to the U.S. embassies and blew themselves up, killing 253 people, mostly Africans but including 12 Americans, and wounding more than 5,000 others, again mostly Africans.

Most of the casualties occurred in Kenya. An al Qaeda operative, Harun Fazul, had rented an upscale residence in Nairobi three months prior to the attacks. Behind the high-walled building, Fazul and his accomplices were able, without detection, to pack a truck with explosives. Two terrorists, Mohammed Rashed Daoud Al-Owhali, a twenty-four-year-old Saudi citizen, and Jihad Mohammed Ali drove the truck toward the embassy, planning to fire a pistol to scare away Kenyan nationals from the scene before blowing up the embassy. If the self-detonated device on the truck bomb failed, Al-Owhali was to manually detonate the bomb.[72]

The plot was foiled when alert Kenyan guards blocked the truck's entrance into the embassy compound. Al-Owhali exited the truck, leaving behind the pistol, launched a grenade at the embassy guards, and fled. He was later arrested and is now serving a life sentence after signing a detailed confession of his participation in the bombings. Ali manually detonated the bomb and was killed instantly. During the few seconds that lapsed between the grenade explosion and the bomb, many embassy employees scrambled to the windows to view the commotion and were killed from flying glass from the explosion. Although the embassy's external structure remained largely unscathed, the shock of the blast damaged the buildings within two blocks of the embassy's radius, killing more than two hundred Kenyan civilians and injuring four thousand others. The accomplice of the suicide bombers, Harun Fazul, remains at large and on the FBI's most-wanted terrorist list.[73]

The attack on the U.S. embassy in the Tanzanian capital of Dar es Salaam mirrored the one in Nairobi. In June 1998, about one month after Harun leased the house in Nairobi, another al Qaeda operative, Khalfan Khamis Mohammed, rented a house in Dar es Salaam. It, too, was located away from the city center and protected by high walls from the gaze of passersby. A garage large enough to accommodate a truck were key fixtures of both houses, and investigations suggest that the homes' garages may have been where the truck bombs were constructed and stored.

The FBI believes that the driver of the truck bomb in Dar es Salaam was an Egyptian, Hamden Khalif Allah Awad, also known as "Ahmed the German" because of his light features. He was unable to enter the compound's perimeter because of a water-tanker vehicle parked in the compound and thus detonated the bomb about thirty-five feet from the outer wall of the embassy, throwing the water tanker three stories into the air. The driver of the water tanker and five unarmed, local contract guards were killed instantly. Another five were killed and eighty-five were injured in the blast; none were American. The FBI believes that both bombings were masterminded by a top bin Laden confidant and operative, Abdullah Ahmed Abdullah (Ali Saleh) who in 2004 remains on the FBI's list of most-wanted terrorists, with a $5 million dollar reward for his arrest still outstanding.[74]

The FBI quickly determined the attacks were the work of Osama bin Laden and his al Qaeda network. These attacks, however, represented a new level of threat, as it was now clear that al Qaeda had the ability to carry out simultaneous attacks inflicting mass casualties. Bin Laden had declared war on America.

Killing Americans is an individual duty

That one terrorist could threaten a superpower was difficult to grasp before September 11. United States policymakers and the bureacracy were geared to state sponsors of terrorism. Yet, the threat from bin Laden was growing. Since his original fatwa in 1996, bin Laden had steadily been increasing his threat to America. In February 1998, he sought to step up support for the al Qaeda network and organized a top-level meeting of all groups associated with al Qaeda in the terrorist training camp of Khost in southern Afghanistan. The meeting generated the widely circulated manifesto entitled "The International Islamic Front for Jihad against Jews and Crusaders," which included a fatwa ruling that the killing of "Americans and their allies—civilians and military—is an individual duty for every Muslim who can do it in any country in which it is possible to."[75] On May 26, 1998 during a press conference, bin Laden discussed "bringing the war home to America."[76]

While the United States was following closely bin Laden's increasing threat to Americans, it failed to seize upon the growing information on the threat to U.S. embassies abroad, much less at home. Although a year prior to the attack, U.S. officials had picked up a report claiming the U.S. embassy in Tanzania would "have to be attacked" after the one in Nairobi was bombed, the threat was discredited because of the questionable integrity of the source. In fact, at the time of the bombings, the State Department considered the threat of terrorism against U.S. interests "low" in Tanzania and "medium" in Kenya. The mention of possible threats to many other

American diplomatic sites and East African targets, as well as the sea of imprecise and conflicting information coming from questionable sources, made it extremely difficult for the embassy security officials to assess the threat of the bombings.[77]

The U.S. ambassador to Kenya, Prudence Bushnell, had, in fact, asked for a new embassy three times in the eight months leading up to the bombing, only to be turned down on the basis of resource constraints. Overall security measures, however, were increased, such as reinforcing the security procedures and training implemented at the embassy at Dar es Salaam. In fact, a security drill that included bomb precautions was completed just thirty minutes prior to the bombing. But in 1998 U.S. embassies abroad were not on a war footing.[78] United States officials still believe the myth of America's invincibility.

7

The Myth of Invincibility

Whoever is winning at the moment will always seem to be invincible.

—George Orwell

America strikes back

Following the al Qaeda attacks against the U.S. embassies, America began to understand the threat of this new breed of terrorism. Suddenly, the superpower was vulnerable, although it took September 11 to understand just how vulnerable. For the next two and a half years, Clinton sought to use the tools of the superpower to eliminate bin Laden and al Qaeda, including attempting to assassinate him. He changed the way the United States fought the war on terrorism and succeeded in preventing many attacks against Americans.

The U.S. Attorney's Office and the FBI quickly attributed the embassy attacks to Osama bin Laden and on November 4, 1998, issued a long and detailed 238-count indictment of bin Laden and his second in command, Mohammed Atef, in a Manhattan federal court for conspiracy to kill Americans. The same day, the State Department announced a reward of $5 million each for information leading to the arrest of the two terrorists. An intercepted mobile phone conversation between two of bin Laden's lieutenants implicated them in the embassy bombings. Court documents later revealed that the U.S. government had actually been tracking an al Qaeda cell operating in Kenya before the bombings, an effort that made it possible to identify and arrest several of the planners in the two attacks.

In October 2000, Ali Mohamed, a forty-eight-year-old Egyptian native and former U.S. Army sergeant, was the first person to plead guilty to charges resulting from the embassy bombings. Mohamed admitted to conducting surveillance of the U.S. embassy and other U.S., British, and French targets in Nairobi. Mohamed delivered pictures, diagrams, and a report to bin Laden in Khartoum, Sudan. Bin Laden reportedly looked at a photograph of the U.S. embassy and pointed to the place where a bomb truck could be driven through. The targets were chosen, Mohamed said, to retaliate against the U.S. intervention in the civil war in Somalia.[1]

With bin Laden's guilt clearly established, Clinton moved to retaliate. He had met with the families of the embassy bombing victims when the bodies had returned to the United States. There was never any doubt he would act. Shortly after the embassy attacks, Berger had created a "small group" of senior officials to develop America's response to the attacks. The group, including Albright, Cohen, Tenet, Reno, Freeh, Fuerth, Clarke, and the chairman of the joint Chiefs of Staff, Hugh Shelton, would meet regularly on terrorism issues for the rest of Clinton's term. The group met in the Oval Office one evening to decide on the targets. Shelton and Cohen went through the proposal to attack bin Laden's camps in Afghanistan and two targets in Sudan, a tannery owned by bin Laden, and a pharmaceutical plant suspected of producing chemical weapons. Clinton took the tannery off the list as it had little value.[2]

The president left as planned on August 20, 1998, for vacation on Martha's Vineyard, because cancelling the long-planned vacation would have tipped off the world that an attack was coming. He also needed to spend some time with his family following the deposition he had just given on the Lewinsky scandal. He returned to Washington shortly after the attacks became public.

On August 20, 1998, Clinton ordered U.S. forces to launch seventy-five missiles at six training camps in Afghanistan and another thirteen missiles at a pharmaceutical factory in Khartoum, Sudan, named al-Shifa, believed to be involved in the production of chemical weapons. The strikes damaged al Qaeda's training camps and killed an estimated twenty terrorists, wounding dozens of others.[3] Unfortunately, bin Laden was not among them. Clinton sent out a warning that would take on new meaning after September 11: "Countries that persistently host terrorists have no right to be safe havens," adding that al Qaeda operatives "are seeking to acquire chemical weapons and other dangerous weapons."[4]

In response to the attacks, the Taliban organized anti-American protests in the streets. When the United States demanded the Taliban turn over bin Laden, the Taliban founder and leader, Mullah Omar Mohammed, responded by declaring that "even if all the countries of the world unite, we [will] defend Osama with our blood."[5]

The first preemptive strike

While few questioned the U.S. decision to bomb the al Qaeda training camps in Afghanistan, the bombing of the al-Shifa pharmaceutical plant was controversial. United States officials believed the plant was producing chemical weapons, possibly for bin Laden, and that the Military Industrial Corporation that owned the plant was an important part of bin Laden's economic network.[6] The Sudanese government vehemently denied these claims, charging that the United States, in an "unprovoked and unjustified act of aggression" not only demolished "Sudan's only pharmaceutical factory" but also "deprived tens of millions of Sudanese and others in neighboring countries of basic medicines for malaria, tuberculosis, and other life-threatening diseases."[7]

At the time, numerous sources reported that bin Laden was seeking chemical weapons and possibly even nuclear weapons. As Sudan had refused to sign the Chemical Weapons Convention Treaty providing for international inspections, the United States had obvious concerns. Thus, in a risky operation, the CIA secretly sent an agent to Khartoum to collect air, water, and soil samples to determine whether the al-Shifa plant might be making chemical weapons. A former CIA official explained that a sample of soil collected outside the al-Shifa plant contained a chemical that is a precursor to the deadly nerve agent VX.

While there were other conceivable reasons for the chemical to exist and some questioned whether the plant was producing nerve gas, officials found no plausible explanation for it to be present at this location in Sudan.[8] A next obvious step was that Sudanese officials might provide their close associate bin Laden with the chemicals. That suspicion was given weight in 2001 when an al Qaeda operative under questioning admitted to traveling to Sudan for bin Laden to follow the work al Qaeda had under way in Khartoum to develop chemical weapons.[9]

As Sandy Berger later explained, "We knew that a chemical only used to make deadly VX had been found near this plant, which was part of the Sudanese Military Industrial Corporation which Osama Bin Laden had helped finance and where Sudan's chemical weapons program was conducted. And we knew Osama bin Laden was trying to obtain chemical weapons. Under these circumstances, not to have destroyed that plant would have been the height of irresponsibility."[10]

Thus, in what became the first preemptive strike against bin Laden, the United States eliminated the plant and a potential source of chemical weapons for bin Laden or other terrorists. The retaliatory strike against bin Laden's camp in Afghanistan was the third such U.S. action against terrorism. Only twice before had the United States used military force to punish a state for terrorism. The first had been in 1986 when President Reagan bombed Libyan President Mohammar Qadhaffi's home in retaliation for the bombing of a West Berlin discotheque that had killed one American serviceman; the second was Clinton's retaliatory strike against Iraq in 1993 for its assassination attempt against the first president Bush. President Reagan never retaliated for the 1983 bombing by Hizbollah of the Marine barracks in Lebanon, or the 1988 downing of Pam Am 103.

Congress quickly lined up to support the strikes. Democrats strongly supported the action, as did the Republican leadership in the midst of seeking to impeach the president. Republican House Speaker Newt Gingrich (R-Georgia), a strong opponent of the president, praised the action, saying, "I think the president did exactly the right thing. . . . By doing this we're sending the signal there are no sanctuaries for terrorists." Senate Majority Leader Trent Lott (R-Mississippi) and House Majority Leader Richard K. Armey (R-Texas) said "the American people stand united in the face of terrorism."[11] According to a poll conducted on August 20, 1998, two-thirds of all Americans approved of the attacks and 61 percent said they had confidence in President Clinton as a military leader. Tellingly, only one-third of all Americans believed that they or someone in their family would fall victim to a terrorist attack.[12]

After the embassy attacks, it was clear to anyone who cared to look that bin Laden had America in his sights—and that the U.S. response would have to include both pursuit of him and his network and strong measures, including the use of force, to discourage states from offering his network shelter and support. While the hegemons would later reflexively belittle the efforts, the administration revamped its comprehensive strategy, seeking to kill bin Laden, foil future plots, and disrupt the financing and hosting of his networks. But the myth of invincibility kept the United States off the war footing necessary to have prevented September 11.

Bin Laden was a challenging adversary—planning multiple plots years in advance, compartmentalizing operations, and developing multiple operational styles such as a top-down approach, employing highly skilled terrorists, as well as training amateurs like the shoe bomber Richard Reid to conduct simple but lethal attacks, helping local groups with their own plans as with the Jordanian plotters during the millennium, and fostering like-minded insurgencies. Bin Laden had imagination, something distinctly lacking among U.S. officials tracking him. Bin Laden's network had tactical flexibility and a willingness to go beyond traditional delivery means and targets that kept him well ahead of U.S. analyses.[13]

Since the mid-1990s, the CIA had tried to collect information on bin Laden and al Qaeda. Collecting human intelligence became an increasingly important priority, using three traditional mechanisms for developing human intelligence (HUMINT): unilateral sources, volunteers, and liaison relationships. Yet, in a testament to bin Laden's success at secrecy, on September 11, 2001, the CIA had *no* penetrations of al Qaeda's leadership.[14]

America's mythology about its invincibility was another handicap. It got in the way of making the changes in bureaucracy, the changes in mind-set, and above all the changes in public opinion that came only after the horrors of September 11. In the late 1990s, the military itself was often opposed to retaliatory action; the intelligence community was mistargeted and reluctant to refocus; no pressing counterweight could be applied to the problem of government coordination; and the public simply did not see terrorism as a central threat, sometimes even perceiving it as a deliberate distraction from the more "serious" issues of Clinton's impeachment.

At the time of Clinton's preemptives strikes against bin Laden in 1998, some made the ridiculous charge that the president had taken the action to divert attention from the investigation over his affair with an intern; an eerily similar plot had been released the prior year in the movie *Wag the Dog*, in which a president fakes a war to divert attention from a sex scandal. Three days before the strike, on August 17, 1998, Clinton had testified to a grand jury about his relationship with the twenty-one-year old White House intern Monica Lewinsky. For instance, Congressman Jim Gibbons (R-Nevada), said, "Look at the movie *Wag the Dog*. I think this has all the elements of that movie. Our reaction to the embassy bombings should be based on sound credible evidence, not a knee-jerk reaction to try to direct public attention away from [the President's] political problems."[15] But the threat from bin Laden was not a movie. It was reality. As the threat rose, so did U.S. efforts.

Killing bin Laden

The strikes against bin Laden in Afghanistan were not only an effort to erode the terrorists' network of support. They were also designed to kill bin Laden. Immediately after the embassy bombings, President Clinton quietly authorized covert and lethal attacks against bin Laden. The expanded authorizations for assassination were issued when it became clear, according to one security official, that "there was no way to avoid killing [bin Laden] if we were going to go after him."[16]

Sandy Berger explained the decision to bomb the Afghan training camps by saying that a meeting of bin Laden's terrorist network leaders at the Afghan training camp the day the missiles were fired "influenced the U.S.' decision to strike the camps at that time."[17] In fact, U.S. officials hoped to kill the terrorists while they slept. Officials believe the missiles missed bin Laden by only a few hours.[18] In the subsequent 2002 Joint Congressional Inquiry into the September 11 attacks, which interviewed the key officials involved in planning the attacks, all confirmed that one objective of the strikes in Afghanistan was to kill bin Laden.[19]

As Berger later explained, from the time of the Africa embassy bombings, the United States was embarked on "a very intense effort to get bin Laden, to get his lieutenants, through both overt and covert means . . . to capture and kill. . . . There was no question that the cruise missiles were not trying to capture him. They were not law enforcement techniques. . . ." The administration made it clear to the people in the field that, in the words of Dick Clarke, we "preferred arrest, but we recognized that that probably wasn't going to be possible."[20]

The United States has been prohibited from conducting assassinations since 1976 when then president Gerald R. Ford issued Executive Order 11905 banning any U.S. government employee from involvement in assassination. Ford's order, which has been upheld by every U.S. president since 1976, remains in effect today.[21] Justice Department lawyers found that the executive order did not prohibit the administration's ability to try to kill bin Laden because, as Berger explained in 2002 "it did not apply to situations in which you are acting in self-defense or you are acting against command-and-control targets against an enemy, which he certainly was . . . as a practical matter, it didn't stop us from doing anything."[22]

In fact, after the August 20, 1998, attacks on Afghanistan and Sudan, Clinton authorized three more precision attacks against bin Laden and top al Qaeda operatives based on the CIA's identification of his location. In each of these cases, however, CIA Director Tenet felt the intelligence was never sufficiently accurate to make a military attack feasible. As Berger later explained, "Unfortunately, after August '98, we never again had actionable intelligence information reliable enough to warrant another attack against bin Laden or his key lieutenants. If we had, President Clinton would have given the order."[23]

Unlike the post–September 11 environment, Clinton also faced a military opposed to "boots on the ground" in Afghanistan. On more than one occasion, Clinton questioned Hugh Shelton, chairman of the joint Chiefs of Staff from 1997 to October 2001 and a former Special Operations commander, about the effectiveness of dropping a small Special Forces team inside Afghanistan to fill intelligence gaps in finding bin Laden.[24] Yet, there was no support in the Pentagon for putting U.S. military operatives in Afghanistan, much less an all-out war. As Dick Clarke explained, "The overwhelming message to the White House from the uniformed military leadership was 'we don't want to do this'. . . . The military repeatedly came back with the recommendations that their capability not be utilized for commando operations in Afghanistan."[25]

In the fall of 2000, after Berger expressed impatience with U.S. efforts to get bin Laden, Shelton, in fact, did prepare a paper containing a dozen options for using military force against bin Laden, including U.S. ground forces in Afghanistan. Shelton and Secretary of Defense Cohen described the military options paper as an effort to "educate" the national security advisor about the "extraordinary complexity of the 'boots-on-the-ground' options."[26] Shelton said the options could have been executed "very quickly" but depended on the intelligence community obtaining actionable intelligence. Shelton said the CIA never provided such intelligence and the military had never been asked to obtain it. For Clinton to strike without a reasonable certainty of hitting bin Laden would have only made the United States look impotent and encourage more terrorists to join al Qaeda.

In 1998, Clinton also ordered the navy to place permanently two Los Angeles–class attack submarines, equipped with Tomahawk cruise missiles, near Afghanistan in the northern Indian Ocean and the Persian Gulf. From these locations, the slow-flying Tomahawk missiles could reach Afghanistan within ninety minutes. When additional preparation and logistics were accounted for, the submarines were poised to launch the missiles at Afghani coordinates within six hours of receiving the attack order. Deployment of these submarines was a significant tactical advantage as it reduced the "strike window" from twenty-four to thirty-six hours down to six hours. It also replaced the need for keeping deploying the Tomahawk missiles to the politically contentious U.S. bases in the Persian Gulf.[27] During his first two years in office, President Bush maintained the readiness of these missile-equipped ships in the North Arabian Sea, and continued to use the intelligence technologies initiative during the later years of the Clinton administration.[28]

While the United States remained reluctant to put U.S. soldiers into Afghanistan, in 1999, the United States trained sixty Pakistani commando soldiers to hunt for and capture bin Laden.[29] The mission was eventually abandoned when Pervez Musharraf overthrew Pakistani president Nawaz Sharif in October 1999.[30] Although some considered arming the Afghan warlords, particularly Ahmed Shah Massoud of the Northern Alliance, to seek the overthrow of the Taliban, such a strategy was controversial. For instance, as former chairman of the joint Chiefs of Staff Hugh Shelton explained, the Northern Alliance "had its own baggage, and when you attach the U.S. flag to their formation, and you become a partner with them, then you also become one who can be held accountable for their actions."[31] As was shown in the 2001 overthrow of the Taliban regime, success would require a substantial U.S. military commitment—one that had no support prior to September 11.

Clinton approved every operation recommended by the military. Yet, other than the one strike in August 1998, the CIA and Pentagon could never reach "a substantial probability of success," which was necessary to justify the launching of an attack. CIA Director George Tenet lamented in small group meetings that "I can tell where [bin Laden]'s been, I can tell you where he's going . . . the problem is, can I tell you where he'll be for the next six to ten hours?"[32]

By February 1999, the intelligence community believed that Osama bin Laden posed the single greatest terrorist threat to the country. He was actively planning to attack U.S. interests and an attack could occur any day. By late 2000, the U.S. military was coming to the same conclusions as the intelligence community: getting bin Laden meant dealing with the Taliban regime first and shutting down the sanctuary in Afghanistan.

Yet, prior to September 11, there was no support in the United States, not in the administration, not in Congress, nor among the American people, for the overthrow of the Taliban. While Clinton regularly spoke of the threat of terrorism to the American people, they did not feel directly threatened at home and thus did not see the need for such drastic measures. The administration did, however, pursue virtually every method short of invasion.

Every method short of invasion

As the threat from bin Laden escalated, President Clinton and his advisors planned increasingly sophisticated methods to kill or capture him. Especially during the later years of his presidency, Clinton repeatedly urged the intelligence community to employ new methods and technologies to find and locate bin Laden and his network. As former national security advisor Sandy Berger described Clinton's focus on aggressively seeking out bin Laden, "We were continually looking at new techniques . . . in February 2000, for example, I sent a memo to President Clinton outlining what we were doing. And he wrote back, 'This is not satisfactory . . . we have got to do more.' And that prompted us to work with the intelligence community and the military on a new technique for detecting bin Laden . . . actually it was very promising as a way of determining where he would be if we had one strand of human intelligence."[33]

Recognizing the need for real-time intelligence to locate and take out bin Laden, and pressed by Clinton's constant demand for innovation and creativity, Richard Clarke began toying with the idea of arming the unmanned drone, dubbed the Predator, that had proved extraordinarily useful in gathering intelligence during the Balkan wars. The drone gathered full-area video data in both day and night cruises from a safe, midaltitude flight. Clarke also sought to arm the small 950-pound drone, an idea that was tested in 2000.

Yet, prior to September 11, the proposal remained controversial and the Predator was deployed only as an observation tool in Afghanistan in September and October 2000. The CIA opposed the idea of arming it, citing flaws in the drone's surveillance mechanisms and accompanying firepower. It indicated that the small plane, equipped with only minimal horsepower akin to a motorbike, would be hard-pressed to lug a hundred-pound Hellfire missile, normally used by attack helicopters, across the expansive terrain of Afghanistan.[34] Like a hot potato tossed away as quickly as possible, the CIA and the air force argued about who should run and fund the operation. The CIA also felt that the air force should be responsible for taking out bin Laden, indicating that CIA agents would face retaliation if responsibility for the operation were linked to the CIA. The critics were silenced after September 11. The drone ultimately became a key intelligence tool in 2001 and was used in Afghanistan to help identify and kill al Qaeda's military chief, Mohammed Atef, on November 16, 2001.[35]

Over eight years, the Clinton administration undertook worldwide manhunts to track down terrorists, apprehending more than fifty important terrorist fugitives from overseas, including the conspirators of the first World Trade Center bombing, perpetrators of the attack on CIA headquarters in 1993, conspirators of the bombings of the U.S. embassies in Kenya and Tanzania, and several who had plotted attacks during the millennium. Called renditions, the arrest and detention of terrorist operatives for return to the United States or another country for prosecution, often led to confessions and disrupted terrorist plots by shattering cells and removing key individuals. Not all of them succeeded. For instance, in 1997, the United States was poised to apprehend Imad Mugniya, the Hizbollah leader responsible for the 1983 Marine barracks in Lebanon. Mugniya was believed to be on a ship crossing the Atlantic.[36] The operation was called off at the last minute when intelligence indicated he was not on the ship. Mugniya was unfortunately allowed to slip away when the Saudi authorities refused to hand him over as he was in transit to Saudi Arabia in 1997.[37] The administration also came up with more creative ways of seeking the apprehension of terrorists. Following the first World Trade Center bombing, the United States launched a worldwide manhunt for the operation's mastermind, Ramzi Yousef. I remember sitting in the situation room when Richard Clarke passed out matchbooks with Yousef's photo on it, advertising a $2 million reward for his arrest. The matchbooks, along with posters, flyers, and paid ads in local newspapers, were distributed throughout Asia.[38]

Where possible, the United States worked with foreign nations to arrest al Qaeda operatives and dismantle their terrorist cells, launching a worldwide effort to thwart attacks. The disruption effort involved dozens of foreign intelligence services, which detained suspected radicals, minimally to keep them off the streets, but also in the hope of gaining confessions or intimidating them into aborting planned attacks. Although results were mixed, since 1997, the CIA and FBI foreign cooperation efforts have led to the disruption of dozens of al Qaeda cells in twenty countries. Since September 11, the number of renditions has increased substantially.[39] Additionally, the FBI was successful in disrupting the sources of terrorist financing, including freezing $113 million from sixty-two organizations and conducting seventy investigations, twenty-three of which have resulted in convictions.[40]

Money moves in mysterious channels

One of the most difficult challenges Washington faced was breaking up bin Laden's vast and complex financial network. Bin Laden has claimed that he has access to four ways of transferring money: smuggling cash, the global banking system, the Islamic banking system, and *hawalas*, or informal money-transfer networks. He once boasted to a Pakistani newspaper that the cracks in the Western financial system were as familiar to him and his al Qaeda colleagues as the lines on their own hands.[41] Tracking his finances was a difficult challenge for the United States.

Reports indicated that he made billions of dollars in opium earnings through his dealings with the Taliban. He funneled his money through holding companies in Luxembourg and Amsterdam, paying non–al Qaeda affiliates to serve as his front men. In addition to money laundering, bin Laden also maintained a network of legitimate businesses, including a European fertilizer wholesaler called Wadi al-Aqiq, a Sudanese road contracting firm called Al-Hiraj, as well as banks, venture capital firms, and export-import ventures.[42] As one former State Department counterterrorism official described the challenge, "Money moves through mysterious channels. . . . A good deal of it moves in suitcases, and it's not always easy to track what flows for terrorist purposes."[43]

President Clinton recognized that an open and rich society like the United States would be a potential hotbed for terrorist money laundering. He attempted to stem this flow of financial resources to terrorists by creating the National Asset Tracking Center, a center Bush's Treasury secretary, Paul O'Neill, would later decide not to fund.[44] Following the 1998 attacks on the U.S. embassies, the United States added bin Laden's name to a list of terrorists whose funds were to be targeted by the U.S. Treasury for seizure.[45] Clinton also used his executive powers to block the financial transactions of terrorists to include bin Laden and others in al Qaeda's network. In 1999, he issued an executive order freezing an estimated $255 million in Taliban assets.[46] Internationally, Clinton pushed the G-8 and OECD nations to form a multilateral financial action taskforce to urge countries with loose banking regulations to tighten their banking laws. Under Clinton, more than thirty countries actively worked to clean up their banking laws.

Richard (Rick) Newcomb, the former director of the Office of Foreign Assets Control (OFAC) until 2004, worked with Dick Clarke to develop an understanding of terrorists' support networks and followed their money trails. He explained, "Tracking the operational infrastructure of al Qaeda involved analyzing its activities in Afghanistan, the Balkans, and other key areas of operation. This effort helped us to understand how al Qaeda used deep-pocket donors and facilitators, nongovernmental organizations, safe havens around the world, and training camps. We also sought to understand their payment for families of operatives who lived abroad, often for years."[47]

Yet, to many officials, tracking terrorist financial funds seemed like searching for a needle in a haystack, especially given the wide array of funds, aliases, and legitimate businesses used by terrorist groups and the small cost of carrying out terrorist attacks. The 2002 Joint Congressional Inquiry (much of which was in use in the 2004 9/11 Commission Report) criticized the intelligence agencies for the lack of formalized systems to separate terrorists from their finances, although noting that the White House was more focused on tracking terrorist financing and assets.[48] Without support from the intelligence agencies, the mechanisms for tracking terrorist assets were incomplete prior to September 11.

FBI investigations, for example, were inconsistent and performed on a case-by-case basis only, and intelligence agencies were reluctant to use financial databases to track the funds of terrorist suspects. Despite these capacities, the FBI did not search for the banking and financial data of the hijackers until after the attacks. In his memoir, Dick Clarke is scathing in his criticism of the FBI's failure to seriously address financing and tracking of al Qaeda funds in the United States. "Nobody from FBI could ever answer even our most basic questions about the number, location, and activities of major *hawalas* in the U.S.—much less take action." He criticized FBI Director Freeh's focus on foreign-based terrorism and that the bureau was "consumed with Russian and Chinese espionage, the case of FBI agent Robert Hanssen [caught spying for the Russians], and the case of Wen Ho Lee [accused of spying for China at the nuclear labs]." He also noted the reluctance of the FBI to send written reports to the White House, in contrast to the CIA, NSA, and State, which flooded Clarke's e-mail with reports.[49]

As Clarke summed it up in 2002, the intelligence community was "unable to tell us what it cost to be bin Laden, what it cost to be al Qaeda, how much was their annual operating budget within some parameters, where did the money come from, where did it stay when it wasn't being used, how it was transmitted."[50]

Overall, the Joint Congressional Inquiry investigation found that the U.S. government was unable to disrupt financial support for bin Laden's terrorist activities effectively.[51] Prior to September 11, "no single U.S. Government agency was responsible for tracking terrorist funds, prioritizing and coordinating government-wide efforts, and seeking international collaboration in that effort."[52] There was no coordinated strategy for tracking and closing down financial networks and sharing information on financial investigations between agencies. The report also found a reluctance to take actions, such as seizures of assets and bank accounts and arrests of those involved in the funding, out of a fear by the Treasury Department that such activity could adversely affect the international financial system.[53] However, as Newcomb explained, Treasury officials are and always have been willing to consider ways to do so that do not risk disrupting the international financial systems.[54]

"We are at war."

In December 1998, Director of Central Intelligence George Tenet sent a memo to senior CIA officials that read "we must now enter a new phase in our effort against bin Laden. . . . We are at war. . . . I want no resources or people spared in this effort, either inside [the] CIA or the Community."[55] He moved the threat from bin Laden up to the highest priority category and then in 1999 ordered a baseline review of the CIA's operational strategy against bin Laden. In response, the CIA produced in 1999 a new comprehensive operational plan of attack against bin Laden and al Qaeda inside and outside Afghanistan, dubbed simply, "The Plan." It included a strong and focused intelligence collection program to track and act against bin Laden and his associates in terrorist sanctuaries. It was a blend of aggressive human source collection—both unilateral and with foreign partners—and enhanced technical collection.

The CIA's Counterterrorism Center (CTC) developed a program to, as one CIA official described it, "select and train the right officers and put them in the right places." Between the August 1998 embassy attacks and September 11, the number of CIA personnel working on al Qaeda almost doubled.[56] The CIA brought the best and most experienced operations officers into the effort and initiated a nationwide program to identify, vet, and hire qualified personnel for counterterrorist assignments in hostile environments. The plan was geared toward increasing the CIA's capacity to gather intelligence on bin Laden and his associates. The CIA sought highly skilled officials, well-versed in Middle Eastern and South Asian languages and cultures. The CTC trained these select agents in eight-week counterterrorism operations courses, teaching them skills for operating within hostile environments.[57] The plan included covert action and technical collection aimed at capturing bin Laden and his principal lieutenants.[58]

In contrast, Director Louis Freeh never put the FBI on a war footing before September 11. Although Clinton increased FBI funding for counterterrorism dramatically in the mid-1990s, including a 250 percent increase in the number of agents involved with counterterrorism and an increase in the FBI budget for these purposes of nearly 350 percent, the agency failed to make the issue a priority. The FBI counterterrorism budget rose from

$118 million to $286 million and the agency allocated 2,650 agents to the task, more than doubling the number of counterterrorist specialists since 1998.[59] The number of special agent and support positions dedicated to terrorism more than doubled from 1993 to 1999.[60] In 1999, the FBI created the Bin Laden Unit at its headquarters, with about nineteen people working in the unit prior to September 11.[61]

Several initiatives domestically also enhanced the intelligence community's ability to handle counterterrorism investigations. One of the key difficulties in a comprehensive plan of attack against bin Laden was the lack of coordination between the CIA and FBI. To address the problem, the administration placed a top-level FBI official at the CIA's Counterterrorism Center and a top CIA official at the FBI. In addition, Joint Terrorism Task Forces (JTTF) were created to facilitate collaboration between the FBI and municipal police departments. Officials from the CIA joined the task forces as they were implemented in thirty-five cities. These task forces brought together federal, state, and local agencies to provide valuable expertise to counterterrorism investigations.[62] Such cooperation was critical to tracking down suspects at home and abroad.

A governmentwide strategy

The administration sought to establish an integrated, comprehensive, governmentwide strategy for countering the threat from bin Laden. Just prior to the 1998 bombing of the African embassies, Clinton built on his 1995 Presidential Decision Directive, PDD-39, by strengthening the authority to apprehend terrorists outside the United States and ways to address terrorist attacks involving weapons of mass destruction. In May 1998, he signed a new directive, PDD-62, "Protection Against Unconventional Threat to Homeland and Americans Overseas." The PDD created a ten-program counterterrorism strategy and assigned specific tasks to agencies within the intelligence community. The directive gave the Department of Justice responsibility for mitigating foreign-terrorist threats in the United States and the authority to apprehend, extradite, and prosecute suspected terrorists and collaborators within the United States. The task of disrupting terrorist cells was assigned to the CIA, while the National Security Council was charged with preventing terrorists from acquiring weapons of mass destruction and protecting critical infrastructure and cyberspace.[63] Clinton's PDD-62 was the first integrated and comprehensive counterterrorism strategy put forth by the federal government. The initiative created a framework for dealing with terrorism and emphasized the need for an interagency process to facilitate information-sharing among intelligence agencies.

Also in May 1998, Clinton signed PDD-63 to protect the nation's key national infrastructure, particularly transportation and energy, from the growing threat of unconventional and cyber attacks. The directive sought to protect and fortify these "critical infrastructures," including telecommunications, energy, banking and finance, transportation, water systems, and emergency services. The directive assigned government agencies with the task of assessing the risks and developing plans to protect their critical structures, and it emphasized close cooperation between federal, state, and local government officials to implement the plans. In developing the first National Critical Infrastructure Plan, the administration sought to energize public–private sector cooperation and attention on security of such systems as power grids, electricity, and computer networks. The Gore Commission on Aviation Security, for example, ordered new measures to increase the safety and security of air travel on international and domestic flights, including the establishment of federally mandated standards for security enhancements, such as the use of Explosive Detection System machines and the development of manual and automated profile programs; enhanced passenger check-in and security procedures at airports; and a directive to encourage the FAA to work with the Department of Defense and the Department of Energy on programs to "anticipate and plan for changing threats, such as chemical and biological agents."[64] Lead agencies within the federal government were charged with overseeing especially vulnerable targets.[65]

As the threat grew of a terrorist attack in the United States, the administration sought to ensure America's first-responders were prepared. It initiated the first training of firefighters and other first responders in more than 150 cities to react in the event of a chemical or biological attack. The administration created National Guard Rapid Reaction teams that could surge to an American city attacked by chemical or biological weapons and organize the flow of federal or military assistance. Over Clinton's last three years, there was an increase of over 500 percent in the Federal Emergency Management Agency (FEMA) budgets for preparation and response to weapons of mass destruction–related threats.

Clinton also created a national stockpile of drugs and vaccines, including the CIPRO stockpile of antibiotics that were available when anthrax attacks took place in 2001. The administration also developed and acquired new vaccines and antidotes to cope with chemical or biological attacks and established the first contract to develop smallpox vaccines as part of a $300 million program to produce 40 million doses. Clinton increased funding for public health infrastructure related to counterterrorism to $600 million in FY 2001, a 475 percent increase over 1998 spending levels. He also ensured a substantial budget increase for the Health Department's bioterrorism initiative for prevention, consequence management, and research and development from $16 million in 1998 to $265 million by the end of the administration.[66]

Overall spending for counterterrorism programs more than doubled from $5 billion in FY 1996 to over $11 billion in FY 2000, despite the strong push to balance the budget during this period. For the first time, the budget targeted counterterrorism funds for front-line agencies involved in responding to potential attacks, such as the Heath and Labor departments and FEMA, which was for the first time recognized as part of the national security framework.

In developing a more systematic approach to fighting terrorism by designating federal agencies' missions and roles, Clinton also established a new White House position of national coordinator for security, infrastructure protection, and counterterrorism. The position was given principal status, meaning a seat at the Principals Committee table, although in this case, not cabinet rank. Dick Clarke assumed the position. Clarke ran the Counterterrorism Security Group (CSG), which included representatives of all key federal agencies that met at least once and often several times a week to coordinate counterterrorism activities among key intelligence and law enforcement agencies. The CSG reviewed significant threat information for action and follow-up. The group often met weekly, sometimes daily, especially from 1998 to 2001 to address the growing threat from terrorism. The interagency group still exists under Bush and meets regularly.

They weren't planning terrorism, they were planning a revolution

On November 30, 1999, in Amman, Jordanian intelligence listened as one of bin Laden's top lieutenants, Abu Zubaydah, gave orders for an attack he called "the day of the millennium." At 2 A.M., Jordanian officials raided several houses, arresting sixteen individuals suspected of planning a massive attack against the Radisson Hotel and various other sites expected to be populated by Americans visiting for the millennium. On December 5, with the help of one of those arrested in the November 30 raid, Jordanian police raided another house and found seventy-one plastic containers of nitric acid and sulfuric acid, the equivalent of sixteen *tons* of TNT, enough to destroy most of the neighborhood. Officials also learned that the terrorists intended to release cyanide gas inside a crowded movie theater that was popular with foreigners."[67] They also planned to bomb Mount Nebo, one of the holiest sites in Jordan, a pilgrimage site popular among American Christians, the site where Moses is believed to be buried. As the Jordanian crown prince remarked, "They weren't planning terrorism, they were planning a revolution."[68]

Jordan was not al Qaeda's only target for the millennium. Throughout the fall of 1998 until the plot was broken up, U.S. intelligence agencies were picking up signs that a major terrorist plot was under way to inflict mass casualties against Americans around the time of the millennium celebrations on December 31, 2000. For instance, in the fall of 1998, U.S. officials received information concerning a bin Laden plot involving aircraft in the *New York and Washington, D.C. areas,* an eerie prediction of September 11. Other reports in November 1998 indicated a bin Laden terrorist cell was attempting to recruit a group of five to seven men from the United States to travel to the Middle East for training in conjunction with a plan to strike U.S. domestic targets. There was real concern al Qaeda would seek to disrupt the country's computer and telecommunications networks.

In the spring of 1999, the United States received information about a planned bin Laden attack on a government facility in Washington, D.C. In August 1999, there were reports indicating that al Qaeda had decided to assassinate the U.S. secretary of State, secretary of Defense, and director of Central Intelligence. By September 1999, there was information that bin Laden and others were planning a terrorist act in the United States, possibly against landmarks in California and New York City. By late 1999, U.S. officials received information regarding possible al Qaeda network plans for between five and fifteen attacks in the United States, including targets in Washington, D.C., and New York City during millennium celebrations.[69] It was clear America was under threat, but where, when, and how—no one knew.

Dick Clarke and National Security Advisor Sandy Berger swung into high gear in the lead up to the millennium. Clarke's CSG prepared for the worst and canceled all holidays. The principals met daily during the month before New Year's Eve, scouring all available intelligence to discover the plot. Berger told Attorney General Janet Reno, FBI Director Louis Freeh, and CIA Director George Tenet, "This is it, nothing more important, [use] all assets." Thousands of agents fanned out across the country, searching for any piece of evidence they could link together to discover the plot. There were more wiretaps a week than normally took place in the course of the year. Disaster units and nuclear-weapons detectors were positioned across the nation, the Coast Guard sent cutters to New York's harbors and rivers. The administration sent a warning of a possible al Qaeda attack to federal, city, and state law enforcement agencies.[70]

The breakup of the Jordanian cell prevented major attacks overseas. But it was not until two weeks before the millennium that the United States got a break regarding possible attacks within the United States. On December 14, 1999, an Algerian extremist, Ahmed Ressam, was arrested as he tried to enter the United States from Canada with bomb-making chemicals and detonator equipment. He was caught after an alert Customs agent asked to search his car and he attempted to flee. The investigation revealed that his target was Los Angeles International Airport and he was an operative with ties to bin Laden's network.[71] Ressam agreed to cooperate with investigators and helped U.S. officials piece together a dramatic plot to attack targets around the United States on the millennium.

Thus, the largest counterterrorism operation in U.S. history worked. There were no explosions, no attacks, no massive computer failures. The U.S. and Jordanian officials thwarted multiple attacks by al Qaeda in the United States and Jordan, including planned attacks against the Los Angeles International Airport and the Amman Radisson Hotel in Jordan, as well as the Mount Nebo pilgrimage site in Jordan. Yet, the plot revealed a frighteningly extensive al Qaeda network in the United States. For instance, information provided by Ressam led to the arrest in Brooklyn of an al Qaeda operative. The investigation of the plot in Jordan revealed the head of a cell of the plot in Jordan had been a Boston cab driver and another operative had lived not far from Los Angeles International Airport.

As Dick Clarke said, "For anyone who doubted it before, the Boston taxi driver, the Los Angeles airport, the Brooklyn connection, the Montreal cell had all said one thing: they're here."[72]

Trying diplomacy

From the bombing of the U.S. embassies in Africa to September 11, administration officials directly and personally warned the Taliban that the United States would hold the leaders responsible for bin Laden's actions. Senior U.S. officials pressed the Taliban to hand over bin Laden and for those with influence in Kabul to do the same. Should the Taliban refuse, the United States would push for an end to landing rights for the Afghan airline, a freezing of their assets, and a prohibition on visas to prevent the travel of the Taliban leadership.[73] Left purposefully vague was what military actions the United States might take should another attack occur.

The response of the Taliban was either open defiance, calling on President Clinton to resign and for U.S. forces to vacate Saudi Arabia, or it was equivocal. They argued that it would violate cultural etiquette to mistreat their guest, that bin Laden was a hero to Afghans because of his role in the 1980s opposing the Soviet rule, or that the regime would be toppled if they handed bin Laden over.[74] In response to the $5 million U.S. bounty for bin Laden and Mohammed Atef, bin Laden placed a bounty of $9 million each for the assassination of four "top" U.S. intelligence agency officers.

Undersecretary of State Tom Pickering, State's third-ranking official, warned Pakistan of the consequences of its continued support for the terrorist-supporting Taliban state. In April 2000, he summoned Pakistan's intelligence chief, Mahmoud Ahmed, to tell him that people who killed Americans were enemies and "people who support those people will also be treated as our enemies."[75] A month later, in May 2000, Pickering met again with the Pakistanis, this time with Deputy Foreign Minister of the Taliban Mullah Ahmed Jalil, to convey the seriousness of the message. Again the Taliban refused to take action against bin Laden.

The United States also pressed Pakistan to assist in the handing over of bin Laden and his supporters. It also sought access to Pakistan's territory to launch either "snatch-and-capture" missions or accurate bombing strikes against bin Laden. Pakistan's support was only sporadic, as the military considered bin Laden a useful resource in its effort to support militants in Kashmir. For instance, Pakistan used bin Laden's terrorist camps to train militants to be sent into Kashmir.[76] Ultimately, Pakistan never cooperated in any significant way with the U.S. requests.

The United States sought the aid of Saudi Arabia, which, along with Pakistan and the United Arab Republic (UAE), was the only other country to recognize the Taliban. In addition, the Saudis were key funders of radical Islamic schools and other institutions favored by the Taliban. While the Saudis did provide the United States with some information on al Qaeda activities outside Afghanistan and agreed to press the Taliban to hand over bin Laden, they did little to crack down on Saudi citizen support for the terrorist. In 1998, on behalf of the United States, Saudi Prince Turki al-Faisal visited Kandahar, a key al Qaeda stronghold in Afghanistan, to press Mullah Mohammed Omar, the Taliban's one-eyed leader, to hand over bin Laden. Omar refused, accusing both the prince and the royal Saudi family of being beholden to U.S. interests. In response, Saudi Arabia suspended all diplomatic relations and aid to the Taliban and denied visas to Afghans traveling for nonreligious reasons.[77]

Against the advice of the Secret Service, President Clinton traveled to Pakistan in 2000 to press Musharraf to cooperate on our efforts to capture or kill bin Laden. The first U.S. president to visit South Asia since 1978, Clinton stopped briefly in Islamabad. Several members of Congress, prominent representatives of the Indian American community, and much of the press criticized Clinton's decision to meet with General Musharraf, arguing that such a visit would be seen as legitimating his then recent coup. They urged Clinton to skip the stopover in Pakistan because of General Musharraf's refusal to cut links with international terrorist groups, his resistance to treaty commitments to curb Pakistan's nuclear weapons problem, and his opposition to taking steps toward restoring democratic rule.[78] Yet it was precisely for these reasons that the president and his advisers believed he *had* to go. Pakistan still refused to end its support to the Taliban.

Attack on the USS Cole

On October 12, 2000, al Qaeda struck again, attacking the USS *Cole*, an American destroyer docked in Yemen's Aden Harbor. Seventeen U.S. soldiers were killed. Detonated from a small, heavily armed boat that had cruised up alongside the $1 billion ship, the explosion, designed to explode forcefully in one direction tore a forty-foot hole in its side. In hindsight, the decision to refuel the ship in Yemen was inexcusable as, at the time of the attack, only Afghanistan was higher on the list of states harboring terrorists. The navy later conceded that the *Cole*'s commanding officer had no specific intelligence, preparation, or security equipment to anticipate or prevent the attacks on the ship. The ship's watch team was not prepared with a force protection plan, and there was little attention heeded to the boat traffic within the harbor.[79]

Two days after the attacks, a team of two hundred FBI agents went to Yemen to investigate the attack. High restrictions placed on the team by the Yemeni government hindered the investigation, and by the end of October the majority of investigators were forced to depart, leaving behind only a small team of fifty investigators to finish up the work.[80] In the spring and summer of 2001, there were growing indications that al Qaeda was planning an attack against Americans, most likely abroad. Because of such a concern, FBI agents in Yemen were told to leave the country.[81]

Thus, at the time of Bush's inauguration, the investigation was ongoing, although most officials assumed the attack was the work of al Qaeda. Although some have criticized Clinton for not retaliating against al Qaeda before he left office, Clinton believed it prudent to wait for the results of the investigation (which never came before the end of his term) and thus leave the decision to the next president. In his first eight months in office, President Bush took no action against al Qaeda for the attack on the *Cole*. Bush first linked al Qaeda to the *Cole* bombing publicly in his speech to Congress after the September 11 attacks.

UN Sanctions

As the diplomacy failed, the United States sought to increase its pressure against the Taliban. In December 1998, the UN Security Council had condemned the Taliban regime for harboring terrorists, drug trafficking, and continued support for terrorism and threatened to impose sanctions. In the face of continued Taliban intransigence, in July 1999 the United States imposed unilateral sanctions and, in October 1999, secured a unanimous UN Security Council vote imposing sanctions in an effort to pressure the Taliban to hand over bin Laden and shut down the terrorist network. The sanctions included a ban on landing rights for the Afghan airline that was being used to ferry terrorist material, personnel, and finances; a freezing of their assets; and a prohibition on visas to prevent the travel of the Taliban leadership except for religious purposes. The resolution also called for states to freeze funds and other financial resources controlled directly or indirectly by the Taliban or its associated entities.[82]

Still defiant, the Taliban refused to hand over bin Laden, despite the obvious fact that he was plotting to kill Americans. Thus, following the attack on the USS *Cole*, the administration sought to raise the pressure on the Taliban by imposing international sanctions against the regime, including an arms embargo, reducing diplomatic relations with the Taliban, and freezing bin Laden and al Qaeda assets. It was December 2000, a month before Clinton was to leave office. At the time, I was finishing up my three years as a U.S. representative in the Security Council during which I had responsibility for negotiating the U.S. mission's policy toward the Taliban in the Security Council. President Clinton had appointed me to the post in his second term.

Sitting in the UN Security Council that December, behind the famous sign marked "United States," I worked to secure agreement on a resolution imposing sanctions against the Taliban. The real work of the council is not done in the famous chamber with the horseshoe table, but in a small room across the hall called the "informal chamber." There, a smaller horseshoe table brings diplomats closer to each other. Although some delegations still insisted on using the translators, most speak perfect English. Although the room has a beautiful view of the East River, the blinds are always drawn for security reasons. Diplomats rush in and out, aides scurry back and forth. Translators look down on the room from their glass booths along the sides of the room.

In the informal chamber, I worked to get the agreement of my colleagues around the table on the text of the resolution sent from Washington. As usual, I was the only woman at the table, the men nearly all twenty years my senior. But I wasn't just a young woman negotiating; I was representing the United States of America. And following the 1998 bombings of the U.S. embassies by al Qaeda and the USS *Cole* just two months before, no country was willing to block our effort to put sanctions on the Taliban as long as the regime harbored bin Laden. Although support at the UN for sanctions in general had deteriorated because of the controversial sanctions against Iraq, in this case, other states recognized they could not oppose actions against a state so blatantly supporting an active terrorist. Even the Russians, usually opposed to involvement of other states in Afghanistan, which they still viewed as their sphere of influence, did not object.

Sitting with the small white plastic translation earpiece hanging on my ear, I listened to the Russian and Chinese representatives, the two delegations most wary of sanctions. Russia had long been seeking to undermine the UN sanctions in Iraq and had resisted tough measures against the Taliban in the past. Over the past several days, I worked with my colleagues in Washington to meet the Russians' concerns, mostly to ensure that the sanctions would be aimed at the leadership, not the people of Afghanistan. Finally, the Russian representative, Sergey Lavrov, who also happened to be serving as president of the council, ended his statement by saying he would vote to pass the resolution. That meant the others would follow and we would get the tougher sanctions. With the agreement in hand, the other delegates and I walked across the hallway to the large, famous chamber.

I sat in the same chair made famous by Adlai Stevenson as he revealed the satellite photographs of the Cuban missiles in 1962. The other fourteen representatives gathered around the table, with a variety of noncouncil representatives sitting in the red chairs to the side. As the UN had never recognized the Taliban's legitimacy to rule Afghanistan, that country's delegate remained a representative of the former regime of President Burhanuddin Rabbani, who had been ousted in 1996 when the Taliban took Kabul. I raised my hand as the resolution passed 13 to 0, with China and Malaysia abstaining.[83]

Speaking after the vote, I said, "The Taliban leadership harbors the world's most wanted terrorist—Osama bin Laden. Over a year ago, this body enacted sanctions with a single, simple demand to the Taliban leadership: turn over Osama bin Laden without further delay to appropriate authorities in a country where he will be arrested and effectively brought to justice."

Arguing that the terrorists in Afghanistan remained a threat, I reiterated the administration's warning that Clinton would leave to his successor in the White House, that the "Taliban cannot continue to flout the will of the international community and support and shelter terrorists without repercussions. As long as the Taliban leadership continues to harbor terrorists—in particular Osama bin Laden—and to promote terrorism, it remains a threat to international peace and security."

At the time, the country did not know if Al Gore or George Bush would be charged with addressing that growing threat. Much had been done to put U.S. military, intelligence, and diplomatic institutions on a war footing to meet it. But very few understood the gravity or imminence of the threat. The intelligence and law enforcement agencies were still in the mindset of the superpower's invincibility. The threat of terrorism seemed distant from America's shores. The myth of America's invulnerability, kept the United States from an all-out war against al Qaeda before September 11, 2001.

8

Failure to Be
on a War Footing

You're going to spend more time on al Qaeda than any other issue.

—Briefing to Condoleezza Rice by Samuel Berger, January 2001

George Bush took office in January 2001, when the planning for the September 11 attacks was well under way. Why the new team failed to take the threat as seriously as they should have remains hard to discern. The slowness and lack of urgency with which the Bush administration approached the terrorist threat before September 11 contrasts dramatically with its quick and forceful response to al Qaeda in the immediate aftermath—Bush's voice of reassurance and leadership for the traumatized American public, the creation and use of an international coalition, the rapid drive through Afghanistan, and equally rapid moves to involve the UN and turn the government of the country back over to its people. The simplest explanation is that, for a brief moment, the administration set politics aside and focused on the threat of terrorism.

What September 11 could not provide, however, was a sustained shift in the same mindset that allowed too many warnings to go unnoticed before September 11—the hegemons' certainty that America's military might, largely on its own, can keep America safe. This same certainty, which handicapped us in the critical months leading up to September 11, reared its head shortly after the overthrow of the Taliban. Adherence to the hegemons' myth led to dangerous failures, including the missed opportunities that could have done more to stem the threat of terrorism and nonproliferation. Its ideological abhorrence to nation building led to mistakes in the effort to build Afghanistan into a genuinely peaceful and even democratic society, where threats would no longer arise against its own citizens—or us. Had the hegemons learned the lesson of September 11—that America cannot protect itself on its own—the administration might have avoided many costly mistakes in the war in Iraq, successfully addressed the growing threats from North Korea and Iran, and convinced more of the world to follow our lead.

What will you wish then that you had already done?

With the outcome of the 2000 presidential elections in question until December 13, George W. Bush lost nearly half his transition time to prepare for office. During the legal battles over the Florida election, however, Bush had assembled a transition team. Once the Supreme Court intervened and gave the presidency to Bush, Clinton and his administration began to brief the new team. "I told Rice," Berger recalled, "that the number-one issue she will work on is terrorism, and al Qaeada specifically. I joined Dick Clarke's briefing on transnational threats and specifically said, 'Condi, I'm here to emphasize how important this is.' I did everything I could to dramatize to her they had to pay attention. But these were people who hadn't been in government in years, in some cases since the 1980s, and they did not understand the phenomenon of stateless terror. They could only imagine state-sponsored terror. They could not get their heads around the fact that guys in caves with beards could do bad things to us."[1] Berger also met privately with Rice to convey the same message.

Nevertheless, once in office, Bush and his advisors had other priorities. As with most new presidents, the administration took months to conduct policy reviews, wanting to set its own course. For the new team, the priority was building a national missile defense, the containment of China as a rising threat, and establishing a relationship with U.S. allies.

Despite the warnings from Clinton's national security team of the urgent threat from bin Laden, Bush's advisors did not begin their major counterterrorism review until April 2001. By September 11, the administration had yet to finalize its review of terrorism and how to deal with the imminent threat bin Laden posed to the United States.[2] While Rice kept Clinton's point man on terrorism, Richard Clarke, on her National Security Council staff, she demoted him, stripping him of his seat at the principals' table, questioning whether she wanted to keep all of Clarke's broad terrorism portfolio in the White House.[3] The 2002 Joint Congressional Inquiry found that "significant slippage in counterterrorism policy may have taken place in late 2000 and early 2001. At least part of this was due to the unresolved status of Clarke as national coordinator for counterterrorism and his uncertain mandate to coordinate Bush administration policy on terrorism and specifically on bin Laden."[4]

The policy review considered how the Bush administration could take a tougher stand against bin Laden. The goal was to move beyond Clinton's policy of "containment, criminal prosecution, and limited retaliation for specific attacks," as the new officials derisively described Clinton's anti-terrorism efforts. Instead, they sought an as yet undefined way to attempt to "roll back" al Qaeda.[5] Despite Clarke's urgent request for a Principals Committee meeting on the issue, Rice insisted Clarke first have the issue reviewed by the deputies. As Clarke summarized it, "the Principals Committee was meeting with a full agenda and a backlog of Bush priority issues: the Antiballistic Missile Treaty, the Kyoto environment agreement, and Iraq. There was no time for terrorism."[6]

The first Deputies Committee on terrorism did not occur until April 30. At that meeting, Clarke reports, Deputy Secretary of Defense Paul Wolfowitz focused not on the stark threat posed by bin Laden that Clarke laid out, but rather on Iraq. "I just don't understand why we are beginning by talking about this one man bin Laden . . . there are others that [threaten the United States] as well, at least as much. Iraqi terrorism for example." In response to Clarke's and the CIA deputy's response that there had been no Iraqi-sponsored terrorism directed at the United States since the 1993 U.S. retaliation for the attempted assassination of former president Bush, Wolfowitz replied that the officials gave bin Laden "too much credit. He could not do all these things like the 1993 attack on New York, not without a state sponsor. Just because the FBI and CIA have failed to find the linkages does not mean they don't exist."[7]

The deputies took until August to prepare options for the principals' consideration, distributing an options paper to the principals for comments on August 13, 2001. Conscious of the threat from al Qaeda, the principals tried to meet in mid-August to agree on a policy; however, the meeting was not scheduled until September 4, 2001.[8] On that date the principals met for the first time to discuss the new approach, eight months into the administration.

Richard Clarke's briefing and proposals put forth many of the ideas he had been advocating in recent years. He argued for a threefold strategy to eradicate al Qaeda. The approach included arming the Northern Alliance, mobilizing anti–bin Laden fighters in Uzbekistan, and arming an unmanned forty-nine-foot, nine-hundred-fifty-pound flying drone equipped with precision video and infrared cameras to find and attack bin Laden. As had been the case with the Clinton team, however, the threefold plan was controversial and received only fragmented support from the CIA and the principals.[9] As part of broader discussions on the new administration's counterterrorism policy, the administration was close to increasing authority for the CIA to carry out covert investigations when September 11 occurred.[10]

The September 4 principals' meeting concluded without any decisions on how to meet the rising threat from bin Laden. Clarke urged National Security Advisor Rice, the meeting's chair, to consider how she might feel should al Qaeda kill hundreds of Americans, asking, "What will you wish then that you had already done?" Yet, the meeting, in Clarke's words, was largely a nonevent. Again, officials, especially Secretary of Defense Donald Rumsfeld, pressed for action, not on al Qaeda, but on Iraq. The CIA still maintained it "could not find a single dollar in any other program to transfer to the anti-al Qaeda effort," despite the fact that Tenet had told Clarke in June he felt an attack was coming, saying "This is going to be the big one."[11] The CIA and Defense still argued about who would run the Predator program. The principals never got agreement on a policy to go after al Qaeda. The meeting ended with Rice simply asking Clarke to send a policy directive on al Qaeda to the president.[12]

Thus, when the September 11 attacks occurred, the Bush administration still had no comprehensive policy in place to combat the terrorist threat, despite increasing signs of an imminent attack against America.[13]

A gathering threat

Throughout the spring and summer of 2001, the United States received increasingly alarming reports that al Qaeda was planning an attack against America. In response, during their first eight months in office Bush administration officials took a number of limited steps to sound an alert about the possible threats and to arrest suspected terrorists. Between January and September, the administration issued nine warnings, five of them global. Three of the rounds of warnings occurred between late May and August 2001. In each case, the warnings were unspecific and alluded only to credible threats with no specific information.[14]

Most U.S. officials assumed the attacks would occur abroad. The State Department issued worldwide travel cautions, and the FAA warned of a possible hijacking plot. The Defense Department issued four terrorism warning reports or extensions, primarily to alert U.S. military forces to signs that bin Laden's network was planning a near-term, anti–United States terrorist operation. Troops in the Persian Gulf continued to be on Delta alert.[15]

As reports of impending al Qaeda attacks increased in the spring and summer of 2001, the administration intensified its focus on renditions and disruptions of possible attacks. Working with the FBI and foreign liaison services, the United States succeeded in thwarting attacks on the U.S. embassies in Paris, Albania, and Yemen, U.S. facilities in Saudi Arabia, and operations to kidnap U.S. citizens. CIA Director Tenet claims the United States approached twenty countries with specific targets for disruption, prompting arrests.[16]

The State Department continued, unsuccessfully, to push the Taliban to hand over bin Laden. For instance, on June 26, 2001, the department warned Taliban representatives in Pakistan that the Taliban would be held responsible for terrorist attacks carried out by bin Laden or al Qaeda and specifically noted the threats to Americans emanating from Afghanistan.[17]

On June 25, the intelligence community issued a terrorist-threat advisory, warning government agencies that there was a high probability of an imminent terrorist attack by Sunni extremists associated with al Qaeda resulting in numerous casualties against U.S. interests abroad. In early July, a briefing prepared for senior government officials asserted: "Based on a review of all-source reporting over the last five months, we believe that [bin Laden] will launch a significant terrorist attack against U.S. and/or Israeli interests in the coming weeks. The attack will be spectacular and designed to inflict mass casualties against U.S. facilities or interests. Attack preparations have been made. Attack will occur with little or no warning."[18]

The CIA worked overtime, trying to coordinate with other intelligence services for information. As Deputy Secretary of State Richard Armitage explained, George Tenet "was around town literally pounding on desks saying, 'Something is happening, this is an unprecedented level of threat information.' He didn't know where it was going to happen, but he knew it was coming."[19]

Bin Laden actively planning against U.S. targets

One of the key mistakes made in the pre–September 11 period was that U.S. officials did not seriously consider an attack inside U.S. territory to be a real concern. As CIA director George Tenet admitted in 2002, "Essentially, we all believed that it would never happen here. [W]e were so busy overseas. . . . They were looking here the whole time and steadily planning in terms of what they were doing. So they were operating on two fronts." The FBI's assistant director for counterterrorism at the time said that the intelligence he was seeing led him to believe with a high probability, "98 percent," that an attack would occur overseas.[20]

A review of the available information prior to September 11 makes it difficult to understand how such a belief could have prevailed among policymakers in the face of much evidence to the contrary. In the eight years between the two World Trade Center attacks, bin Laden left numerous clues he intended to strike America at home. In addition to the discovery over the years of bin Laden's links to those involved in the 1993 attack on the World Trade Center and his *fatwas* and other threats, the millennium plot was an obvious advertisement of his intention to strike America.

In addition, starting in 1998, the U.S. government received a steady stream of intelligence indicating bin Laden intended to attack the United States at home. In October 1998, the United States received information that al Qaeda was trying to establish an operative cell within the United States, suggesting an effort to recruit Islamist U.S. citizens and United

States–based expatriates from the Middle East and North Africa.[21] Shortly after bin Laden's May 1998 press conference threatening to bring the war home to America, the intelligence community obtained information from several sources that bin Laden was considering attacks in the United States, including Washington, D.C., and New York City; the information was disseminated throughout the intelligence community and to senior U.S. policymakers.

Many of these reports were not taken as seriously as they should have been because they did not contain specific information as to where, when, and how a terrorist attack might occur and generally were not corroborated. In addition, officials did not believe terrorists would strike at home. But the sheer volume of the reports should have alerted U.S. officials to the growing danger. In fact, by the end of 1998, the intelligence community's own assessment was that bin Laden was "actively planning against U.S. targets."

The indications of an attack on U.S. soil increased substantially in the first eight months of the Bush administration. In March 2001, intelligence sources claimed that a group of bin Laden operatives was planning to conduct an unspecified attack in the United States in April 2001. That same month, authorities received information on the types of targets al Qaeda might strike. The list included the Statue of Liberty, skyscrapers, ports, airports, and nuclear power plants.[22] Between May and July, the National Security Agency reported at least thirty-three communications suggesting a possibly imminent terrorist attack. One of them was thought to perhaps constitute a signal to proceed with the terrorist operations. However, it was not clear that any persons involved in the intercepted communications had first-hand knowledge of where, when, or how an attack might occur, casting doubt on the urgency of the threat.

During the spring and summer of 2001, the intelligence community detected a significant increase in information that bin Laden and al Qaeda intended to strike against U.S. interests in the very near future. In June, there was information that key operatives in bin Laden's organization were disappearing, while others were preparing for martyrdom. In July, the CTC became aware of a person who had recently been in Afghanistan who reported, "Everyone is talking about an impending attack." Some reports described the increase in the threat as unprecedented. While the reports provided no specific detail that could be acted on, there were "numerous signs of an impending terrorist attack, some of which pointed specifically to the United States as a target."[23]

In an action blatantly contradictory to the claims that it did not know al Qaeda would strike at home, during the summer of 2001, the intelligence community disseminated information to a wide range of senior government officials at all federal agencies and military commands about the potential for imminent terrorist attacks *in the United States*. For instance, on July 2,

2001, the FBI advised federal, state, and local law enforcement agencies of increased threat-reporting about groups aligned with or sympathetic to bin Laden. Following the White House's Counterterrorism Security Group review of possible disasters, a warning was issued to all domestic law enforcement about the possibility of an impending attack, especially as the July 4 holiday approached. A meeting on July 5 was held between domestic law enforcement, FBI, Customs, FAA, Coast Guard, and Civil Service in which the planning phases of an attack were verified as being still in the works.[24]

The FBI even asked for increased authority to use surveillance on individuals with plausible connections to al Qaeda. Yet, until September 11, the FBI maintained that the majority of the reports suggested attacks would occur against U.S. targets abroad, and that the FBI had no information suggesting a credible threat of terrorist attack in the United States, although the bureau always added the caveat that the possibility could not be discounted.[25]

In July and August 2001, alert field FBI officials discovered clues to the impending September 11 attacks, yet, tragically, bureaucratic bungling kept officials from piecing together the plot. On July 10, an FBI agent based in the Phoenix field office sent a memo to FBI headquarters urging an investigation of reports of Islamic radicals receiving training at U.S. flight schools.[26] The memo, perhaps the strongest lead in the 9/11 plot, outlined the agent's "first-hand" knowledge of bin Laden's initiative to send operatives to the United States for flight lessons. The agent indicated that an "inordinate number of individuals worthy of FBI investigation, who may commit future terrorist activity via aircraft," should be investigated. The memo, sent via "Electronic Communication" to four employees of the FBI's Radical Fundamentalist Unit, two analysts in the bin Laden investigative unit at FBI headquarters, and two agents on New York's international terrorism squad, recommended that headquarters alert all civil aviation flight schools in the United States to possible al Qaeda infiltration as well as seek authority to investigate the visa information of students seeking to attend flight school.[27]

Yet, the memo was essentially ignored. It was never sent to the FBI's analytic unit or the CIA. Only three of the eight agents who received the memo actually recalled reading it.[28] The head of the Radical Fundamentalist Unit did not see the memo until after September 11 and told the Joint Inquiry that the memo "should have been disseminated to all field offices and to our sister agencies, and it should have triggered a broader analytical approach."[29] Even the author of the memo realized at the time of writing that his memo might not be met with vigilance from headquarters. The memo did not set off alarms there, partly because the agents knew that persons connected to al Qaeda had already received training in the United States. Before September 11, many agents believed that bin Laden needed pilots to operate aircraft he had purchased in the United States to move men and material.[30]

The second key clue came on August 16, 2001, when the Immigration and Naturalization Service detained Zacarias Moussaoui in Minneapolis, Minnesota. His conduct had aroused suspicions about why he was learning to fly large commercial aircraft. The local flight school contacted the local FBI field office, which believed Moussaoui might be intending to hijack a plane and asked Washington for authority to obtain a warrant to search Moussaoui's belongings. But FBI headquarters turned down the request, claiming there was not enough evidence for a search warrant.

By July 2001, however, the threat-reporting was already beginning to decline. Many officials assumed the attacks were planned for the July 4 celebrations, thus breathed a sigh of relief when the national holiday passed without incident. By August, much of the intelligence "chatter" on terrorist activity had died down, although in August 2001, senior government officials were given a report that members of al Qaeda, including some U.S. citizens, had resided in the United States for years, or traveled there, and that the group maintained a support structure in the United States. The report cited uncorroborated information that bin Laden wanted to hijack airplanes to gain the release of United States–held extremists. On September 10, the nation's eavesdropping agency, the National Security Agency, intercepted two communications suggesting imminent terrorist activity, but they were not translated into English and disseminated until September 12.[31]

A few arrests of al Qaeda operatives in the Persian Gulf, combined with the uneventful passing of July 4, led many people in government to believe falsely that the plots of al Qaeda had been stymied. The president and his chief aides were able to get away for their usual summer vacations.[32]

No one could have predicted use of an airplane as a missile

Following the attacks of September 11, National Security Advisor Condoleezza Rice defended her administration's inaction prior to the terrorists attacks, claiming, "I don't think anybody could have predicted that these same people would take an airplane and slam it into the World Trade Center . . . that they would try to use an airplane as a missile."[33] Yet, before September 11, the intelligence community had produced numerous reports over a seven-year period suggesting that terrorists might use airplanes as weapons. While the credibility of sources was sometimes questionable and information often sketchy, over time, the reports made clear the idea was seriously considered a possibility by some terrorists.

Terrorists are first known to have contemplated using airplanes as a weapon in December 1994, when the Algerian Armed Islamic Group terrorists hijacked an Air France flight in Algiers and threatened to crash it into the Eiffel Tower in Paris.[34] In a 1995 National Intelligence Estimate (NIE), intelligence analysts recognized that if "terrorists operating in the [United States] are similarly methodical, they will identify serious vulnerabilities in the security system for domestic flights." The NIE was updated in 1997, stating that civil aviation "remains a particularly attractive target."[35]

The information obtained in the 1995 raid disrupting the Bojinka plot in the Philippines suggested the terrorists' intention to crash an airplane into the CIA headquarters. In addition, in January 1996, intelligence agencies received information concerning a planned suicide attack on the White House. Later in 1996, there were reports regarding an Iranian plot to hijack a Japanese plane and crash it into Tel Aviv. Other reports in 1997 indicated that terrorists had purchased an unmanned aerial vehicle (UAV) for use in terrorist attacks.

In September 1998, the United States received information that bin Laden's next operation might involve flying an explosive-laden aircraft into a U.S. airport and detonating it. In November 1998, a Turkish Islamic group, believed to have cooperated with bin Laden, planned a suicide attack to crash an airplane packed with explosives into the tomb of the founder of modern Turkey, Mustafa Kemal Ataturk, during the celebrations marking his death. In March 1999, the United States learned of a plot by an American al Qaeda member to fly a hang glider into the Egyptian presidential palace and detonate explosives. He had received hang glider training in the United States.[36]

In an eerie prediction of September 11, in August 1998, the intelligence community received information that a group of unidentified Arabs planned to fly an explosive-laden plane from a foreign country into the World Trade Center. While the information was passed to the FBI and FAA, the agencies thought the plot unlikely, or that it would in any case be detected in a foreign country before it reached the United States. The FBI's New York office took no action on the information, simply filing it.

The intelligence community often has individuals enter its field offices unannounced and provide information to U.S. intelligence officials, so-called walk-ins. In April 2000, one such walk-in went to the FBI's office in Newark, New Jersey, and told officials of a bin Laden plot to hijack a Boeing 747, claiming he had learned hijacking techniques and received arms training in a Pakistani camp. He also claimed he was to meet five or six persons in the United States, some of whom were training to be pilots who had been instructed to take over a plane, fly to Afghanistan, or, if they could not make it there, blow it up. A year later, in April 2001, one source said that bin Laden was interested in commercial pilots as potential terrorists. The source warned that the United States should not focus only on embassy bombings, that terrorists sought "spectacular and traumatic" attacks, and that the first World Trade Center bombing would be the type of attack that would be appealing. Because the source was offering personal speculation and not hard information, the information was not disseminated within the intelligence community. In August 2001, U.S. officials obtained information about a plot to bomb the U.S. embassy in Nairobi from an airplane or crash the airplane into it.[37]

Before September 11, Tenet, FBI Director Louis Freeh, and the rest of the intelligence community failed to piece together the vast body of available information. As implausible as it seems in retrospect, the intelligence community did not produce any specific assessments of the likelihood that terrorists would use airplanes as weapons, and U.S. policymakers remained unaware of the potential threat."[38] Prior to September 11, there was no effort to catalogue information regarding the use of airplanes as weapons as a terrorist tactic; no request for additional information on this threat; no consideration of the likelihood that al Qaeda or any other terrorist group would attack the United States or U.S. interests in this way.

In fact, the administration's December 2000 report to Congress fulfilling a requirement that the FAA and FBI conduct joint threat and vulnerability assessments of security at select high-risk U.S. airports, stated that the intelligence community reporting did "not suggest evidence of plans to target domestic civil aviation. Terrorist activity within the U.S. had focused primarily on fundraising, recruiting new members, and disseminating propaganda. While international terrorists have conducted attacks on U.S. soil, these acts represent anomalies in their traditional targeting which focuses on U.S. interests overseas."[39] Former National Security Advisor Sandy Berger, Condoleezza Rice, and Deputy Undersecretary of Defense Paul Wolfowitz all testified in 2002 that they were not informed of any specific threat information regarding the use of aircraft as weapons.[40]

In the spring of 2004, much was made of a report in the president's Daily Brief (PDB) of August 6, 2001.[41] It included information about bin Laden's methods of operation from a historical perspective dating back to 1997, saying "Bin Ladin since 1997 has wanted to conduct foreign terrorist attacks on the U.S." The report also said:

> Al Qa'ida members—including some who are U.S. citizens—have resided in or traveled to the U.S. for years, and the group apparently maintains a support structure that could aid attacks. . . . We have not been able to corroborate some of the more sensational threat reporting, such as that from a [deleted] service in 1998 saying that Bin Ladin wanted to hijack a U.S. aircraft to gain the release of "Blind Shaykh" Umar 'Abd al-Rahman and other U.S.-held extremists. Nevertheless, FBI information since that time indicates patterns of suspicious activity in this country consistent with preparations for hijackings or other types of attacks, including recent surveillance of federal buildings in New York. The FBI is conducting approximately 70 full field investigations throughout the

U.S. that it considers Bin Ladin–related. CIA and the FBI are investigating a call to our Embassy in the UAE in May saying that a group of Bin Ladin supporters was in the U.S. planning attacks with explosives.

Why President Bush, a faithful PDB reader, saw the report but took no action on it has been a matter of great speculation. The PDB is prepared overnight by CIA officers and shown to the president and a very select few senior government officials. It is tightly held in order to give CIA analysts more freedom to put sensitive information in it, with less fear of leaks. Starting with the transition in Little Rock in 1992, I received the document six days a week until I left the White House in 1997. Most items are a page long, three pages at most, designed to alert the president to important information anywhere in the world. The August 6 item on bin Laden in the PDB was no more alarmist than many other frightening things the president and his top advisors read every morning. Usually bad news, the PDB items range from impeding coups, reports of missing components of weapons of mass destruction, foreign leaders' strategy on upcoming negotiating strategies, success or failure of U.S. military operations, and a range of political, military, and economic developments, the latter added in 1993 at Clinton's request. Some items are prepared in response to the president's questions.

That bin Laden was trying to attack America was known by most officials; thus it is not surprising this one item did not set off particular alarm bells. The PDB in fact made it clear it could not corroborate the information that bin Laden wanted to hijack a U.S. aircraft. It also gave the impression that the FBI was on the case, claiming that the agency was conducting approximately seventy full field investigations, a claim that later proved to be false. During his testimony before the 9/11 Commission, acting FBI director Tom Pickard said that the number seventy referred to individuals rather than whole cases—he could only provide details for twenty-seven cases—and the investigations entailed monitoring fund-raising activities and conducting surveillance rather than full-fledged investigations.[42] By indicating the CIA and the FBI were investigating the report that bin Laden's supporters were in the United States planning attacks with explosives, the report implied there was no urgent action needed. Like so many alarming PDB reports, they may or may not come true. Bush had already been briefed repeatedly, starting with the departing Clinton team in 2001, that bin Laden wanted to attack the United States. This report did not give Bush the impression he was about to succeed.

What is surprising is that across the Bush administration there was no plan to counter the range of threats from bin Laden to U.S. interests. Even if Bush did not believe bin Laden would succeed in attacking America, it is inexcusable that for the first eight months in office he and his top officials took no action against the terrorist and his network. More focus on the threat may not have prevented September 11, but it might have disrupted parts of it and saved some lives.

Despite the vast body of knowledge indicating the possibility of an attack like the ones that occurred on September 11, senior officials never imagined such a plot. President Bush stood at the podium with the widow of a 9/11 pilot in March 2004 and stressed, "Had I known that the enemy was going to use airplanes to strike America, to attack us, I would have used every resource, every asset, every power of this government to protect the American people."[43]

When nineteen hijackers downed four planes on September 11 in the deadliest attack in America's history, U.S. officials possessed information that, had they coordinated among each other, may have prevented at least some of the terrorist attacks. Why and how did they fail to fulfill that most basic of responsibilities?

Failure to be on a war footing

The failures in coordination, prioritization, and attention to the threat stemmed from the basic fact that on September 11, 2001, America was not at war against al Qaeda, although bin Laden was at war against America. Thus, the intelligence community never developed an estimate of the threat bin Laden's network posed to U.S. interests at home or abroad; the counterterrorism effort lacked significant participation by elements of the intelligence community other than the CIA; resources and intelligence priorities were never balanced to counter the threat from bin Laden; and the FBI was never fully engaged in combating the threat to America from al Qaeda.[44]

In fact, while the CIA had declared war against bin Laden, officials at the FBI and Defense Department were not even aware of the declaration. As the Joint Inquiry summarized the problem, "Despite the Intelligence Community's growing recognition that Afghanistan was churning out thousands of radicals, the U.S. government did not integrate all the instruments of national power and policy—diplomatic, intelligence, economic, and military—to address this problem."[45] The failure to do so was most acute at the FBI.

Throughout the years leading to September 11, as the intelligence community repeatedly warned that al Qaeda had both the capability and the intention to threaten the lives of thousands of Americans and wanted to strike within the United States, the FBI's role in the efforts to combat terrorism gradually increased. The FBI has traditionally investigated all terrorist acts on U.S. territory, including the 1993 World Trade Center bombing, the Oklahoma City bombing, and the 1996 Olympics. As the al

Qaeda threat grew, so did more general threats of terrorism against Americans at home. Thus, FBI resources were increasingly called upon.

The FBI took several important steps to improve its counterterrorism capabilities throughout the 1990s, including more than doubling the number of personnel working on counterterrorism and more than tripling its counterterrorism budget. In 1999, the FBI made counterterrorism a separate headquarters division, elevating its importance within the bureau. It also created a separate operational unit focused on bin Laden. The Bureau initiated personnel exchanges with the CIA and increased stationing of FBI representatives in U.S. embassies overseas, in order to deepen the FBI's ability to link domestic and international threats.[46]

Joint Terrorism Task Forces (JTTFs), originally created to improve coordination between the FBI and the New York Police Department (NYPD), were expanded to other cities after the first World Trade Center attack and throughout the 1990s were given increasing prominence. These task forces were designed to combine federal and local law enforcement and intelligence capabilities into a cohesive unit to address complex international and domestic terrorism investigations. By September 11, 2001, thirty-five of the fifty-six U.S. FBI field offices had JTTFs.[47]

As a result of these improvements, the FBI prevented a number of major terrorist attacks, no doubt saving many lives. Bush's FBI director, Robert Mueller, testified that throughout the 1990s the FBI foiled schemes including plots to attack New York City landmarks, bomb U.S. aircraft, place pipe bombs in New York City subways, and bomb the Los Angeles Airport. Bureau sources proved invaluable in preventing the Day of Terror plot and prosecuting the perpetrators of the first World Trade Center bombing. The FBI had numerous wiretaps and several human informants in its effort to target various radical Islamic organizations.[48]

Increased counterterrorism responsibilities within the FBI strained the organization. Increasingly, the FBI was given the task of providing security against terrorism at trials, special events, and meetings of world leaders. Cyber threats and weapons of mass destruction also demanded FBI attention. Although FBI Director Louis Freeh claimed "the allocations were insufficient to maintain the critical growth and priority of the FBI's counterterrorism program,"[49] the Joint Inquiry asserted that the FBI failed to shift adequately its priorities toward counterterrorism and potential attacks within the United States. The problem was more a misallocation of resources, not lack of funds as Freeh has charged. At the time of the September 11 attacks, 6 percent of the FBI's personnel, about 1,300, worked on counterterrorism. The FBI had fewer than ten tactical analysts and only one strategic analyst assigned to al Qaeda. Analysts instead focused on critical infrastructure, case support, and domestic terrorism.[50]

The FBI never gathered intelligence across cases nationwide to produce an overall assessment of al Qaeda's presence in the United States.[51] Across FBI field offices, there was a wide range in the priority placed on bin Laden and al Qaeda. Richard Clarke, former NSC special coordinator for counterterrorism, described how, other than the New York office, FBI field offices around the country were "clueless" about counterterrorism and al Qaeda. Former national security advisor Berger testified to the Joint Inquiry that the FBI was not sufficiently focused on counterterrorism before September 11. Even the New York office, which headed up investigations of bin Laden, concentrated primarily on investigating attacks against Americans overseas.[52]

The FBI director throughout the gathering threat of bin Laden, Louis Freeh, has come under little scrutiny for his stewardship of the bureau he left on June 22, 2001, less than three months before the attacks on September 11. While his counterpart at the CIA had declared war on al Qaeda, Freeh never developed a plan against the terrorist organization. For example, the assistant director of the FBI's Counterterrorism Division described to the Joint Inquiry that "absolutely, we did not" have a plan to deal with bin Laden at the time. He did not know how the FBI's counterterrorism program fit into the overall intelligence community's program.[53] The FBI did not inform policymakers of the extent of terrorist activity in the United States, although Freeh met regularly with senior government officials to discuss counterterrorism.

Of the problems encountered by the FBI in effectively combating terrorism before September 11, some were structural. For example, as a primarily investigative and law enforcement organization, the FBI's strengths tend to lie in reacting to crimes committed, rather than taking preventative measures. The terrorist threat was viewed through a more narrow lens because of the FBI's case-based approach. Analysts were sent to operational units to assist in case work rather than assess data gathered by the various field offices. The Joint Inquiry describes how the FBI's decentralized structure and inadequate information technology contributed to a failure to synthesize the intelligence and data gathered by its fifty-six U.S. and forty-four overseas offices. In addition, FBI counterterrorism training was extremely limited before September 11, and the bureau often lacked linguists for the languages and dialects spoken by al Qaeda radicals.

Because the United States was not on a war footing, terrorism, as the Joint Inquiry found, remained only "one concern of many and counterterrorism efforts had to compete with other priorities. The process for setting intelligence priorities was also vague and confusing, and neither the Clinton nor the Bush administration developed an integrated counterterrorism strategy that drew on all elements of national power before September 11."[54]

Despite the White House's effort to prioritize intelligence through its Presidential Decision Directive 62, none of the witnesses interviewed by the Joint Inquiry, other than the directive's author Dick Clarke, pointed to it as the guiding policy in the government's response to the growing al Qaeda threat.[55] Without strong direction at the top of each agency, which was probably only possible had America truly been at war, the coordination, focus, and resource prioritization necessary to have discovered and thwarted the September 11 plot did not exist.

Someday someone will die, wall or not

While the FBI and other agencies suffered from a lack of concrete counterterrorism strategy, the relationship between these institutions and their roles clearly exacerbated the problem. The dysfunctional relationship between the FBI and CIA is the result of restrictions between and within agencies constructed over sixty years as a result of legal, policy, institutional, and personal factors. The "walls" separate foreign from domestic activities, foreign intelligence from law-enforcement operations, the FBI from the CIA, communications intelligence from other types of intelligence, the intelligence community from other federal agencies, and national security information from other forms of evidence. Following WWII, the National Security Act of 1947 created the CIA, the first U.S. peacetime civilian intelligence organization. In doing so, the leadership held two key considerations: the United States would not establish an organization that coupled foreign and domestic intelligence functions; and the FBI's domestic jurisdiction would be preserved. Thus, the act provided that the CIA would not have police, subpoena, or law-enforcement powers and would not perform internal security functions.[56]

The CIA and National Security Agency follow events overseas. They are leery of activity that suggests they are monitoring U.S. citizens or conducting assessments linked to the activities of persons in the United States, a task they believe belongs exclusively to the FBI. This division of responsibility made coordination difficult. In addition, the FBI does not have the analytic capability to prepare assessments of U.S. vulnerability and relied heavily on the CIA for much of its analysis.

The legacy of this wall between the two agencies led to a relationship that prevented the agencies from "connecting the dots" that might have prevented the tragedy of September 11. For instance, in late August 2001, the CIA told the FBI, State, INS, and Customs that Khalid al-Mihdhar, Nawaf al-Hazmi, and two other "bin Laden-related individuals" were in the United States, yet the FBI headquarters refused to accede to the New York field office recommendation that a criminal investigation be opened.

The FBI intransigence was based on the FBI headquarters' reluctance to utilize intelligence information to draw the connections between al-Mihdhar and the USS *Cole* bombing necessary to open a criminal investigation. FBI attorneys took the position that criminal investigators "CAN NOT" (emphasis original) be involved and that criminal information discovered in the intelligence case would be "passed over the wall" according to proper procedures. An agent in the FBI's New York field office responded by e-mail, "Whatever has happened to this, someday someone will die and, wall or not, the public will not understand why we were not more effective in throwing every resource we had at certain problems."[57]

A similar attitude prevented the FBI from acting on the arrest of Zaccarias Moussaoui one month before the September 11 attacks, after Minneapolis FBI agents had reason to believe he might attempt to hijack a plane. FBI headquarters advised the Minnesota agent that the evidence was insufficient to link Moussaoui to a foreign power and thus obtain a Foreign Intelligence Surveillance Act warrant.[58] They also failed to link this information to other intelligence on planned terrorism involving airliners. Similarly, the July 10, 2001, Phoenix field memo urging FBI headquarters to investigate reports of Islamic radicals receiving training at U.S. flight schools failed to generate a response. The problems ranged from gaps in the perceived jurisdiction of the intelligence agencies, to divisions between criminal and intelligence investigations, to information and technology gaps.

During the spring and summer of 2001, no one at FBI Headquarters saw a connection between the Moussaoui case, the Phoenix communication, the possible presence of al-Mihdhar and al-Hamzi in the United States, and the flood of warnings about possible terrorist attacks in the United States, some using airplanes as weapons.[59] A review of the intelligence clues leading up to September 11 reveals many fragmented intelligence reports that were not combined and shared between intelligence agencies. For instance, the author of the Phoenix memo testified that while he was aware of the thwarted attempt to crash aircraft into a CIA building, he was not aware of the other reports of potential use of aircraft as weaponry.[60] In addition, had the FBI run an analysis on the airline tickets purchased by the September 11 terrorists, as well as the form of payment they used, it might have discovered the network of relationships among the hijackers. Two of the hijackers were on the State Department watch list as suspected terrorists. A check for common addresses, phone numbers, and frequent flier numbers might have led to some arrests prior to the attacks.[61] In retrospect, the intelligence community failed to sufficiently recognize the significance of various pieces of information and failed to disseminate information that may have produced telling evidence when combined with the knowledge of other agencies. The Joint Inquiry concluded that the failure of the intelligence community to consider the transnational nature of terrorism led to dismissal of key intelligence clues in the vast flows of intelligence information received.[62]

Whose fault was September 11?

No U.S. government official has been held responsible for the failure to prevent September 11. Richard Clarke, who quit the Bush administration out of frustration in 2003, was the first—and to date only—official to apologize to the families of those who died on September 11. Turning around to face the families of the 9/11 victims gathered in the large room in the Senate's Hart Building to hear the testimony to the 9/11 Commission, he said, "Your government failed you. Those entrusted with protecting you failed you. And I failed you . . . I would ask . . . for your understanding and for your forgiveness."[63] CIA Director George Tenet remained in his post until June 3, 2004, even though the Joint Inquiry harshly concluded in December 2002 he was "either unable or unwilling to enforce consistent priorities and marshal resources across the [Intelligence] Community."[64] He announced his resignation after reading the harsh conclusions of the 9/11 Commission Report. FBI Director Louis Freeh has made a successful career in the business sector as senior vice chairman for administration at MBNA Corporation, the world's largest independent credit card lender, with little pressure for him to account for the failures under his watch to recognize the threat of al Qaeda in America. No White House official has been targeted for blame.

The reason is that the failure to prevent September 11 was a systematic governmentwide failure to understand the threat bin Laden posed to America. United States government agencies move slowly; unless a threat is viewed as real and imminent, other priorities take precedent. As Director of the National Security Agency Lieutenant General Michael Hayden put it, "The war against terrorism was our number-one priority. We had about five number-one priorities."[65]

Had the government not been distracted by the disputed 2000 elections, had Rice not sought to demote Richard Clarke, had the CIA and FBI truly been on a war footing, had the FBI traced the terrorists' addresses, credit cards, and coordinated with the State Department's watch list, or had President Bush made al Qaeda his number-one priority rather than China and the National Missile Defense, could September 11 have been prevented? With luck, in a perfect world, perhaps some of the hijackers could have been stopped. But the governmentwide failures to understand the vulnerabilities of the openness of U.S. society and the fact that bin Laden had learned how to exploit them were simply too vast to enable the United States to stop all nineteen hijackers. No government is capable of shifting its mindset or its priorities as quickly as such a threat would have required. It is not even clear that had the United States succeeded in killing bin Laden, the long-planned plot would have been thwarted.

Asked in 2002 what should have been done differently, CIA director Tenet replied that the U.S. should have taken down that sanctuary provided bin Laden by the Taliban "a lot sooner." Yet, the 9/11 Commission Report found that every official they questioned in both the Clinton and Bush administrations said an invasion of Afghanistan was "almost unthinkable" or "inconceivable," absent a provocation such as the September 11 attacks.[66] With hindsight, the only sure way to have prevented September 11 would have been for the United States to invade Afghanistan well before September 11 or have been lucky enough to kill bin Laden well before the attacks were planned. The question now is, how has the Bush administration faced the threat from bin Laden after the attacks?

Last chance for the Taliban

Following the attacks of September 11, the United States declared war on al Qaeda and bin Laden. On September 15, President Bush declared, "We're at war . . . we will find those who did it, we will smoke them out of their holes, we will get them running and we will bring them to justice."[67] Speaking at the Pentagon just two days later, Bush framed the war in terms of a hunt for bin Laden and his terrorist allies, saying, "I want justice. And there's an old poster out West, that I recall, that said, 'Wanted, Dead or Alive.'"[68]

The brash early language was polished into a strategic declaration of the administration's intentions and presented to a joint session of Congress and the American people on September 20. "Our war on terror begins with al Qaeda, but it does not end there," the president said. "It will not end until every terrorist group of global reach has been found, stopped and defeated. . . . This is the world's fight.[69] President Bush wasted no time in preparing a military strategy for combating al Qaeda forces. On September 14, the same day Congress passed its resolution supporting a possible war against al Qaeda and Afghanistan, Bush was briefed on the military and covert options for pursuing bin Laden and the al Qaeda network, as well as the existing CIA plans for containing al Qaeda. On September 15, President Bush met with his top advisors at Camp David and made a series of critical decisions to launch a massive air campaign, followed if necessary by a large ground campaign.[70]

In stark contrast to the war with Iraq a year and a half later, Bush and his team worked to garner strong international support for military action should the Taliban refuse to hand over the al Qaeda leaders. President Bush and Secretary Powell worked the phones, pressing world leaders for support—open or even secret—for a campaign against al Qaeda and the

Taliban. Donald Rumsfeld conducted shuttle visits to critical Middle Eastern and Central Asian capitals, galvanizing support for United States military action and commitments for intelligence and logistical support assistance from Saudi Arabia, Egypt, Oman, Turkey, and Uzbekistan. Meanwhile, UK prime minister Tony Blair visited Russia, Pakistan, and India to shore up support for the impending mission.[71] The world lined up behind the United States.

On October 2, NATO Secretary-General Lord George Robertson declared that the United States had provided its eighteen NATO allies with "clear and compelling" evidence of Osama bin Laden's involvement in the attacks.[72] Russian president Vladimir Putin assured President Bush that Russia would share its intelligence, provide an air corridor for humanitarian missions to Afghanistan, and carry out search-and-rescue missions. Putin also pledged to supply arms to the Northern Alliance to support its fight against the Taliban.[73]

The strongest message was to Pakistan, Afghanistan's neighbor and one of only three nations that had formally recognized the Taliban as the rightful government of Afghanistan.[74] United States officials told Pakistani officials in blunt terms, "Help us and breathe in the 21st century along with the international community or be prepared to live in the Stone Age."[75]

Even before the Taliban seized power in 1996, Pakistan's military was the chief sponsor of the regime, providing military, political, and financial support.[76] As a result, many were skeptical of whether Pakistani President Pervez Musharraf would bow to U.S. pressure after September 11 and assist with the toppling of his former ally. Nevertheless, faced with the U.S. ultimatum, Musharraf pledged to deliver full cooperation with the United States, agreeing to grant it the right to use Pakistani airspace for bombing raids, cease supplies of fuel to the Taliban, close the borders to prevent the escape of fleeing hostile parties, and augment the level of intelligence sharing.[77] Over time, however, Islamabad's support faltered. Pakistan failed to seal the border with Afghanistan, and Musharraf's government refused to allow U.S. forces to pursue the Taliban and al Qaeda into Pakistani territory.[78] Furthermore, a number of reports suggested that members of the Pakistani intelligence service, the ISI, were working with the mullah-dominated border provincial governments secretly assisting members of al Qaeda and the Taliban.[79] As one observer noted in May 2003, "Pakistan may be allowing its provincial governments to conduct their own foreign security policy, to support the Taliban rather than hand them over, which is convenient for the federal government."[80]

On September 20, in an address to a joint session of Congress, President Bush put the world and the Taliban on notice, declaring that "either you are with us, or you are against us. From this day forward, any nation that continues to harbor or support terrorism will be regarded by the United

States as a hostile regime." To the Taliban, Bush put forth a firm ultimatum, demanding the leadership "hand over every terrorist . . . or share in their fate." The president called on the Taliban to deliver to the United States "all the leaders of al Qaeda" and close "immediately and permanently every terrorist training camp in Afghanistan," emphasizing the demands were not open to negotiation or discussion.[81]

Following the 1989 departure of Soviet forces, Afghanistan had tumbled into anarchy. The Taliban, supported by Pakistani intelligence forces, took the capital, Kabul, in 1996 and had gradually expanded their reach at the expense of the warlords formerly supported by the United States in an effort to oust Soviet forces. By 2001, the Taliban controlled 90 percent of the country. But the stability the Taliban brought came at a great cost. They implemented a very radical interpretation of Muslim religious Sharia law, oppressed minorities, condemned television, film, singing and dancing, and imposed capital punishment for a wide array of crimes. For Afghan women, the restrictions were particularly harsh. Besides having to wear a long veil (burqa) covering their bodies from head to toe, all women, including teachers, doctors, and engineers, were prohibited from working outside the home or attending any kind of educational institution. Any woman who flouted these rules could be publicly beaten or whipped.[82]

When he arrived in 1996, Osama bin Laden found a ready safe haven in Afghanistan. The Taliban approved of his strict Muslim beliefs; he in turn provided the Taliban with troops, weapons, and funding to fight the Northern Alliance.[83] As CIA director George Tenet noted in 2002, the relationship turned the notion of state-sponsored terrorism on its head. In Afghanistan he said, "What we had was something completely new: a *terrorist* sponsoring a *state*.[84] In exchange for his logistical and financial support, the Taliban gave bin Laden a safe haven and the freedom to establish terrorist training camps in Afghanistan. Both the Taliban and bin Laden are believed to have enjoyed profits from the lucrative Afghan drug trade, although the 9/11 Commission Report found no reliable evidence that bin Laden was involved in or made his money through drug trafficking. The Taliban also assigned him guards for security and refused to cooperate with efforts by the international community to extradite him.[85]

Following September 11, the Taliban leaders repeatedly and defiantly rebuffed President Bush's demands that they hand over Osama bin Laden. The Taliban's supreme court conducted a so-called inquiry to determine whether bin Laden financed and supported Islamic terrorists. The Afghani court determined that the evidence did not warrant bin Laden's extradition to the United States. Afghanistan's deputy interior minister Mohammed Khaquar declared, "America wants bin Laden without providing any evidence or proof. America is just trying to show how powerful it is."[86] In rebuffing American requests, the Taliban declared that in keeping with

Afghan tradition, bin Laden was an honored guest in the country and could not be turned away without evidence against him to justify the extradition.[87] Diplomacy was failing.

In the week before the war started, Bush reiterated his demands several times. In a White House meeting of Republican and Democratic congressional leaders on September 30, Bush warned the Taliban of consequences if it failed to meet American demands. "There are no negotiations. There is no calendar. We'll act on our time."[88]

By October 6, diplomacy had been exhausted. More than thirty thousand U.S. and twenty-three thousand British troops were deployed in the region and ready.[89]

America strikes back

On October 7, American and British military forces unleashed a military campaign against the Taliban in Afghanistan, with the goal of eradicating both the al Qaeda network and the Taliban regime that coddled it. The strategy involved coordinated air strikes against Kabul and the key centers of Taliban support in Kandahar in the south and Jalalabad to the east to establish air supremacy prior to the insertion of ground troops. As the operation unfolded, other troops joined the effort, including those from Austria, Australia, Britain, Canada, Denmark, France, Germany, and Norway. More than forty countries in the Middle East, Africa, Europe, and across Asia granted air transit or landing rights; many more shared intelligence.[90] Even Syria, a staunch anti-Western nation, assisted by providing the United States with valuable information about lead September 11 hijacker Mohammad Atta and substantial intelligence on al Qaeda, which U.S. officials later said helped save American lives.[91]

The United States had also turned to the warlords it had supported twenty-five years earlier against the Soviets, planning to use them in the front lines to oust the Taliban. The United States relied most heavily on the twenty thousand troops of the Northern Alliance, a predominantly Tajik group,[92] which had been led by Ahmed Shah Massoud until his assassination by two men posing as a television news crew and probably linked to al Qaeda, just two days before September 11. Other warlord forces fought alongside the Northern Alliance, including Ismail Khan's twenty thousand troops from the west and warlord General Abdul Rashid Dostum's ten thousand from the north. These warlords had been at war for a generation—first with the support of the United States against the Soviet occupiers, then among themselves for control of the country, and finally against the Taliban regime that had seized control of the country in 1996. Finally, they had their chance at victory.

On display in the Afghanistan war was an array of new war-fighting capa-bilities, technology, and strategies developed over the prior decade. Despite the Bush campaign's statements criticizing Clinton's reductions in military spending, Bush's military review released on September 30, 2001, essen-tially continued the programs of the prior administration. According to Michael O'Hanlon of the Brookings Institution, "It [was] still Bill Clinton's military that [was] winning this war [in Afghanistan]. The Bush adminis-tration had barely started to make its mark on defense policy before hostil-ities in Afghanistan began. [In the] spring, it provided a $5 billion supplemental appropriation for the 2001 defense budget, but that consti-tuted less than 2 percent of defense spending for the year and had hardly begun to be noticed before the war began."[93] As one retired four-star gen-eral commented on the success of the Afghan war, "You can't do that with a hollow army."[94] B-52 bombers covered vast areas of terrain, while preci-sion B-2 bombers dropped bombs directed by global positioning systems. The Taliban's archaic military structure, however, provided a tough chal-lenge for an American military trained against more sophisticated armies. Thus, the Northern Alliance forces provided allied forces with essential expertise in mountain combat and intelligence data about local terrain and troops.

In early November, coalition and anti-Taliban forces increased their pressure on the Taliban, including the use of Special Forces and U.S. gun-ship helicopters to attack Taliban military positions near Kabul. By November 9, the Northern Alliance had captured the key northern city of Mazar-i-Sharif, its previous base of support. The victory, and those in five surrounding towns, gave anti-Taliban forces control of one-third of Afghanistan and offered a gateway for U.S. forces to establish bases in the north, facilitating ground assaults into Kabul and southern Afghanistan. With a formidable alliance of American, British, and anti-Taliban Afghan fighters, the Taliban fled Kabul without a fight. On November 13, the elated Northern Alliance claimed victory over Kabul.

Following the ouster of the Taliban from Kabul, the allies continued to confront Taliban forces in its remaining strongholds. On November 24, the fatigued Taliban surrendered Kunduz, retreating to the mountains and stag-ing limited resistance. On November 25, 2001, American ground troops surrounded Kandahar, the remaining stronghold of the Taliban and spiri-tual center of Afghanistan. In keeping with the initial plan of deploying mas-sive air strikes before inserting ground troops, U.S. B-52 bombers heavily bombed Kandahar for eight days and nights. Next, American and anti-Taliban forces surrounded Kandahar, preparing to act. Before the soldiers even set foot in Kandahar, the Taliban fled, heading to the rugged moun-tains bordering Pakistan called Tora Bora.

The fall of Kandahar in early December marked a virtual defeat of the Taliban, but not al Qaeda. Afghan intelligence experts correctly predicted "Al Qaeda will never surrender . . . the only way that remains for them is to be killed, or die slowly of cold and starvation in the mountains."[95] The key figure in the war, Osama bin Laden, remained at large. Information on his whereabouts had been sketchy throughout the war, with rumors circulating in mid-November that he had fled Afghanistan. In early December, the United States believed he and as many as two thousand of his fighters were in Tora Bora. In November, the United States raised from $5 million to $25 million the reward for bin Laden's capture and advertised the offer in the pamphlets dropped over Afghanistan.

The menacing terrain of caves, tunnels, and steep hills of Tora Bora presented a significant challenge to American and British fighters. As the United States stepped up the bombing campaign, anti-Taliban eastern alliance forces issued an ultimatum to the al Qaeda operatives in Tora Bora to surrender or die.[96] Two thousand Afghan fighters, with intimate knowledge of the Tora Bora terrain gained through fighting Soviet forces, went to help root out al Qaeda, but U.S. ground forces inexplicably did not join them. After sixteen days of intensive bombing, the area was under the alliance's control. However, Osama bin Laden, his number two man, Mohammed Atef (who would later be killed by the United States in November 2001), and the Taliban leader Mullah Mohammed Omar all were able to escape. Had U.S. ground forces joined the Afghan fighters, perhaps they could have blocked bin Laden and his al Qaeda operatives from fleeing.

The two-month war had destroyed the base of support for al Qaeda and scattered bin Laden's terrorist network. Ninety American soldiers had died. No reliable figures on Afghan deaths exist. The investment in technology of the last decade had proven itself. Bin Laden and his operatives were on the run and America was safer. The international community was strongly supportive of America's actions and prepared to continue to provide unprecedented support in the war against terrorism. George W. Bush had emerged as a strong, resolute leader with overwhelming support from the American people and America's allies around the world.

We will do our part in the rebuilding of Afghanistan

Following the United States–led overthrow of the Taliban regime in October 2001, President Bush promised that "America and her allies will do our part in the rebuilding of Afghanistan." At a ceremony at the National Museum of Women in the Arts on December 13, 2001, Bush pledged that "We learned our lessons from the past. We will not leave until the mission is complete. We will work with international institutions on the long-term development of Afghanistan."[97] In April 2002, the president even invoked the need for the United States to work "in the best traditions of George Marshall," making a parallel between the U.S. efforts in Afghanistan and General Marshall's plan to rebuild Europe after World War II.[98]

The administration moved quickly to establish security in the capital of Kabul and an Afghan interim government led by Hamid Karzai. The United States chose Karzai because he had been an anti-Soviet fighter, was a royalist, and a Pashtun from the south—all key traits that drew support from much of the population. Again, in stark contrast to Bush's later sidelining of the United Nations, the United States turned quickly to the United Nations to create a government seen as legitimate by Afghans. In late 2001, the United Nations convened a wide array of Afghan factions in Bonn, Germany, to build a new government. The process resulted in the Bonn Agreement signed on December 5, 2001, which established an interim power-sharing arrangement and a road map for the subsequent establishment of the Afghanistan transitional administration and a constitution.

In a decision that would vastly complicate the challenges of the new government, the United States left the control of security and valuable resources in the hands of the country's warlords. Despite the grave security concerns, the Bonn Agreement called for only a small international force that would secure solely the Kabul area rather than the entire country, severely limiting the control that Karzai's new government would have over warlords outside the capital.[99] With the need for immediate stability and the goal of rooting out terrorists taking precedence over the country's long-term stability, the United States bolstered regional leaders who could best support its immediate aims. Many of those leaders had no real interest in maintaining peace at the expense of their own power.[100] The warlords quickly snubbed the demands of Karzai's government that they surrender to the central authority.

The removal of the Taliban and the introduction of international aid money brought dramatic improvements in the first year of the transitional administration. From October 2001 to the end of 2002, the United States contributed $350 million in aid assistance in Afghanistan,[101] and the Afghanistan Freedom Support Act authorized $3.47 billion for Afghanistan over fiscal years 2003 to 2006. As of January 2004, over four hundred thousand metric tons of food had been delivered; the international community has helped Afghanistan repair more than seven thousand kilometers of roads, reconstruct more than seventy bridges, and rehabilitate over eleven thousand wells, canals, dams, and water systems.[102]

Over two million Afghani refugees returned to the country following the defeat of the Taliban, and UNHCR continues to assist them with food, housing, and integration. Food production had improved substantially as of late 2002, and those made vulnerable by food insecurity and the harsh Afghan winter were being targeted with assistance from UN and international agencies. Demobilization and police training began in some parts of the country, although progress was slow.[103]

Overall, the process worked in establishing a system that set the country on the path to elections in 2004. As one UN official told me in the spring of 2004, comparing the process of establishing a new government to the one seen as illegitimate in Iraq, "It was far from perfect but it was seen as legitimate in the eyes of Afghans. In the end, that is what counted."[104] On June 13, 2002, within seven months of the Taliban's ouster, President Hamid Karzai was sworn into office. For the first time in a generation, Afghanistan had a real chance of peace.

Yet, rather than continue the pursuit of Osama bin Laden and al Qaeda in the mountains of Tora Bora, continue to ensure the stability of Afghanistan, and strengthen the worldwide coalition against terrorism, President Bush chose to invade Iraq.

9

Iraq: A Decade of Deceit

There is no worse mistake in public leadership than to hold out false hopes soon to be swept away.

—Winston Churchill

On February 5, 2003, Secretary of State Colin Powell sat before the UN Security Council in an attempt to convince skeptics that Iraq had been actively deceiving UN weapons inspectors. Launching into an indictment of Iraq's failure to comply with the demands of the international community, Powell declared, "I cannot tell you everything that we know but what I can share with you, when combined with what all of us have learned over the years, is deeply troubling." In his hour-and-a-half presentation, Powell provided satellite photos, electronic intercepts, and other intelligence to prove that the Iraqis were undermining UN weapons inspectors' efforts toward disarmament. He played cryptic audiotapes of Iraqi officers implying a campaign to hide information from inspectors and put forward a sober laundry list of biological and chemical weapons possessed and used in the past.[1]

Furthermore, for the first time Powell detailed the connection between Saddam Hussein and terrorist organizations such as al Qaeda, saying that Iraq harbored and trained al Qaeda terrorists. "Iraq today harbors a deadly terrorist network headed by Abu Musab al-Zarqawi, an associate and collaborator of Usama bin Laden and his al-Qaida lieutenants. . . . Iraqi officials deny accusations of ties with al-Qaida. These denials are simply not credible."[2]

Powell provided detailed diagrams of mobile production facilities for biological weapons disguised as trucks or train cars and a detailed discussion of aluminum tubing believed to be intended for enriching uranium. Powell acknowledged that there was still debate in the intelligence community over the significance of this evidence. He nonetheless expressed confidence that Iraq constituted a threat, both in terms of weapons of mass destruction and terrorism. "Some believe, some claim, these contacts do not amount to much. They say Saddam Hussein's secular tyranny and al Qaida's religious tyranny do not mix. I am not comforted by this thought. . . . When we confront a regime that harbors ambitions for regional domination, hides weapons of mass destruction, and provides haven and active support for terrorists, we are not confronting the past; we are confronting the present. And unless we act, we are confronting an even more frightening future."[3]

Powell sought to make the case that by acting as though they had something to hide, Iraq must have weapons of mass destruction. "The United States will not and cannot run that risk for the American people. Leaving Saddam Hussein in possession of weapons of mass destruction for a few more months or years is not an option, not in a post–September 11th world."[4]

Powell hoped that the presentation would convince the other council members that Iraq was already in material breach of UN Resolution 1441. "We have an obligation to this body to see that our resolutions are complied with. . . . We must not shrink from whatever is ahead of us. We must not fail in our duty and our responsibility to the citizens of the countries that are represented by this body." By portraying Saddam as the outcast who had violated his UN obligations and the United States as the multilateral leader defending the UN's importance and relevance, President Bush thought he could rally the world behind his effort. He did—for a time. He would lose that world coalition when the U.S. goal clearly became overthrowing Saddam Hussein, not enforcing UN resolutions.

A decade in the planning

The United States has a long and difficult history with Saddam Hussein's regime. Established as an independent kingdom in 1932 by the departing British colonial powers, Iraq is comprised of two dominant ethnic groups, Kurds and Arabs, and two distinct Muslim sects, Sunni and Shia. Population figures are imprecise: 75 to 80 percent of Iraqis are Arab, while Kurds predominantly live in the north and make up 15 to 20 percent of the population. Sunni Muslims live in and around Baghdad and make up 32 to 37 percent of the Muslim population; Shia Muslims live in the south and constitute 60 to 65 percent of the Muslim population.[5] When Saddam Hussein seized power in 1979, he proposed a political platform of moderate social democracy based on the European model and a goal of holding together the varied ethnic and religious groups of the country. Over the course of three administrations, the U.S. government looked to Saddam Hussein to check the Islamic fervor in neighboring Iran and to help secure a stable oil supply. Despite his brutal authoritarian rule and use of chemical weapons against the Kurds in 1988, the United States counted his regime as an ally in the region.

The relationship changed dramatically in 1990. Burdened with an enormous debt from the eight-year Iran–Iraq war, low oil prices, and reluctance by his OPEC partners to curb oil production, over the summer of 1990 Saddam Hussein amassed seven military divisions on the Iraq–Kuwaiti border. The United States sent mixed signals on how it would respond to an invasion of Kuwait. In a now infamous conversation that ultimately ended her career, U.S. Ambassador to Iraq April Glaspie met with President Saddam Hussein on July 25, 1990. While the United States has never released notes of the meeting, Glaspie apparently told Hussein that the United States had little to say about Arab border disputes and was eager to improve relations with Iraq.[6] She did reportedly express concern and ask "in the spirit of friendship" what his intentions were.[7]

In the early morning of August 2, one hundred twenty thousand Iraqi troops with two thousand tanks invaded Kuwait.[8] The same day, the UN Security Council passed Resolution 660 condemning the invasion and calling for the complete withdrawal of Iraqi forces.[9] In stark contrast to the 2003 Iraq war, the United States launched one of the most successful diplomatic campaigns ever, gathering strong international support, including the crucial support of the Arab world. President Bush declared on August 5, that the act of aggression would "not stand." Less than one week after the Iraqi invasion, on August 8, Saddam Hussein announced Iraq's annexation of Kuwait as the nineteenth province of Iraq.[10]

On Monday, August 6, the UNSC passed Resolution 661, imposing economic sanctions on Iraq.[11] The same day Secretary of Defense Richard Cheney met with King Fahd in Riyadh to discuss the presence of U.S. troops in Saudi Arabia. During the course of the two-hour meeting, Cheney convinced the Saudis of the need to begin the immediate mobilization of U.S. forces on Saudi territory if they were to protect the lucrative oil fields from possible Iraqi aggression.[12] The next day, President George Bush ordered warplanes and ground forces to Saudi Arabia as the start of Operation Desert Shield. (President Bush kept the world united over the principle of Kuwaiti sovereignty. The administration was also motivated by oil.)

In a surprisingly unguarded comment, Senate Republican leader Robert Dole, speaking on the Senate floor in October 1990, explained, "We are in the Mideast for three letters: O-I-L."[13] Within days of the Iraqi occupation of Kuwait, an unnamed senior American official, believed to be Secretary of State James Baker was quoted as saying, "We are talking about oil. Got it? Oil, vital American interests."[14] By the end of November, the Security Council had passed Resolution 678 authorizing member states, in cooperation with Kuwait, to use "all necessary means" to uphold Resolution 660 as well as the ten previous resolutions[15] to restore international peace and security to the region. The resolution provided a deadline of January 15, 1991, for full compliance.[16]

On January 9, 1991, Baker met with Iraqi foreign minister Tariq Aziz in Geneva in a final effort to find a peaceful solution. As Baker later described the purpose of the meeting, "Unless we could show that we'd done everything we could, diplomatically and politically, to achieve Iraq's withdrawal from Kuwait we could be criticized maybe for going to war precipitously."[17] In contrast to his dismissal of diplomacy a decade later, Dick Cheney said the meeting "demonstrated conclusively to the public and to the Congress that we in fact were deadly serious about trying every last option to get him out [of Kuwait] and we would only use force as a last resort."[18]

The Geneva meeting failed to make progress. On January 12, the U.S. Congress authorized the president to use force to compel Iraqi compliance with the United Nations resolutions. "We would not have won the [congressional] vote without Geneva," Baker explained. "We simply wouldn't."[19] The UN deadline of January 15 passed with Iraqi failing to meet the UN demands.

On January 16, Operation Desert Storm began with the aerial bombardment of Iraq. For forty-three days, coalition air forces conducted thousands of flights, or sorties, per day, attacking more than twenty-seven thousand targets.[20] For the first time, Americans watched their war on television, broadcast by CNN. The United States–led ground invasion began on February 24 when coalition forces broke through Iraqi lines along a three-hundred-mile front and penetrated deep into southern Iraq. Kuwait was liberated by February 27. President Bush declared a ceasefire on February 28, bringing an end to the hundred-hour ground offensive. One hundred forty-eight Americans died from combat and another 145 from disease or accident, with 467 wounded.[21]

The first Bush administration handled the situation deftly, giving diplomacy six months and working hard to keep America's friends and allies together. The result was a strong international coalition during and in the aftermath of the war to contain Saddam Hussein. In 2003, the second Bush administration would try diplomacy only halfheartedly and fail dramatically.

Ceasefire

On March 2, 1991, the Security Council passed Resolution 686 establishing the terms of the ceasefire between Iraq and Kuwait. It demanded Iraq implement the prior twelve resolutions, rescind any actions purporting to annex Kuwait or other hostile acts, pay compensation to Kuwait and others suffering damages from the war, and take a number of humanitarian steps.[22] Representatives from the Iraqi government formally accepted the terms of the ceasefire from U.S. military leaders on March 3, and signed a permanent ceasefire agreement on April 6.

President Bush's decision not to continue the war to Baghdad and topple Saddam Hussein was a controversial one. He had eviscerated departing Iraqi forces but had stopped his attack at the border. I remember traveling to Kuwait in March 1991, when a dark cloud hung over the city from burning oil wells spewing flames hundreds of feet high. The road leading out of Kuwait City to Iraq was still littered with Iraqi army tanks, trucks, and bodies bombed by U.S. forces as they fled. Many had pushed Bush to continue the war and remove Saddam Hussein from power. Yet, Bush understood that he would lose his Arab coalition were he to do so. The president also appreciated the high costs in terms of American blood and treasure that a U.S. occupation of Iraq would entail. As he explained, presciently, in 1998, "We would have been forced to occupy Baghdad and, in effect, rule Iraq. The coalition would instantly have collapsed, the Arabs deserting it in anger and other allies pulling out as well. . . . Had we gone the invasion route, the U.S. could conceivably still be an occupying power in a bitterly hostile land. It would have been a dramatically different—and perhaps barren—outcome."[23]

Secretary of State James Baker also pointed out the costs of ousting Hussein, predicting accurately the difficulties of the 2003 invasion. "I think that if we had marched to Baghdad, we would have fractured the coalition, the Arab members would have left, the countries in the region are fearful of the Lebanization of Iraq . . . we didn't want to lose a whole lot more American lives that probably would have been lost if we had occupied Iraq, and had to fight . . . a guerrilla war there. . . . There really is no argument to be made for going to Iraq—for going to Baghdad."[24] Baker added that the progress in the Arab-Israeli peace process would not have been achieved. "There would be no peace process in the Middle East today."[25]

An avid champion of toppling Saddam Hussein a decade later, in 1991, then secretary of defense Dick Cheney agreed with Baker's rationale. "I think if we had done that we would have been bogged down there for a very long period of time with the real possibility we might not have succeeded."[26] Colin Powell explained, "What we came to do, and what the UN authorized us to do, and what the American Congress authorized us to do, was to kick the Iraqi army out of Kuwait, restore the legitimate government of Kuwait, bring about a new relationship in the region and please try to do it with minimum loss of life. All of that was accomplished."[27]

For the next decade, the United States would contain Saddam Hussein, continuing to support the goal of his departure by means other than U.S. military invasion. While often frustrating, this policy successfully protected U.S. interests, containing any threat from Saddam Hussein.

Sanctions

Throughout the 1990s, the United States and UK used United Nations–backed economic sanctions, no-fly zones, and UN weapons inspections to contain the threat Saddam Hussein posed. The sanctions brought into effect by Resolution 661 on August 6, 1990, remained in place until the 2003 war and were specifically linked to the elimination of weapons of mass destruction (WMD) in Resolution 687, passed on April 3, 1991.[28] Before the Gulf War, as Iraq objected to a strong mandate, UN weapons inspectors had failed to discover the full extent of Iraq's WMD programs. Only after the war's end in 1991 did inspectors uncover significant evidence of WMD facilities, in particular a nuclear weapons program. From then on, the inspectors insisted on more stringent inspections. At the time, most observers believed that Saddam would comply with the disarmament demands within a reasonable period and that the sanctions would be lifted.

The economic sanctions imposed against Iraq since 1990 have constituted the most comprehensive international sanctions regime in history.[29] The Security Council made it clear that if Iraq wished to import or export any type of goods (save medical supplies and humanitarian necessities) it would have to fully disarm its chemical, biological, and nuclear facilities. In March 1991, the UN concluded that "the Iraqi people may soon face a further imminent catastrophe, which could include epidemic and famine, if massive life-supporting needs are not rapidly met."[30] In response, the United States proposed a program to exchange Iraqi oil for food and humanitarian goods.

The Iraqi regime initially resisted the plan, but finally agreed to the conditions in 1995 after nearly *five years* of delay.[31] By then calorific intake had fallen below 1,000 calories per day.[32] The program went into effect in December 1996, allowing Iraq to resume exporting oil up to a quantity of $2 billion semiannually to buy food, medicine, and other humanitarian goods. This UN "oil-for-food" program was unique in that it represented the first time a state subject to economic sanctions was compelled to use its own revenues to address the humanitarian needs of its citizens.[33]

Although the sanctions regime included provisions for providing humanitarian relief to the Iraqi people, Saddam Hussein instead spent billions constructing an estimated forty-eight presidential palaces and a sprawling lakeside vacation resort containing stadiums, an amusement park, hospitals, parks, and 625 homes to be used by government officials. This project cost hundreds of millions of dollars.[34] In July 1999, *Forbes* magazine estimated Saddam Hussein's personal wealth at $6 billion, acquired primarily from oil and smuggling.[35]

Saddam Hussein successfully convinced most of the world that the sanctions were the cause of the suffering of the Iraqi people, not his failure to use the billions made available to him to provide food and medicine to the population. Yet, in the north, which was controlled by the Kurds and not Saddam Hussein, the UN program essentially worked. In giving speeches, both in the United States and abroad, there was almost always someone who asked me why the United States was killing Iraqi babies. As Saddam built palace after palace, the Iraqi people suffered, with sharp rises in infant mortality, malnutrition, and disease. One study estimates that between one hundred thousand and two hundred twenty-seven thousand children under the age of five died between 1991 and 1998 as a result of the Gulf War and subsequent sanctions. A UNICEF report estimated that five hundred thousand children under five had died.[36] The deteriorated infrastructure, a result of the Iran-Iraq war and Operation Desert Storm, also caused an increase in disease, malnutrition, and death.[37] Certainly, sanctions further contributed to Iraq's deterioration by limiting the availability of certain dual-use items; yet, Saddam Hussein held the key to their lifting. He refused to turn it.[38] The sanctions were finally lifted by the UN Security Council on May 22, 2003, following the overthrow of Saddam Hussein.

Throughout the 1990s, pressure built for the UN to drop the sanctions, not for Saddam Hussein to comply. My colleague, Ambassador A. Peter Burleigh, and I tag-teamed the Security Council on various issues. Brilliant, gentle, apolitical, and well liked at the UN and in Washington, he had the difficult UN Iraq portfolio at the United Nations from 1998 to 1999. When he arrived at the UN in August of 1997, the consensus on sanctions in the council had already evaporated. His first effort to address Iraq's lack of full cooperation with the UN inspectors was to seek to impose sanctions. The provisions included a ban on visas to senior Iraqi officials. "We negotiated away tougher penalties," Burleigh recalled, "on the wrong assumption that the French and the Russians would vote in favor if we did so." Instead, Russia, China, France, Egypt, and Kenya abstained on the resolution. "It was a disaster for us," Burleigh recalled, "reflecting the already well-advanced dissolution of the council's consensus on Iraq. [The failure of that resolution] was a prelude to those horrible years of 1998, 1999, and 2000 when France and Russia opposed every effort to get tough with the Iraqis."[39]

The reasons for the security council's breakdown are many. Certainly, the increased suffering of the Iraqi people was an important one. But, as Burleigh explained, "The international attempts to inhibit [or] end Iraq's weapons of mass destruction programs were futile; further, [Russia and France] both had lucrative contracts with Iraq and the Iraqi authorities were clever at manipulating those contracts, and involving friends of important political leaders in both countries in the contracts; finally, I think they both calculated (correctly) that if there was really an imminent threat from Iraq, that the U.S. would take care of the problem."[40]

Francois Bujon de L'Estang, France's ambassador in Washington at the time, explained that there was no disagreement on the substance, but rather the tactics. "It is like two doctors called to a sick bed who agree on the diagnosis but are prescribing different treatments. The U.S. was being tough; we were trying to explain we could be successful if we could attract some good will and cooperation from the Iraqis, such as by promising a lifting of sanctions. We were always of the opinion that we should keep pushing inspections by showing the light at the end of the tunnel. The U.S. was not ready to do that."[41]

Burleigh perhaps best summed up the attitude, explaining "that the French and Russians, and to some extent the Chinese, and others, see the UN Security Council as the one place where they can rein in the hyper-power U.S., get us bogged down in consensus-building, negotiate the pants off us, and then decline to go along [as the French did with Colin Powell in 2003 and earlier], ensuring that international legitimacy is lacking from subsequent U.S. actions."[42]

In addition to the sanctions regime, the "no-fly zones" proved an issue of great disagreement. In 1991 the United States, UK, and France began to patrol northern Iraq by air in order to protect the Kurds, creating a no-fly zone north of the thirty-sixth parallel. After continuing attacks on the Shia population in the south and troubling moves by Saddam indicating he contemplated another attack on his neighbors, the United States and its allies imposed a similar no-fly zone south of the thirty-second parallel on August 26, 1992. NATO extended this zone to 33 degrees latitude September 3, 1996, just south of Baghdad, but only French, U.S., and UK forces enforced it. For twelve years, the U.S. Air Force, along with the Navy and Marine corps, worked alongside the Royal Air Force, flying nearly four hundred thousand sorties to enforce the no-fly zones. As the air force's vice chief of staff said in March 2004, "Throughout this period, our airmen honed their war-fighting skills, gained familiarity with the region, and were able to establish favorable conditions for [the war in Iraq]. For more than a decade, American airmen rose to one of our nation's most important challenges, containing Saddam Hussein."[43]

The no-fly zones were hotly contested, with Iraq, supported by Russia, China, and eventually France, claiming there was no authority in existing UN resolutions for them. The United States and Britain, on the other hand, contended that there was enough authorization in previous resolutions that allowed force to maintain peace and security in the region.[44] Following the withdrawal of the UN inspections in 1998, France ended participation in enforcing the no-fly zones, arguing that they had become an extension of U.S. strategic operations in the region and were not an effective means of protecting people in southern Iraq. British and U.S. aircraft never ceased to patrol these zones until the war in 2003. In 1998, they began a more aggressive operation that entailed periodic bombing of air defenses in response to increased Iraqi targeting of aircraft enforcing the zones. At times, the United States and the UK conducted air strikes against suspected weapons sites that were in violation of the UN agreements. For instance, between February 2000 and February 2001, allied pilots entered the southern zone ten thousand times; the Iraqis fixed their radar on the jets or engaged them with antiaircraft weapons five hundred times.[45]

In 1998, I visited the USS *Eisenhower* carrier strike group while it was on predeployment work-up exercises off the coast of Puerto Rico, preparing to deploy to the gulf to enforce the no-fly zones. Nuclear powered with over one hundred aircraft, the "*Ike*" is one of the largest warships in the world. Its 4.5 acres obviated the need for foreign basing of its planes and personnel, enabling the United States to keep a lighter footprint in an Arab world sensitive to the presence of U.S. forces. Landing in a C-2 transport aircraft, the plane stopped abruptly as it caught the third of the deck's four large steel cables, called trapping aboard. We left by a steam catapult, or "CAT," that flung the C-2 off the ship at 150 miles an hour in less than two seconds. In naval aviator–speak, I did a TRAP and a CAT on the C-2.[46]

After my tour of the ship, I joined one of the fighter squadrons from Carrier Airwing Seven in its "ready room" where pilots prep and get final instructions before missions. Becoming a fighter pilot is one of the most competitive processes in the U.S. military, and few units have a more "can do" attitude. This squadron had dubbed itself the "World Famous Pukin Dogs." An appropriately tough image of a dog was on patches on their jackets and painted on their F-14 Tomcat aircraft. Following my talk on U.S. policy toward Iraq, one pilot stood up in the back and asked, "Ma'am, why doesn't anyone pay attention to our mission?"

I was taken aback by such a sensitive question from such a tough guy. I explained that while the press may not pay attention, "I can assure you the president of the United States does." Reports of the no-fly zone operations were in the morning PDB and other intelligence summaries circulated each day to U.S. officials. One of my worries throughout my eight years in the administration was always that a plane would be shot down and the pilots killed or taken hostage. I am still amazed such a tragedy did not occur in twelve years of enforcing the no-fly zones. The United States did not lose a single pilot or plane despite flying hundreds of thousands of sorties over Iraq.[47] That it did not is a testament to the Pukin Dogs and every other aviator, airman, and sailor flying or supporting that mission. The missions continued under President Bush. On February 2001, for the first time since the no-fly zones had been established, the United States struck Baghdad and other installations outside the zones, dramatically escalating the raids.

A decade of hide-and-seek

Following the Gulf War, the Security Council set up a system for monitoring and verifying Iraq's compliance with the ban on weapons of mass destruction and missile production. The investigative body, called the UN Special Commission (UNSCOM), worked closely with the International Atomic Energy Agency (IAEA). Following the failure to find Iraq's prewar programs, the IAEA secured new robust rules that provided it greater freedom to conduct random, unscheduled searches, which revealed frighteningly sophisticated chemical and biological poisons, warheads equipped to deliver these poisons, and a blossoming nuclear program.[48] The UNSCOM inspectors conducted the first inspections of Iraqi chemical weapons facilities on June 9, 1991, but by the end of the summer, Iraq was blocking inspections. Throughout the 1990s, Iraq lied, obfuscated, and failed to cooperate with the UN inspectors. For instance, a 1994 UNSCOM review declared that Iraq was pursuing the development of biological weapons despite having denied such a program existed. In August 1995, Iraq officially admitted that it had concealed important information from UNSCOM and IAEA but cooperation with the inspectors never followed.[49]

As has become clear since the 2003 war, UN inspections, coupled with U.S. and UK targeted strikes against weapons sites, eroded Iraq's weapons of mass destruction program. The IAEA and UNSCOM reports of the 1990s show a worrisome array of weapons materials seized from Iraq. Since 1991, UN inspectors confirmed the existence of a biological warfare program as well as the deadly chemical nerve agent VX. Furthermore, the UN seized missiles, chemical warheads, 38,500 chemical munitions, 690 tons of chemical weapons agent, over 3,000 metric tons of precursor chemicals, and a variety of materials and equipment used to produce biological weapons.[50] Analysts believed that Iraq was developing long-range missiles that could be tipped with chemical or biological warheads; realization of such a program would be the greatest threat Iraq posed to its neighbors. Having seen the intelligence reports on Iraq since 1993, I, like most Bush administration officials, was convinced Saddam Hussein had a covert program to produce chemical and biological weapons, although most likely not nuclear. I was as surprised as the Bush administration when none were discovered following the 2003 war.

Iraq's failure to cooperate with the inspectors reached a crisis in October 1997 when Iraq required all U.S. personnel working for UNSCOM to leave Iraq immediately. Iraq claimed that the United States was putting too much pressure on the Security Council to increase sanctions.[51] Rather than permit Iraq to distinguish among the UN inspectors, the UN rightly withdrew most UNSCOM personnel. Iraq also declared it would not let UN inspectors into certain sites it deemed "presidential" on the grounds of national sovereignty and in January 1998 announced it was withdrawing its cooperation with the inspection team on the pretext that the team included too many American and British inspectors.

In a gamble that eventually failed, Secretary-General Kofi Annan visited Iraq in February 1998 in an effort to secure Iraq's cooperation with the inspectors. He did so against the wishes of the Clinton administration, which did not fully trust the secretary-general to negotiate a sufficiently tough deal. Annan's defiance of the United States was a difficult decision for him, as the United States was the most powerful member of the UN and had gotten Annan his job. He felt, however, his responsibility was to avoid what he knew would be U.S. military action should he fail to resolve the confrontation.

Annan's trip resulted in the signing of a Memorandum of Understanding (MOU) between the United Nations and the Republic of Iraq on February 23, 1998.[52] In the agreement, Iraq reconfirmed its acceptance of all relevant resolutions of the Council and pledged "immediate, unconditional and unrestricted access" for the UN and IAEA inspectors. In exchange, the UN reiterated the commitment of all member states to respect the sovereignty and territorial integrity of Iraq, and that UNSCOM would "respect the legitimate concerns of Iraq relating to national security, sovereignty and dignity."[53] The MOU also established special procedures for so-called presidential sites. The inspectors returned March 26.

The agreement was short-lived. In August 1998, Iraq decided to halt cooperation with UNSCOM and the IAEA pending Security Council agreement to lift the oil embargo, reorganize the commission, and move it to either Geneva or Vienna. In October 1998, Iraq announced it would cease all forms of cooperation with UNSCOM. It repeatedly accused the UN of spying for the United States and Israel (the UN later admitted it had allowed its inspectors to pass intelligence to the United States). On November 4, UNSCOM informed the Security Council that as a result of Iraq's actions, the commission was unable to determine whether Iraq was complying with its obligations. The stage was set for a confrontation.

Operation Desert Fox

I was sitting in the informal chamber of the UN Security Council on December 16, 1998, when suddenly, cell phones began to ring. Ambassadors and staff alike moved out of the room to make or take calls. Our discussion on maintaining peace and security and postconflict peace-building was abruptly suspended. The Brazilian ambassador Celso Amorim was the first to tell me the United States had begun a bombing campaign. They are calling it "Desert Fox," he told me with a bemused smirk.

The night before, Peter Burleigh had received a call from Washington telling him to instruct the UN to evacuate its staff from Baghdad. He was also told to keep the tightly controlled decision to launch the military campaign to himself. Once the UN staff was out, the United States, with British support, launched the operation to destroy Iraq's nuclear, chemical, and biological weapons program. The operation involved over thirty thousand troops in the theatre of operation and another ten thousand in support roles outside of the area. There were six hundred sorties in four days, half of which were at night. Forty ships performed strike-and-support roles, with ten of them launching over three hundred Tomahawk Land Attack Missiles and ninety cruise missiles. Thousands of U.S. ground troops were deployed to protect Kuwait and to respond to any counteraction.[54]

Secretary of State Albright explained the purpose of the operation: "Month after month we have given Iraq chance after chance to move from confrontation to cooperation. We have explored and exhausted every diplomatic option. We will see now whether force can persuade Iraq's misguided leaders to reverse course and to accept at long last the need to abide by the rule of law and the will of the world." Albright also stated what many in the administration had come to believe, that Saddam Hussein had to go, "We have now made quite clear that we are prepared to work with these opposition groups for a regime change."[55] While the threat did not warrant an invasion, the U.S. action made it clear the United States would use military force against the threat of WMD.

The military action ended any semblance of consensus in the Security Council on Iraq. As one senior French official close to President Chirac explained, "December 1998 was a disaster. Like toothpaste, once the inspectors were out, they would never go back in. Clinton was ready to fight a war to have the inspectors back." He explained the French position that a preferable solution would have been to lift the sanctions in exchange for permanent monitors on the ground. The regime would have crumbled more from opening than closing, like Cuba. "Maybe we are wrong but in our view, sanctions helped the regime to find a culprit for all its difficulties."[56]

Operation Desert Fox, with some one hundred targets across Iraq, succeeded in degrading Iraq's ability to produce weapons of mass destruction. As General Anthony Zinni, commander in chief of the Central Command, explained, "Our objectives for this operation were: reduce Iraq's capability to produce weapons of mass destruction, degrade strategic and tactical command and control facilities, damage industrial infrastructure used for the smuggling of gas and oil; and the overall reduction of Iraq's capability to threaten its neighbors in the region."[57] In Zinni's assessment, Iraq's ballistic missile program was set back one to two years. While the Clinton administration did not know how well it had set back Iraq's weapons program at the time, it is now clear that the operation did effectively eliminate much of its remaining program. As Sandy Berger commented, "I pressed both Hugh Shelton and George Tenet for more WMD on the target list, high value targets. With the attacks, Saddam's WMD was set back and the attack shook up his power position. He spent the next two years in a bunker. He was far more quiescent than he otherwise would have been."[58]

From 1991 to 2001, the United States sought to contain Saddam Hussein from developing weapons of mass destruction and threatening the region. As has since become clear, it largely succeeded in doing so, although the process was messy, frustrating, and far from ideal. Still, it increasingly became evident that Saddam Hussein would never fully comply with the Security Council demands. The United States, therefore, sought alternatives to bring about his fall from power, focusing on giving support to Iraqi opposition groups to do the job themselves.

Although several attempts were made after 1998 to secure a return of the inspectors, including a revamped mission renamed the United Nations Monitoring Verification and Inspection Commission (UNMOVIC) in December 1999, they did not return until President Bush secured a unanimous resolution in November 2002 under the threat of war.

The Bush administration debates Iraq

When Bush took office in January 2001, Iraq was not a major focus. His top officials were divided on how to address the continued threat of Saddam Hussein. On the one hand, State Department officials argued for an improved containment policy. Secretary of State Colin Powell was not a cheerleader for toppling Saddam Hussein. When he became secretary of state in 2001, he worked to improve the sanctions and opposed efforts by his colleagues to prepare for war.

The hegemons, led by Vice President Cheney, Secretary of Defense Rumsfeld, and his deputy Paul Wolfowitz, came to office focused on regime change in Iraq. Supported by conservative think tanks, the lead champion for war was Richard Perle as well as Iraqi exiles such as Ahmed Chalabi. These men had spent much of the last decade calling for action and belittling the UN inspections. Once in office, they pressed for action. According to former Treasury secretary Paul O'Neill, from the start they were "building the case against Hussein and looking at how we could take him out and change Iraq into a new country. And, if we did that, it would solve everything. It was all about finding *a way to do it*. That was the tone of it. The President saying, 'Fine. Go find me a way to do this.'"[59] President Bush let the debate between Powell and his colleagues play out, making no decision.

The attacks of September 11, 2001, essentially ended the debate in the administration over Iraq. While it would take a year and a half to crystallize, the terrorist attacks gave the upper hand to the hegemons who argued America now had no choice but to take the fight to Saddam Hussein.

Immediately after the attacks, Rumsfeld and Wolfowitz escalated their campaign to go to war. Richard Clarke describes returning to the White House for an emergency meeting in the middle of the night following the September 11 attacks, expecting a discussion on the attacks. "Instead, I walked into a series of discussions about Iraq. At first I was incredulous that we were talking about something other than getting al Qaeda. Then I realized, with almost a sharp physical pain that Rumsfeld and Wolfowitz were going to try to take advantage of this national tragedy to promote their agenda about Iraq."[60]

The hegemons' disconnection with reality—and obsession with Saddam Hussein—were evident in the days and months following September 11. On the afternoon of September 12, Rumsfeld discussed the possibility of broadening the objectives of the response to the attacks and "getting Iraq," arguing oddly that there were relatively few good air targets in Afghanistan. Wolfowitz, in particular, was convinced that Iraq must have been al Qaeda's state sponsor, despite the lack of support for the theory in the intelligence community. For instance, in April 2001, he said to colleagues, "You give bin Laden too much credit. He could not do all these things like the 1993 [World Trade Center] attack on New York, not without a state sponsor. Just because the FBI and CIA have failed to find the linkages does not mean they don't exist."[61]

President Bush initially heeded Secretary Powell's advice that the focus should remain on al Qaeda.[62] The discussion over whether to invade Iraq was put on hold, while the United States focused on ousting the Taliban from Afghanistan. Yet, it was a short-lived victory for Powell as the hegemons quickly returned to the issue as soon as the Taliban fled from Kabul. Open disagreements over U.S. policy toward Iraq began to surface in December 2001, with Wolfowitz and Rumsfeld pushing for an invasion and Powell and his deputy, Richard Armitage, losing ground on maintaining the diplomatic route. By early 2002, the debate was over methods and timing, more than over whether regime change in Iraq was justified. As one senior U.S. official described it, "The question is not if the United States is going to hit Iraq; the question is when."[63] A former senior military official explained that the planning for the war was under way by early 2002 when he visited the European Central Command (CENTCOM) in charge of the planning. He was surprised to find the planners working on the assumption of the robust participation of the European nations. He told the planners they had better "get a grip on this. We are going to have only the U.K., possibly Turkey." "By November," he said, "we were so far leaning forward that it would be hard to call it off, given our threats and that we had five carriers out there."[64]

Axis of evil

Although Osama bin Laden remained at large and the war on terrorism was far from over, proponents of war against Iraq made their move and began to build their case inside the administration and publicly. The United States would now seek out terrorists and their supporters before they could act. This aggressive strategy was sold to President Bush as an essential element in the effort to protect Americans in the new war on terrorism. Saddam Hussein was its primary target.

President Bush set forth the new doctrine of preemption in his January 29, 2002, State of the Union Address. Declaring the United States must pursue terrorists, "wherever they are," Bush said that America will not allow terrorist training camps to operate or nations to harbor terrorists. Even more importantly, the president made it clear that enemies, be they terrorists or hostile regimes providing support to terrorists, would be confronted by the United States before it suffered at their hands. Bush specifically named Iraq, Iran, and North Korea as constituting an "axis of evil, arming to threaten the peace of the world."[65] The policy was the realization of the 1992 Defense Planning Guidance document stating that the United States would retain the "preeminent responsibility for addressing selectively those wrongs" which threaten U.S. interests. The hegemons would finally have the chance to implement their vision.

While not labeling it as such at the time, Bush then put forward his new doctrine of preemption in the war against terrorism, evoking the title of Winston Churchill's first volume of the history of World War II, "The Gathering Storm," declaring, "I will not wait on events, while dangers gather. I will not stand by, as peril draws closer and closer." In a graduation address at West Point on June 1, 2002, President Bush refined the theory and made the case for preemption explicit, rejecting the cold war doctrines of containment and deterrence. "Our security will require all Americans to be forward-thinking and resolute, to be ready for preemptive action when necessary to defend our liberty and to defend our lives."[66]

The preemption doctrine was more a justification for toppling Saddam Hussein than a realistic policy of seeking out and preventing terrorism. As early as March, the administration was making Iraq the focus of its new doctrine. In a March 13 press conference, President Bush continued making the case against Saddam Hussein and Iraq. Repeating the now familiar accusations regarding chemical weapons and noncooperation with UN inspectors, Bush called Saddam Hussein "a problem," stating "we're going to deal with him. But the first stage is to consult with our allies and friends, and that's exactly what we're doing."[67]

In explaining the need for war, the administration typically cited Iraq's threat of weapons of mass destruction, noncompliance with inspectors, oppressive and belligerent regime, and gross human-rights abuses against the Iraqi people. United States officials belittled the risks of deposing Saddam and occupying Iraq. In March 2003, White House Press Secretary Ari Fleischer asserted that "the Iraqi people are yearning to be free and to be liberated, 500 people will rejoice" and that "there's no question" that we have evidence and information that Iraq has weapons of mass destruction, biological and chemical particularly.[68] They also greatly exaggerated the possible benefits to U.S. interests in the region. For instance, on August 26, 2002, Vice President Cheney, speaking in Nashville to the Veterans of Foreign Wars, explained, "Regime change in Iraq would bring about a number of benefits to the region. . . . Our ability to advance the Israeli–Palestinian peace process would be enhanced just as it was following the liberation of Kuwait in 1991. . . . Our goal would be an Iraq that has territorial integrity, a government that is democratic and pluralistic, a nation where the human rights of every ethnic and religious group are recognized and protected."[69] Rice's goal for Iraq was for it to become a democratic, self-governing, free-trading state to ensure a "balance of power that favours freedom" in the Middle East.[70]

President Bush continued his public campaign against Saddam Hussein, invoking the supposed al Qaeda connection regularly. "We know that Iraq and al Qaeda have had high-level contacts that go back a decade," Bush said in October 2002, "and we know that after September the 11th, Saddam Hussein's regime gleefully celebrated the terrorist attacks on America."[71] While Bush never claimed directly that Iraq was behind the al Qaeda attacks, he and his advisors relentlessly spoke of links between the two. The American people understood his message, with 53 percent believing throughout 2003 that Saddam Hussein was "personally involved" in the September 11 attacks, although the number dipped to 44 percent in 2004.[72] As one former four-star general quipped in July 2004, "Every intel group in the world thought he had chemical weapons. But not nukes and not al Qaeda. There are al Qaeda groups in Flint, Michigan. That doesn't mean Bush is in cahoots with bin Laden."[73]

By the fall of 2002, President Bush was nearing a decision to topple Saddam Hussein. Cheney, according to one former official, "was beyond hell-bent for action against Saddam. It was as if nothing else existed."[74]

Let's try the United Nations

The hegemons in Bush's administration strongly opposed a return of the UN inspectors, seeing the effort as weak and feckless and delaying the war. As Powell tried to convince the president to take the issue of Iraq back to the Security Council, Rumsfeld and Cheney sought to undermine the case.[75] Vice President Cheney declared on August 26, "Simply stated, there is no doubt that Saddam Hussein now has weapons of mass destruction. There is no doubt he is amassing them to use against our friends, against our allies, and against us. . . . Nothing in the last dozen years has stopped him." Cheney then linked Iraq to the September 11 attacks, "This nation will not live at the mercy of terrorists or terror regimes."[76]

Powell prevailed in the short term and President Bush took the issue to the United Nations—if only briefly. Addressing the United Nations the day after the one-year anniversary of September 11, President Bush challenged the UN to remain relevant by enforcing past resolutions insisting that Iraq disarm. Declaring Iraq "a threat to peace," Bush said the world now faced a test, with the United Nations "facing a difficult and defining moment. Are Security Council resolutions to be honored and enforced, or cast aside without consequence? Will the United Nations serve the purpose of its founding, or will it be irrelevant?"[77]

A diplomatic blitz

As the United States had done in 1991, it sought world support for action against Iraq and sought a new resolution on Iraq demanding Saddam Hussein disarm. Powell went to work immediately, meeting with over a dozen foreign ministers of major nations, including all fifteen members of the Security Council, as well as the foreign ministers of Japan, Canada, and Qatar, a gulf state whose cooperation would be essential to any military campaign.[78] But this time, the world was skeptical. Foreign leaders began to realize the message behind Bush's speech: the United States was prepared to go to war to oust Saddam Hussein. They started lining up in opposition, led by the French.

On September 16, the French foreign minister Dominique de Villepin adamantly argued against the U.S. call for war. "We feel that Europe needs the United States, but the United States also needs Europe. You just cannot go out and do things alone," he said. At a press conference at the UN, Russian foreign minister Igor S. Ivanov, sharing the same platform as Powell, contradicted Powell's view that the Security Council needed a new resolution on Iraq. On September 17, 2002, Ivanov said: "On the question of the work of the international inspectors and the work of UNMOVIC, from our standpoint we don't need any special resolution for that to occur. All the necessary resolutions, all of the necessary decisions about that are at hand."[79]

German chancellor Gerhard Schroeder vociferously opposed the war, in part to garner support among the German populace during his difficult reelection campaign. Schroeder was unequivocal declaring, "Under my leadership, Germany will not take part in an intervention in Iraq."[80] Critical not only of war with Iraq, but also of America's handling of the issue, "In the past it was always said: Before we do anything, we will consult with our principal allies—at least with those who take an active—very active—part in the fight against international terrorism. But consultation cannot mean that I get a phone call two hours in advance only to be told: We're going in. Consultation among grown-up nations has to mean not just consultation about the how and the when, but also about the whether."[81] The German justice minister Herta Daeubler-Gmelin went so far as to compare President Bush's tactics on Iraq to those of Hitler by saying, "Bush wants to divert attention from his domestic problems. It's a classic tactic. It's one that Hitler used."[82]

President Bush phoned French president Jacques Chirac on October 10 to make his pitch for the U.S. resolution. France wanted to slow the path toward war by proposing a two-step process. First, the Security Council would adopt one resolution strengthening the weapons inspection process without threatening force. Second, if Iraq blocked inspectors, the council would then vote on taking further action. French worries were not limited to Iraq. "Even beyond Iraq, we are talking about the future of the international order," said French UN ambassador Jean-David Levitte. He warned that relations between the major powers, rich and poor, Arab and non-Arab, were all affected by this decision.[83] Wary of becoming bogged down in a bureaucratic quagmire, the United States rejected the two-step process.

Negotiating UN resolutions is one of the most arcane processes in diplomacy. While at the UN, I often watched in amazement as officials spent hours haggling over the placement of commas, whether to use the word "or" or "and," then found myself doing exactly that. In the end, each nation interprets the resolution differently so in drafting, diplomats often cede certain ambiguities in order to garner broader support. This resolution was no different. The United States insisted that it include the term "material breach," which it could then use as a trigger for war. The United States also pressed for a firm timetable, specifying that Iraq must accept the new resolution within seven days and make a full report of all materials for weapons of mass destruction within thirty days. If Iraq did not comply with these guidelines, or if it blocked inspectors, it would be found in violation of the resolution. "We're hard core on these issues," said one U.S. official.[84] The Russians and French proposed their own resolution with much weaker provisions.

A breakthrough occurred November 7 following a phone conversation between Presidents Bush and Chirac. They agreed on two modifications to the U.S. resolution. First, the original draft of paragraph four stated that a "material breach of Iraq's obligations" would be reported to the Security Council "in accordance with paragraph 11 or 12." At the request of France and a number of other representatives, the "or" was replaced with "and" giving them confidence that the Security Council would have to convene again following a reported violation to authorize further action.[85] Secondly, the phrase "restore international peace and security" was changed to "secure international peace and security."[86] The changes were interpreted by France and others to mean that inspectors, not Washington, would determine whether Iraq had committed an infraction. These semantic changes assuaged French fears of U.S. "hidden triggers."

The next day, November 8, the UN Security Council unanimously approved UN Resolution 1441. The resolution stated that Iraq was in material breach of its international obligations under previous Security Council resolutions. Resolution 1441, however, gave Iraq "a final opportunity to comply with its disarmament obligations" by submitting to the Council "a currently accurate, full, and complete declaration of all aspects" of its weapons of mass destruction programs within thirty days of the resolution's adoption.[87] As a final warning, the resolution declared that failure to cooperate, by lying to the council or restricting inspections, would amount to a further material breach. Finally, the Security Council reiterated that Iraq had been warned "that it will face serious consequences as a result of its continued violations of its obligations."[88] In short, the resolution demanded unfettered access for UN inspectors to search for weapons of mass destruction throughout Iraq.[89] In a surprising turn, even Syria, the only Arab nation on the council, voted for the resolution.

The passage marked an impressive diplomatic victory for the Bush administration, and in particular Secretary of State Colin Powell. After almost eight weeks of negotiations, the United States had gotten what it wanted: a unanimous vote for a resolution demanding Iraq disarm. As with most UN resolutions, the language left room for different interpretations. The majority of the council's members stressed that the resolution did not authorize war. French president Chirac claimed that the resolution now gave Iraq "a chance to disarm peacefully."[90] To make their point even clearer, China, France, and Russia took the unusual step of issuing a separate statement insisting that it was the UN weapons inspectors' prerogative to determine whether Iraq had violated the resolution and up to the council to decide what to do next.[91] Immediately following the vote, President Bush sent the opposite message, declaring Iraq would face "the severest consequences" if it failed to comply with the resolution.[92]

While they had lost the battle not to go to the UN, the hegemons, led by Vice President Dick Cheney, lost no time in laying the foundation for war. Having no faith in the ability of UN inspectors to contain Iraq, Cheney set forth the public rational for toppling Hussein, always linking him to al Qaeda and the war on terrorism. For instance, on December 2, Cheney gave a speech at the Air National Guard Senior Leadership conference in which he stressed the connection between terrorism and confronting Iraq. "There is also a grave danger that al Qaeda or other terrorists will join with outlaw regimes that have these weapons to attack their common enemy, the United States of America. That is why confronting the threat posed by Iraq is not a distraction from the war on terror. It is absolutely crucial to winning the war on terror." Cheney declared, "Saddam Hussein is harboring terrorists and the instruments of terror" and claimed that "the war on terror will not be won till Iraq is completely and verifiably deprived of weapons of mass destruction."[93] Defense secretary Rumsfeld belittled the UN resolution just passed by the UN, saying "the minute that Saddam Hussein and his small ruling clique sense that they're out of danger, I suspect that they'll have no further incentive to [cooperate] and any UN inspection and disarmament efforts could then fail." Rumsfeld added that the United States was still preparing for the possibility of a post–Saddam Iraq.[94]

In Washington, the administration had also been preparing for war. On October 2, 2002, Congress overwhelmingly passed a Joint Resolution authorizing the use of force against Iraq. With the House of Representatives voting 296 to 133 and the Senate voting 77 to 23, the message was clear: when the president decided it was time for war, he had a preauthorized blank check. The most passionate opponent of the war, Senator Ted Kennedy, declared: "The question of whether our country should attack Iraq is playing out in the context of a more fundamental debate about how, when and where in the years ahead our country will use its unsurpassed military might. . . . The administration's doctrine is a call for 21st-century imperialism that no other nation can or should accept."[95] But the vast majority in Congress voted to give the president the authority he sought, largely because of WMD intelligence that later proved staggeringly wrong.

The return of the UN inspectors

The UN inspectors returned to Iraq on November 18, 2002, the first time since they were withdrawn in 1998. They spent the first week conducting examinations of sites they had previously visited before they left in 1998, and then moved on to more sensitive sites likely to meet Iraqi resistance. When Iraq sent in a twelve-thousand-page document ostensibly making a full disclosure of its programs and capabilities as required by the November resolution, observers dubbed it a "swiss cheese" declaration because it was so full of holes.

Why Iraq did not cooperate with the inspectors remains perplexing. As has become clear since the war, Iraq had no weapons of mass destruction, yet Saddam Hussein failed to account for what he had done with the stockpiles he had after the 1991 war. Had he done so during the mid-1990s, he might have succeeded in securing a lifting of UN sanctions. Had he done so following the UN vote in November 2002, he might have avoided the war. It was evident that Iraq would not meet the conditions demanded by the Security Council. Some posit that Saddam was misled by his sycophantic advisors who told him the weapons existed. Others suggest he believed that he could reassemble in weeks defunct programs that would really take years to rebuild. Others believe he was intent on maintaining the fiction as a deterrent to Iran. We may never fully understand his actions.

A key turning point came on December 19, when UN chief weapons inspector Hans Blix and the Director of the IAEA, Mohammed ElBaradei, made highly critical assessments of Iraqi cooperation to the Security Council, saying Iraq had failed to provide "much new significant information."[96] In response, Secretary Powell asserted that Iraq was in material breach of UN resolutions and that the world would not wait forever for Iraq to comply with its obligations, setting off an impromptu debate. Barely concealing his frustration, Russian ambassador to the UN, Sergei Lavrov, demanded that the Bush administration provide hard evidence to prove that Saddam Hussein was hiding weapons of mass destruction. "To say 'We know, but we wouldn't tell you,' is not something that is persuasive. This is not a poker game, when you hold your cards and call others' bluff."[97] But by early January 2004, the United States had made the decision to go to war. On January 14, President Bush expressed his growing impatience. "So far I haven't seen any evidence that he is disarming. Time is running out on Saddam Hussein. He must disarm. I'm sick and tired of games and deception."[98] The stage was set for a showdown.

The normally staid and courteous Security Council then broke into open verbal warfare. On January 20 Powell attended a Security Council session, called by French foreign minister Dominique de Villepin, intended to discuss terrorism and the progress of the Security Council Counter-Terrorism Committee that had been set up after the September 11 attacks. The meeting quickly deteriorated into an open debate over the possibility of war with Iraq. Departing from the meeting's stated agenda, several delegates condemned the possibility of war with Iraq. De Villepin summed up the impasse, "If war is the only way to resolve this problem, we are going down a dead end."[99]

Caught off-guard by the comments, Powell departed from his prepared remarks on terrorism and challenged the UN to remain relevant. Such a breach of UN etiquette not only deviated from the announced topic but also launched a broadside at a fellow state that was highly unusual.[100] As the former French ambassador in Washington, Francois Bujon de L'Estang explained, the session was a key turning point that went beyond Powell's pique at the ambush. "Chirac and his close associates believed Bush had made the decision to go to war. The UN had become a smoke screen."[101] Another senior French official close to Chirac said, "Chirac was preoccupied by the consequences of the war."[102] The divergence of the United States and France on Iraq had broken into the open. De Villepin announced that France would not support a resolution for military action against Iraq in the coming weeks.

Freedom fries

It was clear that the United States was losing any chance of keeping France in support of an early U.S. decision to go to war. That meant others would oppose the United States as well. The Russians would follow the French lead, not wanting to oppose the United States on its own. The Chinese would follow the Russian lead for the same reason. That meant that, of the key five permanent members of the council, the United States had only the British on its side. Passage of another resolution looked unlikely.

The French have long been a thorn in America's side on issues ranging from refusal to join NATO to U.S. and British frustration with French President Charles de Gaulle during World War II. "Oh, let's don't speak of him," said Churchill in 1943. "We call him Jeanne d'Arc and we're looking for some bishops to burn him."[103] Relations reached an historic nadir during the Washington–Paris disagreement over the war with Iraq. As one former British diplomat explained the French position, there was a "very strong wish on Chirac's side that the single superpower should not act unilaterally. It should be made to work within the system." He added that Chirac felt particularly strongly about Iraq, as he had been the architect of the close French-Iraq relationship in the seventies and eighties.[104]

In January 2003, Secretary of Defense Rumsfeld bluntly dismissed French and German opposition to the war, declaring those countries represented "old Europe."[105] Then, in March 2003, the U.S.–France quarrel reached a low when U.S. representatives decided to take on a real threat: the french fry. In February, a fast-food restaurant in North Carolina renamed its french fries "freedom fries" in a revolt against France's antiwar stance. The move inspired Representative Walter Jones (R-North Carolina) to circulate the idea in Congress. In a move that prompted fodder for late-night talk shows across the United States and Europe, Representative Bob Ney (R-Ohio), chairman of the Committee on House Administration, announced he was changing the name of "french fries" to "freedom fries," in the House of Representatives cafeteria.[106]

Nearing the end of the long road

In his second State of the Union Address before Congress, on January 28, 2003, Bush made it clear that he was ready to use force to disarm Saddam. "A brutal dictator, with a history of reckless aggression, with ties to terrorism, with great potential wealth, will not be permitted to dominate a vital region and threaten the United States."[107] Bush again linked Saddam

Hussein to al Qaeda, declaring that he "aids and protects terrorists, including members of al Qaeda. Secretly, and without fingerprints, he could provide one of his hidden weapons to terrorists or help them develop their own." The president argued that after September 11 America could no longer rely on containing Saddam Hussein as "chemical agents, lethal viruses and shadowy terrorist networks are not easily contained. Imagine those 19 hijackers with other weapons and other plans and this time armed by Saddam Hussein. . . . Trusting the sanity and restraint of Saddam Hussein is not a strategy and it is not an option."[108] Bush had just ordered thirty-seven thousand additional soldiers to the Persian Gulf region, bringing the number of troops deployed to the area to about one hundred twenty-five thousand since Christmas.[109]

Secretary of State Powell's now infamous briefing to the UN Security Council on February 5 failed to persuade his colleagues on the need to go to war. The slides and intercepted recordings were meant to dramatize the situation, as Adlai Stevenson had done when he showed the world the satellite photos of the Soviet missiles in Cuba. The majority of the council members believed Saddam Hussein could be contained. Much of Powell's presentation would later prove to be inaccurate; the CIA's analysis was shown to be flat wrong.

It is rare for UN and other international officials to openly challenge the United States in the Security Council. Yet, on February 14, 2003, fearing an imminent war, UN and IAEA inspectors Blix and ElBaradei did just that, directly disputing a number of Powell's assertions. Blix refuted Powell's statement that Iraq had been alerted to UN visits. He also questioned the U.S. analysis of some of the satellite photos Powell presented as evidence that Iraq was camouflaging its weapons program, saying the reported movement of prohibited weapons away from inspectors "could just as easily have been routine activity."[110] Similarly, ElBaradei reported that the IAEA had finished examining two thousand pages of documents seized from an Iraqi scientist's home on January 16 and had concluded that, thus far, his agency had no reason to believe Hussein had reconstituted a nuclear program.[111] In late January, I happened to be moderating a think-tank discussion with ElBaradei during his visit to New York. As we sat waiting for the program to begin, he commented, "you know, they are simply wrong about the nuclear issue."[112]

France responded to the inspectors by proposing that they report to the council again on March 14, an effort Washington ignored. Support for giving inspectors more time was so strong that remarks by French foreign minister de Villepin and Russian foreign minister Ivanov, each received applause, a rare occurrence in the council.

Over the next month, there were a flurry of proposals and counterproposals seeking to break the impasse. Yet, with Washington bent on war, there was never any real chance of holding the council together. In addition, the composition of the council had changed since the unanimous vote last November, with Washington losing key allies.[113] If Washington and the UK could convince the other three permanent members (France, China, and Russia) not to veto the resolution, they could secure passage of the resolution by a vote of nine members. Washington thus launched an offensive to win the seven additional votes it would need among the other non-permanent members of the council that might vote with the United States, Angola, Bulgaria, Cameroon, Guinea, Pakistan, and Spain looked like possibilities. Chile, Germany, Mexico, and Syria were not. The votes simply were not there.

Ignoring reality, the United States still made a quixotic diplomatic push toward gaining the nine Security Council votes necessary to pass a resolution declaring Iraq in breach of past UN resolutions and authorizing military force. The tentative strategy was to get nine votes lined up, which would then force France, China, and Russia to confront a majority in the council and thus perhaps refrain from using their veto. Some U.S. officials also stressed that a resolution passed even with a weak majority would carry the needed authority to go to war.

It's time to deal with the problem

National Security Advisor Condoleezza Rice then upped the ante. Speaking in front of a White House painting of Theodore Roosevelt, Rice admitted that the only way to avoid military confrontation at that point would be for Saddam Hussein to relinquish power of Iraq. "It's time to deal with the problem," Rice said.[114] When pressed on the subject, White House Press Secretary Ari Fleischer admitted that disarmament was the UN's goal while regime change was the president's.[115] Such statements killed what little chance remained for a second resolution. Blix called for more time, saying, "it would not take years, nor weeks, but months."[116]

Meanwhile, President Bush continued appealing to the American public for support, linking Iraq to September 11. In his radio address on March 8, Bush said Iraq "provides funding and training and safe haven to terrorists who would willingly deliver weapons of mass destruction against America and other peace-loving nations. The attacks of September the 11, 2001, showed what the enemies of America did with four airplanes. We will not wait to see what terrorists or terror states could do with weapons of mass destruction."[117]

To push back on Washington, the French, Russians, and Chinese advocated giving Iraq more time to show compliance with Resolution 1441. In another rare protest, UN Secretary-General Kofi Annan warned that if the

United States attacked Iraq without approval from the Security Council, it would be in violation of the UN charter. "If [members of the Security Council] fail to agree on a common position and action is taken without the authority of the Security Council, the legitimacy and support for any action will be seriously impaired."[118] Annan's remarks drew sharp criticism from Washington. Press secretary Fleischer responded by saying that "from a moral point of view," if the United Nations failed to support the new resolution, it will have "failed to act once again," as it did in the case of Kosovo and Rwanda.[119]

Valiant UK effort

As it became clear the United States' diplomatic effort was failing and war was imminent, the British made one last attempt to keep the council together. The UK representative, Sir Jeremy Greenstock, combined the U.S. half-willingness to put forward benchmarks for Iraq's compliance and the French, Russian, and Blix's proposal for additional time for inspections, and suggested a set of specific tests for Iraq within a tight timeframe.[120]

In the end, Washington agreed to putting forward six tests to Iraq but would only agree to extend the deadline for Iraq to disarm to March 24 at the very latest. As Greenstock later explained, "At the time, this was being rushed in a way that didn't allow for a wider coalition, and it still feels that way. . . . The whole thing would have been handled better if we had that extra six months." Greenstock explained that regarding his benchmarks proposal, "Blair was looking for the end of April, the Canadians came back with twenty-eight days. But the worry in Washington was that any delay would lead to an endless series of half performances. Deep down, they [the Americans] weren't into benchmarks. They just wanted to get on with it."[121]

As one senior French diplomat explained, "Success was possible without war. With a little more patience and cohesion between Western countries and Arabs, we could have ousted Saddam Hussein without a war. The U.S. had all the troops there. If we had maintained them, saying we want this guy out, maybe it could have been possible. Force was a last resort. France did not exclude the use of force. . . Saddam was in a box for 10 years. He could not move one finger. We were ready to accept a consensus on two more months, even one month if the inspectors recommended it."[122] When asked if he could see France ever supporting the war, Ambassador Bujon de L'Estang, replied, "Yes, probably if complete bad faith had been clearly established."[123]

Whether the French would have ever joined the United States in another war against Saddam Hussein is difficult to judge. But had Washington been willing to agree to keep the UN inspection process going for three to six more months, it possibly could have kept the council united, or at least had a better understanding of the threat Saddam actually posed—or did not pose. It certainly would have had much broader support for the war.

Instead, Washington abandoned diplomacy and went to war.

Operation Iraqi Freedom

The second war with Iraq began on March 19, 2003. In preparation for ground troops, the American and British air forces bombed specific military targets and dropped millions of warning pamphlets; civilians were urged to avoid military targets and soldiers were encouraged to surrender. The next day three hundred thousand coalition troops invaded.[124] Air strikes initially targeted the northern cities of Baghdad, Kirkuk, and Mosul, with troops working their way up from Kuwait toward the capital. In the south, coalition forces focused on seizing the oil fields near Basra.[125] Because the administration failed to win Turkish approval for deployment of U.S. forces in its territory, they had to transit the Sunni Triangle, an area traditionally loyal to Saddam Hussein that harbored strong anti-American sentiments. Initially, Iraqi opposition was thin, with many instances of surrender. Hussein's regime was even more of a house of cards than most people had expected. U.S. and coalition forces entered Baghdad on April 5, 2003.

The man who perhaps best exemplifies the regime's lack of touch with reality was the minister of information, Mohammad Al-Sahaf. As U.S. forces entered Baghdad, he repeatedly insisted there were no U.S. troops in Iraq. When CNN and other networks filmed Iraqi soldiers surrendering to American forces, Al-Sahaf alleged the surrendering men were not Iraqi, saying "Who were these people?" and "Where were they?" When coalition forces were broadcast in armored columns he implied that the images were false, being filmed outside Iraq; "Well, where is this desert? Which desert are they in?"[126] Eventually, CNN ran split scenes of him making these claims and U.S. soldiers clearly in Baghdad. Al-Sahaf became the butt of late-night comedy talk shows.

On April 10, 2003, President Bush delivered a message translated into Arabic directly to the people of Iraq: "The goals of our coalition are clear and limited. We will end a brutal regime. . . . Coalition forces will help maintain law and order, so that Iraqis can live in security. We will respect your great religious traditions. . . . We will help you build a peaceful and representative government that protects the rights of all citizens. And then our military forces will leave. Iraq will go forward as a unified, independent and sovereign nation that has regained a respected place in the world."

American, UK, and other coalition forces successfully overthrew the Iraqi regime. Saddam Hussein was eventually found hiding in a hole in the ground on December 13, 2003, and was captured. Winning the peace, however, would prove much more difficult.

10

The Hegemons'
Failed Peace

*No one starts a war—or rather, no one in his senses ought to do so—without
first being clear in his mind what he intends to achieve by that war and how
he intends to conduct it.*

—Carl von Clausewitz

On August 19, 2003, the United Nations Special Envoy to Iraq Sergio
Vieira de Mello and a number of his staff members were meeting in his office
in Baghdad with Arthur Helton of the Council on Foreign Relations and
Gil Loescher from the London-based International Institute for Strategic
Studies.[1] De Mello was a rising star in the United Nations, openly discussed
in the hallways as a possible successor to Secretary-General Kofi Annan.
Disarmingly handsome with white stylishly short hair, fit and athletic, always
cheerful, oozing enthusiasm, and down-to-earth in the presence of both
kings and peasants, he had risen through the ranks of the UN staff, first as
a humanitarian worker, rising to head the United Nations Office for the
Coordination of Humanitarian Affairs in 1998. Annan had next tapped de
Mello to run the mission in Kosovo and then East Timor.

On September 12, 2002, Annan appointed de Mello to the coveted
post of UN High Commissioner for Human Rights, based in Geneva. He
had become one of Annan's most trusted aides. The secretary-general valued his astute political judgment, constant optimism, and his tireless commitment to getting the job done. He was also well liked throughout the
organization. De Mello was irrepressibly upbeat about living in war zones
and was regularly chided for always being immaculately dressed, without a
hair out of place, in the midst of refugee camps and some of the most des-
olate spots on earth. De Mello and I had become friends during my tenure
at the U.S. mission to the UN in New York. We had kayaked to the Statue
of Liberty together, with him pushing me to "paddle harder!" the whole

way. He had asked me to join him in East Timor as his deputy. While I declined the opportunity, we had stayed in touch.

Following the overthrow of Saddam Hussein, Kofi Annan had turned once again to de Mello, asking him to take up the difficult mission of running the United Nations operation in Iraq. At the time, the Bush administration was openly derisive of the United Nations, refusing to give it a significant role in the political development of the post–Saddam era. Yet, Annan understood he would need a skilled diplomat in Baghdad and, despite de Mello's criticisms of the Bush administration's treatment of the prisoners held at the U.S. detention center at Guantanamo Bay, Cuba, he had charmed President Bush when they first met at the White House in March 2003.[2] De Mello arrived in Iraq in early June, bringing with him some of the best and the brightest staff from UN headquarters in New York. The UN's formal role in Iraq had been restricted to primarily humanitarian endeavors, with little support from the coalition authorities that marginalized the United Nations. De Mello, however, was able to forge a good relationship with the head of the U.S. Coalition Provisional Authority (CPA), L. Paul Bremer, and was becoming a close political advisor to him. Annan had promised de Mello he would return to his post as high commissioner for human rights in Geneva after four months.

In July, de Mello briefed the Security Council on the situation in Iraq, and while he said that the Iraqi Governing Council "can be viewed as broadly representative of the various constituencies in Iraq,"[3] de Mello warned that the Americans and the British must first restore security. "In the current context, the coalition has the primary obligation of restoring and maintaining security, law, and order. Iraq today finds itself in an awkward situation: post-conflict, but with hostilities occurring every day; awash with weapons, many legitimately present, many more not; and under military occupation."[4]

On August 19, 2003, at 4:30 P.M. on a cloudless afternoon in Baghdad, a truck filled with explosives barreled through a wire fence surrounding the Canal Hotel, which had been transformed into the UN's local headquarters, and smashed into the building, just beneath the third-floor office of Sergio Vieira de Mello. The explosion shattered the windows and collapsed the ceiling of the third floor, crushing most of the people in the room. The force of the explosion thrust de Mello and the others to the first floor, burying them in the building's rubble. Sergio de Mello was wounded and trapped underneath the rubble for nearly three hours.[5]

On that day, I was sitting in a television studio in Jacksonville, Florida, where I had gone to write this book and recuperate from a recent foot operation. I had been invited to discuss Iraq on a variety of news shows and had just commented on how the United States would be well advised to engage the United Nations more seriously. I had finished the interviews when the producer asked if I could stay on for a minute. Then I saw the picture of the UN complex in rubble on the screen. My heart sank.

I quickly called a friend at the UN in New York who said Sergio had been making phone calls right after the blast, but that no one had heard from him in the last fifteen minutes. My friend was worried. Somehow, I knew de Mello would survive; it was inconceivable that the man with unbounded energy would do anything but climb smiling out of the rubble asking what he could do to help others. Then the news came. Sergio Vieira de Mello had died.

The producer asked if I would comment on his death. While feeling physically ill, I wanted to pay tribute to my friends. Fifty-five-year-old de Mello and twenty-one other UN staff had been killed, including one of the most talented UN staffers, Rick Hooper, also a friend. I put the earpiece back in and sat down in the chair facing the camera. "These were the best and the brightest of the UN system," I said. They were in Iraq with no political agenda. Most of them were personally opposed to the war. They were just there to help the Iraqi people and to see such horrible carnage with such fine servants is a shock to everyone." I then called on the United States to return to the UN for a new resolution and additional troops, pointing out that India had offered seventeen thousand troops.

It is hard to overstate the impact on Kofi Annan and the United Nations community of the death of de Mello and his colleagues, as well as the one hundred fifty who were severely wounded and disfigured.[6] It was the UN's September 11. Today, pictures of de Mello and his fallen colleagues still hang in the halls of the United Nations, as well as around the world, including in de Mello's favorite restaurant in Geneva. On October 30, Annan pulled all non-Iraqi UN personnel from the country and has since resisted U.S. efforts to send them back. He will not do so until security conditions improve.

The secretary-general is deeply angry at himself for having sent de Mello to Baghdad, knowing the United States had fundamentally misunderstood the politics of the situation. Until August 19, 2003, the United Nations personnel considered their political neutrality as protection from attack. While the UN had known the situation was dangerous, de Mello and others believed they were less vulnerable because of their blue flag and white vehicles that had always represented "good." Yet, the Iraqis so resented the U.S. occupation that they made no distinction among foreigners. The United Nations was an easy target. An independent panel investigating the bombing later found that, "The UN security management system failed in its mission to provide adequate security to U.N. staff in Iraq," calling the procedures "sloppy" and that noncompliance with security rules was commonplace."[7]

While the UN, including de Mello, was careless about its own security, the violence was largely triggered by the hegemons' naive and ideological decisions following the war. The United States had made colossal mistakes on almost every key decision following the overthrow of Saddam Hussein. The president and his top advisors believed the myth of the hegemons that the United States could act alone and bend the world to its will. The cost has been high in terms of UN, American, coalition, and Iraqi blood and of American treasure.

Mission accomplished

No action symbolized the administration's failure to grasp the gravity of occupying Iraq more than President Bush's now infamous visit to the USS *Abraham Lincoln* aircraft carrier on May 1, 2003. Bounding out of the cockpit in a pilot's flight suit, Bush stood in front of a banner that read "MIS-SION ACCOMPLISHED," and declared the war over. "My fellow Americans, major combat operations in Iraq have ended. In the battle of Iraq, the United States and our allies have prevailed."[8]

While 138 American soldiers had died in the war as of Bush's carrier appearance, by November 2004, nearly one thousand more soldiers had lost their lives and more than 7,700 had been wounded. Although the Pentagon does not track Iraqi deaths, one estimate put the Iraqi civilian deaths as high as one hundred thousand,[9] while others suggest that closer to thirty thousand had been killed during and after the war.[10]

Understanding the mistakes the Bush administration made offers important lessons on how the policy must be changed, as well as important lessons for American policy in the future. The reality of Iraq ended the hegemons' supremacy within the administration and paved the way for the beginning of a more balanced, reasoned U.S. foreign policy. Years of policy ruminations on how the United States could unilaterally shape the world to its image fell apart as chaos reined in the streets of Baghdad.

A year into the U.S. occupation of Iraq, law and order remained elusive, the installed interim government was neither representative nor considered legitimate, nor did the United States have a workable plan to end its occupation. The Bush administration had failed to anticipate that the Iraqis would deeply resent the American-led occupation and that they would begin a guerrilla campaign against the foreign presence. Stunningly, virtually no planning had been done for the key challenges the United States would face, including providing security for Iraqis, developing a government that would be seen as legitimate in the eyes of Iraqis, and creating a capable Iraqi police and military which could take over the task of security from American forces.

The president and his advisors deeply believed their own rhetoric about how only good things would blossom from an overthrow of Saddam Hussein. Out of government for a decade or more, the hegemons had fumed over the failure of the first President Bush to topple Saddam Hussein.

Harshly dismissive of peacekeeping and nation building, the administration believed it could simply will the Iraqis a stable democracy. Having convinced themselves theirs was a just goal, Bush, Rice, Cheney, Rumsfeld, Wolfowitz, and others took for granted that the Iraqis would welcome the overthrow of Saddam Hussein and greet American troops as had the people of Europe in the Second World War.

While U.S. policy has slowly shifted course, during the first year of occupation the United States made a number of costly mistakes because of the misguided hegemonic ideology of those in charge of Iraq policy. With Colin Powell largely sidelined, Secretary of Defense Donald Rumsfeld, his deputy Paul Wolfowitz, and Vice President Cheney largely drove the decision making. National Security Advisor Condoleezza Rice did little to coordinate the Pentagon's activities with those of the State Department. The result was a disaster for American policy in Iraq and the region, at great cost in terms of lives, money, and American interests around the world. The key mistakes involved a failure to provide for adequate security, a failure to grasp the complexity of the Iraqi political situation and to develop an interim government that had legitimacy, and a failure to involve the international community, particularly the United Nations, in the full range of post-invasion challenges.

First exhausting all available alternatives

Winston Churchill once observed, "The Americans will always do the right thing . . . after they've exhausted all the alternatives." Nowhere is that more true than in Iraq. While by mid-2004, the United States had shifted course, its early efforts were inexcusably ham-handed and shortsighted. For the second time in two years, the administration, which so adamantly opposed peacekeeping, undertook a major operation following Afghanistan. While stridently denying the U.S. interests in failed or failing states, it suddenly was occupying two. It quickly became clear that America had neither the troops nor the legitimacy to accomplish its goals through unilateral force. The administration's most egregious error was the failure to provide adequate security.

While the overthrow of Saddam Hussein was a successful, if relatively simple, military operation, the Bush administration failed to grasp the magnitude of the difficult challenges of postwar Iraq. Secretary of Defense Donald Rumsfeld had long believed in higher-tech, smaller armies and insisted on testing his unproven theory in Iraq. Dismissive of peacekeeping and nation building, Rumsfeld fundamentally misjudged the task at hand in Iraq. Rejecting the hard lessons learned during the 1990s of the need for a strong, robust peacekeeping force in the immediate aftermath of a war, Rumsfeld sent a grossly inadequately sized force to Iraq of one hundred fifty thousand to keep the peace. While estimates of the correct size vary, had Iraq been provided with the same per capita troop density as had been sent to the Balkans, there would have been several hundred thousand U.S. troops on the ground.[11] In fact, before the war, Army Chief of Staff Eric Shinseki told Congress that "several hundred thousand soldiers" would be needed to secure Iraq in the postwar period. Rumsfeld and Deputy Secretary of Defense Paul Wolfowitz briskly dismissed Shinseki's estimations as "wildly off the mark." Soon after, Pentagon officials leaked the name of Shinseki's replacement, fifteen months before his term was slated to end, essentially making him an early lame duck.[12]

The impact of shortchanging troop deployment and poor planning was felt immediately on the ground. One key lesson of the peacekeeping missions of the 1990s is the need to control looting in the early stages of deployment. Predictably, following the ouster of Saddam Hussein, looters took to the streets. The widespread lawlessness resulted in millions of dollars of damage to the nation's remaining infrastructure, caused the destruction of priceless national monuments, and impeded the delivery of vital humanitarian supplies.[13] Shops were destroyed, homes were pillaged, valuable state assets and cultural institutions were destroyed, and priceless artifacts were stolen. For instance, the Iraqi National Museum, home to the priceless tablets on which is engraved the code of Hammurabi and the original text of the *Epic of Gilgamesh*, was plundered by looters and vandals who stole and destroyed artifacts up to seven thousand years old.[14] Many Iraqis were enraged that U.S. forces took no action to stop the looters or to protect key national monuments and museums. Said one Iraqi archaeologist, "If a country's civilization is looted, as ours has been here, its history ends. . . . Please remind [President Bush] that he promised to liberate the Iraqi people, but that this is not a liberation, this is a humiliation."[15]

There are provisions within the international laws of warfare, specifically in the Hague and Geneva conventions, that protect sites of cultural importance, such as ancient monuments and museums, but Secretary Rumsfeld eschewed responsibility, saying, "Bad things happen in life, and people do loot."[16] He also blamed the media for exaggerating the situation. "The images you are seeing on television you are seeing over and over and over, and it's the same picture of some person walking out of some building with a vase, and you see it twenty times, and you think, 'My goodness, were there that many vases? Is it possible that there were that many vases in the whole country?'"[17] Nevertheless, potential insurgents were emboldened by an apparently unresponsive U.S. presence.

It was the job of the civilian leadership of the administration to ensure that planning for the postwar period was done right. In fairness to the Pentagon's military leadership, it was consumed by planning for a worst-case scenario of the war. One former four-star general commented that General Tommy Franks, commander in chief of U.S. Central Command, "had to focus on a war plan, involving the possibility of torched oil wells, chemical weapons against the troops, and chemical SCUDs being launched into Israel. There were some rather severe things that could have gone wrong. . . . Imagine being around a table talking about these scenarios and someone speaking up and saying, 'I'm worried about the looting of museums.' He would have been told to get out of the room."[18]

Despite the growing violence, Rumsfeld *withdrew* troops from Iraq. He reduced the one hundred fifty thousand U.S. troops deployed in Iraq in May 2003 to only one hundred fifteen thousand by February 2004.[19] Allies predictably declined to make up the difference. The failure by the Bush administration to gain international support for the war kept the major powers out of Iraq. In fact, the "international coalition" referred to repeatedly by the Bush administration was largely a United States–UK effort. The forty-nine-nation coalition, including Afghanistan, the Dominican Republic, Honduras, Palau, the Marshall Islands, Mongolia, Rwanda, and Tonga, looked far more like a list of nations that *received* support from the United States than a list of those that could provide it.[20] Of the 162,000 troops in Iraq a year after the war, 138,000 were American, 8,500 were British, with only 33 of the 48 coalition countries contributing approximately 15,500 troops, largely from Australia, Italy, Poland, Ukraine, and the Netherlands.[21] A year after the war, nearly nine out of ten military personnel in Iraq were American. By the fall of 2004, a number of these had pulled their troops out of the coalition.[22]

In one of its more ill-advised efforts, the administration sought in the fall of 2003 to invite Turkish troops into Iraq. Another basic lesson of peacekeeping is that neighboring troops are not well suited for peacekeeping, as they almost always have political problems that keep them from being, or being perceived as, neutral. Turkey has a particularly difficult relationship with the Kurdish population, following centuries of opposing Kurdish efforts to establish an independent state and discrimination of its own Kurdish minority. It should have come as no surprise that the Kurdish leadership balked at the U.S. proposal to send Turkish troops to Iraq. As Jalal Talabani, a key Kurdish leader, said, "No one wants [Turkish troops] here. We call for all neighboring countries to stay out, not only Turkey, but Syria, Iran, Jordan, Kuwait, and Saudi Arabia."[23] Adnan Pachachi, a Sunni member of the interim Iraqi Governing Council (IGC), agreed: "No troops from any of our neighbors, please."[24] Yet, the United States pressured the fragile Turkish government into agreeing to send troops and on March 20, the Turkish parliament passed a law that would allow thousands of Turkish troops to enter Iraqi territory.[25] As Turkish troops began to move into northern Iraq, the U.S. belatedly recognized the political problem, shifted its position, and began urging Turkey to refrain from doing so.

Short-staffed, the coalition forces' inability to maintain security and protect the Iraqi borders proved costly in terms of the deaths of U.S. soldiers, international aid workers, and Iraqi and foreign civilians. In addition to the coalition deaths following the end of the war and the 22 UN workers killed in the bombing that took de Mello's life, as many as 214 foreign civilians had been killed as of November 2004.[26] As one study put it, "Every U.S., allied, and Iraqi casualty since late April [2003 was] to some extent the fault of inadequate military preparation for the tasks at hand."[27] The violence continued to escalate.

A deadly insurgency

Throughout the summer and fall of 2003, Iraqi insurgents increased their guerrilla attacks against the coalition forces. Reminiscent of anti-French tactics immortalized in Pontecorvo's *Battle of Algiers*, the insurgency consisted primarily of hit-and-run ambushes, often in broad daylight, using rocket-propelled grenades and small machine guns. A number of American soldiers were assassinated in public areas at close range.[28] The winter of 2003 brought a shift in the insurgents' tactics, whereby they significantly expanded their attacks to include any Iraqis seen to be cooperating with Americans, such as journalists, translators, and police officers. During the initial postwar period, the Bush administration made important progress on the provision of basic services to the Iraqi people, yet the insurgency threatened this accomplishment.

Increasingly, the attacks were attributed to Abu Musab al Zarqawi, a terrorist the administration had linked to al Qaeda in its effort to justify the war. In response to the growing violence in late spring 2003, the United States began to strike back at suspected insurgents. The first major strike, "Operation Desert Scorpion," was launched on June 15, 2003, to defeat remaining pockets of resistance throughout the country.[29] Insurgents continued to intensify their attacks on coalition forces, killing an average of more than sixty coalition soldiers a month. Although the United States had overthrown a hated dictator, Iraqis increasingly resented the American and other foreign presence. The United States had no plan to hand over authority to the Iraqis. As with Somalia more than a decade before, rather than address the political causes of the insurgency, the United States increasingly struck back militarily.

One particular danger was posed by Moktada al Sadr, a Shia leader who sought to rival the most popular Shia leader, Grand Ayatollah Ali al Sistani. He commanded a militia of fifteen hundred to three thousand, although for a time, al Sadr called for nonviolent demonstrations against the U.S.–led occupation. On March 28, 2004, however, the U.S. forces closed his newspaper, *al Hawza*, accusing it (accurately) of spreading lies that enflamed anti-American sentiment. On April 3, coalition authorities arrested one of his aides for the killing of a rival cleric a year earlier and said they intended to arrest al Sadr on similar charges. Literally overnight, al Sadr's rhetoric turned violent. He demanded an immediate U.S. withdrawal from Iraq, calling on his supporters to "Terrorize your enemy, as we cannot remain silent over its violations."[30] What followed were the first large-scale assaults by Shias on U.S. forces and the commandeering of police stations in Sadr City—a neighborhood of Baghdad controlled by al Sadr—and several southern cities. The uprising jarred assumptions that Shias would not revolt and also suggested a surprising Shia-Sunni alliance in opposing the U.S. occupation.[31] People on the streets yelled. "We are now controlled by Sadr. The Americans should stay out."[32]

Reminiscent of the failed raids in Somalia a decade ago, on May 5, U.S. forces shifted their attention to "capture or kill" Sadr and eject his militia from the Shia holy city of Najaf, located ninety miles south of Baghdad. In Najaf, the goal was to avoid the sacred shrines in the city center, the cemetery, and civilian casualties. The U.S. strategy failed. Militants used the cemetery to stage and launch attacks, so eventually U.S. forces knocked down two hundred feet of its wall, angering local citizens. Al Sistani aides, who had generally called for cooperation with U.S. troops, now called for the immediate withdrawal of U.S. forces from Najaf. Eighty-one per cent of Iraqis polled had an improved opinion of Sadr in May from three months earlier.[33] Security broke down not only in Sadr city, a neighborhood of Baghdad, but in many cities throughout Iraq.

By early September 2004, the U.S. forces had lost control of, or abandoned, not only the cities of Karbala and Najaf, but also the cities of Falluja, Samarra, Bukhara, and Ramadi, which became "no go" cities for U.S. forces; these cities were under the clear control of insurgents. One observer noted that, while it was commonplace for Iraqis to prefer the Americans leave their cities, "What is new, however, is that the Americans, in certain cases, appear to agree or have decided that the cost to prove otherwise would be too high."[34] Kidnapping of foreigners surged during the first eighteen months of the insurgency, with over 150 foreigners kidnapped, at least 32 of whom have been killed. The insurgents began the gruesome practice of beheading foreigners, often on camera. Most of these murders were attributed to al Zarqawi.

Violence against American forces surged in April 2004 to its highest level since the war began in 2003, with over 130 U.S. troops and roughly 700 Iraqi civilian deaths.[35] One independent study found that two months after the United States transferred sovereignty, Iraq remained embroiled in an insurgency, with security problems overshadowing other efforts to rebuild Iraq's fragile society in the areas of governance and participation, economic opportunity, services, and social well-being.[36] The United States was forced to shift $3.4 billion from the reconstruction of Iraq to security.[37]

As early as April 2004, the administration admitted it had not anticipated the level of insurgency. For instance, Secretary of Defense Rumsfeld said he "certainly would not have estimated that we would have had the number of individuals lost that we have had lost in the last week."[38] Secretary of State Colin Powell said the United States had "miscalculated the strength of insurgents in Iraq" and that it was "clear we did not expect an insurgency that would be this strong."[39] President Bush also acknowledged that he had made a "miscalculation of what the conditions would be" in a postwar Iraq.[40] The lack of security threatened the Bush administration's goal of a secure Iraq. Elections scheduled for early 2005 were at risk.

By the spring of 2004, it was obvious to all but the hegemons that the United States was failing in Iraq. President Bush described the insurgency in April 2004 as isolated acts of terrorism, claiming that "most of Iraq is relatively stable."[41] The administration also sought to hide images of the returning coffins. While all of Italy participated in the mourning of the nineteen Italian soldiers killed on November 12, 2003, the Bush administration banned any television coverage of the returning bodies of U.S. soldiers. Bush declined to travel to Dover, Delaware, to pay respect to the returning dead.

Bremer takes charge

A few months before the war, retired lieutenant general Jay Garner was put in charge of the Office of Reconstruction and Humanitarian Assistance, which would administer the postwar reconstruction effort (and would later become the Coalition Provisional Authority). In early March 2003, Garner traveled to the still shell-shocked United Nations and met with Deputy Secretary-General Louis Frechette and other top officials to discuss postwar aid and reconstruction.[42] While Garner was congenial and likeable, UN officials were taken aback by his failure to grasp the size of the task ahead. As one senior UN official described the meeting, "I was left with the impression that Garner was planning to go in as soon as possible, 'fix things,' and get out, all with the assurance and the flair of an American general."[43]

Garner rightly sought to put Iraqis quickly in charge of their own government. On April 15 in the southeastern city of Ur, a cradle of Iraqi civilization, Garner brought together seventy local Iraqi leaders from several tribal, religious, and civil factions. The group called for an immediate end to the looting and lawlessness and agreed to work together to create democracy in Iraq.[44] Two weeks later, the momentum continued as three hundred local leaders met on April 28 and agreed to reconvene in one month to do something that would have gotten them killed only two months before—select a representative government for the people of Iraq. Looking back one year later, General Garner reflected, "My preference was to put the Iraqis in charge as soon as we [could], and do it with some form of elections . . . I just thought it was necessary to rapidly get the Iraqis in charge of their own destiny."[45]

Garner, however, never gained the support of the Pentagon and he was abruptly forced out. His tenure was marred by controversy and agency infighting between the Pentagon and State Department, both with very different approaches to the postwar Iraq. Powell pressed for more international involvement; Rumsfeld and Wolfowitz insisted on shunning the UN. Wolfowitz and others at the Pentagon were critical of Garner's efforts at Iraqi reconstruction, primarily his failure to restore adequately and rapidly vital electricity, water, and sewage operations. Many charged that the infighting and differing views among the various U.S. agencies compromised Garner's chance of success. As one former CPA official put it, "In fairness, they never gave him a chance."[46] On May 6, 2003, President Bush abruptly replaced Garner with L. Paul Bremer III, a civilian and seasoned diplomat, ostensibly to speed reconstruction. Bremer, who had studied at Yale and Harvard, joined the U.S. Foreign Service in 1966, served as President Reagan's ambassador at large for counterterrorism, and had worked in the private sector since 1989, including as the managing director of Kissinger Associates and as head of a consulting firm. He assumed control of the U.S. Coalition Provisional Authority on May 12, 2003.[47]

The CPA was the temporary governing body, created by the United States and designated by the United Nations as the lawful government of Iraq. Bremer's powers in Iraq were absolute although somewhat murkey. "The lack of a clear, authoritative, and unambiguous statement about how this organization was established and its status . . . leaves open many questions, particularly regarding the area of oversight and accountability." The CPA appeared to be accountable only to the U.S. president and reported to the secretary of Defense. Ambassador Bremer's salary was paid by the U.S. Army.[48]

Bremer brought great energy, drive, and leadership to the job, working eighteen-hour days, and was constantly on the move. Jeremy Greenstock had left the UN in July and gone to Iraq in September 2003 as the UK's special representative for Iraq and Bremer's UK counterpart in the CPA. Sir Jeremy Greenstock said, "Jerry's dynamism kept the show on the road." Bremer inherited a difficult situation in which key decisions had already been made, such as the limited role of the United Nations, the lack of postwar planning, and the decision to send too few troops to Iraq. In addition, Bremer had little influence over the actions of the U.S. military, "that was Rumsfeld and Wolfowitz territory," Greenstock explained. "Overall, Bremer succeeded in handing power over to the Iraqis under very difficult circumstances. For that important achievement he deserves great credit."[49]

While Bremer brought great skill, charm, and leadership to the job, he also fell into the hegemonic myth. Close to the hegemons in Washington, especially Rumsfeld and Wolfowitz, he sought to make their myth a reality. In doing so, he made serious mistakes, particularly regarding security and in misjudging much of the Iraqi political situation.

Disbanding the Iraqi army and the banning of the Baathists

On May 23, 2003, Bremer dissolved the four hundred thousand–strong Iraqi army, a decision he apparently took without even consulting the joint Chiefs of Staff at the Pentagon.[50] Overnight, Bremer unleashed hundreds of thousands of angry—and armed—young men into the volatile Iraqi landscape. The move destroyed an important national organization and marginalized many Sunnis who had made clear their willingness to participate in the rebuilding of a new Iraq. Anti–United States sentiment ballooned among the very men who could have helped to mitigate the Iraqi people's perception of the United States as an imperial occupier.

As one report found, "Hundreds of thousands of former soldiers, most of whom had displayed no loyalty to the regime and many of whom were too young to have participated in the atrocities in which the army played a part, found themselves without pay, future, and honor. . . . The CPA's decision to undo this last remaining symbol of sovereignty and national unity contributed to the perception that the liberators were in fact occupiers."[51] As Iyad Allawi, a Shia member of the IGC who would later be chosen to run the transitional government in Iraq, observed in October 2003: "Any American-led military presence, even if complemented by the United Nations, will never have the credibility and legitimacy that the Iraqi Army has among the people."[52] The United States in part recognized its mistake when it agreed in June 2003 to pay monthly stipends of between $50 to $150 per month, depending on rank, to approximately two hundred fifty thousand Iraqi soldiers who had previously been dismissed.[53]

The disbanding of the army not only alienated a significant portion of the Iraqi population, it also deprived U.S. forces of hundreds of thousands of trained, locally knowledgeable reinforcements who could have helped quell the growing violence and patrol the borders. Absent the help of the Iraqi army, it fell entirely upon coalition forces—the vast majority of which were American—to maintain security throughout Iraq and protect the country's 2,200-mile border, much of which is shared with Iran and Syria.

The United States did begin to address the need for a local police and security force—a key prerequisite for the U.S. departure from Iraq. On August 8, 2003, the Coalition Provisional Authorities (CPA) created the New Iraqi Army (NIA) that together with new police, civil corps, border patrol, and facilities protection divisions would comprise an entirely new Iraqi security force.[54] Political problems immediately emerged. Many Iraqis were outraged by the recruitment of former security and intelligence officers who were known to be loyal to Saddam Hussein. Tensions between Shias, Sunnis, and Kurds complicated the process. For instance, some soldiers refused to patrol in the Sunni triangle—known for its loyalty to Saddam Hussein—and Kurdish recruits refused to serve in any Arab areas at all.[55]

These problems were compounded by the CPA's failure to provide adequate pay, training, and equipment to new soldiers. By the end of March 2004, only 19 percent of the 80,000 new police officers—and 68 percent of the entire new security force numbering 211,000—had received *any* training at all.[56] Only two months after being recruited, half of the NIA's first battalion resigned, largely over frustrations that they were being paid less than their police counterparts.[57] And in the NIA's first real test, during heavy fighting in April 2004, General John Abizaid, the top U.S. general in Iraq, observed, "Some of them did very well and some of them did not . . . a number of units, both in the police force and also in the [Iraqi Civil Defense Corps] did not stand up to the intimidators . . . and that was a great disappointment to us."[58]

Nonetheless, the establishment of the new Iraqi security forces is the key exit strategy for U.S. forces from Iraq. While the United States will no doubt ultimately succeed in establishing such a force, it will take years until there is a capable domestic force that can maintain at least basic law and order. Until that time, American troops are in Iraq to stay.

Another key mistake was Bremer's decision to ban members of Saddam Hussein's Baath Party from participating in the new government. Overnight, the decision eliminated the very pool of trained and talented Iraqis available to run the country. Created long before Saddam Hussein, the origin of the Baath Party can be traced to the populist movements driven by the rise of Arab nationalism and the desire for social change.[59] Under Hussein, membership in the party was a *sine qua non* for most jobs in his regime. Thus, some Iraqis had been long-standing members of the party, with little affection for Hussein. Others joined it out of necessity for the opportunity for employment that membership offered. Lastly, there were Hussein loyalists who willingly joined the party as a way of cozying up to the dictator. United States policy from the start should have been to bar these sycophants, not all Baath Party members. Nearly a year into the policy, on April 22, 2004, the United States reversed course and eased the ban on former Baathists in the Iraqi government.[60] But during that year, the United States had lost critical time in developing talent for the new Iraqi government.

Washington also fundamentally misjudged the political situation among Iraqis in choosing an interim Iraqi Governing Council (IGC). Overly reliant on exiled Iraqis with their own agendas and deeply skeptical of nation building, the Bush administration greatly complicated the task of establishing a legitimate government in Iraq.[61] Pentagon officials steadfastly ignored the extensive planning for a postwar Iraq that had been done not only in many respected think tanks but its own government. Designed to develop a strategy for the post Saddam Hussein political transition, the Future of Iraq project had been set up a year before the war and involved seventeen federal agencies, led by the State Department, and involved hundreds of Iraqis at a cost of $5 million. The program engaged Iraqis representing the country's different ethnic and religious groups.

Yet, as David Phillips, a participant in the project recalled, "Pentagon officials thought the endeavor was too academic." He explained that "Secretary Donald Rumsfeld and his inner circle thought they could liberate a nation without even talking with those they were liberating. The Pentagon never had a policy or a program. All it had was a person— Ahmed Chalabi."[62] Ignoring the important political players in Iraq and shunning the United Nations were particularly costly mistakes. Much of the problem was in the way the CPA chose the Iraqis meant to be its partners during the occupation.

Relying on exiles

The story of Ahmed Chalabi, the first president of the IGC, is particularly illustrative of the hegemons' failure to grasp the complex politics of Iraq. Chalabi, the son of a prominent Iraqi businessman and government official, had not been in Iraq since 1956, except for a period in the mid-1990s when he helped organize resistance to topple Saddam's regime. In 1995, with CIA funding and approval, Chalabi led a failed uprising in the Kurdish areas of northern Iraq that was to attack Saddam's forces simultaneously in three cities. Word of the plan leaked and the scheme failed.[63] The CIA was furious that it had funded the disaster, which became known as the "Bay of Goats,"[64] (Iraqi Muslims do not have pigs) and stopped supplying Chalabi in 1996 after he went public with complaints about the CIA's operation in northern Iraq.[65] Chalabi was, however, one of the most outspoken opponents of Saddam Hussein before the war and had formed the Iraqi National Congress, a group dedicated to the overthrow of Saddam Hussein. From his London perch, Chalabi had developed close ties to key conservative members of Congress, the Pentagon, and influential Republicans such as Paul Wolfowitz and Richard Perle.

The administration put Chalabi front and center in its Iraq strategy— both behind the scenes and publicly. Following the overthrow of Saddam Hussein, the Pentagon flew Chalabi and around a hundred of his private security force into southern Iraq. He commanded a seven-hundred-man militia, the Free Iraqi Fighters. Paul Bremer relied heavily on Chalabi for advice on how to establish an interim government in Iraq, leading Washington to create an interim government council that was overly reliant on the exile community. As a sign of support for Chalabi, President Bush gave him the honored seat behind the First Lady during his January 20, 2004, State of the Union address. When President Bush addressed the United Nations in September 2003, Chalabi was in the Iraqi seat at the UN.

The U.S. reportedly made monthly payments of $335,000 to his Iraqi National Congress (INC), totaling $32 million during the Bush administration. Bush's two predecessors had also supported Chalabi, although at two-thirds the level.[66] In exchange, the INC provided intelligence on Iraq, including its weapons of mass destruction programs, recommendations for Saddam Hussein's removal, and, postwar, on suspected insurgents.[67] Violating one of the most important rules in intelligence gathering, U.S. officials ignored the obvious fact that Chalabi had his own agenda of hoping to return to Iraq to seek office and thus a motive to exaggerate the dangerous nature of the Iraqi regime.

Chalabi's friends in Washington also chose to ignore his checkered past. Chalabi had fled Jordan in 1989 after being tipped off about his impending arrest for criminal behavior as head of the country's second-largest bank, Petra Bank. In April 1992, a military tribunal in Jordan found Chalabi guilty of thirty-one charges, including embezzlement, theft, forgery, currency speculation, making false statements, and bad loans. He was sentenced to twenty-two years of hard labor and repayment of $32 million in embezzled funds. An audit by Arthur Anderson found that the bank had overstated its assets by $300 million. Additionally, $150 million had disappeared from the bank's accounts. Chalabi claims the charges were contrived due to his open criticism of Saddam Hussein, to whom he alleged Jordan was beholden for oil and economic aid. Jordanian banking officials deny this, pointing out that, in addition to illegal activities in that country, almost all of Petra Bank's listed American assets were worthless. Its one real "office" was an estate in Virginia where the Chalabi family lived.

Incredibly, despite this past, the CPA put Chalabi in charge of the *finance* committee of the IGC. Washington looked the other way when Chalabi used his position to provide lucrative jobs and contracts to his friends and family. For instance, a $327.5 million contract to equip the New Iraqi Army (NIA) was awarded in December 2003 to Nour, a firm with close ties to Mr. Chalabi. As head of the IGC's Finance Committee, Chalabi proved effective at political cronyism as well. He was instrumental in installing the oil, finance, and trade ministers, as well as the Central Bank governor. Chalabi's nephew, Ali Allawi, became minister of trade and defense. Nadeel Musawi, former INC spokesman, was appointed a deputy on the governing council.[68]

While Chalabi was popular in certain powerful circles in Washington, he had virtually no support in Iraq. In a 2004 poll asking who among a list of politicians Iraqis do "not trust at all," Chalabi topped the list, even beating Saddam Hussein.[69] Problems with Chalabi quickly emerged. In May 2004, after a long-running probe, the INC was charged with theft of government property and money, misrepresentation, and abuse of power. An INC–affiliated company was accused of profiting from the introduction of a new currency by recalculating old money it was obligated to destroy. Chalabi, also in charge of the De-Baathification Committee, was accused of blackmailing Iraqis, threatening to list them as Baath Party members if they did not support the INC's business. In one case, a senior official in the Ministry of Science and Technology was listed and received a letter claiming that "you're a Baathist and you'll be eliminated" after he refused to sign off on a contract brought in by the INC.[70]

It was not until June 2004 that the United States finally openly broke with Chalabi, following accusations that he passed sensitive intelligence secrets to Iran. On June 30, 2004, the United States cut off payments to the INC and did not interfere when Iraqi authorities put out arrest warrants for certain INC leaders and raided Chalabi's home.[71]

As the hegemons' favorite Iraqi, Chalabi was instrumental in convincing Washington to invade Iraq and to make political postwar decisions that overly favored the exile community, some of whom, Chalabi included, had not been in Iraq in four decades. This overreliance on Chalabi alienated the United States from many Iraqis who had endured the regime of Saddam Hussein, further complicating Washington's already very difficult political challenges in Iraq. Chalabi was also responsible for much of the faulty intelligence that led the CIA to conclude Iraq had weapons of mass destruction. As one exile who collected information about Iraq from defectors put it, the INC "intentionally exaggerated all the information so they would drag the United States into war."[72]

Yet, the fault lies not with Chalabi but with the officials in Washington whom Chalabi successfully duped. Defending himself, Chalabi said, "We didn't mislead anyone," he said. "We said we had information. We didn't say the information was great. We thought it would be useful. . . . How can we be blamed for the failure of the entire world's intelligence?"[73] It was the job of U.S. officials to treat Chalabi's information with appropriate skepticism, given that he had his own ambitions and a reason to mislead Washington. Yet, he provided supporters of the war in Iraq with what they were looking for: support for the costly myth that it would be easy to topple Saddam Hussein and establish democracy in Iraq.

Collaboration with al Qaeda?

By the spring of 2004, the violence in Iraq was severely hampering U.S. efforts at reconstruction, and deaths of U.S. soldiers surged to a monthly high of 139 in April, with another 84 killed in May. As the violence in Iraq grew, so did the presence of foreign terrorists. Although the total number of foreign terrorists in Iraq is unknown, as of late August 2003, 250 of 9,000 detainees in U.S. custody were foreign.[74] As of April 2004, the U.S. military estimated that number to be "several thousand," many of whom entered though Syria, often with the assistance of the Assad regime. The jihadists form cells and often join local insurgents to pursue their common goal of expelling the United States.[75] While details on all the insurgent organizations were sketchy, forces opposed to U.S. occupation probably included a mix of common criminals released by Saddam prior to the war, Saddam loyalists, Baath Party hard-liners, Sunni tribal members who feared a loss of their former dominance, and Iraqi nationalists.[76]

While much has been made of the link between terrorism and the necessity of going to war in Iraq, prior to the war there was scant evidence of any terrorist threat emanating from Iraq that threatened the United States.[77] Once in Iraq, however, the United States and its allies became a target, especially for Abu Musab al Zarqawi and his Tawhid and Jihad movement. Born in Jordan, al Zarqawi fought the Soviets in Afghanistan as a teenager, where he may have met bin Laden. He returned to Jordan in the early 1990s but fled back to Afghanistan in 1999 when he was accused of plotting to overthrow the monarchy and blow up a tourist hotel. Intelligence officials say that he ran a terrorist training camp in that country and experimented with chemical weapons. Until spring and summer of 2004, U.S. intelligence agencies believed he had lost a leg in an American missile attack in Afghanistan and received medical treatment in Baghdad.[78] Al Zarqawi, a Sunni, probably also spent time in Iran and northern Iraq, working with Ansar al-Islam developing chemical weapons.

Al Zarqawi is a prime suspect in some of the worst attacks around the world in recent years, including the March 11, 2004, Madrid bombings, which killed 191 people, and the murder of USAID official, Laurence Foley, in Jordan in October 2002.[79] In February 2004, U.S. authorities intercepted a letter by al Zarqawi in which the author claims to have masterminded twenty-five successful attacks against the coalition forces in Iraq.[80] Al Zarqawi was also increasingly viewed as the force behind attacks on Shias, including those in April 2004 in Basra that killed at least fifty Iraqis, including twenty children, and the March 2, 2004, attacks in Baghdad and Karbala that killed over 180 Shia pilgrims on the holiest day of their religious calendar.[81] He is believed to be behind the gruesome strategy of beheading at least six foreign captives and probably the one who first shocked the world by decapitating American Nicolas Berg before cameras. In the video of the horrific Berg murder, the American is seated before five masked men as a statement is read condemning American treatment of Iraqi prisoners. He is then pushed to the floor, screaming. Putting a knife to Berg's neck, a man yells, "God is Great!" He then decapitates Berg.[82]

Al Zarqawi has variously called for getting the United States out of the Arab heartland, promoting Sunni over Shiite predominance within the Islamic community, targeting Israel as the basis of evil, as well as instigating fundamentalist Islamic rule in the Middle East.[83] Al Zarqawi also sought to incite Sunnis to violence against Shias, to undermine both the U.S. occupation and the possibility of a Shia-dominated future Iraq. Although he represented a threat to America's goal of establishing a stable, democratic Iraq following the invasion, how much of a threat he was to America before the war is a matter of debate. Administration officials repeatedly referred to him in justifying the war, with President Bush first publicly mentioning him in October 2002 as a terrorist associated with al Qaeda who was receiving medical treatment in Baghdad.[84] During his February 2003 UN Security Council meeting, Powell claimed al Zarqawi headed a deadly terrorist network in Iraq and was an associate of and collaborator with Osama bin Laden.

Certainly, al Qaeda and al Zarqawi shared a common hatred of America and found common cause in opposing the U.S. occupation of Iraq. But the evidence suggests that the two have not collaborated. For instance, German intelligence interrogated members of a militant cell who claim that al Zarqawi headed their group, set up "especially for Jordanians who did not want to join al Qaeda."[85] Al Zarqawi's targeting of Shiites, including the assassination of the Shia cleric, Ayatollah al Hakim, runs counter to bin Laden's desire to unify the Muslim world against the West. It is now believed that al Zarqawi operates independently, and even in competition with bin Laden.[86] There may have been contacts and pleas on the part of al Zarqawi for al Qaeda's assistance, but evidence of substantive cooperation is lacking. In fact, American intelligence picked up signs in late February 2004 that al Qaeda operatives outside of Iraq had refused al Zarqawi's request for cooperation, leading analysts to conclude a significant divide exists between the actors.[87]

Beyond al Zarqawi, the Bush administration also sought to establish a link between Iraq and al Qaeda, implying to the American public Saddam Hussein was somehow involved with the attacks of September 11, although it was careful not to make that spurious claim directly. Bin Laden made overtures to Saddam for assistance as he did with leaders in Sudan, Iran, Afghanistan, and elsewhere in seeking to build an Islamic army. Saddam reportedly dispatched a senior Iraqi intelligence official to Sudan to meet with bin Laden in 1994 to discuss bin Laden's hope of procuring weapons and establishing a training camp in Iraq. Iraq apparently never responded. While bin Laden and Iraqi officials apparently made repeated contacts during the 1990s, no collaborative relationship ever developed. Another of the administration's "smoking guns," an alleged April 2001 meeting between Iraqi intelligence and Mohammed Atta in Prague, likely did not happen, as phone records indicate that Atta was in Florida at the time.[88]

When Congressional inquiries concluded in June 2004 that there was "no credible evidence" that Saddam Hussein helped al Qaeda target the United States, administration officials quickly deployed to point out that it had never claimed such a linkage. Yet, they had deliberately created that exact impression in the American mindset. And it worked. For instance, right after the September 11 attacks, 78 percent of Americans suspected Iraq's involvement and in the years that followed, the administration reinforced that belief.[89] By August 2002, 86 percent thought Baghdad was giving support to terrorist groups planning to strike America.[90] In March 2003, 88 percent believed Hussein supported terrorist groups that planned to attack the United States,[91] and in August of 2003, seven in ten Americans believed that Saddam Hussein had a role in the attacks.[92] In a testament to the power of the president's bully pulpit, even after it emerged that Iraq had no weapons of mass destruction and no link to al Qaeda or the September 11 attacks, Americans clung to the link between Iraq and al Qaeda. In late April 2004, 49 percent of Americans still believed that "clear evidence that Iraq was supporting al Qaeda has been found."[93] In June 2004, even after 9/11 Commission staff reports to the contrary, 62 percent still thought Iraq provided direct assistance to al Qaeda.[94]

The administration had to keep the American people believing the war was one of necessity, not choice. Particularly as the administration headed into its reelection campaign in 2004, it sought to keep up that fiction in spite of the mounting evidence that Iraq had no weapons of mass destruction and that there was no linkage to al Qaeda. For instance, in June 2004, Vice President Dick Cheney continued to claim that the Iraqi dictator "had long established ties with al Qaeda," calling the evidence "overwhelming."[95] His claims flatly contradicted preliminary findings of the National Commission on Terrorist Attacks upon the United States investigating the attacks of September 11. When asked directly if he knew things the commission members did not, Cheney replied, "probably."[96] Cheney declined to provide such information to the commission. He continued to cling to the theory that the Iraq–al Qaeda meeting in Prague might have occurred, saying, "We just don't know."[97] In June 2004 he defended the administration against charges it had fabricated links between September 11 and Iraq, saying, "We did say there were numerous contacts between Saddam Hussein and al Qaeda.[98] President Bush, speaking before the United Nations General Assembly in September 2004, persisted in linking al Qaeda and Iraq, saying "a terrorist group associated with al Qaeda is now one of the main groups killing the innocent in Iraq today."[99]

Having chosen to go to war in Iraq, President Bush had to ensure the American people continued to believe it was a necessary war. Its credibility rested on the hegemonic myth that Iraq presented an imminent threat to the United States, and that the lone superpower could take care of the problem on its own. With the failure to find weapons of mass destruction, the administration's primary justification for the war was terrorism. Despite the mounting evidence to the contrary, the administration stuck to the line that the links between Saddam Hussein and al Qaeda were such that they constituted a threat to America, justifying the more than $100 billion the war had cost so far, as well as the over one thousand Americans who have died during the war and after. As the White House communications director explained, "We'll continue to talk about how Saddam Hussein was a threat, and his ties to terrorism, and we will not give an inch on what we've said in the past."[100] An outside advisor to the White House explained that making the linkage was important to the administration's "long-term credibility on the issue of the decision to go to war. . . . If you discount the relationship between Iraq and Al Qaeda, then you discount the proposition that it's part of the war on terror. If it's not part of the war on terror, then what is it—some cockeyed adventure on the part of George W. Bush?"[101]

While the administration succeeded in keeping September 11 linked to the need to go to war in the minds of the American people, it could not hide the fact that it had quickly lost the peace in Iraq. Washington realized it needed the help of the body it has so derided, the United Nations. The long experiment of the hegemons' foreign policy was over.

The United Nations to the rescue

January 19, 2004, Administrator of the Coalition Provisional Authority Paul Bremer, met with UN Secretary-General Kofi Annan to solicit a role for the United Nations in Iraq. Shortly afterwards, in an Oval Office meeting with Secretary-General Annan on February 3, 2004, President Bush made a personal appeal for the UN's help in breaking the logjam between Bremer's proposal for Iraq's largest Shia caucuses and leader Ali al Sistani's call for direct elections. Bush sought to put a positive spin on his abysmal relations with the United Nations. "I have always said that the United Nations needs to play a vital role and it's an important role. . . . I look forward to working with the Secretary General to achieve that."[102]

The initial expectations for a quick, easy, and peaceful transfer to democracy in Iraq promoted primarily by Cheney, Rumsfeld, and Wolfowitz had proven to be wildly unrealistic. Their expectation of a warm embrace by the Iraqi people of victorious U.S. troops had been a fantasy. The hope that a democratic Iraq would promote reform in the Arab world was a distant pipe dream. Rather than promoting peace between the Israelis and Palestinians, the war further divided the Arab world from the United States. Arab resentment of America has never been higher. Rather than viewing the United States and coalition troops as liberators, 92 percent of Iraqis viewed it as an occupying force in mid-June 2004. Fifty-five percent of Iraqis said they would feel safer if U.S. troops left immediately, nearly double the 28 percent who felt that way in January. More than half believe that all Americans behave like those portrayed in the Abu Ghraib prisoner-abuse photos.

Three and a half years into the Bush administration, the hegemons' easy victory in Iraq was clearly a myth. A more realistic, balanced, and internationalist approach toward Iraq began to emerge. Having called the United Nations irrelevant, the Bush administration now saw it as its only way to success in Iraq, and ultimately to bring the troops home.

Initially, the United States hoped the UN could essentially take the mess in Iraq over from the United States. After shunning the UN aside in Iraq, U.S. officials were practically begging for the United Nations to get involved. Suddenly, the names of UN officials tripped off the president's tongue, surprising observers of the usually foreign name–phobic president. United Nations officials' jaws dropped when President Bush repeatedly referred by name to the hitherto obscure director of the Electoral Assistance Division, Carina Perelli. But the fact he knew her name underscored just how much the United States was counting on the United Nations to pull its chestnuts out of the fire.

While the UN could not reverse the U.S. administration's past mistakes, Secretary-General Annan agreed to help in two significant ways: first, to help chart a political consensus on the way to Iraqi sovereignty, something the United States had lost the credibility to do, and second to assist in elections, a key element to Washington's exit strategy from Iraq. The UN's most able official, Lakhdar Brahimi, first traveled to Iraq as the secretary-general's special advisor in February 2004 to break the logjam over elections between Washington and al Sistani. With Washington's legitimacy largely nonexistent, Brahimi consulted broadly with the key political actors and proposed the mechanism for the transfer of authority that would take place on June 30. With seven election experts on his team, Brahimi evaluated the feasibility of elections prior to the U.S. imposed June 30 deadline for transfer of power, assessed the time frame and conditions required, and determined other options of representing the will of Iraqis within the time frame laid out in an agreement reached in November 2003. Encouragingly, al Sistani had indicated that he would accept the UN's decision, even if it meant no direct elections prior to transfer of sovereignty.[103] The group met with large numbers of political leaders, religious leaders, tribal leaders, nongovernmental organizations, women's groups, professional associations, human rights groups, journalists, and the CPA leadership. Security concerns, however, limited his contacts outside Baghdad.[104]

Through extensive consultations, Brahimi's team determined that Iraqis wanted a return of their sense of dignity as soon as possible and, hence, maintain to the June 30 transfer of power deadline Bremer had set. While the deadline was an arbitrary early one, Bremer chose it to keep the pressure on the IGC for progress, to underscore that the U.S. occupation would be short-lived, and probably to ensure President Bush could point to some political progress as he ran for reelection in the fall of 2004. "I can make all kinds of arguments about why we need to establish democracy in Iraq on an urgent basis," said one administration official. "But when you hear from on high that this is what we must do, and there can be no questioning of it, it sounds like politics."[105]

Following his consultations, Brahimi determined a way forward that kept the major players in Iraq on board and kept the June 30 deadline. It was clear that holding elections before June 30 was unrealistic. Election preparations would take eight months *after* a legal and institutional framework was established. So, a consensus emerged that a provisional government would have to be established by means other than direct elections which would require more time or the caucus system that had been rejected by a large portion of Iraqis. Ultimately, Brahimi proposed that a single legislative and constitutional assembly be selected. A prime minister, a cabinet of twenty-five ministers, a ceremonial president, and two vice presidents would compose the government that would take over on June 30, 2004. Its primary task would be to prepare for elections in January 2005.

Only the United Nations could have brokered the political agreement among the parties in Iraq. The impasse created by Washington's gross misreading of the political situation on the ground, its failure to provide adequate security, and deep Iraqi resentment over the occupation eliminated the chance for U.S. officials to be seen as honest brokers. As Greenstock summed up Bremer's approach, "against the background of things not going right, Jerry produced a perfectly acceptable political program."[106] But when things went horribly wrong, the United States could not handle the situation on its own.

Brahimi's great skill proved crucial in coming to agreement on the way forward. He, together with the IGC and Paul Bremer, ultimately settled on Iyad Allawi, a Shia, to serve as prime minister. An exile with reported ties to the CIA and the British intelligence service MI6, he had supported the U.S. invasion and was considered less likely to request removal of coalition forces. In an ironic twist demonstrating how wrong Bremer's de-Baathification policy had been, Allawi had been a member of the Baath Party.[107] As president, Brahimi chose Ghazi Mashal Ajil al Yawer, a Sunni, and two vice presidents, Ibrahim al Jaafari, a Shia and Rowsch Shaways, a Kurd.[108] Rounding out the new cabinet was an ethnically balanced mix of thirty-one members, six of them women.[109] Al Zarqawi quickly pledged to assassinate Allawi.[110]

On June 8, 2004, the United Nations passed Resolution 1546 that endorsed the interim government of Iraq proposed by Brahimi, as well as the timetable for the transfer of sovereignty and elections. The unanimous vote represented the end of the Bush administration's ill-advised sidelining of the United Nations and an important shift from the unreal world of the hegemons.

The resolution authorizes the UN to play "a leading role" in convening a national conference in July, to "advise and support" the various Iraqi authorities on the process for holding elections, and to promote national dialogue and consensus-building on the drafting of a national constitution. In addition, the UN is assigned a role in advising Iraq on developing civil and social services; contributing to the coordination and delivery of reconstruction, development, and humanitarian assistance; promoting human rights, national reconciliation, strengthening the rule of law; and planning for a comprehensive census.[111]

The ongoing security crisis will prevent the UN from fulfilling much of those responsibilities. At the secretary-general's strong insistence, the resolution also says the UN will assume these tasks "as circumstances permit." With the UN deaths of August 2003 on his conscience, the secretary-general is determined not to make that mistake again, warning the Security Council in December 2003 that "bad resolutions kill people."[112] Thus, the UN has declined to return to Iraq in large numbers, instead continuing the practice of sending short missions to Iraq for specific tasks, such as those by Lakhdar Brahimi, his elections team, led by Carina Perelli, and the Volker team investigating corruption of the Oil-for-Food program. Annan's special representative to Iraq has only a small staff of thirty-five; the UN will not return to Iraq in large numbers absent an improvement in the security situation. Washington's mistakes made the UN as much of a target as the occupying U.S. forces. As one UN official put it, "Because the UN role has been unclear, it looked to most Iraqis as part of the occupation."[113] Secretary-General Annan insisted on "symmetry between the risks the UN was asked to accept and the substance of the role we were being called upon to play."[114]

Despite a joint declaration by President Bush and Prime Minister Blair on April 8, 2003, that the United Nations could play a "vital role" in postwar reconstruction,[115] the UN was never asked to play such a role in Iraq until early in 2004—eight months after the end of the war. But as the United States turned to the UN for help, it was never willing to give up the control necessary to enable the UN to operate effectively in Iraq. "The U.S. has never understood that the UN derives its legitimacy from the fact that the UN represents everyone, not just the U.S.," one top UN official explained in June 2004. "The U.S. wants us to pour holy water on it. But what we need is a process with clear authority and independence."[116] Had the U.S. ceded a greater role in the political process to the UN in the immediate aftermath of the war, the UN might have been able to effect a more legitimate transition process than the one that has triggered today's dangerous insurgency.

Getting back to reality

In an embarrassing testament to the failure of the United States to ensure a stable Iraq, the formal transfer of power was secretly moved up two days and performed in front of about a few dozen people. While the move was a necessary one given the security concerns, the symbol of the United States having to hand power over in secret underscored the vast task ahead. Brahimi characterized the new government, saying it was "the best that we can reach right now . . . one may choose to look at it as half full or half empty."[117]

The new government faces significant challenges. First, its legitimacy is not accepted by the Iraqi people. While not solely chosen by the United States as was the IGC, the interim government was still hand-picked, albeit by the UN, which has more legitimacy in the eyes of Iraqis. According to polls, Allawi enjoys almost no support among Iraqis; with 61 percent opposing him and only 22 percent expressing any support for him.[118] Brahimi himself pointed out in his February 2004 report that legitimacy can only come about through elections, saying that the Iraqis recognized that direct elections were indeed the source of legitimacy for a representative body.[119]

Second, the security situation threatens the election schedule, as the insurgency has shown no early signs of abating. Certainly, as secretary-general Kofi Annan reports, "You cannot have credible elections if the security conditions continue as they are now."[120] The insurgency demands the withdrawal of foreign forces, yet it is its own violence that puts at risk the development of institutions and security forces that will enable the coalition forces to depart. While the UN believes the process can work, the ongoing violence in the country may make it difficult to hold elections as scheduled in early 2005.

Third, the institutions of government in Iraq are so debilitated that it will be impossible to meet the high expectations of the Iraqi people for a better life following the ouster of Saddam Hussein. Brahimi emphasizes the challenges, saying "This government will have its work cut out for it . . . it will not be easy for them to prove the skeptics wrong."[121]

The hegemons' experiment had failed in Iraq. Historians and politicians will continue to debate whether President Bush was right to go to war against Iraq in order to protect American interests. The main justification for the war, Iraq's weapons of mass destruction, was a fiction. On July 7, 2004, the Senate Select Committee on Intelligence released a scathing report indicating that the intelligence community's assessment that Iraq had chemical and biological weapons was "unfounded and unreasonable" and that the CIA's assertion that Iraq was reconstituting its nuclear program was "not supported by the intelligence." David Kay, former head of the Iraq Survey Group, the body assigned the task of finding weapons of mass destruction, resigned in January 2004 with the admission that "we were all wrong" about Iraq's programs.

The report also refuted the administrations effort to link Saddam Hussein to September 11 finding that contacts between Iraq and al Qaeda "did not add up to an established formal relationship" and that there was no evidence proving Iraqi complicity or assistance in an al Qaeda attack. Following the release of the report, President Bush shifted his justification of the war, no longer claiming Iraq possessed WMD but rather that Iraq had the "capability of producing weapons of mass destruction and could have passed that capacity to terrorists bent on acquiring them. In the world after September 11, that was a risk we could not afford to take."[122] Many senators said they would not have voted to authorize the war had they been aware of the facts from the congressional report.

Whether other benefits of the war cited by the administration will materialize, such as promoting democracy and reform in the Middle East and a resolution of the Israeli-Arab conflict will take years to evaluate. Early signs indicate the war set back rather than promoted these goals. Objective observers will agree that the poor planning and ideological approach taken by the president and his advisors seriously undermined the United States' interests in the Middle East and around the world, at great cost in terms of American lives and treasure. Certainly, anger over the war has put American security at greater risk. A third as many Americans have already died in Iraq as were killed on September 11. The toll continues to rise. As of June 2004, American taxpayers had already spent over $100 billion for military operations with another $50 billion expected to be approved. In addition, $21 billion is pledged for reconstruction. Future costs will include a continued American military presence, rebuilding Iraq's infrastructure, and training and paying Iraq's security forces, all of which could be exacerbated if insurgents continue disrupting recovery efforts.[123] Most tragically, hundreds, perhaps thousands more Americans will die before the war is over.

The United States will remain in Iraq until the job is done. Having invaded Iraq, it can only leave once there is some semblance of security and an Iraqi force to maintain it. But it will have to do it largely on its own. While the Bush administration succeeded in gaining Security Council authorization for its activities in Iraq, most nations are not assisting the United States in the task. For instance, at the NATO summit in Georgia on June 10, 2004, leaders made it clear they would not send troops to Iraq. As the former French ambassador to Washington Francois Bujon de L'Estang said, "NATO is not going into Iraq to clean up the mess, although it can help."[124] On June 28, the day of the transition of U.S. sovereignty, the allies only pledged to "encourage" members to contribute training the new security forces, with most insisting on doing it outside of Iraq, which contradicted the U.S. position that it should be done in the country. French President Chirac said that "any NATO footprint on Iraqi soil would be unwise."

While it will take many years, the Iraqi people will be better off without Saddam Hussein and for the vast American investment in the country. As Greenstock commented, "People will have to make their own judgment on whether it has been worth it." Regarding the overall conduct of the United States following the attacks of September 11, he said "The opportunity that was opened up after September 11 in terms of other countries' sympathy and willingness to be partners has to some extent been dissipated. . . . Above all, there was an expectation of an environment in Iraq that would be much more benign than actually proved to be the case." As far as whether the U.S. policy in Iraq will succeed, he said, "the Iraqis as a society will have to decide that they are fed up with violence. The cost will continue, in terms of lives lost and ongoing violence, the elections in early 2005 are going to be difficult in that respect."[125] Former national security advisor Anthony Lake observed that the invasion of Iraq has proven to be the greatest humanitarian intervention in history. "Bush has become a humanitarian president, while letting threats to our security, such as Iran and North Korea, fester."[126]

Whether the Bush administration will take to heart the lessons for American foreign policy of the failed hegemonic approach in Iraq remains to be seen. Although throughout the election campaign of 2004 administration officials clung to hegemonic rhetoric, U.S. policy began to shift back to reality on a variety of issues. In the Balkans, Bush worked with the allies for an orderly transfer of security to the Europeans, abandoning his earlier pledges to pull U.S. troops quickly. He began to find ways to strengthen international arms-control treaties. The administration dropped in June 2004 their much touted insistence in the Security Council on an exemption of U.S. soldiers from the International Criminal Court in every peacekeeping resolution.[127] Laura Bush even went to Paris to kiss and make up with President Chirac, and pictures of the two embracing made front pages around the world.

The realization slowly emerged that a responsible U.S. policy must return to the proven policies of U.S. leadership, international engagement, and sharing of the burden of the lone superpower—coupled with zero tolerance for terrorism and proliferation. Only a new policy of tough engagement will protect America's interest in the post–September 11 world. The shift was dangerously slow in the making with the crisis in North Korea.

11

Are We Really Going to War?

I can almost hear the ticking of the second hand of destiny.
We must act now.

—General Douglas MacArthur, August 23, 1950

The crisis in January 2003 was all too familiar. North Korea had announced it would withdraw from the Nuclear Non-Proliferation Treaty (NPT), expel international inspectors, and restart the nuclear weapons program it had agreed to freeze in the 1994 Agreed Framework deal negotiated by the Clinton administration. The CIA reiterated its belief that North Korea already had one or two nuclear weapons and estimated that it could produce five or six more within months. North Korea once again threatened to turn Seoul into a "sea of fire" and hurled invectives at the United States, calling Americans "infinitely greedy and beastly."[1]

North Korea had taken virtually the same actions in 1993 and 1994, bringing the international community to the brink of what could have been a bloody war. As the 2003 crisis escalated, I recalled the chilling briefing given during the previous crisis by the chairman of the joint Chiefs of Staff, John Shalikashvili. The costs of a war with North Korea were staggering. The Pentagon had "run the numbers" on potential troop casualties: thirty thousand Americans and four hundred fifty thousand South Koreans in the first ninety days. Hundreds of thousands of Seoul's ten million residents living a mere twenty-five miles from the demilitarized zone between North Korea and South Korea could be slaughtered.[2] I knew these figures would be the same in 2003. In addition, any war with North Korea would destabilize Asia, creating a refugee crisis. The United States again faced a difficult choice: try to negotiate another deal to stop North Korea's nuclear program, knowing it might again cheat or risk a war with a million-man army and a leader prepared to use nuclear weapons, possibly triggering World War III.

Clinton's 1994 deal with North Korea had never been accepted by the conservative wing of the Republican Party, although it stopped North Korea from making enough plutonium to mass-produce nuclear bombs. Experts estimate that without the deal, the North Koreans could have had enough plutonium to make more than *fifty* bombs by 2003.[3] Calling the deal blackmail, opponents objected to the $4.5 billion in assistance to be provided by the international community as part of the agreement, including five hundred thousand tons of fuel and the provision of two light-water reactors that, while expensive, involve less weapons-grade material and thus a lower risk of diversion to a nuclear program.

When he took office in 2001, President Bush did not support the 1994 deal, accepting the view of his national security advisor, Condoleezza Rice, that Clinton had failed to act "resolutely and decisively" in dealing with North Korea and had threatened to use force only to back down. Yet, the Bush administration failed to offer any workable alternative, especially one that would garner the crucial support of the allies in the region that was necessary for any credible threat of force. Instead, Rice approached the issue as the United States had approached the Soviet Union during the cold war, stating "the first line of defense should be a clear and classical statement of deterrence—if they do acquire WMD [weapons of mass destruction], their weapons will be unusable because any attempt to use them will bring national obliteration."[4] While such an outdated approach of mutual assured destruction (MAD) had worked with the rational Soviet leaders, it fundamentally misjudged the only realistic way to handle North Korea: a sophisticated balance of the threat to use force and the willingness to negotiate. There is simply no guarantee that the North Korean leaders would refrain from war if threatened or that deterrence would dissuade the North from exporting nuclear material.

For an administration that believed its superpower status enabled it to threaten other countries into submission, North Korea presented a difficult challenge. Still immersed in classic state-to-state rivalry, administration officials clung to hegemonic policies that relied primarily on force to protect American interests. That myth left no room for a failed nuclear state undeterred by the threat of annihilation by the superpower. North Korea's ability to use nuclear "blackmail" against the United States contravened the myths about U.S. power, as well as the sensibility of not rewarding rogue regimes for bad behavior. As unpleasant a prospect as it may seem, however, the only practical way to shut down the North Korean program is through negotiations, inspections, and working with U.S. allies in the region. As with Iraq, the challenge of confronting the North Korean leg of the axis of evil would prove more complex than the Bush administration anticipated.

While Bush took the wrong approach to North Korea, it is the only problem he correctly identified at the start as a priority. It is the last cold war state-against-state kind of problem. Yet, lumping it with the very different problems of Iraq and Iran only underscored how little Bush and his team understood the challenge. The superpower myth led Bush to diagnose the problem as an evil challenge to America; his response was to call for regime change and missile defenses. Clinton's approach led him to correctly identify the problem as an unstable and failing state that could undermine America's interests. He therefore pressed North Korea into the world community of rules and regulations that would contain the unstable regime, and he got America's allies to help bear the burden.

I have a gut feeling about this

National security advisor Condolezza Rice arrived at the White House determined to take a tougher approach to North Korea and Clinton's 1994 deal but failed to inform the new secretary of state, Colin Powell, of the shift. Powell recognized the merits of the previous administration's approach and set out to continue it, including negotiations with the North Koreans. On the eve of the first visit to the White House of South Korean president Kim Dae Jung in March 2001, Powell stated that the administration planned "to engage with North Korea to pick up where President Clinton and his administration left off."[5]

The White House, however, was not about to pursue any path taken by Clinton. The day after Powell spoke, he had to eat his words and admit he had been a "little forward on my skis."[6] President Bush announced in the presence of President Kim that he was "skeptical" of North Korean leader Kim Jong Il, saying he couldn't be trusted to keep agreements.[7] The administration made it clear it did not intend to support the 1994 Framework Agreement and that it would undertake a "full review" of the policy toward North Korea. That was a public repudiation not just of Powell but also of President Kim, who in 2000 had won the Nobel Peace Prize for his "sunshine" policy of engagement with and increased assistance for North Korea.

President Bush and his advisors resisted the reality that the 1994 Framework Agreement was the most practical way to keep North Korea's nuclear weapon ambitions in check. Lacking a workable alternative, the administration pursued two inconsistent policies simultaneously over the next two years, with the State Department continuing Clinton's policy of engagement, the Pentagon and the White House pressing a policy of isolation, and President Bush oscillating between the two.

Powell completed the policy review in three months and President Bush appeared to endorse Powell's recommended course of engagement with the North Koreans. Officials in the interagency process could not agree on a policy; thus, as our participant described it, hurried efforts by State and NSC officials resulted in an ill-defined proposal designed primarily to inoculate the administration from criticism over its lack of a policy.[8] On June 6, 2001, Bush announced that the administration would "undertake serious discussions with North Korea on a broad agenda" calling for a "comprehensive approach."[9] The administration emphasized that the approach differed from Clinton's because it demanded reductions in North Korea's conventional forces and pressed for progress on humanitarian issues. Naively, it also, it soon became apparent, did not involve negotiating with the North.

The comprehensive approach continued Clinton's policy of food and fuel shipments to the regime and—in response to allied objections—ending the call for a halt to construction of reactors promised under the 1994 Agreed Framework.[10] On February 16, 2002, President Bush reversed his earlier opposition and endorsed the South Korean "sunshine" policy during a visit to Seoul, emphasizing the United States has no intention of attacking North Korea. But in early April, as the North Koreans indicated a willingness to enter into talks, President Bush rejected the comprehensive approach, saying "I don't want to get involved in long-term negotiations. I have a gut feeling about this."[11] Bush ordered a second review of the policy, which resulted in a so-called "bold initiative." While the details have never been spelled out, it is believed to resemble the earlier comprehensive approach.

The first high-level, albeit brief, meeting finally took place on July 31, 2002, on the margins of the Association of Southeast Asian States (ASEAN)[12] conference in Brunei between Secretary Powell and North Korean foreign minister Paek Nam-sun. By September 2002, no substantive progress had been made on the United States–North Korea agenda. Thus, seventeen months into the administration, the North Korea policy remained adrift, although the administration continued to press for talks. On September 19, White House spokesman Ari Fleischer reiterated support for the administration's comprehensive approach, saying that, "there's a lot to talk to North Korea about."[13]

I've got a visceral reaction to this guy

While this policy of stumbling engagement was proceeding, the administration heightened its anti–North Korean rhetoric and threatened North Korea with a preemptive attack. Following the terrorist attacks of September 11, the administration sought to show resolve against rogue regimes, shifting emphasis across the board away from a negotiations strategy in favor of the use of force. The harshest salvo came in President Bush's second State of the Union address to Congress on January 29, 2002, when he referred to Iraq, Iran, and North Korea as the "axis of evil." The line was apparently inserted by White House advisors at the last minute, without consultation with the State Department or consideration of the diplomatic impact of the statement. Colin Powell only saw the statement very late and "no one below him had any idea it was coming."[14] The phrase caused an uproar in Washington and around the world. Not only was there no "axis" of terrorist supporting efforts between the three countries, the line, coupled with other policy statements by the administration, implied the administration was prepared to attack each of the three countries. As the administration had overthrown the Taliban regime in Afghanistan the previous October, the possibility appeared more than theoretical.

The "axis of evil" remark set off a flurry of concern in Asia, where leaders opposed any military action in the Korean peninsula. South Korean foreign minister Han Seung Soo sought to reassure the region by telling Seoul's MBC Radio that "President Bush's remarks do not necessarily mean that the United States will launch military action against North Korea."[15] President Bush himself also sought to dampen concerns over a possible military strike against North Korea, saying in a press conference with South Korea's President Kim Dae Jung that "We're peaceful people. We have no intention of invading North Korea. South Korea has no intention of attacking North Korea, nor does America. We're purely defensive."[16]

In isolation, the axis-of-evil line would have been viewed over time in context as a rhetorical, if unwise, embellishment. Yet, the statement was followed by a series of derogatory remarks by the president against the North Korean leader, more bellicose rhetoric, and a new military doctrine advocating preemptive military strikes against North Korea. On May 23, 2002, during a meeting with Republican senators, President Bush referred to Kim Jong Il as a "pygmy," and compared him to a "spoiled child at a dinner table."[17] Three months later, he told a journalist in an on-the-record interview that he "loathes" the North Korean leader, saying "I've got a visceral reaction to this guy."[18] Not surprisingly, both remarks became public.

On March 10, 2002, the administration released the Nuclear Posture Review, which listed North Korea as a possible target for a nuclear strike intended to destroy underground complexes of chemical and biological arms.[19] Coupled with other Pentagon efforts to resume nuclear testing and develop new types of tactical nuclear weapons, this rhetoric made any peaceful resolution of the crisis more difficult. The so-called bunker busters were "designed to be used" in the words of one member of the influential Defense Policy Board.[20] The fact that Washington's official policy now emphasized a possible nuclear strike against North Korea fueled concern in an already paranoid regime. Pyongyang was also a Pentagon target in the National

Security Strategy, released in September 2002, which identified North Korea as a "rogue regime" and declared the United States must be prepared to stop such states "before they are able to threaten or use weapons of mass destruction."[21]

Thus, twenty months into President Bush's term, North Korea policy involved a widening gap between State Department and Pentagon approaches to North Korea. The State Department sought meaningful talks to continue the Agreed Framework, expanding talks to include conventional arms reductions and human rights issues. The Pentagon sought to stop the threat of possible terrorism from North Korea through undefined, yet strongly hinted at, military action. No effort appears to have been made to synchronize the two policies, much less reach a workable compromise. While that task is clearly the responsibility of the national security advisor, Condoleezza Rice failed to carry it out. Thus, in the words of one participant, rather than hammer out a policy, Rice would simply tell State and Defense officials, "You guys fight it out and tell us what the answer is."[22] As another senior official complained, "We ended up with a policy that could best be described as hostile neglect."[23]

Finally, over the summer of 2002, information came out that would put this confused, split, and failing policy to a serious test. The Bush administration confirmed what intelligence agencies had suspected for some time: North Korea was developing a second, covert nuclear program. While keeping their plutonium processing plant frozen as required by the 1994 Agreed Framework, the North Koreans had secretly started another nuclear program, one based on highly enriched uranium (HEU).[24] The administration had a major crisis on its hands.

In the late 1990s, North Korea and Pakistan apparently had cut a deal that met both of their perceived needs. North Korea provided Pakistan with its blueprints for Nodong missiles and Pakistan in return provided uranium enrichment designs and technology to North Korea. In the summer of 2002, U.S. satellites watched a Pakistani plane pick up its cargo in North Korea, but U.S. officials could not figure out how cash-strapped Pakistan had paid for such missiles. Discovery of the nuclear barter solved the mystery. The deal was probably initiated by Pakistan when it could not pay for the North Korean missiles.[25]

Playing the nuclear card

Although the news of the new program made headlines around the world, Korea watchers inside and outside the administration had long suspected Pyongyang was reneging on its international obligations. North Korea has a history of cheating on its nuclear deals since it first began negotiating with the international community in the late 1970s. It had learned early on it could gain international benefits in exchange for reining in its nuclear program. As the implementation of promised assistance lagged, North Korea would resume its nuclear programs and demand more international aid to once again end them.

North Korea had been pursuing a nuclear energy program since the end of the Korean War (1950–1953) when it signed a nuclear research cooperation agreement with the Soviet Union. Under the agreement, North Korean scientists visited Soviet nuclear research centers and the Soviet Union gave North Korea an experimental nuclear reactor and put it at the now infamous site of Yongbyon, sixty miles north of Pyongyang. Concerned even then that the North Koreans might use the reactor to build nuclear weapons, the Soviet Union asked inspectors from the International Atomic Energy Agency (IAEA), a Vienna-based autonomous UN organization,[26] to monitor the program, even though North Korea had not yet signed the Treaty on the Non-Proliferation of Nuclear Weapons (NPT). The treaty commits "each non-nuclear-weapon State Party . . . not to manufacture or otherwise acquire nuclear weapons or other nuclear explosive devices." It limits to five—China, France, Russia, the United Kingdom, and the United States—the nations legally permitted to have nuclear weapons. It also prohibits the transfer of nuclear weapons, materials, or technology.[27] North Korea finally signed the NPT in 1985.

No one outside North Korea knows exactly when the country moved from a nuclear energy program to a nuclear weapons program. It might have been in response to the secret program by South Korea begun in the 1970s to develop the capability to build nuclear weapons. Regardless of when North Korea first began its drive for nuclear weapons, by the mid-1980s, the North Koreans began pushing hard for nuclear power stations from the Soviet Union, and their nuclear intentions were clear. From then on, the North Koreans pursued a dual strategy of moving forward toward nonproliferation restraints, only to step back and blackmail the international community for rewards in exchange for continued compliance with such nonproliferation agreements.

The question for policymakers has never been, "Will they cheat?" but whether a deal can be made that addresses the immediate threat, while working to contain any longer-term threat until the regime collapses. Policymakers must always assume the reclusive, paranoid North Korean regime will seek to cheat on its agreements. Yet, given its nuclear status and its intent to remain in power at all costs, irrespective of the human toll, North Korea could well choose war if it feels threatened. Thus, the international community faces the real prospect of a costly and bloody war should diplomacy fail.

President Bush's nuclear deal

When George H. W. Bush became president, North Korea had nuclear plants producing dangerous plutonium, no light-water reactors, and no inspectors. The United States finally began to press for an IAEA agreement, and the Bush administration succeeded in securing North Korea's signature of a nuclear safeguards accord on January 30, 1992. But by then, the North Koreans had upped the ante: in exchange for signing the IAEA accord, North Korean President Kim Il Sung wanted the United States to remove its nuclear weapons from the Korean Peninsula, cancel the annual joint United States–South Korea "Team Spirit" military exercises, sign a nonaggression pact, and agree to direct talks.[28] Although President Bush never called it a quid pro quo deal, throughout the fall of 1991, he took most of these steps. The steps sparked heated debates within the administration. However, President Bush understood the need to make North Korea feel more secure in order to convince it to rein in its nuclear program. It worked. North Korea signed the IAEA nuclear inspection accord.

The IAEA deal committed North Korea to allow the IAEA to inspect the nuclear plant and reprocessing facility at Yongbyon, and the North at first appeared to cooperate. But soon, serious problems emerged. Most importantly, the IAEA determined that North Korea had produced more plutonium than it acknowledged when it shut its nuclear reactor facility in Yongbyon for a hundred days in 1989.[29] While the focus of the discussions was the Korean deception, the North Koreans also started to lay down their price for abandoning their efforts to reprocess plutonium: IAEA assistance in acquiring light-water reactors and nuclear fuel.

In an effort to press North Korea to comply with its IAEA obligations, the Bush administration threatened to withdraw some of the "carrots" it had put on the table. On October 8, 1992, the South Korean and United States defense ministers announced preparations for the resumption of Team Spirit in March 1993. Predictably, Pyongyang reacted angrily to the decision, warning that the dialogue with South Korea could not proceed "while a large scale thermonuclear war rehearsal is conducted." In November, it warned that it might disrupt IAEA inspections if Team Spirit were held.[30] Without inspectors, North Korea would mostly likely seek to produce nuclear weapons.

A better-than-even chance they have nuclear weapons

Faced in February 1993 with continued North Korean obstruction of the IAEA inspectors, the organization informed North Korea it would take the issue to the UN Security Council, warning of "further measures," UN–speak for sanctions. New presidents had just taken office in Washington and Seoul. Both Bill Clinton and Kim Young Sam followed their predecessors' leads and agreed to move forward with Team Spirit, which began on March 8. In addition, the new South Korean president signaled an overall tougher line than that of his predecessor.[31]

Four days later, North Korea announced its intention to withdraw from the NPT, which meant that North Korea might reject IAEA inspections and begin once again to produce nuclear weapons. Such a development had serious implications for South Korean and U.S. troops stationed there, as well as the possibility of a transfer of materials and know-how to terrorists. Although North Korea eventually decided to suspend its withdrawal from the NPT, this cycle of events marked a pattern that would last for the next year and a half and be repeated starting in 2002. In response to what it perceived as lagging commitments by South Korea or the United States, the North would renege on its inspections commitments; the United States would respond by ratcheting up the pressure by suspending bilateral talks, rescheduling Team Spirit, and supporting discussion of the imposition of UN sanctions. North Korea would threaten once again to pull out of the NPT, expel inspectors, and talk of war. During the bargaining process, it would also repeat its demand for light-water reactors, a nonaggression pact, and additional food and fuel aid.

By November 1993, it was clear that North Korea was not going to cooperate with the IAEA. Washington called off the next round of talks planned with North Korea and began discussing an effort to impose sanctions to pressure North Korea back into compliance. Clinton and his advisors hoped a diplomatic solution could be found. As a precaution, however, the Pentagon had begun to dust off its military plans for the peninsula. Then in December 1993, the CIA circulated some alarming information that meant the situation on the Korean peninsula might be much more dangerous.

The CIA circulated a National Intelligence Estimate (NIE), which quickly leaked to the press in mid-December, assessing that North Korea had probably developed *one or two nuclear bombs*. The sensitive document stated that there was a "better than even" chance that North Korea had a nuclear bomb. As North Korea is the world's most secretive nation, U.S. officials have little first-hand knowledge of its activities. As opposed to areas where the United States has spies, informants, and eavesdropping capabilities, in North Korea, much of the intelligence is guesswork. Thus, this NIE was not based on any hard evidence, but rather on officials' extrapolation of the number of weapons North Korea could make with the estimated 12 kilograms of plutonium taken from its reactor during the 1989 shutdown. It also argued that diplomatic efforts or economic sanctions were unlikely to succeed, saying that sanctions could lead the North to attack the South. There was also concern North Korea might trade bombs for oil with countries like Iran. The majority of the intelligence community agreed with the

NIE, although the State Department's Bureau of Intelligence and Research disputed the conclusion, arguing the estimate as a "worst case" analysis.[32] At any rate, the United States could not dismiss the possibility they now might face war with a probable nuclear power.

We're in a pickle if the IAEA bell rings

On December 6, 1993, with the situation deteriorating daily, Clinton was sitting at the head of the table in the Situation Room, surrounded by his top national security advisors. Robert Gallucci, the chief U.S. negotiator with the North Koreans and ambassador at large, was discussing the latest report from the IAEA Board that the North Koreans were blocking inspections, that the "safeguards had lapsed," in IAEA jargon. The head of the IAEA, Hans Blix, was handling the situation with great caution, trying to buy time. "Blix *meant* to mince words," Gallucci explained in his typical pithy fashion, explaining Blix "said they are at the very point of breaking the continuity of safeguards, i.e., they are not *yet* broken."

"Blix is finding every way he can *not* to find a way to say safeguards have been broken," Clinton interjected. "We're in a pickle if the IAEA bell rings. We will have to go to sanctions." The principals all agreed. "We need to look like we've turned over every rock," said Clinton, pushing for greater diplomatic effort. Lake, always looking for the witty comment, added, "Yes, we have to turn over every R-O-K," using the government's abbreviation for the South, "Republic of Korea (ROK)."

Always trying to understand the motivation of his adversaries, Clinton asked, "What's in it for North Korea?" Gallucci responded, "They can avoid sanctions. It will get them to broad and thorough negotiations," meaning a comprehensive change in relations with the United States and South Korea. Ultimately, that meant the possibility of normalizing relations.

But by early January 1994, it was increasingly clear that the North Koreans were not prepared to negotiate. By February, the U.S. armed forces were on high alert—the first time since Desert Storm. The prior December, Clinton had asked to review the Pentagon plans to defend South Korea.[33] The Pentagon had drawn up new war plans, taking account of the lessons learned during the Persian Gulf War. In the event of a North Korean attack, the plan called for American and South Korean forces to slow the assault, allow reinforcements to arrive, and then repulse the invaders. The next stages involved invading North Korea and occupying Pyongyang.[34] Tens of thousands of U.S. soldiers and hundreds of thousands of Korean soldiers and civilians could die. The Pentagon also drew up a plan to attack the Yongbyon facility with precision-guided bombs. Secretary of Defense Perry summed up the approach, "The best way to avoid a war is to make sure they see our resolve."

In early 1994, war with North Korea was a real possibility. All indications—trench digging in the demilitarized zone (DMZ), between North and South Korea, fishing vessels laying mines—indicated the North Koreans wanted the United States to know they were ready to go to war. United States analysts thought they had probably resumed the reprocessing of nuclear materials as well. By March, North Korea was threatening that "we are ready to respond with an eye for an eye and a war for a war. Seoul is not very far from here. If a war breaks out, Seoul will turn into a sea of fire."[35]

On March 19, tensions ran high in the Situation Room. Lake had limited attendance to "principals only," complaining there had been leaks "within two hours" of the last meeting. The principals agreed to proceed with the joint military exercises with South Korea and to "take prudent steps" on the next level of intensity when the UN moved to sanctions. A few days later, they agreed to send Patriot missiles to South Korea and to begin work on a UN resolution to apply economic sanctions against North Korea. As NSC aide Dan Poneman explained it, Shali knew North Korea could well do something violent and big, but it also knew it would not have a regime left.[36] Perry emphasized the United States could not dismiss the possibility of war.

Nevertheless, throughout the crisis with North Korea, President Clinton made it clear that the North Koreans could avoid sanctions and more confrontation, if only they would live up to their commitments. "There's still time for North Korea to avoid sanctions actually taking effect if we can work out something on the nuclear inspections," he declared on June 4 during a meeting in Britain with Prime Minister John Major. "This is in their hands."[37] While preparing for the use of force, he kept the door to diplomacy open.

To the brink

On a cool summer evening on June 13, 1994, the president hosted the Emperor Akihito and Empress Michiko of Japan on their first visit to the United States since ascending to the largely ceremonial post called the "Chrysanthemum Throne." It was the first white-tie event since the Reagan administration. While mostly White House life is unglamorous hard work, State dinners provide a rare exception, with evenings of forced relaxation and elegance. Movie stars, authors, and artists mingle with government officials, each slightly envious of the others' profession.

This night was especially luxurious, especially as the evening's entertainment was an East Room concert of one of the all-time great cello players, Mstislav Rostropovich. He had played for President and Mrs. Kennedy at the height of their charmed presidency. I had worn long gloves for the first and only time in my life and, as I stood in the receiving line, mentioned to a friend that I had no idea whether to keep them on or off during cock-tails and dinner. Luckily, a woman behind me tapped me on the shoulder, saying, "I got the briefing on the gloves." I turned around to see Oprah Winfrey, who told me to keep the gloves on during cocktails but remove them during dinner.

Belying the gaiety of the evening, the president and his foreign policy team were tense. A few hours earlier, North Korea had announced its inten-tion to shut down its reactor, remove the spent fuel, and withdraw from the NPT, deepening the crisis. Such a step meant the North Koreans would begin making nuclear weapons and preparing for war. In response, South Korea had called up 6.6 million reservists earlier in the day. The CIA again warned that North Korea might already possess two nuclear weapons.

The United States was preparing for war, while still hoping lesser meas-ures would succeed in convincing North Korea to pull back, including nego-tiations and possibly sanctions. A few days earlier, the principals had agreed on a phased-sanctions approach to the crisis, starting with reductions in cul-tural and diplomatic ties and a small UN aid program, moving to a ban on all financial sanctions, and eventually a reinforced arms embargo if the North Koreans failed to respond. The end state was enforced sanctions. As Secretary Perry told his colleagues during the June 10, 1994, principals' meeting, if they were to stop a North Korean ship forcibly, "that's an act of war."

The Japanese had a key role to play in the strategy. One of the largest sources of funds in North Korea comes from an organization of Korean res-idents in Japan called "Chosen Soren"[38] that sends substantial funds directly to North Korea. Any sanctions strategy would need the full cooperation of Japan. In addition, the United States would need the support of Japan in a possible war with North Korea.

The presence of many high-level Japanese officials that evening at the White House was fortuitous. Japanese prime minister Hata was wavering on Clinton's decision to keep sanctions against North Korea on the table. The spat had leaked to the press and Japanese officials were quoted as say-ing Tokyo would not support a decision by the United States to refer the issue to the UN Security Council. During the State dinner, Lake shuttled between diplomats seeking to secure Japan's agreement for the sanctions strategy. He pulled Clinton out for a call to Hata, emphasizing the need to be unified and firm against the North.[39]

On June 14, the United States, Japan, and South Korea pledged sanc-tions against North Korea. The stage was set for war.

The Carter gambit

Calls for a military strike against the reprocessing plant were increasing, including one by the respected former national security advisor, Brent

Scowcroft, who in June called on the United States to threaten a military strike to "remove its capacity to reprocess" if Pyongyang failed to cooperate with the inspectors.[40] Clinton knew that any such strike might not eliminate the dispersed nuclear materials or weapons already in North Korea's possession and could well trigger a broader war. As the president reviewed the various options for war, he also continued the search for a diplomatic solution.

As Clinton searched for alternatives, he began to consider seriously the use of former president Jimmy Carter. "You know," Clinton commented to his foreign policy team on June 10, 1994, "he's never violated an understanding I've had with him." While a relationship between two former presidents is always somewhat tense, Clinton respected the fellow Southerner and had found his diplomacy useful in Haiti. Clinton knew Carter was eager to go to North Korea and had secured an invitation to visit on behalf of his center in Atlanta. Clinton had secretly sent a letter to the North Korean president, Kim Il Sung via his friend the Reverend Billy Graham, but as a former president Carter was a more credible interlocutor on this issue. With strong beliefs of his own and deeply skeptical of the use of force, Carter could also be a bit of a loose cannon, making his own policy.[41] As commander in chief, Clinton bore the responsibility of defending the United States, with war as a last resort. He agreed Carter should go to Pyongyang.

On June 15, 1994, Carter, his wife Rosalynn, and a small delegation arrived in Pyongyang, the same day the United States began circulating a draft resolution calling for phased sanctions at the UN. There remains disagreement on exactly what Carter had authority to discuss with the North Koreans. Carter's version was that he left virtually uninstructed. He says he "wrote out my talking points . . . read them to Gallucci, and he had no suggestions for changes. We left home . . . as well briefed as possible but without any clear instructions or official endorsement. In effect, we were on our own."[42]

In fact, Lake had met Carter at National Airport outside of Washington, D.C., as Carter was leaving. Clinton had decided Carter was to listen carefully to the North Koreans and restate existing policy. Lake made it clear that the president had decided Carter was to have no negotiating authority. "I defined for him clearly and carefully our policy and where things stood," Lake recalled. "He was to make it clear that he was acting as a private citizen, but we expected him to act consistently with our policy."[43] "He had zero authority to say anything beyond existing U.S. policy," Dan Poneman later recalled.[44] Bob Gallucci claims Carter was authorized to describe Clinton's "firmness on issues," including sanctions, but also that President Clinton was interested in improving political and economic relations as he resolved the nuclear issues. Yet, as a former president, Carter felt empowered to follow his own instincts rather than such specific guidelines.

According to Carter's later recollection, at his meeting on June 16 with President Kim Il Sung and his foreign ministry team, he "outlined the entire situation" and ultimately got Kim to accept his proposals to end the North Korean nuclear program. Kim had two major requests: that the United States support North Korea's acquisition of light-water reactor technology, realizing that the funding and equipment could not come directly from America; and that the United States guarantee that there be no nuclear attack against his country. Kim also wanted to resume the next round of talks with the United States to resolve all the outstanding nuclear issues. Carter also claimed Kim was willing to freeze North Korea's nuclear program during the talks and to consider a permanent freeze if their aged reactors could be replaced with modern and safer ones. If such a freeze also meant the North Koreans would commit to not reprocessing the spent fuel or restarting its problematic reactor, it represented a major breakthrough. The problem was, Washington had no details and no sense of how real the deal was.

Later that evening, Carter called Gallucci on an open line to report the apparent agreement with President Kim Il Sung and told Gallucci he intended to announce the deal on CNN. It was morning in Washington and the principals were meeting in the Cabinet Room. Gallucci briefed the principals on what Carter had told him. Lake quickly asked Gallucci whether he had asked Carter not to announce any deal before the principals had a chance to review it. Unfortunately, Gallucci had not, feeling it was difficult for him to tell a former president what he could and could not say to the press. Lake rushed to try to reach Carter but could not.

So the principals huddled around the television in the small anteroom between the Cabinet Room and the Oval Office to hear what Carter had to say. Around 11:30 A.M., Wolf Blitzer explained on CNN that Carter had achieved a breakthrough. Carter then told the world by telephone from Pyongyang that "President Kim Il Sung has committed himself to maintain the inspectors on site . . . and also to guarantee that the surveillance equipment would stay in good operating order. The other point . . . is a denuclearized peninsula." He did not mention the crucial requirement that North Korean freeze its nuclear program—a major omission. In a statement that enraged those watching back in Washington, Carter said he hoped the United States would pull back from its sanctions efforts, adding that he was trying to prevent the "irreconcilable mistake" of imposing sanctions, a direct slap at Clinton's policy.

Carter then went on to talk about the possibility of normalizing relations between the two countries and to suggest a meeting at the foreign ministry level, and even a direct conversation between President Clinton and Kim Il Sung.[45] Clinton's advisors all winced. Such proposals were out of the question in 1994 as they would be viewed as appeasement. Carter made it worse the next day in earshot of reporters when he said to Kim Il

Sung the administration had "stopped the sanctions activity in the United Nations,"[46] while, in fact, Albright was still pushing the issue in New York. Although Carter had technically followed the "ET" rule of diplomacy—phone home—the fact that he was announcing a suspension of the sanctions was stunning. Not only was that step directly opposed to Clinton's policy of keeping the pressure of sanctions on, Carter had been explicitly told he had no authority to make such a statement, especially without first discussing it with the White House. Lake recalls that Carter had not been authorized to discuss normalization; "We never used the word normalization," Lake recalled. "Rather, over time as the North Koreans did certain things, the U.S. would take measures that would lead to more normal relations."[47] Contradicting a sitting president showed chutzpah, even if Carter had once occupied the Oval Office. The main problem was that Carter did not support Clinton's policy of imposing sanctions against North Korea if it violated its nonproliferation commitments. As Carter later commented, he had "always believed that the North Koreans are incapable of accepting peacefully the insult of international sanctions."[48]

Vice President Gore pressed the principals to "make lemonade out of this lemon."[49] The administration had not verified the North Korean statement and hoped to secure more than Carter had announced, such as a commitment that the North Koreans would not restart the reactor at Yongbyon or reprocess the spent fuel. Clinton understood the opportunity Carter's possible breakthrough offered but did not know whether the North Koreans would come through and felt the step was not sufficient to justify an end to the push for sanctions. As Dan Poneman later explained, Clinton could not go back to the status quo ante for a resumption of negotiations, as the North Koreans had crossed a red line. "The only firm commitment Carter had was for the North Koreans to let the inspectors stay," said Poneman. Lake explained that Carter had not dealt with two key aspects the United States sought, a commitment by North Korea not to process the spent fuel or restart the 5 megawatt reactor.[50]

At 5:45 P.M., Clinton strode into the White House press briefing. "Today," Clinton explained with caution, "there are reports that the North Koreans, in discussions with President Carter, may have offered new steps to resolve the international community's concerns. . . . If North Korea means by this, also, that it is willing to freeze its nuclear program while talks take place, this could be a promising development." Clinton avoided saying definitively that this in fact *was* a promising development. The administration quickly sent the North Koreans a letter demanding these additional steps.

A week later, on June 22, the administration received confirmation from Gallucci's counterpart, Kang Sok Ju, that North Korea would freeze its nuclear program while talks proceeded, reiterating that sanctions and dialogue were "absolutely incompatible."[51] The president announced that he was suspending the sanctions effort at the UN during the discussions, emphasizing that the developments were not a solution to the problem, but rather "a new opportunity to find a solution."[52] In the meantime, he continued military preparations, and Shalikashvili kept under review sending another twenty-five thousand troops to Korea, worrying whether the Pentagon could sustain the deployment of the estimated four hundred thousand troops needed for full war preparations.

Getting to yes

Then, suddenly, the "Great Leader," Kim Il Sung, died on July 8, the day talks on the agreement began in Geneva. As Kim had been the only man empowered to make major decisions in North Korea, no one knew what his death meant for the agreement he had just reached with the United States. U.S. intelligence had never been able to penetrate the closed society. Thus, U.S. policymakers had little idea of whether his son, Kim Jong Il, would continue his policy now that he had succeeded him. The United States had virtually no information on the son and knew next to nothing about why the father had suddenly died. The United States did know that Kim's son was in charge of nuclear programs, and that he had some kind of health problems. His mouth would drop and his eyes roll, prompting Korea watchers to speculate that the son had a neurological problem, possibly epilepsy. He was also rumored to have diabetes and heart trouble.

Yet, the new North Korean leader did eventually pick up where his father had left off. Negotiations with North Korea finally concluded on October 17, 1994. Four days later, the president announced the signing of the 1994 United States–North Korea Agreed Framework in a press conference in the East Room of the White House, reserved for momentous occasions. "This is a good deal for the United States. North Korea will freeze and then dismantle its nuclear program. . . . The entire world will be safer as we slow the spread of nuclear weapons." Clinton also pointed out that South Korea, Japan, and other nations would bear most of the cost of providing North Korea with fuel.[53]

The Agreed Framework involved three phases spread over ten years, in each of which the United States, Japan, South Korea, and others would finance aid to North Korea—fuel, food, and two light-water reactors—in exchange for steps North Korea would take to freeze and dismantle its nuclear program, under a strict IAEA inspections regime. North Korea would receive no significant nuclear components until it complied fully with the IAEA's requirements, in particular inspections. Japan and South Korea were to bear the bulk of the cost of $4 billion to $5 billion for the reactors, targeted for completion in 2003. The United States and its allies would also provide five hundred thousand tons of free heavy fuel annually to North

Korea to compensate for the energy equivalent to that produced by the frozen reactors.

The United States also pledged to provide formal assurances to North Korea against the threat or use of nuclear weapons by the United States. Both North Korea and the United States also pledged to "move toward full normalization of political and economic relations." While many have since come to believe the agreement required North Korea to send the spent fuel rods out of the country, the issue was left for later discussions.[54]

Republicans wasted no time in criticizing the deal. Paul Wolfowitz, who would become the number two official at the Pentagon under the second president Bush, declared, "It seems to me that we are in a situation where we are paying more and more for less and less."[55] The Republican Party's "Contract with America," a platform it used to win control of the House of Representatives—giving the Republican party control of both houses of Congress for the first time in forty years—contained sharp criticism of the Agreed Framework deal. Many Republicans, such as Maine's senator William Cohen, whom Clinton chose as his secretary of defense in 1997, claimed the Agreed Framework had "little prospect of successfully addressing the North Korean threat."[56] Another, Alaska's senator Frank Murkowski declared that it did nothing more than extend "the life of the North Korean regime by providing vast sums of free oil and expensive nuclear reactor technology."[57]

Clinton's own CIA director, James Woolsey, commented to his colleagues as the deal was being negotiated that "this is a policy fraught with danger because of its uncertainty. I think we should face the fact that they won't stop processing nuclear materials," arguing the administration should support sanctions. Woolsey and Clinton always had a difficult relationship, not, as Woolsey has charged, because Clinton was not interested in intelligence issues. Rather, Clinton came to distrust the smart but very opinionated official's objectivity. He also felt Woolsey did not fully grasp the complexity of the challenges Clinton faced. When the small Cessna plane crashed into the White House in 1994, jokes circulated in Washington that the pilot was Woolsey trying to get in to see the president. He resigned in 1995 and endorsed Republican candidate Bob Dole in the 1996 presidential race.

To his credit, former president Bush did not criticize the deal, although in private he said to Gallucci and Poneman, "It looks like we are just paying them off to do what they should have done anyway." He added that the issue might be a "Vandenberg-like" issue, where bipartisan support would be appropriate, referring to former Michigan Senator Arthur Hendrick Vandenberg who had argued that politics should stop at the waters' edge. But Bush was skeptical the North Koreans would live up to their word, saying he did not trust them. "I really don't. I don't think that the old man turned nice at the end. And his son should stay out of the photographs."[58]

The best of bad options

Following the Agreed Framework, progress was made on a range of issues of concern to the United States. President Clinton and South Korean President Kim Young Sam initiated the Four Party Korean Peace Talks, among two Koreas, China, and the United States, in April 1996 to reduce tensions on the peninsula. In October 2000, Clinton sent his secretary of state, Madeleine Albright, to North Korea; she remains the highest-ranking U.S. official ever to visit the secretive country. During her visit to Pyongyang, Albright met with Kim Jong Il for six hours. In October 2000, Clinton met with a North Korean special envoy in the Oval Office, following which both countries signed a communiqué declaring neither had hostile intent toward the other.[59] Clinton seriously considered visiting North Korea, but in the end decided against doing so, instead inviting Kim Jong Il to the White House. Kim declined.

Substantial progress was made through these encounters on an end to the North's missile program. In September 1999, North Korea pledged to refrain from testing long-range missiles. It reiterated its respect for this moratorium in June 2000 and, in response, Clinton eased the sanctions against North Korea that had been in place since 1948. Trade was reopened, as well as direct personal and commercial financial transactions, investments, cargo shipments, and commercial flights. Trade in military goods and sensitive technology, however, remained prohibited.[60] Progress on the recovery of remains of soldiers missing from the Korean War was made as well. And the two presidents of North and South Korea held their first summit, in June 2000, in Pyongyang.

In the end, the 1994 Agreed Framework deal succeeded in keeping North Korea from using its plutonium to mass-produce nuclear bombs, a major accomplishment. But there were problems in implementing the agreement throughout. Lee Sigal, a longtime Korea watcher, argues that the United States "did not fully meet any of its obligations under the accord in the critical 1994–1997 period."[61] As Dan Poneman described it, "North Korea thought it was buying a different kind of relationship. While it was always looking for ways out, when they didn't get that relationship, their efforts took on a new meaning."[62] South Korea and Japan were also slow to put up the money for new reactors. In 1997, North Korea repeatedly warned U.S. officials that if Washington did not live up to the accord, it was not obligated to either. In 1998, the North began acquiring the means to enrich uranium from Pakistan.

While the slow U.S. and allied implementation in no way justifies North Korean actions, it does shed some light onto the secretive regime's logic. By 2002, the promised light-water reactors had yet to be delivered to North Korea, although ground had been broken in preparation for their construction. Difficulties in funding for the reactors and the major logistical challenge of building such complex facilities in such an undeveloped nation created major hurdles. By May 2003, the target date for the two reactors had shifted from its original target date of 2003 to 2008 for the first reactor and 2009 for the second.[63] While the international community did honor its pledge to deliver annually the five hundred thousand tons of heavy fuel oil to North Korea, the shipments were chronically behind schedule.[64]

For their part, North Korea complied in some areas and violated the agreement in others. It kept its plutonium program frozen, halted construction of the new reactors, and permitted IAEA inspectors access to most of its facilities. However, it blocked the IAEA access to some facilities, including an isotope production laboratory and the stored plutonium. It also failed to implement the declaration on denuclearization and failed to improve its relations with South Korea, although South Korean President Kim Dae Jung visited Pyonyang.[65] In addition, the second stage was never reached, when the North Koreans would be obliged to dispose of the fuel rods in a safe manner that did not involve reprocessing in North Korea. And most importantly, it apparently started its HEU program in late 1997 or 1998, one the North Koreans are believed to have accelerated in late 2001 and 2002. In late 2002, Secretary of State Powell stated that he now believed they have had nuclear weapons for years.[66] North Korea might be capable of producing a bomb's worth or more of HEU by mid-decade, in addition to its plutonium-based program already under way, with probably six to eight nuclear weapons by late 2004.

In response to the news of the HEU program, the United States, Japan, and South Korea suspended further shipments of heavy fuel oil in December 2002. Future fuel shipments would depend on North Korea's "concrete and credible actions to dismantle completely its highly enriched uranium program" as well as its prompt elimination of "nuclear weapons program in a visible and verifiable manner." Future relations with these countries would depend on "complete and permanent elimination of its nuclear weapons program."[67]

While the United States has always formally kept the issue of food aid separate from the nuclear issue, the Bush administration has dramatically scaled back on food aid, despite continued need in North Korea—roughly 41 percent of children under the age of seven in North Korea are severely malnourished. The World Food Program indicated that the restriction on food aid caused by tensions between North Korea and its three largest donors (the United States, Japan, and South Korea) led to an almost 50 percent cut in food assistance to the nation. Between September and December 2002, the World Food Program had to drop approximately 3 million of the 6.4 million North Korean beneficiaries from its food programs.[68]

On January 10, 2003, North Korea announced it was withdrawing from the NPT. History was set to repeat itself. The U.S. response this time, however, was different, driven largely by the hegemon myth and not reality.

We won't play

Faced with a crisis almost identical to the 1994 situation, the Bush administration was intent on not negotiating with North Korea or offering any inducements whatsoever. White House spokesman Ari Fleischer declared on January 13, 2003, "North Korea wants to take the world through its blackmail playbook and we won't play. It's up to North Korea to come back into international compliance with their obligations."[69] For the next year and a half, the administration struggled to avoid negotiating with North Korea, naively expecting the North would back down in the face of tough talk from Washington.

Rather than back down, however, North Korea escalated its threats. In mid-April, North Korean officials told their American counterparts that the country already possessed two bombs, had reprocessed the previously stored spent fuel, and hinted it might test a nuclear weapon to prove its capabilities. To reverse this course, North Korea demanded that the United States provide four types of benefits similar to what it had demanded in the lead up to the 1994 Agreed Framework deal: security assurances, a pledge not to seek regime change, economic assistance, and energy assistance.[70] When it received no response from the administration, North Korea once again upped the ante, claiming in August 2003 it was capable of, and prepared to test, a nuclear weapon to prove its capability.[71] In July 2003 it also threatened to make its supplies of plutonium available to the highest bidder.[72]

The threat to the United States was not just rhetorical. In February 2003, CIA Director George Tenet testified in Congress that North Korea had missiles that could hit the West Coast of the United States with a nuclear warhead.[73] In July, the respected Carnegie Endowment for International Peace estimated that by 2010, an unchecked North Korea could produce enough weapons-grade material to produce up to 235 plutonium-based weapons and up to 18 HEU weapons.[74] By continuously running its 5-megawatt reactor, it was possible that North Korea could be adding one additional nuclear bomb to its stockpile per year. If Pyongyang could complete construction on its medium (50-megawatt) and large (200-megawatt) reactors, it would eventually be able to produce enough plutonium to create 55 nuclear weapons to its arsenal per year. The full extent and capacity of North Korea's uranium program is largely unknown.[75]

As the crisis escalated throughout the spring and summer of 2003, Bush administration officials sent confusing signals on whether it would negotiate with North Korea. The White House spokesman had announced on January

8 that the administration will talk but had "no intention of getting into any negotiations or offering any inducements."[76] Yet on January 13, the same day his spokesman stated the United States "won't play," Bush in effect offered to negotiate, saying he would consider restarting the "bold initiative" Colin Powell had begun if North Korea agreed to end its nuclear program.[77]

Assistant Secretary James A. Kelly, while in Seoul that January, elaborated the economic incentives the administration would consider were North Korea to end its nuclear programs. "We are of course willing to talk," Kelly explained. "Once we get beyond nuclear weapons, there may be opportunities with the United States, with private investors, with other countries to help North Korea in the energy area."[78] Kelly reportedly also told his South Korean counterparts that neither sanctions against North Korea nor a military attack were currently being contemplated.[79]

The administration faced strong political pressure not to negotiate. Many prominent Republicans opposed any negotiations or incentives. Senator John McCain commented in January 2003, "After first responding appropriately to North Korean violations of the agreement and refusing even to discuss with North Korea its extortion demands, the administration now appears to have embraced, and in some respects exceeded, the style and substance of Clinton's diplomacy."[80] Some in the Bush administration also sought to squelch any negotiations, including Undersecretary John Bolton, who publicly berated Kim Jong Il as a "tyrannical dictator."[81] Yet, the administration had no other sensible options. A military strike against the facility was not a feasible option as such action would not eliminate North Korea's dispersed and well-hidden program.

Not a crisis?

As the North Korean crisis escalated, the administration sought to avoid attention on the issue, preferring instead to focus its effort on the war on terrorism and on building the case for war against Iraq. While U.S. defense doctrine maintains that the U.S. force level be sufficient to fight two wars simultaneously, the senior Bush administration officials made a concerted effort to downplay the Korean crisis, in effect denying it was a crisis at all. On January 20, 2003, Secretary of Defense Rumsfeld called the situation on the Korean Peninsula "fairly stable," but oddly also said it was "teetering on the verge of collapse."[82] In February 2003, as North Korea expelled inspectors, restarted its nuclear power, and threatened war, Secretary of State Powell stated that North Korea was not a "crisis situation."[83]

While Iraq readmitted international inspectors and repeatedly stated it did not possess nuclear weapons, North Korea took the opposite tack, and the administration was hard pressed to explain to the American people why Iraq presented a crisis and North Korea did not. Rice tried to draw the distinction with Iraq, indicating Iraq's twelve-year history of defying the international community and seventeen United Nations resolutions. Rice made it clear that Saddam's use and possession of weapons of mass destruction "posed a threat to the security of the United States and the world," making confrontation with his regime "essential."[84]

In his January 28 State of the Union address, a year after the "axis of evil" reference, Bush barely mentioned North Korea, saying that he was "working with the countries of the region . . . to find a peaceful solution, and to show the North Korean government that nuclear weapons will bring only isolation, economic stagnation and continued hardship." In contrast, regarding Iraq, Bush declared that Saddam Hussein had "pursued chemical, biological, and nuclear weapons, even while inspectors were in his country. . . . If Saddam Hussein does not fully disarm, for the safety of our people and for the peace of the world, we will lead a coalition to disarm him."[85]

The administration tried unsuccessfully to balance the political opposition to talks within its own party and the administration and the obvious growing imperative to engage with the North Koreans. The result was an incoherent approach of agreeing to meet, but refusing to negotiate on substance. For example, in early 2003, the administration offered to meet with North Korean officials to talk about their return to compliance with their international obligations, but emphasized that negotiations would occur only once North Korea had dismantled its nuclear programs. President Bush reiterated the approach in May 2003, stating that before the United States would consider any steps, North Korea must achieve "complete, irreversible, and verifiable" dismantlement of its nuclear weapons.

The incoherent policy triggered the inevitable snide jokes. One journalist likened the administration's effort to draw the distinction between talks and negotiations as "basically the difference between foreplay and sex."[86] As the administration struggled for a workable policy that did not resemble that of his predecessor, political pundits joked that Clinton's policies appeared to be the fourth leg of the "axis of evil."

The United States is the main obstacle

While refusing direct negotiations, Bush urged China to take the lead in the multilateral negotiations. But pushing China presented the administration with a major problem: neither China, nor the rest of the Asian leaders supported the administration's confrontational approach. China, South Korea, Japan, and Russia were all pushing for negotiations as the crisis escalated through the spring and summer of 2003.

The United States did succeed in securing a series of regional talks including China, Russia, South Korea, and Japan, first hosted by Beijing August 27 to 29, 2003. During that meeting, the group formulated a unified message to let North Korea know that it had no choice but to abandon its nuclear program. While the Bush administration was right to push for more leadership from the Asian countries, especially China, absent a realistic U.S. policy, the talks went nowhere. In addition, North Korea will not make a deal until it knows what the position of the United States will be. The United States insisted it would not discuss any economic or political benefits until North Korea unilaterally dismantled its nuclear program. North Korea, for its part, demanded that the United States first agree to a nonaggression treaty and threatened to test a nuclear weapon. China and the other regional leaders pushed the United States to negotiate. While stressing the need for an immediate dismantling of nuclear weapons, Japan attempted to smooth the way for negotiations by insisting that "No country, including the United States, has a hostile policy toward North Korea."[87]

Japan and South Korea also indicated it would be willing to help North Korea have alternative access to fuel once it dismantled its nuclear program. China and Russia emphasized the need for economic cooperation with North Korea. While Kim Dae Jung left office in February 2003,[88] his successor, Roh Moo Hyun largely continued the engagement policy, urging moderation and dialogue between the United States and North Korea, while opposing any effort to impose sanctions against North Korea. Parliamentary elections in 2004 strengthened the peace camp in South Korea even further.

In an unusually frank statement for the normally reserved Chinese officials, in August 2003, the Chinese vice foreign minister, Wang Yi, declared that the United States was the "main obstacle" in settling the nuclear issue peacefully. China's foreign ministry spokesman, Kong Quan complained that the United States was threatening North Korea and referred to Washington's "negative policy" toward North Korea.[89] South Korean and the State Department officials warned the White House that talks could break down if Washington could not describe some vision of how relations could improve in the future.[90]

Charles L. Pritchard is the former special envoy for negotiations with North Korea who handled Korean issues for the White House and State Department from 1996 to 2003, and an army colonel until 2000. He characterized the policy: "Once I realized how the Bush team operated, it was amazing. They came across as religious zealots. There was no interagency process, never any effort to compromise to develop a workable policy. Anytime there was progress toward talks, the President and his key advisors would seek to kill it. It was scary."[91]

Getting to yes (again)

By the fall of 2003, the Bush administration began to face the harsh reality that it would have to negotiate with North Korea to end the crisis and moderate its unsustainable position on no negotiations until the North Koreans had abandoned their nuclear campaign. Having no realistic military options, diplomacy once again came to the fore, although the administration did not put forward a semblance of a policy until June 2004.

While reports were premature that Bush had authorized his negotiators to say the United States was prepared to take a range of steps to assist North Korea, the administration slowly backed down from its policy of insisting that the North Koreans give up their weapons before the United States took any steps at all. The administration began to talk of benefits for North Korea, while emphasizing that help would come only after North Korea allowed unplanned "challenge inspections" of suspected nuclear sites and the relocation out of the country of its weapons-grade materials and equipment.[92]

The key shift in strategy was pushed by Secretary of State Colin Powell and his deputy Richard Armitage while they were at the president's Texas ranch in August 2003. Armitage had headed the National Defense University study in 1999, which had endorsed the "more for more" approach.[93] He and Powell further developed the approach without the involvement of Rumsfeld and his Pentagon staff. "It helped that a lot of them were on vacation, or thinking about Iraq," one official commented. Senior U.S. officials began telling reporters that when negotiations started to meet reality, positions had to evolve. "Everybody is realistic enough to know that you can't have a negotiation where one side does everything before the other side does nothing," commented another senior official.[94]

The inept, ideological handling of the crisis with North Korea is not without costs to U.S. interests. As one respected journal noted, there "is increasing concern about whether the USA is a partner capable of playing the multiplicity of roles that international relations requires in Northeast Asia." It went on to say that Bush's actions have already started to shift alliance patterns in Asia. "China and Russia are about as close to each other as they have ever been . . . South Korea continues to shift politically towards an alignment of interest with both Russia and China."[95] Anti-Americanism in South Korea is growing, with 58 percent responding to a poll in May 2003 that they were disappointed that Iraq armed forces had not put up more of a fight against American and coalition forces. Three in ten said they had considered boycotting U.S. products to protest American foreign policy.[96] The revelation in August 2004 that South Korea had conducted secret uranium-enrichment experiments in 2000 as well as in 1982, although it has halted the activity, sparked threats of a nuclear arms race by North Korea. And while the administration focused on Iraq, which had no weapons of mass destruction, North Korea most likely processed enough plutonium to make several more bombs and is now believed to have six to eight.

A deal has been on the table for some time. A senior North Korean diplomat laid it out in a meeting I attended in May 2003, as well as on its news agency Web site. North Korea wants assurances that the United States will not interfere in its internal affairs or seek regime change, will provide assurances of nonaggression, and will not impede its economic development, for example, through denying it access to international financial institutions. If Washington gives such assurance, North Korea is prepared to give up its nuclear weapons programs, rein in its conventional and missile programs, and agree to a more aggressive inspection regime, including United States inspectors.[97] Some form of economic assistance, paid for by South Korea and Japan, will likely also be part of the deal.

Despite the difficulties of negotiating with North Korea, the alternatives remain less attractive. Just as Clinton discovered in 1994, Bush eventually will have to accept the harsh reality that the best way to contain North Korea's nuclear ambitions is to work with it to address its leaders' paranoid fears, while keeping a close eye on its nuclear and proliferation activities. While tough talk of preemptive action, sanctions, and a possible regime collapse played well politically with the administration's hard-line supporters, none of these options were any more realistic in 2004 than they were in 1994. Particularly following the difficulties in Iraq, the administration realized that negotiations were far preferable to a war.

In the end, the administration had little choice but to negotiate a new deal with North Korea. Put forward in June 2004, the Bush plan called for a two-stage effort. In the first, North Korea would fully disclose its nuclear activities, submit to inspections, and pledge to begin eliminating nuclear programs after a three-month period. In exchange, North Korea would receive shipments of heavy fuel oil and have some sanctions lifted. In addition, the United States would provide a provisional security guarantee. Should North Korea comply with the three-month stage, a broader stage could occur, including the lifting of some sanctions, improved diplomatic relations, the removal from the U.S. list of states sponsoring terrorism, and increased economic assistance.[98] Yet, once again, the administration pulled back from negotiations and did not engage the North Koreans. No action was taken on the plan as Bush headed into the fall presidential campaign. North Korea's nuclear program continues unabated.

The hegemons' myth had been destroyed in Iraq and now in North Korea. As both cases make clear, America can only protect its interests by imbedding its policies and actions in the international community's principals, rules, and capabilities. As a superpower, America must lead, but it must also share the burden of that leadership. That principle applies particularly to the many challenges faced in Africa.

12

The African
Intervention Gap

*Nobody should feel he has a clear conscience in this business. If the
pictures of tens of thousands of human bodies rotting and gnawed on
by dogs do not wake us up out of our apathy, I don't know what will.*

—Then Undersecretary Secretary-General Kofi Annan,
commenting on Rwanda, May 1994

Resolving the crisis with North Korea was clearly in the "strategic interest"
of the United States. There was never any doubt that we would intervene,
that we would risk war to protect our interests. The actions taken to resolve
that crisis stand in stark contrast to the dithering courses the United States
adopts toward crises in Africa. There is agreement among the American
people and its leaders on the need to use force to defend United States'
interests in the war on terrorism and in strategic areas, such as Korea, the
Middle East, and Europe, but Africa remains outside the intervention zone,
not only for the hegemons but for every U.S. president to date.

Much of the world looks to the United States, as the lone superpower,
to act everywhere. The myth of America as the world's police force persists.
While the United States cannot solve all the continents' problems, the crises
in Africa demand that a reluctant Washington engage and lead, intervening at times and assisting others to do so when not. The two post–cold war
presidents, Clinton and George W. Bush, did seek innovative and energetic
ways to alleviate African suffering. But both were cautious about sending
UN troops to address Africa's ills and opposed sending U.S. troops to
engage in containing the region's many conflicts.

No conflict symbolized the U.S. reluctance to engage in Africa's crises
more than Rwanda. Yet, despite the criticism of the UN and Clinton administration during those horrible months of 1994 and the collective world
guilt for having failed to act, America remains reluctant today to intervene
in Africa. The Bush administration, while continuing to make Africa a polit-

ical priority, is even more unwilling to engage militarily in Africa, illustrated by Bush's refusal to put any meaningful U.S. troop presence on the ground following the departure of Charles Taylor in Liberia in the fall of 2003 and the halting response to the genocide that occurred in Darfur, Sudan, in 2003 to 2004. Despite the pledges of "never again," Africa remains outside the United States' view of strategic importance.

The hegemonic view of America's priorities affords no place for any U.S. military role in Africa's many challenges. The demands of the war on terrorism and the crisis in Iraq make any such intervention even more improbable. Yet, as the continent continues to grapple with the HIV/AIDS epidemic, humanitarian crises, and civil and interstate wars, America is increasingly called upon to respond. Certainly, it must now realize the danger of letting states fail and possibly become another Afghanistan-style haven for terrorists. The continent's many wars pose a threat to the United States—each risks spawning more failed states. It was, after all, in Sudan that bin Laden was able first to develop his al Qaeda network, in Africa that two U.S. embassies were blown up, and in Somalia that a failed state offers continuing opportunities to today's terrorists.

Much of President George Bush's foreign policy is couched in terms of fighting evil; yet he, like his predecessors, is all too willing to stand on the sidelines as evil attacks much of Africa. Particularly given its refusal to put U.S. troops on the ground in Africa, America must use its superpower status to lead the world in addressing the challenges faced by Africa of infectious disease, continuing wars, and failed states. Much can be achieved short of requiring military intervention if the United States is willing to lead and invest in developing institutions, trade, and security in Africa.

Engaging in the many challenges in Africa must be seen as central to protecting America's interests. Sadly, the United States is failing to rise to that challenge. The seemingly endless televised carnage—and the developed nations' seeming indifference to it—risks creating cynicism in the developing world about whether America's great promise really stands for anything at all. Much of the problem is represented in the world's failure to respond to the 1994 Rwandan genocide.

How could we let this happen?

On a bright, sunny December day in 1994, I stepped off the white UN helicopter onto the grassy field of a churchyard. It was lined by the lush trees characteristic of the hills of Rwanda, known as "the land of a thousand hills."[1] I had arrived in the western village of Nyarbuye as part of a delegation led by National Security Advisor Tony Lake on an eight-nation African tour.[2] With the helicopter's rotors still whirling, I shuffled away, head down to avoid the blades. As I straightened up, I took in the scene.

Exotic plants crept up to man-made buildings nearly engulfing them. A rich assortment of birds sang from the trees. Monkeys screeched in the distance. Walking over to the church we had come to visit, the day seemed no different from any other day in this part of Africa. Crossing a grassy field, I stepped over a large bone, assuming at first it was a cow bone left by a dog. Then suddenly, I realized it was a human femur bone, left in the field after the horrific genocide in which hundreds of thousands of people had been hacked to death by their fellow machete-wielding Rwandans. Suddenly, a place that a minute before had been teeming with life seemed eerily silent.

Inside the church, there were bodies everywhere of men, women, and children strewn over the floor—little girls in pretty dresses, men in suits, still lying where the killers had struck them down. Their heads were split, their arms slashed, and their bodies hacked apart. They were here, in this house of peace, because they had sought refuge from the killers. The local officials who led us through the carnage knew exactly who was responsible for the violence, including the mayor of their town and many of their former neighbors, killing an estimated fifteen thousand people at this single site. Right there and then we all vowed to ourselves to use the power of the United States government to help bring those responsible to justice. Some of the killers were brought to trial, yet today, it is far from clear that the world stands prepared to stop the next genocide.

During the killing spree, the United States had not acted to end the massacres; instead it pushed for a withdrawal of the United Nations peacekeeping force. The genocide in Rwanda became a symbol of the West's unwillingness to intervene in Africa's conflicts. Those of us involved in the events at the time still struggle with understanding our actions. But to date, the accounts of the decision-making have been told largely by outsiders, with little understanding of the real choices faced by policymakers at the time. Understanding what happened provides important—and realistic—policy prescriptions for United States policy in Africa.

Is it Hutus or Tutsis?

Rwanda, with a population of 7.4 million today, gained independence from Belgium in 1962, and in the four decades since then, there has been a violent relationship between its two main ethnic groups, Hutus and Tutsis. While the categories used are less than exact, roughly 85 percent of Rwanda is considered Bantu Hutu, and 15 percent is considered Tutsi. As with much of Africa, European colonialists exploited ethic differences that today continue to fuel conflict. In Rwanda's case, the Belgians favored the Tutsis, choosing them to run the provincial government and administer the colony on their behalf. The Hutus still resent what they viewed as the arrogance of the Tutsis and their privileged status.

Periodic power struggles erupted between the two ethnic groups, costing tens of thousands of lives. In 1959, the Hutus seized power, driving many Tutsis into exile. Descendants of those exiled would later form the Rwandan Patriotic Front (RPF) army, now leading the country. Fighting had most recently erupted in February 1993, triggering the killing of more than forty thousand civilians and causing the exodus of approximately a million people. In August 1993, with the support of the United States and activists such as Jesse Jackson, the parties reached the Arusha peace accord.

Hutu president Juvenal Habyarimana and the leaders of the opposition Tutsi RPF, Paul Kagame and Alexis Kenyarengwe, signed the accord in Arusha, Tanzania. The agreement, which initially had an overly ambitious mandate for the UN to "guarantee the overall security of the country," called for a forty-five-hundred-member United Nations peacekeeping force to support the Arusha ceasefire.[3] In what would prove to be perhaps the biggest mistake it made, the United States, citing cost and danger to the troops, succeeded in pressing for what it considered a more realistic mandate, limited to monitoring and observing the situation, investigating noncompliance with the peace accord, and limiting the force to twenty-five hundred members. That smaller mission would later prove wholly inadequate in the face of genocide. For a few months, the accord appeared to be holding and the United Nations force and mandate sufficient.

Then, on April 6, 1994, the plane carrying President Habyarimana and the newly elected president of Burundi, Cyprien Ntaryamira, was shot down as it was approaching the airport in Rwanda's capital, Kigali. The two presidents—both Hutu—were killed instantly. The attack was most likely carried out by extremist Hutu militants opposed to the peace accord. It was the signal to the killers to start carrying out the genocide that they had been carefully planning throughout late 1993 and early 1994. Yet, at the time, no one in Washington expected a genocide to break out.

The morning after the death of the two presidents, I asked my morning CIA briefer what was likely to happen. "Another cycle of violence," the briefer replied.

"Is it Hutus killing Tutsi? Or vice versa?" I asked.

"It is likely to be both," he said.

"How many are likely to die?"

"Probably tens of thousands," I was told. The State Department assessment at the time was that "there is a strong likelihood that widespread violence could break out."[4] In a slaughter that received virtually no international attention, *one hundred thousand* had died the previous October in neighboring Burundi. That was viewed as the limit of possible casualties.

There has been much debate in the international community over what the White House knew of the impending genocide and when it knew it.

The answer is, in short, that we knew tens of thousands might die in the wake of the deaths of the two presidents. We did not know that close to a million people would be slaughtered over a hundred days in a premeditated genocide that surpassed even the Nazi attempt to exterminate the Jews in speed and horrible efficiency. Until mid-April, when a shocking two hundred thousand people had been killed, most policymakers thought the peace process could be put back on track.

In twenty minutes, my men can kill up to a thousand Tutsis

While the failures to pick up on clues following the signing of the Arusha peace accords are many, one of the most egregious was not to take seriously the reports of a possible genocide in the fall of 1993 and in early 1994. The possibility that a genocide could occur was never seriously considered. Policymakers instead focused on keeping the peace process on track. Nowhere is this myopic view better demonstrated than in the now famous "genocide fax" of early 1994.[5]

On January 11, 1994, the United Nations force commander in Rwanda, Canadian Lieutenant General Romeo A. Dallaire, sent a cable to the United Nations military advisor in New York entitled "Request for Protection for Informant." The prime minister designate, a Hutu, Mr. Faustin Twagiramungu, had put Lieutenant General Dallaire in contact with an informant who was a top-level trainer in the Hutu militia, called the Interahamwe, meaning "those who fight together." The informant told Dallaire three key things—all of which would soon come true. First, the Hutu militia was planning to target and assassinate opposition deputies and to kill Belgian soldiers serving in the United Nations mission, hoping they would then withdraw. Second, the informant said the militia had trained seventeen hundred men who were scattered in groups of forty throughout Kigali. Their objective was to register all Tutsis, most likely for their extermination. Providing chilling detail, the informant said his militia could kill up to one thousand Tutsi in twenty minutes. Third, the informant told the United Nations of a major weapons cache with at least 135 weapons. He asked for protection for his family if he showed the United Nations the cache.[6]

Although Dallaire's cable became known as the "genocide fax" when Philip Gourevitch first described it four years later in *The New Yorker* on May 11, 1998, at the time, the United Nations and government officials who were aware of the information focused not on the threat of extermination of Tutsis but rather on the request by Dallaire to seize the arms cache. At the United Nations headquarters, the Department of Peacekeeping, led at the time by Kofi Annan, rejected his request to seize the arms and instead instructed Dallaire to raise the issue of the weapons cache with key foreign governments as well as the interim Rwandan government—which was right then planning the genocide. United Nations Special Representative Jacques-Roger Booh Booh and Dallaire met in Kigali with the Belgian, French, and American chiefs of missions on January 12, 1994, to discuss a coordinated response to the informant's information.

Booh Booh and Dallaire explained that they had sought guidance from United Nations headquarters because they sensed the possibility of a diplomatic or military "trap" in the offing, in effect questioning the motives of the informant. During the conversation, the arms cache, not the threat of genocide, was the focus of discussion. A confidential embassy cable back to Washington reporting on the meeting was entitled, "UN Special Representative asks for Support on Security Demarche." What it should have said in hindsight: "RED ALERT! GENOCIDE BEING PLANNED! MOBILIZE THE TROOPS!"[7] It did not even mention training the militia or plans for the extermination of the Tutsis. During the months the genocide was being planned, the international community was overly focused on the establishment of an interior government and upholding the Arusha peace process. For instance, on February 3, Dallaire briefed a visiting U.S. official that the UN mission in Rwanda was still "a winner." Dallaire said Rwandans still had the will to implement the peace accords and remained supportive of UNAMIR, although he did push for a UN reserve of rapidly deployable forces to "maximize the good will."[8] A review of the cables from the U.S. embassy in Kigali reveals that the primary focus of U.S. officials at the time was the peace process as well. Officials drew Washington's attention to threats of violence but believed the best way to address those threats was to support the peace process.

No one focused on the impending genocide. As with Bosnia and so many other conflicts, the international community put its energy into negotiating peace, missing the broader picture of an impending total collapse. The pressure to make the peace work meant the international community was not attuned to the signs of impending genocide. Sadly, it took the United States three years to intervene in Bosnia; there was never any chance it would mobilize quickly in Rwanda.

A fatal withdrawal

By April 10, the nongovernmental organization Doctors without Borders estimated that eight thousand people had been killed in Kigali alone. It soon became clear that government-backed Hutus were systematically targeting Tutsis and moderate Hutus. They were assassinating government officials, Catholic clerics, and Rwandan employees of foreign aid agencies. Hutus abducted and executed Prime Minister Agatha Uwilingiyimana while she was under the supposed protection of Belgian troops. Ten Belgian United Nations peacekeepers were taken to Rwandan barracks and executed. On April 21, officials of the International Committee of the Red Cross had estimated that more than a hundred thousand Rwandans had been killed during the prior two weeks and called it a "human tragedy on a scale we have rarely witnessed."[9]

Even with so many reported dead, the international response and the use of the word genocide were slow to come. The RPF rebels first used the term genocide on April 13, charging that the Hutu-led Presidential Guard was on a campaign to "exterminate the Tutsi minority and liquidate the politicians who are not in the presidential movement."[10] The United Nations Secretary-General did not term the killing a genocide until May 4[11]; the Clinton administration inexcusably did not do so until May 21, fearing that might obligate it to act to stem the violence under the genocide convention.[12] The United States looked to the UN and the Rwandans to restore the peace, not to the Pentagon to stem the killing. On April 22, National Security Advisor Lake called on Rwandan military leaders to "do everything in their power to end the violence immediately."[13]

In the days after the death of the two presidents, United Nations Lieutenant General Dallaire asked for troop reinforcements. Yet, his April 10 message from the field revealed his own ambivalence about their effectiveness, saying, "If we see another three weeks of being cooped up watching them pound each other then we have to seriously assess the risk of keeping these soldiers here." He was well aware the refugees at locations like the Red Cross and various churches were in danger of a massacre if the United Nations left, but added, they "have been in this danger without result so far for the last week even with UNAMIR on the ground."[14] Such comments did not encourage Washington to seek to strengthen the United Nations force. Given the ongoing violence and the death of the Belgian peacekeepers, the United States and other members of the Security Council did not give serious consideration to reinforcing the United Nations troops; they thought drawing down the force to be the prudent option, while seeking to negotiate a renewed peace.

At the time, all the principals agreed that the United Nations force in its current configuration was a failure, although there was never a formal principals' meeting on the issue. In fact, virtually no high-level attention was given to the decision to draw down the UN force. Although Lake and his colleagues were preoccupied with Bosnia and Korea at the time, their lack of attention to Rwanda was principally due to the fact that there was no senior-level disagreement at the time over the proposed course of action. Midlevel officials at the State Department and Richard Clarke of the National Security Council, then the White House point man on peacekeeping issues, recommended to their bosses that the mission be drawn down until a cease-fire could be restored. No decision maker in the U.S. government proposed sending in U.S. or other troops in the middle of the genocide. Thus, much like the lead-up to the loss of the U.S. soldiers in Mogadishu, no one saw a need for a high-level discussion of the issue. Even Monica Mujawamariya, the Rwandan human rights activist who narrowly escaped death during the genocide, did not raise the issue of U.S. ground troops when she met with Lake on April 22. She did ask Lake to name those responsible publicly, which he quickly did.[15]

Secretary-General Boutros-Ghali put forward three options for the Council's consideration, including a reinforced and strengthened mission, a drastic reduction of the force, and a complete withdrawal. However, he failed to push for any of the options. The African delegations of the UN, including Nigeria, which held a rotating seat on the Security Council, did not push for intervention and only mildly opposed a total withdrawal. Africa's other rotating seats were held by Oman and ironically Rwanda. The African states were generally skeptical of non–United Nations intervention due to lingering resentment of their colonial period. Nigeria's UN Ambassador Ibrahim A. Gumbari explained that Nigeria was slow to grasp the genocide and that "events were moving so rapidly . . . the organization of African Unity did not have the opportunity to organize diplomatic lobbying efforts." Gumbari now believes Nigeria should have abstained on the resolution, as it did on the later one authorizing the French intervention.[16] On April 21, the UN Security Council, with strong support from the United States, voted unanimously to reduce UNAMIR to just 270 troops, leaving only a symbolic presence to ostensibly demonstrate its willingness to return once peace was reestablished.

Lake summed up the administration's approach to the crisis on April 26, 1994, at the White House Conference on Africa, a session ironically designed to underscore the administration's commitment to the continent. The first sitting national security advisor to visit Africa and the first to have a serious commitment to assisting the continent, Lake described Rwanda as a "test case" of one of the great security challenges of the post–cold war era: conflicts within rather than among nations. "And it is a warning of what can happen if African nations and all of us do too little to stop simmering conflicts before they boil over."[17] Lake, in essence, was arguing that the international community's only real choice had been to act prior to the genocide. When the sheer scale of the killing emerged in mid-April, however, Lake and his colleagues did act to save lives, although short of intervening to stop the killing through force.

No one is willing to fight a war to stop genocide

Within a week of the fateful decision to pull out the United Nations troops, the massive scale of the carnage became clear and the administration began to realize that, in fact, it should act to save lives where it could, although it still opposed sending troops to stop the genocide. In a May 18, 1994, meeting with a U.S. diplomat, UN High Commissioner for Human Rights Ayala Lasso described the situation in Rwanda as "dramatic and terrible," and he said that he feared that magnitude of the tragedy was far worse than the reported two hundred thousand dead.[18] Thousands of bodies were floating down the Kagera River into Tanzania at the rate of twenty-five bodies an hour.[19] We could now all see that the carnage was worse than any of us had imagined was possible. More than two hundred fifty thousand refugees fled to Tanzania in a twenty-four-hour period, in what the United Nations high commissioner for refugees called "the largest and fastest exodus" ever seen.[20] While the international community hoped the killing spree would end, Boutros-Ghali warned of "strong evidence of preparations for further massacres of civilians . . . [and noted that] massacres continue on a large scale in the countryside, especially in the south."[21]

The administration was skeptical a United Nations peacekeeping mission was the right answer. It had just issued a new policy paper on peacekeeping, called Presidential Decision Directive (PDD) 25. In the wake of the failed operation in Somalia and in response to a Congress hostile to any peacekeeping, the policy laid out a series of conditions for United States support for or participation in United Nations peacekeeping operations. These included, for missions in a permissive environment, under Chapter VI in which peace was expected,[22] the existence of a ceasefire and consent of the parties, and, more generally, a requirement "that the operation's anticipated duration [be] tied to clear objectives and realistic criteria for ending the operation."[23]

On May 17, the United States agreed to support a new mandate for a force of fifty-five hundred troops not to stop the violence, but rather to create secure areas to protect refugees, support the distribution of food supplies, and enforce an arms embargo. The mandate was under Chapter VI and not the more robust Chapter VII under which UN troops would be authorized to take military action. The force therefore would not intervene to stop the genocide, but rather attempt to care for those who could survive it. Rwanda, which in a bizarre twist of history held one of the rotating seats on the Security Council, voted against the resolution.[24]

Given the ongoing violence and the fact that no Western troops would participate in the new mission, it is not surprising that virtually no African nations volunteered troops for the mission, either. By late May, Secretary-General Boutros-Ghali had approached more than thirty heads of state asking for troops. He said it was a "scandal" the world had not acted, and was still not acting; he blamed the whole international community for this failure.[25] On July 25, over two months after the passage of the new resolution, the United Nations force in Rwanda consisted of only five hundred fifty troops. The mission did not reach its full authorized strength of fifty-five hundred until *October* 1994.[26] In early July, the RPF took control of Kigali, effectively ending the war. On July 19, the RPF formed a Government of National Unity consisting of both Hutus and Tutsis. The nightmare was abating, thanks not to the international community but to the Rwandan Patriotic Front.

At the Naval Academy commencement address at the end of May, President Clinton explained in blunt terms yet why the United States would not intervene militarily in Rwanda. Discussing the world's conflicts "from Rwanda to Georgia," Clinton declared, "We cannot solve every such outburst of civil strife or militant nationalism simply by sending our forces. We cannot turn away from them, but our interests are not sufficiently at stake in so many of them to justify a commitment of our folks. Nonetheless, as the world's greatest power, we have an obligation to lead and, at times when our interest and our values are sufficiently at stake, to act." Clinton then spoke not of Rwanda, but of the effort to end the war in Bosnia.[27]

The United States was not yet prepared to act purely on the "values" at stake in Rwanda, such as the deep respect for freedom and human life. Instead, it was the lack of "interests sufficiently at stake" that were at the heart of why the superpower stood by. In 1994, Clinton was still struggling to define America's role in the world and resisting the post–cold war pressure to have the United States serve as the world's policeman.

The aftermath

Throughout July and August, the crisis was no longer of genocidal proportions, but the millions of refugees and displaced persons had immense needs. By July, there were an estimated 2.2 million Rwandan refugees in neighboring countries. Thousands had already died from disease, hunger, exhaustion, and dehydration. An estimated three thousand a day were dying of cholera.[28] Journalists visiting the area described refugee camps as "concentration camps" because of the deplorable living conditions.[29] Lake ran an ad hoc interagency meeting of senior third-tier officials to make sure that, while unwilling to send troops to save Rwandans from the genocide, the United States would do all it could to save lives in the aftermath, becoming in effect a desk officer for the relief effort. "Operation Support Hope," designed to ensure the United Nations had the international logistical support it needed in real time, involved four thousand U.S. military personnel.

In stark contrast to earlier dithering, U.S. forces began deploying on July 22 to Kigali and neighboring Zaire and Uganda to assist those who had fled the genocide, although also inevitably assisting some genocidaires as well. It could do so because it knew how to provide basic services quickly, whereas there were no off-the-shelf, ready-to-go plans to stop a genocide. The United States took responsibility for four of the eight "service packages" requested by the United Nations high commissioner for refugees, including airport services, logistic base services, water management, and site planning. The United States delivered thousands of tons of equipment, food, water, and medicine, increasing safe water production and distribution from nothing to a hundred gallons a day by the end of July.

The one nation to take bold action, albeit too late, was France. French President Francois Mitterrand announced on June 18 that he would dispatch two thousand troops to Rwanda to provide humanitarian assistance until the newly authorized UN peacekeeping force could be brought up to its full strength. The French "Operation Turquoise" brought in troops already in neighboring Zaire to establish a safe humanitarian zone in Rwanda to aid victims of the genocide. While the operation was endorsed by the Security Council on June 22, five Security Council members abstained, including Nigeria, Brazil, China, New Zealand, and Pakistan, concerned over France's history of support for Rwanda's Hutu regimes and wary of any European intervention in the continent.

Initially designed to assist Tutsis fleeing the genocide, the French instead ended up assisting many of the more than 1.5 million Hutu refugees fleeing the Tutsis who had just seized power, many of whom were considered perpetrators of the genocide. Operation Turquoise ended in August 1994 following international outrage over the effort's support for thousands of genocidaires, effectively creating a safe zone for them. While it ended up saving an estimated twenty thousand lives, the poorly handled effort left France reluctant to intervene in future Great Lakes conflicts. For instance, a senior French diplomat explained to me in June 2004 that French troops could not intervene in the deteriorating situation in eastern Congo because of its history in Rwanda.[30] In May 2001, the same official told me that France had learned the lesson of "never again." I had asked him if France would respond to the UN's call for troops to deploy to Burundi, which was at risk of genocide. "Never again," he said, "would France intervene in Africa."[31] General Dallaire, however, later commented that he had only the highest praise for the French operation and that in his estimate it achieved its aims and saved lives.[32]

In the end, American and French resources were only mobilized to assist survivors in the aftermath of the genocide. At the time, "it was unthinkable" that the United States would have sent troops to intervene, Lake later explained.[33] There never was a real possibility that the United States and its allies would be prepared to deploy troops during the first weeks of the genocide, when the killing was taking place and the international community had a chance to stop it. Nor are they today.

Peacekeeping mandate failure

The key mistakes in Rwanda were designing a United Nations peacekeeping mission ill-prepared to deal with a worst-case scenario, having too much optimism on the peace process, and not reinforcing the United Nations force to save those in its care. "All of us must bitterly regret that we did not do more to prevent it," UN Secretary-General Annan said in 1999. "On behalf of the United Nations, I acknowledge this failure and express my deep remorse."[34]

As the United Nations' independent inquiry on Rwanda found, "the mission's mandate was based on an analysis of the peace process which proved erroneous, and which was never corrected despite the significant warning signs that the original mandate had become inadequate. . . . The United Nations mission was predicated on the success of the peace process. . . . The overriding failure to create a force with the capacity, resources and mandate to deal with the growing violence and eventual genocide in Rwanda had roots in the early planning of the mission."[35]

A Carnegie Commission study said there was a "window of opportunity . . . from about April 7 to April 21" when the introduction of a combat force "could have stemmed the violence in and around the capital, prevented its spread to the countryside, and created conditions conducive to the cessation of the civil war."[36] Half the victims died during this period. Yet, the United States, the only country with sufficient capabilities to perform the function, was not prepared to act, especially within that two-week period. The chaotic situation, emphasis on the peace process, and opposition to putting troops into the midst of a genocide doomed any such move.

Those who argue the United States should have mobilized its troops to stop the genocide within days after it had begun fundamentally fail to understand what is required in such decisions. Even assuming President Clinton had realized within a few days that the fastest genocide in history was occurring and had ordered the deployment of troops over the stringent opposition of the Pentagon and the Congress, developing the plans and deploying the troops to Rwanda to stop the killing would have taken weeks under the best of circumstances. One study by Alan Kuperman of the Massachusetts Institute of Technology has looked at possible interventions and found none that would have stopped the genocide early on, although, tragically, they could have saved seventy-five to one hundred thousand Rwandan lives in May and June.[37] In the past, when it has intervened, the United States has deployed roughly twenty thousand troops, as it did in 1965 in the Dominican Republic, 1989 in Panama, and 1994 in Haiti.[38] The Pentagon would have insisted on at least similar numbers for Rwanda during a genocide and would have needed weeks to draw up a plan to intervene into such violence. By the time the killing began, it was too late for an early intervention on this scale. There was no off-the-shelf plan for such an intervention.

Nor could UN forces be deployed in time to stop the killing, absent a willingness by the United States, France, or Britain to airlift troops into the genocide, and absent volunteers of such troops to deploy. Even had the UN Security Council agreed to Dallaire's request for more troops, it is unlikely the troops would have reached Rwanda in time to stop the genocide. By the time a decision to deploy troops by the UN would be decided, reinforcement troops recruited and deployed—probably a month at best—most of the others would have already perished as well. Even when the world realized the extent of the genocide in late April, it took until May 13 to decide on the force and until October for the full fifty-five hundred troops to be deployed.

This is not to excuse the inaction of the United States. Smaller, faster interventions should have been considered. In late April about three hundred thousand of the previous population of 1.1 million Tutsis in Rwanda were still alive, half of whom might have been saved.[39] Innovative approaches, such as airborne assistance to fleeing refugees, should have been used.[40] Certainly, the twenty-five hundred United Nations troops already in the country had a responsibility to protect the twenty-five thousand Rwandans who had sought refuge in United Nations locations around the country. United Nations safe zones could have been established. Had the force stayed in country and been reinforced by a force already on standby, those Rwandans probably would have lived.

The only realistic way to stop the genocide in a large-scale way would have been to reinforce UNAMIR several months prior to the genocide and to have additional troops on standby to augment the force if necessary. In effect, the international community should have prepared for the worst-case scenario and developed plans to address it early on. In early 1994, Belgium had, in fact, urged reinforcements and a new mandate for the mission, arguing that UNAMIR could not maintain order. Making perhaps the most egregious mistake of the whole period, the United States and Britain blocked the Belgian request, citing the cost of more troops and the danger to the peacekeepers. Another thirty-five hundred high-quality troops in Kigali, with armed personnel carriers, helicopters, adequate logistics, and the authorization to use force to ensure security could probably have stopped the genocide. As Kuperman points out, this would have been the five-thousand-man force that Dallaire had envisioned, but one deployed *prior* to the genocide.[41]

In addition to ensuring that the peacekeeping mission in Kigali was larger and tougher, the international community could have also taken other meaningful steps to slow the genocide. It should have branded the crimes genocide much earlier and publicly and frequently denounced the slaughter, making clear the perpetrators would be prosecuted. It certainly should have expelled Rwanda's representation from the Security Council.

Commenting on the failure of the world to respond to the genocide on its tenth anniversary, President Clinton reiterated that the United States had not acted quickly enough after the killing had begun. He said the United States should not have allowed the refugee camps to become safe havens for the killers, nor waited so long to have used the term genocide. He called on the world to improve its "intelligence-gathering capabilities, increase the speed with which the international intervention can be undertaken and muster the global political will required to respond to the threat of genocide wherever it may occur."[42] Is the world prepared to do so?

Never again?

Writing in 1998, a broken Lieutenant General Dallaire lamented the world's continuing reluctance to intervene to stop large-scale slaughter. "I remain mystified that human life, the security of noncombatants, and the prevention of such horrors as the genocide in Rwanda are sadly not sufficient to act as a catalyst for a swift and determined response from the international community."[43] The general's complaint is shared by all of us involved at the time. Yet, his words remain an accurate description of today's international system. The sad but true fact is that at the dawn of the twenty-first century, most, if not all, nations are not prepared to put their own troops at risk outside their own sphere of influence. Rwanda was in 1994—or even today—well outside America's sphere. Washington still believes it would not be our responsibility to stop the killing.

The trauma of the genocide still haunts the officials involved in the events of April and May 1994, as it will for the rest of our lives. Each of us still struggles to understand our inaction; the pictures of the hacked bodies are seared in our memories. In 1994, the world assumed that the tragedy in Somalia had made the United States gun shy about African crises. True. It had. But even had the tragedy in Somalia never occurred, it is unlikely President Clinton would have ordered U.S. troops to deploy to Rwanda or supported a United Nations–authorized force to enter the country to try to stop the killing once it began. Despite the many later apologies and pledges to stop the next genocide, the world is not yet committed to doing so. The ugly truth is that at the root of the failure to act is a belief—perhaps only slightly less prevalent in Washington today than it was in 1994—that the United States has little responsibility to protect the lives of the victims of an ongoing genocide. As Lake, the most humanitarian action–friendly national security advisor in history, explained in 2000, "With the heightened perception of military omnipotence, so may come a sense of ex post facto omniresponsibility. . . . But the possession of such power does not bring with it an automatic responsibility to use it. . . . The perception of unparalleled American strength has led us to be viewed as an 'Atlas that shrugged' in indifference whenever we've chosen not to use it."[44] America the superpower can intervene anywhere. The task is deciding where and when it should.

While the United States cannot be the world's policeman, it can and must lead the world in solving not only strategic conflicts but also humanitarian crises. While the myth that they do not affect America's interests persists, Washington must begin to understand that wars creating economic degradation, massive flows of refugees and displaced persons, and regional instability directly affect us. Not only do they create havens for criminals and terrorists, the United States is ultimately called upon to help with the aftermath.

A decade after the Rwandan genocide, it is far from clear that the world has accepted its responsibility to act.

Responsibility to protect

Secretary-General Kofi Annan, the man in charge of the United Nations peacekeeping department during the failures of the early mid-1990s, broke many United Nations barriers when he called on the international community to unite to stop egregious human rights violations. He declared to the General Assembly on September 20, 1999, that the sovereign state "is being redefined by the forces of globalization and international cooperation. The state is now widely understood to be the servant of its people, and not vice versa." He spoke of a "developing international norm in favour of intervention to protect civilians from wholesale slaughter" as a profound challenge.[45]

A year later, in his Millennium Report to the General Assembly, Annan took the issue a step further, stating "if humanitarian intervention is, indeed, an unacceptable assault on sovereignty, how should we respond to a Rwanda, to a Srebrenica—to gross and systematic violations of human rights that affect every precept of our common humanity? . . . Surely no legal principle—not even sovereignty—can ever shield crimes against humanity."[46] Speaking to the United Nations delegates on September 20, Annan announced his plan to establish a distinguished panel to develop his "responsibility to protect" doctrine further and to try and mold world opinion to accept it.

In 2001, the United Nations Commission on Humanitarian Intervention, cochaired by former Australian foreign minister Gareth Evans[47] and an Algerian diplomat and close advisor to Annan, Mohammed Sahnoun, issued its findings. The groundbreaking study called on the world to accept its responsibility to protect lives at risk. The commission held that "where a population is suffering serious harm, as a result of internal war, insurgency, repression or state failure, and the state in question is unwilling or unable to halt or avert it, the principle of nonintervention yields to the international responsibility to protect."[48] The commission issued a challenge to the world community that it could no longer ignore human rights abuses under the cover of sovereign rights; nor could it stand aside claiming it did not have a responsibility to intervene in the face of grave human rights abuses. Yet, as was brought brutally to light by recent events in Liberia and Sudan, the United States and the world has yet to respond to that call.

Taylor's Liberia

Of all the nations of Africa, Liberia looks most to the United States for support. Established in 1822 as a haven for freed American slaves, Liberia became Africa's first black-run republic in 1847. Until the 1970s it was a peaceful country, but since then, Liberia has deteriorated into a failed state run by a series of repressive rulers. The latest of these was Charles Taylor, who has been involved in Liberia's bloody civil wars since 1989 and became the country's president in 1997.

Aptly dubbed the "Milosevic of West Africa" by Ambassador Richard Holbrooke, Taylor succeeded in destabilizing the entire West African region in his bid to remain in power. In a complicated web of support to neighboring militias, Taylor fomented war in neighboring Sierra Leone, the Ivory Coast, and Guinea, in order to keep his neighbors from supporting his opponents and to secure access to his neighbors' lucrative diamond resources. Taylor was in large part responsible for some of the worst atrocities in Sierra Leone, where Taylor-backed rebels made a practice of cutting off the limbs of thousands of victims, including both arms of a *two-year-old* girl I held on a visit to Sierra Leone in 1999.

While keeping the issue of military intervention off the table, the international community sought to isolate Taylor as his threat to the region became clear. With the little two-year-old girl's image seared in my mind, I worked at the United Nations to secure sanctions against Liberia, often over the strong objection of the representatives of Taylor's African allies on the Security Council, such as Mali. The United Nations Security Council imposed an arms embargo against Liberia in 1992 and later strengthened it in 2001, adding a ban on diamonds and travel. Between 1997 and 2000, the Council also sought to restrict Taylor's fomenting of violence and theft in nearby Sierra Leone by passing bans on petroleum, arms, and diamonds there. The poorly enforced sanctions did little to stop the flow of arms and funds to Taylor. In negotiating the establishment of the war-crimes tribunal for Sierra Leone in August 2000, I worked with the State Department's talented lawyer, Pierre Prosper, to draft the language specifically to include Taylor in those eligible for indictment by the court.[49]

It was not until the summer of 2003 that the international community began to realize Taylor had to go. He was finally indicted on June 4, 2003, for war crimes and crimes against humanity. The United States joined in the effort to secure his departure on June 26, 2003. On the eve of his first trip to Africa, President Bush declared, "President Taylor needs to step down, so that his country can be spared further bloodshed."[50] This action changed the dynamics in Liberia overnight. Until Bush's statement, the international community remained engaged in tactical negotiations with Taylor, in the vain hope that peace was possible with Taylor still in office. In yet another instance in which the international community lost sight of the need for an endgame strategy, the negotiators had failed to grasp the fact that Taylor himself was the principle obstacle to peace and would ultimately scuttle any of their short-term tactical ceasefires or other weak agreements. But the indictment and Bush's call changed the dynamics. Nigerian president Olusegun Obasanjo offered Taylor asylum and he fled to southern Nigeria on August 11.[51]

Double standard

President Bush pledged to work with regional governments to reach a comprehensive peace agreement and to map out a secure transition to elections, adding that the United States was "determined to help the people of Liberia find the path to peace."[52] What kind of help the United States would offer remained unclear. Pressure immediately began to build for the United States to lead a peacekeeping force to ensure stability in Liberia and to support a transition from Taylor to a democratically elected government. With major operations in both Iraq and Afghanistan under way, charges of a double standard quickly emerged. Texas congresswoman Shelia Jackson Lee said, "I believe there is a question of whether or not we treat Africa differently because of its race of people as opposed to other areas. [The president and Secretary Powell] need to look at this very, very carefully."[53]

The United States was under particular pressure to send a peacekeeping force to Liberia, not only because of its historical ties to Liberia but also because European allies had done their part in the region. In May 2000, Britain had sent a thousand troops to shore up the faltering UN peacekeeping mission in neighboring Sierra Leone and in October 2002, the French did the same to stem the civil war in Ivory Coast, sending initially twenty-five hundred and then a total of four thousand troops. In both cases, the peace was fragile as Taylor continued to support rebels opposing the governments now supported by French and British troops. Additionally, in June 2003, a coalition led by the French and including troops from Britain, Sweden, Norway, South Africa, Canada, and Brazil, with Belgium and Germany providing only noncombat troops, sent eighteen hundred troops into Bunia in the northeast region of the Democratic Republic of the Congo in an attempt to stem the swelling violence.[54] The United States was a natural first choice to assist in Liberia.

Despite President Bush's leadership in calling for Taylor's departure, United States officials quickly sent signals opposing American participation in any Liberian peacekeeping mission, pushing instead for African forces to take the lead. For instance, Deputy Secretary of Defense Paul Wolfowitz said in July that the United States sought to "assist the United Nations and the countries of West Africa to stabilize the situation to avert a humanitarian disaster . . . our job is to set the conditions for other people to step up to their responsibilities."[55]

The calls for the United States to assist the African-led effort continued as the violence escalated, despite a peace agreement signed on August 18. On July 25, 2003, the United States sent twenty-three hundred marines to anchor offshore, refusing to place Americans on Liberian soil in any significant numbers. A total of two hundred U.S. soldiers entered Monrovia, primarily to protect the United States embassy and the airport, and to act as liaisons with the African peacekeeping forces. The ground forces stayed only eleven days.[56] The United Nations, regional African leaders, Liberian officials, and nongovernmental organizations pleaded with the United States to increase its presence, to do more to assist the thirty-five hundred African peacekeepers, and to remain in the country until the United Nations force of fifteen thousand was in place to take over. As the head of one relief agency in Liberia said, "While Americans sit offshore and the United States Ambassador claims the conflict is over, tens of thousands of desperate people are streaming toward the capital in search of safety."[57]

In the end, the meager United States intervention may prove to have been adequate to secure the departure of Taylor and ensure the insertion of a peacekeeping operation that will "assist the transitional government, in conjunction with [the Community of West African States] ECOWAS and other international partners, in preparing for national elections scheduled no later than the end of 2005."[58] But thousands of lives outside Monrovia could certainly have been saved had the United States deployed troops in larger numbers, equipped the African forces, and assisted in their deployment. The response to the 2004 crisis in Sudan was only slightly more encouraging in judging whether the United States and the international community are recognizing their responsibility to protect.

Darfur

On May 11, 2004, I sat across from the French ambassador to the United Nations, Jean-Marc de La Sablière in the modern conference room of the French Mission on the forty-fourth floor of a building overlooking Manhattan. Around the table sat ambassadors from most of the Security Council members who had come to hear a briefing from one of my colleagues at the International Crisis Group on the crisis of ethnic cleansing in Darfur, Sudan.

Over the last two decades, a little noticed civil war has raged in Sudan between the Muslim government in the north and the Christian and animist south, with 2 million dead and a million regularly at risk of famine.[59] It is Africa's longest-running war. Pressed by the Christian community in the United States, concerned over the persecution of Christians in southern Sudan, President Bush has made the pursuit of a peace agreement in Sudan a priority. In 2001, five days before September 11, he appointed an envoy for peace in Sudan, former senator and Episcopalian priest John C. Danforth. The first step toward a lasting peace came about in July 2002 with the Machakos Protocol, which guarantees the people of southern Sudan the right to hold a referendum on their future relationship to northern Sudan after a six-year interim period. It also established that northern Sudan will be governed in accordance with sharia law, while southern Sudan will have a secular judicial system. Building upon this initial document, a security protocol was adopted in September 2003, which guaranteed that southern Sudan could have its own army during the interim period. Negotiations, organized and facilitated by the Intergovernmental Authority on Development, led by Kenya,[60] resulted in the signing of peace protocols for each of the three disputed areas of the country involved in the north-south war on May 26, 2004, in Naivasha, Kenya. A comprehensive peace agreement detailing these framework protocols remains elusive.[61]

As this fragile peace process moved forward, rebels in the western region of Darfur saw a chance to make their own demands, and in February 2003 rebels seized the capital of a regional province, demanding more development projects for the underdeveloped region.[62] Although uniformly Muslim, Darfur's population, Arab and non-Arab, consists of an array of tribal groups of ancestry, the latter derogatorily known as "Zurga" or "blacks." Since the 1980s, the Khartoum government has sought to favor groups of Arab background, causing resentment among those identified as non-Arab.[63] With the government making peace with the rest of the country, they saw a chance at righting the wrongs of the past two decades. The two rebel groups in Darfur, the Sudan Liberation Army/Movement (SLA/M) and the Justice and Equality Movement (JEM) called for an end to the region's marginalization, better representation, and more power-sharing with the central government.[64]

Khartoum regarded the insurgency as a grave threat to its long struggle to preserve and consolidate power. The Sudanese government unleashed a brutal campaign of ethnic cleansing, assuming the world would look away, as it had for most of the twenty-year war with the south. The government recruited and armed over twenty thousand Muslim militiamen, called Janjaweed, or "evil men on horseback," to carry out attacks on the Muslim civilian population. In a swift campaign, approximately one million people were uprooted in the first fourteen months and were displaced within Sudan, while about two hundred thousand fled across the border into neighboring Chad, one of the world's poorest countries.

Despite all the pledges to learn the lesson of Rwanda, the international community has failed to respond adequately to Khartoum's brutal campaign to crush the rebellion. By September 2003, there were sixty-five thousand refugees in Chad and at least half a million people in Darfur in need of assistance. Yet, major international actors—including neighboring governments and the four most involved Western countries (the United States, UK, Norway, and Italy)—chose quiet diplomacy over any significant pressure.[65] My colleagues and I began to press the United Nations and key members of the Security Council to act in early 2004. The group I had joined after the Clinton administration, the International Crisis Group (ICG), is a nonprofit organization, based in Brussels, that seeks to prevent and contain deadly conflict. In mid-February 2004, the group's special advisor on Africa, John Prendergast, and I had briefed UN officials and a number of ambassadors on his recent trip during which he had witnessed the ethnic cleansing. The brilliant and passionate Prendergast spent most of 2004 prodding the world to act. He deserves high praise for his major contribution in raising the world's conscienceness on Darfur. Starting in early 2004, Prendergast had also briefed editorial staff, Congress, and humanitarian organizations and warned that three hundred thousand people were at risk of death by the end of 2004. In April, UN officials briefed the Security Council that seven hundred thousand internally displaced people and an estimated one hundred ten thousand refugees in neighboring countries were at risk as government-sponsored militias continued to burn, pillage, and abuse civilians. The council, however, did not act, considering the issue an "internal matter" and therefore off-limits.

By May, the crisis had worsened while the international community continued to sit on the sidelines. The meeting at the French mission was aimed at changing that mindset and spurring some action. My colleague Stephen Ellis, then ICG's Africa program director, and I argued that the crisis in Darfur presented a challenge to the international community: "Were the pledges of 'never again' meaningful?" we asked. Ironically, the world had just finished commemorating the tenth anniversary of the Rwandan genocide. Here was a chance to prove the world was prepared to act. Yet, the discussion around the table indicated clearly the answer was no, that the world had not substantially progressed on the need to protect those at risk.

The reasons we heard around the table varied. The Pakistani representative said that the international community had to tread carefully. "We can't press the Sudanese too hard. This may destabilize the government with unforeseen consequences." The French representative cautioned that, while the Darfur crisis was still raging, the United Nations could not efficiently or reasonably ensure compliance with a peace agreement between the north and south. The Chinese representative opposed any formula that might "further complicate the situation." The Algerian representative urged us to let the Africans take the lead, and the UK representative argued that we needed an overall approach to Sudan to tackle both the Naivasha process and Darfur. The U.S. representative, Stuart Holliday, was the only one at the table who argued on the need to act through diplomacy and possible sanctions, although actual intervention remained off the table.

The international community, having worked for years for an end to the civil war in the south, feared that concerted strong action on Darfur might upset those negotiations. Yet, peace in the south would prove impossible if violence raged elsewhere in the country. In effect, the Sudanese were playing a very sophisticated game of talking about signing a peace deal with the south—just enough to forestall serious council action—while "solving" the Darfur problem militarily. In this case, the Security Council knowingly watched as the Sudanese ethnically cleansed the area with no sanction on the government from the international community, only threats and calls for action.

On May 13, Secretary-General Kofi Annan called for Sudan's president to act immediately to end the crisis in Darfur. In late May, UN Emergency Relief Coordinator Jan Egeland called the situation in Darfur "the biggest humanitarian drama of our time."[66] In June, the U.S. ambassador-at-large for war crimes, Pierre Prosper, said he saw "indicators of genocide" in Darfur and criticized the Sudanese government for continuing to create "artificial obstacles" to humanitarian relief deliveries. "The Bush administration believes that we have a responsibility to help prevent and punish genocide, war crimes and other serious abuses that occur in Africa and worldwide."[67] On September 9, 2004, Secretary of State Colin Powell announced the administration considered the situation to be one of genocide. He blamed the government of Sudan and the Janjaweed militias. Evoking the language of the genocide convention, President Bush urged the international community to work with us to prevent and suppress acts of genocide."[68]

The administration's declaration of genocide in Sudan invokes Article 8 of the Convention on the Prevention and Punishment of the Crime of Genocide, which calls on states to prevent genocide and punish the perpetrators.[69] Yet, it is far from clear what exactly states are required to do once the provision is triggered. Secretary Powell in fact said that "no new action is dictated by this determination," claiming the administration was already doing all it could. "Call it civil war. Call it ethnic cleansing. Call it genocide. Call it 'none of the above.' The reality is the same. There are people in Darfur who desperately need the help of the international community."[70]

The United States had in fact been the most active country opposing the genocide in Darfur. Powell, with Secretary-General Annan, had visited the region in June, the United States had succeeded in pressing the Security Council to issue press statements and pass resolutions in the Security Council, and had threatened sanctions. The Security Council called on the

Sudanese government to end its campaign of violence, disarm the Janjaweed militia, and end its obstruction of humanitarian workers, particularly as the summer rainy season approached. In July 2004, the council passed an ineffective arms embargo against the government-backed Janjaweed, rather than the government of Sudan.

By the fall of 2004, the Security Council had threatened to sanction the government of Sudan if it failed to live up to its commitment to end the violence, disarm the Janjaweed, and allow humanitarian aid. Yet, the Security Council refused to impose sanctions on the government or to send a UN force to Darfur. Instead, each month, it noted the Sudanese failure to fully comply with the council's demands and simply kept threatening sanctions. The Russians publicly stated they will not support sanctions. The Chinese even threatened to veto any sanctions resolution. Both nations presumably are concerned about possible international intervention in their own domestic problems, as well as protecting their financial interests in Sudan. Other members of the council continued to call for caution, lest the Sudanese break off any cooperation. In fact, it was only international pressure that secured any positive action from Khartoum.

It is unlikely that the Security Council will ever take strong action against the Sudanese genocide, such as imposing tough sanctions or authorizing an intervention force to protect the people of Darfur. The majority of the countries represented on the council oppose such action, believing instead that engagement with Khartoum will secure better results. The more cynical reason is that they do not want to set a precedent for UN meddling in their own abuses or risk their financial interests in Sudan.

Another reason for the weak response from the council is that no member was prepared to send its own troops to Darfur, particularly over the continuing objections from the Sudanese. As one diplomat told me, "How can we authorize intervention when there is no one prepared to intervene? The Americans and the British are embroiled in Iraq; the French are going to go to Ivory Coast, and the Africans can't do it."[71] In the end, Sudan took minor steps to end its support for the militias, disarm them, and to end its obstruction of humanitarian aid. By the fall of 2004, an estimated fifty thousand people had been killed, with another two hundred thousand refugees in Chad, and 1.5 million displaced people in Darfur at risk.[72]

In September 2004, the Security Council did endorse an African monitoring mission of 3,320 to Darfur—a year and a half after the genocide began. However, doubts remain over whether the international community will provide the necessary support to make the mission feasible and whether the Sudanese will cooperate with it. "The African mission risks turning into a cynical joke if the U.S. and others do not support it," one senior UN official warned in September 2004.[73] In the end, the world's response to the genocide in Darfur is likely to be a few thousand poorly trained and equipped African monitors and threats of sanctions but no actual imposition or forceful action to prevent or suppress the genocide as the convention requires. The government of Sudan will have essentially had a free hand since February 2003 to conduct genocide. The Security Council demands and threats will have pressured the Sudanese to rein in the violence but not end it. As of November 2004, the sole concrete measure that has occurred is the deployment of eighty African Union observers (protected by six hundred African Union troops) to Darfur, a country the size of France.

Has the world learned from the Rwandan crisis? A bit. The crisis in Darfur demonstrates that genocide can prompt criticism and threats, but the world is still far from forceful action in the face of genocide. As Evans, the intellectual author of the concept of the "Responsibility to Protect" doctrine, said in July 2004, "It's getting a little harder than it used to be for governments to avoid taking effective action when conscience-shocking situations expode." He believes that the responsibility to protect principle is gaining "a real conceptual toehold," but he added that the "instinct and capacity to avoid doing the right thing is still depressingly alive and well. We have a long way to go."[74]

The intervention gap

As Secretary-General Annan recognized in 1999, the willingness of the international community to intervene "varies greatly from region to region and crisis to crisis."[75] Asked on the tenth anniversary of the Rwandan genocide whether the world had learned the lessons from Rwanda, Annan replied, "I really don't know . . . I am not convinced that we will see the kind of political will and the action required to stop it."[76] In discussing whether the world would intervene in the next Rwanda-type crisis, a senior UN diplomat told me in the spring of 2004, "I seriously doubt it. Maybe if it were a former French colony, the French would act. They are more intervention prone."[77]

The Bush administration's extreme reluctance to deploy troops in Africa—and to a lesser extent that of Clinton before him—underscores the harsh reality that the United States and the major capable powers are, for the most part, unwilling to send troops into harm's way for humanitarian missions outside of their sphere of influence, even ten years after Rwanda. George Bush has stuck to the statement he made in his 2000 campaign that he will not act to prevent genocide, declaring "I don't like genocide. But I would not commit our troops."[78] Over time, and with strong U.S. leadership, that fact may change, and capable states may eventually be willing to send their troops abroad beyond their own currently perceived areas of interests. In the meantime, however, the immediate challenge for policymakers is to develop alternatives to protect those at risk.

The need is urgent to develop more capacity for UN peacekeeping, as the United States has essentially opted out of that important function. In 2004, the UN faced new and potential operations in Burundi, Haiti, Ivory Coast, Liberia, and Sudan, and a doubling of the mission in the Congo. Yet, increasingly, developed countries are opting out of UN peacekeeping. The participation of U.S. troops in United Nations peacekeeping essentially ended in 1999 when the UN mission in Macedonia closed. The permanent members of the Security Council, Britain, China, France, Russia, and the United States, contribute a paltry 3.7 percent of the 53,240 UN peacekeepers currently deployed abroad.[79] Of those peacekeeping troops and military observers, the United States contributes a paltry twenty-five soldiers, most serving as military advisors not troops on patrol.[80] The majority of today's UN peacekeepers are made up of soldiers from the developing world. Increasingly, the rich pay and the poor deploy.

Enforcement operations are unevenly undertaken as well. With a few notable exceptions, such as the recent interventions by former colonial powers Britain and France in Africa and NATO's deployment to Afghanistan, American and European leaders share a core principle of sending troops into harm's way only in one's own sphere of regional interest. For instance, the United States intervened in Haiti in 1994 and 2004 and the Balkans in 1995 and 1999; Australia led the intervention into East Timor in 1999; and Nigeria intervened in 1998 in Sierra Leone. Only South Africa answered the secretary-general's 1999 call for troops in Burundi. Yet, as the proposed African deployment to Sudan demonstrates, for the most part, Africa lacks well trained and equipped troops to deploy quickly to stem violence in its own sphere of influence. Thus, there is an intervention gap in Africa, one that is largely driven by a capability gap.

To address that gap, developed nations, especially NATO, U.S., and European Union forces, should build up such a capability in Africa that might prevent future genocides. After the Rwandan genocide, out of concern for a possible genocide in Burundi, President Clinton and his advisors sought to address the reality that neither the United States nor any other capable force was likely to deploy troops to stem crises in Africa. The administration began enhancing the ability of African troops to deploy when crises on the continent erupt. In October of 1996, the administration launched the African Crisis Response Initiative (ACRI) designed to provide training and equipment to African nations that seek to enhance their peacekeeping capabilities and are committed to democratic progress, principles, and civilian rule.[81] The French, initially wary of the United States effort, eventually developed a parallel program in 1997, called Reinforcement of African Peacekeeping Capabilities (RECAMP), which included but was not limited to francophone countries. Britain has also committed to developing a similar program.

In another lesson learned from the Rwanda tragedy, a Multi-National Stand-By-High Readiness Brigade for United Nations Operations (SHRIB-RIG) was created. This force, headquartered in Denmark, has been called on to assist the UN force in Ethiopia and Eritrea (2000 and 2001), to assist the West African regional force, the Economic Community of West African States (ECOWAS), in Cote D'Ivoire (2003), and the UN mission in Liberia (2003).[82] Although it is too early to assess the success of this force, it is undeniably a step in the right direction in terms of recognizing the need for a well-prepared and readily deployable force.

The African Crisis Response Initiative includes three components: peacekeeping training for African soldiers; subregional training exercises that bring African troops together; and the equipping of troops. To date, these various training programs are taking effect. While not yet an intervention force, African nations are developing significant capabilities. The ACRI has trained eighty-six hundred peacekeepers from six countries.[83] Senegal, Ghana, Benin, and Mali have deployed to support United Nations and regional peacekeeping missions. Senegal, Malawi, and Uganda have all sent troops to participate in peacekeeping training exercises. The program has promoted interoperability, standard communication technology, and a common doctrine among African forces ready for rapid deployment to crises in the region.

President Bush has continued the program since taking office, initially supporting ACRI at the level of $20 million, keeping it at the basic level of his predecessor. In the spring of 2002 the Bush administration renamed this program the Africa Contingency Operations Training Assistance (ACOTA), adding training for offensive military operations, including light-infantry tactics and small-unit tactics, to enhance the ability of African troops to conduct peacekeeping operations in hostile environments.[84]

Regrettably, Bush in 2003 cut the program in half as the war against terrorism took precedence, a short-sighted action that was reversed as the administration slowly began to understand the essential role of peacekeeping. In June 2004, the administration indicated it would seek $660 million over five years for training for African peacekeepers and meet more regularly with G8 countries to coordinate peacekeeping support.[85]

With American forces bogged down in Iraq and Afghanistan, it is in the United States' interest to assist Africans in addressing their own problems. Until the United States and other capable countries fulfill their "responsibility to protect," this type of cooperation could very well be the best hope for preventing future genocides and failed states.

These actions demonstrate the world learned a little from the Rwanda genocide. While still reluctant to send troops into the midst of violence, Europeans have demonstrated a willingness to deploy troops in their former colonies in Africa during a crisis. Had it not been for Rwanda, British troops may not have deployed in May 2000 to Sierra Leone, and French troops perhaps would not have deployed to the Ivory Coast in 2002. Yet each of these deployments, and the reluctant minimalist U.S. deployment to Liberia in 2003, were very little, very late. Had the international community acted earlier to confront Charles Taylor, or moved more quickly to stem the ethnic cleansing in Darfur, many more lives would have been saved.

Meeting the challenges of the future

As Africa remains at risk, so does America when policymakers are caught between the myth that the United States can ignore Africa and the myth that it can solve all of Africa's problems. Today, there are more failed states in Africa than in any other region. Addressing the root concerns in the post–September 11 environment is essential to preventing terrorists from finding new safe havens. America is threatened by the ongoing wars, the human toll of HIV/AIDS, and the wasted human and economic potential of the continent. United States leadership in addressing these concerns will remain critical, including meeting its responsibility to protect those in need in Africa.

As a superpower, America has the responsibility to lead in addressing the conflicts of Africa. The United States must realize that Africa can become a threat, even though its states are not a direct enemy of the United States. These weak, failing, and failed states must be considered threats, especially given the free flow of terrorism and WMD. Nonstate actors are often the prime menace. Military intervention can at times help save lives, but only the building of a system of lawfulness and stability will truly protect U.S. interests and make the need for intervention obsolete.

The war on terrorism is placing new strains on U.S. policy toward Africa. Attention is diverted from peace negotiations, the administration is ever more reluctant to deploy United States troops to the region, and scarce aid resources to the region are at risk. Yet, the stakes are too high to ignore Africa. While the pledges of "never again" may not be fulfilled in the near future, the United States must lead the international community in preventing and containing the region's many conflicts. Washington must begin to see addressing these conflicts not simply as humanitarian altruism but rather as vital to America's national security. That means overcoming the myth that Africa doesn't matter and working with the continent's leaders to improve security and head off problems before they develop. Military solutions will not solve the next Somalia or Rwanda. But long-term engagement might.

13

Winning the War on Terrorism

This is the world's fight. This is civilization's fight. This is the fight of all who believe in progress and pluralism, tolerance and freedom.

—President Bush, Address to a Joint Session of Congress, September 20, 2001

Three and a half years after the attacks of September 11, America remains at risk. The threat from al Qaeda is growing more diffuse and potentially more dangerous. America and its allies in the war in Iraq are a particular target, and Iraq has become a magnet for terrorists. Afghanistan remains at risk of war and the Taliban. An unrestrained North Korea continues to churn out nuclear weapons, concerns over Iran's nuclear intentions are increasing, and Africa remains at risk. The effort to create a global effort to drain the swamp of terrorists and their support networks is faltering. Osama bin Laden remains at large.

There have been successes. The administration has shown that it can fight and win two wars, and that intelligence, military, and law enforcement agencies can work together to detect and disrupt planned attacks. Yet abroad and at home, the administration has yet to show it has mastered—or even fully understands—the need for the coalition-building, cooperation, and long-term change processes that the challenge demands. The fixed ideas of the hegemons are still blinding them from pursuing the most effective ways to protect Americans and, long term, to building a world that is not hostile to U.S. interests.

America's interests abroad remain at risk from a backlash over the war in Iraq, the escalating Israeli Palestinian conflict, and rising Muslim fundamentalist hostility toward the United States. An unvanquished al Qaeda has splintered and regrouped; al Qaeda and its allies are networked, global, twenty-first-century organizations. The administration's military vision has proven inadequate to combat the political and financial side of terrorism; and the administration's efforts to remake the domestic legal framework and security apparatus have generated mixed success and gross injustices, while the mistreatment of prisoners abroad has caused considerable embarrassment and fueled anti-American sentiment.

As with Iraq, the lack of security in Afghanistan threatens the gains made there since the overthrow of the Taliban in 2001. Once again, the hegemons' superpower myth focused too heavily on military solutions; the rest of the problem, including the root causes of the failed state, did not warrant sustained U.S. engagement. Once the U.S. military ousted the Taliban from Kabul, the administration believed it had won the war and could ignore the challenge of peace. Again, the more nuanced challenge of winning the peace was dismissed as not worthy of the lone superpower's focus. The myth is dangerous. Today, despite the successful presidential elections in October 2004, Afghanistan is at risk of again becoming a failed state that could once again threaten the region and the United States. The problem is evident to anyone who travels in the country outside of Kabul.

Enough with the burqa, I need a job

I sat in a small room surrounded by twenty Afghan women in October 2002, part of a visit on behalf of the International Crisis Group to the town of Herat on Afghanistan's western border with Iran. Their burqas, all made of the same blue cheap polyester material, hung on a hanger in the corner. They sat on the floor, giving me the one chair in the room. Each worked on embroidering white sheets, pillows, and handkerchiefs, part of an internationally funded aid project seeking to teach war widows employable skills. Women in an adjacent room were weaving richly colored rugs. I asked them, through a translator, how they could stand to wear the burqas, telling them a bit about my own life working side by side men every day. They giggled as I tried on one of the burqas, finding it hilarious to see a Western woman in one.

Sitting down again, I asked the women about their lives. None of them hesitated to tell me the challenges they face. "Forget about the burqa," one said. "My problem isn't wearing the burqa, it is that I don't have a husband, have four children, and can't live with my mother-in-law." These women's husbands had all died in the many Afghan wars, leaving them no way to support themselves. Often, the families of their husbands beat them or used them primarily as slave labor. This project was their only hope for providing themselves and their families with the most basic of needs. They all feared that funding for the project would end and leave them even more destitute.[1]

In fact, since the 2001 overthrow of the Taliban, these women's lives have seen little improvement, although efforts have been made. A ministry of women's affairs was established and significant international donor money for women and girls followed, including the funding of school and university programs for girls and young women. The government made efforts to promote a visible female presence in government posts and other public spaces. These early efforts have been followed by tremendous challenges that threaten genuine advancement of the status of Afghani women. There have been important strides in some areas, such as the central highlands. In other cases, the harsh policies of the religious extremists are applied to both men and women.

However, many women still fear reprisals from religious extremists if they move freely in public. Women and girls are reportedly targeted by soldiers as well, particularly in rural areas, limiting school attendance and meaningful participation in civil society.[2] Police question and detain women seen traveling alone, imposing restrictions on women's ability to work outside the home, and even to listen to music. Girls' schools have been set on fire.[3] In a stark example of women's desperation, human rights groups and media organizations documented the pervasive pattern of immolation and other forms of suicide among women who were trapped in forced marriages and abusive or neglectful households.[4]

The risk to women is symptomatic of the risk of a return to a Taliban-style rule across Afghanistan. Many mistakes made by the Bush administration have put at risk the opportunity created by the overthrow of the Taliban in 2001. The short time line put forward by the United States for the creation of an Afghan government necessitated an overreliance on the existing power structures well before the central Karzai government had security forces capable of enforcing its rule over the rest of the country. That decision could have been ameliorated by a robust peacekeeping mission throughout the country, while the central authority established its new army and police force. But instead, the United States wrongly opposed expanding peacekeeping beyond the capital of Kabul, and local leaders are free to enforce national laws or not as they will.

Security, security, security

The refusal of warlords to submit to the authority of the central government, much less to send resources back to the capital, threatens the stability of Afghanistan and its transition to full democracy. The problems were obvious when I traveled to Herat, where conditions contrasted starkly with the poverty and chaos in Kabul. The capital city in October 2002 had no basic services, heavy pollution, little electricity, and unemployed men lingering in the streets. Large parts of the city still lay in rubble from the 1992–1993 fighting among the mujahadeen. The streets had no traffic lights, electrical wires were jerryrigged throughout the city, and traffic jams were legend.

Traveling to the western city of Herat on the Iranian border, however, was like going to another country. Electricity flowed, buildings were repaired, and roads were being rebuilt. Construction was occurring everywhere. Buildings and bridges were being reconstructed, and the city's famous horse-drawn taxis, cheerfully decorated with red pom-poms, jingled through the city. To make all this happen, the local warlord, Ismail Khan, made only sporadic payments to Kabul, keeping the lucrative revenues from trade with neighboring Iran for his own city. With no army, there was very little President Karzai could do about it.

For security beyond Kabul, the Bush administration steadfastly refused to support a countrywide peacekeeping effort, leaving Hamid Karzai essentially little more than the mayor of Kabul, not the president of Afghanistan. Like the real estate mantra, "location, location, location," success in Afghanistan depends on security, security, security. Following the overthrow of the Taliban, the United States supported the creation of a forty-five-hundred-strong International Security Assistance Force (ISAF)—sanctioned by the UN Security Council in December 2001—to keep the peace and help build a new Afghan national army and police.[5]

The United States chose not to participate in ISAF, wanting to leave the U.S. military free to concentrate on the hunt for bin Laden. The December 2001 Bonn Agreement called for the progressive expansion of the ISAF beyond Kabul to "other urban centres and other areas."[6] But the United States opposed any expansion of the ISAF. As in Iraq, the United States fundamentally failed to anticipate and provide for the peace following U.S. military action. Ideology trumped the practical need for security beyond the capital. It was not until August 2003 that the United States finally relented and agreed to drop its objections, after the economic reconstruction and democratic transition preparations had been undermined. The United States–led coalition forces have focused on the effort to locate terrorists at the expense of broader stabilization and democratization efforts throughout the country, when they should have done both, through an expanded peacekeeping force of soldiers from other nations. The result has been a dangerous ceding of control of the country to the warlords that puts Afghanistan once again at risk.

Provisional reconstruction teams

Despite opposition in Washington to expanding the peacekeeping mission, U.S. commanders on the ground in Afghanistan clearly understood the need for it. United States military officials developed an innovative way to expand the peacekeeping mission in small ways, without calling it expansion. As the commander of U.S. forces in Afghanistan, Lieutenant General Dan K. McNeil, explained it to me in the fall of 2002, "I can send eighty guys to do construction outside a warlord's turf, and he doesn't know whether another two thousand are around the corner." Starting in early 2003, U.S. teams of forty to eighty soldiers were deployed to key sites of instability outside Kabul to provide a presence. Called Provisional Reconstruction Teams (PRTs), the troops carry out civil-military operations, supporting development programs, and providing protection to aid agencies as well as carrying out security functions. By early 2004, the United States had established seven PRTs. By July, NATO had assumed control over PRTs in four northern towns, with plans for an additional one in the northeast. The PRTs were not ideal, however, as many humanitarian organizations felt more at risk as the PRTs blurred the line between military and humanitarian organizations.

While the PRTs helped the security situation, they were no substitute for an expanded peacekeeping mission. Predictably, security conditions in much of the country, especially the south and east, continued to deteriorate. In 2003, attacks on aid workers increased from one per month to one every two days. From January to June 2004, thirty-five humanitarian workers had been killed or wounded. In one brutal incident, Taliban militants beheaded an interpreter for U.S. forces and an Afghan soldier.[7] Afghan soldiers beheaded four Taliban in revenge. The violence led to the withdrawal of international humanitarian staff from project sites in more and more parts of the country.[8]

Responding to the need for expanded security and with an interest in regaining its military relevance in the war on terror, NATO took full command and coordination of ISAF in August 2003, under a mandate from the UN. In October 2003, the United Nations Security Council called for the expansion of ISAF to areas outside of Kabul. But five months elapsed before some of the fifty-seven hundred NATO troops moved beyond Kabul. Even then, the troops only went to Kunduz, a hotbed of stability and security. Expansion is stumbling as NATO member states remain reluctant to commit troops, especially to areas of instability without certainty of continued reinforcement should full-blown conflict break out.[9]

Just when U.S. troops were needed to ensure the capture of key al Qaeda operatives, the Bush administration shifted its focus to Iraq. Security and reconstruction efforts have suffered the consequences. In May 2004, in contrast to the nearly 150,000 U.S. troops deployed throughout Iraq, there were only 10,000 U.S. troops and another 5,700 NATO troops stationed in all of Afghanistan, the larger of the two countries.[10] And, by March 2004, only 9,000 new Afghani police and 7,000 soldiers had been trained, although the original goal had been 20,000 and 10,000, respectively by June 2004.[11] Equally important, by June 2004, only 9,000 of Afghanistan's 100,000 militiamen had been disarmed; the goal had been 40,000, or 40 percent, by the end of June.[12] By the presidential elections in October 2004, only sixteen thousand had been disarmed.

Ambassador Lakdar Brahimi, the UN envoy to Afghanistan until January 2004, expressed his frustration four months after the death of his colleague Sergio Vieira de Mello in Iraq: "Countries that are committed to supporting Afghanistan cannot kid themselves and cannot go on expecting us to work in unacceptable security conditions," he said. "[T]hey seem to think that our presence is important here. Well, if they do, they have got to make sure that the conditions for us to be here are there. If not, we will go away."[13] Concerns for the safety of international personnel mirrored ongoing frustration and fear among Afghan citizens that their lives were in danger from uncontrolled warlords, unmonitored police, and efforts by the Taliban to reestablish its draconian rule.

Hamid Karzai did take several steps to remove some warlords from power, such as negotiating with them over government posts and economic aid in exchange for decommissioning tanks and troops.[14] The lack of disarmament of these troops, however, remains a serious problem. The fighting in Herat in March 2004 is illustrative of the program. When the assassination of the civil aviation minister, a son of warlord Ismail Khan, led to a clash between forces loyal to Ismail a commander Fourth Corps militia, Karzai deployed a battalion, the newly trained Afghan National Army, to keep the violence from spiraling out of control, although Ismail quickly regained control. The action indicated that the new Afghan army was making progress as it successfully defused the situation with only the assistance of American military advisors. But the threat remains throughout the country as government forces are far from capable of maintaining security throughout the country.

Like Iraq, security remains the key challenge for Afghanistan. The consequences of troop and funding shortfalls have obviously put Afghanistan at risk. Despite Secretary Rumsfeld's rosy assertion on March 22, 2004, that Afghanistan was "a success story,"[15] realities on the ground point to a precarious situation. A more accurate description came in June 2004 from the UN Secretary-General's special representative for Afghanistan, Jean Arnault, who concluded that "if anything it has become more volatile."[16]

On June 9, amidst this ongoing violence, Karzai postponed parliamentary elections until April 2005 due to the security threat, while keeping presidential elections to their October 2004 time table.[17]

A Taliban comeback?

Incredible as it may seem to contemplate, it is not impossible that the Taliban or other Islamic radicals could regain power in Afghanistan. As U.S. attention shifted from Afghanistan to Iraq in the fall of 2002, the threat of instability from the warlords, lack of a peacekeeping mission beyond Kabul, and the vast challenges of poverty began increasingly to threaten the U.S. goal of establishing a stable, democratic Afghanistan. Many parts of the country still resemble the environment in which the Taliban first came to power.

Senior Taliban officials, who see the way to power as keeping the country in chaos, have reemerged near the Pakistani border, reconnecting with fundamentalist leaders who have traditionally supported them, and they are now in positions of power in the Pakistani provinces bordering Afghanistan.[18] They are joining warlords opposed to the Bonn process like Gulbuddin Hekmatyar, a hardline mujahadeen leader. Their goal is to seize power from the Karzai government.[19] Their attempts at perpetuating instability and instilling fear in the Afghan population have made it difficult for people to return to daily activities, such as planting and selling crops. They distribute leaflets calling on the local population to oppose the Americans and the government of Hamid Karzai.

The Taliban vowed to disrupt any electoral process, viewing it as legitimizing the United States–backed government. Taliban leaders in Pakistan have issued orders and provided funding for attacks on reconstruction and aid teams as well as government and elections officials. A senior intelligence official said that Taliban senior commander Mullah Mujahid admitted distributing over $1 million to supporters.[20] The Taliban have proven effective in carrying out their plans: 180 died in Taliban-related attacks in the first half of 2004, including the bombing of a bus carrying 15 women elections workers[21] and the killing of 16 Afghans in June for carrying voter registration cards.

Yet, defying these threats, on October 9, 2004, after two decades of war, over ten million Afghans went to the polls to vote, despite the intimidation and the logistical challenges. The day passed with few reports of serious violence. While there were some problems, including multiple registrations, indelible ink washing off too easily, and several legal challenges to the process, Hamid Karzai was officially declared president on November 3, 2004. The hard work of the Afghan government and the international community paid off. The Afghan people's desire for freedom triumphed.

Efforts to get women to vote were also surprisingly successful. Forty-one percent of the registered voters were women who responded to civic education programs, female election workers, and special efforts, such as allowing women to get voter registration cards without photographs. Burqa-clad women, for the first time incorporated into mainstream politics over the objections of the Taliban, courageously went to the polling places. While security threats, inadequate monitoring, and staffing problems kept some women away, especially in the south, overall women came out in larger numbers than expected.[22]

Meeting the Afghans' high expectations that democracy will improve their lives will be difficult. The next test of the strength of their democracy will be the parliamentary elections planned for April 2005. These elections are crucial to Afghanistan's future because the legislature alone can legitimize the president's determination of future state policies. A particularly urgent task is the reconstitution of the Supreme Court, currently stacked with Islamic extremists. Women will face particular challenges in the next election. Although the new Afghan constitution guarantees a quarter of the seats in the parliament to women, continued threats from warlords, the Taliban, and social pressures may keep many women from running. Addressing the overall security environment and the disarmament of armed factions is identified by many women's rights activists as the most significant step that the Afghan government and the international community can take to ensure women's participation in the new democracy.[23]

Meeting this ongoing challenge will require engagement and leadership from the United States. The war in Iraq drew the Bush administration's focus away from Afghanistan during the critical two years following the overthrow of the Taliban, making the job there infinitely harder. The October 2004 elections proved that it is not too late to take steps to ensure that Afghanistan becomes a stable democracy. The key will be a continued focus on the threats posed by weak states, weak economies, and weak institutions. The hegemons' focus on military power cannot address such threats, but sustained international engagement and assistance can.

Challenges ahead

It is not too late for the post-Taliban transition to succeed. But for it to do so, the United States will have to refocus its efforts on a number of key issues. First, it must put its full weight behind the expansion of the ISAF beyond Kabul. While it need not participate itself, the United States must be actively involved in recruiting first-rate, combat-capable troops and ensuring ISAF deployments to areas of instability, not just stability. Factional conflict between the warlords including those represented in Karzai's cabinet, threatens not only the stability of the central government, but also impedes the delivery of much-needed humanitarian supplies to the Afghani people and creates an unsafe environment for both Afghanis and foreign aid workers. In contrast to Iraq, this and other efforts in Afghanistan can be shared with America's friends and allies.

Second, the United States must do more to ensure adequate funding for the development of Afghanistan. To date, the U.S. commitment to Afghanistan of $3 billion pales in comparison to the more than $21 billion in U.S. aid pledge to reconstruction in Iraq.[24] In a stunning testament to the administration's diverted attention, it forgot to provide for humanitarian aid or reconstruction for Afghanistan in the 2003 budget. Congress quickly added the necessary $300 million allocation. Even if one accepts that the United States must invest more heavily in Iraq than in Afghanistan, aid provisions remain well below efforts elsewhere. For instance, in

September 2003, the administration launched a program in Afghanistan entitled "Accelerating Success" proposing $1.76 billion. Yet six months later, aid to Afghanistan was still only $67 per capita, far lower than aid to Kosovo ($814 per capita), Bosnia ($249), Rwanda ($114), and Haiti ($74) during their postconflict reconstruction periods.[25] In contrast, Iraq, an oil-producing country, receives $1,300 per capita.[26]

Despite significant public pledges, congressional reviews found USAID received "very little funding" until the second half of fiscal year 2003— almost two years after the U.S. invasion of Afghanistan. Officials were therefore "unable to develop and plan for long-term resource-intensive reconstruction projects and instead focused on short-term projects that required less money."[27] Many locals turned to the drug trade.

Third, Afghanistan is still producing 70 percent of the world's opium— a figure buoyed by a bumper crop in 2003 and farmers' plans to further expand production in 2004.[28] This, in turn, provides regional warlords with annual drug revenues of roughly $1.3 billion, which are used to augment their already dangerous militias that threaten the stability of Afghanistan and the authority of the central government.[29]

Fourth, while the international community has a responsibility to assist in providing security for the 2005 parliamentary elections, ultimately it will be up to the Afghan people to select leaders and policies for the future, not the past. When Afghanistan's new constitution came into effect on January 6, 2004, U.S. ambassador Zalmay Khalilzad called it "one of the most enlightened constitutions in the Islamic world," noting the requirement for women to hold 25 percent of the seats in the Wolesi Jirga (the lower house of Parliament).[30] The progressive constitution of January 2004 gives Afghans new opportunities, but implementation and enforcement of its provisions are vulnerable to conservative interpretation by Islamic judges.[31] It will be up to the Afghans to make the right choices about their future.

It will also be up to the Afghan people to stand up to the warlords and the Taliban, who exploit the bleak economic and political circumstances to rally increasing support for their extreme policies. Drawing from a pool of more than 2 million Afghan refugees, and the many millions more lacking any real prospect for economic advancement, militant groups successfully expanded their enrollment and operations—so much so that in 2004 the head of the U.S. Defense Intelligence Agency lamented that Taliban attacks had reached "their highest levels since the collapse of the Taliban government" in December 2001.[32]

Fifth, the administration has undermined its interest by turning a blind eye to Pakistan's president Pervez Musharraf's running roughshod over democratic institutions in Pakistan. After September 11, the administration rightly pressed Musharraf to end its support for the Taliban, which he did to some extent. But the administration failed to see the risk of a rise of

Islamic extremism in the wake of a democratic outlet for political expression. By failing to prioritize democratic issues in relations with the Musharraf administration, America may have contributed to the creeping religious radicalization of Pakistan.

Following his 1999 coup and 2001 seizure of the powers of the presidency, Musharraf repeatedly pledged to return the country to civilian rule after elections in October 2002. Yet in April of 2002, Musharraf tightened his grip on power, extending his self-declared presidency for five years, and in 2004 reneged on his pledge to give up the post of army chief. The military has targeted Pakistan's moderate secular parties. Not surprisingly, extreme Islamic parties have gained in popularity. In October 2002, the MMA Islamist Alliance rose from 2 to 45 of the 272 seats in the National Assembly. They also gained control of the Northwest Frontier Province, bordering the Taliban's home province of Kandahar in Afghanistan, where they began to enforce strict Islamic laws and formed a coalition with Musharraf's political party. Throughout 2003 the MMA introduced mandatory prayer calls for government employees, banned shirts and trousers as school uniforms in favor of the loose-fitting traditional *shalwar kameez*, announced that male doctors will not be allowed to treat women, and passed a bill calling for the imposition of Sharia law. The United States must press Pakistan to address this resurgent Islamism that threatens stability in Pakistan and encourages support for al Qaeda in the country.

With Pakistan and Afghanistan at risk, America's war on terror is at risk. After nearly three years of U.S. involvement, Afghanistan is still marked by rampant violence, lawlessness, extreme poverty, and fragile government. Such conditions resemble the conditions that enabled the emergence of the Taliban in the 1990s. They also enable bin Laden and al Qaeda to continue to threaten the United States from inside Afghanistan and along the border with Pakistan.

Al Qaeda: Hunted but not vanquished

CIA director George Tenet summed up the war against al Qaeda in 2002 by saying, "In this struggle, we must play offense as well as defense. The move into the Afghanistan sanctuary was essential." He continued, "We have disrupted the terrorists' plans, denied them the comfort of their bases and training facilities and the confidence that they can mount and remount attacks without fear of serious retribution."[33]

Since the invasion of Afghanistan in October 2001, U.S. forces have sought to hunt down, capture, or kill al Qaeda operatives in Afghanistan and in dozens of countries around the world. Today, 70 percent of al Qaeda senior leadership and more than thirty-four hundred lower-level al Qaeda operatives or associates have been detained or killed.[34] The masterminds of

many major al Qaeda strikes, including September 11, are among those captured or killed.

Other nations have also taken steps to crack down on terrorist cells and
their financial support networks. Since September 11, 2001, 173 countries
have ordered the freezing of terrorist assets in more than 1,400 accounts,
netting $200 million as of September 2003, over half of which was outside
the United States. Over 80 countries have created intelligence units to share
information on terrorist financing and 100 have passed laws to prevent such
cash flows.[35] After initial problems, key countries such as Indonesia and
Saudi Arabia have begun to take steps to crack down on international terrorists operating in their countries. At the June 2003 G-8 summit in Evian,
France, world leaders came to agreements on the international Counterterrorism Action Group, on transport security, and on controls on the proliferation of surface-to-air missiles and weapons of mass destruction.[36] At
the 2004 Sea Island Summit, G-8 leaders agreed on the Secure and
Facilitated International Travel Initiative to protect international travelers
from terrorist attacks and to facilitate trade.[37] Yet, these steps have not eliminated the threat from al Qaeda.

Appearing in early 2004 before Congress for the first time since the Iraq
invasion, CIA director George Tenet warned that al Qaeda "remains as committed as ever to attacking the U.S. mainland," and that "this enemy remains
intent on obtaining and using catastrophic weapons."[38] FBI director Robert
Mueller said during the same Senate meeting that the agency had "strong
indications" that al Qaeda still planned to target strategic U.S. facilities such
as the White House and the Capitol, noting that al Qaeda "retains a cadre
of supporters within the United States," and is actively recruiting more.[39]
Osama bin Laden, his top lieutenant Ayman al Zawahiri, head of Islamic
Egyptian Jihad, and the Taliban leader Mullah Omar remain at large, most
likely along the Afghanistan-Pakistan border.

As U.S. forces shifted to the war in Iraq, al Qaeda regrouped along the
Pakistan border, using traditional tribal areas as a safe haven. An October
2003 tape of bin Laden reiterated his threats against America, calling for
the youth of the Islamic world to join the "jihad" in Iraq, saying "You are
God's soldiers and the arrows of Islam," and specifically threatening attacks
against countries that were members of the "Coalition of the Willing" in
Iraq.[40] In an early 2004 tape, bin Laden's deputy, al Zawahiri, denied Bush's
assertion that two-thirds of the al Qaeda network had been captured and
promised a continued assault on the United States and its allies, saying
"Bush, fortify your defenses and intensify your security measures, because
the Muslim nation, which sent brigades to New York and Washington, has
decided to send you one brigade after another, carrying death and seeking
Paradise."[41] Just before the third anniversary of the September 11 attacks,

al Zawahiri appeared in a video again threatening to send "successive brigades to sow death and inspire to paradise."[42]

Not until March 2004 did the United States begin a serious effort to hunt down bin Laden in the border region between Afghanistan and Pakistan. Task Force 121, an elite unit of Special Forces and CIA operatives, which had played a role in the capture of Saddam Hussein, arrived in 2004 to spearhead a spring offensive to search for bin Laden.[43] For the first time, Pakistan provided significant military involvement as well, sending five thousand troops into the mountains on the Afghan border to push foreign fighters toward Afghanistan and American troops.[44] But from his hiding spot, bin Laden, believed still to be alive, and his operatives continued to record video and radio tapes threatening America and its allies. Al Qaeda also remains active in the United States.

Since 2001, numerous suspected al Qaeda supporters have been arrested in the United States, including in Seattle, Detroit, Buffalo, and Portland, Oregon. The Department of Justice has charged over 260 individuals, with 140 convictions or guilty pleas as of September 2003. But the record of success is questionable. Too many of those whose arrests were trumpeted as significant victories in the war on terrorism have been found guilty of little more than visa irregularities, found to be victims of unscrupulous informers, or had their cases irreparably marred by improper Justice Department procedures. For example, a December 2003 review of the over 260 terrorism-related prosecutions cited by the Justice Department revealed that many of those included in the tally were originally detained as terrorist suspects but later actually charged only for petty crimes unconnected to terrorism, such as twenty Pittsburgh men involved in a scam to obtain commercial drivers' licenses, or two men convicted of accepting stolen breakfast cereal in their stores.[45] Similarly, a Syracuse University study showed that the median sentence for defendants in international terrorism cases won by the Justice Department is two weeks.[46] Whether these arrests represent any real blow to al Qaeda's threat to the United States is difficult to judge.

The administration continues to warn the American public of a grave threat to the United States. But the color-coded threat advisory system, modeled after the military's defense condition, or DefCon, threat scale, has been disconcerting to the American public and unaccompanied by any specific information on how the public should respond when alert levels are raised.[47] As one Israeli major general observed in 2003, drawing on his knowledge of his country's vast experience with the constant threat of terrorism, "We would never just raise an alert level without specific instructions to the public."[48]

Airplanes, too, remain part of bin Laden's terror plots. While beefed up U.S. security appears to have deterred additional al Qaeda airline attacks within the United States, overseas flights, particularly those headed for the United States, continue to be al Qaeda targets. After initially proposing to place armed U.S. air marshals aboard several flights from Europe to America, U.S. officials opted instead to ground any flights of concern following international objections to the air marshals. Throughout 2003 and 2004, intelligence led to the cancellation of numerous flights from Europe, Saudi Arabia, and Mexico to the United States, as well as flights between the UK and Kenya and Saudi Arabia. British Airways and some U.S. airlines have also explored missile-defense shields for their aircraft following concerns over missile attacks.[49]

Since September 11, bin Laden and his operatives have made good on many of their threats. In late 2002, a shoulder-fired missile narrowly missed a plane carrying Israeli tourists in Kenya, and minutes later, the Paradise Beach resort in Mombasa was rammed with a truck full of explosives, killing three Israelis and eleven Kenyans. In May 2003, a suicide bombing was carried out in a suburb in Riyadh, Saudi Arabia, that housed mainly Westerners, killing twenty-five residents in addition to the nine bombers. Al Qaeda took responsibility for multiple terrorist attacks in Istanbul, Turkey, in the fall of 2003, which targeted synagogues, the British Consulate, and an office of the British bank HSBC. Attacks linked to al Qaeda have been documented from the Philippines to Indonesia, Pakistan, and Iraq.[50]

The next wave of the terrorist threat

CIA director George Tenet said in early 2004 that the al Qaeda threat had "splintered" as a result of U.S. efforts to dismantle the group, creating smaller al Qaeda cells that will be "the next wave of the terrorist threat."[51] As one observer noted, the now dispersed al Qaeda is linking up with smaller terrorist groups, such as Salifiya Jihadia in Morocco, which have "gained momentum because these high-quality al Qaeda members joined them," referring to the core military trainers, recruiters, and financiers who were displaced from Afghanistan and Pakistan with the invasion of U.S. forces. Al Qaeda's capacities to attack have expanded, and its influence has spread as far as the Philippines, Yemen, Chechnya, Somalia, and Georgia, among others.[52]

There are also some links with the Indonesia-based Jemaah Islamiya, which was responsible for bombing a Bali nightclub in October 2002 that killed more than two hundred people, mostly vacationing Australians. While Jemaah Islamiya has kept its distance from al Qaeda and operates with its own local decision-making process and specific agenda for establishing an Islamic state in Indonesia, the organization has received direct financial support from al Qaeda and shares much of the same ideology and emulation of bin Laden.[53] The group's leader, Hambali, was captured in Thailand on August 13, 2003.[54]

In October 2003, bin Laden threatened that his network would "maintain our right to reply, at the appropriate time and place," to states involved in the United States–led war in Iraq, "particularly Britain, Spain, Australia, Poland, Japan, and Italy."[55] Spain would suffer the consequences.

Ground zero Madrid

An eerie 911 days after the attacks of September 11, 2001, Europe suffered its deadliest attack since World War II. More than 190 innocent people were killed and fifteen hundred were wounded when ten bombs tore into commuter trains during the morning rush hour in Madrid, Spain. It was Spain's September 11.

Initially, many assumed that the Basque terrorist group ETA was behind the attacks.[56] Through connections I had made during the Irish peace process, I had been in touch with some Basque groups seeking to convince ETA to declare a ceasefire. A month before the Madrid bombs, they told me that ETA was considering a ceasefire following the elections and had made it clear that it wanted to do so in an atmosphere that would not look like a defeat. At first, I thought ETA, like the IRA when it broke its 1994 ceasefire with its 1996 bombing of Canary Wharf, might perversely have felt such a "spectacular," as the IRA called large attacks, would send the Spanish government a signal ETA was not defeated. The fact that the bombings took place just three days before Spain's general elections also seemed to suggest the involvement of a group with domestic political motivation, such as the ETA.

Yet, it quickly became clear that ETA was not behind the attack. Large-scale bombings with no warning to the civilian population had never been an ETA tactic. Spanish authorities soon determined the bombings were the work of al Qaeda affiliates. Bin Laden appears to have made good on his October 2003 threat. Prime Minister Aznar, conscious of the fact that 90 percent of the population opposed his decision to go to war, clung irresponsibly to the ETA theory in a blatant effort to bolster his conservative Popular Party in the elections. Combined with rising discontent over Aznar's perceived arrogance, his close alignment of Spain with the United States, and his mishandling of an oil tanker spill off the coast of Spain two years before led to his ouster, the move backfired.[57] Spain's Socialist Party, led by Jose Luis Rodriguez Zapatero, who had campaigned against the war in Iraq and pledged to withdraw Spain's thirteen hundred troops from Iraq and redirect Spain's foreign policy, won the March 14 elections. Zapatero withdrew the last Spanish troops from Iraq in May 2004. The Socialist win sent shock waves around Europe and in the United States, where many fretted that Zapatero's antiwar message and troop withdrawal would undermine the coalition's efforts in Iraq. Many feared al Qaeda would take credit for the ouster of Aznar, Bush's key ally in the war, and seek to undermine America's allies elsewhere through terrorism.

The attack demonstrated Europe's vulnerability and the world's failure to stop al Qaeda. Despite strong pledges in 2001 to galvanize support for implementing the twelve UN conventions against terrorism, at the time of the Madrid bombings, "many states are not yet party to these legal instruments, or are not yet implementing them," according to the UN Office on Drugs and Crime.[58] Immediately following the 2001 attacks, the UN Security Council pressed all states to implement fully the UN conventions. It put its most able diplomat, Sir Jeremy Greenstock, at the head of the terrorism committee responsible for pressing states to deal with terrorism. "Actually, we got going with considerable momentum," Greenstock recalled in June 2004. "Only seven states failed to respond to our badgering. We set up regional activity, global seminars, and approached the operational institutions, such as the OECD, INTERPOL, and regional institutions."[59] While in recent years, the committee has lost momentum, especially after Greenstock left for Iraq, it is still making a contribution. As the then director of the U.S. Treasury Office of Foreign Assets Control, Rick Newcomb, explained, "the UN Committee is working to target, identify, and block the assets of al Qaeda and its support structure. It is working better and is more coordinated and effective than I ever thought possible. However, with the UN focusing only on al Qaeda and not all terrorists groups . . . , it is not a truly global war on terrorism, as we now have in the U.S., in so far as Hezbollah, Hamas, and other such non–al Qaeda terrorist groups are not included in its mandate."[60]

At the time of the Madrid bombings, five European countries had failed to make extradition of terrorist suspects part of their national law; only nine had implemented joint investigation teams to trace cross-border crimes; eleven nations had failed to enact laws enabling police to make cross-border requests on communications and banking. Three had not even approved the EU's common definition of terrorism. Cooperation among European intelligence and law enforcement agencies was fraught with difficulties. An action plan to cut off funding to terrorists has frozen only one hundred bank accounts, netting a paltry 1.6 million euros.[61] It was not until March 2004, after the Madrid bombing, that Europe finally appointed an antiterror czar, Gijs de Vries. As one German official put it, Europe woke up after September 11, "and then hit the snooze button."[62]

With the transatlantic rift over the war in Iraq, the U.S. administration has been reluctant to work with Europe in a pragmatic and effective way. The administration's overall ideological resistance to international engagement and sharing of sensitive intelligence information also hampered progress on the war on terrorism. For instance, the roommate of one of the September 11 hijackers walked free in Germany from lack of evidence because the United

States could not find a way to share evidence with the Germans and refused to allow testimony in German court from an al Qaeda suspect in U.S. custody.[63] Such an approach undermines the law enforcement cooperation necessary to run al Qaeda assets and operatives to the ground.

Europe and America remain vulnerable to another al Qaeda attack. Following the Madrid bombings, a French official said that another attack was "imminent." Scotland Yard's chief said that a strike against London was "inevitable." The FBI director Robert Mueller declared in March 2004 that he fears terrorist attacks in both Europe, especially around the Olympics and the U.S. political conventions.[64] Thankfully, none occurred.

Both sides of the Atlantic must do more together. The United States and Europe must add a crackdown on informal financial networks, including those masquerading as charities, to their efforts in the formal financial sector. They can do more to make the UN antiterrorism conventions strong and relevant, and more to build cooperation with its third-country partners. And both sides must work through the institutions they built together, the UN, NATO, and WTO chief among them. The United States must realign itself to address the threat within its borders as well.

USA PATRIOT Act

At home, President Bush has sought to make vast changes in the way the United States fights terrorism. Following the attacks of September 11, the administration had unprecedented and extraordinary political support to reshape the government's response to terrorism. Sweeping policy reforms were suddenly possible to transform the laws, financial system, and bureaucratic structures countering terrorism. What was not possible prior to September 11, suddenly, was possible. The bureaucratic wrangling that had stymied efforts to "connect the dots" in the lead up to September 11 could be put to rest. Intelligence and military priorities were suddenly clear.

America was under attack and had to respond. In stark contrast to the constraints on President Clinton's efforts to enact tough antiterrorism legislation, the American people and the Congress united behind President Bush's efforts to enhance the government's authority to fight terror following the September 11 attack. The administration's own priorities became clear; first, the legal changes enacted in the USA PATRIOT Act and the Military Order of November 13, 2001; then, when the clamor for it grew too loud to be ignored, a Department of Homeland Security; and finally, increases in counterterrorism funding and activity across the board. The question is whether these measures are making Americans safer.

On October 25, 2001, President Bush stood in the White House East Room surrounded by lawmakers and accompanied by the vice president, who had been largely absent from public life since the September 11 attacks.

There, he signed a bill that gave him sweeping new powers, the Uniting and Strengthening America by Providing Appropriate Tools Required to Intercept and Obstruct Terrorism Act of 2001, called the USA PATRIOT Act.[65] In one of the swiftest actions in its two-hundred-year history, the Congress passed the bill a mere thirty-seven days following the administration's introduction of a draft to Congress on September 19, with no substantive debate or changes.

The act included numerous intelligence and technology provisions that had been proposed before the attacks of September 11 but never enacted due to political opposition. It provides authorities to strengthen law enforcement's abilities to prevent, investigate, and prosecute acts of terror. It gives investigators greater authority to track communications for the purposes of law enforcement or intelligence gathering against terrorism, including roving wire taps and greater ability to monitor e-mail and Internet use. It increases information-sharing opportunities among law enforcement and intelligence bodies and provides unambiguous authority for law enforcement officials to disclose foreign intelligence collected in a criminal investigation. It provides stronger regulatory powers to prevent money laundering for terrorist purposes in U.S. financial institutions. It allows the indefinite preventative detention of non–United States citizens suspected of terrorist activities.

The bill provides extraordinary new powers to the government. Surveillance jurisdiction now permits detectives to search a subject's residence and other property without the subject's knowledge. In searching private residences and businesses, law enforcement officials have the authority to confiscate personal property, without notifying the subject of the search until weeks later. Seeking to eliminate the "wall" between foreign and domestic agencies, the act provides unambiguous authority for the attorney general and other law enforcement officials to disclose to the director of Central Intelligence foreign intelligence collected in the course of a criminal investigation.[66] Terrorist-related crimes are now given maximum penalties and forgo statutes of limitations for their suspects. The act allows the government to seize personal records, including library, medical, and insurance records.

Many of these provisions have no doubt made Americans safer. The administration claims that the act's longer prison terms have forced plea agreements, producing key information on terrorist cells, training, recruitment, and U.S. targets. The Department of Justice notes that along with the FBI and international partners, over one hundred terrorist threats and cells have been neutralized and over 515 individuals have been deported in connection with September 11 investigations, largely due to their expanded powers.[67]

Civil right activists claim the PATRIOT Act has enabled the government to violate the rights of Americans and immigrants in the United States, permitting the government to detain noncitizens indefinitely and without charges, violating due process and aspects of the Vienna Convention on Consular Relations. In the months following September 11, the Bush administration detained thousands of individuals, mostly men of Middle Eastern and South Asian decent. Some were held for as long as two years without having been charged with a crime or provided access to lawyers. The government refused to release the identities of the detained or notify their families, citing security concerns.[68]

Treatment of these detainees also raised the ire of rights advocates. The administration issued an interim ruling on October 31, 2001, allowing intelligence and law enforcement personnel to monitor conversations between designated detainees and their lawyers, a clear violation of attorney-client privilege.[69] Not unlike the scandal at Abu Ghraib prison in Iraq, an investigation into the conditions of detention in one Brooklyn, N.Y., facility found incidents of unprovoked beatings and strip searches of inmates in the presence of female guards.[70] The beatings and other harassment were done to prisoners held in secrecy and without legal representation.

Nearly all of those detained appear to have been deported or allowed to leave the country as of early 2004, but a coalition of civil liberties groups continued to push to have the identities and the charges against the detainees made public, taking the issue all the way to the Supreme Court. The Court ultimately denied their appeal, upholding the decision at the federal level that the administration need not reveal the circumstances or details of the detainees' arrests for fear that the disclosure would threaten national security.[71]

Conscious of the potential civil liberty problems with a bill passed so quickly, Congress included in the PATRIOT Act a sunset provision by which the legislation would expire if not renewed by December 31, 2005.[72] Early in 2004, President Bush made renewal of the bill central to his reelection campaign, asserting it is critical to the war on terror. He stressed that although key provisions of the PATRIOT Act would expire in 2005, "The terrorist threat will not expire on that schedule."[73]

Overall, the PATRIOT Act provides necessary new authorities to the government in fighting terrorism and should be extended, although its violations of civil liberties must be corrected. Strong leadership in ensuring the bill's implementation is critical. Bush rightly sought to realign the superpower to fight the war on terror. With the new tools of the PATRIOT Act, he has the power he needs to combat the war on terror, but he will succeed only if he works with the rest of the world to galvanize a global effort. This is not a battle the lone superpower can win on its own. In addition, in fighting the war on terrorism, Washington must not lose sight of the need to preserve the civil rights embodied in our democracy.

A legal black hole

One of the most controversial policies of the war against terrorism is the President's Military Order of November 13, 2001, titled "Detention, Treatment, and Trial of Certain Noncitizens in the War against Terrorism," which declared the government's right to try by military commission those detained during the course of the war on terror. The administration determined that alleged terrorists such as al Qaeda members are "unlawful combatants," and "enemy combatants"—not prisoners of war—which would have made them eligible for protections under the Third Geneva Convention.[74] The order granted the president the power to incarcerate any noncitizen who he "had reason to believe" may have engaged in terrorist planning, execution, or the harboring of an individual associated with such acts, or simply, if "it is in the interest of the United States that such individual be subject to this order."[75] The order bypassed the role of the U.S. judiciary to uphold the rights of individuals in U.S. custody.

Nearly seven hundred suspects, most of them captured in Afghanistan, but from over 40 countries—including from England, Germany, France, and Australia—have been detained, nearly all without charges. They have been held at Camp X-Ray in Guantanamo Bay, Cuba, a cold war holdover controlled by the United States but not considered U.S. territory where domestic laws would apply. Claiming the prisoners were all "enemy combatants," the administration denied them access to legal counsel or any way to question their open-ended detention. The situation of the Guantanamo detainees has been described by Human Rights Watch as "a legal black hole."[76]

While touring Guantanamo, Rumsfeld explained the administration's rationale; "They are not POWs. . . . They will not be determined to be POWs . . . there is no ambiguity in this case."[77] Rumsfeld later defended the use of interrogation techniques such as dietary changes, sleep deprivation, forcing prisoners to sleep naked, and forcing them into "stress positions" as justified for use on unlawful combatants: "Terrorists don't comply with the laws of war. They go around killing innocent civilians," he said.[78] Vice President Cheney also supported this harsh approach: "They may well have information about future terrorist attacks against the United States. We need that information. We need to be able to interrogate them and extract from them whatever information they have."[79] Similar practices were later repeated on Iraqi prisoners. The policy sparked outrage only after photos of abuse of Iraqi prisoners leaked to the press in 2004.

On June 28, 2004, the Supreme Court upheld the right of the president to detain "enemy combatants," including U.S. citizens, but ruled that actions of the executive in the war on terror affecting individual rights are not immune from judicial review. In other words, detainees now have the right to lawyers and to contest the case against them in front of a judge.

The court also ruled that all Guantanamo detainees had the right to ask a U.S. judge to be released.

The decision to consider the United States outside the standards and norms of human rights, demonstrates yet again the myth that the lone superpower can write its own rules. The abuses in Guantanamo Bay and the prisons of Iraq, directly attributable to the climate of impunity set by Defense Secretary Rumsfeld and Vice President Cheney, have greatly damaged America's standing in the world and put U.S. soldiers and citizens at risk abroad. As with so many international norms and treaties, the hegemons chose to ignore or undermine the international standards. The superpower is worse off because of it. Over the decades, America has supported international laws and standards. Upholding such standards is in the interest of the United States. They pressure other states to live by the rules and provide some protection for Americans abroad.

The difference between a mule and an 8-cylinder Chevy

Winning the war on terrorism will require more than new legal powers. It will require looking at terrorism in a systematic, twenty-first-century way. One of the most difficult challenges is to deny terrorist funds to support their networks and finance attacks. Shortly after September 11, President Bush pledged to "direct every resource at our command to the war against terrorists," including a targeted campaign to "starve the terrorists of funding."[80] On September 23, 2001, he signed an executive order to target terrorist assets and funding. Since the order was signed, the U.S. government has successfully blocked terrorist assets, seized smuggled cash, arrested terrorist financiers, and closed front companies, charities, banks, and *hawala* conglomerates—the informal money-exchanging associations that support the al Qaeda network.[81] The FBI implemented a comprehensive national strategy for tracking terrorist funds by using financial data from a common database to "investigate, disrupt and prosecute" and freezing a reported $133 million in assets and conducted more than seventy investigations into terrorist financing.[82]

The United States has expanded efforts to build alliances to track terrorist financing, pressing Saudi Arabia in particular to do more, and it has pushed the UN to create a designation for organizations known to be terrorist financers that would serve as a green light for freezing the assets of those organizations. As the Treasury general counsel described it, "The difference between the activity before 9/11 and after 9/11 is the difference between a mule and an 8-cylinder Chevy."[83] Yet, whether the Bush administration is succeeding in drying up terrorist resources remains unclear.

Several studies have found vast deficiencies in the administration's efforts at disrupting al Qaeda's financial network. One 2002 study found that, while the administration has succeeded in disrupting parts of al Qaeda's financing network, it had not made the effort a high enough priority. Its approach was "strategically inadequate" and had not taken the necessary approach of a "mix of incentives and coercion" to build political will among the international allies.[84] Another study in 2004 documented unrealistic goals, weak information-sharing plans among key agencies such as the IRS and the Treasury and Justice Departments, and complaints of lagging resources and inadequate commitment to the problem at higher levels. One Justice Department official working on terror financing explained that tracing money "in the best of circumstances is very, very difficult, and when you're talking about terrorist operations that can be carried out for $50,000 or $75,000, it's almost impossible."[85] As of January 2004, the Treasury Department reported that it had blocked virtually no new funding since January 2003, and that it had only blocked $139 million overall, $100 million of which was blocked in the first six months after September 11, 2001.[86]

As Rick Newcomb, the man in charge of drying up terrorist funding for the U.S. Treasury Department until he resigned in September 2004, explained, "the issue is less how much money is blocked. The biggest stick we have is in making terrorist parties and their support structure, including deep-pocket donors from wealthy nations, public. In fact, terrorists themselves do not have a lot of money. Rather, the names of the donors and their support infrastructure are key. Unless you are dealing with an oil-rich terrorist-supporting nation, the trick is how much pressure you can bring on those who pay for, harbor, and support them to stop doing so." Newcomb had been in charge of tracking international financing since 1987, when he had only ten people on staff. Working closely with Dick Clarke throughout the 1990s, he developed ways to track finances and gain an understanding of how they work—quiet diplomacy, seeking international cooperation, and public sanction if needed. One key improvement to OFAC's capability to track terrorists' financing was the new coordination after September 11 in which OFAC places officials in each of the military's regional command centers. "It works for us nicely in identifying targets, Newcomb explained. "They really know what is going on out there."[87]

By 2004, he had a staff of 150. Newcomb credits Dick Clarke with developing the policy of tracking terrorism financing that is in use today. "Dick and his group were working on this in the 1990s—and it works." While I was interviewing him for this book, he reminded me that we happened to be in the U.S. embassy in Belgrade together on September 11. I had turned to him as we watched the towers fall and said, "Dick was right. It is al Qaeda. We should just take out bin Laden."[88]

Drying up the source of terrorist financing is less about the amount one seizes than in breaking the link with states willing to harbor them, deep-pocket donors willing to finance them, and nongovernmental organizations willing to provide a safe haven and cover for them. It requires international cooperation with allies and friends, and pressure on reluctant nations. But to succeed, the United States will need to better engage in the hard work of convincing others to join us in the fight. In the world of open economies, instant communications, and easy world travel, only a world coalition can stop the terrorists. America cannot win the fight at home without a strong coalition behind the effort. Lastly, the United States must reshape its WWII–era institutions to be better able to tackle the challenges of terrorists seeking to attack its cities and its citizens.

Department of Homeland Security

The 9/11 Commission found that one of the government's "most serious weaknesses" was that no domestic agency had as its first priority the job of defending America from domestic attacks.[89] Following September 11, the superpower sought to realign itself to the twenty-first century threat from terrorism. Formally established in February 2003, the new cabinet-level Department of Homeland Security (DHS), was the most extensive reorganization of the federal government since the 1940s. It brought together twenty-two different agencies given the task of protecting America, in addition to the Secret Service and the Coast Guard, with a total of one hundred eighty thousand employees falling under its umbrella by its one-year anniversary.

Several large agencies were transferred from other departments to enable better coordination, including the Immigration and Naturalization Service, the Justice Department, the Coast Guard, the Department of Transportation, the Customs Service, the Federal Emergency Management Agency, and parts of the Justice and Treasury departments.[90] Former Pennsylvania governor Tom Ridge, previously appointed to handle the issue from the White House as Homeland Security director, was appointed secretary of Homeland Security with cabinet rank, making him the twenty-first member of Bush's cabinet.

Among other things, the new department creates the U.S. Customs and Border Protection organization, consolidating all border activities into a single agency to create "one face at the border" instead of three disparate agencies. Since September 11, 2001, the Coast Guard has conducted more than 124,000 port security patrols, 13,000 air patrols, boarded more than 92,000 vessels, interdicted over 14,000 individuals attempting to enter the United States illegally, and created and maintained more than 90 maritime security zones. Hundreds of thousands of first responders across America have been trained to recognize and respond to the effects of a weapons-of-mass-destruction attack.[91]

The federal government has now taken responsibility for airport security, having hired, trained, and deployed more than forty-five thousand federal security screeners. While often frustrating to the millions of American air travelers who face inconsistent guidelines, having to check nail clippers in one airport but not another, air travel has been safe. However, with over 1.7 million passengers a day, airline security in the United States will remain an enormous challenge. Despite the billions of dollars spent in improving security systems and the thousands of extra federal employees, in April 2004 the House Aviation Subcommittee began to voice concerns. Government investigations for the panel concluded that dangerous objects were continuing to pass through airport security checkpoints. The panel's chairman, Representative John Mica (R-Florida), described the findings as "pretty scary."[92]

One of the toughest challenges involves screening the twenty thousand containers that enter the United States each day. The DHS screens only *information* regarding nearly 100 percent of all containerized cargo before it arrives in the United States. Higher risk shipments are physically inspected for terrorist weapons and contraband prior to being released from the port of entry. Yet, Customs inspects only 4 to 5 percent of all containers coming into the United States, and the sheer volume of cargo makes it essential that most security checks are done at the point of loading in foreign ports, which requires coordination with other governments.[93] Goods from trusted countries, such as Canada, are not inspected at all once they arrive in U.S. ports. Thus, as one observer noted, "we have basically made Canadian ports our American ports."[94]

According to a recent report card on the new Department of Homeland Security, released in March 2004 by the respected Century Foundation, its first year included some successes, but it still receives mixed reviews, with an overall grade of C+. In particular, DHS received high praise for tracking international students, hiring checkpoint screeners, expanding the federal air marshal system, and instituting the Information Analysis and Infrastructure Protection Directorate, which acts as a center for collection, assessment, and dissemination of information about threats and how to respond to them.[95] Not surprisingly, given the monumental task of changing the bureaucracy, the report claimed it is in the realm of coordination that the new department has been weakest. Criticism was targeted specifically at air cargo security, coordination with states and municipalities, relieving the immigration and naturalization case backload, and coordinating with Congress to develop coherent policy goals.[96]

The way forward

In late 2002, President Bush signed legislation to create the National Commission on Terrorist Attacks Upon the United States, referred to as the 9/11 Commission. It was an independent bipartisan group of ten former and contemporary state governors, senators, lawyers, college presidents, and others. The commission was charged with accounting for the events of September 11, 2001, and understanding how and why those attacks were not prevented. On July 22, 2004, the commission released its report, which offered a valuable blueprint for future counterterrorism policy by setting forth forty-one recommendations.

First, the commission urged a focus on root-cause prevention, and recognized that terrorism, per se, is not the primary enemy threatening the United States. Rather, it is the ideology of Islamist terrorism, which bolsters such networks as al Qaeda, that must be suppressed. To do so, the commission advised that all resources—diplomacy, intelligence, economic and foreign aid policy, and homeland security—be utilized to combat this ideological zealotry.

Within the United States, the commission urges America to prepare better for a terrorist attack, mostly focusing on how to improve the government's intelligence capabilities and bureaucracy. In this regard, the most significant recommendations is to unify the nation's intelligence gathering and planning resources under a National Intelligence Director (NID), who would coordinate all intelligence—CIA, FBI, Counterterrorism—operations. Under the NID there would be a new organization, the National Counterterrorism Center, headed by a Senate-confirmed national counterterrorism director. Simultaneously, the commission argues for greater congressional oversight to ensure accountability as well as stronger FBI and Homeland Security operations. The National Counterterrorism Center would be placed within the executive branch, and would incorporate the counterterrorism-oriented branches of the FBI, CIA, and Homeland Security Department.[97]

President Bush has selectively accepted the commission's recommendations, initially opposing the creation of a national intelligence director position. In response to strong congressional pressure, however, the president changed his position and submitted legislation to Congress to establish the NID post. Regrettably, despite the urgency, the bulk of the commission's recommendations would not be taken up until after the November 2004 election.

While the reorganization of the government is an important step forward, it will not enable the United States to defeat the war on terrorism alone. Success will require coordination at all levels of government on a scale never before imagined, as well as stronger cooperation from abroad. America cannot protect its cargo ports without robust control efforts at ports of origin. Without strong sharing of intelligence on terrorists and their financial networks abroad, the United States will not be able to win the war on terrorism. Success at home will require engaging America's allies. The myth of America being able to go it alone is dead.

Have these efforts made America safer? Yes. There can be no question that tens of thousands of Americans, from the most senior levels of the Bush administration to everyday workers checking packages, screening passengers, and planning disaster response have made tremendous efforts since September 11 to make Americans safe at home and abroad. The United States has fought two wars, removed two noxious regimes from power, broken up terrorist networks, closed some gaping holes in our domestic security structures, and no doubt prevented attacks. The administration has spent billions of dollars and moved various arms of the federal government faster than many thought possible. More steps are under consideration. Anyone who has served in government appreciates how difficult it is to move bureaucracies. But four years into Bush's term, the American public remains unsettled and unsure of its security. By mid-2004, 61 percent of Americans felt the world was more dangerous than ever before in their lifetime.[98]

The jury is still out on whether we have made the most important investment of all—a change in the attitude of government about threats. Ultimately, this will require recognizing that the superpower myth is outdated and leaving it behind. We cannot win this fight without others. If we foresee that terrorists will set up bases and attack us from poor, weak, and collapsed states, we must work to repair those states before terrorists gain a foothold, not after attacks have been launched. If we foresee that terrorists will use the institutions of our globalized world to transfer money, people, information, and ideas, we must build international law and international institutions to counter them.

Winning the war on terrorism and overcoming the ideology and hatred of Islamic terrorism will require reestablishing general goodwill to defuse tacit support for attacks on the United States by cooperating and leading on global challenges such as global warming, development, and conflict, especially in the Middle East. Reform in the Arab world is also essential.

If we understand, as by now surely we should, that our ocean borders will not protect us, we must continue cooperating with others in ways that are mutually beneficial, not imagine that we can withdraw only to reemerge, guns blazing. The myth of the hegemon reflects a world that does not exist. It hides the reality of a world that can harm us deeply or, if we are prepared, offer us plentiful opportunity. The way forward must be a return to the policy of engagement if America is to become safe once again—but a new, tougher engagement.

14

Lessons for the President

The wave of the future is not the conquest of the world by a single dogmatic creed but the liberation of the diverse energies of free nations and free men.

—John F. Kennedy

As 2005 begins, President Bush faces dangerous challenges that the United States cannot meet alone. The soaring international goodwill following the attacks of September 11, indeed since World War II, has been squandered. Hegemons came to power in 2001 determined to use America's supremacy to reshape the world to match their surreal vision. The failures in Iraq and the war on terror exposed concrete costs of pursuing that hollow myth. They believed that America's vast and unrivaled military and economic power gave Washington the freedom to act alone. In the process, America alienated its friends and allies—just when it needed them most in building a world coalition to combat terror.

America can certainly change the world, but it cannot bend it to its will. The world imagined by the hegemons is one in which not only America's military power but also its absolute authority on political and economic issues shape the world in America's interest. That world does not exist. Rather, a more complex—and often more frustrating—balance of force and diplomacy that will convince allies to follow the United States is the only way America will succeed in defending its interests.

In his time, President Clinton certainly succeeded through his policy of engagement in strengthening the rules of the world to better protect America's interests. And he succeeded in building international coalitions that eased the burden of the lone superpower. When he had to act alone, such as in Kosovo, he did so in ways that ultimately persuaded the rest of the world to follow. Today, one out of every ten soldiers in Kosovo is

American, with Europe taking over the mission; in Iraq almost nine out of every ten foreign soldiers is American, and allies, including Spain, Poland, Honduras, Dominican Republic, and Costa Rica, have or are pulling out.[1] Clinton laid a solid foundation for American policy that recognized it was in America's interest to engage in the world's crises. At the end of his second term, America was respected around the world in ways that enhanced countries' willingness to follow Washington's lead. Countries by and large believed the United States was a force for progress. Yet, the world changed on September 11. So what is the alternative?

First, it is time for America to put to rest the superpower myth of the hegemons. America cannot act alone, primarily through military force, to protect its interests. While Clinton used force to get parties back to diplomacy, President Bush, buying into the superpower myth, primarily used diplomacy to justify force. As the lone superpower, America is powerful enough to act whenever and wherever it wants. But the hegemons' belief that the United States, largely on its own, can spread democracy, end terrorism, prevent nuclear war, transform the Arab world, bring peace to the Middle East, and ignore much of the world's other problems has been proven false by the costly experiments of the presidency of George W. Bush. It has caused deep resentment in Europe and the Middle East that makes it vastly more difficult for the United States to lead.

Getting the balance of U.S. engagement right is difficult. The all-important threat of global terrorism, vastly enhanced by the increasing challenges of drugs, weapons of mass destruction, failed states, refugees, and infectious diseases, increasingly affects America's interests. While no longer fighting another superpower, the United States is equally threatened by these challenges of the twenty-first century. America cannot meet them without leading a world coalition to do so.

Yet, America cannot serve as the world's police force. Scores of conflicts around the globe all demand and deserve attention. Many rightly look to the United States for help. When its interests are sufficiently threatened, the United States must act, including with military measures. In other cases, the United States can—and should—lead others to get involved. But increasingly, other nations must step up to the plate and assume the burden of aid, negotiations, and where necessary, send in ground troops. Working with allies beyond Britain, including in particular the French, Germans, and Russians, can help build a coalition to assist the United States on patrol. Increasingly, the European Union, NATO, and the United Nations can all share the burden and create not necessarily a world police force but at least a 911 rescue squad, aid bank, and support network for democracy. Eventually, other regional organizations can assume these burdens, such as the African Union or ASEAN. They are not yet ready to assume the full burden they should, but with strong U.S. leadership and support, they can do so in the future.

The triumphs and tragedies of the past fifteen years, from the fall of the Berlin Wall to the collapse of the twin towers to the demise of Saddam Hussein's regime, have made it clear that we cannot achieve America's purpose as the world's beacon of freedom without seeing the world as it truly is. Advancing America's interests today demands engaging with others as partners in a common endeavor. It is not too late to change course, from a policy based on mythical hegemony to one based squarely on realism, one that promotes America's ideals.

Tough engagement

Only through a more nuanced policy of tough engagement will America meet its daunting challenges. Today's foreign policy, while it should implement the lessons learned in the 1990s, must do more. The new policy of realism for the twenty-first century must be one in which America engages, leads, and builds coalitions, acting alone only when it must as a last, not first, resort. With the grave threat of terrorism, the new policy must also include a zero tolerance toward terrorism and proliferation. Tough engagement will require the United States to rebuild its fractured relationships with its allies, work within the United Nations and other international and regional institutions to share the superpower burden, and return to its core principles of promoting democracy, rule of law, and justice through building world coalitions and rules of the road. It will also mean building stronger coalitions to end support for and financing of terrorists, and cracking down on those who seek weapons of mass destruction.

The world needs superpower leadership, but as a reliable partner. And America needs the world. It matters to American security that the world is increasingly wary of the United States, less willing to cooperate in helping to realize its international goals. Alarmingly, America is increasingly viewed with distrust as global anti-Americanism has spiked to unprecedented heights. Majorities in seven out of eight Muslim countries worry about a military threat from the United States, including 74 percent in the world's most populous Muslim state, Indonesia.[2] Surprisingly, majorities in most Western countries also consider the United States a threat to world peace, including 61 percent in Spain, 55 percent in Britain, and 52 percent in France.[3] These trends spiked anti-Americanism to unprecedented levels, at an unheard-of speed. For instance, between 2002 and 2003, anti-Americanism jumped in Russia from 33 percent to 68 percent.[4] Stunningly, for the first time, the Irish people—one of the most pro-American in the world—protested President Bush when he visited Ireland in June 2004.

It is not too late to change course. The age of terrorism puts new demands on the lone superpower—also its primary target—and America can only protect its interests through a policy of tough engagement. The necessary policies can be put in place starting immediately. Despite the rancor caused by the policies of the last four years, the world will respond to a fundamental shift back toward engagement and responsible U.S. leadership. The results would reunify Americans at home and forge the coalitions abroad necessary for America to meet the threats and seize the opportunities that lie ahead.

Protecting America's interests in the coming decades will require winning the war on terrorism through a world coalition and strong leadership at home. President Bush will continue to grapple with the challenges of Iraq, but eventually a new Iraq will emerge and U.S. troops can depart. The United States has no choice but to reengage in the search for peace in the Middle East, even if a comprehensive solution remains elusive. Some momentum must be restored. The president will also need to negotiate an end to North Korea's nuclear program and rein in Iran's nuclear ambitions.

Keeping America safe will also require reengaging with the multilateral and regional institutions that can help America share its burden as a superpower. The frustration and minor infractions on American sovereignty are a small price to pay for that support. The United Nations can help implement peace processes, conduct the bulk of the peacekeeping missions around the world, and help tackle the myriad health and development issues around the world that will make America safer. The United States must push NATO to fulfill a role beyond Europe. The deployment to Afghanistan was a welcome first step. Deployments of NATO in Africa and vastly increased training of African peacekeepers must be next on the agenda. Similarly, the United States and European allies must build up regional peacekeeping capabilities in Africa, Latin America, and Asia so that America, France and Britain are not always the first port of call. America must also live by the rules the world has written over the last fifty years. Actions such as exempting itself from the Geneva Conventions, Kyoto protocols, and the International Criminal Court undermine America's interests by encouraging others to flaunt the international rules of the road and thereby increasing the threat to the United States.

Beyond the myth, America's new policy of realism and tough engagement will guide us well through the twenty-first century.

The focus of this book has been major issues in force and diplomacy since the end of the cold war. September 11 shows it is difficult to predict what crises a president will face. But the lessons of the last decade indicate that in early 2005, there are four urgent additional issues that must be addressed. They are areas in which only the lone superpower can lead and make meaningful progress. The four areas requiring urgent action are:

1. addressing the root causes of September 11 by developing a serious policy, implemented with skillful diplomacy, to promote reform and democratization in the Arab world
2. maintaining a coherent and sustained zero-tolerance nonproliferation policy
3. showing consistent support for democracy and human rights in this hemisphere, Russia, and beyond
4. addressing the challenges of the developing world, especially in Africa.

1. Addressing the root causes of September 11

As the 9/11 Commission urged, America must address the root causes of the hatred that drove nineteen young men to hijack four airplanes and attack America on September 11, 2001. While much has been made of the link between American policies toward the Middle East as a cause of that horrific act, it is important to remember that those attacks were planned while an American president was engaged in an unprecedented effort to reach an accord between the Israelis and Palestinians. Certainly, America's support for Israel fuels resentment throughout the Middle East that enhances the terrorists' sense of righteousness in killing innocent civilians. A majority in Islamic countries reported that U.S. support for Israel was the top reason for their dislike of America.[5] In addition, studies find that the conflict is "one of the most pervasive obstacles to security and progress in the region."[6] America's task of engaging the Arab world will be made infinitely easier following meaningful progress on resolving the Arab-Israeli conflict.

Yet, the more pertinent causes of September 11 lie in the failed policies of the Arab governments, particularly Saudi Arabia and Egypt, which were home to sixteen of the nineteen hijackers.[7] Promoting democracy and reform in the Arab world is an urgent task directly related to the security of Americans at home and abroad. Terrorism is on the rise, especially in Saudi Arabia, which faces increasing attacks against foreign and regime interests, including the gruesome beheading of an American citizen.[8] In March 2004, Saudi forces killed Khalid al Hajj, the alleged leader of al Qaeda and coordinator of a campaign of violence that began in 2003. The violence is linked to the growing frustrations of the population. One in five Arabs still live on less than $2 a day. The paltry 0.5 percent annual growth in income per capita over the past twenty years is lower only in sub-Saharan Africa. The Arab region has eighteen computers per one thousand people, compared to the global average of 78.3 per one thousand. The region suffers from an "Arab brain drain," where roughly 25 percent of three hundred thousand Arab university first-degree graduates in 1995 and 1996 have emigrated.[9] Overall, the UN points to three deficiencies that have seriously hindered development in the region: freedom, women's empowerment, and education.

Yet, the history of United States–Arab relations is one in which Washington has turned a blind eye to the need for reform in the Middle East. For decades, the United States has struck a bargain with the moderate Arab states: they provided oil and access to U.S. military to contain Iraq; in exchange, Washington agreed to leave the regimes' domestic situation alone while reinvigorating its efforts to solve the Israeli-Palestinian conflict. One former senior official explained U.S. policy toward the Arab world by arguing, "Pushing hard for political change might not only disrupt the effort to promote peace but could also work against vital U.S. interests: stability in the oil-rich Persian Gulf and in strategically critical Egypt.[10] While the United States lent its support to those Arab nations making some progress on human and democratic rights, such as Jordan, Kuwait, Morocco, Qatar, Oman, and Yemen, it never made achieving real democratic change a priority. Neither President Clinton nor President Bush chose to change this bargain during their time in the White House.

In order for the United States to be able to act as an instigator and guarantor of reform, the administration must pay attention to the deteriorating reputation of America across the Middle East, now at an all-time low following the war with Iraq and Washington's disengagement in the search for peace in the Middle East. Only 12 percent of the region's population believe the United States respects Islamic values and a paltry 7 percent believe the West understands Muslim customs and culture. Only 9 percent believe military action in Afghanistan was morally justified.[11] Only 18 percent believe Arabs carried out the attacks on September 11. Only 3 percent of Saudis hold a favorable opinion of the United States.[12] Egypt's President Mubarak said that "there exists today a hatred [of America] never equaled in the region."[13] The graphic images of torture that emerged from Abu Ghraib prison directly strengthened every misconception of America as a country of double standards and moral corruption that is held in the Middle East. Never has America needed more power of influence in the region, and yet never has America's credibility been so weak.

Today, Washington faces a difficult choice: it must address the failures of the regimes, especially in Cairo and Riyadh, that begat al Qaeda. But if it pushes too hard, it risks having those regimes fall to radical Islamic governments. No president wants to be responsible for another Iran in the region. Having claimed the war in Iraq would help foster reform in the Arab world, President Bush sought to ignite the debate in late 2003 when the administration put forward a plan to promote reform in the Middle East. On December 12, 2003, Secretary of State Powell announced the administration's new Greater Middle East Initiative (GMEI), stating that it "places the U.S. firmly on the side of change, of reform, and of a modern future for the Middle East."[14] It set three priorities: promoting democracy and good governance, building a knowledge society, and expanding economic opportunities. The Arabs rejected the plan.

The two regimes most in need of reform, Saudi Arabia and Egypt, led the charge against the plan. They argued it was a U.S. effort to impose democracy on all Arab countries regardless of their different circumstances and cultural particularities. Saudi Arabian foreign minister Prince Saud al-Faisal claimed the U.S. initiative included "clear accusations against the Arab people and their governments that they are ignorant of their own affairs."[15] Egypt's president Hosni Mubarak and King Abdullah of Jordan made separate tours of Europe to urge Tony Blair and other European leaders not to support the proposal. Bush's invitation to attend the 2004 G8 at Sea Island, Georgia, was rejected by several Arab countries, including Egypt and Saudi Arabia.[16]

Some do not believe the Arabs see reform as in their own interest. For instance, Major General Giora Eiland, Israeli prime minister Ariel Sharon's national security advisor, believes that the Arab states do not see democratization and human rights reform as in their interest. So long as the Palestinian conflict continues, the Arabs can use it as an "excuse not to make reforms," explained Eiland. "The reality, especially after September 11, is that they do not want to solve the conflict."[17]

The key challenge is to convince the Arab leadership that it is in its interest, and quite possibly essential for the survival of its regimes, to institute reforms. The transformation will be far more difficult than those that occurred in Asia or Eastern Europe during the 1980s and 1990s. Lacking a strong middle class that helped fuel the Asian tiger, or some previous experience with democracy that formed the basis of much of the progress in Eastern Europe, Arab states will have to nurture a democratic base largely from scratch. States must begin to challenge the massive "poverty of opportunity" identified by the UN: serious deficits in freedom, women's empowerment, and education.

Clearly, the United States will be handicapped in any effort to promote reform in the Middle East until the crisis in Iraq subsides and Washington once again shows leadership in pressing for peace between the Arabs and Israelis. The need for progress is urgent. Terrorists will continue to sprout in the region until democratic and economic reforms occur within the Arab societies and the furor triggered by the Arab-Israeli conflict is diffused. So long as the wealth and power in these countries is concentrated in the hands of the few, ambitious young men not in the inner circles will be tempted by terrorist groups that give them a sense of purpose, however warped.

Significant reform of these insular societies will take a generation. One of America's most difficult challenges will be to use its strength as a superpower to build momentum for a long process of reform by pushing governments to initiate real change and delivering on their promises. Success, however, will not depend on America's military might but rather the strength of its ideas in convincing allies to join in the effort and supporting Arab leaders willing to push for progress. The effort will take full use of the broad powers of America's superpower: economic to foster development and education, trade and technical advice; diplomatic to assist in forging international coalitions; and moral to help in convincing Arab leaders that America is acting in their interest as well as its own. Priority must be given in three key areas that will help give the youth hope in their society.

First, Arab regimes should reform the education system by taking back control from the extremists. As one report says, today, "no Saudi ruler can contemplate a significant policy shift without taking into account the likely reaction of the country's religious establishments."[18] Public spending on education in Arab countries has declined since 1985, and enrollment in higher education has fallen. Egypt and Saudi Arabia, in particular, must end the hatred and anti-American propaganda emanating from government-sponsored schools and mosques. The use of the religious Madrassas schools must be reduced by providing a thorough, modern, and successful educational alternative. A narrow religious education is not sufficient for the children of tomorrow. In particular, Saudi Arabia must shift control away from the Wahhabist extremists, develop a more modern curriculum that will enable the next generation of Saudis to compete in the twenty-first-century economy, and refrain from funding extremist religious establishments in other parts of the Muslim world.

Second, governments must loosen their suffocating grip on the economies of the region. For too long, an Arab's prosperity has only come through association with corrupt governments and oil. The region needs a broader economic base to generate jobs, development, and trade. This means governments must make the space for entrepreneurs and innovation and then support these businesses and industries with the financial resources that have previously only served the needs of ruling cliques.

Third, governments must resist crushing any semblance of dissent and civil society within their countries. They must be persuaded that the ambition to control and mold all forms of political participation is futile and detrimental. Real political engagement must be nurtured, democratic oppositions allowed to develop, and freedom of the press and assembly permitted. Unless a peaceful outlet for dissent is created, the Arab regimes remain at risk of continuing violence and instability. They risk fulfilling the words of President Kennedy, "Those who make peaceful revolution impossible will make violent revolution inevitable."

Fourth, women must be given equal rights in Arab societies. No country can successfully compete in the twenty-first century if it disenfranchises half its population from political and economic life.

2. Maintaining a zero-tolerance nonproliferation policy

The Bush administration came to office in 2001 focused on three key issues it saw as a threat to the United States: China, Iraq, and the threat of missiles launched at the United States. While more realistic policies have since emerged toward China and postwar Iraq, the administration is doggedly moving forward with plans to deploy a national missile defense, despite the lack of a system that works. Conservatives spent most of the 1990s hyping the threat and criticizing President Clinton's more reasoned approach to the issue.[19] For instance, Rumsfeld's 1998 commission on assessing the ballistic missile threat ignored informed analysis and exaggerated that threat.[20] It is real, but not what the proponents would have Americans believe.

The most significant threat, North Korea, has tested a missile potentially capable of delivering a heavy payload to Hawaii and parts of Alaska. How much of a threat the missile program actually poses is difficult to determine. In the last six years, North Korea has not tested one with a further reach. It has not developed a warhead small enough to be carried in a long-range missile.[21] No other hostile country has, or will have in the near future, a missile capable of reaching the United States. Yet, four years into the Bush administration, no effort has been made to negotiate any limits on North Korea's missile program. Rather, the administration has focused instead on the illusive goal of a national missile defense.

Three months after September 11, the Bush administration gave formal notice to Russia that it would exercise its right to withdraw from the Anti-Ballistic Missile (ABM) Treaty in six months, declaring the pact "hinders our government's ability to develop ways to protect our people from future terrorist or rogue state missile attacks."[22] Dire predictions of the ramifications of a U.S. withdrawal did not come to fruition as the world rallied behind the United States in the aftermath of the terrorist attacks. Russian president Putin said the decision "does not pose a threat to the national security of the Russian Federation."[23] Whether the ABM withdrawal will have adverse affects on proliferation may only become apparent over time. So far, Russia has scrapped plans to cut more immediately the number of its ballistic missile divisions from fifteen to two. The administration will need to be vigilant to ensure that the withdrawal does not adversely affect disarmament and nonproliferation efforts.

The Bush administration has moved forward with a costly missile defense plan that may or may not work when it is deployed. The plan would entail building up to twenty ground-based interceptors at two sites to intercept long-range missiles, to begin upgrading the Aegis-class destroyers and cruisers to be equipped with sensors, and to begin the fielding of up to about twenty of the sea-based interceptors that could be used against short- and medium-range missiles.[24] Since December 2002, nine tests have been put off or cancelled, and there have been no tests of the interceptor with its current booster rocket.[25] The congressional investigative arm, the General Accounting Office, found that the eight flight intercepts attempted were "repetitive and scripted" and that the technology is "largely unproven." It recommended that operational testing and evaluation be done in realistic conditions.[26]

Certainly, America should pursue a national missile defense, but at a pace that keeps the deployment linked to the reality of a system that works. It would be prudent to pursue vigorous testing and research while deferring a major investment in deployment until it is determined whether a system could work against likely threats. Then, the administration could assess the costs of moving ahead with deployment versus the costs of proceeding with other needed defense programs. For example, we are currently spending $10 billion a year on missile defense and only $1 billion a year on the Nunn-Lugar Threat Reduction program, which helps former Soviet states secure nuclear, chemical, and biological weapons and materials. If the more direct threat to U.S. security is from terrorists inside the United States attacking with weapons of mass destruction, the administration must consider whether dollars are better spent on augmenting port security, increasing customs and border security, and continuing support for the Nunn-Lugar program to keep weapons of mass destruction out of terrorists' hands. If the threat merits and a system works, the United States should move ahead with a missile defense as well.

An Armageddon of our own making

One of the most dangerous threats to America today is posed by the possibility that weapons of mass destruction might fall into the hands of terrorists bent on attacking the United States. The most dangerous legacy of the cold war superpower struggle is the presence of thirty thousand intact nuclear warheads in the United States and Russia. Seventeen thousand five hundred of them are operational, with the others in reserve, retired, and awaiting dismantlement.[27] Russia and the United States still have thousands of nuclear weapons on hair-trigger status. In addition, the technology revolution has made information on how to construct nuclear, biological, and chemical weapons readily available to terrorists anywhere. Rogue states, including Iran and North Korea, may pass sensitive materials to terrorists. Al Qaeda's next attack could include weapons of mass destruction.

Progress has been made in addressing the legacy of the cold war's stockpiles of nuclear, chemical, and biological weapons, but additional steps must be taken to assure global security. One of the most critical counter-proliferation efforts is the Nunn-Lugar program which has succeeded in substantially reducing the threat from Soviet weapons. Since 1991, all nuclear weapons from Ukraine, Kazakhstan, and Belarus have been removed; over twenty thousand nuclear scientists have found peaceful work; and 6,252 nuclear warheads have been deactivated.

Despite these steps, the threat of these weapons, especially from theft or terrorism, is real. In Russia, over seven thousand operational nuclear warheads remain, as well as ten thousand nonoperational ones, and the Russians have barely begun to eliminate their forty-thousand-metric-ton stockpile of chemical weapons.[28] Security of much of the former Soviet Union's nuclear weapons remains terrifyingly inadequate, with only 40 percent of facilities housing nuclear materials having received security improvements, and only half of which received complete security systems. Former senator Sam Nunn, cochairman of the Nuclear Threat Initiative, summed up the danger of these weapons in June 2004: "We are running the risk of an Armageddon of our own making."[29] America must work with Russia to urgently secure these remaining stockpiles.

Another urgent issue with respect to residual cold war stockpiles is their alert status. While campaigning in the summer of 2000, George Bush called for "the United States to remove as many weapons as possible from high alert, hair-trigger status—another unnecessary vestige of cold war confrontation."[30] Unfortunately, since coming to office, he has done little to reduce the number of nuclear weapons on hair-trigger alert, instead adopting a policy that reemphasizes the role of nuclear weapons. The Bush administration cut funding for the Nunn-Lugar program by $40 million in its 2005 budget, refused to push for ratification of the Comprehensive Test Ban Treaty, advanced the readiness of the Nevada Nuclear Weapons Test Site, and budgeted $485 million for the bunker-buster nuclear weapon.[31] These policies all must be reversed. Although in May 2002, the United States and Russia agreed to further reduce their operationally deployed warheads to between 1,700 and 2,200, the Strategic Offensive Reductions Treaty does not set that goal until 2012. Demonstrating the administration's skepticism of arms control, the treaty contains no verification provision (reversing Ronald Reagan's maxim of "Trust, but verify"). It also excludes nonoperational and nonstrategic warheads, those weapons perhaps most vulnerable to theft by a terrorist group.[32] Those deficiencies should be corrected.

Taking these steps will help erode the threat these weapons of mass destruction will reach terrorists plotting to attack America. Washington must work with the United Nations, the international arms control agencies and regimes, Europe, and other allies to forge a new world policy of zero tolerance for proliferators. In one interesting area, the Bush administration has begun to do so.

A new zero tolerance

One positive area in which the administration is breaking new ground is in illicit trafficking of arms and sensitive materials. The Bush administration has utilized an atypical strategy of arms control, one which circumvents the cumbersome treaty process and instead uses the UN Security Council to reinforce existing regimes and strengthen norms against the proliferation of WMD. However, its initial approach was flawed. In May 2003, President Bush announced a new approach to nonproliferation, a coalition of the willing, rather than a new international treaty. His Proliferation Security Initiative (PSI) declared that the United States and its partners would take measures, either alone or with other willing states, to stop the transfer or transport of weapons of mass destruction, their delivery systems, or related materials to and from states and nonstate actors of proliferation concern.[33] The PSI's focus would be to keep materials from rogue states and terrorist organizations.

Rather than seeking to establish new international laws governing the rights of such interdiction, the administration sought to build a coalition of like-minded states that would join it. Initially, only eleven nations signed up.[34] Notably South Korea, Russia, China, and most of the Middle East, Africa, and Latin America refused to participate in the PSI. Critics questioned its legality under international law, claiming it contradicted the law of freedom of movement.[35] "What are the guidelines, the rules, by which the U.S. will decide to act? It is the legitimization of international piracy?" commented one IAEA official in March 2004.[36] Recognizing reality, the Bush administration then did something unthinkable just a short while before: it brought the issue to the United Nations in late 2003.

In an unconventional approach to arms control, the United States rejected the long-drawn-out negotiations involved with setting up a new international treaty. Instead, it sought the faster, more controllable avenue of the Security Council. The United States began work with Britain and the other permanent members of the Security Council to secure passage of a resolution compelling nations to adopt and enforce laws to prevent terrorists and rogue states from being able to manufacture, possess, transfer, or use weapons of mass destruction or their means of delivery. While the effort has received little attention, throughout the spring, the United States engaged in skillful diplomacy, which gained not only the support of the other permanent members of the council, Britain, China, Russia, and France, but, surprisingly, all ten nonpermanent members of the council. Despite deep concerns over the lack of a U.S. commitment to overall disarmament, a key goal of the developing world, one by one, the members of the council agreed to the resolution. Pakistan was especially wary of the proposal because the discussions came on the heels of revelations that its top nuclear scientist has sold sensitive materials to North Korea and Libya. As the Algerian UN Ambassador Abdullah Baali commented, "What choice did we have? We cannot oppose the United States. At least they were coming to the United Nations."[37]

Demonstrating the strength of the superpower when it chooses to engage constructively, on April 28, 2004, the Security Council voted unanimously to enact the new regime. The U.S. deputy representative, James Cunningham, recognized, "No one nation can meet this challenge alone."[38] Resolution 1540, adopted under Chapter VII—implying the possibility of the use of force—requires all states to "refrain from providing any form of support to non-State actors that attempt to develop, acquire, manufacture, possess, transport, transfer or use nuclear, chemical or biological weapons and their means of delivery." It also called on all states to "take cooperative action to prevent illicit trafficking in nuclear, chemical or biological weapons, their means of delivery, and related materials." The United States had succeeded in internationalizing its controversial PSI.

The proposal represents an important development in arms control and may represent a new way of doing arms control business. The hegemons' unilateral approach failed, but the policy of tough engagement succeeded.

Rogue regimes

There have also been important developments within several states long involved in illicit proliferation, notably Libya and Pakistan, which in the spring of 2003 agreed to end their involvement in such activity. Coupled with the change in regime in Iraq, the sudden willingness of these two nations to reveal their past actions dealt a strong blow to the black market in weapons of mass destruction. While problems still remain in Iran, Syria, and North Korea, the change in attitude is significant.

In a stunning reversal of decades of rejection of international obligations, on December 19, 2003, Libyan leader Col. Mohammar Qaddafi publicly revealed the country's nuclear weapons program and committed to dismantle all weapons of mass destruction programs. Libya invited the IAEA to verify the elimination of nuclear weapon related activities in-country and also pledged to adhere to the Nuclear Non-Proliferation Treaty, which it had ratified in 1975, and to sign the Additional Protocol, which gives IAEA personnel the right to inspect both undeclared and declared nuclear sites in a timely fashion. Libya signed it on March 10, 2004. According to International Atomic Energy Agency Director General Mohamed El-Baradei, who led a December 2003 inspection team to Libya, that country's nuclear weapons program had been in the initial stages, about three to seven years away from producing a nuclear weapon.

The step was a validation of a decade of pressure on the Libyans, and particularly of nine months of intense negotiations between Libya and the Bush and Blair administrations. The Bush administration was quick to claim the preemptive war in Iraq had convinced Qaddafi to act. While the war no doubt played a role, the step was part of a much longer process of negotiations with Libya, dating from the December 1988 bombing by Libyans of Pan Am Flight 103.[39] Disastrous economic policies, mismanagement of oil revenues, and UN and U.S. sanctions that prevented Libya from being able to expand oil production were the underlying cause for Libyan rapprochement with Washington.

Libya's new openness soon embroiled Pakistan in controversy. As a result of the new inspections, the IAEA concluded that Pakistan and Dr. Abdul Qadeer Khan, the "father" of Pakistan's nuclear program, was the direct or indirect source of Libya's bomb-making equipment. The design, one from the 1960s by the European consortium Urenco and engineer Gernot Zippe, was easily identifiable. Khan had been convicted in 1983 of industrial espionage for stealing the design's secret blueprints in 1975, but the verdict was overturned on a technicality. He later used the plans to create Pakistan's nuclear program.[40] Libya's new openness and IAEA investigations into Iran's suspected nuclear program had revealed clear evidence of Pakistani fingerprints in selling sensitive materials to both nations, as well as to North Korea.

On February 4, 2004, Dr. Khan publicly confessed to having delivered secret nuclear information to other states, including Libya, North Korea, and Iran. As one senior U.S. official summarized the new revelations, "These guys are now three for three as supplier to the biggest proliferation problems we have."[41] In what was most likely a bold-faced lie, Dr. Khan made the implausible claim that members of his nuclear team had broken proliferation rules on their own; he sought to "clarify that there was never ever any kind of authorization for these activities by a government official."[42] President Musharraf officially pardoned Dr. Khan, mindful of his country's adoration of the man who brought nuclear weapons capability to the Islamic world. "Crowds dancing in the streets, prayers of thanksgiving in mosques and celebratory gunfire in the air" along with a snap poll showing 97 percent support for the first test of Pakistan's bomb in 1998 illustrate the strong support for a Pakistani nuclear program.[43]

Even more surprising was Washington's reaction to the pardon: total acquiescence. Although the Pakistani nuclear establishment had admitted to aiding some of America's worst enemies gain nuclear weapons capability, Washington was wary of putting too much pressure on President Musharraf. It needed his help in the war on terrorism and gave Pakistan a total pass. The decision will prove to be shortsighted; while the United States welcomes Pakistan's assistance regarding Afghanistan, it must not put its proliferation concerns on the back burner. In the post–September 11 foreign policy, the United States must insist on full compliance by Pakistan with its obligations regarding proliferation. To date, Pakistan has yet to reveal fully the extent of its assistance to Iran, North Korea, and beyond, or to allow IAEA inspectors full access to its programs or reveal the full extent of Pakistan's own activities.[44] As one former U.S. official responsible for nonproliferation policy described Pakistan's proliferation policies, "Over the past decade Pakistan has done more to undermine U.S. security than any single state—and, if a nuclear weapon explodes somewhere in the next decade, it will probably be traced back in some way, shape or form to Pakistan."[45]

Iran's weapons of mass destruction programs remain a challenge for the United States. Although Iran is a party to the Chemical Weapons Convention, the CIA claims that in 2003, Iran sought Chinese expertise in production of nerve agents, and probably has stockpiled blister, blood, choking, and nerve agents. Also a signatory to the Biological Weapons Convention, it has nevertheless likely maintained a biological weapons program and continues to seek dual-use biotechnical materials, equipment, and expertise, although its abilities to weaponize these agents are limited.[46] While much of Iran's activities regarding biological or chemical weapons are unknown, Iran is believed to have the capacity to produce one thousand metric tons of agent per year and may have a stockpile of at least several thousand metric tons of weaponized and bulk agent. Iran possesses five research reactors and two partially constructed power reactors. It claims the right to possess nuclear weapons to counter Israel's weaponry.[47]

For years, the United States has been concerned about the Iranian nuclear facilities thought to be used to enrich uranium not simply provide fuel. The United States has rightly pressed Iran to live up to its commitments under the Treaty on the Non-Proliferation of Nuclear Weapons (NPT). Publicly, Iran claims it is trying to establish a complete nuclear fuel cycle to support a civilian energy program. The concern is that this very same fuel cycle can also provide materials for a nuclear weapons-development program. The issue came to a head in June 2003 when IAEA director General ElBaradei stated that Iran was not meeting the obligations required of it under the Nuclear Nonproliferation Treaty. The worst of numerous identified violations came in a confidential IAEA report, leaked to the media in August, outlining the discovery of trace elements of highly enriched uranium found in an Iranian nuclear facility. According to IAEA officials, the Iranians claim the elements must have originated in Pakistan, from where some of the equipment originated. Pakistan denied the IAEA inspectors access to compare samples.[48]

In seeking an end to Iran's activity, the Bush administration has made clear to the Iranians they would face international sanction should they refuse full cooperation with the inspectors. Yet, the Europeans refused to go along with the U.S. effort, fearing a tough reaction might cause a backlash in Iran. These concerns precipitated an unprecedented October 2003 joint visit by the foreign ministers of Britain, France, and Germany to Tehran. Following talks, Iran agreed to open its nuclear activities to international inspection and voluntarily to suspend its nuclear enrichment activities. This was followed by Iran signing the Additional Protocol in December 2003 allowing undeclared inspections. The United States has kept open the possibility of referring the issue to the Security Council, the first step in imposing sanctions. On September 18, 2004, the board of the IAEA passed a resolution calling for Iran to halt all uranium-enrichment activities, although it declined Washington's push to have the issue referred to the Security Council. Three days later, Iran announced it had begun converting tons of uranium into gas, a crucial step in making fuel for a nuclear bomb.

As Iran struggles with its own internal tensions, exacerbated by an esti-mated two-thirds of the population below the age of thirty, the interna-tional community must work to ensure support for the reformers. But at the same time, it must send a clear signal that Iran's violations of its inter-national commitments can no longer be tolerated. So long as the interna-tional community is divided on the issue, and Iran can avoid sanctions, it is unlikely to stop its programs. Given the tense history with Iran, the United States is ill-placed to lead the charge absent allies. Military action against Iran by the United States, or possibly Israel as it did against Iraq's nuclear facility in 1981, is unlikely given the backlash and uncertainty that such action would eliminate the threat. The United States therefore must work behind the scenes for stronger European leadership in developing a zero-tolerance policy toward Iran. While difficult to achieve, a tough sanctions policy with international support must be put on the table.

To succeed in a zero-tolerance nonproliferation policy, the United States will have to return to a policy of supporting the various international treaties and regimes that enable it to lead a global effort to meet the global threat. Having spent the first three years deriding international arms-control conventions, the Bush administration slowly reversed its earlier dis-missal of existing international nonproliferation conventions. Although very late in Bush's term, to its credit, the administration began to realize the hegemon's approach is unworkable and shifted to a more realistic approach of engagement. In February 2004, Bush laid out proposals to improve the existing multilateral treaty regimes, including the NPT, the Convention on the Prohibition of the Development, Production and Stockpiling of Bacteriological (Biological) and Toxin Weapons and on their Destruction (BWC), and the Convention on the Prohibition of Development, Production, Stockpiling and Use of Chemical Weapons and their Destruction (CWC). He announced that the United States would seek to address some of the existing treaty's problems, such as the NPT's current provisions allowing states to facilitate the development of nuclear technology for peaceful purposes, which has provided loopholes for rogue regimes to divert materials to develop weapons of mass destruction.[49] Additionally, Bush proposed that nuclear-supplier states should refuse to sell enrichment and reprocessing equipment or technology to any state that does not already possess full-scale functioning enrichment and reprocessing plants. The United States must also do more to press states to sign the Additional Protocol of the NPT, strengthening the inspections worldwide. While the proposals have gained little traction, the administration is right to continue efforts to forge a new consensus.

Done right, these proposals can lead to more effective controls on the remaining state proliferators—Iran, Pakistan, North Korea, and Syria—as well as ensuring weapons of mass destruction do not fall into the hands of al Qaeda or other terrorist groups.

3. Showing consistent support for democracy and human rights

Throughout the 1990s, the United States developed a strong record of support for democracy. Today, that reputation is damaged and America's power to advance democracy is diminished. While focused on the wars on terrorism and in Iraq, American policies have eroded the institutions of civil society. Today, democracy is at risk throughout much of Latin America, Russia is increasingly autocratic, and Pakistan's democracy is suffering as Washington turns a blind eye to these troubling trends. Around the world, America's image is declining just when we need strong moral leadership to galvanize world coalitions. Throughout the world, the United States must seek a better balance between the war on terrorism and support for the very institutions that could serve as a bulwark against terrorism. The problem is especially acute in Latin America.

Largely unnoticed, fragile democratic institutions in the Western Hemisphere have been undermined by misguided U.S. policies. The first mistake was U.S. actions when Venezuela's leftist leader was overthrown in a bloodless coup in 2002. In April, Venezuela's president, Hugo Chavez, faced a national strike calling for his resignation. Chavez had alienated the business community the previous November by adopting forty-nine new laws that were contrary to business interests and increased government control over land, hydrocarbons, and commercial fishing. Oil workers went on strike to protest Chavez's decision to appoint a number of his cronies to the board of the state-owned oil industry. Anti-Chavez demonstrations numbering over one hundred fifty thousand supporting the striking oil workers gathered in the capital city of Caracas. On April 12, Chavez was briefly forced to resign by the military.

Rather than condemning the military intervention in Venezuela, the Bush administration appeared to justify it by citing a number of human rights abuses and arguing that President Chavez was becoming increasingly authoritative and repressive.[50] Immediately following the coup, White House spokesman Ari Fleischer said, "We know that the action encouraged by the Chavez government provoked the crisis."[51] Fleisher also announced as fact that Chavez had voluntarily resigned despite reports that he left the presidential palace under military escort[52] and failed to call for the restoration of Venezuela's elected authorities or question the legitimacy of the transitional government.[53] In fact, Assistant Secretary of State Otto J. Reich acknowledged that the administration had engaged in direct contact with Pedro Carmona Estanga, the Venezuelan businessman installed in Chavez's place.[54]

Chavez was returned to power over the course of the weekend and by Monday, the United States struggled to explain why it had supported what amounted to an unconstitutional coup. Philip Reeker, deputy spokesman for the State Department said, "I think if you look at what we said on Friday [April 13], we were reflecting on the need for restraint and respect for peaceful expression of political opinion; we were saddened by the loss of life that took place on Friday; and we were trying to examine the facts as we saw them at the time."[55] Reich asserted that the administration had been operating under an "information blackout" in the first hours of the revolt and its knowledge was limited. He also defended his decision to establish contact with Carmona, saying the administration would have been criticized even more harshly had it failed to inform him of its desire to see democratic processes respected.[56] Today, Chavez remains in power, taunting President Bush with claims that he will outlast him in power. "Let's bet on who will last longer, George W. Bush, you in the White House or me in Miraflores Palace," he said.[57]

Two years later, the administration took a similar stance in Haiti, supporting the unconstitutional calls for President Aristide to resign for his failure to meet opposition demands for new elections. Strongly supported by the business community, armed mobs seized control of Gonaives, the country's fourth-largest city. Fighting and looting quickly spread to a dozen northern cities as the Haitian military and police force slowly ceded control. Many of the thugs were associated to the former Duvalier regime and the Cedras junta. Within three weeks, the situation had reached crisis point. Rebels controlled half of the country and were making their way toward the capital Port-au-Prince.

As Haiti slid further into chaos, the Caribbean leaders stepped in to develop a plan that called on Aristide to share some power with his opposition during the remaining year and a half of his term. The plan called for the appointment of a new government with "a neutral and independent" prime minister who "enjoys the public trust."[58] It also insisted that President

Aristide declare that he would not seek to extend his term or contest another election, and it assured the right to public demonstration while providing for the release of a number of political activists and leaders who had been illegally imprisoned. Aristide accepted the plan, but the opposition did not. Yet, rather than pressure the opposition to accept the region's plan, the administration instead pushed Aristide to leave office.

As he had done a decade earlier, Aristide started calling me, pleading for international intervention to prevent the mobs from entering Port-au-Prince. "We need international troops now," he said to me a week before he was forced into exile, "otherwise, people will be killed." I knew if Aristide was calling me, he had few supporters left in Washington, as I had not spoken with him in years. Shortly afterwards, Aristide told me, U.S. forces showed up at his home in the middle of the night of February 29, 2004, and told him he had to leave Haiti. "We will not protect you," he was told. "You need to leave Haiti now." Aristide and his wife Mildred were escorted onto a U.S. chartered plane and flown out of the country, not knowing where they were headed. Aristide claims he was kidnapped and forced to resign. Vice President Cheney stated the administration's view in March "We're glad to see him go."[59]

The international community had failed Haiti and Aristide failed his country. He never succeeded in building a more moderate political center, and gross human rights abuses, corruption, and drug trafficking continued. The peacekeepers left too soon and international assistance was grossly inadequate to the need. Many Bush administration officials opposed the United States–led return of Aristide in 1994 and the administration froze aid to his government.

Although Aristide was a continuing problem, he still represented the institution of democracy. It is far from clear that Haiti will benefit from the United States undermining the principle of elections. A better course would have been to send an international force to stabilize the country, while negotiating a new sharing of power during a transition to the next government in 2006. Instead, while three thousand international troops are in Haiti, the majority of the population that supported Aristide is alienated, and those who used mob violence are expecting political rewards from the transitional government. Despite continued pressure by the United States, regional leaders have refused to recognize the interim government of Prime Minister Gerard Latortue and designated president Boniface Alexandre, the respected head of the Supreme Court, who will lead the country until new elections occur in 2005.

The Bush administration's actions have real implications for the hemisphere. Throughout Latin America, others seeking to overthrow democratic governments are emboldened, including in Venezuela, Bolivia, and Peru. Popular discontent with failing governments is widespread and the institution of democracy, still recovering from the decades of military rule and dictatorships, is growing. In addition, the thirty-year conflict in Colombia is a growing source of instability for the region. The U.S. Plan Colombia invests billions in the government's effort to defeat the rebels, a goal that remains elusive. Slow economic growth, expanding social inequities, lack of social services, and weak legal systems have eroded confidence in elected governments. A 2004 survey compiled by Latin Americans for the United Nations found that 55 percent of the people supported the replacement of a democratic government with an authoritarian one if it could produce economic benefits; 58 percent agreed that leaders should "go beyond the law" if they have to, and another 56 percent said economic development was more important than maintaining democracy. Since 2000, four elected presidents have been forced to step down: Peru (Alberto Fujimori, 2000); Bolivia (Gonzalo Sánchez de Lozada, 2001); Argentina (Fernando de la Rúa, 2001); and Haiti (Jean Bertrand Aristide, 2004).[60] There is continuing instability in Venezuela, Peru, and Bolivia. During Bush's second term, he must once again put the United States firmly behind democracy in this hemisphere and beyond.

Russia

In Russia, America has stood on the sidelines as President Putin attacked the already fragile pillars of civil society, including the press, political opposition, and business leaders. Bush's early days in office included some tough rhetoric against Russia's increasingly undemocratic actions. Bush had criticized Clinton's strong support of Yeltsin during the campaign. Rice was uncompromising in stating that "our big mistake was in assuming we would have a strategic partnership."[61] She accused Clinton of "happy talk." In the fall of 2001, Bush criticized Putin's crackdown on democracy, declaring Russia "cannot build a stable and unified nation on the ruins of human rights. . . . It cannot learn the lessons of democracy from the textbook of tyranny. We want to cooperate with Russia on its concern with terrorism, but that is impossible unless Moscow operates with civilized self-restraint."[62]

Yet, Bush soon developed a close relationship with his Russian counterpart that brought about a softening of Washington's attitude toward Putin's actions. Putin was the first foreign leader to speak to Bush after September 11 and the first Russian leader to visit NATO headquarters in Brussels. The two leaders bonded when, at their first meeting, Putin showed Bush the christening crucifix that he wears around his neck. He was secretly baptized as a baby and his mother gave the crucifix to him to have it blessed when he visited the holy land some years ago. In an interview with Reuters in 2000 the Russian president said, "I put it on to avoid losing it and haven't removed it since."[63] After the meeting, President Bush said that he had looked Putin in the eye, "was able to get a sense of his soul," and found him "trustworthy."[64]

The close relationship has had benefits for both nations. Bush secured Putin's support for a variety of issues that went against traditional Russian policies. For instance, Putin acquiesced in the Afghan war, provided intelligence, opened airspace, and did not urge Uzbekistan to refuse U.S. military presence. In May 2002, the two leaders signed a nuclear arms treaty cutting their arsenals by two-thirds.[65] Russia accepted the inclusion of Baltic states into NATO, a step it had long opposed. On its part, the United States pledged support for Russia to join the WTO.[66]

Yet, during the last four years, President Putin has also sought to undermine the institutions of democracy and President Bush has turned a blind eye to the dangerous trend. In late October 2003 Putin ordered the arrest of Mikhail Khodorkovsky, the head of Yukos, the second largest oil company in Russia. The move was widely criticized as a thinly veiled attempt to crush a political opponent to Putin. In September 2004, Putin announced a sweeping overhaul of Russia's political system, aimed at strengthening his control of the legislative branch and regional governments. The tragedy of Chechnya continues, with the United States abiding by Moscow's desire to keep the international community out of the issue. As the ongoing violence and chaos in Chechnya, the downing in August 2004 of two civilian planes, and the taking hostage of schoolchildren in September 2004 demonstrate, Russian policy toward Chechnya is a complete failure.

The press has also been subject to harassment. In June 2003, Putin passed a new media law giving the state authority to close news organizations if they publish an article critical of candidates unless it is paid for by an opponent and carries a note to that effect. Previously, media that violated the law risked only a fine. Bush's relationship with Putin also failed to convince Moscow to assist in Iraq and North Korea, or to end its involvement in building Iran's nuclear reactor. In 2002, Moscow and Tehran unveiled a new ten-year plan for nuclear cooperation.

It is in Russia's interest to protect its nascent institutions of democracy. It is also in America's interest to make the issue a higher one in its relationship with Moscow. Only the world's superpower can maintain the support for democracy worldwide necessary to ensure these nations do not become havens for criminals and terrorists.

4. Addressing the challenges of the developing world

Today, instability and disease in much of Africa threaten America's interests. Only the United States can lead a world coalition to address the root causes of Africa's failing states. The link between failing, poor states and conflict is well documented. For instance, the UN's report, *The World*

Social Situation 2003, found that 164 of the violent conflicts that broke out in the last two decades were concentrated in poor countries and took place within rather than between states.[67] The cycle of failed states necessitating international intervention must be broken. Certainly, one of the lessons from Afghanistan and September 11 is that failed states are a clear and direct threat to the United States' interests. As J. Brian Atwood, former head of USAID commented, failed states "threaten our nation. They cost us too much. They create diseases that impact on us. They destabilize other nations. They stymie economic growth and they deny us economic opportunity in the largest new marketplace—the developing world."[68] Africa is hardest hit by the cycle of poverty and violence that leads to state failure. As the UN Development Program's 2003 Human Development Report noted, most of the countries that grew poorer from 1990 to 2000 were in sub-Saharan Africa. Thirty out of the thirty-four countries on the "low" human development index, a composite of life expectancy, education, and income per person, are in sub-Saharan Africa. Life expectancy in Zimbabwe, for instance, plummeted from fifty-six years in the early 1970s to thirty-three today.[69]

Both Presidents Bush and Clinton sought a broad approach to alleviating the underlying causes of conflict in Africa—the continent's challenges of HIV/AIDS, poverty, environmental degradation, underdevelopment, and lack of democracy. Throughout his eight years in office, Clinton strongly supported efforts to expand democracy, trade, and economic development in Africa. He forgave vast amounts of Africa's debt. He built up the capacity of institutions needed to promote justice, foster internal trade, enhance regional cooperation, and consolidate peace efforts. The Africa Growth and Opportunity Act of 2000 broke new ground in expanding duty-free treatment to virtually all of sub-Saharan Africa exports to the United States. Clinton's direct engagement with Africa was unprecedented, including a lengthy trip through the continent in 1998, sending most of his cabinet to Africa at least once, and hosting a United States–Africa ministerial meeting that developed a blueprint for expanded economic engagement.

While many expected President Bush to ignore Africa, he has engaged boldly in some areas, traveling there early in his presidency, unveiling a massive $15-billion package to fight HIV/AIDS, increasing development aid to the continent, and pressing for peace in Sudan. Bush's plan for Africa, building on that of his predecessor, includes five main objectives: "to promote economic growth through support for market reforms and the private sector; help resolve conflicts that are blocking economic and political development; foster democratic reforms, good governance, and respect for human rights; combat the HIV/AIDS pandemic and other infectious diseases, and protect Africa's natural environment and renewable resources"[70]

In March 2002 at an international aid conference in Monterrey, Mexico, Bush called for "an entire new approach to development aid" and announced the "Millennium Challenge Account." Its goal is to increase United States development aid to poor countries by 50 percent, resulting in an annual increase of $5 billion by 2006 to countries following free-market principles, democratic governance, and respect for human rights. The administration has also linked support to Africa to the war on terrorism, increasing military ties to the region and securing basing arrangements, including in Djibouti, Tunisia, Morocco, Algeria, Senegal, Uganda, and Kenya, and allocating $100 million to improve security at East Africa's ports and airports.

A child in Africa has the same importance before God as the president

Today, Africa is perhaps most threatened by HIV/AIDS, which has infected at least 23 million of the continent's 750 million citizens. One child out of every ten in sub-Saharan Africa has lost his or her mother to the disease, and it is estimated that by 2010 there will be 40 million orphans in the region. The disease is eviscerating the skilled working population of the continent, threatening to drive its people further into poverty. Teachers and soldiers are also hard hit. For example, in the Ivory Coast, a teacher dies of AIDS every school day.[71] Ethiopian officials estimate that 5 percent of its soldiers have the disease and Kenyan officials suggested that they are losing eight to ten soldiers to the disease every week.[72] Ninety-five percent of those infected do not even know they carry the deadly virus.[73]

Clinton recognized the threat of the epidemic and in 1999 launched the Leadership and Investment in Fighting an Epidemic (LIFE) initiative to expand the fight against HIV/AIDS in Africa, adding $100 million to the FY 2000 budget, bringing the total spending on global HIV/AIDS assistance to $250 million.[74] In May 2000, Clinton issued an executive order to help make HIV/AIDS–related drugs and medical technologies more accessible and affordable to sub-Saharan countries. The administration also changed the debate on the issue. For instance, in 2000 UN Ambassador Richard Holbrooke broke important new ground when he forced the issue of HIV/AIDS into the Security Council, calling it a security threat. Wary UN diplomats (including myself) wrongly resisted the move. UN representatives considered an internal affair to be dealt with by the traditional humanitarian bodies of the organization. Holbrooke persuaded Vice President Al Gore to chair the Security Council session during which he endorsed Holbrooke's view that HIV/AIDS is "a security crisis because it threatens not just individual citizens but the very institutions that define and defend the character of a society."[75] Holbrooke also pushed a reluctant UN bureaucracy to conduct education and testing for UN peacekeepers on the disease, insisting that each peacekeeping mandate include such a provision.[76]

President Bush has shown vision and leadership on the issue as well. During his January 28, 2003, State of the Union address, Bush unveiled a dramatic increase in funding in the fight against HIV/AIDS. His Emergency Plan for HIV/AIDS Relief committed $15 billion over five years to combat the disease in the fourteen African countries and the Caribbean.[77] He later added Vietnam. Bush's strong support for Africa sparked surprise in many quarters, including Irish rock star Bob Geldof, who pioneered celebrity fundraising through his highly successful Live Aid concerts. Geldof commented, "You'll think I'm off my trolley when I say this, but the Bush administration is the most radical—in a positive sense—in its approach to Africa since Kennedy."[78] Irish rocker Bono of U2, who traveled in May 2002 to Africa with Treasury Secretary O'Neill, said, "I believe the president is sincere in his conviction to put the United States out front in a way that has not been done before on this issue,"[79] Praise came even from French president Jacques Chirac, on the heels of a bitter dispute over the war with Iraq, "the Bush administration has taken a very positive step to increasing the amount of money devoted to the fight against AIDS."[80]

Much of Bush's interest in Africa is driven by his deep religious faith. As Bush's born-again Christian chief speechwriter, Michael Gerson, put it, "It's a fairly radical belief that a child in an African village whose parents are dying of AIDS has the same importance before God as the President of the United States."[81] In addition to pressing Bush to intervene in the peace process in Sudan where Christians in the south are at risk, Christian groups pressed Bush to engage in the global fight against AIDS, in particular to focus on promoting "Abstinence, Being faithful, and Condoms," the so-called A.B.C. approach first tried in Uganda. The A.B.C. model has been very effective in Uganda where the adult rate of infection, which peaked in 1991 at 15 percent, dropped to only 5 percent in 2001, one of the lowest rates in sub-Saharan Africa.[82] Following one meeting with Christian groups discussing the faith-based policy, Bush declared, "You don't have to tell me. I'd still be drinking if it weren't for what Christ did in my life."[83]

Certainly, Bush's policies have come under some criticism, most noticeably for the reinstatement of the Mexico City policy, which hits Africa hardest and the fight against HIV/AIDS in particular.[84] In addition, the funding for Bush's ambitious programs remains in question. While initially pledging $3 billion for his Emergency Plan for HIV/AIDS, Bush has only requested $2 billion. The administration also has put its objections over the International Criminal Court ahead of its development goals in Africa, threatening to cut off military aid to countries if they did not sign ICC impunity statements exempting U.S. citizens from prosecution by the newly created court. To date, at least twenty-two countries have had aid cut off.[85]

The way forward

If the United States is to be seen once again as a force for progress and working for the interests of the international community as a whole, it will have to change course. Four years of the Bush administration's hegemonic policy prescriptions have made America less, not more secure. America is losing support among allies and creating more enemies by clinging to policies proven to have failed.

A new course requires realigning American foreign policy to work in concert with the international community, rather than clashing with it. Far from subjugating America's interests, as some would charge, such a shift would enable the United States to leverage its superpower status and share the burden of progress with its friends and allies. The reality is that despite its superpower status, the challenges of the twenty-first century can only be won by galvanizing world opinion in favor of America's goals and by leading in a way that the world will follow. The damage of the last four years has set back that goal, but it is not too late to chart a new course.

To succeed in making America safe once again, the lone superpower will have to marshal the full strength of its powers, those beyond its unrivaled military. Only a sophisticated blend of economic, moral, and political leadership, coupled with the use of force as a last, not first resort, can restore America's place as the country that inspires change and leads others to improve the international community. That is how America can win the war on terror. It is time for President Bush to take up that challenge in earnest.

Notes

1. Things Fall Apart

1. Quotes from White House meetings are from declassified notes of the author and not footnoted throughout the book.
2. The U.S. military is structured in various units. A platoon (15–40 soldiers); a company is 3–4 platoons (100–200 soldiers); a battalion is 3–5 companies (500–900 soldiers); a brigade is 3 or more battalions (3,000–5,000 soldiers); and a division is 3 brigades (10,000–18,000 soldiers).
3. Peter Hart and Breglio Research Cos., poll conducted April 1–14, 1992.
4. Oberdorfer, Don, *Washington Post*, September 29, 1992, A7. See also: Christopher Madison, *National Journal*, August 15, 1992, 1891.
5. Based on numbers combined by the Gallup Organization. Cited in Casey B. Dominguez, "The President's Honeymoon with Congress: Explaining Reagan's 1981 Victories" (University of California, Berkeley, 2002), Working Paper presented at the Conference on the Reagan Presidency, Santa Barbara, California, March 28–30, 2002, http://repositories.edlib.org/cgi/viewcontent.cgi?article=1003&context=igs. The term "honeymoon" was first used to describe FDR's early months as president.
6. *USA Today*/CNN/Gallup poll conducted May 10–12, 1993. Results available in Richard Benedetto, "Clinton's Job Approval Slips Below 50 Percent, *USA Today*, May 14, 1993, A1. The second figures are from ABC News/*Washington Post* poll conducted February 25–28, 1993, and CBS News/*New York Times* poll conducted June 1–3, 1993.
7. Clark, Wesley K., *Waging Modern War: Bosnia, Kosovo, and the Future of Combat* (New York: Public Affairs Press, 2002), 437.
8. Shawcross, William, *Deliver Us from Evil: Peacekeepers, Warlords, and a World of Endless Conflict* (New York: Simon & Schuster, 2000), 67.
9. Powell, Colin L., *My American Journey* (New York: Random House, 1995), 149.
10. *U.S. News and World Report* poll conducted in September 1993. Results published by Roberts, Stephen V. and Bruce B. Auster, "Colin Powell—superstar," *U.S. News and World Report*, Sept. 20, 1993, 48.
11. Powell, Colin L., "Why Generals Get Nervous," *New York Times*, October 8, 1992, A35.
12. Powell, *My American Journey*, 559.
13. "New Steps toward Conflict Resolution in the Former Yugoslavia," Opening statement by the Secretary of State at a news conference, February 10, 1993. Reprinted in *Dispatch*, vol. 4 (February 13, 1993): 81.
14. Daalder, Ivo, *Getting to Dayton* (Washington, D.C.: Brookings Institution Press, 2000), 19.
15. William, Daniel, *Washington Post*, August 19, 1993, A1.
16. Daalder, 20.
17. Gallup poll conducted May 6, 1993.
18. CBS News poll conducted May 27–29, 1993.
19. Gordon, Michael R., *New York Times*, August 3, 1993, A1. Earlier that year, Clinton had sought but failed to implement his campaign pledge to lift the ban on gays in the military. In a controversial compromise worked out with Congress and the Pentagon, the military would no longer ask soldiers about their sexual preference and permitted gays to remain in the service only if they did not admit to their sexual preference, a policy dubbed "Don't Ask, Don't Tell."
20. Drew, Elizabeth, *On the Edge* (New York: Simon & Schuster, 1994), 275.
21. Ibid., 276–277.

2. Crossing the Rubicon

1. *Public Papers of the Presidents, William J. Clinton*, vol. 2 (1993), 1753.
2. Ibid., 1703–1706.
3. Jackson, Derrick Z., "What Are Americans Dying for Now," *The Boston Globe*, June 18, 2003, http://www.globalpolicy.org/security/issues/iraq/occupation/2003/0618americans.htm.
4. For an excellent review and analysis of Somalia, see William Shawcross, *Deliver Us from Evil*.
5. Shawcross, 221.

6. *Public Papers of the Presidents, William J. Clinton*, vol. 1, (1993), 867.
7. Ibid.
8. Krauss, Clifford, "Many in Congress, Citing Vietnam, Oppose Attacks," *New York Times*, April 28, 1993, A10.
9. The United States was continuing to investigate any reports of living U.S. POWs. The United States had by April 1993 resolved questions about 104 of 196 reports of U.S. POWs living in Vietnam. All 104 were found to have died. See DOD News Briefing, April 21, 1993. In 2004, 1,862 Americans were still considered missing and unaccounted for from the Vietnam War, http://www.pow-mia families.org/powmiastatus.html). As of April 2004, there were fifty unresolved cases of POWs.
10. The Spratly Islands, rich in natural resources, were claimed in whole or in part by Brunei, Malaysia, the Philippines, Taiwan, Vietnam, and China. In February 1993, China served notice that they would be prepared to defend their claim with force.
11. The Vietnamese regularly complained to U.S. officials that they were working hard to find U.S. MIAs but no progress had been made on their own missing Vietnamese soldiers.
12. Taylor's body was exhumed in 1991 and found not to have been poisoned.
13. Weiner, Tim, "Opening to Vietnam: Sense of Relief, and One of Betrayal, Are Evoked," *New York Times*, February 4, 1994, A8.
14. Seabees are U.S. naval forces, which since World War II have built military bases, roads, airways, and a variety of construction projects. Their motto is "We build, we fight." See U.S. Navy Web page.
15. This ship is a Newport Tank Landing Ship (LST) Class capable of storing amphibious assault vehicles and navy helicopters.
16. "Tom Tomorrow Takes Stand on Waffles," *The Comics Journal* no. 172 (November 1994): 36–37.
17. Sciolino, Elaine, "Haiti's Man of Destiny Awaiting His Hour," *New York Times*, August 3, 1993, A1.
18. Stephanopoulos, George, *All Too Human* (Boston: Back Bay Books, 2000), 219.
19. Lake, Anthony, *Six Nightmares: Real Threats in a Dangerous World and How America Can Meet Them* (Boston: Little, Brown, 2000), 132–134.
20. Since October 1, 1986, each chairman has been appointed for a two-year term beginning on October 1 of odd-numbered years. The chair may be reappointed for two additional terms, except in time of war when there is no limit on the number of reappointments. An officer may not serve as chairman or vice chairman if his or her combined service in such positions exceeds six years, http://hrw.org/wr2k3/americas7.htm.
21. Greenhouse, Steven, "Aristide Condemns Clinton's Haiti Policy as Racist," *New York Times*, April 22, 1994, A1.
22. Greenhouse, Steven, "Clinton Policy Toward Haiti Comes Under Growing Fire," *New York Times*, April 15, 1994, A2.
23. CBS News/*New York Times* poll, conducted September 8–September 11, 1994.
24. Sciolino, Elaine, "Invasion of Haiti Would be Limited, Clinton Aides Say," *New York Times*, September 13, 1994, A13.
25. Powell, *My American Journey*, 599–601.
26. Ibid.
27. The UN Human Development Report can be found at www.undp.org/hrd2003/indicator/sty_f_HTI.html. Other statistics are at http://www.countryreports.org/content/haiti.htm.
28. Shawcross, 407.
29. Cooper, Kenneth J., and Helen Dewar, "Congress Urges 'Prompt' Troop Withdrawal from Haiti," *Washington Post*, October 7, 1994, A14.
30. Minzesheimer, Bob, "White House, GOP clash over troops in Haiti," *USA Today*, November 28, 1994, 10A.
31. See: Michael Norton, "UN Mission Leaves Haiti," Associated Press, March 18, 2000.
32. Sachs, Jeffrey, "Don't Fall for Washington's Spin on Haiti," *Financial Times*, February 29, 2004, 13.

3. Go as Peacemakers

1. See: RAND Terrorism Chronology Database, Oklahoma City National Memorial Institute for the Prevention of Terrorism, 2002, http://db.mipt.org/index.cfm. Irish figures are from 1969–2001 from http://www.parliament.the-stationery-.office.co.uk/pa/ld199900/ldhansrd/pdvn/lds01/text/11116w01.htm#11116w01_sb hd5. Middle East figures are from http://www.pbs.org/pov/pov2001/promises/timeline3.html. For American casualties, see U.S. State Department, http://www.state.gov/r/pa/ho/pubs/fs/5902.htm. The most notorious world-terrorist incidents were the 1985 bombing of an Air India flight by Sikh terrorists, which killed 329 people. Middle East–related incidents include the Islamic Jihad's 1983 suicide bombing of the U.S. Marine Corps base in Beirut, Lebanon, killing 241 Americans, the bombing of the U.S. embassy in Beirut, also in 1983, killing 63, and the 1988 bombing of Pan Am flight 103 over Lockerbie,

Scotland, in 1988, which killed 270 and was ultimately attributed to Libya.

2. Statistical information obtained from Steven Erlanger, "Wrestling with Rubles," *New York Times*, July 28, 1993, A8.

3. Bentsur, Eytan, "The Way to Peace Emerged at Madrid: A Decade Since the 1991 Peace Conference," Jerusalem Center for Public Affairs (February 15, 2002), http://www.jcpa.org/jl/vp472.htm.

4. Fagforeningens Forskningsorganisationjon (FAFO).

5. For an excellent background, see: the International Crisis Group Middle East Report No. 1, *A Time to Lead: The International Community and the Israeli-Palestinian Conflict* (April 10, 2002). See also: http://www.palestinefacts.org/pf _1991to_now_oslo_background.php.

6. For an excellent summary of the Oslo process, see Uri Savir, *The Process: 1,100 Days that Changed the Middle East* (New York: Random House, 1998).

7. Haberman, Clyde, *New York Times*, September 10, 1993, A1. It would take some time for Arafat to secure a change to the articles in the original Palestinian charter calling for the destruction of Israel. By 1996, Peres had demanded that Arafat put the revocation of these articles to a vote. Arafat confirmed in April 1996 that the PNC had agreed that the charter would reflect "nullification of all its articles contrary to the letters exchanged between the PLO and the government of Israel on September 9 and 10, 1993." The issue came largely to closure in December 1998, when President Clinton attended the Palestinian Legislative Council vote that renounced the articles.

8. In "A" areas the PA had full responsibility for civil administration, public order, and internal security; "B" areas gave the PA civil control, but Israeli forces would retain over-riding military control; and "C" areas, which were unpopulated pieces of land of strategic importance for Israel and/or its settlements, were under full Israeli military control.

9. http://info.jpost.com/1998/Supplements/Rabin/5.html.

10. "Arabs, Jews Join to Mourn; Killer: 'We Need to be Cold-Hearted.'" *Houston Chronicle*, November 7, 1995, 1a.

11. *Public Papers of the Presidents, William J. Clinton*, vol. 2 (1995), 1720.

12. http://www.usaid.gov/wbg/faq.htm#aa2.

13. Agha, Hussein, and Robert Malley, "Camp David: The Tragedy of Errors," *New York Review of Books*, August 9, 2001.

14. "A Time to Lead: The International Community and the Israeli–Palestinian Conflict," International Crisis Group, *Middle East Report* no. 1, April 10, 2002.

Recounting the conclusions of the Fact Finding Report of the Mitchell Committee, which came to be known as "The Mitchell Report."

15. Today there are about 3.8 million refugees registered with the United Nations Relief and Works Agency. More than 1.7 million Palestinians live in Jordan, and about four hundred thousand live in both Lebanon and Syria, http://www.cesr.org/PROGRAMS/palestine.htm.

16. Agha and Malley.

17. The Taba principles were never formally turned into a legal document. This overview is based on the "Moratinos Non-Paper," a summary that both sides agreed was a relatively fair description of the outcome of the negotiations on the permanent status issues at Taba. (Prepared in January 2001.) Source located at United Nations Information System on the Question of Palestine (UNISPAL), http://domino.un.org/UNISPAL .NSF/9a798adbf322aff38525617b006d88 d7/cea3efd8c0ab482f85256e3700670af8! OpenDocument&Highlight=2,non-paper.

18. By March 1997, $2.714 billion had been committed to specific forms of expenditure by donor countries and $1.527 billion had been disbursed. "Development Under Adversity: The Palestinian Economy in Transition," March 1999, http://lnweb18 .worldbank.org/mna/mena.nsf/Countries/ West+Bank/4DDD0E8FA940D20485256 B02003D548B?OpenDocument.

19. "UN Report Draws Rosy Picture of Palestinian Economy," January 18, 2000, www.arabicnews.com.

20. *The Economist*, January 20, 2000.

21. Garber, Larry (Director of UNAID, Gaza), e-mail exchange, April 19, 2004. Garber left his post in June 2004.

22. Palestine Red Crescent Society: http://www .palestinercs.org/intifadasummary.htm.

23. "Islamic Social Welfare Activities in the Occupied Palestinian Territories," International Crisis Group, April 2, 2003.

24. Morris, Benny, "Camp David and After," *New York Review of Books*, August 9, 2001.

25. "A Time to Lead," International Crisis Group.

26. Sontag, Deborah, *New York Times*, July 26, 2001, A1.

27. "A Time to Lead" International Crisis Group.

28. Ross, Dennis, *The Missing Piece: The Inside Story of the Fight for Middle East Peace* (New York: Farrar, Straus, and Giraux, 2004).

29. Interview with the author, July 9, 2004. Steinberg served under Clinton as director of policy planning at the State Department and as deputy national security advisor at the White House.

30. *Public Papers of the Presidents, William J. Clinton*, vol. 1 (1993), 943–944.
31. Reuters, June 21, 2002.
32. "Sharon Declares 'Roadmap' Dead," Ramallah online, April 29, 2004, http://ramallahonline.com/modules.php?name=News&file=articles&sid=1894.
33. Fandy, Mamoum, discussion on April 21, 2004. Fandy is a senior fellow at the Baker Institute for Public Policy, Rice University.
34. See, for example: Christine Hauser, "Powell Meets With Framers of Symbolic Mideast Accord," *New York Times*, December 5, 2003, http://www.nytimes.com/2003/12/05/international/middleeast/05CNDMIDE.html; http://www.crisisweb.org/home/index.cfm?l=1&id=2391. See also: the International Crisis Group Web site www.crisisweb.org for background on the Geneva Accord.
35. http://www.crisisweb.org//library/documents/middle_east_north_africa/survey resultsfinal.pdf.
36. Thatcher's exact quote is that she would "never concede political status to the hunger strikers," http://irelandsown.net/armagh women.html.
37. http://cain.ulst.ac.uk/events/peace/docs/dsd151293.htm.
38. The Department of State keeps a list of individuals who are considered ineligible for a visa to enter the United States. There are a variety of reasons to be on such a list, i.e., charge of espionage, terrorism, and criminal activity. While the State Department maintains the list, the Justice Department has the authority to waive the visa restrictions. Brodie, Ian, "Irish-American Lobby Angered by Visa Decision." *Times* (London), November 12, 1993.
39. See: *Daily Star* and *The Sun*, February 1995.
40. Clinton also had briefly met Adams at the annual St. Patrick's Day lunch hosted by Speaker of the House Newt Gingrich in 1995.
41. Clinton met with Trimble in both his roles as UUP Leader and as first minister to Ireland, a position he assumed in June 1998.
42. http://www.cec.org.uk/info/pubs/regional/ni/chap1p4.htm.
43. Gallagher, A. M., "Employment, Unemployment, and Religion in Norther Ireland," *Majority Minority Review* no. 2 (Ulster: University of Ulster, 1991).
44. http://www.facilitycity.com/busfac/bf_02_05_intl.asp.
45. http://www.nio.gov.uk.
46. See: *Making Peace* by George Mitchell for his interesting personal account of the negotiations.
47. http://www.rte.ie/news/archive/clinton visit/ahernspeech2.html.
48. Sipress, Alan, *Washington Post*, March 17, 2001, A24.

4. Force and Diplomacy

1. Report of the Secretary-General pursuant to General Assembly Resolution 53/35, *The Fall of Srebrenica*, A/54/549-a, November 15, 1999, 41–42.
2. Echikson, William, *Boston Globe*, July 14, 1995, A8.
3. Burns, Nicholas, U.S. Department of State, Daily Press Briefing, DPB #101, Monday, July 10, 1995.The United States placed ninety U.S. soldiers in Croatia to provide logistical support.
4. The Senate voted on July 26, 1995, 69 to 29 to lift the arms embargo against the Bosnians. On August 1, 1995, the House of Representatives voted 298 in favor and 128 against. President Clinton vetoed the legislation on August 11 and Congress made no attempt to override the veto.
5. Among the negotiators appointed to bring peace in former Yugoslavia: the former British foreign secretary Lord Carrington (for the European Community 1991–1992), then replaced by David Owen (1992–1995); the former U.S. secretary of state Cyrus Vance (for the UN 1993–1999); Carl Bildt, former Swedish prime minister, as European Union peace envoy's high representative in Bosnia (1999–2001); Thorvald Stoltenberg, as UN representative to the International Conference on the Former Yugoslavia from 1993 to 1996.
6. Shawcross, William, *Deliver Us from Evil*, 161. Only half were infantry soldiers; the rest were in support capacities.
7. For a detailed account of the tragedy of Srebrenica, see: the Report of the Secretary-General pursuant to General Assembly resolution 53/35.
8. Quoted in Mark Danner, "The Killing Fields of Bosnia," *New York Review of Books*, September 24, 1998.
9. The administration declassified spy photos for the UN Security Council on August 10, 1995. "Daily Reports on the Balkan Conflict," CNN Online, August 10, 1995, http://www.cnn.com/WORLD/Bosnia/updates/august95/8-10/massgraves.jpg.
10. Crossette, Barbara, "U.S. Seeks to Prove Mass Killings," *New York Times*, August 11, 1995, A3.
11. Darnton, John, "Conflict in the Balkans: Policy—Allies Warn Bosnian Serbs of 'Substantial' Air Strikes If UN Enclave Is

Attacked; Accord in London" *New York Times*, July 22, 1995, p. A1.

12. See: *Report to the OSCE: The International Helsinki Federation for Human Rights Fact-Finding Mission to the Krajina*, August 17–19, 1995, 1. See also: Ivo H. Daalder, *Getting to Dayton, the Making of America's Bosnia Policy*, 120–123.

13. The Croats and Bosnians were partners in a federation, with the Bosnians controlling 30 percent and the Croats 21 percent. See: UN report A/54/549-a 91.

14. Burg, Steven L., "Coercive Diplomacy in the Balkans," in *The United States and Coercive Diplomacy*, edited by Robert J. Art and Patrick M. Cronin (Washington, D.C.: United States Institute of Peace Press, 2003), 60.

15. Wirthlin Quorum, June 1995. Gallup public opinion survey released February 1, 1995.

16. "Clinton Fatigue Undermines Gore Poll Standing," Pew Center for People and the Press. New Interest Index: Final Topline No. 1, 786, March 1999. http://people-press.org/reports/print/php3?Page1K=309.

17. The commitment at the Air Force Academy, written by Lake, was broader than the principals had agreed. After his colleagues objected, the president restated the commitment in narrower terms. The May 31 language stated, "We should be prepared to assist NATO if it decides to meet a request from the United Nations troops for help with a withdrawal or a reconfiguration and a strengthening of its forces." The June 3 language was: "If our allies decide they can no longer continue the UN mission and decide to withdraw . . . we should help them to get out," dropping the reference to any assistance should the UN stay.

18. For an excellent summary of the evolution of Clinton's Bosnia policy, see: Daalder, *Getting to Dayton.*

19. Lake, Anthony, *Six Nightmares: Real Threats in a Dangerous World and How America Can Meet Them* (Boston: Little, Brown, 2000), 147.

20. Woodward, Bob, *The Choice* (New York: Simon & Schuster, 1996), 263.

21. British prime minister John Major chaired the conference with EU, UN, NATO, Contact Group, and other UN troop contributors.

22. Daalder, 75–77.

23. See: Daalder, 111, and Lake, *Six Nightmares*, 149.

24. Daalder, 131.

25. Shawcross, 13.

26. Holbrooke, Richard, *To End a War* (New York: Random House, 1998), 132.

27. Robert C. Frasure, U.S. deputy assistant sec-retary of state for European and Canadian affairs, Joseph Kruzel, U.S. deputy assistant secretary of defense for international security affairs, and Lieutenant Colonel, S. Nelson Drew, U.S. Air Force; National Security Council.

28. Holbrooke, 138–141.

29. Holbrooke, 142–152. Quote from 152.

30. See: Fact Sheet Operation Deliberate Force in the NATO Regional Headquarters Allied Forces Southern Europe's Web site http://www.fas.org/man/dod-101/ops/docs/DeliberateForceFactSheet.htm.

31. Daalder, 129–134.

32. Holbrooke, 363.

33. Daalder, 180.

34. "Serbian Reform Stalls Again," International Crisis Group, Balkans Report no. 145, July 17, 2003; See also: "Bosnia's Nationalist Governments: Paddy Ashdown and the Paradoxes of State Building," International Crisis Group, Balkans Report no. 146, July 22, 2004.

35. Neuffer, Elizabeth, *Boston Globe*, December 1, 1995, 10.

36. One thousand five hundred eighty U.S. troops remain in Bosnia as part of the eighteen-thousand-member international forces. In addition, the Europeans started the European Union Police Mission (EUPM) in Bosnia and Herzegovina. The mission is comprised of five hundred police officers from over thirty countries, including the fifteen EU member states. The European Union will assume command of the peacekeeping force in Bosnia from NATO early 2005. NATO, "SFOR Organization," updated June 1, 2004, http://www.nato.int/sfor/organisation/sfororg.htm.

37. Report of the Secretary-General, A/54/549-a, 93.

38. Ibid., 94.

39. Ibid., 97.

40. Ibid., 103–104.

41. Contrary to common beliefs, Khrushchev did not pound his shoe on the table.

42. United States–UN Press Release #155 (98), September 23, 1998, available at http://www.un.int/usa/98_155.htm.

43. Daalder, Ivo H., and Michael E. O'Hanlon, *Winning Ugly: NATO's War to Save Kosovo* (Washington, D.C.: Brookings Institution Press, 2000), 43.

44. Silverman, Jon, "Racak massacre haunts Milosevic trial," BBC, February 14, 2002, http://news.bbc.co.uk/1/hi/world/europe/1812847.stm.

45. The Contact Group consisted of the foreign ministers of France, Germany, Italy, Russia, the UK and the United States.

46. Daalder and O'Hanlon, 75.

47. Clark, Wesley K., *Waging Modern War*. In

his memoirs, Clark provides an excellent, detailed description of the Kosovo campaign and fighting a war in the post–cold war era.

48. Daalder and O'Hanlon, 108–109.

49. *Newsweek* poll conducted April 21–22, 1999, by Princeton Research Associates, http://www.pollingreport.com/serb9904 .htm.

50. "World: Europe Nato vows to 'tighten the screw'" BBC, http://news.bbc.co.uk/1/ hi/world/europe/326924.stm. See also: William Drozdiak and Thomas W. Lippman, "Clinton Joins Allies on Ground Troops; Milosevic's House, Serb TV Struck as NATO Heads Meet," *Washington Post*, April 23, 1999, A1.

51. Clark, xxii.

52. Daalder and O'Hanlon, 156.

53. NATO's KFOR Web site, http://www .nato.int/docu/facts/2000/kosovo.htm.

54. "NATO Waits, Russians Head for Kosovo," Associated Press, published in *Chicago Tribune*, June 11, 1999, 1C. KFOR stands for Kosovo Force.

55. NATO, "NATO's Role in Relation to Kosovo." August 9, 2000, http://www .nato.int/docu/facts/2000/kosovo.htm.

56. http://news.bbc.co.uk/2/hi/europe/ 3522230.stm; UNMIK figures as of November 2003, available at http://www .un.org/Depts/dpko/dpko/home.shtml.

57. Berger, Samuel R., "Power and Authority: America's Path Ahead," chapter in upcoming book.

58. The International Crisis Group has long advocated conditional independence for Kosovo.

59. "Ready or Not," *The Economist*, May 24, 2003.

60. McCullough, David, *Truman* (New York: Simon & Schuster, 1994).

61. Fukuyama, Francis. *The End of History and the Last Man* (New York: Free Press, 1992); Huntington, Samuel P. *The Clash of Civilizations and the Remaking of World Order* (New York: Simon & Schuster, 1998).

62. Schweid, Barry, "Helms Says U.S. Should Withdraw From UN If Reforms Aren't Adopted," Associated Press, August 20, 1996.

63. *A Foreign Policy for the Global Age: The Clinton Administration Record 1993–2001*, internal NSC working document.

64. Ibid.

65. Berger, Sandy, "A Foreign Policy for the Global Age," *Foreign Affairs* (November/ December 2000): 24.

66. Information obtained from White House Fact Sheet, issued December 6, 2000, available at http://hongkong.usconsulate .gov/uscn/wh/2000/120602.htm.

67. Berger, Sandy, "A Foreign Policy for the Global Age," 29.

68. Summers, Lawrence, as quoted in Samuel P. Huntingon's "The Lonely Superpower," *Foreign Affairs* (March/April 1999): 38.

69. Prestowitz, Clyde, *Rogue Nation: American Unilateralism and the Failure of Good Intentions* (New York: Basic Books, 2003), 21.

5. A Realistic Foreign Policy?

1. Keen, Judy, "Dole Sharply Critical of President's Foreign Policy Record," *USA Today*, October 4, 1996, 6A.

2. Eilperin, Juliet, and William Claiborne, "Troop Deployment Narrowly Approved," *Washington Post*, March 12, 1999, A28.

3. Kissinger, Henry, *Does America Need a Foreign Policy?* (New York: Touchstone, 2002), 29–30.

4. The Contract with America was a ten-point legislative program that focused on reducing the size and scope of the government. Spearheaded by House Speaker Newt Gingrich and endorsed by many Republican candidates, the program involved immediate cutback in government programs, and a congressional audit for waste and fraud. In addition, the program promised to bring to a vote within one hundred days issues such as a balanced budget amendment, tax cuts, and a bill to prohibit U.S. troops from serving under UN command. See: http://usinfo.state.gove/ products/pubs/archive/elect00/congress .htm. The full text of the Contract is available at http://www.whitehouse.gov/house/ Contract/CONTRACT.html.

5. Kristol, William, and Robert Kagan, *Foreign Affairs* vol. 75:4 (July/August 1996): 19.

6. Project for a New American Century (PNAC), "Statement of Principles," June 3, 1997.

7. PNAC, "Letter to Pres. Clinton," January 26, 1998, http://www.newamericancen tury.org/iraqclintonletter.htm.

8. Gellman, Bart, *Washington Post*, March 11, 1992, A1.

9. Mann, James, *Rise of the Vulcans: The History of Bush's War Cabinet* (New York: Viking, 2004), 211.

10. Sciolino, Elaine, "Bush's Foreign Policy Tutor; An Academic in the Public Eye," *New York Times*, June 16, 2000, A1.

11. Bush, Governor George W., "A Distinctly American Internationalism," speech at the Ronald Reagan Presidential Library, Simi Valley, California, November 19, 1999,

http://www.fas.org/news/usa/1999/11/991119-bush-foreignpolicy.htm.

12. Rice, Condoleezza, "Promoting the National Interest," *Foreign Affairs,* (January/February 2000).

13. Rice, Condoleezza, "How to Pursue the National Interest," *Hoover Digest* no. 2 (November 6, 2004), http://www.hooverdigest.org/002/rice/html.

14. Bush, "A Distinctly American Internationalism."

15. Op. cit., 61.

16. Ibid., 62.

17. Quoted in the Atlantic Monthly, http://www.theatlantic.com/doc/200401/fukuyama.

18. Gordon, Michael, *New York Times,* October 21, 2000, A1.

19. Bush, George W., speech given at The Citadel in Charleston, South Carolina, September 23, 1999. Full text of speech available at http://usinfo.state.gov/topical/pol/terror/01121002.htm.

20. Kissinger, *Does America Need a Foreign Policy?,* 268.

21. Bush, Citadel speech.

22. *CNN.com,* "With eye on polls, Bush addresses military readiness," September 7, 2000, http://www.cnn.com/2000/ALLPOLITICS/stories/09/07/campaign.wrap/index.html.

23. *The Weekly Standard,* September 7, 1998, 7.

24. Perle, Richard, "New Weapon for a New World Order," *American Enterprise* (April 2001).

25. Presidential debate at Wake Forest University, North Carolina, October 11, 2000, http://www.issues2000.org/2000/Wake_Forest_debate_Foreign_Policy.htm.

26. Rice, Condoleezza, "Promoting the National Interest."

27. Gore received 51,003,894 votes to Bush's 50,459,211. However, with Florida awarded him by the Supreme Court, Bush was declared the winner with 271 electoral votes to Gore's 266.

28. Carney, James, and John F. Dickerson, "Man in Charge," *Time* (December 1, 2000).

29. Tyler, Patrick E., "After the War; U.S. Juggling Iraq Policy," *New York Times,* April 13, 1991, 5.

30. Hartmann, Robert Trowbridge, *Palace Politics: An Inside Account of the Ford Years* (New York: McGraw-Hill, 1980), 283, quoted in James Mann *The Rise of the Vulcans.*

31. Lemann, Nicholas, "Without a Doubt: Has Condoleezza Rice Changed George W. Bush, Or Has He Changed Her?," *The New Yorker* (October 14, 2002): 164.

32. Text of Colin Powell's speech available *New York Times,* December 17, 2000, 51.

33. Daalder, Ivo H., and James M. Lindsay, *America Unbound* (Washington, D.C.: Brookings Institution Press, 2003), 54.

34. Steinberg, James B., "The Bush Foreign Policy Revolution," *New Perspectives Quarterly* (Summer 2003).

35. Comptroller General of the United States, B-229069, September 30, 1987, http://www.gwu.edu/~nsarchiv/NSAEBB/NSAEBB40/04287.pdf.

36. Dobbs, Michael, "Back in Political Forefront: Iran-Contra Figure Plays Key Role on Mideast," *Washington Post,* May 27, 2003,. http://www.washingtonpost.com/ac2/wp-dyn/A41843-2003May26?language=printer.

37. McGeary, Johanna, *Time* (September 10, 2001): 24.

38. Sipress, Alan, *Washington Post,* March 17, 2001, A24.

39. Statement made following Bush's meeting with UK Prime Minster Tony Blair, February 23, 2001. See: *Public Papers of the President, George W. Bush,* vol. 1 (2000), 128.

40. Presidential debate at Wake Forest University, North Carolina, October 11, 2000, http://www.issues2000.org/2000/Wake_Forest_debate_Foreign_Policy.htm.

41. Fee, Florence C., "Russia and Iraq: The Question of the Russian Oil Contracts," *Middle East Economic Survey Report* (April 7, 2003).

42. Shribman, David, *Boston Globe,* March 12, 2002, A3.

43. McGeary, Johanna, "Odd Man Out," *Time* (September 10, 2001).

44. Perlmutter, Amos, *Washington Times,* March 15, 2001, A17.

45. Gordon, Michael R., *New York Times,* October 21, 2000, A1.

46. Garamone, Jim, "Rumsfeld Reflects on Military Service," American Forces Press Service, Washington, May 20, 2002.

47. Hassan-Gordon, Tariq, "Washington's decision on Sinai forces still uncertain," *Middle East Times,* May 11, 2001.

48. Ricks, Thomas, "Possible Military Overhaul Outlined," *Washington Post,* May 18, 2001, A1.

49. Dannheisser, Ralph, "Powell Says U.S. Troops Could Help at Macedonia Disarmament Points Secretary Briefs Senate Panel after Europe Trip with Bush," *Washington File Congressional Correspondent* (June 21, 2001), http://www.uspolicy.be/Issues/Balkans/powmace062101.htm.

50. Marc Lacey, "Powell Fails to Persuade NATO on Antimissile Plan," *New York Times,* May 30, 2001, A14.
51. Ibid.
52. "US troops will remain in Bosnia, Kosovo: Bush," *Agence France-Presse,* July 24, 2001.
53. "Bush Keeps Troops Option Open on Macedonia," *Washington Post,* June 28, 2001, A23.
54. "Macedonia Peacekeeping," *Online NewsHour,* PBS, August 22, 2001, http://www.pbs.org/newshour/bb/europe/july-dec01/macedonia_8–22.html.
55. Holt, Douglas, "Army to close Peacekeeping Institute," *Chicago Tribune,* April 14, 2003, http://www.tallahassee.com/mld/tallahassee/news/politics/5634135.htm.
56. Bush, Citadel speech.
57. Deans, Bob, "Bush Tougher Stance on Foreign Policy, Reflects New 'Realism,'" Cox News Service, March 22, 2001.
58. Cottrell, Robert, "The partners who returned to the cold: The US-Russia spy row has exposed the cracks in an already fragile relationship" *Financial Times,* March 26, 2001, 21.
59. Bush, "A Distinctly American Internationalism."
60. *Public Papers of the President, George W. Bush,* vol. 1 (2000), 355.
61. Allen, Mike, and Steven Mufson, "U.S. Voices Regret Over Chinese Pilot," *Washington Post,* April 5, 2001, A1.
62. Allen, Mike, and Steven Mufson, "Bush Backs Diplomacy, But Also Warns China," *Washington Post,* April 10, 2001, A1.
63. Barber, Ben, "Bush's remarks leave in doubt U.S. policy on Taiwan," *Washington Times,* April 26, 2001, A12.
64. Bering, Helle, "No Aegis shield for Taiwan; Bush White House defers to China," *Washington Times,* April 25, 2001, A19.
65. Raum, Tom, "Bush words on Taiwan trigger new controversy," Associated Press, April 25, 2001.
66. Sammon, Bill, "White House sees 'no change' in Taiwan policy; Tougher stance angers Beijing," *Washington Times,* April 26, 2001, A1.
67. Editors, "The End of Strategic Ambiguity," *Washington Times,* April 27, 2001, A20.
68. Ricks, Thomas E., "Rumsfeld Outlines Defense Overhaul; Reorganization May Alter, Kill Weapons Systems," *Washington Post,* March 23, 2001, A1.
69. Arkin, William M., "Rumsfeld Stumbles," *Washingtonpost.com,* March 26, 2001.
70. Roedemeier, Chad, "GOP vice presidential nominee brings pro-military message to Georgia," Associated Press, August 30, 2000.
71. White House briefing, Press Secretary Ari Fleischer, January 31, 2001.
72. Kondracke, Morton M., "After China Crisis, Bush Must Explain His Foreign Policy," *Roll Call,* April 9, 2001.
73. Bush, Citadel speech.
74. O'Hanlon, Michael, "Rumsfeld's Defence Vision," *Survival,* vol. 44, no. 2 (Summer 2002): 103–117.
75. Ibid., 112.
76. Rumsfeld's $5.6 billion through a supplemental appropriation request and additional $18.4 billion, almost entirely devoted to added training, spare parts, and military pay, brought the total to $335 billion. Before September 11, the Bush administration proposed a budget roughly $25.5 billion higher than Clinton's proposal. During the campaign, Bush had proposed increasing by $45 billion to a total of $341 billion.
77. Kagan, Robert, and William Kristol, editorial, *Weekly Standard,* July 23, 2001.
78. Clark, Wesley, "Iraq: What Went Wrong," *New York Review of Books,* vol. 50, no. 16 (October 23, 2003).
79. Interviews with a retired four-star general, July 12, 2004.
80. Sanger, David E., "After ABM Treaty: New Freedom for U.S. in Different Kind of Arms Control," *New York Times,* December 15, 2001, A8.
81. "National Missile Defense Act of 1999," sec. 2, at CDI Web site, http://www.cdi.org/hotspots/missiledefense/act.html.
82. See: Elisabeth Becker, "U.S. Seeks Missile System Despite Treaty Risk," *New York Times,* November 6, 1999, A8.
83. Gertz, Bill, "ABM Treaty update apt to be next fight," *Washington Times,* October 14, 1999, A15.
84. Gertz, Bill, "Missile Test Fails, But System Solid," *Washington Times,* July 9, 2000, C1.
85. *Public Papers of the President, George W. Bush,* vol. 1 (2000), 472.
86. Rice, Condoleezza, remarks at the National Press Club, July 12, 2001.
87. Public Papers of the President, 644.
88. Ibid., 472.
89. "George Bush's Revolution," *Economist* (May 5, 2001).
90. Public Papers of the President, 644.
91. http://www.whitehouse.gov/news/releases/20010123–5.html.
92. Bone, James, "Republicans to Block War Crimes Treaty," *Times* (London), January 2, 2001.
93. BBC News Online, "Dismay over US germ warfare stance," July 25, 2001, http://news.bbc.co.uk/2/low/americas/1457324.stm.
94. *Public Papers Bush,* vol. 1 (2000), 634.

95. The protocol was to only enter into force after it has been ratified by at least fifty-five members of the United Nations Framework Convention on Climate Control, including developed countries representing 55 percent of the total 1990 carbon dioxide emissions. The U.S. produces 36 percent of these emissions and its absence makes it difficult to bring the protocol into force. In July 2001 in Bonn, Germany, more than 180 nations adopted the Bonn Agreement, resolving most of the high-profile issues. The Bonn Agreement that was adopted was a watered-down version of the original vision. The new agreement reduced the average cut in greenhouse gas emissions required by the year 2012 from 5.2 percent below 1990 levels to 1.8 percent below 1990 levels, and it incorporated a number of the negotiating positions previously advanced by the Clinton administration, such as crediting nations for maintaining large forests to serve as "carbon sinks" to soak up the offending gas. The United States was not an adopting party. The November 2001 Marrakech Accords then set the stage for countries to ratify the protocol and bring it into force. The United States participated in the conference but reaffirmed that it did not intend to ratify the Protocol.

96. Evans-Pritchard, Ambrose, and Charles Clover, "Europe Fights to Save Kyoto Treaty," *Daily Telegraph*, April 6, 2001, 19.

97. Prestowitz, Clyde, *Rogue Nation: American Unilateralism and the Failure of Good Intentions* (New York: Basic Books, 2003), 113.

98. "Sharp European reaction to Bush repudiation of Kyoto," *Agence France-Presse*, March 29, 2001.

99. Allen, Mike, and Eric Pianin, "Bush Raises Doubts on Global Warming Causes," *Washington Post*, June 12, 2001, A1.

100. McGeary, Johanna, "Odd Man Out," *Time* (September 10, 2001): 24, http://www.time.com/time/asia/news/printout/0,9788,173496,00.html.

101. See: Eric Pianin, "160 Nations Agree To Warming Pact—U.S. Was on Sidelines in Morocco Talks," *Washington Post*, November 10, 2001, A1.

102. McGeary, Johanna, "Odd Man Out," *Time* (September 10, 2001): 24, http://www.time.com/time/asia/news/printout/0,9788,173496,00.html.

103. Prestowitz, Clyde, *Rogue Nation: American Unilateralism and the Failure of Good Intentions* (New York: Basic Books, 2003), 139.

104. Knowlton, Brian, "Bush Gets Low Marks in Europe; Poll Finds Wide Disapproval of President's Conduct of Foreign Policy," *International Herald Tribune*, August 16, 2001, 1.

105. "Doubts on Both Sides of the Atlantic," *The Economist* (March 31, 2001).

106. Woodward, Bob, *Bush at War* (New York: Simon & Schuster, 2002), 13.

107. Wilson, Brian, "Secretary Rumsfeld Interview with Fox News," News Transcript, U.S. Department of Defense, September 10, 2001, http://www.defenselink.mil/news/Sep2001/t09172001_t0910fox.html.

108. Allen, Mike, and Dana Milbank, "Cheney's Role Offers Strengths And Liabilities," *Washington Post*, May 17, 2001, A1.

6. A New Breed of Terrorists

1. As of August 30, 2004, 2,992 people were presumed dead as a result of the four September 11 attacks. This includes the casualties at the World Trade Center, the Pentagon, on the four airplanes, and the hijackers. Source: Wikipedia, http://en2.wikipedia.org/wiki/Wikipedia. On December 7, 1941, 2,395 people were killed and 1,178 were wounded in the Pearl Harbor attack. Source: Pearl Harbor Memorial, http://my.execpc.com/~dschaaf/pearl2.html.

2. Federation of American Scientists Online, "Communications, Command, Control and Intelligence," last updated on October 2, 2000; available online at http://www.fas.org/nuke/guide/usa/c3i/peoc.htm.

3. "Cheney Recalls Taking Charge From Bunker," *CNN.com*, September 11, 2002, http://www.cnn.com/2002/ALLPOLITICS/09/11/ar911.king.cheney/.

4. September 11 News: Online Archives, "President Bush," November 16, 2003, http://www.september11news.com/PresidentBush.htm.

5. Statement by the president in his address to the nation, September 11, 2001, http://www.whitehouse.gov/news/releases/2001/09/20010911-16.html.

6. Remarks by the president in photo opportunity with the National Security team, White House Press Release, September 12, 2001, http://www.whitehouse.gov/news/releases/2001/09/20010912-4.html.

7. Erlanger, Steven. "Day of Terror: The World's Reaction," *New York Times*, September 12, 2001, A23.

8. Ibid.

9. Ibid.

10. On September 12, 2001, NATO invoked the principle of collective defense as articulated in Article V of the Washington Treaty.

The Council agreed that if it were determined that the attack had been conducted from abroad, it would then be regarded as an action covered by Article V of the Washington Treaty. Under this article, "the Parties agree that an armed attack against one or more of them in Europe or North America shall be considered an attack against them all."

11. Rozenberg, Joshua, "A Nation Challenged: The Diplomacy: World Leaders List Conditions On Cooperation," *Daily Telegraph*, September 18, 2001, 21.

12. UN General Assembly Resolution A/RES/56/1. September 12, 2001, http://www.un.org/documents/ga/doc/56/agresolution.htm.

13. Tyler, Patrick E., and Jane Perlez, *New York Times*, September 19, 2001, A1. The quote refers to German foreign policy advisor Karl Kaiser.

14. Rosenbaum, David E., "A Nation Challenged: The Lawmakers. Congressional Leaders Offer Strong Endorsement of Attack," *New York Times*, October 8, 2001, B11. The lone dissenting vote was cast by Representative Barbara Lee (D-CA). Lee feared that a rapid counter-attack would lead to unnecessary civilian casualties in the war on terror. She also expressed concern that U.S. military retaliation would spark anti-American sentiment and that the resolution would lead to an open-ended war with no clear focus or exit strategy. "Rep. Barbara Lee's Speech Opposing the Post 9-11 Use of Force Act," Nuclear Age Peace Foundation, September 14, 2001, http://www.wagingpeace.org/articles/2001/09/14_lee-speech.htm (accessed January 29, 2004).

15. Rosenbaum, "A Nation Challenged," B11.

16. Toner, Robin, and Neil Lewis, "A Nation Challenged: the Legislation; Bill Greatly Expanding Surveillance Power in Terrorism Fight Clears Senate," *New York Times*, October 12, 2001, B11. Wisconsin Democrat Russ Feingold was the lone vote against the bill.

17. CNN/*USA Today*/Gallup poll, September 2–4, 2002, http://www.pollingreport.com/terror3.htm. Only five U.S. presidents, including George W. Bush, have enjoyed job ratings of over 80 percent: Franklin Delano Roosevelt scored 84 percent after the Japanese attack on Pearl Harbor; Harry Truman hit 87 percent upon assuming the presidency; John F. Kennedy scored 83 percent in the wake of the Bay of Pigs incident; and George H. W. Bush peaked at 89 percent during the Gulf War, http://www.campaignline.com/commentary/index.cfm?id=70 (accessed February 4, 2004).

18. U.S. Congress: U.S. Senate Select Committee on Intelligence and U.S. House Permanent Select Committee on Intelligence, *Joint Inquiry into Intelligence Community Activities Before and After the Terrorist Attacks of September 11, 2001* (December 2002), 236. Referred to subsequently as the *Joint Inquiry*.

19. America's experience with international terrorism in the 1980s began with the bombing of the U.S. embassy in April 1983 in Beirut and the Marine barracks that October; Islamic Jihad claimed responsibility for both. In March 1984, a CIA official in Beirut, William Buckley, was kidnapped and murdered, and a number of other Americans were also held hostage. In April 1984, the Iranian-backed terrorist group Hizbollah claimed responsibility for bombing of a restaurant frequented by U.S. service members in Spain, and in September 1984, the U.S. embassy annex in Beirut, Lebanon, was bombed. In 1985, there was a flurry of terrorist activities against U.S. citizens and interests, including the cruise ship *Achille Lauro* in October 1985, the November 1985 hijacking of an Egypt Air jetliner from Athens to Malta, and the December 1985 attacks by Abu Nidal's organization against the Rome and Vienna airports. See *Joint Inquiry*, 229.

20. In August 2003 Libya handed over a letter at a United Nations Security Council meeting formally taking responsibility for the Lockerbie bombing. In December 2003, Libya's leader Qaddafi agreed to give up his weapons program and allow international inspectors full access to his previously clandestine programs.

21. *Joint Inquiry*, 192. See also: "Terrorists Targeted Disneyland, Space Needle," United Press International, February 1, 2001, http://www.newsmax.com/archives/articles/2001/2/20/160738.shtml.

22. Opposed to U.S. forces in Somalia, bin Laden operatives sought to blow up two hotels in Yemen believed to be host to American soldiers supporting the humanitarian operation in Somalia. An alert security guard had stopped a terrorist from blowing up the Aden Hotel; a bomb did explode in the Goldmore Hotel, killing a janitor and an elderly guest at the hotel, but no Americans. Links to bin Laden would also later be discovered in the October 1993 fight in Mogadishu, Somalia, in which 18 American soldiers died. See: Richard Miniter, "Losing Bin Laden: How Bill Clinton's Failure Unleashed Global Terror," Regency Publishing 2003, 1–4. See also:*The 9/11 Commission Report: Final Report of the National Commission on Terrorist Attacks*

upon the United States (New York: W. W. Norton, 2004), 60, 341, 468. Hereafter referred to as the 9/11 Commission Report.

23. Al Gamat al Islamiya is an Egyptian-based fundamentalist network once headed by Sheikh Omar Abdel Rahman. It is believed responsible for the November 1997 massacres of fifty-eight foreign tourists and four Egyptians at Luxor.

24. *Joint Inquiry*, 191–192. See also: John Miller, "Terrorism: a Family Business. Leading al Qaeda Operative Captured by Anti-Taliban Forces," *ABCNews.com*, November 21, 2001, http://abcnews.go .com/sections/wnt/WorldNewsTonight/ rahman_captured011129.html (accessed February 4, 2004).

25. *Joint Inquiry*, 193–194.

26. Miller, Judith, *New York Times*, March 19, 1993, B1.

27. In October 2001, George W. Bush appointed Clarke to be the special adviser for cyberspace security within the National Security Council. In July 2003, he joined Arlington, Virginia–based Good Harbor Consulting LLC as chairman.

28. "Remarks by National Security Adviser Condoleezza Rice at a White House news conference on terrorism intelligence shared with the president prior to the Sept. 11 attacks," Associated Press, May 16, 2002, http://newsandviews.tripod.com/news/ 051702.html (accessed January 29, 2004).

29. Lewis, Anthony, *New York Times*, February 24, 1995: A29.

30. Blumenthal, Sidney, *The Clinton Wars* (New York: Farrar, Straux and Giroux, 2003), 133.

31. Car bombs first appeared in 1976 when the Ulster Volunteer Force, the Northern Ireland Loyalist Group, detonated a car bomb in Dublin and in Monaghan.

32. Harris, John F., "Clinton Signs 'Mighty Blow' Against Terrorism," *Washington Post*, April 25, 1996, A4. "Anti-Terrorism Legislation Expected to Pass This Week," *Pittsburgh Post-Gazette*, April 16, 1996, A6. A summary of the provisions in the legislation is available at Jurist: The Legal Education Network Web site, University of Pittsburgh School of Law, http://uspoli tics.about.com/gi/dynamic/offsite.htm?sit e=http%3A%2F%2Fjurist.law.pitt.edu%2Fter rorism%2Fterrorism3.htm (accessed February 20, 2004).

33. In October 1997, then secretary of state Madeleine K. Albright approved the designation of the first thirty groups as Foreign Terrorist Organizations. U.S. State Department Web site, http://www.state .gov/s/ct/rls/rpt/fto/2001/5258.htm.

34. The list included: Armed Islamic Group (Algeria); Khmer Rouge (Cambodia); Manuel Rodriguez Patriotic Front Dissidents (Chile); National Liberation Army and Revolutionary Armed Forces of Colombia; Holy War (Egypt); Revolutionary Organization 17 November and Revolutionary People's Struggle (Greece); Islamic Group and Mujahedeen Khalq (Holy Warriors of the World) (Iran); Kach (Thus) and Kahane Lives (Israel); Japanese Red Army and Aum Shinrikyo (Supreme Truth) (Japan); Shining Path and Tupac Amaru Revolutionary Movement (Peru); Harakat ul-Ansar (Supporters Movement) (Pakistan); Abu Sayyaf Group (Philippines); Kurdistan Workers Party and Revolutionary People's Liberation Party-Front (Turkey); Euzkadi ta Azkatasuna (ETA: Basque Land and Liberty) (Spain); Liberation Tigers of Tamil Eelam (Sri Lanka). The following groups operating in the Middle East support the Palestinians: Abu Nidal Group; Democratic Front for the Liberation of Palestine, Hawatmeh Faction; Hamas (Islamic Resistance Movement); Palestine Islamic Holy War, Shaqaqi Faction; Palestine Liberation Front, Abu Abbas Faction; Hizbollah (Party of God); Popular Front for the Liberation of Palestine; Popular Front for the Liberation of Palestine, General Command. Steven Erlanger, "U.S. Labels 30 Groups As Terrorists; Omits I.R.A.," *New York Times*, October 9, 1997, A13.

35. As to the interception of oral communications, the government may seek authorization without specifying the location(s) of the interception when it can be shown that it is not practical to do so. See: http:// www.usdoj.gov/usao/eousa/foia_reading _room/usam/title9/7mcrm.htm#9-7.111.

36. Identification taggants have yet to be implemented, although their use has been debated three times during the last ten years. Taggants are miniscule plastic chips that can be mixed into explosive powder. Identification taggants, when viewed with a microscope, provide investigators with data about when and where the explosive material was manufactured. Detection taggants enable security offers to detect explosives. This is especially important for plastic explosives, which are virtually undetectable without the marking (and therefore dangerous in the hands of terrorists). The Antiterrorism and Effective Death Penalty Act of 1996 requires detection agents for plastic explosives. While detection taggants are less controversial, the cost effectiveness of identification taggants in conventional explosives, however, are highly contested by explosive makers, and by the National Rifle Association, due to the high cost of adding them to each explosive. Institute Makers of

Explosives Web site, http://www.ime.org/CurrentPolicies/taggantsinExplosives2003.PDF (accessed January 29, 2004).

Also, several lobbyist groups including the NRA, Institute of Makers of Explosives, and the Bureau of Alcohol, Tobacco, Firearms, and Explosives (BATFE) are opposed to mandating the use of identification taggants due to their high cost and dubious effectiveness. Editorial, "One more Weapon Against Terrorism," *Buffalo News*, November 8, 2001, C18. See also: the President's statement on signing the bill, *Presidential Papers of the Presidents, William J. Clinton*, vol. 1 (1996), 630–631.

37. http://www.s-t.com/daily/11-96/11-21-96/c06op052.htm.

38. Miller, Judith, Jeff Gerth, and Don Van Natta Jr., "A Nation Challenged: The Response; Planning for Terror but Failing to Act," *New York Times*, December 30, 2001, A1.

39. Ibid., A1.

40. Brzezinski, Matthew, "Bust and Boom," *Washington Post Magazine*, December 30, 2001, W9.

41. See: Benjamin, Daniel, and Steven Simon, *The Age of Sacred Terror* (New York: Random House, 2002), 21. Also: Matthew Brzezinski, *Washington Post*, December 30, 2001, W9, www.worldhistory.com and http://www.time.com/time/asia/features/malay_terror/hambali4.html. Some wrongly claim that the word *bojinka* means "loud bang" or "explosion" in Serbo-Croatian. In asking several native speakers, none had heard the word.

42. Miniter, Richard, *Losing Bin Laden* (Washington, D.C.: Regnery Publications, 2003), 81–82.

43. *Joint Inquiry*, 192.

44. 9/11 Commission Report, 60.

45. Unless otherwise noted, most of the information in this section is taken from declassified personal notes of the author, based on my time at the National Security Council from 1993 to 1997.

46. *Joint Inquiry*, 194.

47. According to reports, Hassan al-Turabi was working for an Islamic revolution in Egypt planning the assassination of Mubarak. He approached bin Laden to participate in the early planning of the assassination during a PAIC conference in Khartoum at the end of March 1995. Some believe bin Laden's network helped in the planning of the assassination. Bodansky, Yosset, *Bin Laden: The Man Who Declared War on America*, (Rocklin, Calif.: Forum, 1999), 120–125.

48. Colvin, Marie, Stephen Grey, Matthew Campbell, and Tony Allen-Mills, "Clinton Gambles All on Revenge," *Sunday Times*, August 23, 1998.

49. 9/11 Commission Report, 60.

50. Benjamin, Daniel, and Steven Simon, *The Age of Sacred Terror* (New York: Random House, 2002), 242. See also: the *Joint Inquiry*, 195, and http://www.globalsecurity.org/military/agency/dod/opm-sang.htm.

51. Clarke, Richard, *Against All Enemies*, 111–118.

52. 9/11 Commission Report, 60.

53. For an investigation into the lack of U.S. security at Khobar, see the Downing Commission report at: http://www.fas.org/irp/threat/downing/unclf913.html. The Khobar bombing has roots as early as 1993 when members of the Saudi Hizbollah, one of a number of Hizbollah terrorist organizations operating in Saudi Arabia, Lebanon, Kuwait, and Bahrain, began surveilling Americans and American targets. Al-Nasser, chief of the military wing of the Saudi Hizbollah, worked with Al-Mughassil to begin regular surveillance of Khobar Towers in 1995. According to the indictment finally handed down in 2001, the attack was intended to promote Iran's interests by driving the Americans from the Gulf region. See also: http://www.fbi.gov/pressrel/pressrel01/khobar.htm.

54. Laden, Osama bin, "Declaration of War Against the Americans Occupying the Land of the Two Holy Places" (August 23, 1996), http://www.pbs.org/newshour/terrorism/international/fatwa_1996.html.

55. Reiland, Ralph R., PittsburghLive.com, "The will but not the power—yet," December 31, 2001, http://www.pittsburghlive.com/x/tribune.review/opinion/reiland/s_10329.htm.

56. Declassified notes of the author.

57. The full list, since declassified from author's notes, was
- Information on and/or extradition to Ethiopia of three Gamat al Islamiyya (GI) suspects who sought refuge in Sudan following the Mubarak assassination attempt.
- Repudiation of support for GI and its expulsion; date certain by which Hamas members would leave Sudan, the use of Sudan's influence with Hamas to end terrorist attacks in Israel.
- The detention or extradition to Saudi Arabia of Osama bin Laden.
- Provision of the names, dates of arrival, departure, destination, and passport data on the Mujahedeen that bin Laden had brought to Sudan.
- Information on activities of Iranian

MOIS in Sudan, a list of all official and unofficial Iranians in Sudan. Information on key terrorist figures, such as Imad Mugniya, Abu Nidal and Osama bin Laden.

• Information on license plates of cars surveilling the U.S. embassy and some residences in Khartoum.

• Information on personnel installations, activities in Sudan of Abu Nidal's organization, Palestinian Islamic Jihad (PIJ), Eritrean Islamic Jihad, Hizbollah, and Hamas. Passport information and visa on members of GI, Algerian Islamic Jihad, and Hamas.

• Bulldozing of Merkhiyat terrorist training camp.

• Reorientation of the Pan-Arab Islamic Conference (PAIC) away from its present role as a forum for meetings of various Islamic extremist groups engaged in terrorism. Sudan's role in leading and supporting the PAIC must diminish or cease.

58. Goshko, John, "UN Remains Reluctant to Impose Tough Sanctions on Sudan for Terrorist Links," *Washington Post*, November 24, 1996, A32.

59. *Sudan Fact Sheet, Use of Sanctions Under Chapter VII of the UN Charter*, Office of the Spokesperson for the Secretary-General, United Nations, http://www.un.org/News/ossg/sudan.htm (accessed February 5, 2004).

60. Executive Order No. 13067, http://www.tres.gov/offices/eotffc/ofac/sanctoins/t11sudan.pdf.

61. "In 2001, a Sudanese-born suspect arrested in a foiled plot to bomb the U.S. embassy in New Delhi told Indian investigators that Sudanese diplomats had given him explosives and detonators." Source: "Terrorism: Q&A, Council of Foreign Relations," http://www.terrorismanswers.com/sponsors/sudan_print.html.

62. CNN *Crossfire*, December 10, 2001.

63. Clarke, 142.

64. 9/11 Commission Report, 109–110.

65. Gellman, Barton, "U.S. Was Foiled Multiple Times in Efforts To Capture Bin Laden or Have Him Killed; Sudan's Offer to Arrest Militant Fell Through After Saudis Said No," *Washington Post*, October 3, 2001, A1.

66. Ibid.

67. Miller et al., *New York Times*, December 30, 2001, A1.

68. *Joint Inquiry*, 230.

69. Ibid., 295.

70. Ibid., 387.

71. Prepared testimony, March 24, 2004, by former national security adviser Samuel L. Berger, to the National Commission on Terrorist Attacks Upon the United States, http://www.msnbc.msn.com/id/4593926/.

72. Details of the bombings and investigation are drawn from the FBI's "Executive Summary of the Status and Findings of the FBI Investigation into the Embassy Bombings" November 18, 1998, http://www.pbs.org/wgbh/pages/frontline/shows/binladen/bombings/summary.html. See also: "Report of the Accountability Review Boards, Bombings of the US Embassies in Nairobi, Kenya and Dar es Salaam, Tanzania on August 7, 1998," http://www.state.gov/www/regions/africa/board_nairobi.html.

73. FBI's Most Wanted Terrorist List, http://www.fbi.gov/mostwant/terrorists/termohammed.htm (November 23, 2003).

74. Ibid.

75. Rashid, Ibid., 134. The text includes the following threat: "The ruling to kill the Americans and their allies—civilians and military—is an individual duty for every Muslim who can do it in a country in which it is possible to do it, in order to liberate the al-Aqsa Mosque and the holy mosque [Mecca] from their grip, and in order for their armies to move out of all the lands of Islam, defeated and unable to threaten any Muslim." The February 23, 1998, document was put forward in the name of the World Islamic Front, including bin Laden and representatives from the Jihad Group in Egypt, the Egyptian Islamic Group, the Jamiat-ul-Ulema-e-Pakistan, and the Jihad Movement in Bangladesh. For the full text, see http://www.fas.org/irp/world/para/docs/980223-fatwa.htm.

76. *Joint Inquiry*, 195.

77. Crowe, Admiral William J., Chairman. "Press Briefing on the Report of the Accountability Review Boards on the Embassy Bombings in Nairobi and Dar es Salaam," January 8, 1999.

78. Ibid. In January 1999, a panel of experts headed by Admiral Crowe released the findings of their "Report of the Accountability Review Boards on the Embassy Bombings in Nairobi and Dar es Salaam" aka "The Crowe Report." In addition to detailing the circumstances of the embassy bombings, the report cited two disturbing trends: "1) the inadequacy of resources to provide security against terrorist attacks; and 2) the relative low priority accorded security concerns throughout the U.S. Government..." What Crowe found most distressing was "how similar the lessons were to those drawn by the Inman Commission," a similar review of embassy security conducted fourteen years earlier. Both embassies were found to have complied with the Department of State's

guidelines for diplomatic security required for the threat levels the embassies faced. In the wake of the terrorist attacks, these guidelines were reviewed and strengthened to tighten diplomatic security overseas. Congress appropriated more than $1 billion in supplemental funds to tighten security at diplomatic posts throughout the world. See: http://www.state.gov/www/policy_remarks/1999/990108_emb_rpt.html (accessed March 5, 2004). An electronic version of the report is available at: http://www.state.gov/www/regions/africa/accountability_report.html.

7. The Myth of Invincibility

1. Zill, Oriana, "The U.S. Embassy Bombing—A Summary," in "Hunting bin Laden," PBS *Frontline*, September 2001, http://www.pbs.org/wgbh/pages/frontline/shows/binladen/bombings/summary.html (accessed March 14, 2004).
2. Interview with Sandy Berger, July 16, 2004.
3. Albright, Madeleine K., *Madam Secretary: A Memoir* (New York: Miramax Books, 2003) 368.
4. McKinley, James C., "U.S.-Sudanese Tensions Finally Erupt into Open Warfare," *New York Times*, August 21, 1998.
5. Risen, James, "U.S. Seeks Means to Bring Suspect from Afghanistan," *New York Times*, August 20, 1998, A6.
6. Mintz, John, "Bin Laden's Finances Are a Moving Target; Penetrating Empire Could Take Years," *Washington Post*, August 28, 1998, A1.
7. Embassy of Sudan, "Time for the United States to take responsibility: the 1998 American attack on the al-Shifa Pharmaceutical Plant," press release, August 19, 2003, http://www.sudanembassy.org/default.asp?page=viewstory&id=196.
8. Pillar, Paul R., *Terrorism and US Foreign Policy* (The Brookings Institution, 2001). The author is a former deputy chief of the Counterterrorist Center at the CIA.
9. Clarke, 145–177.
10. Berger, Samuel, e-mail to the author, February 28, 2004. For an excellent summary of the debate surrounding the bombing of the al-Shifa plant, see Daniel Benjamin and Steve Simon's article, "A Failure of Intelligence?" *New York Review of Books*, September 20, 2001.
11. Gugliotta, Guy, and Juliet Eilperin, "Tough Response Appeals to Clinton Critics," *Washington Post*, August 21, 1998, A17, http://www.washingtonpost.com/wp-srv/politics/special/clinton/stories/react082198.htm.
12. Holland, Keating, "Most Americans Support Sudan, Afghanistan Strikes," CNN, August 21, 1998, http://www.cnn.com/ALLPOLITICS/1998/08/21/strike.poll/.
13. U.S. Congress, U.S. Senate Select Committee on Intelligence and U.S. House Permanent Select Committee on Intelligence, *Joint Inquiry into Intelligence Community Activities Before and After the Terrorist Attacks of September 11, 2001* (December 2002), 196–197. Referred to subsequently as the Joint Inquiry. Much of the information in this inquiry was used for the 2004 9/11 Commission Report.
14. Ibid., 386–388.
15. "Wag the Dog Back in Spotlight," CNN *All Politics*, http://www.cnn.com/ALLPOLITICS/1998/08/21/wag.the.dog/ (accessed March 2, 2004). While some outsiders charged that the Lewinsky scandal distracted the president, anyone talking to White House officials during the period knows, in fact, that the president worked harder on policy issues then than perhaps any other time. Although I had moved to the United Nations, my friends at the NSC repeatedly expressed surprise at the extent of Clinton's comments on memos they had prepared, asking for more detailed questions than usual and reading every attachment.
16. Gellman, Barton, "The Covert Hunt for bin Laden: Broad Effort Launched After '98 Attacks," *Washington Post*, December 19, 2001, A1, http://www.washingtonpost.com/ac2/wp-dyn/A62725-2001Dec18?language=printer.
17. Payton, Jack, "US Missiles Target Terror," *St. Petersburg Times* (Florida), August 21, 1991, 1A.
18. Gellman, A1.
19. *Joint Inquiry*, 297, 282.
20. Ibid., 283.
21. The order came in the wake of post-Watergate revelations that the CIA considered assassination a legitimate policy tool, having staged multiple attempts on the life of Cuban president Fidel Castro. It was also later revealed that the United States had planned to kill leftist leaders in Guatemala, including former president Jacobo Arbenz, and had strongly supported the overthrow of Chilean president Salvador Allende in 1973. Section 5(g) of the order, entitled "Prohibition on Assassination," maintains that "no employee of the United States Government shall engage in, or conspire to engage in, political assassination." In 1978, President Carter signed an executive order reaffirming the prohibition, and in 1981, President Reagan issued Executive Order 12333, upholding the assassination prohibition. It remains in effect today since no piece

of legislation or executive order has been passed reversing the prohibition. See: "U.S. Policy on Assassinations," *CNN.com*/Law Center, November 4, 2002, http://www.cnn.com/2002/LAW/11/0 4/us.assassination.policy/ (accessed March 1, 2004).

22. *Joint Inquiry*, 283–284.
23. Ibid., 305.
24. Gellman, A1.
25. *Joint Inquiry*, 105.
26. Ibid., 306.
27. Gellman, 6.
28. *Joint Inquiry*, 108.
29. Gillan, Audrey, "On the Brink of War: Covert plots: Pakistani hit squad was trained by CIA to kill Bin Laden: US history of failure," *The Guardian*, October 4, 2001, 9.
30. Hussain, Zahid, and Stephan Farrell, "Clinton Sent Hit Squad to Kill or Catch bin Laden," *Times* (London), September 24, 2001, 7.
31. Coll, Steve, *Ghost Wars: The Secret History of the CIA, Afghanistan, and Bin Laden*, from *The Soviet Invasion to September 10, 2001* (New York: Penguin Press, 2004), 502.
32. Gellman, 7–8.
33. *Joint Inquiry*, 301.
34. Gellman, 7–8.
35. Benjamin, Daniel, *The Age of Sacred Terror* (New York: Random House, 2002), 349.
36. Transcript, *Sixty Minutes II*, May 1, 2002.
37. Clarke, 153.
38. http://www.state.gov/secretary/rm/ 2001/dec/6844.htm.
39. *Joint Inquiry*, 225.
40. http://www.iwar.org.uk/news-archive/ 2003/02–11.htm.
41. *Joint Inquiry*, 308.
42. Mintz, A1.
43. Ibid.
44. Paul O'Neill worried that these measures would be seen as coercive and contrary to American interests overseas and thus cut the funding for the National Asset Tracking Center. See: Adam Cohen, "Banking on Secrecy," *Time* (October 22, 2001): 73, and William Wechsler, "Follow the Money," *Foreign Affairs* (July/August 2001): 40.
45. Mintz, A1.
46. In 1998, Clinton signed Executive Order 12947, blocking the financial transactions of terrorists to include bin Laden and others in Al Qaeda's network. In 1999, he issued Executive Order 13129 to freeze Taliban assets.
47. Interview with author July 13, 2004.
48. *Joint Inquiry*, 308–309.
49. Clarke, 192–193, 216–217.
50. *Joint Inquiry*, 117.
51. Ibid., 113.
52. Ibid.

53. Ibid., 114.
54. Interview by author, August 13, 2004.
55. *Joint Inquiry*, 114.
56. Ibid., 261.
57. Ibid., 231.
58. Ibid., 98.
59. Rashid, Ahmed *Taliban: Militant Islam, Oil and Fundamentalism in Central Asia* (London: IB Tauris, 2000), 135.
60. *Joint Inquiry*, 256.
61. Ibid., 230.
62. Ibid., 5.
63. Ibid., 119. The ten included: apprehension, extradition, rendition, and prosecution (DOJ); disruption (CIA); international cooperation (State); preventing terrorist acquisition of weapons of mass destruction (NSC); consequence management (FEMA); transportation security (Transpiration); protection of critical infrastructure and cyber systems (NSC); continuity of operations (NSC); countering the foreign terrorist threat in the United States (DOJ); and protection of Americans overseas (DOD and State).
64. Vice President Al Gore, chairman, White House Commission on Aviation Safety and Security, *Final Report to President Clinton* (February 12, 1997), http://www.fas.org/ irp/threat/212fin~1.html (accessed March 13, 2004).
65. PDD 63 on Infrastructure, May 1998, http://www.uhuh.com/laws/pdd63.htm# PDD%2063%20White%20Paper%20May%2 022,%201988 (accessed January 4, 2004).
66. Prepared testimony, by former national security adviser Samuel L. Berger to the National Commission on Terrorist Attacks Upon the United States (March 24, 2004), http://www.msnbc.msn.com/id/ 4593926/.
67. Coll, *Ghost Wars*, 482.
68. Clarke, 211.
69. *Joint Inquiry*, 195–200. Information also taken from talking points drafted for Berger's testimony to congressional inquiries.
70. Clarke, 211–213.
71. *Joint Inquiry*, 201.
72. Clarke, 211–212.
73. Albright, *Madam Secretary*, 369.
74. Ibid.
75. Gellman.
76. Rubin, Barnett R., "The Flash Point Where Afghanistan Meets Pakistan," *International Herald Tribune*, http://www.iht.com/ articles/124546.html.
77. Rashid, 139.
78. "Troubled Trip to Pakistan," editorial, *New York Times*, March 8, 2000, A28.
79. Benjamin, 323.
80. Thompson, Paul, *9/11 Timeline*, Center for

Cooperative Research, http://www
.cooperativeresearch.org/searchResults.jsp
?searchtext=USS+Cole&events=on&
entities=on&articles=on&topics=on&
timelines=on&projects=on&titles=on&
descriptions=on&dosearch=on&search=
+Go+.

81. *Joint Inquiry*, 208.
82. Text of resolution available at http://
www.un.int/usa/sres1267.htm.
83. Both China and Malaysia abstained on the
resolution, out of a general opposition to
sanctions and any discussion of any country's
internal affairs. China and others are concerned that the UN might investigate their
own abuses as well.

8. Failure to Be on a War Footing

1. Interview with the author and Samuel
Berger, July 16, 2004.
2. Ibid., 218.
3. Richard Clarke was appointed director of
cyber security at the National Security
Council in October 2001. Becker,
Elizabeth, and Elaine Sciolino, "A New
Federal Office Opens Amid Concern That
Its Head Won't Have Enough Power,"
New York Times, October 9, 2001, B11.
4. *Joint Inquiry*, 218.
5. Ibid.
6. Clarke, 234.
7. Clarke, 231-232.
8. Benjamin, Daniel, *The Age of Sacred Terror*,
343.
9. Clarke, 234.
10. *Joint Inquiry*, 104.
11. Clarke, 235.
12. Clarke, 237.
13. With special thanks to Elizabeth Bistrong
for helping organize the many press sources
used for this and the following two chapters on Iraq.
14. Benjamin, 341.
15. Ibid.
16. *Joint Inquiry*, 226.
17. Ibid., 120.
18. Ibid., 205.
19. Ibid., 8.
20. Ibid., 119.
21. Ibid., 198-200.
22. Ibid., 201.
23. Ibid., 203.
24. Benjamin, 341.
25. *Joint Inquiry*, 207.
26. Benjamin, 349
27. *Joint Inquiry*, 20.
28. Ibid., 325.
29. Ibid., 21-22
30. Ibid., 329.
31. The reports, however, were unspecific and
not necessarily related to the September 11
attacks.
32. Benjamin, 342-343.
33. *Joint Inquiry*, 209.
34. Ibid.
35. Ibid., 213.
36. Ibid., 211.
37. Ibid., 201.
38. Ibid., 212.
39. Ibid., 214.
40. Ibid., 10.
41. The August 6, 2001, PDB item, as released
on April 10, 2004, is entitled, "Bin Laden
Determined to Strike U.S." [The text is
from http://fpc.state.gov/fpc/31435
.htm.] The text is:
Clandestine, foreign government, and
media reports indicate Bin Ladin since 1997
has wanted to conduct foreign terrorist
attacks on the U.S. Bin Ladin implied in U.S.
television interviews in 1997 and 1998 that
his followers would follow the example of
World Trade Center bomber Ramzi Yousef
and "bring the fighting to America." After
U.S. missile strikes on his base in Afghanistan
in 1998, Bin Ladin told followers he wanted
to retaliate in Washington, according to a
[deleted] service.
An Egyptian Islamic Jihad (EIJ) operative
told an [deleted] service at the same that Bin
Ladin was planning to exploit the operative's
access to the U.S. to mount a terrorist strike.
The millennium plotting in Canada in 1999
may have been part of Bin Ladin's first serious attempt to implement a terrorist strike
in the U.S. Convicted plotter Ahmed
Ressam has told FBI that he conceived the
idea to attack Los Angeles International
Airport himself, but that Bin Ladin lieutenant Abu Zubaydah encouraged him and
helped facilitate the operation. Ressam also
said that in 1998 Abu Zubaydah was planning his own U.S. attack. Ressam says Bin
Ladin was aware of the Los Angeles operation. Although Bin Ladin has not succeeded,
his attacks against the U.S. embassies in
Kenya and Tanzania in 1998 demonstrate
that he prepares operations years in advance
and is not deterred by setbacks. Bin Ladin
associates surveilled our Embassies in
Nairobi and Dar es Salaam as early as 1993,
and some members of the Nairobi cell planning the bombings were arrested and
deported in 1997. Al Qa'ida members—
including some who are U.S. citizens—have
resided in or traveled to the U.S. for years,
and the group apparently maintains a support structure that could aid attacks. Two al
Qa'ida members found guilty in the conspiracy to bomb our Embassies in East Africa
were U.S. citizens, and a senior member
lived in California in the mid-1990s.

A clandestine source said in 1998 that a Bin Ladin cell in New York was recruiting Muslim-American youth for attacks. We have not been able to corroborate some of the more sensational threat reporting, such as that from a [deleted] service in 1998 saying that Bin Ladin wanted to hijack a U.S. aircraft to gain the release of "Blind Shaykh" Umar 'Abd al-Rahman and other U.S.-held extremists. Nevertheless, FBI information since that time indicates patterns of suspicious activity in this country consistent with preparations for hijackings or other types of attacks, including recent surveillance of federal buildings in New York. The FBI is conducting approximately 70 full field investigations throughout the U.S. that it considers Bin Ladin-related. CIA and the FBI are investigating a call to our Embassy in the UAE in May saying that a group of Bin Ladin supporters was in the U.S. planning attacks with explosives.

For the President Only
6 August 2001.

42. Eggen, Dan, and Walter Pincus, "Ashcroft's Efforts on Terrorism Criticized, Ex-FBI Official Doubted Priorities," *Washington Post*, April 14, 2004, A1. See also: Charlie Savage, "FBI overstated investigations, Shortcomings attributed to lack of resources," *Boston Globe*, April 14, 2004.

43. President George W. Bush, remarks at New Hampshire Community Technical College, March 25, 2004, http://www.whitehouse.gov/news/releases/2004/03/20040325-1.html.

44. *Joint Inquiry*, 237–238.

45. Ibid., 121, 232.

46. Ibid., 243.

47. Today, all fifty-six U.S. FBI field offices operate joint terrorism task forces.

48. *Joint Inquiry*, 243, 246.

49. Ibid., 246.

50. Ibid., 266–267. See also: "Law Enforcement, Counterterrorism, and Intelligence Collection in the United States Prior to 9/11," Staff Statement No. 9, National Commission on Terrorist Attacks Upon the United States," http://www.9-11commission.gov/hearings/hearing10/staff_statement_9.pdf.

51. Ibid., 245.

52. Ibid., 244.

53. Ibid., 238.

54. *Joint Inquiry*, 215.

55. Ibid., 220, 235.

56. Ibid., 363.

57. Ibid., 367.

58. Bash, Dana, and Terry Frieden, "FBI Agent Blows Whistle on Moussaoui Probe," *CNN.com*, May 23, 2002, http://www.cnn.com/2002/US/05/23/fbi.minnesota.memo/.

59. *Joint Inquiry*, 324.

60. Ibid., 10.

61. *Protecting America's Freedom in the Information Age*, a report of the Markle Foundation Task Force (October 2002).

62. *Joint Inquiry*, 10.

63. Shenon, Philip, and Richard W. Stevenson, "Threats and Responses: The Overview; Ex-Bush Aide Says Threat of Qaeda Was Not a priority," *New York Times*, March 25, 2004, A1.

64. *Joint Inquiry*, 236.

65. Ibid., 42, 233, 239.

66. Ibid., 137, 349.

67. Miga, Andrew, and Joe Battenfeld, "Bush: 'We're at War'—President Points Finger at bin Laden," *The Boston Herald*, September 16, 2001, 3.

68. Buzbee, Sally, "Rumsfeld: bin Laden Hard to Catch," Associated Press, October 26, 2001.

69. President George W. Bush, "Address to a Joint Session of Congress and the American People" (September 20, 2001), http://www.whitehouse.gov/news/releases/2004/01/20040120-7.html (accessed February 14, 2004).

70. Baltz, Dan, and Bob Woodward, "A Day to Speak of Anger and Grief: After Bush's Pivotal Speech and New York Visit, Time to Decide Strategy," *Washington Post*, January 30, 2002, A1. See also: Baltz and Woodward, "At Camp David, Advise and Dissent, Bush Aides Grapple with War Plan," *Washington Post*, January 31, 2002, A1.

71. "Fighting on Two Fronts: a Chronology," PBS *Frontline*, http://www.pbs.org/wgbh/pages/frontline/shows/campaign/etc/cron.html (accessed February 14, 2004).

72. *September 11th News.Com*, http://www.september11news.com/DailyTimelineOct.htm (accessed January 27, 2004).

73. Sipress, Alan, "U.S., Russia Recast Their Relationship: Anti-Terror Agenda Appears To Be Framework for Future," *Washington Post*, October 4, 2001, A1.

74. The three states that recognized the Taliban as the legitimate government of Afghanistan were: the United Arab Emirates (UAE), Saudi Arabia, and Pakistan. The UAE severed its official ties with the Taliban on September 22, 2001, and Saudi Arabia broke its diplomatic relations on September 25, 2001. Pakistan was the last to withdraw recognition, breaking relations with the Taliban in November 2002. Dunoff, Jeffrey Stephen Ratner, and

David Wippman, *International Law: Norms, Actors, Process* (New York: Aspen Publishers, 2002), 941.

75. Rind, Ahmed, "New World Disorder: Unholy Ends," *LA Weekly*, November 9–15, 2001, http://www.laweekly.com/ink/01/51/new-rind.php (accessed January 28, 2004).

76. Rashid, Ahmed, "Pakistan, the Taliban and the U.S.," *The Nation* (September 20, 2001). See also: Ted Galen Carpenter, "Uncooperative Pakistan Rates Less U.S. Aid," *Newsday* (July 10, 2003).

77. Ibid.

78. Carpenter, "Uncooperative Pakistan Rates Less U.S. Aid."

79. Ibid.

80. Baldauf, Scott, and Owais Tohid, "Taliban appears to be regrouped and well-funded," *Christian Science Monitor*, May 08, 2003, quoting Barnett Rubin of New York University.

81. Bush address to Congress, September 20, 2001.

82. Revolutionary Association of the Women of Afghanistan, *Restrictions Placed on Women by the Taliban*, http://www.islamfortoday.com/afghanistanwomen4.htm.

83. The Dossier Against Bin Laden, *Responsibility for the Terrorist Atrocities in the United States, September 11th, 2001*, http://image.guardian.co.uk/sys-files/Guardian/documents/2001/11/14/Culpability_document.pdf (accessed September 9, 2004).

84. *Joint Inquiry*, 227. Emphasis in the original.

85. Ibid., 171, 227.

86. Associated Press, "Taliban Rejects U.S. bin Laden Bid," *USA Today*, http://www.usatoday.com/news/world/bomb164.htm September 2001 (accessed January 26, 2004).

87. Ibid.

88. "NATO Finds that Terrorist Attacks Against U.S. Were Directed from Abroad," U.S. Department of State Information International Information Programs (October 1, 2002), http://usinfo.state.gov/topical/pol/nato/01100201.htm (accessed February 5, 2004).

89. Burgess, Lisa, "Bush sends Rumsfeld to Middle East for 'wide-ranging conversations,'" *Stars and Stripes*, October 3, 2001, http://www.stripes.com/01/oct01/ed100301q.html and http://www.operations.mod.uk/veritas/statements/press_brief_08oct.html. Hoon, Geoff, UK secretary of state for defence, and Admiral Sir Michael Boyce, chief of the defence staff, press conference, October 8, 2001, http://www.operations.mod.uk/veritas/statements/press_brief_08oct.htm.

90. Bush, George W., "Presidential Address to the Nation," the White House, http://www.whitehouse.gov/news/releases/2001/10/20011007-8.html (accessed February 14, 2004).

91. "Q&A: U.S.-Syrian Relations," *New York Times* Web site. Published from the Council on Foreign Relations, April 2, 2004. See also: Nikolas Gvosdev, "The Road to Damascus?" *The National Interest* (April 16, 2003), http://news.bbc.co.uk/1/hi/world/middle_east/786287.stm.

92. While the Northern Alliance was predominantly ethnic Tajik, key figures in the Alliance's leadership were ethnic Uzbek, including most notably, Uzbek General Abdul Rashid Dostum.

93. O'Hanlon, Michael, "Winning With the Military Clinton Left Behind," *New York Times*, January 1, 2002, A21.

94. Author's interview with a retired senior military officer, July 12, 2004.

95. Gordon, Michael R., "Shifting Fronts, Rising Danger: The Afghanistan War Evolves," *New York Times*, December 9, 2001. Accessed online.

96. Tyson, Ann Scott, "US worries bin Laden will escape," *Christian Science Monitor*, December 12, 2001, 1.

97. Donnelly, John, *Boston Globe*, January 9, 2002, A1.

98. President George W. Bush, remarks by the president to the George C. Marshall ROTC Award Seminar on National Security, Virginia Military Institute, April 17, 2002, http://www.whitehouse.gov/news/releases/2002/04/20020417-1.html.

99. Gordon, Michael, "Less Ambitious Security Force Is Favored by Afghan Leaders," *New York Times*, December 5, 2001, B2.

100. International Crisis Group, *The Afghan Transitional Administration: Prospects and Perils*, July 30, 2002.

101. United States Agency for International Development, press release, September 2002.

102. The White House Office of the Press Secretary, "Progress in the War on Terror," January 22, 2004, http://www.fas.org/irp/news/2004/01/wh012204.html (accessed April 25, 2004).

103. United Nations Assistance Mission in Afghanistan, press briefings and fact sheets, 2003.

104. UN official, interview with author, April 14, 2004.

9. Iraq: A Decade of Deceit

1. One intercept that Powell played for the Council was between a colonel and a brigadier general of Iraq's elite Republican Guard discussing preparations for a visit by UN weapons inspectors. In the U.S. translation, one official says, "We have this modified vehicle. What do we say if one of them sees it?" The other official says, "I'll come to see you in the morning. I'm worried. You all have something left." The other official then replies, "We evacuated everything. We don't have anything left." White House, Office of the Press Secretary, "U.S. Secretary of State Addresses the U.N. Security Council," February 5, 2003, http://www.whitehouse.gov/news/releases/2003/02/iraq/20030205-1.html.

2. Powell, Colin, remarks to the United Nations Security Council, New York City, February 5, 2003. http://www.state.gov/secretary/rm/2003/17300.htm.

3. Ibid.

4. Ibid.

5. "Iraq," CIA World Factbook (updated January 1, 2004), http://www.cia.gov/cia/publications/factbook/geos/iz.html.

6. Gup, Ted, "History 'A Man You Could Do Business With,'" Time (March 11, 1991).

7. "Excerpts From Iraqi Document on Meeting with U.S. Envoy," New York Times, September 23, 1990, 19. The Iraqi government provided ABC News with what they claim is a transcript of the conversation:

Glaspie: I admire your extraordinary efforts to rebuild your country. I know you need funds. We understand that and our opinion is that you should have the opportunity to rebuild your country. But we have no opinion on the Arab-Arab conflicts, like your border disagreement with Kuwait. My assessment after 25 years' service in this area is that your objective must have strong backing from your Arab brothers. I now speak of oil. But you, Mr. President, have fought through a horrific and painful war. Frankly, we can only see that you have deployed massive troops in the south. Normally that would not be any of our business. But when this happens in the context of what you said on your national day, then when we read the details in the two letters of the Foreign Minister, then when we see the Iraqi point of view that the measures taken by the U.A.E. and Kuwait is, in the final analysis, parallel to military aggression against Iraq, then it would be reasonable for me to be concerned. And for this reason, I received an instruction to ask you, in the spirit of friendship—not in the spirit of confrontation—regarding your intentions.

8. "Operation Desert Shield," Global Security.org., http://www.globalsecurity.org/military/ops/desert_shield.htm.

9. UNSC Resolution 660, August 2, 1990.

10. Op. cit.

11. UNSC Resolution 661, August 6, 1990, http://www.fas.org/news/un/iraq/sres/sres0661.htm.

12. Cheney, Dick, interviewed on "The Gulf War," PBS Frontline, published on Web site in January 1996; last updated July 2002, http://www.pbs.org/wgbh/pages/frontline/gulf/oral/cheney/1.html.

13. McCartney, James, "Oil and Honesty at Stake," Hobart Mercury, October 27, 1990.

14. Friedman, Thomas L., "The Iraqi Invasion; Battle for the Saudi Soil," New York Times, August 4, 1990, A1.

15. Resolution 661 of August 6, 1990, 662 of August 9, 1990, 664 of August 18, 1990, 665 of August 25, 1990, 666 of September 13, 1990, 667 of September 16, 1990, 669 of September 24, 1990, 670 of September 25, 1990, 674 of October 29, 1990, and 677 of November 28, 1990, http://www.un.org/Docs/sc/committees/Iraq Kuwait/IraqResolutionsEng.htm.

16. UN Security Council Resolution 678 passed 12 to 2 (Cuba and Yemen against). China abstained.

17. "Oral History: James Baker," interview with Secretary of State James Baker, Frontline: The Gulf War. PBS Online, Accompaniment to broadcast of January 9, 1996, http://www.pbs.org/wgbh/pages/frontline/gulf/oral/baker/1.html.

18. Cheney, Dick, interviewed on "The Gulf War."

19. Baker, James, ibid.

20. "Operation Desert Storm," Global Security.org., http://www.globalsecurity.org/military/ops/desert_storm.htm.

21. "Statistical Summary: America's Major Wars," The United States Civil War Center of Department of Veteran Affairs, http://www.cwc.lsu.edu/cwc/other/stats/warcost.htm.

22. UNSC Resolution 686, March 2, 1991.

23. Bush, George H. W., and Brent Scowcroft, A World Transformed (Alfred A. Knopf, 1998). Excerpted in: "Why We Didn't Remove Saddam," Time (March 2, 1998).

24. Baker, James, "James Baker on Foreign Policy," interviewed by David Gergen on The Newshour, PBS, October 11, 1995.

25. Ibid.

26. Cheney, Dick, interviewed on "The Gulf War."

27. Powell, Colin, ibid.

28. UNSC Resolution 687, April 3, 1991.

29. Pickering, Thomas, Undersecretary of

State, testimony before Committee on Foreign Relations, Committee on Energy and Natural Resources, May 21, 1998, http://www.state.gov/www/policy_re marks/1998/980521_pickering_iraq.htm l. Resolution 661, adopted in 1990 under Chapter 7 of the UN Charter, called upon states to prevent the import of any Iraqi goods and made illegal the export of any products or economic resources to Iraq, except those sent for medical or humanitarian purposes. Additionally, Resolution 661 established the Security Council Sanctions Committee to monitor state compliance with the resolution. Resolution 687 reiterated the expansive sanctions outlined in Resolution 661, while unequivocally demanding that Iraq open itself to inspections and pursue true disarmament.

30. "About the Programme," *(S/22366, para. 37)* and Oil-for Food Programme Official Web site, http://www.un.org/Depts/oip/background/index.html.

31. "Oil-for-Food Program," US Department of State Fact Sheet, December 20, 2002. http://www.state.gov/r/pa/prs/ps/2002/16176.htm.

32. "Former U.N. Humanitarian Coordinator for Iraq Denis Halliday opposes U.N. Sanctions," *CNN Online*, January 16, 2001.

33. Seventy-two percent of the proceeds funded the humanitarian assistance, 25 percent went toward war reparation payments, 2.2 percent for UN administrative and operational costs, and 0.8 percent for the weapons inspection program. In 1998, the ceiling on oil exports was raised to just over $5 billion every six months. In December of 1999 the Security Council removed the ceiling altogether, although strict controls remain on imports of "dual use" items that could potentially be used to manufacture weapons of mass destruction. See: "About the Programme," Oil-for-Food Programme Official Web site; "Timeline: Saddam's Iraq," BBC *News,* http://news.bbc.co.uk/1/shared/spl/hi/middle_east/03/v3_iraq_timeline/html/oil_food.stm.

34. "When Sanctions Don't Work," *Economist* (April 8–14, 2000).

35. U.S. Department of State, *Saddam Hussein's Iraq* (September 13, 1999). In another example of what the Iraqis did with the humanitarian account, the government in October 2002 submitted orders under the Oil for Food program for "22,000 tons of chewing gum machines, 12,000 tons of mobile phones, 36,000 dishwashers and over three quarters of a million TVs." See:

"'Time To Kill the Lie that the West Is Responsible for the Iraqi People's Suffering'-Straw," Foreign and Commonwealth Office Press Release, November 24, 2002, http://www.fco.gov.uk/servlet/Front?pagename=OpenMark et/Xcelerate/ShowPage&c=Page&cid=1 007029391638&a=KArticle&aid=10379 87757885.

36. "When Sanctions Don't Work." Quoting study by Richard Garfield, a public-health expert at Columbia University, http://www.globalpolicy.org/security/sanction/iraq1/iraq34.htm.

37. NGO letter to Security Council, http://www.globalpolicy.org/security/sanction/iraq1/ngolettr.htm.

38. One of the most telling facts of Saddam Hussein's culpability for his people's suffering is that in areas where he was not in control, such as the northern part of the country controlled by the Kurds, the people fared much better. According to a British Foreign and Commonwealth Office report, "in northern Iraq, where the UN administers the programme directly, child mortality rates are lower than before sanctions were imposed." See: "Time To Kill The Lie."

39. E-mail exchange with the author, July 7, 2004.

40. Ibid.

41. Interview with the author, July 9, 2004.

42. E-mail exchange with the author, July 9, 2004.

43. Moseley, General T. Michael, Testimony before the United States House of Representatives Committee on Armed Services Subcommittee on Readiness, March 11, 2004.

44. UNSC Resolution 678, adopted to expel Iraq from Kuwait, authorizes force "to restore international peace and security in the area." The U.S. and U.K. delegates also argued that resolution 688 authorized the use of force; the resolution contains language condemning the persecution of the civilian population, especially the northern Kurds, by the national government. See: Lobel, Jules, and Michael Ratner, "Bypassing the Security Council: Ambiguous Authorizations to Use Force, Cease-Fires and the Iraqi Inspection Regime," *The American Journal of International Law* 93 (January 1999).

45. "Operation Southern Watch," Global Security.org, http://www.globalsecurity.org/military/ops/southern_watch.htm.

46. With special thanks to Commander Steve Brock then-military advisor to the U.S. mission to the UN, who accompanied me

on the trip and helped me get the details of the story right.

47. Cody, Edward, "Under Iraqi Skies, a Canvas of Death," *Washington Post*, June 16, 2000, A1.

48. "In Praise of Weapons Controls: And the Will to Enforce Them," *Economist* (May 10, 1997): 15.

49. UN Document S/1996/848, "Report of the Secretary-General on the activities of the Special Commission established by the Secretary-General pursuant to paragraph 9 (b) (i) of resolution 687 (1991)," October 11, 1996.

50. Tyrangiel, Josh, "What Saddam's Got," *Time* (May 16, 2002), http://www.time .com/time/covers/1101020513/weapons .html.

51. UNSC Resolution 1137 was passed November 12, 1997. It banned travel of Iraqi officials who were responsible for Iraq's obstruction of UNSCOM. The Iraqi declaration that all Americans had to leave came the day after this tougher resolution passed the Security Council.

52. UN Document S/1998/166.

53. "UNSCOM: Chronology of Main Events," United Nations Special Commission Web site, http://www.un.org/Depts/unscom/ Chronology/resolution1137.htm.

54. Zinni, Anthony C., commander in chief, U.S. Central Command, Department of Defense press briefing, December 21, 1998.

55. Albright, Madeleine K., Secretary of State, "Remarks on Air Strikes Against Iraq," U.S. State Department Office of the Spokesman, December 16, 1998.

56. Interview with the author, July 7, 2004.

57. Zinni press briefing.

58. Interview with the author, July 16, 2004.

59. Suskind, 86.

60. Clarke, Richard, *Against All Enemies: Inside America's War on Terror* (New York: Simon & Schuster, 2004), 30.

61. Ibid., 232.

62. Ibid., 31.

63. Dickey, Christopher, and John Barry, "Next Up: Saddam," *Newsweek* (December 31, 2001): 24.

64. Interview with the author, July 12, 2004.

65. Bush, George W., State of the Union Address, January 29, 2002.

66. Bush, George W., remarks by the President at 2002 Graduation Exercise of the United States Military Academy at West Point, June 1, 2002.

67. George W. Bush Press Conference, from Lou Dobbs Moneyline, March 13, 2002, http://www.cnn.com/TRANSCRIPTS/ 0203/13/mild.00.html.

68. Fleischer, Ari, White House press briefing, March 21, 2003.

69. Warren, David, "Signals of war directed mainly at Saddam: U.S. prepared to send in troops, and Iraqi dictator knows it," *Ottawa Citizen*, August 28, 2002, A10. For instance, on August 26, 2002, Vice President Cheney, speaking in Nashville to the Veterans of Foreign Wars, explained, "Regime change in Iraq would bring about a number of benefits to the region. . . . Our ability to advance the Israeli-Palestinian peace process would be enhanced just as it was following the liberation of Kuwait in 1991. . . . Our goal would be an Iraq that has territorial integrity, a government that is democratic and pluralistic, a nation where the human rights of every ethnic and religious group are recognized and protected."

70. Rice, Condoleezza, quoted in Harding, James, and Richard Wolffe, *Financial Times* (London), September 23, 2002.

71. Bush, George, address at the Cincinnati Museum Center, Cincinnati, Ohio, October 7, 2002.

72. Gallup poll, July 8-11, 2004.

73. Interview with former senior military official, July 12, 2004.

74. Clarke, 265.

75. Rumsfeld, Donald, secretary of defense, interviewed on *The News Hour*, PBS, September 18, 2002. Epitomizing this attitude, Secretary Rumsfeld said that disarmament through inspections "only works if you have a cooperative partner. You can't go in and inspect a country that's resisting those inspections and expect to find very much, because so much of it is mobile, so much of it is underground . . . and we've seen the situation with Iraq where they've violated some 16 U.N. resolutions, and finally threw the inspectors out."

76. Cheney, Dick, remarks by the Vice President to the Veterans of Foreign Wars 103rd National Convention, August 26, 2002.

77. Bush, George, president's remarks at the United Nations General Assembly, September 12, 2002.

78. Woodward, Bob, "A Struggle for the President's Heart and Mind," *Washington Post*, November 17, 2002, A1.

79. Ivanov, Igor S., Russian Foreign Minister, press conference with representatives of the "Quartet"—the United States, the Russian Federation, the European Union, and the United Nations (unofficial transcript), September 17, 2002.

80. "Iraq: Schroeder Shuns Blair, U.S.," *CNN Online*, September 4, 2002.

81. "Interview with Gerhard Schroeder," *New York Times*, September 4, 2002.

82. Daeubler-Gmelin, Herta, German Justice Minister, quoted in *Schwaebisches Tagblatt*, and cited in "US Attacks German Hitler Jibe," *BBC News*, September 19, 2002.

83. Preston, Julie, "Threats and Responses: United Nations; Negotiators Seeking a Deal Retreat Behind Closed Doors," *New York Times*, October 20, 2002, 13.

84. Ibid.

85. Wurst, Jim, "Iraq: Security Council Unanimously Gives 'Final Opportunity' to Iraq." *Global Security Newswire*, November 8, 2002.

86. "UN Passes Iraq Resolution on Weapons Inspectors," *CNN Online*, November 8, 2002.

87. SC Resolution 1441, paras. 2–3.

88. Ibid., para. 13.

89. Ibid., para. 5: "Decides that Iraq shall provide UNMOVIC and the IAEA immediate, unimpeded, unconditional, and unrestricted access to any and all, including underground, areas, facilities, buildings, equipment, records, and means of transport which they wish to inspect, as well as immediate, unimpeded, unrestricted, and private access to all officials and other persons whom UNMOVIC or the IAEA wish to interview in the mode or location of UNMOVIC's or the IAEA's choice pursuant to any aspect of their mandates; further decides that UNMOVIC and the IAEA may at their discretion conduct interviews inside or outside of Iraq, may facilitate the travel of those interviewed and family members outside of Iraq, and that, at the sole discretion of UNMOVIC and the IAEA, such interviews may occur without the presence of observers from the Iraqi government."

90. Neuffer, Elizabeth, "Confronting Iraq: Resolution on Iraq Passes Security Council; Vote Unanimous," *Boston Globe*, November 9, 2002, A1.

91. Preston, Julie, "Threats and Responses: United Nations; Security Council Votes, 15–0, For Tough Iraq Resolutions; Bush Calls it a 'Final Test,'" *New York Times*, November 9, 2002.

92. "UN passes Iraq resolution on weapons inspectors," *CNN Online*, November 8, 2002. According to President Bush, "If Iraq fails to fully comply, the United States and other nations will disarm Saddam Hussein.... If we're to avert war, all nations must continue to pressure Saddam Hussein to accept this resolution and to comply with his obligations."

93. Cheney, Dick, remarks by the Vice President at the Air National Guard Senior Leadership Conference, Denver, Colorado, December 2, 2002.

94. "U.N. passes Iraq resolution," *CNN Online*.

95. Kennedy, Ted, quoted in Michael Kelly, "A Doctrine of Armed Evangelism," *Washington Post*, October 9, 2002, A31.

96. Blix, Hans, quoted in "In Blix's Words, Unresolved Issues," *New York Times* December 20, 2002, A16.

97. Preston, Julie, "Threats and Responses: United Nations; Diplomatic Strain on Iraq: Allies See U.S. as Hasty," *New York Times*, December 22, 2002, A22.

98. Bush, George W., remarks by President Bush and Polish President Kwasniewski in Photo Opportunity, Washington, D.C. January 14, 2003, http://www.state.gov/p/eap/rls/rm/2003/16637.htm.

99. Kessler, Glenn, and Colum Lynch, "France Vows to Block Resolution on Iraq War; U.S. Schedule Put at Risk By UN Debate," *Washington Post*, January 21, 2003, A1.

100. Powell, Colin, remarks at the United Nations Security Council Ministerial Session on Terrorism," January 20, 2003. In his speech before the Security Council, Secretary Powell responded, "In the very near future, this council will meet again to determine what to do about this situation.... We cannot be shocked into impotence because we're afraid of the difficult choices that are ahead of us."

101. Interview with the author, July 9, 2004.

102. Interview with the author, July 7, 2004.

103. Meacham, Jon, "D-Day's Real Lessons," *Newsweek* (May 31, 2004): 46.

104. Interview with the author, June 23, 2004 and email exchange July 28, 2004.

105. "Rumsfeld: France, Germany are 'Problems' in Iraqi Conflict," *CNN Online* (January 23, 2003).

106. With special thanks to Jake Bistrong for reminding me of this episode.

107. Bush, George W., State of the Union Address, January 28, 2003.

108. Ibid.

109. Kessler, Glenn, and Colum Lynch, "France Vows to Block Resolution on Iraq War; U.S. Schedule Put at Risk By UN Debate," *Washington Post*, January 21, 2003, A1.

110. Lynch, Colum, and Peter Slevin, "U.S. Faces Deep U.N. Doubts on Iraq War; Support for Expanding Inspections Increases," *Washington Post*, February 16, 2003, A1.

111. Ibid.

112. Discussion with the author, January 30, 2004.

113. Colombia, Ireland, Mauritius, Norway, and Singapore were replaced in the council's

two-year rotation by Bulgaria, Cameroon, Guinea, Mexico, and Syria.

114. Barringer, Felicity, and David E. Sanger, "Threats and Responses: Diplomacy; U.S. and Allies Ask the U.N. to Affirm Iraq Won't Disarm," *New York Times*, February 25, 2003, A1.

115. Ibid.

116. Blix, quoted in "Oral introduction of the 12th quarterly report of UNMOVIC," Security Council, March 7, 2003, http://www.un.org/Depts/unmovic/SC 7asdelievered.htm.

117. Bush, George W., President's Radio Address, March 8, 2003.

118. Barringer, Felicity, and Patrick E. Tyler, "Threats and Responses: United Nations; Annan Says U.S. Will Violate Charter If It Acts Without Approval," *New York Times*, March 11, 2003, A10.

119. Ibid.

120. The benchmarks would include a television appearance in which Hussein would admit he had concealed weapons of mass destruction and was prepared to turn them over to the weapons inspectors. He would also agree to allow thirty scientists and their families to be interviewed outside of Iraq; to surrender all remaining stocks of anthrax and other biological and chemical weapons; to account for all unmanned aerial vehicles; to destroy all missiles that exceeded UN range limits; and to hand over all mobile chemical and biological weapons facilities. See also: Deans, Bob, and Shelly Emling, "Bush off to Iraq talks; U.S., Britain, Spain start last-ditch bid to craft proposal U.N. will approve," *The Atlanta Journal-Constitution* Metro Ed. March 15, 2003, LexisNexis.

121. Interview with the author, June 23, 2004 and e-mail exchange July 28, 2004.

122. Interview with the author, July 7, 2004.

123. Interview with the author, July 9, 2004.

124. "War Against Iraq," *Global Policy Forum Online*, http://www.globalpolicy.org/security/issues/iraq/attackindex.htm.

125. "Iraq: the War's First Few Days," *Council on Foreign Relations Online*, http://www.cfr.org/background/background_iraq_strategy.php.

126. "Iraqi officials deny soldiers have surrendered," *CNN*, March 21, 2003.

10. The Hegemons' Failed Peace

1. Loescher, Gil, "Sole Survivor: August 19, 2003," *Notre Dame* (April 2004), http://www.nd.edu/~ndmag/sp2004/iraq4.html.

2. Lynch, Colum, "Diplomat Will Be 'Acutely Missed,' Says U.N.'s Annan" *Washington Post*, August 20, 2003, http://www.washingtonpost.com/ac2/wp-dyn?pagename=article&contentId=A16095-2003Aug19&notFound=true.

3. "Security Council welcomes Iraqi Governing Council, sets up new UN mission." UN News Service, August 14, 2003.

4. Ibid.

5. Loescher, Gil, "Sole Survivor."

6. McMahon, Robert, "Iraq: Report Says UN Ignored Warnings, Basic Procedures Before Attack," Radio Free Europe, October 23, 2003, http://www.globalsecurity.org/wmd/library/news/iraq/2003/10/iraq-031023-rferl-162401.htm.

7. Brookings Institution, *Report of the Independent Panel on the Safety and Security of UN personnel in Iraq*, October 20, 2003, 1.

8. "Bush makes historic speech aboard warship" CNN, May 1, 2003, http://www.cnn.com/2003/US/05/01/bush.transcript/index.html.

9. Reaney, Patricia, "Civilian Death toll in Iraq Exceeds 100,000," Reuters, October 28, 2004. The poll was published by the *Lancet* medical journal.

10. O'Hanlon, Michael E., and Adriana Lins de Albuquerque, *Iraq Index*, Brookings Institution, updated November 3, 2001. Available online at http://www.brookings.edu/iraqindex.

11. Betts, Richard, speech at Columbia University, April 20, 2004. See also: O'Hanlon, Michael, "Shinseki vs. Wolfowitz," *Washington Times*, March 4, 2003. http://www.brookings.edu/views/op-ed/ohanlon/20030304.htm.

12. See: Eric Schmitt, "Pentagon Contradicts General on Iraq Occupation Force's Size," *New York Times*, February 28, 2003, and Pamela Hess, "Abizaid has requested more forces," United Press International, April 9, 2004.

13. "Looting Delays Food Aid Delivery" *CBS News*, April 15, 2003, http://www.cbsnews.com/stories/2003/03/31/iraq/main547047.shtml.

14. Gumbel, Andrew, and David Keys, "US Blamed for Failure to Stop Sacking of Museum," *The Independent*, April 14, 2003.

15. Burns, John F., "Pillagers Strip Iraqi Museum of Its Treasure," *New York Times*, April 12, 2003.

16. Gugliotta, Guy, "U.S. Urged to Save Iraq's Historic Artifacts," *Washington Post*, April 14, 2003. See 1954 the Hague Convention for the Protection of Cultural Property in the Event of Armed Conflict (1954) and its

two additional protocols: Protocol I, Article 53; Protocol II, Article 16. While the United States has not ratified these treaties, it has signed both the 1954 Hague Convention and the two Additional Protocols to the Geneva Conventions. Given the overwhelming number of states that are party to these treaties, they are widely held to be binding as international customary law.

17. "Damage Done: Who's to Blame for Looting of Iraq's Treasures?", *ABC News Nightline*, April 19, 2003.

18. Interview with retired four-star general, July 12, 2004.

19. O'Hanlon, and Albuquerque, 10.

20. "Who are the Coalition Members?" Policies in Focus: News. The White House Web site. February 4, 2004, www.white house.gov/infocus/iraq/news/20030327 -10.html.

21. Hoon, Geoff, British Secretary of State for Defence, "Iraq: Adjustments To UK Forces In Multinational Division (South East)," Ministerial Statement to the House of Commons, May 27, 2004, http://www .operations.mod.uk/telic/statement_sofs _27may04.htm and "Non-US Forces in Iraq—20 May 2004," Global Security.org., http://www.globalsecurity.org/military/ ops/iraq_orbat_coalition.htm.

22. Those countries withdrawing troops include the Dominican Republic, Honduras, Nicaragua, Poland, Spain, and Ukraine.

23. "Ankara Appeases US by Agreeing to Deploy Troops," *Guardian*, October 8, 2003, http://www.guardian.co.uk/Iraq/ Story/0,2763,1058204,00.html.

24. "Turkish Troops Would Make Things Worse in Iraq," *International Herald Tribune*, October 10, 2003, http://www .iht.com/articles/113111.html.

25. "IRAQ: U.S.-Turkey Relations," Council on Foreign Relations, March 31, 2003, http://www.cfr.org/background/back ground_iraq.php.

26. O'Hanlon and Albuquerque.

27. "The War after the War in Iraq," Center for Strategic and International Studies, August 8, 2003, http://www.csis.org/features/ iraq_warafterwar.pdf.

28. Piore, Adam, "They Hide in Plain Sight," *Newsweek*, July 3, 2003.

29. Operation Desert Scorpion," Global Security.org, http://www.globalsecurity .org/military/ops/desert_scorpion.htm.

30. Gettleman, Jeffrey, "Violent Disturbances Wrack Iraq from Baghdad to Southern Cities," *New York Times*, April 4, 2004, http://www.nytimes.com/2004/04/04/ international/middleeast/04CND-IRAQ

.html?ex=1082520000&en=8a660c2242f 9e616&ei=5070.

31. Gettleman, Jeffrey, and James Risen, "The Struggle for Iraq: Alliances; Ex-Rivals Uniting," *New York Times*, April 9, 2004, http://query.nytimes.com/gst/abstract .html?res=F60C15FB395C0C7A8CDDA D0894DC404482.

32. Op. cit.

33. Penketh, Anne, "Middle East Turmoil: Blow for Bush as Poll Reveals Hostility to America and Support for Rebel Cleric," *The Independent*, June 17, 2004, 5.

34. Filkins, Dexter, "One by One, Iraqi Cities Become No-Go Zones," *New York Times*, September 5, 2004

35. O'Hanlon and Albuquerque.

36. Center for Strategic and International Studies, "Measuring Iraq's Reconstruction Progress," September 2004.

37. Weisman, Steven R., "U.S. Envoy to Iraq Urges Shift of Money to Security," New York Times, August 31, 2004, A9.

38. Rumsfeld, Donald, news conference April 15, 2004.

39. Housego, Kim, "French Hostages in Iraq Given to Sunni Group," Associated Press, September 3, 2004.

40. Sanger, David E., and Elisabeth Bumiller, "Bush Dismisses Idea That Kerry Lied on Vietnam," *New York Times*, August 27, 2004, A1.

41. George Bush televised address, April 13, 2004, http://www.whitehouse.gov/ news/releases/2004/04/20040413-20 .html.

42. Arieff, Irwin, "U.N. draws up plan for postwar Iraq," Reuters, March 5, 2003.

43. E-mail exchange with senior UN official and the author, June 22, 2004.

44. "Iraq Timeline," Council on Foreign Relations, www.cfr.org/publication.php ?id=5351.

45. Garner, Jay, BBC interview reported by *Guardian*, March 18, 2004, http:// www.guardian.co.uk/international/story/ 0,3604,1171689,00.html.

46. Interview with the author and former CPA senior official, June 23, 2004.

47. "Ambassador L. Paul Bremer III," Biographies: March Crisis Academy Web site, http://www.marshcrisisacademy.com/ content/40_thought_leadership/!_bremer _bio.asp.

48. Halchin, L. Elaine, *The Coalition Provisional Authority (CPA): Origin, Characteristics, and Institutional Authorities*, Congressional Research Service, April 29, 2004, 4.

49. Interview with the author, June 23, 2004.

50. "Joint Chiefs Bypassed in Decision to Disband Iraqi Army: Pace" *Agence France-*

Presse, February 18, 2004, http://www
.commondreams.org/headlines04/0218
–06.htm.

51. "Iraq: Building a New Security Structure,"
    International Crisis Group, December 23,
    2003, http://www.reliefweb.int/library/
    documents/2003/icg-irq-23dec.pdf.

52. Allawi, Iyad, "Americans must let Iraq
    rebuild itself: A view from the Governing
    Council," *New York Times*, October 19,
    2003.

53. Peterson, Scott, "US decides to pay Iraqi
    soldiers and form new Army." *Christian
    Science Monitor*, June 24, 2003, http://
    www.csmonitor.com/2003/0624/p01s04
    -woiq.html, and "Good News for Iraqi
    Soldiers," Coalition Provisional Authority
    press release, June 23, 2003, http://
    www.iraqcoalition.org/pressreleases/23
    June03PR6_good_news.pdf, and Arraf,
    Jane, "U.S. dissolves Iraqi army, Defense
    and Information ministries," CNN
    Baghdad Bureau, May 23, 2003,
    http://www.cnn.com/2003/WORLD/
    meast/05/23/sprj.nitop.army.dissolve/.

54. CPA Web site, http://www.cpa-iraq
    .org/regulations/CPAORD22.pdf.

55. "Iraq: Building a New Security Structure,"
    International Crisis Group, December
    23, 2003, 12, http://www.reliefweb.int/
    library/documents/2003/icg-irq-23dec
    .pdf.

56. O'Hanlon and Albuquerque.

57. "Iraqi Army's Mass Walkout," *The
    Guardian*, December 12, 2003, http://
    www.guardian.co.uk/international/story/
    0,3604,1105204,00.html.

58. "Mehdi Army ordered out of Najaf," CNN,
    April 12, 2004, http://www.cnn.com/
    2004/US/04/12/mehdi.army/index.html.

59. "Iraq Backgrounder: What Lies Beneath,"
    International Crisis Group. Report no. 6,
    October 2002.

60. Wong, Edward, "Policy Barring Ex-
    Baathists From Key Iraq Posts Is Eased,"
    New York Times, April 23, 2004.

61. Out of the thirteen Shias, five Sunnis, five
    Kurds, one Turk, and one Assyrian
    Christian who made up the IGC, six Shias
    and three Sunnis were exiles. In total, nine
    out of twenty-five members—more than
    one-third—did not have strong historical
    relationships with the people whom they
    were appointed to govern. In addition, the
    five Kurds represented a group that had
    lived outside of Saddam Hussein's control
    since 1991 and strongly desired continued
    autonomy. Thus, fourteen of twenty-five
    members—more than half—were seen by
    Iraqis as outsiders who did not represent
    the true victims of Saddam Hussein's
    regime. See: "Governing Iraq," Inter-

national Crisis Group, August 25, 2003,
http://www.crisisweb.org//library/docu
ments/report_archive/A401098_250820
03.pdf.

62. Phillips, David L., "Pentagon's Postwar
    Fiasco Coming Full-Circle?" *Christian
    Science Monitor*, May 24, 2004.

63. Mayer, Jane, "The Manipulator," *New
    Yorker*, June 7, 2004, http://www
    .newyorker.com/fact/content/?040607fa
    _fact1_a.

64. Thomas, Evans, and Mark Hosenball, "The
    Rise and Fall of Chalabi: Bush's Mr.
    Wrong," *Newsweek* (May 31, 2004): 22.

65. Op. cit.

66. Tully, Andrew, "US Ends Payments to
    Chalabi's Iraqi National Congress," *Radio
    Free Europe/Radio Liberty*, May 19, 2004,
    http://www.globalpolicy.org/security/
    issues/iraq/election/2004/0519chalabi
    .htm. See also: Jane Mayer and ABC.
    http://more.abcnews.go.com/sections/
    world/cia/rendon.htm. Exact U.S. sup-
    port to the INC is difficult to determine,
    particularly as appropriations included
    other groups supported by the Iraq
    Liberation Act of 1998.

67. Mayer.

68. Ibid.

69. Oxford Research International, Ltd,
    "National Survey of Iraq," February 2004,
    http://news.bbc.co.uk.nol/shared/bsp/
    hi/pdfs/15_03_04_iraqsurvey.pdf.

70. Hirsh, Michael, "Crime and Politics,"
    Newsweek, May 20, 2004, http://
    www.msnbc.msn.com/id/5024660/site/
    newsweek/.

71. Hosenball, Mark, "Chalabi—And the
    Questions Keep Coming," *Newsweek* (June
    7, 2004): 9. See also: Richard A. Oppel,
    "U.S. to Halt Payments to Iraqi Group
    Headed by Ahmad Chalabi," May 18,
    2004, http://middleeastinfo.org/article
    4545.html.

72. Dwyer, Jim, "Defectors' Reports on Iraq
    Arms Were Embellished, Exile Asserts,"
    New York Times. July 9, 2004, http://
    www.nytimes.com/2004/07/09/politics/
    09defe.html.

73. Mayer.

74. "Iraqi Insurgency Groups," GlobalSecurity
    .org, December 5, 2003, http://
    www.globalsecurity.org/military/ops/iraq
    _insurgency.htm.

75. Scarborough, Rowan, "'Several Thousand'
    foreign fighters slip into Iraq," *Washington
    Times*, April 30, 2004, http://www.wash
    times.com/national/20040429-110506-
    4564r.htm.

76. "Iraqi Insurgency Groups" Global
    Security.org

77. The only active indigenous group, Ansar al-

Islam, estimated to number around seven hundred, targeted Iraq's Kurdish politicians, not the United States. In addition to possibly providing refuge to foreign fighters fleeing Afghanistan and links to Abu Musab al-Zarqawi, concrete evidence of cooperation with al Qaeda is sketchy, but possible. The Ansar al Islam leadership denies ties to Osama bin Laden. See: "Ansar al Islam," GlobalSecurity.org, http://www.globalsecurity.org/military/world/para/ansar_al_islam.htm.

78. Gettleman, Jeffrey, and Terence Neilan, "New Clashes Erupt in Falluja and Baghdad Bomb Kills Iraqi," *New York Times*, June 25, 2004.

79. Jehl, Douglas. "C.I.A. Says Qaeda Miltant Decapitated American," *New York Times*, May 13, 2004, http://www.nytimes.com/2004/05/13/international/middleeast/13CND-TERR.html?ex=1087963200&en=59044ef7cf7a087f&ei=5070.

80. "Profile: Abu Musab al-Karqawi," BBC, July 1, 2004.

81. Schmitt, Eric, "Allies Suspect Al Qaeda Link to Bombings in Basra; Death Toll Is Reduced," *New York Times*, April 23, 2004, A10; and Rajiz Chandrasekaran and Karl Vick, "Iraq-Iran Border to be Tightened in Bid to Stem Attacks," *Washington Post*, March 14, 2004, A26.

82. Jehl, "C.I.A. Says."

83. Pincus, Walter, "Terror Suspect's Ambitions Worry U.S. Officials: Zarqawi May be Looking Beyond Iraq," *Washington Post*, March 3, 2004, http://www.washingtonpost.com/ac2/wp-dyn/A24354–2004Mar2?language=printer.

84. Ibid.

85. Burke, Jason, "Terror Cell's UK Poison Plot," *The Observer* (UK), May 25, 2003, http://observer.guardian.co.uk/uk_news/story/0,6903,963314,00.html.

86. Ibid. See also: "Profile: Abu Musab al-Zarqawi," BBC, May 12, 2004, http://news.bbc.co.uk/2/hi/middle_east/3483089.stm.

87. Jehl, Douglas, "Al Qaeda Rebuffs Iraqi Terror Group, U.S. Officials Say," *New York Times*, February 21, 2004, http://www.nytimes.com/2004/02/21/international/middleeast/21INTE.html?ex=1078383407&ei=1&en=baca3c98500f42cd.

88. Shenon, Philip, and Christopher Marquis, "Panel Finds No Qaeda-Iraq Tie; Describes a Wider Plot for 9/11," *New York Times*, June 17, 2004, A1.

89. http://www.washingtonpost.com/ac2/wp-dyn/A32862–2003Sep5?language=printer.

90. http://www.cnn.com/2002/ALLPOLITICS/08/26/time.iraq/.

91. "Panel's Finding Suggest Flawed Justifications for Iraq War," *USA Today*, June 17, 2004, http://www.usatoday.com/news/opinion/editorials/2004–06-17-our-view_x.htm.

92. Milbank, Dana, and Claudia Deane, "Hussein Link to 9/11 Lingers in Many Minds," *Washington Post*, September 6, 2003, http://www.washingtonpost.com/ac2/wp-dyn/A32862–2003Sep5?language=printer.

93. Milbank, Dana, and Walter Pincus, "Al Qaeda-Hussein Link is Dismissed," *Washington Post*, June 17, 2004.

94. Langer, Gary, "Iraq and the Election: Poll Shows Bush Losing Ground on Antiterror Policy," *ABC News*, June 21 2004, http://www.abcnews.go.com/sections/us/Polls/iraq_election_040621.html.

95. Milbank and Pincus, "Al Qaeda-Hussein Link is Dismissed."

96. Shenon, Philip, and Richard W. Stevenson, "Leaders of 9/11 Panel Ask Cheney for Reports That Would Support Iraq-Qaeda Ties," *New York Times*, June 18, 2004, A8.

97. Ibid.

98. Millbank, Dana, "Bush Defends Assertions of Iraq—Al Qaeda Relationship," *Washington Post*, June 18, 2004, A9.

99. Bush, George W., "President Speaks to the United Nations General Assembly," United Nations, September 21, 2004, http://www.whitehouse.gov/newsreleases/2004/09/print/20040912–3/html.

100. Shenon and Stevenson. The official is White House communications director Dan Bartlett.

101. Ibid.

102. "Remarks by the President and U.N. Secretary-General Kofi Annan in Photo Opportunity, The Oval Office," Office of the Press Secretary, White House, February 3, 2004, http://www.whitehouse.gov/news/releases/2004/02/20040203–1.html.

103. Younge, Gary, "Annan Considers Sending UN Mission to Iraq," *Guardian*, January 20, 2004, 2.

104. "The political transition in Iraq: report of the fact-finding mission," United Nations, S/2004/140.February 23, 2004, 3.

105. Weisman, Steven R., "Many Wonder if June 30 Date for Self-Rule in Iraq Is Too Risky," *International Herald Tribune*, February 20, 2004.

106. Interview with the author, June 23, 2004.

107. Chandrasekaran, Rajiv, "Envoy Bowed to Pressure in Choosing Leaders," *Washington Post*, June 3, 2004, A10.

108. Global Policy Forum, "Interim Iraqi Government," http://www.globalpolicy.org/security/issues/iraq/election/2004/0601government.htm.

109. "Al-Yawer Named Iraqi President," *The Washington Times*, June 2, 2004.

110. Chandrasekaran.

111. "Public Opinion in Iraq: First Poll Following Abu Ghraib Revelations," *Newsweek* (May 14–23, 2004). Available online at http://msnbc.msn.com/id/5217741/site/newsweek.

112. United Nations Security Council, S/2004/140, 19.

113. Recknagel, Charles, "Iraq: Debate Grows Over Whether to Hold Iraqi Poll Amid Security Problems," Radio Free Europe, September 17, 2004. Accessed online at http://www.globalsecurity.org/wmd/library/news/iraq/2004/09/iraq-040917-rferl01.htm.

114. Wong, Edward. "Violence Breaks Out Days Before Shift of Sovereignty to Iraqis," *New York Times*, June 24, 2004, http://www.nytimes.com/2004/06/24/international/middleeast/24CND-IRAQ.html?ex=1089082515&ei=1&en=bc26d8adf62b74b4

115. Chandrasekaran.

116. United Nations, S/RES/1546, June 8, 2004.

117. "UN's Return to Iraq is Stalled by Friction," *International Herald Tribune*, December 30, 2003. See also: *New York Times*, April 17, 2004, http://www.nytimes.com/2004/04/17/international/middleeast/17REAX.html.

118. Interview by the author and a senior UN official, June 17, 2004.

119. Statement by Secretary-General Annan to the Security Council, June 7, 2004.

120. Council on Foreign Relations, "Iraq Timeline," http://www.cfr.org/publication.php?id=5351

121. Interview by the author and a senior UN official, June 17, 2004.

122. Jehl, Douglas, "Senators Assail C.I.A. Judgments on Iraq's Arms as Deeply Flawed," *New York Times*, June 10, 2004, A1; and Eric Schmitt and Richard W. Stevenson, "Admitting Intelligence Flaws, Bush Stands by Need for War," *New York Times*, June 10, 2004, A7.

123. Adams, Gordon, "The Price of War," *New York Times*, June 28, 2004, A15.

124. Interview with the author, July 9, 2004.

125. Interview with the author, June 23, 2004.

126. Interview with the author, July 16, 2004.

127. The United States is considering withdrawal of all UN peacekeeping operations following its failure to secure a renewal of its exemption. Ambassador Cunningham refused to say what the United States would do when the next UN peacekeeping operation comes up for renewal in the Security Council. In his statement, he said, "In the absence of a new resolution, the United States will need to take into account the risk of ICC review when determining contributions to UN authorized or established operations," "US Drops Resolution Seeking War Crimes Exemption," CNN, June 23, 2004.

11. Are We Really Going to War?

1. French, Howard W., "The World: Korean Word Games; Carefully Chosen Invective," *New York Times*, January 19, 2003, sec. 4, 3.

2. O'Hanlon, Michael, and Mike Mochizuki, *Crisis on the North Korean Peninsula. How to Deal with a Nuclear North Korea*, a Brookings Institute Book (New York: McGraw-Hill, 2003), 63. The authors note that "1 million troops, 20,000 armored vehicles . . . more than 1 million land mines, abundant chemical weapons, and fortified defensive positions are found between Pyongyang and Seoul." The distance between the two capital cities is approximately 105 miles.

3. Carter, Ashton B., and William J. Perry, *Washington Post*, October 20, 2002, B1. Others have estimated the North Koreans have the capacity to produce "dozens" of nuclear weapons annually, meaning it could have produced between 150 to 200 nuclear weapons had it not frozen the plutonium program in 1994. See: Philip C. Sanders, "Confronting Ambiguity: How to Handle North Korea's Nuclear Programs, March 2003, http://www.arsonctrol.org/act/2003_03/Saunders_mar03; and Robert L. Gallucci, Congressional testimony, "The US-DPRK Agreed Framework," House of Representatives, International Relations Committee, February 23, 1995.

4. Rice, Condoleezza, "Promoting the National Interest," *Foreign Affairs* (January/February, 2000): 45.

5. Excerpts: Powell March 6 Remarks on S. Korea, N. Korea, China. Washington File, Office of International Information Programs, U.S. Department of State, March 7, 2001, http://usembassy-australia.state.gov/hyper/2001/0307/epf309.htm (accessed October 12, 2003).

6. CNN Live Special Event, 09:45, transcript no. 01051401V54, May 14, 2001.

7. Bush's precise words were, "I was forthright in describing my support for [Kim's] vision, as well as my skepticism about whether or not we can verify an agreement in a country that doesn't enjoy the freedoms that our two countries understand. . . .", http://www.whitehouse.gov/news/releases/2001/02/20010301-6.html.

8. Description of the failed interagency process from an interview on December 17, 2003, with a former senior official who participated in it. The policy announced by Bush was developed "at the last moment" by Assistant Secretary of State James Kelly and NSC Senior Director for Counterproliferation Robert Joseph, following the failure of the interagency effort to agree on a policy.

9. "Bush: Broad Agenda for North Korea Talks," *CNN.com*, June 6, 2001, http://us.cnn.com/2001/US/06/06/bush.nkorea/, (accessed October 10, 2003).

10. For instance, in March 2001, the administration announced the continuation of its heavy fuel shipments to North Korea and pledged the following December 105,000 metric tons of food. In February 2002, Bush stated that the U.S. will continue providing humanitarian assistance to the North Korean people regardless of whether dialogue with the North Korean government is resumed. "Humanitarian Aid and Engagement with North Korea," The Friends Committee on National Legislation, April 2002, http://www.fcnl.org/issues/int/sup/nkor_humanitarian.htm (accessed October 10, 2003).

11. Interview December 17, 2003, with former senior official. The comments quote National Security Advisor Rice, relaying Bush's comments to colleagues.

12. ASEAN was created in 1976 to promote economic, social, and cultural development of the region and to enhance regional stability. The association's member states include Brunei Darussalam, Cambodia, Indonesia, Laos, Malaysia, Myanmar, Philippines, Singapore, Thailand, and Vietnam. ASEAN Member States, October 16, 2003, http://www.aseansec.org/home.htm.

13. White House press briefing by Ari Fleisher, September 19, 2001, http://www.whitehouse.gov/news/releases/2002/09/20020919-4.html.

14. E-mail exchange with the author and a former senior state department official, December 15, 2003.

15. Lederer, Edith M., Associated Press, February 8, 2002, http://www.washingtonpost.com/ac2/wp-dyn/A44271-2002Feb8?language=printer.

16. Wolffe, Richard, and Andrew Ward, "Bush to press China over missile sales," *Financial Times*, February 21, 2002, 11.

17. Fineman, Howard, "*I Sniff Some Politics,*" *Newsweek* (May 27, 2002): 37.

18. Woodward, Bob, "A Course of 'Confident Action'; Bush Says Other Countries Will Follow Assertive U.S. in Combating Terror," *Washington Post*, A1, November 19, 2002.

19. GlobalSecurity.Org, Nuclear Posture Review (NPR), excerpts from the NPR submitted to Congress on December 31, 2001, Posted January 8, 2002, http://www.globalsecurity.org/wmd/library/policy/dod/npr.htm (accessed October 17, 2003).

20. Blinken, Antony J., "From Preemption to Engagement," *Survival* vol. 45, no. 4 (Winter 2003–4): 42. Newt Gincrich is the identified official.

21. See: White House publications, September 20, 2002, http://www.whitehouse.gov/nsc/nss.pdf, 14.

22. Interview with a former senior official, December 17, 2003.

23. Sanger, David E., "Nuclear Mediators Resort to Political Mind Reading," *New York Times*, January 12, 2002, A14. For an excellent summary and analysis of the North Korean crisis, see the International Crisis Group's report, *North Korea: A Phased Negotiation Strategy*, August 1, 2003, http://www.crisisweb.org//library/documents/report_archive/A401073_01082003.pdf.

24. Highly Enriched Uranium (HEU) is created by purifying uranium that is naturally found in the environment. Uranium that is 90 percent pure is considered to be 'highly enriched.' Weapons-grade uranium has been enriched to a 20 percent purity level. While it takes approximately three times as much HEU (25 kg) as plutonium (8 kg) to create a nuclear reaction, the most basic method of detonating a nuclear explosion requires HEU as opposed to plutonium. Joseph Cirincione, Jon B. Wolfsthal, and Miriam Rajkumar, "Deadly Arsenals," Carnegie Endowment for International Peace Publication, June 2002, chapter 3, 3, http://www.ceip.org/files/projects/npp/resources/DeadlyArsenals/chapters%20(pdf)/14-NoKorea.pdf (accessed October 17, 2003).

25. Sanger, David E., *New York Times*, November 24, 2002, A1. Note: A former U.S. official commented on December 17, 2003, that the deal was probably initiated by Pakistan when it could not pay for the North Korean missiles. While the administration's bellicose rhetoric may have contributed to North Korea's pace of developing the HEU program, most analysts agree that the North Koreans had started the HEU program before President Bush took office, most likely in 1997 or 1998. Thus, it likely was begun in response to the stalled implementation of the Agreed Framework Agreement under Clinton, not the heightened Bush rhetoric. North Korean officials, however, continue to seek to blame the Bush administration. North Korea's official Web site states it decided "to

build a strong deterrent force," to cope with a hostile Bush administration.

26. The IAEA is an autonomous organization created under the United Nations. It was established in 1957 as an independent intergovernmental, science- and technology–based organization. It is charged with assisting member states in using nuclear technology for peaceful purposes, with developing nuclear safeguards and with verifying that states comply with commitments under the NPT, http://www.iaea.org/worldatom/about/profile/mission.html.

27. The treaty entered into force on March 5, 1970. In addition to committing states to refrain from acquiring nuclear weapons, the NPT also requires each party to commit not to "transfer to any recipient whatsoever nuclear weapons or other nuclear explosive devises . . . and not in any way assist, encourage, or induce any non-nuclear-weapon State to manufacture or otherwise acquire nuclear weapons." It also held that each non-nuclear-weapon State Party should not receive any transfer "whatsoever of nuclear weapons or other nuclear explosive devises . . . [nor] manufacture or otherwise acquire nuclear weapons." Each non-nuclear-weapon state party also undertook "to accept safeguards, as set forth in an agreement to be negotiated and concluded with the International Atomic Energy Agency . . . for the exclusive purpose of verification of the fulfillment of its obligations assumed under this Treaty." The treaty also committed the parties to "pursue negotiations in good faith on effective measures relating to cessation of the nuclear arms race at an early date and . . . nuclear disarmament." See: www.unog.ch/disarm/distreat/npt.pdf.

28. Moffett III, George D., *Christian Science Monitor*, July 27, 1992, 1.

29. Gorden, Michael R., *New York Times*, June 18, 1994, A1. Rather than the 90 grams North Korea claimed it had produced, analysts suspected that North Korea had reprocessed as much as 5–7 kilograms of plutonium; 5 kilograms of plutonium is enough to build a crude nuclear bomb (see: www.isis-online.org/publications/dprk/currentandfutureweaponsstocks.html). The North Koreans also admitted they had started experimenting with plutonium reprocessing in the late 1970s. See: Statement of the IAEA Director General regarding DPRK at informal briefing of UN Security Council, April 6, 1993, http://www.fas.org/news/un/dprk/dgsp1993n10.html.

30. Sigal, *Disarming Strategies*, 46–47.

31. For detail on South Korea's harder line, see Sigal, 84–89.

32. Bill Gertz, "North Korean Nuclear Threat Grows, Intelligence Chiefs Warn Senators," *Washington Times*, January 26, 1994. Burton, John, "U.S. Fingers Crossed Over North Korea," *Financial Times*, January 21, 1994, 5.

33. Gordon, Michael R., "Pentagon Studies Plans to Bolster U.S.-Korea Forces," *New York Times*, December 2, 1993, A1.

34. Gordon, Michael R., and David Sanger, "North Korea's Huge Military Spurs New Strategy in South," *New York Times*, February 6, 1994, A1.

35. Burton, John, "N. Korea's 'Sea of Fire' Threat Shakes Seoul," *Financial Times*, March 22, 1994, 6. North Korea later retracted the statement.

36. Interview with the author, February 4, 2004.

37. *Public Papers of the Presidents, William J. Clinton*, vol. 1 (1994), 1026–1027.

38. "The General Federation of Korean Residents in Japan" (Chosen Soren in Japanese) is an organization of Korean nationals in Japan that sends an estimated between $600 million and $1.9 billion a year to North Koreans. See: http://www.fas.org/irp/world/dprk/chosen_soren.

39. Inteview with Dan Poneman by author, February 4, 2004.

40. Scowcroft, Brent, and Arnold Kanter, *Washington Post*, June 15, 1994, A25.

41. Clinton would later comment to Colin Powell when Clinton proposed Powell join former president Jimmy Carter in a 1994 mission to seek the removal of the junta in Haiti, "I took a chance on him in North Korea, and that didn't turn out too badly." The president told Powell he was concerned that if Carter went to Haiti, "The next thing you know, I'm expected to call off the invasion because he's negotiating a deal." See: Colin Powell, *An American Journey*, 598.

42. Trip report by Carter on his North Korea trip, July 21, 1994.

43. Interview with the author, July 13, 2004.

44. Interview with Poneman, February 4, 2004.

45. CNN transcript, June 16, 1994, 11:27 A.M. ET.

46. CNN transcript, June 17, 1994, 5:46 A.M. ET.

47. Conversation with the author, July 16, 2004.

48. Letter from former President Carter to President Clinton, March 30, 1995.

49. Sigal, *Disarming Strategies*, 159–160.

50. Interview with Poneman, February 4, 2004, and with Anthony Lake on July 16, 2004.

51. Translation of June 22, 1994, letter from

Kang Sok Ju, Head of the DPRK Delegation to the DPRK-USA Talks and First Vice-Minister of Foreign Affairs.

52. *Public Papers of the Presidents, William J. Clinton*, vol. 1 (1994), 1117.

53. Ibid., vol. 2 (1994), 1819.

54. Agreed Framework of the United States of America and the Democratic People's Republic of Korea, Geneva, October 21, 1994, Part II, Part III, 1, http://www .kedo.org/pdfs/AgreedFramework.pdf. In the first phase, North Korea was to shut down its five-megawatt nuclear reactor at Yongbyon and stop building other reactors. Fuel rods containing plutonium that had already been removed were to be put in special containers and subject to regular inspections. In short, the North agreed to shut down facilities that in a few years' time could be producing thirty bombs' worth of plutonium a year. In exchange, the international community would build two light-water reactors at a cost of $4 billion to 5 billion, with a target date for completion of 2003. Each would produce 1,000 megawatts, roughly enough energy for one million typical American households—a significant energy source for a country of 22 million very poor people. The United States and its allies would also provide 500,000 tons of free heavy fuel annually to North Korea until the reactors were completed.

The second phase of the plan would begin when the United States provided North Korea "assurances for the provision of [light-water reactors] and for arrangements for interim energy alternatives." North Korea would then freeze its graphite-moderated reactors and related facilities and will eventually dismantle these reactors and related facilities." The freeze on the reactors and related facilities was to be "fully implemented within one month" of the signing of the Agreed Framework. During that month "and throughout the freeze" the International Atomic Energy Agency (IAEA) would be allowed to monitor this freeze, and the DPRK would provide full cooperation to the IAEA for this purpose.

In the third phase, North Korea would dismantle its old graphite reactors and the reprocessing plant that could convert the spent nuclear fuel into weapons-grade plutonium. The dismantling of North Korea's graphite-moderated reactors and related facilities was to correspond with the completion of the light-water reactor project. Together, the United States and North Korea would "cooperate in finding a method to store safely the spent fuel from the 5 MW(e) experimental reactor during the construction of the LWR project, and to dispose of the fuel in a safe manner that does not involve reprocessing in the DPRK."

55. Gordon, Michael R., *New York Times*, October 6, 1994, A7.

56. U.S. Congress, Senate, February 22, 1995, "Peace and Freedom" Senator William Cohen (R-Maine), 104th Congress 1st Session, 141 Cong Rec S 3320, vol. 141, no. 39.

57. Murkowski, Frank, (R-Alaska), Remarks of U.S. Congress, Senate, June 4, 1996. "Defend America Act of 1996-Motion to Proceed" 104th Congress 2nd Session, 142 Cong Rec S 5715, vol. 142, no. 80.

58. Declassified notes of the author of NSC memo on Bush meeting.

59. On October 10, 2000, President Clinton met with Special Envoy Vice Marshal Cho Myong-nok, first vice chairman of the National Defense Commission of North Korea, in the Oval Office. The joint communiqué was issued on October 12, 2000.

60. "North Korea Ban Eased," *New York Times*, June 20, 1999, A8. Reprinted from Reuters.

61. Interview with the author, December 9, 2003. Lee Sigal is currently director of the Northeast Asia Cooperative Security Project at the Social Science Research Council in New York.

62. Interview with Dan Poneman, February 4, 2004.

63. Interview with senior KEDO official, May 12, 2003.

64. International Crisis Group, *North Korea: A Phased Negotiation Strategy* (August 1, 2003). The cost to the American taxpayers of the program was $1 billion. In the eight years of the program, the United States spent $401 million on fuel and contributed approximately $4 million per year to the consortium given the task of building the light-water reactors. Had the reactors been built, Japan and South Korea would have put up most of the approximately $4.5 billion deal for the reactors. The United States also provided $591 million on food aid, although the aid was not directly linked to the deal. Washington did follow through on its commitments to lift economic and trade sanctions but did not normalize relations or provide formal assurances that it would not use or threaten to use nuclear weapons against it, http://www.crisisweb.org// library/documents/report_archive/A4010 73_01082003.pdf. From 1995–2002, Japan contributed $386 million and South Korea $940 million to KEDO.

65. Ibid, 10.

66. "Secretary Colin Powell discusses North Korea," *Meet the Press*, NBC News, December 29, 2002.

67. The Executive Board of the Korean

Peninsula Energy Development Organization (KEDO), led by the United States, South Korea, and Japan issued this statement following a board meeting in New York on November 14, 2002. See the press release issued following KEDO negotiations on November 14, 2002, http://www.kedo.org/news_detail.asp?NewsID=10.

68. In 1998, the United States donated 300,000 tons of food to North Korea, with another 400,000 tons donated in 1999. In 2002, the Bush administration cut the program to about 155,000 tons a year, about half of what it had donated in 2001. In 2003, the aid was reduced to 40 tons a year, with the administration saying only that it would consider another 60,000. The Bush administration has linked the aid reduction not to the North Korean's nuclear program but to the Korean failure to agree to the presence of international monitors of food distribution. "World in Brief; New U.S. Food Aid to N. Korea," *Atlanta Journal and Constitution*, September 22, 1998, A9; Associated Press, "U.S. Agrees to Ship 400,000 tons of Food to North Korea," *St. Louis Post-Dispatch* (Missouri), May 18, 1999; Mohammed, Arshad, "U.S. Offer Food Aid to North Korea but Cuts Amount," Reuters, February 5, 2003; Struck, Doug, "Aid Used as Lever With Pyongyang; Foreign Food Donations Drop Sharply As North Korea Again Faces Severe Crisis," *Washington Post*, December 5, 2002, A18.

69. French, Howard, "Aides Declare the U.S. 'Willing to Talk' in Korea Dispute," *New York Times*, January 14, 2003, A1.

70. International Crisis Group, *North Korea: A Phased Negotiation Strategy*, 13.

71. Kahn, Joseph, "Korea Arms Talks Close With Plans For a New Round," *New York Times*, August 30, 2003, A1.

72. Woo, James R., and Thomas McInerney, "The Next Korean War," *New York Times*, August 4, 2003, A8.

73. U.S. Congress, Senate Armed Services Committee, *Committee Hearing on Worldwide Threats to US Security*, George Tenet: director, Central Intelligence Agency; February 12, 2003.

74. The numbers are high-range estimates and assume that North Korea possesses "full production capability, construction/expansion of additional reprocessing capacity, early operation of facilities." Low-end estimates of weapons potential by 2010 include 97 plutonium-based weapons and 15 HEU weapons. Low-end estimates assume "late completion of reactors, no increase in reprocessing capabilities and late completion of HEU capability. Jon B. Wolfsthal, "Estimates of North Korea's Unchecked

Nuclear Weapons Production Potential," July 28, 2003, http://www.ceip.org/files/projects/npp/pdf/JBW/nknuclearweaponproductionpotential.pdf.

75. A Carnegie Endowment report released in June 2003 states that minimal amounts of HEU may have first been processed in 2001. Although U.S. sources do not know exactly where the processing takes place, they believe North Korea probably has three sites. See: Carnegie International Endowment for Peace and Nautilus Institute for Security and Sustainability, *Verifying North Korean Nuclear Disarmament: A Technical Analysis* (June 2003), http://www.ceip.org/files/pdf/wp38.pdf, HEU: 20–21; plutonium: Table 1, 11. The report indicates that North Korea's construction of the 50 MWe and 200 MWe reactors would be completed within several years from the date of publication (June 2003).

76. "North Korea Holds Hard Line," *CBSNews.Com*, January 8, 2003, http://www.cbsnews.com/stories/2003/01/09/world/main535804.shtml (accessed October 17, 2003)

77. "US Dangles Energy Aid to North Korea," *CBSNews.Com*, January 13, 2003, http://www.cbsnews.com/stories/2003/01/14/world/main536385.shtml (accessed October 17, 2003). See also: David E. Sanger, "Threats and Responses: East Asia; Bush Says Shift By North Korea Could Bring Aid," *New York Times*, January 15, 2003, A1.

78. "Kelly Says Talks with North Korea, Energy Aid Possible," press statement by James A. Kelly, assistant secretary of state for East Asian and Pacific Affairs, January 13, 2003 (Washington File), http://usembassy-australia.state.gov/hyper/2003/0113/epf107.htm (accessed October 15, 2003).

79. French, Howard W., "Threats and Responses: Asia; Aides Declare US 'Willing to Talk' In Korea Dispute," *New York Times*, January 14, 2003, A1.

80. McCain, Senator John, "Rogue State Rollback," *Weekly Standard*, January 20, 2003.

81. Smith, Hazel, "Northeast Asia frustrated by US Pyongyang policy," *Jane's Intelligence Review*, November 2003, 34.

82. United States Department of Defense, news release, "Rumsfeld Says Iraq, North Korea Require Different Approaches," January 20, 2003.

83. *Meet the Press*, NBC News, February 9, 2003. Secretary Colin L. Powell interview with Tim Russert. Powell says "U.S. Still Hopes to Avoid War with Iraq."

84. Remarks by National Security Advisor Condoleezza Rice at 28th Annual

Convention of the National Association of Black Journalists, Office of the Press Secretary, August 7, 2003, http://www.whitehouse.gov/news/releases/2003/08/20030807-1.html (accessed October 15, 2003).

85. Bush, President George W., "State of the Union Address," US Capital, January 28, 2003, Office of the Press Secretary, http://www.whitehouse.gov/news/releases/2003/01/20030128–19.html.

86. Keller, Bill, "At the Short End of the Axis of Evil: Some F.A.Q's," *New York Times Op-Ed*, January 11, 2003.

87. The Ministry of Foreign Affairs of Japan, "Six-Party Talks on North Korean Issues," Overview and Evaluation, September 2003, http://www.mofa.go.jp/region/asia-paci/n_korea/6party0308.html (accessed October 16, 2003).

88. Kim Dae Jung, the architect of the sunshine policy, left office on February 25 amidst reports that he had authorized a secret payment of nearly $200 million to North Korea before his June 2000 summit with his counterpart. "South Korean Sorry for Payments to North," *Washington Post*, February 14, 2003, A32.

89. Kahn, Joseph, "U.S. Stand Could Stall Korea Talks, Chinese Say," *New York Times*, September 3, 2003, A7.

90. Sanger, David E., "U.S. said to Shift Approach in Talks with North Korea," *New York Times*, September 5, 2003, A1.

91. Interview with Charles L. Pritchard, December 17, 2003. Pritchard also served as the U.S. Representative to KEDO, with the rank of ambassador, as special assistant to the president and senior director for Asian affairs, and as a Colonel in the army, serving twenty-eight years before retiring from active military service in June 2000. He is currently at the Brookings Institution in Washington, D.C.

92. Sanger, David E., "U.S. Said to Shift Approach in Talks with North Korea," *New York Times*, September 5, 2003, A1.

93. Sanger, David E., "U.S. Sees Quick Start of North Korea Nuclear Site," *New York Times*, March 1, 2003, A1.

94. Weisman, Steven R., "Bush Foreign Policy and Harsh Reality," *New York Times*, A1.

95. Smith, Hazel, 32–35.

96. Pew Global Attitudes Project, "Views of a Changing World," June 2003, http://people-press.org/reports/pdf/185.pdf.

97. Interview for ICG report, together with another ICG colleague and Lee Sigal, with a senior North Korean diplomat on May 14, 2003.

98. Kahn, Joseph, "North Korea Is Studying Softer Stance from the U.S.," *New York*

Times, June 24, 2004, A12. See also: editorial on same day, "Movement on North Korea, Finally," A22.

12. The African Intervention Gap

1. The hate radio that fueled the 1994 genocide was cynically named "A Thousand Hills" or "Milles Collines."

2. This trip comprised of visits to Rwanda, Ethiopia, Burundi, Mozambique, Angola, Zambia, Benin, and Senegal.

3. *Report of the Independent Inquiry into the Actions of the United Nations during the 1994 Genocide in Rwanda*, s/1999/1257, 3 (hereafter *United Nations Rwanda Report*).

4. Powers, Samantha, "Bystanders to Genocide," *Atlantic Monthly* (September 2001): 8.

5. The "genocide fax" can be viewed at http://www.gwu.edu/~nsarchiv/NSAEBB/NSAEBB53/rw011194.pdf.

6. *United Nations Reports*, 7.

7. State Department confidential cable (1994 KIGALI 000157), UN Special representative asks for support on Security Demarche, declassified January 23, 2004.

8. State Department confidential cable (1994 KIGALI 00475), General Dallaire's comments on UNAMIR operations to A/S Bennet, declassified January 23, 2004.

9. Preston, Julia, *Washington Post*, April 22, 1994, A1.

10. Richburg, Keith B., *Washington Post*, April 10, 1994, A1.

11. The United Nations's own high commissioner for human rights, Jose Ayala Lasso, who visited Rwanda on May 1 to 12, stopped short of characterizing the situation as genocide, noting that more than two hundred thousand civilians had been killed. He said the situation was one where "extremely serious violations of human rights had taken place" and were continuing.

12. Article 8 of the genocide convention states: "Any Contracting Party may call upon the competent organs of the United Nations to take such action under the Charter of the United Nations as they consider appropriate for the prevention and suppression of acts of genocide or any of the other acts enumerated in article III," http://www.preventgenocide.org/law/convention/text.htm#VIII.

13. Statement by the press secretary, White House, April 22, 1994.

14. United Nations Rwanda report, 18.

15. *Frontline* interview with Anthony Lake, December 15, 2003, http://www.pbs.org/wgbh/pages/frontline/shows/ghosts/in

terviews/lake.html: "Let me recall when [Monique Mujawamariya] visited. I met with them and was moved and terrified for her by her story of barely escaping—hiding in the attic for a while, and then getting out. I remember at the end, saying, 'We want to do what we can do to protect those under U.N. protection, and what we can do more generally. What can we do?' As I recall, they did not say, 'You need to look at intervention. You need to get the U.N. forces in there.' Of course, human rights activists [did] not necessarily automatically think, in those days, in terms of military interventions. But what they said, I remember clearly, 'Publish the names, or broadcast the names of the people who are responsible for this, and it may deter them.' I asked for the names, and it was on the airwaves very quickly."

16. Gumbari, Ibrahim A., "The Security Council and the (mis)handling of the tragic situation in Rwanda (1994–95): an African perspective," paper presented for forthcoming book, February 24, 2003.

17. U.S. Department of State Dispatch, vol. 5, no. 27 (Bureau of Public Affairs, July 4, 1994), http://dosfan.lib.uic.edu/ERC/briefing/dispatch/1994/html/Dispatchv5no27.html.

18. State Department Confidential Cable (1994GENEVA04608, May 18, 1994). "High Commissioner for Human Rights Reports on Visit to Rwanda, Intentions for UNHRC's Special Session," declassified January 22, 2004.

19. Richburg, Keith B., Washington Post, May 1, 1994, A34.

20. http://www.dispatchesfromthevanishingworld.com/pastdispatches/rwanda/rwanda3.html.

21. Preston, Julia, Washington Post, April 29, 1994, A1.

22. Chapter VI of the United Nations Charter, "Pacific Settlement of Disputes," encourages nations to settle cross-border disputes peacefully through negotiation, mediation, arbitration, or by whatever "pacific" means seem workable. Under Chapter VI, the United Nations can facilitate an end to hostilities through diplomacy, but it cannot coerce the hostile parties to make peace. In contrast, Chapter VII, "Action with Respect to Threats to the Peace, Breaches of the Peace, and Acts of Aggression," envisions a range of decidedly coercive Security Council actions—from imposing economic sanctions to dispatching troops and tanks—if there has been a "threat to the peace, breach of the peace, or an act of aggression." In theory, the UN Security Council can make war to end war, although in practice it has failed at enforcement operations. Drawn from

http://www.thebulletin.org/issues/1995/ma95/ma95.peacekeeping.html.

23. See: http://www.mikenew.com/pdd25.html.

24. It was not until June 3 that the RPF wrote to the Secretary-General requesting the Security Council to declare the atrocities were genocide, to jam or destroy Radio Milles Collines, and to suspend Rwanda from the council.

25. http://news.bbc.co.uk/1/hi/programmes/from_our_own_correspondent/3757211.stm.

26. http://www.un.org/Depts/dpko/dpko/co_mission/unamirS.htm.

27. Public Papers of the Presidents, William J. Clinton, vol. 1 (1994), 986.

28. State Department Cable (1994STATE 201161, July 27, 1994), press guidance released January 23, 2004.

29. State Department Confidential Cable (1994STATE144915, May 31, 1994), official-informal declassified January 22, 2004.

30. Interview with the author, June 21, 2004.

31. Author's interview of senior French official, May 31, 2001.

32. State Department confidential cable (1994USUNN03783, September 12, 1994), "Rwanda: General Daillaire Address Troop Contributors" declassified January 23, 2004.

33. Interview with Lake, July 16, 2004.

34. http://www.un.org/News/ossg/sgsm_rwanda.htm.

35. United Nations Rwanda Report, 26–27.

36. Feil, Scott R., Preventing Genocide (Carnegie Corporation of New York, April 1998), 3.

37. Kuperman, Alan J., "Rwanda in Perspective," Foreign Affairs (January/February 2000), 508.

38. Ibid., 9.

39. Only an estimated one quarter of the Tutsi population survived, according to the Paris-based International Federation of Human Rights Leagues and the U.S.-based Human Rights Watch. See: http://cnnstudent news.cnn.com/WORLD/africa/9903/31/rwanda.01/.

40. Kuperman.

41. Ibid., 10.

42. Clinton, Bill, "Learn from Rwanda," Washington Post, April 6, 2004, A21. During a visit to Kigali in 1998, Clinton said, "We did not act quickly enough after the killings began. We should not have allowed the refugee camps to become safe havens for the killers. We did not immediately call these crimes by their rightful name: genocide. . . . Let us work together as a community of civilized nations to strengthen our ability to prevent and, if necessary, to stop genocide. . . . Never again must we be shy in the

face of evidence." See also: *Public Papers of the Presidents, William J. Clinton*, vol. 1 (1998), 432.

43. Feil, *Preventing Genocide*, vi.

44. Lake, Anthony, *6 Nightmares*, 93.

45. United Nations General Assembly, 54th Session, A/54/PV.4.

46. *We the Peoples: The role of the United Nations in the Twenty-First Century*, (United Nations General Assembly, 54th Session), A/54/2000, 34.

47. Gareth Evans is president of the International Crisis Group and the author's boss.

48. *The Responsibility to Protect*, report of the International Commission on Intervention and State Sovereignty (December 2001), http://www.dfait-maeci.gc.ca/iciss-ciise/report-en.asp.

49. United Nations Security Council Resolution 1315 reaffirms that persons who "commit or authorize serious violations of international humanitarian law are individually responsible and accountable for those violations." The resolution also recommends "that the special court should have personal jurisdiction over persons who bear the greatest responsibility for the commission of the crimes referred to in paragraph 2, including those leaders who, in committing such crimes, have threatened the establishment of and implementation of the peace process in Sierra Leone." The entire resolution can be found at http://ods-dds-ny.un.org/doc/UNDOC/GEN/N00/605/32/PDF/N0060532.pdf?OpenElement.

50. Hutcheson, Ron, "Ahead of a Visit Bush Shares Ideas for Africa," *Philadelphia Inquirer*, June 26, 2003, http://www.philly.com/mid/inquirer/news/nation/6180223.htm.

51. While Obasanjo was right to do what it took to get Taylor out of Liberia and avoid further bloodshed, pressure is rightly mounting on Nigeria to hand Taylor over to the court, with the United States Congress appropriating a $2 million reward for Taylor's capture.

52. Remarks by President Bush to the Corporate Council on Africa's US-Africa Business Summit, June 26, 2003.

53. Robinson, Dan, "African-American Lawmakers Look Carefully at US Involvement in Liberia," July 10, 2003, Capitol Hill, taken from *VOAnews.com*, www.globalsecurity.org/military/library/news/2003/07/mil-030711-voa03.htm.

54. Operation Artemis in the Democratic Republic of the Congo was a EU-led force of eighteen hundred troops, including France, Britain, Sweden, Norway, South Africa, Canada, and Brazil, with Belgium and Germany providing only noncombat troops. Hungary and The Netherlands provided headquarter support in Paris. The mission ended in Septebmer 2003.

55. Fox News, July 27, 2003. http://japan.usembassy.gov/e/p/+p-20030729a8.html.

56. http://www.news24.com/News24/Africa/News/0,6119,2-11-1447_1406489,00.html.

57. "Thousands of Civilians Flee Rebel Attacks One Day After US Declares Nightmare Over," Oxfam International (Boston), September 4, 2004, http://www.oxfam.org/eng/pr030904_liberia_civilians_stmt.htm.

58. http://www.un.org/Depts/dpko/missions/unmil/mandate.html.

59. The "first" Sudan civil war ended in 1972; the "second" began in 1983.

60. IGAD members are Djibouti, Eritrea, Ethiopia, Kenya, Somalia, Sudan, and Uganda. Friends of IGAD include 16 mostly European countries (such as the United States, Norway, the UK, Italy), UNDP, EC, and the World Bank.

61. The three areas are the Nuba Mountains, Southern Blue Nile, and Abyei. Percentages of a future government are given each party. An expected six-month "pre-interim" period is expected before the establishment of an interim government for Sudan.

62. http://www.unsudanig.org/News/Data/Press/2003/Feburary/DPR0227.pdf.

63. "Darfur Rising: Sudan's New Crisis," ICG Africa Report #76, March 25. 2004, 4–5.

64. "Sudan: Darfur Destroyed," Human Rights Watch Report, http://www.hrw.org/campaigns/darfur/.

65. "Darfur Rising," i.

66. "WHO Seeks Urgent Action to Avert Sudan Crisis" (June 2, 2004), http://www.cnn.com/2004/WORLD/africa/06/02/sudan.who/index.html.

67. U.S. Department of State, "Prosper Reports 'Indicators of Genocide' in Darfur," June 24, 2004.

68. Weisman, Steven R., "Powell Says Rapes and Killings in Sudan Are Genocide, *New York Times*, September 10, 2004, A3.

69. Text of the Convention on the Prevention and Punishment of the Crime of Genocide, December 9, 1948, http://www.unhchr.ch/html/menu3/b/p_genoci.htm.

70. Ibid.

71. Interview with senior European diplomat, June 22, 2004.

72. Abramowitz, Morton, and Samantha Power, "A Broken System," *Washington Post*, September 13, 2004, A21.

73. Interview with the author, September 9, 2004.

74. Evan, Gareth, e-mail exchange with the author, July 12, 2004.
75. Annan, Kofi, speech to United Nations General Assembly, September 20, 1999.
76. "Ghosts of Rwanda," PBS *Frontline*, April 1, 2004, http://www.pbs.org/wgbh/pages/frontline/shows/ghosts/.
77. Interview with senior UN official by the author, February 18, 2004.
78. *This Week*, ABC, January 23, 2000.
79. http://www.un.org/Depts/dpko/dpko/contributors/CountriesSummaryApril2004.pdf.
80. The U.S. threatened to withdraw these troops after it was forced in July 2004 to withdraw its effort to get an ICC exemption for U.S. forces in every peacekeeping resolution.
81. The program was initially called the African Crisis Response Force, but "Force" was dropped in favor of "Initiative" a year later out of sensitivities in Africa over the possible military intervention implied. The author led the initial 1996 trip to present the proposal in Europe, NSC Senior Director for African Affairs Susan Rice led the delegation to consult with African leaders. The program's current name is Africa Contingency Operations Training Assistance (ACOTA).
82. http://www.shirbrig.dk/.
83. http://www.defenselink.mil/news/Apr2002/t04022002_t0402dasdaa.html.
84. http://www.prairienet.org/acas/military/miloverview.html#acota.
85. http://www.africafocus.org/docs04/us0406a.php.

13. Winning the War on Terrorism

1. My husband and I have since provided support to the war widows of Herat. We encourage others to do so through the International Organization for Migration (IOM), http://www.iom.int.
2. *Country Report, Afghanistan*, Human Rights Watch (January 2004).
3. *Afghanistan: Women Still Not 'Liberated*, Human Rights Watch (December 17, 2002).
4. Gall, Carlotta, "For More Afghan Women, Immolation Is Escape," *New York Times*, March 8, 2004, A1.
5. Huang, Reyko, *Fact Sheet: International Security Assistance Force (ISAF) in Afghanistan*, CDI Terrorism Project (updated February 14, 2002), http://www.cdi.org/terrorism/isaf.cfm.
6. *Agreement on Provisional Arrangements in Afghanistan Pending the Re-establishment of Permanent Government Institutions*, United Nations Assistance Mission in Afghanistan (December 2001), http://www.unama-afg.org/docs/bonn/bonn.html.
7. "Afghans behead Taliban in revenge for beheadings," Reuters, June 22, 2004, http://www.alertnet.org/thenews/newsdesk/ISL14858.htm.
8. Agency Coordinating Body for Afghan Relief (ACBAR) press release, Kabul, June 22, 2004.
9. Sciolino, Elaine, "Drifting NATO Finds New Purpose with Afghanistan and Iraq," *New York Times*, February 23, 2004, A6.
10. Afghanistan is a country of 250,000 square miles and 28.5 million people. In contrast, Iraq is 168,754 square miles, with a population of 25.4 million. See: CIA World Fact Book, 2004.
11. *NATO in Afghanistan Factsheet*, NATO (July 7, 2004), http://www.nato.int/issues/afghanistan/040628-factsheet.htm. See also: *Afghanistan Reconstruction: Deteriorating Security & Limited Resources Have Impeded Progress; Improvements in U.S. Strategy Needed*, GAO (June 2004), 40 and 43, http://www.gao.gov/new.items/d04403.pdf.
12. Arnault, Jean, special representative of the UN secretary-general for Afghanistan, press conference, June 21, 2004, http://www.unama-afg.org/news/press%20conferences/srsg/2004/SRSG04jun22.htm.
13. Graham, Stephen, "U.N. May Pull Out of Afghanistan," Associated Press, December 12, 2003, http://seattletimes.nwsource.com/html/nationworld/2001814064_unafghan13.html.
14. Constable, Pamela, "Karzai Attempts Diplomacy with Afghan Warlords," *Washington Post*, May 19, 2004, A12, http://www.washingtonpost.com/wp-dyn/articles/A37736-2004May18.html.
15. U.S. Department of Defense news briefing, March 22, 2004.
16. Arnault, Jean, "Afghanistan: National Army Delays Deployment to Ghor Province" RFE/RL, June 22, 2004, Synovitz, Ron, http://www.globalsecurity.org/military/library/news/2004/06/mil-040622-rfer104.htm.
17. Gall, Carlotta, and David Rohde, "Afghan President Describes Militias as the Top Threat," *New York Times*, July 12, 2004, http://www.nytimes.com/2004/07/12/international/asia/12AFGH.html?hp.
18. *Afghanistan: The Problem of Pashtun Alienation*, International Crisis Group (August 5, 2003).
19. Constable, Pamela, "Afghan's Goals Facing Renewed Threats; Worsening Security Could Undercut Progress Toward Democracy, Reconstruction," *Washington Post*, September 9, 2003, A9.

20. "Taliban commander seized," *Financial Times*, July 8, 2004, 1.

21. Gall, Carlotta. "2 Bombings Seen as Part of New Drive By Taliban," *New York Times*, July 1, 2004, A13.

22. Human Rights Asia Special Report, "Women and Elections in Afghanistan," August 28, 2004. Available online at http://hrw.org/campaigns/afghanistan/index.htm.

23. Ibid.

24. *The Costs of War and Reconstruction in Iraq: An Update*, House Budget Committee Democratic Staff (September 2003), http://64.233.167.104/search?q=cache:f P99pHycHhsJ:www.house.gov/budget _democrats/analyses/iraq_cost_update.pdf +omb+aid+afghanistan+iraq+2005&hl=en.

25. *Building a New Afghanistan: The Value of Success, the Cost of Failure*, NYU, Center on International Cooperation (March 2004), 9.

26. Zingales, Luigi, "For Iraq, a Plan Worthy of Zambia," *Washington Post*, November 9, 2003, B2.

27. *Afghanistan Reconstruction: Deteriorating Security & Limited Resources Have Impeded Progress; Improvements in U.S. Strategy Needed*, GAO (June 2004), 48.

28. Op. cit., 13, and *Afghanistan Reconstruction: Deteriorating Security & Limited Resources Have Impeded Progress; Improvements in U.S. Strategy Needed*, GAO (June 2004), 40.

29. Ibid., 43.

30. Morrison, Dan, *Christian Science Monitor*, January 6, 2004, 6.

31. "Islamic Democracy," Editorial, *New York Times*, January 6, 2004.

32. Simpson, Cam, "Taliban attacks at their highest since collapse of regime," *Chicago Tribune*, February 24, 2004, http://www.sunherald.com/mld/sunherald/news/politics/8032284.htm.

33. *Joint Inquiry*, 225.

34. Black, Ambassador Cofer, Coordinator for Counterterrorism, testimony before the House International Relations Committee, Subcommittee on International Terrorism, Washington, D.C., April 1, 2004, http://www.state.gov/s/ct/rls/rm/2004/31018.htm.

35. Bowers, Faye, "Headway on the Al Qaeda Money Trail," *Christian Science Monitor*, October 10, 2003, 2.

36. *Progress Report in the Global War on Terrorism*, The White House (September 2003), http://www.whitehouse.gov/homeland/progress/progress_report_0903.pdf.

37. *G8 Secure and Facilitated International Travel Initiative (SAFTI)*, Summit Documents, G8 Information Centre, http://www.g7.utoronto.ca/summit/2004seaisland/travel.html (accessed July 12, 2004).

38. Jehl, Douglas, "Tenet Says Dangers to U.S. are at Least as Great as a Year Ago," *New York Times*, February 25, 2004, A15.

39. Miller, Greg, "Small Terrorist Units Now the Biggest Threat, Tenet Warns," *Los Angeles Times*, February 25, 2004, A17.

40. Risen, James, *New York Times*, September 10, 2004, A10.

41. El Deeb, Sarah, "Bin Laden Tape Vows Attacks vs. U.S.," Associated Press, October 19, 2003.

42. MacFarquhar, Neil, "A Top bin Laden Aid Threatens New Attacks Against the U.S.," *New York Times*, February 25, 2004, A8.

43. Rowan, Scarborough, "Agencies unite to find bin Laden," *Washington Times*, March 15, 2004, A1, http://www.washington-times.com/national/20040315-122940-5507r.htm.

44. BBC, "Pakistan offensive 'un-Islamic,'" March 25, 2004, http://news.bbc.co.uk/2/hi/south_asia/3569359.stm.

45. Schmitt, Richard B., "Flaws Seen in War on Terror Data: Authorities Include Dismissed Cases as Proof US is Winning," *Los Angeles Times*, December 22, 2003, http://www.boston.com/news/nation/articles/2003/12/22/flaws_seen_in_war_on_terror _data/.

46. Ibid.

47. Miller, Bill, "National Alert System Defines Five Shades of Terrorist Threat; Ridge Expects U.S. to Stay at Heightened Awareness for Years," *Washington Post*, March 13, 2002.

48. Discussion with Major General Giora Eiland, Israeli national security advisor to Israeli prime minister Ariel Sharon, September 23, 2004.

49. Chrisafis, Angelique, "BA Plans Anti-missile shields for Planes," *Guardian* (London), September 6, 2003, 2.

50. "Terror List: Previous Attacks," *Guardian*, May 14, 2003. On Iraq, see: Nicolas Blanford, "Huge Blasts Attack Iraq Unity," *Christian Science Monitor*, March 3, 2004.

51. Miller, Greg, "Small Terrorist Units Now the Biggest Threat, Tenet Warns," *Los Angeles Times*, February 25, 2004, A17.

52. Statement of Dr. Rohan Gunaratna, author of "Inside Al Qaeda," in Faye Bowers, "Scattered Al Qaeda Harder to Target," *Christian Science Monitor*, May 21, 2003, 1.

53. *Jemaah Islamiyah in Southeast Asia: Damaged but Still Dangerous*, International Crisis Group Asia Report no. 63 (August 26, 2003), 1, http://www.crisisweb.org/home/index.cfm?id=2613&l=1.

54. *CNN.com*, "Asia's most wanted in U.S.

hands," August 15, 2003, http://www.cnn.com/2003/WORLD/asiapcf/southeast/08/15/hambali.capture/.

55. Quoting an audiotape attributed to bin Laden that was broadcast on the Al Jazeera television network. "Bin Laden Tape Warns US," *BBC World News Online*, October 18, 2003, http://news.bbc.co.uk/2/hi/middle_east/3203878.stm.

56. ETA stands for Euskadi Ta Askatasuna, or Basque Homeland and Freedom.

57. Frankel, Glenn, "Madrid Bombs Shook Voters; Distrust of the Government, Anger at U.S. Fueled Upset," *Washington Post*, March 16, 2004, A1. Thanks also to Robert Templer for comments on the issue.

58. UN Office on Drugs and Crime (UNODC) informational Web page on conventions against terrorism, http://www.unodc.org/unodc/terrorism_conventions.html (accessed June 30, 2004). For information on the UN conventions, see http://www.unodc.org/unodc/terrorism_conventions.html.

59. Interview with the author, June 23, 2004.

60. Interview with the author, July 13, 2004. Newcomb resigned his position on September 13, 2004, after 17 years at the Treasury Department's Office of Foreign Assets Control.

61. For more information on Europe's antiterrorism actions, see http://europa-eu-un.org/article.asp?id=1587 and http://europa-eu-un.org/article.asp?id=175.

62. *Time, Europe* (March 29, 2004): 24–29.

63. Butler, Desmond, "Faulting US, Germany Frees a 9/11 Suspect," *New York Times*, February 6, 2004, A1.

64. McAllister, J. F. O., "Now What Do We Do?" *Time* (Europe) (March 29, 2004): 24–29.

65. The Uniting and Strengthening America by Providing Appropriate Tools Required to Intercept and Obstruct Terrorism (USA PATRIOT) Act of 2001, HR3162.

66. 9/11 Commission Report, 79.

67. Department of Justice, www.lifeandliberty.org (accessed February 23, 2004).

68. *Civil Rights Concerns in the Metropolitan Washington, D.C., Area in the Aftermath of the September 11, 2001, Tragedies*, chapter 5, "Implementing the USA Patriot Act of 2001: Civil Rights Impact," U.S. Commission on Civil Rights (June 2003), http://www.usccr.gov/pubs/sac/dc0603/ch5.htm

69. *National Security; Prevention of Acts of Violence and Terrorism; Final Rule*, 28 CFR parts 500 and 501. Bureau of Prisons, Department of Justice, 55062, http://www.cnss.org/attorneyclientorder.htm.

70. von Zielbauer, Paul, "Threats and Responses: Prisons; Detainees' Abuse is Detailed," *New York Times*, December 19, 2003, A5.

71. Greenhouse, Linda, "Supreme Court Roundup; Justices Allow Policy of Silence on 9/11 Detainees," *New York Times*, January 13, 2004, A1.

72. Doyle, Charles, "USA Patriot Act Sunset: A Stretch," Congressional Research Service, January 7, 2004, http://www.fas.org/irp/crs/RS21704.pdf.

73. President George W. Bush, "Address to a Joint Session of Congress and the American People," January 2004, http://www.whitehouse.gov/news/releases/2004/01/20040120-7.html.

74. http://www.whitehouse.gov/news/releases/2001/11/20011113-27.html.

75. President George W. Bush, "Military Order on the Detention, Treatment, and Trial of Certain Non-Citizens in the War Against Terrorism," November 13, 2001.

76. *US Detentions Undermine the Rule of Law*, Human Rights Watch (January 9, 2004). The term dates back to a Supreme Court ruling of 1942 in which eight German spies were given up to the FBI as saboteurs by two members of their team upon arrival on U.S. shores. President Roosevelt's establishment of military commissions to try the spies was defended by the Supreme Court *Ex Parte Quirin*, 1942, 217 US 28.63 S. Ct. 11.

77. Seelye, Katherine Q., "A Nation Challenged: Captives; Detainees are not P.O.W.s, Cheney and Rumsfeld Declare," *New York Times*, January 18, 2002, A6.

78. "The Geneva Conventions," *CBC News*, May 13, 2004, http://www.cbc.ca/news/background/iraq/genevaconventions.html.

79. Op. cit.

80. President George W. Bush, remarks on Executive Order, Washington, D.C., September 24, 2001, http://www.whitehouse.gov/news/releases/2001/09/20010924-4.html.

81. *Joint Inquiry*, 116.

82. Department of Justice, www.lifeandliberty.gov. (accessed February 23, 2004).

83. *Joint Inquiry*, 309.

84. "Terrorist Financing: Report of an Independent Task Force Sponsored by the Council on Foreign Relations," October 17, 2002, http://www.cfr.org/pdf/Terrorist_Financing_TF.pdf.

85. Lichtblau, Eric, and Timothy O'Brien, *New York Times*, December 12, 2003, A1.

86. Andrews, Edmund, *New York Times*, January 23, 2004, A4.

87. Interview with the author, July 13, 2004.

88. Interview with the author, July 13, 2004.

89. 9/11 Commission Report, 395.

90. "Washington's Mega-merger," *The Economist*, November 23, 2002.

91. Department of Homeland Security Web site, www.dhs.gov.

92. Miller, Leslie, "Airport security still lacking despite billions of dollars spent since 9/11," Associated Press, April 22, 2004.

93. Orzag, Peter R., "Protecting the American Homeland: A Second Look at How We're Meeting the Challenge," Brookings Institution Briefing, Washington, D.C., January 23, 2003.

94. Daalder, Ivo, "Protecting the American Homeland: A Second Look at How We're Meeting the Challenge," Brookings Institution Briefing, Washington, D.C., January 23, 2003.

95. Gips, Micheal A., "Shared Intelligence Makes Everyone Smarter," *SecurityManagement Online*, January 2004, http://www.securitymanagement.com/library/001550.html.

96. Kettl, Donald, *The Department of Homeland Security's First Year: A Report Card*, Overview, 13–16.

97. 9/11 Commission Report.

98. Yankelovich, Dan, discussion hosted by the Center for National Policy, Washington, D.C., April 21, 2004.

14. Lessons for the President

1. KFOR press release, Pristina, January 21, 2004: total of 18,500 KFOR troops. Also see: Wes Allison, "No end in sight for U.S. in Iraq," *St. Petersburg Times*, March 21, 2004: 2000 US troops in Kosovo, and Brookings Institution, "Iraq Index," June 16, 2004: 138,000 US troops, 162,000 total coalition troops.

2. The Pew Research Center, "Views of a Changing World 2003," June 3. (The Pew Global Attitudes Project surveyed 16,000 people in 20 countries and the Palestinian Authority in May 2003 and more than 38,000 people in 44 nations in 2002.)

3. Taylor Nelson Sofres/EOS Gallup Europe, Public Opinion Poll, October 2003. Fifty-three percent of EU citizens viewed the United States as a threat, as well as North Korea and Iran.

4. Pew Global Attitudes Project, "Views of a Changing World," June 2003.

5. The Pew Research Center, "A Year After Iraq War," March 16, 2004.

6. United Nations Development Programme, *Arab Human Development Report 2003*.

7. Other hijackers were from Yemen and UAE.

8. See: *Can Saudi Arabia Reform Itself?*, ICG Middle East Report no. 28 (July 14, 2004) www.crisisweb.org.

9. United Nations Development Programme, *Arab Human Development Report* (2002).

10. Indyk, Martin, "Back to the Bazaar," *Foreign Affairs* (January/February 2002): 77.

11. Gallup poll. (Researchers conducted face-to-face interviews with 9,924 residents of Pakistan, Iran, Indonesia, Turkey, Lebanon, Morocco, Kuwait, Jordan, and Saudi Arabia to gauge public opinion in those countries following the September 11 attacks.)

12. Levinson, Charles, "$50 Billion Later, Taking Stock of US Aid to Egypt," *Christian Science Monitor*, April 12, 2004.

13. "Sharon Strategy Backfires," *Los Angeles Times*, May 4, 2004.

14. Ottaway, Marina, "Thinking Big: Democratizing the Middle East," *Boston Globe*, January 5, 2003.

15. Michael, Rebecca, "Analysis: U.S. reform plan faces flak," United Press International, April 9, 2004.

16. Sea Island Summit, *G8 Extended Invitees* (www.g8usa.gov/extended.htm). The only Arab leaders in attendance were from Algeria, Bahrain, Iraq, Jordan, and Yemen.

17. Discussion with the author, September 23, 2004.

18. *Can Saudi Arabia Reform Itself?*, 6.

19. See chapter 5 for a more detailed discussion of Clinton's plan.

20. See, for instance, Greg Thielmann, "Rumsfeld Reprise? The Missile Report that Foretold the Iraq Intelligence Controversy," *Arms Control Today* (July/August 2003). See also: William D. Hartung, "Rumsfeld Reconsidered: An Ideologian Moderates Clothing," Foreign policy in Focus, January 2001, Hartung concludes: "The Rumsfeld Commission . . . basically massaged existing U.S. intelligence data to come up with new conclusions that fit the political needs of its creators for a quasi-official endorsement of their exaggerated views of the missle threat to the United States."

21. Ibid.

22. Manuel Perez-Rivas, "US Quits ABM Treaty," CNN, December 14, 2001.

23. Statement by Russian President Vladimir Putin on ABM Treaty, *Official Kremlin Int'l. News Broadcast*, December 13, 2001.

24. Missile Defense Deployment Announcement briefing, Department of Defense, December 17, 2002.

25. "Dubious Threat, Expensive Defense," editorial, *Washington Post*, April 26, 2004, A23.

26. Graham, Bradley, "Missile Defense Agency Faulted On Testing and Accountability,"

Washington Post, Saturday, April 24, 2004, http://www.washingtonpost.com/ac2/wp-dyn?pagename=article&contentId=A37828–2004Apr23&notFound=true.

27. "Global Nuclear Stockpiles, 1945–2002," *Bulletin of the Atomic Scientists* (November/December, 2002), http://www.thebulletin.org/issues/nukenotes/nd02nukenote.html.

28. Ibid.

29. Nunn, Sam, "A New Triumph of Sanity," presented at the Carnegie International Non-Proliferation Conference on June 21, 2004.

30. Ibid.

31. Ibid. See also: Miles A. Pomper, "Bush Stresses Importance of Nunn-Lugar Programs but Cuts Funds in 2005 Budget Request," *Arms Control Today,* Arms Control Association, March 2004, http://www.armscontrol.org/act/2004_03/NunnLugarFunding.asp.

32. Ibid.

33. *White House Statement, Fact Sheet on Proliferation Security,* Washington File (September 5, 2003).

34. The Acronym Institute for Disarmament Diplomacy, *Proliferation Security Initiative (PSI) Meeting, Paris, September 3–4,* http://www.acronym.org.uk/docs/0309/doc06.htm. The eleven core signatories included Australia, France, Germany, Italy, Japan, The Netherlands, Poland, Portugal, Spain, the UK and the United States.

35. Alex Rodriguez, *Chicago Tribune,* January 31, 2004.

36. Interview with senior IAEA official by the author, March 25, 2004.

37. Interview with the author April 7, 2004 and confirmed September 13, 2004.

38. Leopold, Evelyn, "UN Council Unanimously Adopts Terrorist Arms Ban," Reuters, April 28, 2004.

39. Libyan representatives had in fact offered to surrender WMD programs in May 1999, during secret negotiations with U.S. officials. See: Martin S. Indyk, "The Iraq War Did Not Force Gadaffi's Hand," *Financial Times,* March 9, 2004.

40. Traynor, Ian, "Investigators have uncovered a sophisticated black market in components with Islamabad at its centre: Pakistan's nuclear hero throws open Pandora's box," *Guardian,* January 31, 2004, Foreign Pages 16.

41. Tyler, Patrick E., and David E. Sanger, "Pakistan called Libyans' Source of Atom Design," *New York Times,* January 6, 2004, A1.

42. Text of Dr. Khan's Statement, Islamabad, February 4, 2004, www.infopak.gov.pk/statement_dr_a_q_khan.htm.

43. Kifner, John, "Nuclear Anxiety: In Pakistan; Complex Pressures, Dominated by Islam, Led to Testing," *New York Times,* June 1, 1998, A6.

44. Slevin, Peter, "Libya's Uranium Linked to Pakistan," *Washington Post,* May 29, 2004, A21.

45. Interview with Steve Andreasen, former NSC Director for Defense Policy and Arms Control 1993–2001.

46. CIA, "Unclassified Report to Congress on the Acquisition of Technology Relating to Weapons of Mass Destruction and Advanced Conventional Munitions. 1 January Through 30 June 2003." http://www.cia.gov/cia/reports/721_reports/jan_jun2003.htm.

47. http://www.nti.org/e_research/profiles/Iran/index.html.

48. Interview with the author and senior IAEA officials, March 25, 2004.

49. George W. Bush, "President Announces New Measures to Counter the Threat of WMD," remarks at the National Defense University, February 11, 2004.

50. Valenzuela, Arturo, "Bush's Betrayal of Democracy," *Washington Post,* April 16, 2002, A19.

51. Press Briefing by Ari Fleischer Office of the White House Press Secretary, April 12, 2002 and Peter Slevin, "Chavez Provoked His Removal, U.S. Officials Say," *Washington Post,* April 13, 2002, A17.

52. DeYoung, Karen, "Bush Officials Defend Their Actions on Venezuela," *Washington Post,* April 18, 2002, A01.

53. Valenzuela, A19.

54. DeYoung, A01.

55. Philip T. Reeker, Deputy Spokesman, State Department Press Briefing, Washington, D.C., April 15, 2002.

56. Marquis, Christopher, "Combative Point Man on Latin Policy—Otto J. Reich," *New York Times,* April 18, 2002, 8.

57. Forero, Juan, "Venezuelan Leader, Battling a Recall, Mocks Bush," *New York Times,* March 1, 2004, 3.

58. "CARICOM Prior Action Plan," Rev. 6, developed at the CARICOM meeting on Haiti in Kingston, Jamaica, January 31, 2004, http://www.oas.org/OASpage/Haiti_situation/PriorActionPlan-HA_version6bis1.pdf.

59. Weiner, Tim, "Life is Hard and Short in Haiti's Bleak Villages, *New York Times,* March, 14, 2004.

60. "Latin America's Half-Term Presidents," editorial, *New York Times,* February 26, 2004.

61. Interview with Condoleezza Rice, John

McLaughlin's *One on One*, Federal News Service, August 3, 2000.

62. "Bush, Putin Comments," Associated Press, November 12, 2001. Rice's "happy talk" comment can be found in: Condeleezza Rice, "Exercising Power Without Arrogance," *Chicago Tribune*, December 31, 2000.

63. "Schoolboy Putin tried to join KGB," *The Tribune* (India) and Reuters, Sunday, March 12, 2000.

64. Applebaum, Anne, "Beneath the skin, it's the same old Russian Bear," *London Times*, March 15, 2004, and Keller, Bill, "God and George W. Bush," *New York Times*, May 17, 2003.

65. "Russia and US agree arms cuts," *BBC News*, May 13, 2002, http://news.bbc.co.uk/1/hi/world/americas/1984995.stm and White House Fact Sheet: *Moscow Treaty on Strategic Offensive Reductions*, May 24, 2002.

66. Rebecca Santana "RUSSIA: Equal status is the goal," *Atlanta Journal-Constitution*, May 2, 2004, 4C.

67. http://www.unwire.org/UNWire/20031009/449_9280.asp.

68. From Esman and Herring, editors, *Carrots, Sticks, and Ethnic Conflict; Rethinking Development Assistance* (University of Michigan Press, 2001), chap. 3 USAID and Ethnic Conflict: An Epiphany? by Heather S. McHugh, 54.

69. http://www.undp.org/hdr2003/.

70. Budget priorities for sub-Saharan Africa, http://www.state.gov/p/af/rls/rm/20249.htm.

71. Annan, Kofi, speech to United Nations General Assembly, September 20, 1999, 17.

72. www.wfn.org/2003/06/msg00017.html.

73. Holbrooke, Richard, and Richard Furman, *New York Times*, February 10, 2004, 25.

74. http://www.usembassy.it/file2000_11/alia/a0113014.htm.

75. http://usinfo.state.gov/journals/itgic/0700/ijge/gj02.htm).

76. http://ods-dds-ny.un.org/doc/UNDOC/GEN/N00/536/02/PDF/N0053602.pdf?OpenElement.

77. Bush's plan will focus the resources on those countries in Africa and the Caribbean that are the most affected: Botswana, Cote d'Ivoire, Ethiopia, Guyana, Haiti, Kenya, Mozambique, Namibia, Rwanda, South Africa, Tanzania, Uganda, and Zambia. These countries have the highest rates of HIV/AIDS and account for 70 percent of the total in all of Africa and the Caribbean. In FY 2005, the president asked for an additional $2.8 billion for international AIDS relief.

78. "Now for Africa," *Economist*, July 3, 2003.

79. http://www.worldmag.com/world/issue/07–19-03/opening_3.asp.

80. "Bush, hero or hypocrite?" *Economist* (May 29, 2003), http://www.economist.com/displayStory.cfm?Story_ID=S')HL-Q!%3F%20%20%40%23T%0A.

81. Bumiller, Elisabeth, "Evangelicals Sway White House on Human Rights Issues Abroad," *New York Times*, 1.

82. http://www.eldis.org/static/DOC10759.htm.

83. Op. cit.

84. The Mexico City policy prohibits foreign nongovernmental organizations (NGO) that receive U.S. funds from providing abortion, abortion counseling referral, or related services, even *with their own funds*, even if provided in countries where abortion is legal and the NGO's practices are consistent with local law, policy, and standards of medical practice. The policy goes way beyond simply limiting access to abortion as the 1973 Helms amendment to the Foreign Assistance Act of 1961, had previously prohibited the use of any U.S. funds for abortion services except in the case of rape, health risks to the life of the pregnant woman, or incest. See: http://www.plannedparenthood.org/library/facts/030416_global gag.html. See also: chapter 5 for more on Bush's policy.

85. As of May 27, 2004, the following countries have not concluded a bilateral immunity agreement and have lost aid: Benin, Brazil, Costa Rica, Croatia, Eastern Caribbean (Barbados, Dominica, Saint Vincent, and the Grenadines), Ecuador, Lesotho, Malta, Mali, Namibia, Niger, Paraguay, Peru, Republic of the Congo, Samoa, South Africa, Serbia and Montenegro, Tanzania, Trinidad and Tobago, Uruguay, and Venezuela. An additional thirty countries have not concluded a bilateral immunity agreement. However, these countries have not lost aid because they do not receive aid from the United States or they are exempted under the American Servicemembers' Protection Act (ASPA). These counties are Argentina, Australia, Belgium, Bulgaria, Canada, Czech Republic, Denmark, Estonia, Finland, France, Germany, Greece, Hungary, Ireland, Italy, Japan, Jordan, Latvia, Lithuania, Luxembourg, Netherlands, New Zealand, Poland, Portugal, Republic of Korea, Slovakia, Slovenia, Spain, and the United Kingdom. More information can be found at http://www.iccnow.org/documents/other issues/impunityart98/BIAWaiversWICC24Nov03.pdf.

Index